A School Administrator's Guide to the Family and Medical Leave Act

Carl C. Bosland, Esq.

Published in partnership with the
Association of School Business Officials International

Rowman & Littlefield Education
Lanham, Maryland • Toronto • Plymouth, UK
2007

Published in partnership with the
Association of School Business Officials International

Published in the United States of America
by Rowman & Littlefield Education
A Division of Rowman & Littlefield Publishers, Inc.
A wholly owned subsidiary of
The Rowman & Littlefield Publishing Group, Inc.
4501 Forbes Boulevard, Suite 200, Lanham, Maryland 20706
www.rowmaneducation.com

Estover Road
Plymouth PL6 7PY
United Kingdom

British Library Cataloguing in Publication Information Available

Library of Congress Cataloging-in-Publication Data

Bosland, Carl C.
A school administrator's guide to the Family and Medical Leave Act / Carl C. Bosland.
p. cm.
Includes bibliographical references and index.
ISBN-13: 978-1-57886-557-4 (hardcover : alk. paper)
ISBN-10: 1-57886-557-3 (hardcover : alk. paper)
1. Parental leave—Law and legislation—United States. 2. Leave of absence—Law and legislation—United States. 3. Teachers—Legal status, laws, etc.—United States. 4. School management and organization—Law and legislation—United States. 5. School administrators—United States—Handbooks, manuals, etc. 6. United States. Family and Medical Leave Act of 1993. I. Title.
KF4188.B67 2007
344.7301'25763—dc22 2006035123

∞™ The paper used in this publication meets the minimum requirements of American National Standard for Information Sciences—Permanence of Paper for Printed Library Materials, ANSI/NISO Z39.48-1992.
Manufactured in the United States of America.

Contents

Expanded Contents

Preface

School administrators face employee requests for leave from work on a daily basis. Employees request leave from work, for example, because they are ill, because they have been hurt at work, or because they need to care for a sick family member. Whether to grant employee leave requests, however, has long ceased to be a matter in the unfettered discretion of school administration. Rather, an ever-growing array of federal and state laws, as well as the requirements of collective bargaining agreements, provide school employees with legal or contractual rights to job-protected leave. These laws also place numerous limitations and responsibilities on school administrators when addressing leave requests. The Family and Medical Leave Act of 1993 (federal FMLA or FMLA) is perhaps the most notable example of these leave laws.

The FMLA was enacted by Congress on February 5, 1993, to address a growing tension between the time demands placed on employees by work and by family responsibilities. Congress sought to rebalance these competing time demands by providing certain eligible employees with the right to take a reasonable amount of job-protected leave under specified circumstances. When it enacted the FMLA, Congress was not legislating on a blank slate. Prior to the enactment of the federal FMLA, many states had their own family and medical leave laws. As discussed throughout this book, these state family and medical leave laws both interact with and vary in scope from the federal FMLA in many ways.

The goal of this book is to provide school administrators with an up-to-date guide to the rights and responsibilities of public and private sector school administration and employees under the federal FMLA.

Up-to-date information on the requirements of the FMLA is important both to ensure legal compliance and to avoid substantial financial legal liability. Significantly, the federal FMLA has been interpreted to permit individual manager liability for even inadvertent violations. Courts have awarded damages in the hundreds of thousands of dollars against employers and individual managers for errant FMLA leave decisions.

Compliance with the FMLA, however, is not an easy task. As a product of compromise, the FMLA is often less than clear. Similarly, the U.S. Department of Labor (DOL) regulations implementing the federal FMLA are numerous, complex, and all too often incomplete. As discussed throughout this book, the regulations frequently fail to define critical terms, leaving employees and school administrators to guess at what is required.

The confusion stemming from a lack of clarity in the statute and implementing regulations is reflected in the varied interpretations of the law over the past decade in thousands of court decisions. Indeed, the U.S. Supreme Court has twice rendered major decisions interpreting the FMLA while it was still a relatively new law. In one of those decisions, the Court struck down some of the implementing regulations as constitutionally invalid. Additionally, the FMLA does not exist in a vacuum. Rather, FMLA leave decisions must take into account the requirements of other federal and state laws. To assist school administrators with the difficult task of FMLA compliance in this complex and ever-changing environment, this book provides guidance based on up-to-date information regarding the requirements of the FMLA.

The book is organized in a manner intended to facilitate the determination of FMLA coverage, rights, and responsibilities. Chapter 1 provides an overview of state and federal family and medical leave laws, with particular emphasis on the core entitlements of the federal FMLA. Chapter 2 addresses employer coverage of the federal FMLA and state family and medical leave laws. Chapter 3 examines employee eligibility requirements. Chapter 4 explains which family members are covered by the FMLA. Chapter 5 discusses the conditions that permit an eligible employee to take FMLA leave. Chapter 6 discusses employee and employer notice requirements. Chapter 7 addresses the right of employers to require documentation to support an employee's request for FMLA leave. Chapter 8 explains the method for calculating the amount of leave available to an eligible employee and the manner in which the leave may be taken. Chapter 9 examines the interplay of paid leave with FMLA leave. Chapter 10 sets forth the FMLA requirements governing the maintenance of health and other employment benefits during leave. Chapter 11 addresses the rights and responsibilities of employees and employers regarding an employee's return to work from FMLA leave. Chapter 12 discusses FMLA record-keeping requirements. Chapter 13 explains the interaction of the FMLA with other laws, employment practices, and the requirements of collective bargaining agreements. Finally, Chapter 14 discusses prohibited actions, the methods employees may use to enforce FMLA rights, and the remedies available for FMLA violations.

I am hopeful that you will find this book to be a useful resource in your administration of FMLA leave.

CHAPTER 1

Introduction

1.01 OVERVIEW

Public and private schools may concurrently be subject to federal and state family and medical leave laws. The core entitlements of applicable federal and state family and medical leave laws, moreover, may be quite different. Significantly, compliance with the requirements of the Family and Medical Leave Act of 1993 (federal FMLA or FMLA) may not ensure compliance with state family and medical leave laws, and vice versa. Generally, where both federal and state family and medical leave laws apply, school administrators must comply with the provisions of the law that gives the employee the greater benefits and protections. Determining which law, federal or state, provides the employee with greater family and medical leave protections is, however, often a difficult undertaking.

This book focuses on the federal FMLA as it applies to public and private schools.[1] In so doing, it will compare the requirements of the federal law with the requirements of state family and medical leave laws. It is intended to provide school administrators with a clear understanding of this complex entitlement.

The purpose of this chapter is twofold: (1) to introduce the reader to federal and state family and medical leave entitlements and (2) to provide the reader with a series of questions to efficiently analyze and resolve FMLA issues.

1.02 THE SOURCES

As indicated above, there are two sources of family and medical leave laws applicable to public and private schools: federal and state.

[1] Federal Law: The Family and Medical Leave Act of 1993

Title I of the Family and Medical Leave Act of 1993 is the sole source of federal family and medical leave law applicable to public and private schools. The law is codified in the U.S. Code at 29 U.S.C. §§ 2601, 2611–2619, 2631–2636, and 2651–2654. The federal FMLA is supplemented by implementing regulations issued by the U.S. Department of Labor (DOL). The regulations are contained in Title 29 of the Code of Federal Regulations, 29 C.F.R. pt. 825. Both the U.S. Code and the DOL implementing regulations are available at most federal depository libraries, as well as federal, state, and local court law libraries. Many local libraries also carry the U.S. Code and the Code of Federal Regulations. Both the FMLA and the implementing regulations are available on my website: www.fmlacounsel.com.

School administrators subject to the federal FMLA are strongly encouraged to have immediate access to a copy of Title I of the FMLA and the regulations. *WH Publication 1419*, available from your local DOL regional office, is helpful in that it contains the text of the final version of the FMLA implementing regulations along with comments that provide further insight into the meaning of the regulations.

> **Resource Recommendation**
>
> Get a hard copy of *WH Publication 1419* from the DOL. You should also download a copy of the final regulations. The final regulations are available on my website at http://www.fmlacounsel.com/resources.asp. The advantage of a downloaded copy is that you can quickly perform "find" searches using key words for the issue that you are addressing.

[2] State Family and Medical Leave Laws

State family and medical leave legislation preceded enactment of the federal FMLA—in some cases, by decades. According to the legislative history, at the time the FMLA was enacted approximately thirty states, the District of Columbia, and the Commonwealth of Puerto Rico had some form of family and medical leave legislation.[2]

Exactly what constitutes "family and medical leave" legislation is not entirely clear. The lack of clarity is due to the absence of a uniform definition of the term. The federal FMLA defines "family leave" as leave provided by an employer covering "the particular circumstances for which the employee seeks leave for either the birth of a child and to care for such child, placement of a child for adoption or foster care, or care for a spouse, child, or parent with a serious health condition.[3] Ironically, the federal FMLA fails to define what constitutes "medical leave." Given the definition of "family leave," by process of elimination it would appear that "medical leave" concerns leave due to the employee's own serious health condition.

State family and medical leave laws take two forms. Some states have enacted a general family and medical leave law or regulation. States with general family and medical leave laws include Alaska, California, Connecticut, the District of Columbia, Florida, Hawaii, Maine, New Jersey, North Dakota, Oklahoma, Oregon, Rhode Island, Texas, Vermont, Virginia, West Virginia, and Wisconsin.[4] Several states, including Arizona, Colorado, Idaho, Kentucky, Massachusetts, Utah, and Wyoming, provide family and medical leave benefits to state employees by regulation.[5] One state, Washington, has ceased administration and enforcement of its family and medical leave law as a result of the enactment of the federal FMLA.[6] I presume that each state allows state employees to take leave due to their own illnesses.

State family and medical leave laws may also take the form of separate laws that, cobbled together, address some or all of the leave benefits set forth in the federal FMLA. These states generally do not have a single, unified family and medical leave law. For example, many states have laws requiring employers to provide leave for maternity, adoption, foster care, parenting, and organ, blood, or bone marrow donation. States with maternity and pregnancy leave laws include Arkansas, Indiana, Iowa, Kansas, Louisiana, Maryland, Massachusetts, Montana, Nevada, New Hampshire, Tennessee, and Washington.[7] States with laws allowing leave for adoption or parenting include Delaware, Illinois, Kentucky, Maryland, Minnesota, Missouri, Montana, Nebraska,

Nevada, New York, Ohio, Pennsylvania, South Carolina, South Dakota, Tennessee, and Texas.[8] States with laws requiring leave for bone marrow, blood, or organ donation or for other reasons due to an employee's (or someone else's) illness include Arkansas, the District of Columbia, Illinois, Indiana, Louisiana, Maryland, Minnesota, Mississippi, Missouri, Nebraska, New York, Ohio, Oklahoma, Oregon, South Carolina, South Dakota, Utah, Virginia, and Wisconsin.

In addition to the types of conditions covered, state family and medical leave laws vary widely on employer and employee coverage, how much leave is available, eligibility requirements before the right to leave may be invoked, employee and employer notice and documentation requirements, record-keeping requirements, whether the leave is paid or unpaid, the effect of leave on the maintenance of health and other employment benefits, and limitations on an employee's return to work from family and medical leave. As stated earlier, state family and medical leave legislation often differs from the analogous requirements under the federal FMLA.

In making decisions on employee family and medical leave requests, school administrators must consider the applicable provisions of both the federal FMLA and any applicable state family and medical leave laws. This is because the federal FMLA interacts with state family and medical leave laws. As discussed throughout this book, in some instances the federal FMLA mandates the application of the more generous requirements of state family and medical leave laws for federal FMLA purposes. To comply with the federal FMLA, therefore, school administrators must know when to apply the more generous provisions of applicable state family and medical leave laws.

1.03 HISTORICAL DEVELOPMENT OF THE FAMILY AND MEDICAL LEAVE ACT OF 1993

Congress passed the Family and Medical Leave Act of 1993 to relieve employees of growing pressures resulting from the increased and often conflicting demands of work and family responsibilities. Congress felt that the existing patchwork of state legislation and employer policies was inadequate to relieve employees of the burden of choosing between work and family. Congress felt this was particularly true in light of increased time pressures resulting from revolutionary changes in the demographic makeup of the family and workforce.

This section provides an overview of the demographic context and legislative responses to work-family conflicts. It also addresses the legislative history of the federal FMLA and postenactment developments. Knowing the reasons that gave rise to the FMLA will help you understand the FMLA as it currently exists and anticipate future changes to the law.

[1] Demographic Context of the FMLA

Congress's rationale for the FMLA was its finding that the family unit was being threatened by the competing demands on employee time resulting from the confluence of four long-term work and demographic trends: (1) the increased time employees spend at work, (2) the rise of women in the workplace and two-earner families, (3) the increase of single-parent families, and (4) the elder care needs incident to an aging population. A brief review of the demographic forces shaping the enactment of the FMLA follows.[9]

(i) Longer Work Hours

Measured by time at work, Americans are the hardest-working employees in the world. Employees in the United States average more work hours each year (1,966) than do employees in Japan (1,889), Canada (1,732), Britain (1,731), and Norway (1,399), the next four contenders.[10] On average, Americans work 350 hours more per year (almost 9 full workweeks) than Europeans.[11]

Of course, the dubious distinction of being the hardest workers in the world does not come without sacrifice. Researchers agree that American employees are putting in more hours at work and fewer at home.[12] Studies have shown that the average American worker today puts in a month more at work than 25 years ago.[13] One study has shown that the extra time spent at work has resulted in a 14 percent decrease (22 hours per week) in time available to working parents to spend with their children.[14]

(ii) The Dramatic Increase of Women in the Workforce

In addition to increased work hours, changes in the composition of the workforce have added to the competing time pressures of work and family experienced by American employees. In particular, Congress noted the profound effects on working men and women and their families resulting from the dramatic increase in the number of women who entered the workforce in the decades before the 1993 enactment of the FMLA:[15]

- Between 1950 and 1990 the female civilian labor force more than tripled, growing at a rate of one million women workers a year.
- In 1900, women constituted 19 percent of the labor force; by 1993, 74 percent of women aged 25 to 54 were in the labor force.
- Women were responsible for 62 percent of the increase in the civilian labor force from 1979 to 1993; that figure was expected to increase to 66 percent by the year 2000.
- In 1993, 96 percent of fathers and 65 percent of mothers worked outside the home.
- In 1993, 56 percent of mothers with children under the age of 6 and 51 percent of mothers with children under the age 1 were in the labor force.
- The Families and Work Institute predicted that by 1995 nearly two-thirds of women with preschool children and three-quarters of women with school-age children would be in the workforce.

The dramatic increase in the participation of women in the workforce, Congress found, had an adverse impact on family stability. Women, according to Congress, historically stayed home and performed crucial unpaid caretaking services such as caring for young children, ill family members, and aging parents.[16] With the dramatic rise in the number of women in the civilian workforce, there was no one left to perform the crucial caretaking services.[17] As a result, Congress found that families suffered.[18]

(iii) The Rise of Single-Parent Families

The substantial increase in the number of single-parent households was a third major demographic trend noted by Congress in support of the need for family and medical leave legislation.[19] Due to divorce, separation, and out-of-wedlock births, between 1970 and 1988 the number of single-parent families increased more than 120 percent, from 11 percent to 27 percent of all family groups with children under 18 years of age.[20] Moreover, many of these single-parent families were headed by women who struggled to keep their families above the poverty line. In 1987, 20 percent of all children under the age of 6 lived with single mothers. The poverty rate among these children was 61.4 percent, more than five times the poverty rate among children living in two-parent families.[21]

Congress found that single-parent families that were already struggling financially could be devastated by the loss of a job due to absences necessitated by the illness of the working parent or of another family member who required care.[22]

(iv) Increased Parental Care Responsibilities

The fourth demographic trend cited by Congress in support of the need for national family and medical leave legislation was the dramatic rise in employee parental care responsibilities due to the aging of the American population.[23] Because of advances in health care, individuals over the age of 65 were the fastest-growing segment of the American population.[24] According to estimates of the National Council on Aging, 20 to 25 percent of the more than 100 million American workers have some caregiving responsibility for an older relative.[25] Women assume a disproportionate share of adult caregiving responsibilities. According to the National Council on Aging, two-thirds of the nonprofessional caregivers for older, chronically ill, or disabled persons are working women, the most common caregiver being a child or spouse.[26] Without responsive policy, Congress concluded that "the heightened need for elder care will continue to exert enormous pressures on working families and the economy."[27]

(v) Effect of Confluence of Four Demographic Changes

Congress summarized the effect on American workers of the confluence of these four demographic trends as follows:

> The effect of these demographic changes has been far reaching. With men and women alike as wage earners, the crucial unpaid caretaking services traditionally performed by wives—care of young children, ill family members, aging parents—has become increasingly difficult for families to fulfill. When there is no one to provide such care, individuals can be permanently scarred as basic needs go unfulfilled. Families unable to perform their essential function are seriously undermined and weakened. Finally, when families fail, the community is left to grapple with the tragic consequences of emotionally and physically deprived children and adults.[28]

[2] Legislative Responses to Workplace-Family Conflicts

In addition to studying the work-family conflicts that resulted from broad demographic changes, Congress also compared and contrasted family and medical leave legislation around the world with legislation in the United States.[29] Generally speaking, Congress found the patchwork of state leave legislation wanting compared with the family and medical leave benefits enjoyed by employees in most other industrialized countries around the world. The federal FMLA, Congress opined, was necessary to close the gap between the family and medical leave legislation in the United States and that in other Western industrialized countries.[30]

(i) Family Leave Laws in Other Countries

Congress observed that the United States was one of the few countries in the world that did not have a law setting a standard for family leave.[31] "With the exception of the United States, virtually every industrialized country, as well as many third world countries, have national policies that require employers to provide some form of maternity or parental leave."[32] When it passed the federal FMLA, Congress noted that 135 countries provided some form of maternity benefits; 127

provided some wage replacement.[33] Moreover, family and medical leave legislation is well established in Europe, with France, Great Britain, and Italy having had family and medical leave legislation since World War I.[34] Most other European nations have had maternity leave policies since 1919, when 33 countries signed the Maternity Protection Convention providing a minimum of 12 weeks of leave, job protection, and wage benefits.[35] In 1992, the European Community Commission directed that all member countries provide a standard minimum of 14 weeks' paid maternity leave.[36] In 1996, the European Union, successor to the European Community Commission, enacted its Directive on Parental Leave, which guarantees all employees a minimum of 3 months of unpaid, job-protected leave.[37]

Congress further noted that family and medical leave in most industrialized countries is paid leave. "Among the major industrialized countries, the average minimum paid leave is 12 to 14 weeks, with many also providing the right to unpaid, job-protected leave for at least 1 year."[38] Congress noted that Sweden guaranteed 18 months of paid family leave at 90 percent of gross pay.[39] Leave for elder care, Congress noted, was made specifically available in some European countries. Where it is not specifically available, such leave is available through generous paid vacation and sick leave programs and a national health system.[40] Typically, new employees enjoy a mandatory 4 weeks of paid annual leave in most European countries. By comparison, new employees in the United States typically receive only 2 weeks of annual leave.[41]

(ii) State Family Leave Laws

Congress observed that between 1985, when federal family leave legislation was first introduced, and 1993, when the federal FMLA was passed by Congress, approximately thirty states, the District of Columbia, and Puerto Rico adopted some form of family and medical leave legislation.[42] However, the protections afforded by these state leave laws, Congress noted, varied greatly. All thirty states extended family and medical leave to public employees, with two-thirds covering some employees in the private sector.[43] Coverage of private sector employees, moreover, varied greatly by employer size. For example,

Vermont's leave law covers private sector employers with as few as 10 employees; Minnesota covers employers with 21 or more employees; Oregon's and Maine's laws apply to employers with at least 25 employees; and California's and Wisconsin's leave laws apply to employers with at least 50 employees.[44]

Congress also noted that the state leave laws differed significantly in the amount of family and medical leave available to a covered employee and the circumstances under which an employee could take that leave. For example, Pennsylvania law provides state employees with 6 months of parental leave for the birth or adoption of a child.[45] The California law, in contrast, provides up to 16 weeks of leave to be taken over 2 years for the birth or adoption of a child or for the serious health condition of a child, spouse, or parent.[46] Wisconsin ties the amount of leave available to the reason for the leave, allowing 6 weeks of leave for the birth or adoption of a child, 2 weeks to care for a family member with a serious health condition, and 2 weeks of personal medical leave.[47] Finally, Congress felt that the federal FMLA was necessary to set a uniform minimum national family and medical leave standard to more equitably distribute the burden of compliance on all employers.

[3] The Creation of the Federal Family and Medical Leave Act

The Family and Medical Leave Act is the federal government's ultimate response to the increasing tensions between work and family caused by the confluence of major work and demographic trends discussed above. The federal FMLA as it exists today is the product of 8 years of interest group, legislative, and executive branch wrangling and political compromises. During that time, the name of the Act changed several times, as did the scope of coverage and leave entitlements. Outstanding summaries of the legislative history of the federal FMLA include *Family Leave Policy: The Political Economy of Work and Family in America*, by Steven K. Wisensale, and *The Moderation Dilemma: Legislative Coalitions and the Politics of Family and Medical Leave*, by Anya E. Bernstein.[48]

The original impetus for family and medical leave legislation arose from a 1984 decision by a California federal court invalidating a California state maternity law that permitted up to 4 months of job-protected leave to women. The court held that the law violated equal protection (i.e., the law did not grant men the same right to leave) and could subject employers who abided by the law to reverse sex-discrimination lawsuits by men. Groups representing women and labor organizations who were supportive of the maternity-leave legislation were outraged by the decision but were split on tactics. Some groups focused their support on the maternity legislation. Other groups opposed the maternity legislation because it gave women special treatment. These groups favored leave legislation that applied to both men and women as the best means to advance women's issues in the workplace. This tactical clash would play itself out in the formation of the FMLA, with the equal-treatment advocates ultimately prevailing.[49]

Howard Berman, a freshman congressman from California, floated the first legislative proposal addressing the maternity-leave decision of the California federal court. Before entering Congress, Mr. Berman was the California state legislator who authored the maternity-leave law that was later struck down by the federal court. Congressman Berman initially moved to enact federal maternity-leave legislation along the lines of the state maternity-leave legislation struck down by the federal court. Because they believed that such legislation singled women out for special treatment, the equal-treatment women's and labor groups lobbied Berman to turn the issue over to the Congressional Caucus on Women's Issues led by Congresswomen Patricia Schroeder, from Colorado, which he did.

Another congressman from California, George Miller, also contributed to laying the groundwork for federal family and medical leave legislation through the creation of the Select Committee on Children, Youth, and Families. Select committees do not have real political power but provide a forum where issues can be raised and vetted. In 1984, Congressman Miller's Select Committee held hearings on issues involving families and child care, which culminated in a report that, among other things, recommended the need for policies providing expanded family leave with job security. The issuance of the Select Committee's report kicked off serious debate on the need for national family leave legislation.

On April 4, 1985, Congresswoman Patricia Schroeder introduced the first bill proposing national family and medical leave legislation.

Named the Parental and Disability Leave Act of 1985, the legislation applied to all employers and provided job-protected leave that could be taken in different amounts calculated over a 2-year period depending on the basis for the need for leave.[50] For example, both men and women could take up to 18 weeks of leave to care for a newborn or newly adopted child. Up to 26 weeks of leave was available for a temporary disability or to care for a seriously ill child. Although a few hearings were held, the legislation stalled. The legislation, however, was reintroduced the following year. Now called the Parental and Medical Leave Act of 1986 to assuage advocates for the handicapped, the new law included several changes; most notably it was limited to employers with 5 or more employees.[51] The Democratic leadership decided that the law was not ready for a floor vote before the 1986 elections and, again, tabled the legislation.

The 1986 elections saw the Democrats take control of the Senate and retain control of the House. The House Democrats quickly reintroduced the newly named Family and Medical Leave Act of 1987. The bill was substantially changed in committee with the adoption of a substitute bill offered by Representative Marge Roukema of New Jersey. The Roukema amendments further limited the reach of the legislation by increasing the minimum number of employees needed before it applied to a particular employer. The amendments also reduced the amount of leave available, added eligibility requirements before employees were entitled to exercise FMLA rights, and exempted certain highly compensated employees from the right to return to their jobs from FMLA leave.[52] Even with these significant changes, the Democratic leadership decided not to release the bill for a floor vote.[53]

Every year from 1988 to 1991, family and medical leave legislation was introduced with changes and additions. The 1988 legislation died after Senator Strom Thurmond attached an antipornography bill to it. In 1990 and 1991, President George H. W. Bush, as promised, vetoed significantly modified versions of the Family and Medical Leave Act that passed both the House and Senate. Modifications added during these years reduced the amount of leave to 12 weeks a year for all covered conditions, increased the eligibility threshold from 1,000 to 1,250 hours of work, added employee notice requirements, and permitted employers to require employees to submit medical certification substantiating the need for job-protected leave.

In November 1992, William Jefferson Clinton was elected President of the United States. As a candidate, Clinton had made passage of the Family and Medical Leave Act a centerpiece of his campaign. After both the House and the Senate passed the Family and Medical Leave Act of 1993, President Clinton signed the measure into law on February 5, 1993, making the Family and Medical Leave Act the first bill of his administration.

[4] Findings and Purposes of the Federal FMLA

Congress identified the findings underlying the need for legislation and the congressional purpose of the federal FMLA in the body of the statute. As discussed previously, those findings and purposes reflect the major demographic changes in the American workforce. Specifically, Congress found as follows:

(1) The number of single-parent households and two-parent households in which the single parent or both parents work is increasingly significantly;
(2) It is important for the development of children and the family unit that fathers and mothers be able to participate in early child rearing and the care of family members who have serious health conditions;
(3) The lack of employment policies to accommodate working parents can force individuals to choose between job security and parenting;
(4) There is inadequate job security for employees who have serious health conditions that prevent them from working for temporary periods;
(5) Due to the nature of the roles of men and women in our society, the primary responsibility for family caretaking often falls on women, and such responsibility affects the working lives of women more than it affects the working lives of men; and
(6) Employment standards that apply to one gender only have serious potential for encouraging employers to discriminate against employees and applicants for employment who are of that gender.[54]

Not surprisingly, in its statement of the purposes of the FMLA, Congress sought to redress the work-family conflicts it identified in the findings. Congress identified the purposes of the federal FMLA as follows:

(1) To balance the demands of the workplace with the needs of families, to promote the stability and economic security of families, and to promote national interests in preserving family integrity;

(2) To entitle employees to take reasonable leave for medical reasons, for the birth or adoption of a child, and for the care of a child, spouse, or parent who has a serious health condition;
(3) To accomplish the purposes described in paragraphs (1) and (2) in a manner that accommodates the legitimate interests of employers;
(4) To accomplish the purposes described in paragraph (1) and (2) in a manner that, consistent with the Equal Protection Clause of the Fourteenth Amendment, minimizes the potential for employment discrimination on the basis of sex by ensuring generally that leave is available for eligible medical reasons (including maternity-related disability) and for compelling family reasons, on a gender-neutral basis; and
(5) To promote the goal of equal employment opportunity for women and men, pursuant to such clause.[55]

Note the reference in paragraphs (4) and (5) to the need to provide family and medical leave in a manner consistent with equal protection and equal employment between men and women. The language confirms the triumph of the equal-protection faction of the labor and women's lobby over the special-treatment faction in the battle to shape what would ultimately become the federal Family and Medical Leave Act.

[5] Impact of the FMLA: Reports of the Commission on Family and Medical Leave

The federal FMLA created the Commission on Family and Medical Leave.[56] The Commission was charged with submitting a report to appropriate congressional committees on the impact of the FMLA and other voluntary family medical leave policies on employers and employees. The Commission presented its initial report to Congress in 1996, reporting favorably on the impact of the FMLA:

> The Family and Medical Leave Act has had a positive impact on employees overall. It has succeeded in replacing the piecemeal nature of voluntary employer leave policies and state leave statutes with a more consistent and uniform standard. The FMLA has not been the burden to business that some had feared. For most employers, compliance is easy, the costs are nonexistent or small, and the effects are minimal. Most pe-

> riods of leave are short, most employees return to work, and reduced turnover seems to be a tangible positive effect. The FMLA, with its signature features of guaranteed job protection and maintenance of health benefits, begins to emerge, even now, as a significant step in helping a larger cross-section of working Americans meet their medical and family care-giving needs while still maintaining their jobs and their economic security—achieving the workable balance intended by Congress.[57]

Noteworthy observations from the 1996 Report include the fact that although over 89.2 percent of private sector employers are not covered by the FMLA, over half (59.5 percent) of the U.S. labor force was covered by the FMLA in 1995. Obviously, most employers are relatively small, and most private sector employees work for relatively large employers. All public sector establishments, including schools, are covered by the FMLA.

The 1996 Report further found that over 90 percent of covered employers reported that the FMLA was relatively easy to administer, that few or no additional costs were associated with its implementation, and that the Act had no noticeable effect on business or employee performance. During the survey period, one-fifth of the workforce (20.2 percent) needed leave for a covered condition, but only 16.8 percent actually took FMLA leave. Inability to afford leave was the number one reason cited by those who needed FMLA leave but did not take it. The most common reason for taking FMLA leave was to care for one's own serious health condition (61.4 percent). Men were more likely than women to take leave for their own health and to care for an ill spouse. Women were more likely than men to take FMLA leave and to take longer periods of leave. The median leave length was 10 days, and 90 percent of leaves lasted for 12 weeks or less. Most employees (84 percent) who took leave returned to their jobs. Six percent did not return to their jobs, while 10 percent were still on leave at the time covered by the 1996 Report.

In 2000, Congress funded, and the DOL commissioned, new employee and employer family and medical leave surveys to update the studies supporting the 1996 Commission Report.[58] The 2000 Study concluded: "Seven years after the FMLA came into effect, this report finds that family and medical leave is becoming a more important part of the experience of establishments and employees."[59] More employees are using family and medical leave. However, a substantial number of employees cited financial concerns as constraining their ability to take needed FMLA leave. Employees were worried they would not be able to pay the bills. The Study further found that more establishments offered family and medical leave policies—in many instances more generous policies than what is required by the FMLA. On the other hand, compared with the 1996 Report, more employers now reported that the FMLA was difficult to administer, although a larger majority of establishments reported that the FMLA had no adverse effects on their business or employees.

[6] Amendments to the Federal FMLA

Although there have been many bills introduced to amend the federal FMLA, to date none have been passed. Some amendments have sought to expand the reach of the FMLA by lowering the number of employees required for private sector coverage from 50 to 25. Others have focused on expanding the covered conditions to include a limited period of time to attend school functions. On the other end of the spectrum, amendments have been proposed that would narrow the definition of covered serious health conditions, thereby decreasing the reach of the FMLA.

In 1999, President Clinton attempted to modify the federal FMLA by executive directive. As detailed in Chapter 9, *Paid Leave Substitution*, President Clinton directed the DOL to draft regulations that would permit states to use surplus unemployment funds to subsidize parents who use unpaid FMLA leave to care for a newborn or newly adopted child. The DOL dutifully drafted such regulations but subsequently rescinded them after it became clear that none of the states was going to enact legislation to use surplus unemployment funds in this way.

More recently, on December 1, 2006, the DOL announced that it was seeking information and public comment on possible changes to the regulations implementing the federal FMLA.[60] The DOL identified twelve specific areas for comment, although the notice emphasized that the public was not limited to addressing just those areas.[61] Comments are due by February 2, 2007.

The DOL explained that the need to consider regulatory changes was the result of a confluence of factors, including the invalidation of some FMLA regulations by courts and confusion in the courts regarding the meaning of key regulatory terms.[62] The DOL also cited statutory and regulatory developments that interact with the FMLA as another reason for a review of the FMLA regulations, including the enactment of the Health Insurance Portability and Accountability Act of 1996 (HIPPA)[63] and recent Equal Employment Opportunity Commission guidance on the Americans with Disabilities Act (ADA) regarding the privacy of employee medical information.[64] These issues are addressed in detail in Chapter 13, *Coordination of the FMLA with Other Employee Rights and Benefits*.

The DOL solicitation did not offer any proposed changes to the FMLA regulations. Nor is the DOL required to make any changes as a consequence of the solicitation for public comment. However, by soliciting public comment, the DOL has clearly signaled its interest in making some changes to the current FMLA regulations. The DOL has not set a time frame for taking action after the public comment period closes on February 7, 2007. School employers would be well advised to keep current on FMLA regulatory developments in light of the DOL's solicitation for public comment. Developments can be monitored on The FMLA Blog, a site I maintain.[65]

1.04 CORE ENTITLEMENTS OF THE FEDERAL FMLA

The federal Family and Medical Leave Act provides eligible employees of covered employers with up to 12 workweeks of job-protected, unpaid leave each 12-month leave year due to their own serious health condition or to care for a son, daughter, spouse, or parent suffering from a serious health condition. Leave is also available due to the birth, adoption, or foster care placement of a child with the employee. Chapter 2 discusses school coverage. Chapter 3 discusses employee eligibility requirements. Chapters 4 and 5 explain which family members and conditions are covered by the FMLA. Chapter 8 sets forth the amount of leave available to an employee and how that leave may be taken.

To initiate their right to FMLA leave, employees must provide their employers with timely and adequate advance notice of their need for

FMLA leave. The failure of an eligible employee to provide such timely and adequate notice may result in the delay or denial of FMLA leave. Employers also have FMLA notice obligations. Employers must post notice of FMLA rights, include FMLA information in employee handbooks, manuals, or other written information regarding employment benefits, and provide specific notice of FMLA rights and responsibilities to employees requesting leave. The failure of an employer to provide such notice constitutes a violation of the Act. Chapter 6 addresses employee and employer notice requirements.

Employers may also require employees to substantiate their need for FMLA leave with documentation. Both medical and nonmedical documentation may be required. When requested, employees must timely provide adequate documentation to gain the protections of the FMLA. The FMLA also requires employers to maintain records relevant to the FMLA. Chapter 7 reviews documentation requirements. Chapter 12 discusses record-keeping requirements.

While FMLA leave is unpaid, an employee may elect, or an employer may require an employee, to substitute accrued paid leave for unpaid FMLA leave. Chapter 9 discusses the substitution of paid leave. During the employee's FMLA leave, covered employers are required to maintain employee health benefits at the same level and on the same terms as existed prior to the commencement of leave. Chapter 10 discusses the maintenance of health benefits during FMLA leave.

The FMLA entitlement guarantees that an employee on qualifying leave has the right to return to the same or an equivalent position (e.g., equivalent pay, benefits, and other tangible terms and conditions of employment) at the conclusion of that leave. An employer may condition an employee's return from FMLA leave for that employee's own serious health condition on the presentation of medical documentation confirming that the employee is able to return to work. Absent a request for return-to-work medical documentation, an employer may not delay or deny an employee's return to work from FMLA leave. Special exceptions for school employees and "key employees," however, may permit an employer to delay or deny an employee's return to work from FMLA leave. Chapter 11 addresses the requirements governing an employee's return to work from FMLA leave.

The FMLA prohibits covered employers from interfering with an employee's FMLA rights or from discriminating or retaliating against an employee for exercising his or her FMLA rights. The violation of any DOL implementing regulations, whether or not intentional, constitutes interference with FMLA rights. Aggrieved employees may file a complaint with the DOL for violations of their FMLA rights. Alternately, an employee may sue an employer, including individual managers or supervisors, in federal or state court for violations of FMLA rights. The filing of an administrative complaint with the DOL is not a prerequisite for filing a civil action. Employees may recover damages in the form of lost wages and other benefits, double damages for "willful" violations, and attorneys' fees and costs. Chapter 14 discusses prohibited acts, enforcement, and remedies available for violations of the FMLA.

Finally, the federal FMLA does not exist in a vacuum. Rather, compliance with the FMLA may be affected by school administration personnel policies, including the requirements of collective bargaining agreements and the requirements of any applicable state family and medical leave laws. Moreover, while it may not supersede the requirements of other federal employment laws (e.g., the Pregnancy Discrimination Act of 1978, the Americans with Disabilities Act of 1990), the FMLA does interact with these laws. Chapter 13 addresses the interaction of the FMLA with other laws, employment practices, and collective bargaining agreements.

1.05 DETERMINING WHETHER LEAVE QUALIFIES FOR PROTECTION UNDER THE FMLA: ESSENTIAL QUESTIONS

To expedite the determination of whether the federal FMLA applies to any given leave situation, I ask the following series of questions. The questions address what I consider to be the issues central to determining the application of the federal FMLA. The questions, moreover, are ordered in a way intended to quickly identify when the federal FMLA does and does not apply. For example, the first question is whether the employer is covered by the federal FMLA. If not, the federal FMLA inquiry is over. Of course, simply because you have ruled out application of the federal FMLA does not mean that the leave request may be summarily denied. State family and medical leave laws may apply, as may employer polices, the terms of collective bargaining agreements, or the requirements of other federal or state laws.

After over 10 years of responding to FMLA queries, I have found these basic questions helpful in organizing my thoughts and in systematically addressing most FMLA issues. Of course, I make no claim that this is the best or most logical series of questions, only that it has worked for me. Every FMLA issue is unique and will require consideration of all relevant facts.

[1] Is the School an "Employer" within the Meaning of the FMLA?

All public schools and all private elementary and secondary schools are covered "employers" within the meaning of the federal FMLA. Other types of private sector educational institutions, such as colleges and universities, trade schools, and preschools, are covered employers only if they meet the so-called 50/20 test. Pursuant to that test, a person or entity is considered a covered "employer" within the meaning of the FMLA if that entity employs 50 or more employees for each working day of at least 20 calendar workweeks in a calendar year (either the current calendar year or the preceding calendar year).

Individual school administrators may also be covered "employers" within the meaning of the federal FMLA. This is because the definition of a covered "employer" includes any person acting, directly or indirectly, in the interest of a covered employer. The primary significance of defining an FMLA-covered "employer" to include an individual school administrator is liability; the federal FMLA allows suit against covered employers. A school employee whose FMLA rights were violated may bring a civil suit for damages against either the school or the administrative official or both.

If you determine that the school is not covered by the federal FMLA, your FMLA inquiry ends. However, simply because the school falls outside the scope of the federal FMLA does not mean that family and medical leave benefits do not apply. The school may be covered by state family and medical leave laws. For example, a private sector trade school with less than 50 employees during each of 20 or more calendar workweeks in the current or preceding calendar year is not covered by the federal FMLA. You still need to check whether your state has a family medical leave law. In some instances, the applicable state family and medical leave law will reach smaller employers than does the federal FMLA.

[2] Is the Employee "Eligible" for FMLA Leave?

Just because an employee works for a covered "employer" does not mean that the individual is automatically entitled to take FMLA leave. The federal FMLA imposes additional eligibility requirements that an employee must meet before that employee may exercise FMLA rights. All covered school employees, whether in the public or private sector, must meet all three of the following eligibility requirements before they are entitled to take federal FMLA leave:

(1) The individual must have been employed for at least 12 months.
(2) The individual must have worked at least 1,250 hours in the 12-month period immediately preceding leave commencement.
(3) The individual must be employed at a location that has at least 50 employees within 75 miles.

If the individual does not meet all three eligibility requirements, he or she may not be entitled to take job-protected leave under the federal FMLA. Here again, if the state's family and medical leave law has lower eligibility requirements (as many do), the employee may be able to take family and medical leave pursuant to applicable state law.

[3] Does the Leave Involve a Covered Individual?

Once it has been determined that the school is a covered employer and the employee meets the eligibility requirements, the next question is whether the leave involves a covered individual within the meaning of the federal FMLA. The FMLA covers leave to address the needs of certain individuals and only those individuals. Those individuals are

- the eligible employee;
- a spouse;

- a son or daughter; and
- a parent.

If an eligible employee needs leave to address a covered condition of anyone other than himself or herself, a spouse, a son or daughter, or a parent, the leave is not protected by the federal FMLA. Notably absent from the list are brothers and sisters, in-laws, uncles, aunts, cousins, and grandparents. Nor does the FMLA extend to anyone simply because that person is dependent on the employee. If the employee is taking leave for a covered condition for anyone other than himself or herself, that person must fit within the definition of a spouse, a son or daughter, or a parent to come within the protections of the federal FMLA.

The terms "spouse," "son or daughter," and "parent" are defined by the federal FMLA and the DOL implementing regulations. Parents are broadly defined to include biological, legal (e.g., adoptive, foster care placement), and extralegal relationships. The latter category, identified as "in loco parentis," recognizes parent-child relationships in fact, such as where an older sibling takes over day-to-day financial and other parental responsibilities for a younger sibling in the absence of the parent. In this way, an employee might be entitled to take leave for an individual who, at first glance, does not appear to be covered by the FMLA. On the other hand, "spouse" is narrowly defined to cover only a marriage between a man and a woman, thereby excluding legal same-sex marriages or civil unions.

Here again, state family and medical leave law may allow an employee to take job-protected leave for individuals who are not covered by the federal FMLA. School administrators would be well advised to consult applicable state law to determine family and medical leave coverage where it has been determined that the federal FMLA does not apply because the employee needs leave to care for someone other than the employee, a spouse, a parent, or a son or daughter.

[4] Does the Leave Involve a Covered Condition?

Not all employee requests for leave are covered by the federal FMLA. The federal FMLA specifies which conditions are covered for purposes of job and benefits protections. While covered conditions are broadly defined, the permissible reasons for FMLA leave are not limitless (although it often seems that way). For an employee to gain the protection of the law, the reason for the eligible employee's leave must fall within at least one of four broad categories:

- The birth of a son or daughter of the employee and the need to care for such son or daughter
- The placement of a son or daughter with the employee for adoption or foster care and the need to care for such son or daughter
- The need to care for the spouse, parent, or son or daughter of the employee with a serious health condition
- A serious health condition that renders the employee unable to perform the functions of the position

The DOL implementing regulations further refine these four broad statutory categories. The DOL regulations are both surprisingly complex and incomplete. As you will discover throughout this book, the DOL regulations frequently fail to define key terms, leaving employers to guess what is required. These problems notwithstanding, school administrators must become intimately familiar with the DOL regulatory requirements as they form the backbone of FMLA administration and compliance.

A common misconception about the availability of FMLA leave is that the FMLA applies only when someone is sick and where that illness results in an absence of more than three days from work. Actually, FMLA leave is available in the absence of illness. FMLA leave for birth, adoption, or foster care placement does not require illness. Moreover, an employee may be entitled to FMLA leave to drive a parent or child to a doctor's appointment even though the individual is not sick that day. Similarly, the term "serious health condition" has multiple definitions under the federal FMLA, only one of which has a minimum period of incapacity. All of the remaining definitions have no minimum period of incapacity for FMLA coverage.

> There is no list of conditions that are always covered by the FMLA. Rather, school administrators must make the determination of federal FMLA coverage in each case based on the known facts.

Finally, whether any given leave situation constitutes an FMLA-covered condition is highly fact specific. There is no list of conditions that are always covered by the FMLA. Rather, school administrators must make the determination of federal FMLA coverage in each case based on the known facts. The known facts must meet at least one of the definitions for an FMLA-covered condition.

[5] Did the Employee and Employer Both Satisfy Their Respective Notice Requirements?

The federal FMLA imposes notification requirements on employees and employers. Employees must provide timely and adequate notice of their need for FMLA-qualifying leave in order to gain the protections of the FMLA. Whether employee notice is timely depends on the foreseeability of the need for leave. Generally speaking, the more foreseeable the need for leave, the greater the length of advance notice required, and vice versa. Where the need for leave is emergent, notice may be timely after the employee has returned to work from being absent. The only penalty an employer may impose for an employee's failure to provide timely notice of the need for FMLA leave is to delay the start of the leave. The FMLA does not permit an employer to deny leave due to untimely employee notice.

Employees are not required to specifically request FMLA leave in order to gain the protections of the Act. Rather, employees need only state sufficient facts suggesting that the leave may be covered by the FMLA. It is incumbent on the employer to determine whether the leave falls within the coverage of the FMLA based on the facts articulated by the employee. The employer has a duty to inquire further if the facts suggest that the employee may be requesting FMLA leave. Where, however, the employee fails to articulate facts suggesting that the leave may be covered by the FMLA, the employer is not required to inquire further and the leave, if granted, will not be protected by the FMLA.

As employers, schools have multiple notice obligations under the federal FMLA. Covered schools must conspicuously post a notice of FMLA rights on employee bulletin boards. They must include notice of FMLA rights and responsibilities in any written employee handbook, manual, or other materials regarding employee benefits. Schools must also periodically provide an employee requesting FMLA leave with specific notice of FMLA rights and responsibilities. The contents of the posted and specific notices are dictated by regulation. The consequence of a school's failure to provide the required notices varies depending on the type of notice. For example, the failure of a school to post the required FMLA notice may result in a civil fine, and such a failure prohibits the school from delaying the start of an employee's leave because the employee failed to provide timely notice. The failure of a school to provide specific notice of FMLA rights, on the other hand, relieves the employee of responsibility for meeting any of the requirements contained in the notice—a significant penalty.

[6] Did the Employee Provide Adequate Documentation Substantiating the Need for FMLA Leave?

Employers may require employees to substantiate their need for FMLA leave with documentation. The type of documentation an employer may request depends on whether the need for leave is due to a serious health condition or not. Where the need for FMLA leave does not involve illness (e.g., adoptions or foster care placement), the employer may require the employee requesting leave to provide documentation substantiating that leave is needed in furtherance of the adoption or foster care placement. The employer may also require an employee on FMLA leave to report periodically on the status of the leave and when he or she expects to return.

Where the need for leave is due to a serious health condition, three forms of medical certification may be required by an employer:

- Medical certification
- Recertification of the original medical certification
- Certification of fitness to return to duty

While an employer has the right to request medical certification, it is not required to do so. Similarly, absent a request, an employee is generally not obligated to provide medical certification in support of his or her request for FMLA leave.

An employee has a minimum of 15 days to provide FMLA medical certification requested by school administration. The period of time may be extended if the employee is attempting in good faith to secure the medical certification. School administration may also voluntarily grant an employee more time to provide a medical certification. This is typically formalized in school policies or by the terms of a collective bargaining agreement. However, the federal FMLA prohibits a school from requiring an employee to provide medical certification in less than 15 days.

The federal FMLA prescribes the contents of the medical certification. A school may not require the employee to provide more information than is prescribed by the federal FMLA. However, a school may insist that the medical certification provided by the employee be complete regarding all permissible information. Where the employee provides an incomplete certification, a school must identify the deficiency to the employee and give the employee a reasonable opportunity to provide a complete certification.

The federal FMLA has an appeal procedure for resolving disputes regarding the validity of an FMLA medical certification provided by the employee. A school that doubts the validity of a complete FMLA medical certification may require the employee to obtain certification from a second health care provider. If the need for FMLA leave is due to the serious health condition of a spouse, parent, or son or daughter, then these individuals will have to submit to certification by a second health care provider. The second opinion is at the expense of the school. The school, however, gets to select the second health care provider. If the determination of the second health care provider differs from the initial medical certification, the employer, at its expense, may require the employee to undergo review by a third health care provider jointly selected by the school and the employee. The determination of the third health care provider is final and binding on all parties.

FMLA protections may be delayed and ultimately denied to an employee who fails to provide the initial medical certification requested by the school or who fails to cooperate in the medical certification appeal process.

School administrators may also require an employee to update any FMLA medical certifications by recertification. The federal FMLA regulates how frequently a school may require an employee to recertify his or her medical certification. Moreover, once recertified, an employer may be prohibited from challenging the original medical certification through the appeal process described above.

If an employee has taken FMLA leave for his or her own serious health condition, the federal FMLA also permits covered schools to condition the employee's return to work on a medical certification of fitness to return to duty. Generally, this certification need only be a short and simple statement that the employee is certified to return to work. More detailed return-to-work medical certifications are permitted, but only where they are required by state law or the terms of a collective bargaining agreement.

[7] Is the Leave to Be Taken All at Once or Intermittently?

FMLA leave may be taken in one of three ways: (1) in a single block of time, (2) intermittently, or (3) on a so-called reduced leave schedule. Leave is taken in a single block of time where one continuous absence is due to an identified covered condition. Intermittent leave refers to multiple absences arising out of the same underlying covered condition. Similar to intermittent leave, a reduced leave schedule involves multiple absences for the same covered condition taken in a more systematic form, such as going from full-time to part-time employment.

For the most part, FMLA leave on an intermittent or reduced leave schedule basis is treated the same, so knowing the differences between them is relatively unimportant. However, significant differences exist between leave taken in a single block of time and leave taken on multiple occasions for the same covered condition. That is, how FMLA leave is taken impacts employee and school administration rights.

For example, where FMLA leave is taken in a single block of time, all things being equal, a school basically is left with the choice of either granting or denying the leave. Where the employee requests FMLA leave on an intermittent or reduced leave schedule basis, on the other hand, the employee has additional obligations he or she must meet. If the intermittent or reduced leave schedule leave is due to a serious health condition, the need for leave must be medically necessary. That means that an employee, if requested, must obtain a medical certification supporting the claim that leave is medically necessary. Additionally, the employee must make reasonable efforts to schedule the leave so as not to disrupt school operations. While such a reasonable effort does not require success, it requires more than doing nothing. Courts have consistently denied FMLA protections to employees who failed or refused to attempt to schedule their intermittent or reduced leave schedule leave to avoid workplace disruptions.

Where the request for intermittent or reduced leave schedule leave is for the birth, adoption, or foster care placement of a son or daughter, a school can outright deny the leave. The same is not true if the leave request involves a serious health condition. Of course, school administrators will not want to abuse their right to unreasonably deny leave in this situation. For example, if an employee asks for intermittent leave following the birth of a healthy child, the school would be within its rights to deny the request. The employee, however, could turn around and ask for FMLA leave in a single block of time, which the school may not be able to deny. The better course may be for the school to work with the employee to schedule the leave in a way that is least disruptive.

The federal FMLA also allows schools to transfer an employee to an equivalent alternative position that better accommodates the employee's need for FMLA leave on an intermittent or reduced leave schedule basis. A school's right to unilaterally require a transfer, however, is often circumscribed by collective bargaining agreements.

Finally, employee and employer notice requirements are affected by whether FMLA leave is taken in a single block or on an intermittent or reduced leave schedule basis.

[8] Will the Leave Be Paid or Unpaid?

FMLA leave is unpaid. The federal FMLA, however, allows employees or schools to elect to substitute accrued paid leave for unpaid leave under certain circumstances. The substitution of paid leave for unpaid FMLA leave may impact notice, documentation, and other FMLA procedural requirements. For example, if an employee elects to substitute accrued paid annual leave for unpaid FMLA leave, the employee may only have to meet any less stringent notice and documentation requirements governing paid annual leave.

Of course, there are rules governing the circumstances under which an employee or school may elect to substitute paid leave for unpaid FMLA leave. More fundamentally, there is disagreement on what constitutes "substitution." Most courts interpret "substitution" narrowly such that the protections of the FMLA continue with the caveat that the employee is on paid FMLA leave. A few courts have taken a very different approach. They interpret "substitution" more literally to mean that the leave is paid and no longer protected by the FMLA.

1.06 CONCLUSION

Given its modest goal of providing employees with a reasonable period of job-protected leave to attend to family matters, the federal FMLA is a deceptively complicated entitlement to administer. The complexity of the law, coupled with the prospect of substantial school and individual liability for even inadvertent violations of employee FMLA rights, strongly counsels that school administrators exercise great care when addressing employee requests for FMLA leave. In that regard, this guide is intended to aid school administrators responsible for leave and attendance administration by providing a greater understanding of the requirements of the FMLA.

NOTES

1. The book does not address the Family and Medical Leave Act as it applies to schools and school employees employed by the federal government. For a discussion of the application of the FMLA to employees of the federal government, see Carl C. Bosland, *A Federal Sector Guide to the Family and Medical Leave Act & Related Litigation* (Dewey Publications 2003).
2. S. Rep. No. 103-3, at 20 (1993), as reprinted in 1993 U.S.C.C.A.N. 3, 22.
3. 29 C.F.R. § 825.207(b).
4. Alaska Stat. §§ 39.20.305–39.20.330, 39.20.500–39.20.550; Cal. Govt. Code §§ 12945.2, 19072.3; Conn. Gen. Stat. §§ 31-51kk to 31-51qq, 5-248a, 5-248b; D.C. Code Ann. §§ 32-501 to -516, 32-701 to -705; Fla. Stat. §§ 110.221; Haw. Rev. Stat. Ann. §§ 398-1 to -29; Me. Rev. Stat. Ann. tit. 26, §§ 843–848; N.J. Stat. Ann. §§ 34:11B-1 to -16; N.D. Cent. Code § 54-52.4-01 to -10; Okla. Stat. Ann. tit. 74, § 840-2.22; Or. Rev. Stat. Ann. §§ 659A.150–659A.186; R.I.

Gen. Laws § 28-48-1 to -11; Tex. Govt. Code Ann. § 661.912; Vt. Stat. Ann. tit. 21, §§ 470–474; Va. Code Ann. §§ 51.1-1107 to -1108; W. Va. Code § 21-5D-1 to -9; Wis. Stat. Ann. § 103.10.

5. Ariz. Admin. Code §§ R2-5-411 to -413; 4 Colo. Code Regs. § 801; Idaho Admin. Code r. 242.

6. Wash. Rev. Code § 49.78.005.

7. Ark. Code Ann. § 21-4-209; Ind. Code § 20.6.1-6.4; Iowa Code §§ 216.6, 70A.1; Kan. Admin. Regs. § 21–32–6; La. Rev. Stat. Ann. §§ 23:341 to :342; Md. Ann. Code art. 49B, § 17; Mass. Gen. Laws. Ann. ch. 149, § 105D; Mont. Code Ann. § 49-2-310; Nev. Rev. Stat. Ann. § 284.360; N.H. Rev. Stat. Ann. § 354-A; Tenn. Code Ann. §§ 8-50-806, 8-50-802 (paternity leave); Wash. Admin. Code 162-30-020.

8. Del. Code Ann. tit. 29, §§ 5116, 5120; Ill. Admin. Code tit. 80, § 420.645; Ky. Rev. Stat. Ann. § 337.015; Md. Code Ann., Lab. & Empl. § 3-802; Minn. Stat. § 181.941; Mo. Ann. Stat. § 105.271; Mont. Code Ann. § 2-18-606; Neb. Rev. Stat. § 71-4820; Nev. Rev. Stat. Ann. § 284.360; N.Y. Lab. Law § 201-c; Ohio Rev. Code Ann. § 124.136; 16 Pa. Code § 41.104; S.C. Code Ann. § 8-11-155; S.D. Codified Laws § 3-6-7; Tenn. Code Ann. § 8-50-806; Tex. Govt. Code Ann. §§ 661.912, 661.906 (foster parent leave).

9. For a further discussion of the demographic trends that animated the enactment of the Family and Medical Leave Act of 1993, see S. Rep. No. 3, at 5–2(1993), as reprinted in 1993 U.S.C.C.A.N. 3, 7–14.

10. Steven K. Wisensale, *Family Leave Policy: The Political Economy of Work and Family in America* 89 (Sharpe 2001).

11. *Id.*

12. *Id.* at 88.

13. *Id.* at 88–89 (citing Arlie Hochschild, *The Second Shift: Working Parents and the Revolution at Home* (Viking Press 1989) and Arlie Hochschild, *The Time Bind* (Holt 1997)).

14. Council of Economic Advisors, *Families and the Labor Market, 1969–1999: Analyzing the Time Crunch* 12 (1999), available at http://www.newecon.org/ParentingDeficitCEA-May99.html.

15. S. Rep. No. 103-3, at 5–7 (1993), as reprinted in 1993 U.S.C.C.A.N. 3, 7–9.

16. *Id.* at 7, as reprinted in 1993 U.S.C.C.A.N. at 9.

17. *Id.*

18. *Id.*

19. *Id.* at 6, as reprinted in 1993 U.S.C.C.A.N. at 8.

20. *Id.*

21. *Id.* at 6, as reprinted in 1993 U.S.C.C.A.N. at 8.

22. *Id.* at 7, as reprinted in 1993 U.S.C.C.A.N. at 9.

23. *Id.* at 6–7, as reprinted in 1993 U.S.C.C.A.N. at 8–9.

24. *Id.*

25. *Id.* at 7, as reprinted in 1993 U.S.C.C.A.N. at 9.

26. *Id.*

27. *Id.*

28. *Id.*

29. *Id.* at 19–20, as reprinted in 1993 U.S.C.C.A.N. at 21–22.

30. *Id.* at 20, as reprinted in 1993 U.S.C.C.A.N. at 22.

31. *Id.* at 19, as reprinted in 1993 U.S.C.C.A.N. at 21.

32. *Id.*

33. *Id.*

34. *Id.*

35. Wisensale, *supra* note 10, at 118, 127–28.

36. S. Rep. No. 103-3, at 33, as reprinted in 1993 U.S.C.C.A.N. at 35.

37. Wisensale, *supra* note 10, at 221.

38. S. Rep. No. 103-3, at 19, as reprinted in 1993 U.S.C.C.A.N. at 21.

39. *Id.*

40. *Id.*

41. *Id.* at 19, as reprinted in 1993 U.S.C.C.A.N. at 21.

42. *Id.* at 20, as reprinted in 1993 U.S.C.C.A.N. at 22.

43. *Id.*

44. *Id.* at 20–21, as reprinted in 1993 U.S.C.C.A.N. at 22–23.

45. *Id.* at 20, as reprinted in 1993 U.S.C.C.A.N. at 22.

46. *Id.*

47. *Id.*

48. Anya E. Bernstein, *The Moderation Dilemma: Legislative Coalitions and the Politics of Family and Medical Leave* (University of Pittsburgh Press 2001); Wisensale, *supra* note 10; see also Ronald Elving, *Conflict and Compromise: How Congress Makes the Law* (Simon & Schuster 1995); Lisa L. Tharpe, Comment, *Analysis of the Political Dynamics Surrounding the Enactment of the 1993 Family and Medical Leave Act*, 47 Emory L.J. 379 (1998).

49. Bernstein, *supra* note 48, at 92–94; Wisensale, *supra* note 10, at 109–17.

50. Wisensale, *supra* note 10, at 138–40.

51. *Id.* at 141–43.

52. *Id.* at 144–46.

53. Senate Republicans introduced amendments and orchestrated a procedural filibuster. As a result, on October 7, 1988, Senate Majority Leader Robert Byrd accused Republicans of being antifamily and pulled the bill. See Wisensale, *supra* note 10, at 145–46.

54. 29 U.S.C. § 2601(a).

55. 29 U.S.C. § 2601(b).

56. 29 U. S. C. §§ 301–306.

57. Commission on Family and Medical Leave, *A Workable Balance: Report to Congress on Family and Medical Leave Policies, Executive Summary* 8–9 (1996), available at http://www.dol.gov/esa/whd/fmla/fmla/1995Report/family.htm *and* http://eric.ed.gov/ERICDocs/data/ericdocs2/content_storage_01/0000000b/80/26/29/0f.pdf.

58. U.S. Department of Labor, *Balancing the Needs of Families and Employers: The Family and Medical Leave Surveys 2000 Update*, available at http://www.dol.gov/esa/whd/fmla/fmla/toc.htm.

59. *Id.* at section 8.3.

60. Request for Information on the Family and Medical Leave Act of 1993, 71 Fed. Reg. 69504 (Dec. 1, 2006).

61. *Id.* at 69505, 69508 (the 12 items included employee eligibility, the definition of a serious health condition, the impact of the substitution of paid leave on FMLA leave, the impact of the FMLA on employer attendance policies, light duty, essential functions, waiver of FMLA rights, employee and employer notice issues, and medical certification issues).

62. *Id.* at 69505–06.

63. Pub. L. 104-191.

64. Request for Information on the Family and Medical Leave Act of 1993, 71 Fed. Reg. 69504, 69506–07.

65. http://federalfmla.typepad.com/fmla_blog.

CHAPTER 2

Schools as FMLA-Covered Employers

2.01 OVERVIEW

The first question a school administrator must answer when faced with a request for family or medical leave is whether the school is a covered "employer" within the meaning of federal or state family and medical leave laws. A school employee must work for a covered "employer" within the meaning of federal or state family and medical leave laws in order to take job-protected family or medical leave. If the administrator concludes that the school is not an "employer" within the meaning of the federal FMLA, then the leave request is not covered by the protections of the federal FMLA and the federal FMLA inquiry is over. Of course, the leave request may fall within the scope of state family medical leave laws, the provisions of applicable collective bargaining agreements, or school policies, but it is not federal FMLA leave. On the other hand, if the school is an "employer" within the meaning of the federal FMLA, the administrator will have to ask further FMLA-related questions to ensure that the leave falls within the protections of the law.

This chapter addresses the requirements for public and private school employer coverage under federal and state family medical leave laws, with particular focus on the federal FMLA. It will address the difference between local educational agencies and other public and private schools, the treatment of contract and other special employment relationships, individual school administrators as covered "employers," and the effect of more generous school leave policies on FMLA coverage.

2.02 SCHOOL EMPLOYER COVERAGE UNDER THE FEDERAL FAMILY AND MEDICAL LEAVE ACT

[1] Local Educational Agencies and Private Elementary and Secondary Schools: Special Rules

Congress created specials rules for employees of "local educational agencies" and private elementary or secondary schools.[1] "Local educational agencies" and private elementary or secondary schools are "employers" for purposes of the FMLA, regardless of size.[2] Educational institutions covered by these special rules do not have to meet the Act's minimum 50-employee coverage test applicable to private sector employers (including some schools).[3] Employee eligibility requirements, however, are not affected.[4] Congress explained that it created these special rules based "on the belief that schools are a special institution that require special attention."[5] The special rules do not apply to other kinds of educational institutions, such as colleges and universities, trade schools, and preschools.[6] Of course, these institutions may still be covered by the FMLA as public or private employers even though the special rules for elementary and secondary schools do not apply.

The special rules contained in the FMLA define a covered "employer" as any "local educational agency," as that term is defined in the Elementary and Secondary Education Act of 1965, as amended (EASEA).[7] Generally, a "local educational agency" means a public board of education or other legally constituted public entity within a state that is responsible for administrative control or direction of public elementary or secondary schools in a city, county, township, school district, combination of school districts, or other recognized political subdivision of a state.[8]

The EASEA also defines "local educational agency" to include some elementary and secondary schools funded by the Bureau of Indian Affairs,[9] educational service agencies,[10] and state educational agencies.[11] Schools and educational entities that meet these definitions also fall within the coverage of the special rules of the federal FMLA.

As indicated above, all private elementary and secondary schools, regardless of size, are "employers" within the meaning of the FMLA.[12] What constitutes an "elementary or secondary school," however, is not defined by the FMLA or by the DOL implementing regulations. The EASEA defines "elementary school" as "a nonprofit institutional day or residential school, including a public elementary charter school, that provides elementary education, as determined by State law."[13] A "secondary school" is similarly defined by the EASEA as "a nonprofit institutional day or residential school, including a public secondary charter school, that provides secondary education, as determined under state law, except that the term does not include any education beyond grade 12."[14] Note, however, that the FMLA does not incorporate the EASEA definitions for "elementary" or "secondary" schools. They are provided here simply as a frame of reference. Preschools do not fall within the scope of the special school rules.[15]

The FMLA also does not define what the term "private" means in reference to elementary and secondary schools. Presumably it means elementary and secondary schools that are not controlled or administered by the state or other governmental institution. The "private" school reference, by its terms, also does not explicitly exclude for-profit elementary or secondary schools.

[2] Public Schools Other Than Elementary or Secondary Schools

Public schools that are not covered employers under the special rules for "local educational agencies" are covered by the FMLA but are likely not themselves "employers" within the meaning of the Act. Here, we are talking about vocational schools, community colleges, state universities, and any other public school that is not a "local educational agency" or private elementary or secondary school. One of the definitions of "employer" under the FMLA is any "public agency" as that term is defined in section 3(x) of the Fair Labor Standards Act of 1938 (FLSA), 29 U.S.C. § 203(x).[16] In relevant part, a "public agency" is defined by section 3(x) as the government of a state or political subdivision of a state, or any interstate governmental agency.[17]

Whether an entity is a "public agency," as distinguished from a private employer, is determined by whether the agency has taxing authority or whether the chief administrative officer or board (or similar entity) is elected by the voters at large or is appointed by an elected official.[18] A "state" is further defined in section 3(c) of the FLSA (29 U.S.C. § 203(c)) to include any state of the United States, the District of Columbia, or any territory or possession of the United States.[19]

For purposes of the FMLA, a state or a political subdivision of a state constitutes a single public agency and, therefore, a single "employer" for purposes of determining employee FMLA eligibility.[20] For example, a state is a single employer, a county is a single employer, and a city or town is a single employer for purposes of determining employee eligibility.[21] Questions about whether a particular public entity is a separate public agency or a part of another public agency are generally controlled by reference to the U.S. Census Bureau's "Census of Governments."[22] Every 5 years the Census Bureau takes a census of the number, location, and type of state and local governments throughout the United States.[23] The results of this census are available to the general public.[24] For a public entity that was formed after the most recent publication of the census, whether that entity is a single public agency is determined by application of the census criteria, including existence as an organized entity, governmental character, and degree of autonomy of the entity.[25]

All public agencies are covered by the FMLA regardless of the number of employees; they are not subject to the 50-employee threshold that private sector employers (including private sector schools, other than elementary or secondary schools) are subject to.[26] Employees of covered public agencies, however, must still meet all FMLA eligibility requirements, including the requirement that the public agency employ 50 employees at the worksite or within 75 miles.[27]

Given how a "public agency" is defined, most non-elementary/secondary public schools will not be considered separate "employers" for purposes of the FMLA. Rather, these schools will be viewed as part of a larger state, county, town, multijurisdictional, or other "public agency" employer. In any case, non-elementary/secondary public school employees are covered by the federal FMLA. The significance of a public school not being a separate public agency "employer" for FMLA purposes is threefold. First, FMLA obligations are imposed on employers. As such, for most non-elementary/secondary public schools, the rights and responsibilities technically attach to the larger public agency employer, not the individual school. For example, the responsibility to post FMLA notices and to keep required records runs only to FMLA-covered employers, not individual public schools. Of course, there is nothing preventing the larger public agency employer with the FMLA legal responsibilities from delegating those responsibilities as a management matter to local schools within that public agency's jurisdiction.

Second, since only "employers" can be sued for damages for FMLA violations, non-elementary/secondary public schools cannot be named defendants in an FMLA lawsuit by aggrieved employees.[28] Rather, suit would have to be brought against the larger school employer—for example, the city, county, or state. However, as will be discussed in subsection [6] below, individual public school administrators may be sued for federal FMLA violations.

Third, employee eligibility for FMLA leave is based on meeting minimum periods of employment and minimum employee–head count thresholds. If an individual public school does not meet the definition of a "public agency" employer for purposes of the FMLA, those eligibility calculations will necessarily expand to include the larger public school entity.[29]

Finally, I would be remiss if I did not mention that the U.S. Supreme Court recently settled a split in the federal courts in favor of application of the federal FMLA to state and local governments as "public agency" employers. Addressing a growing split in the federal circuit courts, the Supreme Court held, in *Nevada Department of Human Resources v. Hibbs*, that the Eleventh Amendment of the U.S. Constitution does not bar application of Title I of the FMLA to the states.[30] The Supreme Court found that Congress acted within its constitutional authority when it applied the FMLA to state and local governments as public agency "employers."

[3] Private Schools Other Than Elementary or Secondary Schools

Unlike public schools, private non-elementary/secondary schools are not automatically covered by the federal FMLA. Rather, these schools must meet one of the other definitions of "employer" contained in the Act. The primary definition of a covered private sector "employer" for purposes of the federal FMLA is as follows:

> (A) In general. The term "employer"—
>
> (i) means any person engaged in commerce in any industry or activity affecting commerce who employees 50 or more employees for each

> working day during each of 20 or more calendar workweeks in the current or preceding calendar year.[31]

This definition contains several defined terms requiring closer examination.

(i) FMLA-Covered Employer: Three Required Elements

There are three statutory elements of this definition of employer: (1) any person (2) who engages in an activity affecting commerce (3) who employees 50 or more employees for each working day during each of 20 or more calendar workweeks of the current or preceding calendar year. These elements have been liberally interpreted by the courts because Congress intended a broad and inclusive definition of "employer."[32] A review of these essential elements follows.

(A) Any Person

The FMLA defines a "person" by cross-reference to the FLSA definition of "person" contained in 29 U.S.C. § 203(a).[33] The FLSA broadly defines a "person" to include an "individual, partnership, association, corporation, business trust, legal representative, and any organized group of persons."[34] A public agency is also included within the definition of a "person" for purposes of the FMLA.[35] Plainly, private non-elementary/secondary schools, however structured, would fit within the broad definition of a "person."

(B) Engaged in an Activity Affecting Commerce

To be an FMLA-covered private sector employer, the "person" must be "engaged in an activity affecting commerce."[36] "Commerce" and "industry affecting commerce" are defined by cross-reference to the definition of those terms contained in section 501(1) and (3) of the Labor Management Relations Act of 1947, 29 U.S.C. § 142(1), (3).[37] Pursuant to that definition, "commerce" and "industry or activity affecting commerce" mean "any activity, business, or industry in commerce or in which a labor dispute would hinder or obstruct commerce or the free flow of commerce."[38] The Supreme Court has broadly interpreted this language.[39] Schools are "engaged in an industry or activity affecting commerce."[40] Moreover, private non-elementary/secondary schools that meet the so-called 50/20 test are deemed to be engaged in commerce or in an industry or activity affecting commerce.[41]

(C) The 50/20 Test

Pursuant to the so-called 50/20 test, the final requirement for coverage as an FMLA "employer" is that the person engaged in an industry or activity affecting commerce employ 50 or more employees for each working day during each of 20 or more calendar workweeks in the current or preceding calendar year.[42] The FMLA defines "employ" to have the same meaning as that term has under the FLSA (29 U.S.C. § 203(c), (e)).[43] Under the FLSA definition, an individual is "employed" where he or she is "suffered or permitted to work."[44] Under this broad definition, an employer-employee relationship may arise based simply on the employer's knowledge that a person is performing work for the employer.[45] Independent contractors are not "employed" by an employer. Rather, independent contractors are engaged in the furtherance of their own business, as distinguished from an employee "who follows the usual path of an employee and is dependent on the business which he [or] she serves."[46]

The DOL regulations provide the method for counting employees for purposes of the 50/20 test. Excluded from this employee head count are employees located outside the United States. The FMLA applies only to employees who are employed within any state of the United States, the District of Columbia, or any territory or possession of the United States. Employees who are employed outside these areas are not counted for purposes of employer coverage (the 50/20 test) and employee eligibility.[47] For example, a private trade school with offices in Hawaii and Japan would count only the employees in Hawaii for purposes of the 50/20 test.

Any employee whose name appears on the employer's payroll is considered employed each working day of the calendar week and must be counted whether or not compensation is received for the week.[48] Full- and part-time employees are counted.[49] Employees on paid or unpaid leave, including FMLA leave, other leaves of absence, vacation, sick leave, and disciplinary suspension are counted as long as the employer has a reasonable expectation that the employees will later return to active employment.[50]

Where the employment relationship has been severed, such as where the employee has been temporarily or permanently laid off, the employee is not counted for purposes of the 50/20 test.[51] Similarly, an employee who is permanently disabled from work would not reasonably be expected to return to work and, therefore, may be excluded from the employee head count for the 50/20 test.[52] So long as there is a reasonable expectation of return to work, employees on long-term disability count toward the 50/20 test.[53] Whether there is a reasonable expectation that an employee will later return to work is necessarily a fact-specific inquiry.

Employees who work only part of a workweek do not count toward the 50/20 test. For example, a new employee who does not begin to work for an employer until after the first working day of a calendar week, or who terminates employment before the last working day of a calendar week, is not considered employed on each working day of that calendar week and, therefore, does not count toward the 50/20 test.[54]

The 20 workweeks during which 50 or more employees must have been employed need not be consecutive.[55] The test merely requires that, out of the 52 calendar weeks in a calendar year, the employer had 50 or more employees on the payroll for any 20 (or more) of those weeks.[56] Moreover, the requirement that employees be employed for *each working day* of 20 or more workweeks does not mean that every employee actually performs work on each working day to be counted for purposes of the 50/20 test. Again, the test is satisfied so long as the employees are maintained on the payroll for each working day of the week. For example, a private trade school that is open for public business 5 days a week will be considered to have all of its employees, who are regularly maintained on its payroll, "employed for each working day," even though only a few of its employees, such as security guards or maintenance personnel, perform work over the weekend.[57]

Finally, once a private non-elementary/secondary school meets the 50/20 test, the school remains covered by the FMLA for the remainder of that calendar year and all of the next calendar year, even if the school ceases to satisfy the 50/20 test. For example, if a private trade school that met the 50/20 test as of August 5, 2003, subsequently dropped below the 50-employee threshold before the end of 2003 and continued to employ fewer than 50 employees throughout 2004, the employer would continue to be covered by the FMLA throughout calendar year 2004 because it met the 50/20 test during 2003, the preceding calendar year.[58] This result is mandated by the definition of a private sector employer under the Act.[59]

(ii) A Note on Federal FMLA Coverage of Religious Schools

The DOL has observed that there is "nothing elsewhere in the legislation or in the legislative history to suggest that Congress intended religious institutions to be excluded from this definition."[60] Given the broad reach of the "affecting commerce" test, the DOL has opined that churches will almost certainly meet that coverage requirement.[61] As such, FMLA coverage of church employees will be found if the church meets the 50/20 test.[62] There may, however, be cases where, notwithstanding an employer's meeting the "affecting commerce" and 50/20 tests, a religious school or employees of that school fall outside the scope of the federal FMLA pursuant to the Free Exercise Clause of the First Amendment to the Constitution.[63]

The Free Exercise Clause precludes application of the Americans with Disabilities Act of 1990 and all other employment laws to employees of religious organizations, such as ministers, teachers, and other individuals whose duties are "integral to the spiritual and pastoral mission."[64] Identified as the "ministerial exception," the rule is meant to prevent encroachment by the government into an area of religious freedom that it is forbidden to enter under the principles of the Free Exercise Clause.[65] Most federal courts of appeals have embraced the ministerial exception in the context of federal employment laws.[66] State courts have also applied a similar ministerial exception to actions brought pursuant to state employment-discrimination laws.[67] The ministerial exception applies to the federal FMLA.[68]

As a general rule, if the employee's primary duties consist of teaching, spreading the faith, running the church, supervising a religious order, or supervising or participating in religious ritual and worship, he or she should be considered clergy and within the scope of the ministerial exception.[69] Courts are precluded from considering whether the religious entity's motivation for its employment-related decision was religious or secular in nature.[70] The ministerial exception has been found to apply to a professor of canon law at a Catholic university,[71] faculty at a seminary,[72] and a teacher at a private church-affiliated elementary school.[73] It has also been found to apply to the communications director and music director for a church.[74] Where the ministerial exception is found to apply, the First Amendment and Free Exercise Clause preclude a court from exercising jurisdiction over FMLA claims.[75]

School administrators at religious schools should consult with counsel to determine if the ministerial exception applies to the employee asserting the right to leave under the federal FMLA or state family and medical leave laws.

[4] Determining Who Is an FMLA-Covered Employer Where There May Be Multiple Employers

Normally, the legal entity that employs the employee is the "employer" for purposes of the FMLA.[76] For example, a corporation, rather than any of its various divisions, is generally the employer under the FMLA.[77] Sometimes, however, the determination of FMLA employer status in the private sector is clouded due to the presence of separate but related legal entities that both employ employees. For example, ABC Corporation may own a private high school. It may also own an interest in XYZ Corporation, which owns a business school. Generally, where one corporation has an ownership interest in another corporation, each corporation is treated as a separate employer for purposes of the FMLA with two exceptions.[78] Employees of seemingly separate entities may be considered employees of a single employer for FMLA purposes, including the 50/20 test and all other compliance matters, if they are "integrated" or "joint" employers.[79]

Note that the "integrated employer" and "joint employment" tests have limited impact on employer coverage of public or private elementary or secondary schools because those employers are automatically covered regardless of size. For the same reason, these tests have limited impact on the coverage of non-elementary/secondary public school employers because, as public agencies, these schools are covered employers regardless of size. However, the addition of employees by means of the "integrated employer" test or the "joint employment" test may impact public and private school employee eligibility to take FMLA leave. Employee eligibility is addressed in Chapter 3, *Employee Eligibility*.

(i) Integrated Employers

Under the "integrated employer" test, two or more companies may be considered so interrelated that they are deemed to constitute a single employer.[80] The test was not created solely for purposes of the FMLA.[81] Rather, the "integrated employer" test is based on established case law first arising under the Labor Management Relations Act and Title VII of the Civil Rights Act of 1964.[82] Factors considered in determining whether two or more entities are an "integrated employer" include (1) common management, (2) interrelation between operations, (3) centralized control of labor relations, and (4) degree of common ownership or financial control.[83] No single factor is controlling; instead, the entire relationship is reviewed based on the totality of the circumstances.[84] Nor must all factors be present in order for two or more

FMLA Illustrated: Integrated Employer

Early Learning, Inc., is a corporation owned by Derek and Deborah Bok. Early Learning owns and runs six Li'l Einstein preschools in the Denver, Colorado, area. It also owns a 50 percent share in Flat Irons, Inc., which owns and operates two Li'l Einstein preschools in Boulder, Colorado. Early Learning's partner in Flat Irons is the Boks' daughter, Barbara. Derek and Deborah Bok serve on the board of directors for Flat Irons, and Barbara serves on the board of Early Learning. To defray costs, Early Learning and Flat Irons jointly purchase supplies and services. They use the same accountant, although they have separate accounts. Deborah Bok helps her daughter with all hiring decisions and personnel matters, including discipline.

Early Learning has 41 full- and part-time employees. Flat Irons has 10 full- and part-time employees.

Question: Are Early Learning and Flat Irons an integrated employer covered by the FMLA?

Answer: Probably so. Addressing the four factors in 29 C.F.R. § 825.104(c)(2), we see that they share common ownership and management, there is some interrelationship in operations as evidenced by joint purchases of services and supplies, and the participation of Deborah Bok in personnel decisions suggests some degree of centralized labor relations. As an integrated employer, Early Learning and Flat Irons must count the total number of employees at both companies for purposes of determining FMLA coverage. In this case the total number of employees is 51, which is sufficient for FMLA coverage.

entities to be considered an integrated employer.[85] The control of labor relations, however, has been accorded substantially more weight than the other factors.[86]

(ii) Joint Employment: Temporary or Contract Employees

Joint employment refers to the situation in which two or more employers share control over the same employee.[87]Joint employment may arise where the employee performs work that simultaneously benefits two or more employers or where the employee works for two or more employers at different times during the workweek.[88] According to the DOL regulations, a joint employment relationship generally will be considered to exist

- where there is an arrangement between employers to share an employee's services or to interchange employees;
- where one employer acts directly or indirectly in the interest of the other employer in relation to the employee; or
- where the employers are not completely disassociated with respect to the employee's employment and may be deemed to share control of the employee, directly or indirectly, because one employer controls, is controlled by, or is under common control with the other employer.[89]

These employers may be separate and distinct entities with separate owners, managers, and facilities.[90] The employment of an employee from a temporary-help agency or employee-leasing company typically results in a joint employment relationship.[91]

(A) Economic Realities Test

Because the FMLA is a relatively new and, therefore, undeveloped law, the DOL and courts have looked to well-established principles for joint employment developed under the Fair Labor Standards Act.[92] Joint employment for purposes of the FLSA is determined by application of the "economic realities test."[93] The focus of this test is on the economic reality of the whole relationship between two or more entities and is not limited by contractual language or traditional concepts of "employee" or "independent contractor."[94] Rather, whether a joint employment relationship exists depends on the totality of the circumstances.[95] Factors cited by courts to determine the "economic realities" of the relationship between enterprises include

- the nature and degree of control of employees;
- whether the alleged employer had the power to hire employees;
- the extent to which the alleged employer supervised and controlled employee work schedules and other conditions of employment;
- the power held by the alleged employer to determine the method and rates of employee pay; and
- whether the alleged employer prepared the payroll and paid wages.[96]

The factors relied on by the courts are not written in stone.[97] No single factor is determinative of a joint employment relationship.[98] Rather, Congress intended that the definitions of "employer" and "employee" be broadly inclusive in determining whether joint employment exists.[99]

(B) Primary and Secondary Employers

The FMLA responsibilities of each employer in a joint employment relationship depend on whether the employer is determined to be a "primary" or "secondary" employer.[100] Primary employers are responsible for providing required FMLA notices to employees, providing FMLA leave, maintaining health benefits during FMLA leave, and restoring employee jobs at the conclusion of leave.[101] In the typical joint employment relationship, the temporary-help or employee-leasing agency is the primary employer of a joint employee.[102]

Secondary employers are responsible for accepting the return of a joint employee from FMLA leave and complying with the prohibited-acts provisions of the FMLA.[103] The responsibility of a secondary employer to accept the return of a joint employee from FMLA leave, however, is not absolute. The secondary employer is required to accept the return of a joint employee from FMLA leave only if that employer continues to use an employee from the primary employer (e.g., a temporary-help agency) and, in this example, the temporary-help agency elects to place the joint employee with the secondary employer.[104] If the secondary employer discontinues the use of the temporary agency's services altogether or if at the time the joint employee was ready to return to work that employee's services were no longer needed, the secondary employer would not be obligated to accept the return of the joint employee from FMLA leave.[105]

FMLA Illustrated: Joint Employment and Job Restoration

Diana Keel is employed by Substitute Teacher on Call (STOC), an agency supplying temporary substitute teachers for public and private schools. STOC assigns Keel to work for schools in a three-county area. STOC pays Keel directly and bills the schools where she works for her time. STOC assigns Keel to teach a tenth-grade social studies class at Piedmont Academy, a private high school. The assignment is expected to last 8 weeks while the full-time teacher recovers from surgery. Three weeks into the assignment, Keel asks for 1 week of FMLA leave to care for her minor son who was seriously injured a car accident.

Question: For FMLA purposes, identify the primary and secondary employers of Keel.

Answer: Keel's primary employer is STOC. The secondary employer is Piedmont Academy.

Question: Must Piedmont Academy return Keel to her temporary teaching position at the conclusion of her FMLA leave?

Answer: Yes, but only if Piedmont Academy used STOC to replace Keel for the week she was out and STOC decided to return Keel to Piedmont Academy. If Piedmont Academy discontinued using STOC during Keel's absence or if STOC decided to send Keel somewhere else, Piedmont Academy would not be obligated as a secondary employer to accept the return of Keel to her temporary position at the conclusion of her FMLA leave.

Return to work issues are comprehensively addressed in Chapter 11, *Return to Work from Family and Medical Leave*.

(C) FMLA Coverage and Eligibility

Employees jointly employed by two or more employers must be counted by both employers, whether or not the individual is maintained on both employers' payrolls, for purposes of determining FMLA coverage (i.e., the 50/20 test) and employee eligibility.[106] Each joint employer adds the number of joint employees to the number of permanent employees it has to determine whether the employer, primary or secondary, meets the 50/20 test for FMLA coverage. The permanent employees of each joint employer are not counted by the other employer to determine FMLA coverage or employee eligibility.[107]

FMLA Illustrated: Joint Employment and FMLA Coverage

Piedmont Academy has 43 permanent employees. Three of these employees are on paid maternity leave and have been replaced with temporary workers through Academics-On-Call, a temporary-help agency. Academics-On-Call has 25 permanent employees. The school also employs a total of 4 temporary coaches through Academics-On-Call throughout the academic year for various sports programs.

Question: Identify the primary and secondary employers.

Answer: Academics-On-Call is the primary employer of the temporary workers assigned to Piedmont Academy. Piedmont Academy is the secondary employer for these temporary workers.

Question: Does Piedmont Academy meet the requirements for FMLA coverage? How many employees does it have for purposes of determining FMLA coverage?

Answer: Piedmont Academy may meet the 50/20 test for coverage by the FMLA. The 43 permanent employees of Piedmont, including the 3 employees on maternity leave because they remain on the payroll, count toward the 50/20 test. Added to that number are the 3 temporary employees filling in for the employees on maternity leave, as well as the 4 temporary coaches used during the academic year. They are added to Piedmont's employee head count because they are joint employees. The 25 permanent employees of Academics-On-Call do not count toward Piedmont's FMLA employee head count because they are not joint employees.

From the facts given, Piedmont has 50 employees during parts of the academic year. For FMLA coverage, however, Piedmont would have to employ 50 employees for at least 20 workweeks during the calendar year. It is not clear from the facts whether Piedmont has met this requirement.

[5] Successor Employers

The general definition of an FMLA-covered "employer" includes "any successor in interest of an employer."[108] A "successor employer" is one who takes over the operations of another employer that was covered by the FMLA. The "successor in interest" rules define the FMLA responsibilities of the successor employer.

(i) Successor Responsibilities

When an employer is determined to be a "successor in interest," the successor employer is responsible for maintaining FMLA entitlements as if the employment by the predecessor and successor were continuous employment by a single employer.[109] This is true whether or not the successor employer is otherwise a covered "employer" within the meaning of the FMLA.[110] As such, if the predecessor was an FMLA-covered "employer," the successor must honor all of the predecessor's FMLA responsibilities, including allowing eligible employees to take requested FMLA leave and to continue any FMLA leave that began while employed by the predecessor, maintaining benefits during employee FMLA leave, and restoring employees to work at the conclusion of their leave.[111]

Note, however, that the continuing FMLA obligations of the successor employer vis-à-vis predecessor employees are not endless. If the successor employer is not otherwise a covered employer within the meaning of the FMLA, the successor's FMLA obligations are limited to completing the cycle of any FMLA leave requests initiated by the predecessor's employees who met the eligibility criteria at the time the leave was requested.[112] Once the cycle of FMLA leave requests pending at the time of succession has been completed, a successor that is not otherwise covered by the FMLA is not obligated, and indeed has no legal standing, to grant FMLA leave.

If the successor is itself a covered "employer" within the meaning of the FMLA, the successor must count periods of employment and hours worked for the predecessor for purposes of determining employee eligibility for FMLA leave.[113]

Employees have no greater FMLA rights because of the intervention of a successor employer. While, as set forth above, a successor employer is generally obligated to continue FMLA benefits to predecessor employees, the obligation is not without limitation. For example, if a successor employer were to decide to eliminate the position held by a predecessor employee on FMLA leave at the time of the takeover and the job elimination was for legitimate, nondiscriminatory business reasons independent of the taking of FMLA leave, the successor would not be obligated to continue the employee's leave, maintain health benefits, or accept the return of the employee upon completion of FMLA leave. Rather, the successor could terminate the predecessor employee on FMLA leave.[114] Of course, school administrators contemplating such action would want to be doubly sure their legitimate business reasons for terminating the employee could withstand an expected contractual or legal challenge.

If, however, the successor employer decided to continue the position held by a predecessor employee, the successor generally would be obligated to accept the return of that employee upon completion of FMLA leave. The successor employer would also be obligated to maintain that employee's health benefits until the employee returned from FMLA leave, as required by the FMLA.[115]

(ii) Determining Whether an Employer Is a Successor in Interest

The DOL regulations identify eight factors that are relevant in determining whether an employer is a "successor in interest" for purposes of the FMLA:[116]

- Substantial continuity of the same business operation
- Use of the same plant
- Continuity of the work force
- Similarity of jobs and working conditions
- Similarity of supervisory personnel
- Similarity in machinery, equipment, and production methods
- Similarity of products or services
- The ability of the predecessor to provide relief

No one single factor is determinative; rather, the determination is made based on the totality of the circumstances.[117] The factors used for the FMLA successor-in-interest determination are the same as those considered for purposes of Title VII of the Civil Rights Act of 1964 and the Vietnam Era Veterans' Adjustment Act.[118] Courts have also looked to the Labor Management Relations Act to determine FMLA successor-in-interest status.[119]

But whereas notice is a relevant consideration under Title VII, employer notice of a predecessor employee's claim to FMLA rights and benefits is not a consideration for purposes of the FMLA successor-in-interest determination.[120] As such, and as discussed above, a successor employer is obligated to continue the predecessor's FMLA obligations to predecessor employees whether or not the successor was on notice of predecessor employee claims to FMLA rights. However, whether or not the successor employer had notice of predecessor employee claims to FMLA rights is relevant for purposes of determining successor liability for any FMLA violations by the predecessor.[121]

Courts applying these factors have made the successor-in-interest determination shortly before or shortly after the effective date of the succession.[122] One court examined the DOL factors from the aggrieved employee's viewpoint, inquiring whether an employee who has been retained by a successor would understandingly view his or her job as being unaltered.[123]

Finally, the successor-in-interest doctrine applies in both the public and private sectors. While perhaps more prevalent in the private sector where succession is accomplished by the purchase of one business by another, the DOL regulations recognize that a public agency can be a successor in interest for purposes of the FMLA. For example, the DOL recognized that the Resolution Trust Corporation, a federal entity, could be a successor in interest of a covered employer when it assumes control over a failed thrift as part of the resolution process.[124] And a court found that an incoming sheriff was a successor in interest to his predecessor.[125] As such, schools that are purchased (private schools) or taken over or merged (private or public schools) by a public agency are subject to the FMLA "successor in interest" requirements.

[6] Individual School Administrators and Managers as FMLA-Covered "Employers"

The FMLA definition of "employer" includes "any person who acts, directly or indirectly, in the interest of an employer to any of the employees of such employer."[126] In this regard, according to the regulatory history, this definition of "employer" is the same as that under the Fair Labor Standards Act (29 U.S.C. § 203(d)).[127] Under established FLSA case law, corporate officers, managers, and supervisors acting in the interest of an employer can be held individually liable for violations of the law.[128] The FMLA similarly provides that individuals such as corporate officers acting in the interest of an employer are individually liable for any violations of the FMLA.[129] The majority of courts interpreting this FMLA provision have looked to the FLSA for guidance.[130]

The significance of including individuals within the definition of an FMLA-covered employer is that aggrieved employees and the DOL may sue and obtain damages from an "employer."[131] That means that in addition to suing the private or public sector entity employing the employee, the aggrieved employee may bring a suit for monetary damages against individual school administrators and managers involved in the errant decision that deprived the employee of his or her FMLA rights.[132] As set forth more fully in Chapter 14, *Prohibited Acts, Enforcement, and Remedies*, FMLA damage awards and attorneys' fees can easily run into the hundreds of thousands of dollars for even inadvertent FMLA violations.

> Individual school administrators may be personally liable for monetary damages that can reach into the hundreds of thousands of dollars for even inadvertent FMLA violations.

Notwithstanding the seemingly clear language that individuals acting in the interest of a covered employer may be personally liable, courts interpreting the FMLA are split on personal liability of individual managers and supervisors for FMLA violations and whether individual liability can attach to managers in the public sector.

With respect to the private sector, the majority of courts have found that individual managers and supervisors can be held liable as "employers" for violations of the FMLA.[133] A distinct minority of courts have found that the FMLA does not provide for individual manager or supervisor liability in the private sector.[134]

Similarly, the majority of courts that have addressed the issue in public sector cases have found in favor of individual liability of public managers and supervisors as FMLA "employers."[135] However, a minority of courts have found against individual liability under a variety of theories.[136] In *Wascura v. Carver*, for example, the Eleventh Circuit followed one of its prior decisions, which found that individuals are not liable as "employers" for FLSA violations.[137]

In *Lizzie v. Alexander*, the Fourth Circuit found that the Eleventh Amendment barred suit under the FMLA against individual state officials. In light of the Supreme Court's decision in *Nevada Department of Human Resources v. Hibbs* rejecting the argument that the Eleventh Amendment barred FMLA coverage of state and local governments,[138] it is doubtful that the reasoning of *Lizzie* will survive.

Finally, the federal district courts in *Keene v. Rinaldi* and *Johnson v. Runyon* found no individual liability for public sector managers based on an exacting reading of the statutory and regulatory definition of a covered "employer." Essentially, the courts in *Keene* and *Johnson* found that individual liability is not referenced in the "public agency" definition of "employer" and, therefore, individual liability applies only to individual managers in the private sector. This reasoning has been taken to task by several courts.[139]

The courts are split on the individual liability of school employees for FMLA violations. In *Hewett v. Willingboro Board of Education*, the New Jersey federal district court held that individual public school employees could be held personally liable under the FMLA.[140] The court reached that conclusion based on its interpretation of the FMLA's general definition of "employer" at 29 U.S.C. § 2611(4).[141]

In contrast, a federal district court in Illinois recently found that individual school officials are not liable for FMLA violations.[142] In that case, the court found that while the school district was an FMLA covered employer, individual school managers did not fall within the narrower definition of "employer" set forth in 29 U.S.C. § 2618(a)(2). That section refers to the definition of a "local education agency," which does not define an employer to include individual school managers or supervisors.[143]

Of course, private or public sector school officials are not automatically liable for violations of the federal FMLA. In order for liability to attach there must be a nexus between the alleged FMLA violation suffered by the aggrieved employee and the individual acting, "directly or indirectly, in the interest of" the FMLA-covered employer. Here again, courts have looked to decisions interpreting the FLSA to determine what constitutes acting "directly or indirectly in the interest of" a covered employer.[144] Generally, an individual must have supervisory authority over the complaining party and responsibility, in whole or in part, for the alleged FMLA violation in order for that individual to be considered to have acted directly or indirectly on behalf of a covered employer.[145] The individual, however, need not have day-to-day exclusive control over the aggrieved employee, so long as he or she has control over the aspect of employment rights (under the FMLA) alleged to have been violated.[146]

Applying these principles, courts have consistently found that managers and supervisors who made the ultimate decision to terminate the aggrieved employee exercised the requisite supervisory authority to be considered an "employer" within the meaning of the act and therefore subject to personal liability under the FMLA.[147] Similarly, the individual who signed the termination letter has been held to be individually liable as an FMLA-covered employer.[148] Even mere participation by a manager or supervisor in the decision to terminate an employee has been held sufficient to incur individual liability as an "employer" for FMLA violations.[149] On the other hand, absent evidence of participation in the violative conduct, courts have dismissed FMLA suits against individual managers and supervisors.[150] In one case, a court dismissed suit against a temporary supervisor after finding that the supervisor lacked sufficient control over the employee's ability to take FMLA leave.[151]

[7] FMLA Coverage by Voluntary Agreement

Schools that are not covered "employers" within the meaning of the federal FMLA cannot come within the scope of the Act by voluntary agreement. This issue frequently arises where an employer does not meet the FMLA definition of an "employer" but nevertheless voluntarily agrees to be bound by the FMLA as a matter of policy or pursuant to the terms of a collective bargaining agreement.

The issue is complicated by statutory and regulatory language that both requires a covered employer to observe any employment benefit program or plan that provides greater family or medical leave rights to employees than the FMLA[152] and identifies any violation of the Act or the DOL regulations as actionable interference, restraint, or denial of the exercise of FMLA rights.[153] Tying these two requirements together, employees have argued that an employer's voluntary agreement to be bound by the FMLA, where the employer otherwise fails to meet the FMLA definition of an "employer," provides "greater" family and medical leave rights than required by the FMLA and, as such, brings the employer within the scope of the FMLA. Courts have uniformly rejected these arguments.[154]

Of course, the fact that a school cannot, by self-appointment, make itself an FMLA-covered employer if it does not otherwise meet the requirements for employer status does not mean that such voluntary agreement is without effect. A school's voluntary agreement to incorporate the FMLA as a matter of policy or pursuant to the terms of a collective bargaining agreement is as binding on the school as any other employment policy or collective bargaining term. As such, the school will be required to abide by the requirements of the FMLA as interpreted by the DOL and the courts. Violation of that policy would be treated like any other violation of school policy and could result in grievances or suit for breach of contract. As set forth above, an employee suit asserting a violation of the FMLA, however, would be dismissed if the school does not otherwise meet the definition of an FMLA-covered employer.

Finally, given the complexity of the federal FMLA, school administrators who are not otherwise covered by the federal FMLA should think long and hard about voluntarily agreeing to abide by the requirements of the FMLA. A school might be wiser to create its own family and medical leave policy, thereby avoiding some or all of the complexities of the federal FMLA.

2.03 SCHOOL EMPLOYER COVERAGE UNDER STATE FAMILY AND MEDICAL LEAVE LAWS

For purposes of analyzing employer coverage, state family and medical leave laws may initially be divided into three categories: (1) those that apply to public sector employers only, (2) those that apply to private sector employers only, and (3) those that apply to both public and private sector employers.

[1] Public Sector Employers Only

States that have family and medical leave laws that apply only to public sector employers include Alaska, Colorado, Florida, Massachusetts, North Dakota, Oklahoma, Texas, Utah, Virginia, West Virginia, and Wyoming.[155] The state family leave laws differ, however, regarding which public sector employers are covered. For example, Colorado's family and medical leave law applies to all full- or part-time employees in the state personnel system.[156] In Colorado, the state is considered a single employer for purposes of family and medical leave.[157] Similarly, Florida's family and medical leave law covers all state career service employees.[158] In North Dakota, an "employer" means the state but does not include any political subdivision of the state.[159] The Texas family and medical leave law applies only to a state employee employed in the executive or judicial branch of the state government.[160]

Some states define a public sector "employer" in units smaller than the entire state. For example, the Massachusetts family and medical leave law applies to all employees and managers employed in classified positions of the executive branch of the Commonwealth of Massachusetts, except those employees covered by a collective bargaining agreement.[161] The regulations issued by the Massachusetts Human Resources Division delegate the responsibilities for administering family and medical leave to an "appointing authority," defined as "a person, board, or commission with the power to appoint or employ personnel."[162]

The State of West Virginia defines an "employer" for purposes of that state's family and medical leave law to include "any department, division, board, bureau, agency, commission, or other unit of state government and any county board of education in the state."[163]

The State of Alaska defines a public "employer" for purposes of its family and medical leave law as the state and any political subdivision of the state that employed at least 21 employees in the state for each working day during any period of 20 consecutive workweeks in the preceding two calendar years.[164] Excluded from the benefits and protections of the Alaska family and medical leave law are officers, members of the teaching staff, and employees of the University of Alaska.[165] Like Massachusetts, Alaska also excludes from the benefits and protections of the state family and medical leave law persons employed by the state who are covered by a collective bargaining agreement.[166]

[2] Private Sector Employers Only

Hawaii's family and medical leave law covers private sector employers who employ 100 or more employees for each working day during each of 20 or more calendar weeks in the current or preceding calendar year.[167] Prior to July 1, 2002, the Hawaii family and medical leave law also applied to the state, its political subdivisions, and its instrumentalities. That is no longer the case. To determine coverage, an employer must include all workers on the payroll who work within Hawaii, including part-time, temporary, or interim employees regardless of their months of service or eligibility, and employees on paid or unpaid leaves of absence, including family leave or disciplinary suspension.[168] The employee head count does not include employees who are laid off or employees who do not work in Hawaii.[169] The head count is performed at the time an employee gives notice of the need for family or medical leave.[170] Hawaii incorporates the definitions of joint employment and an integrated employer from the federal FMLA.[171] An individual may be an "employer" for purposes of Hawaii's family and medical leave law.[172] Hawaii does not afford local educational agencies special recognition as employers.

[3] Both Public and Private Sector Employers

The family and medical leave laws of a number of states apply to employers in both the public and private sectors. States that include both public and private sector employers within the coverage of their family and medical leave laws include California, Connecticut, the District of Columbia, Maine, Minnesota, New Jersey, Oregon, Rhode Island, Vermont, and Wisconsin. In many cases, the state definitions of a covered employer differ from the federal FMLA definition. For example, the California Family Rights Act applies to the state and all cities and counties in California regardless of size.[173] It also applies to private sector employers who conduct business in California and who employ 50 or more employees in any state. There are no special rules governing local educational agencies. Unlike the federal FMLA, the California Family Rights Act does not define "employer" to include joint employers, successors in interest, or individuals acting in the interest of an employer.

The Oregon Family Leave Act applies to all employers who employ 25 or more persons in Oregon for each working day of 20 or more calendar workweeks in the current or preceding year.[174] Oregon's law does not recognize joint employment, integrated employers, or individuals acting on behalf of employers. Special leave provisions apply to teachers but not to local educational agencies. Interestingly, the Oregon Family Leave Act does not apply to any employer who offers eligible employees a nondiscriminatory cafeteria plan that provides leave at least as generous as the leave required by the Oregon Family Leave Act.[175]

2.04 INTERACTION OF THE FEDERAL FMLA WITH STATE FAMILY AND MEDICAL LEAVE LAWS

The federal FMLA does not supersede any provision of state or local law that provides greater family or medical leave rights than those provided by the FMLA.[176] An employer covered by one law (federal or state) and not the other has to comply only with the law under which it is covered.[177] An employer may also be concurrently covered by both the federal FMLA and state family and medical leave law. In that case, a school employer must comply with the requirements of both laws.

NOTES

1. 29 U.S.C. § 2618(a)(1)(A)–(B); 29 C.F.R. § 825.600(a).
2. 29 U.S.C. § 2618(a)(2)(B); 29 C.F.R. §§ 825.104(a), 825.600(b).
3. 29 C.F.R. § 825.600(b).
4. 29 U.S.C. § 2618(a)(1)(A); 29 C.F.R. § 825.600(b). As discussed more fully in Chapter 3, *Employee Eligibility*, one of the eligibility criteria is that the employee be employed at a worksite where there are at least 50 employees of the employer within 75 miles of the worksite.
5. S. Rep. No. 103-3, at 36 (1993), as reprinted in 1993 U.S.C.C.A.N. 3, 38.
6. 29 C.F.R. § 825.600(a).
7. 29 U.S.C. § 2618(a)(1)(A); 20 U.S.C. § 7801(26).
8. 20 U.S.C. § 7801(26); 29 C.F.R. § 825.600(a).

9. "Local educational agency" includes

> an elementary school or secondary school funded by the Bureau of Indian Affairs but only to the extent that including the school makes the school eligible for programs for which specific eligibility is not provided to the school in another provision of law and the school does not have a student population that is smaller than the student population of the local educational agency receiving assistance under this chapter with the smallest student population, except that the school shall not be subject to the jurisdiction of any State educational agency other than the Bureau of Indian Affairs.

20 U.S.C. § 7801(26)(C).

10. The term "local educational agency" includes "educational service agencies." 20 U.S.C. § 7801(26)(D). The term "educational service agency" means "a regional public multiservice agency authorized by State statute to develop, manage, and provide services or programs to local educational agencies." 20 U.S.C. § 7801(17).

11. The term "local educational agency" includes "the State educational agency in a State in which the State educational agency is the sole educational agency for all public schools." 20 U.S.C. § 7801(26)(E). "State educational agency" means "the agency primarily responsible for the State supervision of public elementary schools and secondary schools." 20 U.S.C. § 7801(41).

12. 29 C.F.R. § 825.600(b).

13. 20 U.S.C. § 7801(18).

14. 20 U.S.C. § 7801(38).

15. 29 C.F.R. § 825.600(a).

16. 29 U.S.C. § 2612(4)(A)(iii); 29 C.F.R. § 825.108(a).

17. See also 29 C.F.R. § 825.108(a).

18. 29 C.F.R. § 825.108(b).

19. See also 29 C.F.R. § 825.108(a).

20. 29 C.F.R. § 825.108(c)(1).

21. *Id.*

22. 29 C.F.R. § 825.108(c)(1)–(2); see also *Rollins v. Wilson County Government*, 967 F. Supp. 990, 993–994 (M.D. Tenn. 1997), *aff'd*, 154 F.3d 626 (6th Cir. 1998).

23. 29 C.F.R. § 825.108(c)(2).

24. Results of the census are available on the U.S. Census Bureau's website, http://www.census.gov/prod/2003pubs/gc021x1.pdf; see also 29 C.F.R. § 825.108(c)(2).

25. 29 C.F.R. § 825.108(c)(1).

26. 29 C.F.R. § 825.108(d).

27. *Id.* FMLA eligibility requirements are discussed in more detail in the next chapter.

28. The ability of school employees to sue their employers for FMLA violations is addressed in Chapter 14, *Prohibited Acts, Enforcement, and Remedies.*

29. FMLA eligibility issues are addressed in Chapter 3, *Employee Eligibility.*

30. 538 U.S. 721 (2003).

31. 29 U.S.C. § 2611(4); see also 29 C.F.R. § 825.104(a).

32. *Torres-Lopez v. May*, 111 F.3d 633, 638 (9th Cir. 1997); *Salgado v. CDW Computer Centers, Inc.*, No. 97-C-1975, 1998 U.S. Dist. LEXIS 1374, at *8 (N.D. Ill. Feb. 5, 1998); *Miller v. Defiance Metal Products, Inc.* 989 F. Supp. 945, 947 (N.D. Ohio 1997).

33. 29 U.S.C. §2611(8); 29 C.F.R. § 825.800 ("person" defined).

34. 29 U.S.C. § 203(a); see also 29 C.F.R. § 825.800 ("person" defined).

35. 29 U.S.C. § 2611(4)(B); 29 C.F.R. § 825.800 (definitions of "person" and "public agency").

36. 29 U.S.C. § 2611(4)(A)(i); 29 C.F.R. § 825.104(a).

37. 29 C.F.R. §§ 825.104(b), 825.800 ("commerce" and "industry or activity affecting commerce" defined).

38. 29 C.F.R. § 825.800 ("commerce" and "industry or activity affecting commerce" defined).

39. *NLRB v. Reliance Fuel Oil Corp.*, 371 U.S. 224 (1963).

40. DOL WH FMLA Advisory Opinion No. 76 (Nov. 30, 1995).

41. 29 C.F.R. § 825.104(b).

42. 29 U.S.C. § 2611(4)(A)(i); 29 C.F.R. § 825.104(a). According to the legislative history, this language parallels language used in Title VII of the Civil Rights Act of 1964 and is intended to receive the same interpretation. See S. Rep. No. 103-3, at 21–22 (1993), as reprinted in 1993 U.S.C.C.A.N. 3, 24.

43. 29 U.S.C. § 2611(3); see also 29 C.F.R. § 825.800 ("employ" and "employee" defined).

44. See 29 U.S.C. § 203(g); see also 29 C.F.R. § 825.800 ("employ" defined).

45. See 29 C.F.R. § 825.105(a); see also *Cunningham v. Gibson Electric Co.*, 43 F. Supp. 2d 965, 975–76 (N.D. Ill. 1999).

46. 29 C.F.R. § 825.105(a).

47. 29 C.F.R. § 825.105(b).

48. S. Rep. No. 103-3, at 22 (1993), as reprinted in 1993 U.S.C.C.A.N. 3, 24; 29 C.F.R. § 825.105(b).

49. S. Rep. No. 103-3, at 22, as reprinted in 1993 U.S.C.C.A.N. 3, 24; 29 C.F.R. § 825.105(c). In comments accompanying the final regulations, the DOL explained that part-time employees were included for purposes of the

50/20 test and eligibility pursuant to congressional intent reflected in the FMLA's legislative history. 60 Fed. Reg. 2180, 2182 (Jan. 6, 1995).

50. S. Rep. No. 103-3, at 22, as reprinted in 1993 U.S.C.C.A.N. 3, 24; 29 C.F.R. § 825.105(c).

51. 29 C.F.R. § 825.105(c).

52. See Comments on Regulations Implementing the Family and Medical Leave Act of 1993 (§ 825.105), 60 Fed. Reg. 2180, 2182 (Jan. 6, 1995).

53. See *id.*

54. S. Rep. No. 103-3, at 22, as reprinted in 1993 U.S.C.C.A.N. 3, 24; 29 C.F.R. § 825.105(d).

55. 29 C.F.R. § 825.105(e).

56. *Id.*

57. See S. Rep. No. 103-3, at 22, as reprinted in 1993 U.S.C.C.A.N. 3, 24.

58. See 29 C.F.R. § 825.105(f).

59. 29 U.S.C. § 2611(4)(A)(i) (defining private sector employer as "any person engaged in commerce or in any industry or activity affecting commerce who employees 50 or more employees of each working day during each of 20 or more calendar workweeks *in the current or preceding calendar year*" (emphasis added)); 29 C.F.R. § 825.105(f).

60. DOL WH FMLA Advisory Opinion No. 76 (Nov. 30, 1995).

61. *Id.*

62. *Id.*

63. *Id.*

64. *Fassl v. Our Lady of Perpetual Help Roman Catholic Church*, No. 05-cv-404, 2005 U.S. Dist. LEXIS 22546, at * 22 (E.D. Pa. Oct. 4, 2005) (quoting *EEOC v. Roman Catholic Diocese of Raleigh*, 213 F.3d 795, 797 (4th Cir. 2000)).

65. *Id.* (quoting *McClure v. Salvation Army*, 460 F.3d 553, 560 (5th Cir. 1972)).

66. *Id.* at * 25 (collecting cases).

67. *Id.* at * 26 (collecting cases).

68. *Id.* at * 34–36.

69. *Id.* at * 22 (quoting *Rayburn v. General Conference of Seventh-Day Adventists*, 772 F.2d 1164, 1169 (4th Cir. 1985)).

70. *Id.* (citing *Alicea-Hernandez v. Catholic Bishop of Chicago*, 320 F.3d 698, 703 (7th Cir. 2003)).

71. *EEOC v. Catholic University of America*, 83 F.3d 455, 461 (D.C. Cir. 1996).

72. *EEOC v. Southern Baptist Theological Seminary*, 651 F.2d 277, 283–85 (5th Cir. 1981), *cert. denied*, 456 U.S. 905 (1982).

73. *Clapper v. Chesapeake Conference of Seventh-Day Adventists*, No. 97-2648, 1998 U.S. App. LEXIS 32554, at *25 (4th Cir. 1998), *cert. denied*, 526 U.S. 1145 (1999).

74. *Fassl*, 2005 U.S. Dist. LEXIS 22546, at *28–29.

75. *Id.* at *36.

76. 29 C.F.R. § 825.104(c).

77. *Id.*

78. 29 C.F.R. § 825.104(c)(1).

79. 29 C.F.R. §§ 825.104(c)(1)–(2), 825.106.

80. 29 C.F.R. § 825.104(c)(2); see also *Hukill v. Autocare, Inc.*, 192 F.3d 437, 442 (4th Cir. 1999), *cert. denied*, 120 S. Ct. 1978 (2000).

81. Comments on Regulations Implementing the Family and Medical Leave Act of 1993 (§ 825.104), 60 Fed. Reg. 2180, 2181 (Jan. 6, 1995).

82. *Id.*; see also *Hukill*, 192 F. 3d at 441–442 & n.7 (4th Cir. 1999), *cert. denied*, 120 S. Ct. 1978 (2000); *Smith v. Allen Health Systems, Inc.*, No. C-99-2128, 2001 U.S. Dist. LEXIS 10547, at *6 (N.D. Iowa Mar. 30, 2001) (FMLA "integrated employer" test adopted directly from National Labor Relations Board test for determining affiliate liability).

83. 29 C.F.R. § 825.104(c)(2).

84. *Id.*; see also *Hukill*, 192 F.3d at 442; *Smith*, 2001 U.S. Dist. LEXIS 10547, at *6.

85. DOL WH Opinion Letter No. 112 (Sept. 11, 2000).

86. See *Hukill*, 192 F.3d 437 (citing fact that employers controlled own day-to-day labor relations as critical to determination that separate employers were not integrated); *Smith*, 2001 U.S. Dist. LEXIS 10547, at *6.

87. 29 C.F.R. § 825.106(a).

88. *Id.*

89. 29 C.F.R. § 825.106(a)(1)–(3).

90. 29 C.F.R. § 825.106(a).

91. 29 C.F.R. § 825.106(b); see also *Moreau v. Air France*, No. C-99-4645-VRW, 2002 U.S. Dist. LEXIS 5665, at *11–*12 (N.D. Ca. Mar. 28, 2002), *aff'd*, 343 F.3d 1179 (9th Cir. 2003). But see *Astrowsky v. First Portland Mortgage Corp.*, 887 F. Supp. 332, 336–37 (D. Me. 1995) (holding that there was no joint employment relationship where employee leasing company did not exercise sufficient control over employee on long-term lease assignment).

92. *Moreau*, 2002 U.S. Dist. LEXIS 5665, at *12–*13; *Harbert v. Health Care Services Group, Inc.*, 173 F. Supp. 2d 1101, 1105 (D. Colo. 2001); *Miller v. Defiance Metal Products, Inc.*, 989 F. Supp. 945, 947 (N.D. Ohio 1997); DOL WH FMLA Opinion No. 113 (Sept. 11, 2000).

93. See *Goldberg v. Whitaker*, 366 U.S. 28, 33 (1961); *Henderson v. Inter-Chem Coal Co.*, 41 F.3d 567, 570 (10th Cir. 1994).

94. *Henderson*, 41 F.3d at 570; *Hale v. Arizona*, 993 F.2d 1387, 1393 (9th Cir. 1992), *cert. denied*, 510 U.S. 946 (1993).

95. 29 C.F.R. § 825.106(b); see also *Moreau*, 2002 U.S. Dist. LEXIS 5665; *Harbert*, 173 F. Supp. 2d at 1104 (D. Colo. 2001); *Miller*, 989 F. Supp. at 948 n.1.

96. See *Torres-Lopez v. May*, 111 F.3d 633, 640 (9th Cir. 1997); *Bonnett v. California Health & Welfare Agency*, 704 F.2d 1465, 1470 (9th Cir. 1983).

97. *Bonnett*, 704 F.2d at 1470.

98. 29 C.F.R. § 825.106(b); see also *Bonnett*, 704 F.2d at 1469.

99. *Miller*, 989 F. Supp. at 947; see also *Nationwide Mutual Insurance v. Darden*, 503 U.S. 318, 326 (1992) (noting that the FLSA's definition of "employ" encompasses "striking breadth"); *Hale*, 993 F.2d at 1393 (explaining that the Supreme Court has instructed that courts interpret the FLSA's definition of "employ" expansively).

100. *Salgado v. CDW Computer Centers, Inc.*, No. 97-C-1975, 1998 U.S. Dist. LEXIS 1374, at *9–*10 (N.D. Ill. Feb. 5, 1998).

101. 29 C.F.R. § 825.106(c), (e).

102. 29 C.F.R. § 825.106(b).

103. 29 C.F.R. § 825.106(e).

104. *Id.*

105. See Comments on Regulations Implementing the Family and Medical Leave Act of 1993 (§ 825.106), 60 Fed. Reg. 2180, 2183 (Jan. 6, 1995).

106. 29 C.F.R. § 825.106(d); see also *Salgado*, 1998 U.S. Dist. LEXIS 1374, at *11.

107. See Comments on Regulations Implementing the Family and Medical Leave Act of 1993 (§ 825.106), 60 Fed. Reg. at 2183.

108. 29 U.S.C. § 2611(4)(A)(ii)(II); see also 29 C.F.R. §§ 825.104(a), 825.107, 825.800 ("employer" defined).

109. 29 C.F.R. § 825.107(c).

110. *Id.*

111. *Id.*

112. See Comments on Regulations Implementing the Family and Medical Leave Act of 1993 (§ 825.107), 60 Fed. Reg. at 2184.

113. 29 C.F.R. § 825.107(c).

114. See Comments on Regulations Implementing the Family and Medical Leave Act of 1993 (§ 825.107), 60 Fed. Reg. at 2184.

115. See *id.* Maintenance of health benefits and return to work issues are addressed in Chapters 10 and 11.

116. 29 C.F.R. § 825.107(a).

117. 29 C.F.R. § 825.107(b); see also *Vanderhoof v. Life Extension Institute*, 988 F. Supp. 507, 513 (D.N.J. 1997); *Rhoades v. FDIC*, 956 F. Supp. 1239, 1252–54 (D. Md. 1997), *aff'd in part, rev'd in part on other grounds*, 257 F.3d 373 (4th Cir. 2001), cert. denied, 535 U.S. 933 (2002).

118. 29 C.F.R. § 825.107(a).

119. See *Vanderhoof*, 988 F. Supp. at 512–14.

120. 29 C.F.R. § 825.107(a).

121. *Id.*; see also Comments on Regulations Implementing the Family and Medical Leave Act of 1993 (§ 825.107), 60 Fed. Reg. 2180, 2184 (Jan. 6, 1995).

122. *Vanderhoof*, 988 F. Supp. at 513 & n.2; *Rhoades*, 956 F. Supp. at 1252–54.

123. *Vanderhoof*, 988 F. Supp. at 512–14.

124. See Comments on Regulations Implementing the Family and Medical Leave Act of 1993 (§ 825.104), 60 Fed. Reg. at 2181; accord *Rhoades*, 956 F. Supp. at 1254.

125. *Joliffe v. Mitchell*, 971 F. Supp. 1039, 1041–42 (W.D. Va. 1997).

126. 29 U.S.C. § 2611(4)(A)(ii); see also 29 C.F.R. §§ 825.104(a), (d), 825.800 ("employer" defined).

127. 29 C.F.R. § 825.104(d).

128. See Comments on Regulations Implementing the Family and Medical Leave Act of 1993 (§ 825.104), 60 Fed. Reg. at 2181 (citing *Reich v. Circle C Investments, Inc.*, 998 F.2d 324 (5th Cir. 1993) and *Dole v. Elliot Travel & Tours, Inc.*, 942 F.2d 962 (6th Cir. 1991)).

129. 29 C.F.R. § 825.104(d).

130. See *Darby v. Bratch*, 287 F.3d 673, 680–81 (8th Cir. 2002); *Wascura v. Carver*, 169 F.3d 683, 685–87 (11th Cir. 1999).

131. 29 U.S.C. § 2617(a)(1)–(2); 29 C.F.R. § 825 400(a), (c).

132. The right to sue individual managers and supervisors for FMLA violations has been criticized as unnecessary to ensure compliance with the law. See Boyd Rogers, Note, *Individual Liability under the Family and Medical Leave Act of 1993: A Senseless Detour on the Road to a Flexible Workplace*, 63 Brook. L. Rev. 1299 (1997).

133. *Longstreth v. Copple*, 101 F. Supp. 2d 776, 778–79 (N.D. Iowa 2000); *Buser v. Southern Food Service, Inc.*, 73 F. Supp. 2d 556, 561 (M.D.N.C. 1999); *Carpenter v. Refrigeration Sales Corp.*, 49 F. Supp. 2d 1028, 1031 (N.D. Ohio 1999); *Bryan v. Delbar Products, Inc.*, 18 F. Supp. 2d 799, 807–08 (M.D. Tenn. 1998); *Mercer v. Borden*, 11 F. Supp. 2d 1190 (C.D. Cal. 1998); *Rupnow v. TRC, Inc.*, 999 F. Supp. 1047, 1048 n.2 (N.D. Ohio 1998). See generally Ann K. Wooster, Annotation, *Individual Liability under the Family and*

Medical Leave Act, 170 A.L.R. Fed. 561 (2001); David R. Mellon, *Individual Liability as an "Employer" under the Family and Medical Leave Act*, 22 Am J. Trial Advoc. 449 (1998).

134. See *Ariba v. Owens-Illinois, Inc.*, No. 1:02CV00111, 2003 U.S. Dist. LEXIS 9429, at *17 (M.D.N.C. June 4, 2003); *Frizzell v. Southwest Motor Freight*, 906 F. Supp. 441, 449 (E.D. Tenn. 1995), *rev'd on other grounds*, 154 F.3d 641 (6th Cir. 1998).

135. See *Darby v. Batch*, 287 F.3d 673, 680–81 (8th Cir. 2002); *Nevada Department of Human Resources v. Hibbs*, 273 F.3d 844, 871–72 (9th Cir. 2001), *aff'd on other grounds*, 538 U.S. 721 (2003); *Luder v. Endicott*, 253 F.3d 1020, 1022 (7th Cir. 2001); *Johnson v. Fayette County*, 271 F. Supp. 2d 1068, 1071–72 (W.D. Tenn. 2003); *Cantley v. Simmons*, 179 F. Supp. 2d 654, 656–58 (S.D.W.V. 2002); *Carter v. USPS*, 157 F. Supp. 2d 726, 728 (W.D. Ky. 2001); *Morrow v. Putnam*, 142 F. Supp. 2d 1271 (D. Nev. 2001).

136. See *Lizzi v. Alexander*, 255 F.3d 128, 136–38 (4th Cir. 2001), *aff'd*, 534 U.S. 1081 (2002); *Wascura v. Carver*, 169 F.3d 683, 686 (11th Cir. 1999); *Billings v. Cape Cod Child Development Program, Inc.*, 270 F. Supp. 2d 175, 177 n.1 (D. Mass. 2003); *Keene v. Rinaldi*, 127 F. Supp. 2d 770, 778 (M.D.N.C. 2000); *Johnson v. Runyon*, No. 1:97-CV-794, 1999 U.S. Dist. LEXIS 5748, at *11–*13 (W.D. Mich. Apr. 22, 1999).

137. The majority of circuits have held that individuals are liable as "employers" for purposes of the FLSA. See *Baystate Alternative Staffing, Inc. v. Herman*, 163 F.3d 668, 676–79 (1st Cir. 1998); *United States Department of Labor v. Cole Enterprises, Inc.*, 62 F.3d 775, 778–79 (6th Cir. 1995); *Brock v. Hamad*, 867 F.2d 804, 808 (4th Cir. 1989); *Riordan v. Kempiners*, 831 F.2d 690, 694 (7th Cir. 1987); *Donovan v. Grim Hotel Co.*, 747 F.2d 966, 971–72 (5th Cir. 1984), *cert denied*, 471 U.S. 1124 (1985); *Donovan v. Sovereign Security, Ltd.*, 726 F.2d 55, 59 (2d Cir. 1984).

138. 538 U.S. 721 (2003).

139. See *Cantley v. Simmons*, 179 F. Supp. 2d 654, 656–58 (S.D. W.Va. 2002); *Morrow v. Putnam*, 142 F. Supp. 2d 1271 (D. Nev. 2001).

140. *Hewett v. Willingboro Board of Education*, 421 Supp. 2d 814 (D.N.J. 2006).

141. *Id.* at 818.

142. *Lombardi v. Board of Trustees Hinsdale School District 86*, No. 06 C 3683, 2006 U.S. Dist. LEXIS 86955 (N.D. Ill. Nov. 29, 2006).

143. *Id.* at *8.

144. See *Buser v. Southern Food Service, Inc.*, 73 F. Supp. 2d 556, 563–64 (M.D.N.C. 1999); *Klivitis v. County of Luzerne*, 52 F. Supp. 2d 403, 412–13 (M.D. Pa. 1999); *Freemon v. Foley*, 911 F. Supp. 326, 330–32 (N.D. Ill. 1995).

145. See *Rollins v. Wilson County Government*, 154 F.3d 626 (6th Cir. 1998); *Evans v. Henderson*, No. 99 C 8332, 2000 U.S. Dist. LEXIS 11907, at *9–*10 (N.D. Ill. Aug. 16, 2000); *Buser*, 73 F. Supp. 2d at 564–65; *Klivitis*, 52 F. Supp. 2d at 412–13; *Bryant v. Delbar Products, Inc.*, 18 F. Supp. 2d 799, 808 (M.D. Tenn. 1998); *Rupnow v. TRC, Inc.*, 999 F. Supp. 1047, 1048 (N.D. Ohio 1998).

146. *Freemon*, 911 F. Supp. at 330–32.

147. See *Buser*, 73 F. Supp. 2d at 564–65 (finding that VP of employer that made ultimate decision to terminate was an FMLA "employer"); *Carpenter v. Refrigeration Sales Corp.*, 49 F. Supp. 2d 1028, 1031 (N.D. Ohio 1999) (holding that HR department head who administered FMLA, spoke with employee about illness, and made decision to terminate was an "employer" for FMLA purposes); *Bryant*, 18 F. Supp. 2d at 808–809 (holding that manager who fired employee was "employer" within meaning of the FMLA).

148. *Klivitis*, 52 F. Supp. 2d at 416.

149. *Evans*, 2000 U.S. Dist. LEXIS 11907, at *9–*10; see also *Cooper v. Harbour Inns of Baltimore, Inc.*, No. L-98-2173, 2000 U.S. Dist. LEXIS 4284, at *14–*15 (D. Md. Mar. 20, 2000) (holding that supervisor not individually liable under FMLA absent evidence of involvement with termination decision).

150. *Evans*, 2000 U.S. Dist. LEXIS 11907, at *9–*10 (dismissing postmaster general and another manager from suit absent allegations of misconduct); *Cooper*, 2000 U.S. Dist. LEXIS 4284, at *14–*15 (holding that supervisor not individually liable under FMLA absent evidence of involvement with termination decision); *Johnson v. A.P. Products, Ltd.*, 934 F. Supp. 625, 629 (S.D.N.Y. 1996).

151. See *Freemon*, 911 F. Supp. 326.

152. 29 U.S.C. § 2652(a); 29 C.F.R. § 825.700(a).

153. 29 C.F.R. § 825.220(b).

154. See *Douglas v. E.G. Baldwin & Associates, Inc.*, 150 F.3d 604, 608-609 (6th Cir. 1998) (rejecting argument that employee was covered by protections of the FMLA where employer did not meet 50/20 test because employer expressly adopted FMLA as a matter of company policy).

155. For state family and medical leave citations, see notes 4–8 in Chapter 1.

156. 4 Colo. Code Regs. §§ 801-1-44B ("employee" defined), 801-5-23 (family and medical leave).

157. 4 Colo. Code Regs. § 801-5-23 (family and medical leave).

158. Fla. Stat. § 110.221(2).

159. N.D. Cent. Code § 54-52.4-01(3) ("employer" defined).

160. Texas Govt. Code Ann. § 661.901.

161. The family and medical leave regulations are contained in the "Red Book" of the Massachusetts Human Resources Division, which is available on the Division's website, http://www.mass.gov/?pageID=hrdhomepage&L=1&L0=Home&sid=Ehrd. Massachusetts Human Resources Division, *Rules Governing Paid Leave and Other Benefits for Managers and Confidential Employees* § 1.04 (1995) [hereinafter Massachusetts Human Resources Division, *Red Book*], available at http://www.mass.gov/?pageID=hrdsubtopic&L=4&L0=Home&L1=Policies+%26+Benefits&L2=Types+of+Leave&L3=Red+Book&sid=Ehrd.

162. *Id.* § 1.07 ("appointing authority" defined).

163. W. Va. Code § 21-5D-2(d) ("employer" defined).

164. Alaska Stat. § 39.20.550(2).

165. Alaska Stat. § 39.20.310(3).

166. Alaska Stat. § 39.20.310(9).

167. Haw. Rev. Stat. Ann. § 398-1 ("employer" defined).

168. Haw. Code R. § 12-27-5(a).

169. *Id.*

170. Haw. Code R. § 12-27-5(c).

171. Haw. Code R. § 12-27-5(d).

172. Haw. Code R. § 12-27-1 ("employer" defined).

173. Cal. Govt. Code § 12945.2(c)(2)(A)–(B).

174. Or. Rev. Stat. Ann. § 659A.153(1).

175. Or. Rev. Stat. Ann. § 659A.153(2).

176. 29 U.S.C. § 2651(b); 29 C.F.R. § 825.701(a).

177. 29 C.F.R. § 825.701(a).

CHAPTER 3

Employee Eligibility

3.01 OVERVIEW

Once it has been determined that the school is a covered "employer" within the meaning of the federal FMLA, the second question a school administrator must ask is whether the employee meets the eligibility requirements for FMLA leave. School employees are not automatically entitled to take FMLA leave simply because the school is an FMLA-covered employer. The federal FMLA imposes additional eligibility requirements that an employee must meet before he or she may exercise FMLA rights. Some state family and medical leave laws impose additional eligibility requirements as well. Federal and state eligibility requirements for family and medical leave are frequently not the same. Accordingly, an employee who meets the eligibility requirements for applicable state family and medical leave may not meet the eligibility requirements of the federal FMLA, and vice versa. An employee who does not meet applicable eligibility requirements is not entitled to the protections afforded by federal or state family and medical leave laws. Of course, the employee's absence may be permitted, and even protected, by other laws, school policies, or the terms of a collective bargaining agreement.

This chapter addresses employee eligibility under federal and state family and medical leave laws, with particular emphasis on the federal FMLA. It summarizes the three eligibility requirements under the federal FMLA. It also discusses different eligibility requirements under state family and medical leave laws and the effect of more lenient eligibility requirements pursuant to school family and medical leave policies.

3.02 ELIGIBILITY UNDER THE FEDERAL FAMILY AND MEDICAL LEAVE ACT

All covered school employees, whether in the public or private sector, must meet the following three eligibility requirements before they are entitled to take FMLA leave:[1]

(1) The individual must have been employed for at least 12 months.
(2) The individual must have worked at least 1,250 hours in the 12-month period immediately preceding leave commencement.
(3) The individual must be employed at a location that has at least 50 employees within 75 miles.

If an employee does not meet all three eligibility requirements, that individual generally will not be entitled to take job-protected leave under the federal FMLA.[2] A school employer could, therefore, discipline an ineligible employee who takes leave, even if the leave would otherwise be covered by the FMLA. A word of caution, however, is in order. As discussed later in this chapter, under certain circumstances an employee may be treated *as if* he or she met the eligibility requirements for FMLA leave. In that case, a school administrator would violate the FMLA if he or she were to discipline an employee who met all of the requirements for FMLA leave save eligibility. School administrators need to rule out these exceptions to the eligibility requirements before determining that the employee is not eligible and, therefore, that the leave is not protected by the federal FMLA.

3.03 EMPLOYEE DEFINED

Generally, FMLA benefits and protections apply only to eligible employees. For example, only eligible employees are entitled to job-protected FMLA leave.[3] A covered employer's responsibility to return an individual from FMLA leave to the same or an equivalent position with accrued benefits is enjoyed only by eligible employees.[4] The right to sue for monetary damages for a covered employer's violation of FMLA benefits and protections is limited to eligible employees.[5] Determining who is an "eligible employee" is, therefore, essential in determining FMLA rights and responsibilities.

[1] FLSA Definition

To be "eligible," an individual must first be an "employee" of a covered employer. The federal FMLA defines "employee" in terms of (1) the individual and (2) who that individual works for. Regarding the former, the federal FMLA defines "employee" to have the same meaning as that term has under the Fair Labor Standards Act of 1938 (FLSA) (29 U.S.C. § 203(e)).[6] The FLSA defines an "employee" as any individual employed by an employer.[7] The federal FMLA also defines the term "employ" by reference to the FLSA (29 U.S.C. § 203(c)).[8] The FLSA broadly defines "employ" as "to suffer or permit to work."[9] Under that broad definition, an individual who is not formally on the employer's payroll may nevertheless be determined to be an "employee" because the employer "suffered or permitted" the employee to perform work. Generally, however, an employee is on the payroll of a covered employer.[10] Whether an individual is an FMLA-covered "employee" is determined on a case-by-case basis.

While broad, the FMLA definition of "employee" is not limitless. Volunteers are not "employees" within the meaning of the FMLA.[11] Partners in a business are not considered "employees" for purposes of the FMLA, because partners are not included within the FLSA definition of "employee," even if their names appear on the payroll.[12] Stockholders of a corporation, on the other hand, may also be employees of the corporation and, as such, when their names appear on the payroll, are employees for purposes of the FMLA.[13] Employees stationed outside the United States (or any territory or possession of the United States) are excluded from the FMLA definition of "employee."[14]

[2] Covered Employer

The DOL regulations generally define an "employee" as any individual employed by a covered employer.[15] The regulations further define who is an "employee" where the employer is a covered public agency. Only certain individuals employed by the government of the United States are considered "employees" within the meaning of the federal FMLA.[16] Most federal employees are covered by Title II of the federal FMLA.[17] There are significant differences between Title I of the federal FMLA, which covers most public and private sector schools, and Title II. For example, Title II does not permit an aggrieved federal employee to file a private lawsuit for violations of his or her FMLA rights. As discussed more fully in Chapter 14, however, Title I of the federal FMLA allows employees to sue covered employers, including most public and private schools, for civil money damages for FMLA violations.[18]

Not all individuals employed by state or local public agencies are covered by the federal FMLA. Generally, the federal FMLA applies to any individual employed by a state, a political subdivision of a state, or an interstate governmental agency.[19] But even individuals who work for a covered state or local public agency may be excluded from federal FMLA coverage if they meet two conditions. First, the individual must not be a subject of the civil service laws of the state, political subdivision, or agency that employs the employee.[20] Second, the individual must also

- hold public elective office of that state, political subdivision, or agency;
- be selected by the holder of such an office to be a member of his personal staff;
- be appointed by such an officeholder to serve on a policy-making level;
- be an immediate adviser to such an officeholder with respect to the constitutional or legal powers of the office of such officeholder; or
- be an employee in the legislative branch or legislative body of that state, political subdivision, or agency but not an employee of the legislative library of such state, political subdivision, or agency.

[3] Independent Contractors

Independent contractors are not "employees" within the meaning of the FMLA. An employee, as distinguished from an independent contractor who is engaged in a business of his or her own, is one who "follows the usual path of an employee" and is dependent on the business that he or she serves.[21] Most courts apply the so-called economic realities test to determine whether an individual is an employee or an independent contractor for purposes of the FMLA.[22] Others apply the common law agency test.[23] There is minimal difference between the two tests.[24] Both tests consider a number of factors, including

- the hiring party's right to control the manner and means by which the work is accomplished;
- the skill required by the hired party;
- the duration of the relationship between the parties (e.g., the length of the relationship and the means by which the relationship can be extended or terminated);
- whether the alleged employer has the power to hire and terminate the employee;
- the hiring party's right to assign additional projects;
- the hired party's discretion over when and how to work;
- the extent to which the hiring party supervises and controls the employee's work schedule or conditions of employment;
- whether the hiring party sets the rate and method of payment;
- whether the work is part of the hiring party's regular business;
- the worker's capital investment;
- the worker's opportunity for profit or loss;
- the hired party's employee benefits;
- whether the hiring party maintains employment records; and
- the tax treatment of the hired party's compensation.[25]

No one factor is controlling. Rather, courts take into consideration the totality of the circumstances to determine whether an individual is an employee or an independent contractor.[26]

[4] Employees of Local Educational Agencies

As addressed in the previous chapter, the federal FMLA contains special rules for employees of "local educational agencies," including public school boards and elementary and secondary schools under their jurisdiction, and private elementary and secondary schools.[27] Employees of these local educational agencies, however, must meet the usual FMLA eligibility requirements.[28]

[5] Applicants and Former Employees

The definition of an "eligible employee" for purposes of the federal FMLA is phrased in terms of an individual currently employed by a covered employer. As a result, an applicant for employment and a former employee are not "eligible employees."[29] As discussed more fully in Chapter 14, *Prohibited Acts, Enforcement, and Remedies*, applicants and former employees may receive some protections for exercising federal FMLA rights.

3.04 12 MONTHS OF EMPLOYMENT

[1] General Rule

To be an "eligible employee" under the federal FMLA, the individual must have been employed by a covered employer for at least 12 months.[30] An employee who has not worked the requisite 12-month period is not entitled to the benefits and protections of the FMLA.[31] The 12 months of required employment is cumulative, not consecutive.[32] For example, a current employee who worked 3 months for a covered school employer this year and worked 10 months for the same employer 5 years ago would satisfy the 12-month eligibility requirement. For purposes of determining whether intermittent or occasional employment qualifies as "at least 12 months," 52 weeks is deemed to be equal to 12 months.[33] If an employee is maintained on the payroll for any part of a week, the week counts as a full week of employment toward the 52-week (12-month) period.[34] Time spent by the employee on paid or unpaid leave during which other benefits or compensation are provided by the employer (e.g., workers' compensation, group health benefits) is considered "on the payroll" and similarly counts toward the 12-month eligibility requirement.[35]

[2] Eligibility Determined at Leave Commencement

The determination of whether an employee has worked for the same covered employer for a total of at least 12 months must be made as of the date leave commences.[36] The determination is not made at any other point in time, such as when the employee requests leave. Where an employee who does not meet the 12-month eligibility requirement requests FMLA leave in advance of the date the leave is to begin, the employer is required to either confirm the employee's eligibility based on a projection that the employee will be eligible on the date leave would commence or advise the employee when the eligibility requirement is met.[37] The issue is addressed more fully in section 3.07 of this chapter, as well as in Chapter 6, *Notice Requirements*.

Neither the Act nor the DOL regulations define what constitutes "leave" and when such leave "commences." The issue is complicated by the fact that FMLA leave may be taken in a single block of time, intermittently, or on a so-called reduced leave schedule.[38] Because a period of FMLA leave may involve multiple absences based on the same underlying covered condition, the question arises whether eligibility is calculated at the start of each and every absence if the absences are related to the same underlying covered condition. As addressed in section 3.05 below, the short answer is that FMLA leave commences at the start of a single absence or series of related absences for the same underlying covered condition.[39] Under this interpretation, eligibility is calculated once for each covered condition as of the date and time of the first absence.

Whether eligibility attaches after FMLA leave has commenced has split the courts. The issue arises where an individual who does not meet the 12-month eligibility requirement at the start of an absence subsequently meets that requirement during the absence. The question is whether the employee may immediately begin applying the protections of the FMLA to the entire absence. Most courts have held that an employee who was not eligible at the commencement of leave may not immediately obtain the benefits and protections of the Act during the absence.[40] At least one court has held otherwise.[41]

[3] Military Leave

The Uniformed Services Employment and Reemployment Rights Act of 1994 (USERRA) is a federal law that provides reemployment rights to veterans and members of the armed services following qualifying military service.[42] The USERRA applies to all employers doing business in the United States, whether public or private, large or small. The USERRA's protections extend to all persons serving in all branches of the uniformed services, including the Army, Navy, Air Force, Marines, Coast Guard, Public Health Service Commissioned Corps, National Guard, and Reserves. The USERRA prohibits employers from discriminating against or punishing employees for military service. Many states have also enacted laws that mirror or supplement the USERRA's protections.

In terms of FMLA eligibility, the USERRA requires all employers to credit uniformed service members who conclude their tours of duty and are reemployed with all benefits they would have obtained had they been continuously employed.[43] If a uniformed service member had been continuously employed, one such benefit to which he or she might have been entitled is leave under the FMLA.[44] Accordingly, the DOL has determined that the USERRA requires that a person reemployed following military service be given credit for the period of military service toward the 12-month FMLA eligibility requirement. Each month performing military service counts as a month actively employed by the employer.[45]

FMLA Illustrated: Military Service and Eligibility

Daryl has been employed by a school district for 9 months when she is ordered to active military service for 9 months. She is reemployed at the conclusion of her military service. On the day she returns to work, Daryl requests FMLA leave. For purposes of FMLA eligibility, the school district must consider Daryl to have been employed by the school district for more than the required 12 months (9 months actually employed plus 9 months while serving in the military service). Remember that the 12 months does not have to be consecutive months to meet this FMLA requirement.

[4] Layoffs, Furloughs, and Suspensions

The layoff, furlough, or suspension of an employee may impact the 12-month eligibility requirement. Where the employer-employee relationship has been severed, such as during a permanent or temporary layoff, the individual is no longer an eligible employee entitled to the benefits and protections of the Act.[46] The employee must be recalled or otherwise reemployed before being eligible for FMLA leave.[47] As such, a laid-off employee does not accumulate time toward the 12-month eligibility requirement (although the time an employee worked before being laid off continues to count toward FMLA eligibility).

A furlough is the public sector functional equivalent of a layoff; a public sector employee may be furloughed because of a lack of funds or work, or for other nondisciplinary reasons. Unlike in the case of a layoff, however, a furloughed employee typically remains on the employer's payroll (even though the employee may not be paid during the furlough period).

With respect to disciplinary suspensions and furloughs, because employees generally remain on the payroll during the period of suspension or furlough, this period generally counts for purposes of the 12-month eligibility requirement.[48]

[5] Long-Term Absences or Disability

It is unclear whether an employee on long-term leave due, typically, to long-term disability continues to accumulate time toward the 12-month eligibility requirement. On the one hand, the eligibility rules strongly suggest that such time does count for purposes of the 12-month FMLA eligibility requirement. The rules clearly provide that if the employee is maintained on the payroll for any part of the week, including any periods of paid or unpaid leave during which other benefits or compensation are provided by the employer (e.g., workers' compensation, group health benefits), the time counts toward the 52-week eligibility requirement.[49]

On the other hand, for the analogous purpose of determining employer coverage, the DOL regulations indicate that the test for evaluating who is an employee is predicated on a "continuing employment relationship."[50] Under that test, an individual is not considered to be an employee where the employer does not have a reasonable expectation that the employee will later return to active employment.[51] The DOL applies the reasonable expectation standard to employees on long-term or permanent disability.[52] The DOL has opined that an employee who is permanently disabled from work would not reasonably be expected to return to work and, therefore, may be excluded from the employee head count for purposes of employer coverage under the federal FMLA.[53]

School administrators would be well advised to check with counsel on this issue before depriving an employee of accumulated time toward FMLA eligibility where the employee remains on long-term leave. Indeed, where the long-term leave is also covered by the FMLA, terminating the employee while on such leave may constitute an independent violation of the FMLA.

[6] Reinstatement to Employment from Termination

Termination severs the employment relationship such that the individual is no longer an "employee" and, therefore, cannot be an "eligible employee" within the meaning of the FMLA. As a nonemployee, the individual would not accumulate time toward the 12-month eligibility requirement during the period of termination. In two common circumstances, however, a terminated individual might accumulate time toward the 12-month eligibility requirement.

Pursuant to applicable state or local law, the terms of a collective bargaining agreement, or school policy, a school might carry a terminated employee on the payroll until exhaustion of any grievances or other internal appeal procedures. If the employee remains on the payroll, including during any periods of paid or unpaid leave during which other benefits and compensation are provided by the employer, a strong argument could be made that the time counts toward the 12-month eligibility requirement. However, a counterargument is available to school administrators that the time would not count.

The counterargument applies, by analogy, the DOL regulations governing the method of counting employees for purposes of employer coverage under the FMLA.[54] As in the case of the eligibility regulations, an employee who remains on the payroll during paid or unpaid leave counts toward employer coverage "*as long as the employer has a reasonable expectation that the employee will later return to active employment*."[55] If there is no employment relationship, such as where an employee is laid off, the individual is not counted.[56] According to the DOL, the test for determining who is an employee is based on a continuing employment relationship.[57] Under that test, where a school employer terminates an employee and, presumably, does not have a reasonable expectation that the employee will return to work, the argument could be made that the individual is no longer an employee for purposes of eligibility.

School administrators would be well advised to check with counsel on this issue before depriving a terminated employee of accumulated time toward FMLA eligibility where the employee remains on the payroll pending resolution of any challenges to the termination.

The authorities are split on the effect on eligibility where a terminated employee has been returned to work with full back pay and benefits by a court, administrative judge, or arbitrator. Most authorities have held that the time a wrongfully terminated employee spent before being returned to work must be must be counted toward the 12-month eligibility requirement.[58] One court has held otherwise.[59] The issue is addressed more fully in section 3.05 below.

[7] Joint Employment and Successors in Interest

The time an employee spent as a joint employee counts toward that employee's 12-month eligibility requirement.[60] For example, the school contracts with a temporary-help agency for clerical assistance during the regular secretary's maternity leave. The temporary-help agency sends Carol, who works with the school for 3 months. The following year, the school hires Carol to fill a full-time vacancy. After 10 months, Carol requests FMLA leave to care for a seriously ill parent. Carol meets the 12-month federal FMLA eligibility requirement because the 3 months she spent as a joint employee added to the 10 months she worked as a full-time employee exceeds the minimum of 12 months required for eligibility.[61] For a further discussion of joint employment, see section 2.02[4] of Chapter 2, *Schools as FMLA-Covered Employers*.

An employer who is a successor in interest to an FMLA-covered employer must count the employee's time with the predecessor employer for purposes of the 12-month federal FMLA eligibility requirement.[62] When an employer is a "successor in interest," an employee's entitlements are the same as if the employment by the predecessor and successor were continuous employment by a single employer.[63] The successor employer's obligation to recognize an employee's 12-month eligibility based on employment with the predecessor continues even where the successor is not an FMLA-covered employer.[64] For a further discussion on the responsibilities of a successor in interest, see section 2.02[5] of Chapter 2, *Schools as FMLA-Covered Employers*.

3.05 1,250 HOURS OF SERVICE DURING THE 12-MONTH PERIOD PRECEDING LEAVE COMMENCEMENT

[1] General Rule

The second requirement for an individual to be an "eligible employee" within the meaning of the federal FMLA is that the employee must have been employed for at least 1,250 hours of service during the 12-month period immediately preceding the commencement of FMLA leave.[65] An employee who has not worked the requisite 1,250 hours in the 12-month period preceding leave commencement is not eligible for FMLA leave or protections.[66]

The 1,250-hour requirement has two components: the employee (1) must have worked at least 1,250 hours and (2) must have worked those hours during the 12-month period immediately preceding leave commencement. These requirements, as well as related issues, are addressed below.

[2] Calculation of 1,250 Hours of Service

The FMLA does not define the term "hours of service."[67] The FMLA does, however, provide that whether an employee has worked the minimum 1,250 hours of service is determined according to the principles established under section 7 of the Fair Labor Standards Act of 1938 (FLSA), 29 U.S.C. § 207.[68] Section 7 of the FLSA does not define the term "hours of service."[69] It does, however, define the "regular rate" standard for determining the rate at which employees must be compensated for engaging in overtime work.[70] For purposes of the 1,250-hours-of-service eligibility requirement, "[t]he determining factor is the number of compensable hours an employee has worked for the employer within the meaning of the FLSA."[71] The status of the employee, whether full-time, part-time, occasional, or seasonal, is not relevant. For purposes of this eligibility requirement, the sole issue is whether the employee worked 1,250 hours in the 12-month period prior to leave commencement.[72]

(i) Basic FLSA Principles

Generally, an employer is required to pay an employee for all time spent performing work for the employer. An employer is also required to pay an employee for not working at all or for waiting for something to happen before the individual is required to work.[73] Compensable on-duty time refers to time an employee is unable to use effectively for his or her own purposes because of work requirements imposed by an employer.[74] Compensable on-duty work time includes time spent by the employee working at the direction of the employer, as well as time spent by the employee on work that was not formally requested by the employer but which the employer knows or has reason to believe that the employee is performing for the employer's benefit.[75] In the latter case, the employer is liable to the employee for compensation for time spent by the employee working, even though the employer did not specifically request the work, because the employer, with knowledge that the employee was working for the employer, "suffered or permitted" the employee to work.

To be compensable, on-duty work time must render an employee unable to use such time effectively for his or her own purposes due to the work requirements imposed by an employer. Conversely, off-duty time is not compensable. Off-duty time is any time that an employee is completely relieved from duty and that is long enough to enable the employee to use the time effectively for his or her own purposes.[76]

The FLSA illustrates the difference between compensable on- and off-duty time as follows:

> A truck driver who has to wait at or near the job site for goods to be loaded is working during the loading period. If the driver reaches his destination and while awaiting the return trip is required to take care of his employer's truck or goods, he is also working while waiting. In both cases, the employee is engaged to wait. Waiting is an integral part of the job. On the other hand, for example, if the truck driver is sent from Washington, D.C., to New York City, leaving at 6 a.m. and arriving at

12 noon, and is completely and specifically relieved from all duty until 6 p.m., when he again goes on duty for the return trip, the idle time is not working time. Instead he is waiting to be engaged.[77]

Under the FLSA, not all idle time at work is compensable. Lunch breaks, other meals, and rest breaks exceeding a half hour are not considered "hours worked" for purposes of the FLSA.[78] Accordingly, such periods of time would not count toward the 1,250-hour federal FMLA eligibility requirement. Short breaks or rest periods of less than 30 minutes, however, must be counted as hours worked for purposes of the FLSA.[79]

Finally, time spent in certain work-related activities is legally excluded from the FLSA calculation of "hours worked." The Portal-to-Portal Act excludes from compensable "hours worked" certain "preliminary" and "postliminary" activities performed prior or subsequent to the workday, where such activities are not compensated by contract, custom, or practice.[80] For example, whether washup time before an employee begins his or her principal work activities counts as FLSA "hours worked" will depend on whether such time is compensable pursuant to the terms of a collective bargaining agreement, custom, or the practice of the employer. If an employer has agreed to compensate an employee for washup time pursuant to the terms of a collective bargaining agreement, the wash-up time counts as "hours worked" for purposes of both the FLSA and the 1,250-hour federal FMLA eligibility requirement. Note, however, that only the amount of time allowed by contract, custom, or practice counts as "hours worked." In our example, if the contract permits an employee 15 minutes of washup time, the employee is credited with having worked only those 15 minutes, even if the employee actually took 20 minutes to wash up.

Several courts have addressed the interaction of the federal FMLA eligibility requirements with "preliminary" and "postliminary" activities covered by the Portal-to-Portal Act. For example, a medical technician met the 1,250-hour eligibility requirement after a court found that the 15 minutes spent by the employee preparing the office to open each morning counted as "hours worked." Although the employer did not authorize the technician to perform this work, because the employer knew or should have known that the employee was, in fact, performing the work for the benefit of the employer, the court concluded that time spent on such work should count as "hours worked." As this was the custom or practice at that office, the Portal-to-Portal Act did not exclude such preparatory time.[81] Another court counted time spent by an airline stewardess who assisted with deplaning and debriefing activities after her last flight of the day as "hours worked" toward the 1,250-hour FMLA eligibility requirement. The court opined that because these postliminary activities were predominately for the benefit of her employer, they were not excluded by the Portal-to-Portal Act.[82]

(ii) Treatment of Overtime and Other Premium Pay

The time spent by an employee working overtime is considered "hours worked" within the meaning of the FLSA and, therefore, counts toward the 1,250-hour FMLA eligibility requirement.[83] However, only the actual time spent on overtime is counted toward meeting the 1,250-hour eligibility requirement. Payment of overtime at a premium rate, typically time and a half, does not add to the number of hours actually worked for purposes of FMLA eligibility.[84] The same is true for any premium-pay system such as night-shift differentials, out-of-schedule premium pay, and Sunday premium pay. For example, if an employee worked 40 hours of straight time at $10.00 an hour and 20 hours of overtime at $15.00 an hour (time and a half), for purposes of FMLA eligibility, the employee is credited with 60 hours toward the 1,250-hour requirement. With the addition of premium pay for overtime, the employee is paid as if he or she worked 70 hours; however, the employee is not credited with the premium-pay differential for purposes of the 1,250-hour FMLA eligibility requirement.

(iii) Paid or Unpaid Leave

Leave, whether paid or unpaid, does not count toward the 1,250-hour FMLA eligibility requirement because leave is not considered "hours worked" within the meaning of the FLSA.[85] Time spent on vacation, holidays, personal leave, sick leave, leave without pay (LWOP), disability leave, medical leave, maternity leave, FMLA leave, and sabbaticals, whether paid or unpaid, do not count toward the 1,250-hour FMLA eligibility requirement.[86]

Note the difference in treatment of leave for purposes of FMLA eligibility between the 12-month eligibility requirement and the 1,250-hour eligibility requirement. For purposes of the 12-month eligibility requirement, leave, whether paid or unpaid, counts. For purposes of the 1,250-hour eligibility requirement, however, paid or unpaid leave does not count.

(iv) Time Spent on Union Business and Grievance Adjustments

Pursuant to FLSA principles, time spent during the workday adjusting grievances between an employer and employee counts as "hours worked" toward the 1,250-hour eligibility requirement.[87] Where, however, a bona fide union is involved, the terms of the governing collective bargaining agreement, custom, or past practice will determine whether time spent adjusting grievances counts as "hours worked" toward the 1,250-hour eligibility requirement.[88]

(v) Military Leave

The time an employee spends on qualifying military leave counts toward the 1,250-hour requirement for FMLA eligibility.

The DOL has issued guidance on the effect of the USERRA and leave eligibility under the federal FMLA.[89] With respect to the 1,250-hour requirement, the DOL Q&A Guidance provides the following:

> 6. How should the 1,250 hours-of-service requirement be calculated for returning service members?
>
> An employee returning after military service should be credited with the hours-of-service that would have been performed *but for* the period of military service in determining FMLA eligibility. Accordingly, a person reemployed following military service has the hours that would have been worked for the employer added to any hours actually worked during the previous 12-month period to meet the 1,250 hour requirement. In order to determine the hours that would have been worked during the period of military service, the employee's preservice work schedule can generally be used for calculations. For example, an employee who works 40 hours per week for the employer returns to employment following 20 weeks of military service and requests leave under the FMLA. To de-

termine the person's eligibility, the hours he or she would have worked during the period of military service ($20 \times 40 = 800$ hours) must be added to the hours actually worked during the 12-month period prior to the start of the leave to determine if the 1,250-hour requirement is met.[90]

(vi) Layover Time

Whether or not layover time counts toward the 1,250-hours-worked eligibility requirement depends on the agreement of the parties, the nature and extent of restrictions, if any, placed by the employer on the employee's free use of time during layover, and all surrounding circumstances. In *Rich v. Delta Airlines, Inc.*, the employee, an airline flight attendant, was terminated for absenteeism.[91] She sued, alleging that the absences that formed the basis of her removal were covered by the FMLA. The employer moved to have the case dismissed, alleging that the employee was not an eligible employee as she did not satisfy the 1,250-hours-worked requirement. It was undisputed that if layover time (time spent between flights) were included, the employee would have satisfied the 1,250-hour eligibility requirement. The court concluded that the employee's layover hours did not count as "hours worked" for FMLA eligibility. The court observed that the employee was generally free to use her layover time as she pleased. The restrictions placed on the employee—not consuming alcohol or drugs for certain periods and having to call in to notify the airline if she would be away from the hotel for more than 6 hours—were insufficient to convert the layover time to "work hours."

(vii) Employee Training Time

Time spent by an employee receiving education or training outside of the workplace may count as "hours worked" toward the 1,250-hour FMLA eligibility requirement. FLSA regulations (29 C.F.R. § 785.27) provide that an employer need not count the time an employee spends at lectures, meetings, training programs, and similar activities if

- attendance is outside of the employee's regular working hours;
- attendance is in fact voluntary;

- the course, lecture, or meeting is not directly related to the employee's job; and
- the employee does not perform any productive work during such attendance.

Where, however, those conditions are not met, the time spent by an employee attending training will count as "hours worked." For example, where an employer required an employee to retain professional certification, enrolled her in courses, paid for the courses, and paid for some of her time at the courses, one court held that the time the employee spent at the courses counted toward the 1,250-hour FMLA eligibility requirement.[92] In those circumstances, the court found that attendance at the courses was not voluntary and was related to her job.[93]

(viii) Disciplinary Suspensions

The period of time an employee serves on disciplinary suspension does not count toward the 1,250-hour eligibility requirement because the employee has not performed work for the employer during this period.[94] This contrasts with the 12-month eligibility requirement, which would count the time an employee spent on disciplinary suspension because the employee would continue on the employer's payroll during the suspension.

(ix) Reversal of Suspension or Termination

As addressed previously in section 3.04[6] regarding the 12-month eligibility requirement, the courts are split on the effect of the reversal of a disciplinary suspension or termination on the 1,250-hour FMLA eligibility requirement. The issue in *Plumley v. Southern Container, Inc.* was whether the time an employee would have worked but for being erroneously discharged, as reflected in an arbitration back pay award, counts for purposes of the 1,250-hour eligibility requirement.[95] The court concluded that because the employee did not perform any work for the employer during the discharge period, under generally recognized FLSA principles, the time he was compensated for as back pay did not count for purposes of the FLSA and, therefore, did not count toward the 1,250-hours-worked FMLA eligibility requirement.

Faced with the same issue, the Sixth Circuit in *Ricco v. Potter* found that the period of time the employee was discharged counted for purposes of the 1,250-hour eligibility requirement.[96] In that case, after a two-year period, a U.S. Postal Service employee was brought back to work by an arbitrator with make-whole relief. Within a few months of her return, she requested FMLA leave. The Postal Service denied Ricco's requests for FMLA leave on the grounds that she did not meet the 1,250-hour eligibility requirement. The Postal Service subsequently terminated Ricco for failure to maintain a regular work schedule. The Sixth Circuit reasoned that the FLSA does not strictly prohibit such hours from being considered and that the failure to give employees credit toward the hours-of-service requirement for hours that they would have worked, but for their unlawful termination, rewards employers for their unlawful conduct.

Given the split in judicial authority, school officials should consult with counsel before deciding not to count the hours an employee would have worked but for an erroneous suspension or termination that is overturned with make-whole relief.

(x) Layoffs and Furloughs

The period of time during which an employee is laid off from work does not count toward the 1,250-hour FMLA eligibility requirement because a laid-off employee does not incur any "work hours" for an employer.[97] Similarly, because a furloughed employee is not performing work during the furlough, the time spent on furlough does not count toward the 1,250-hour FMLA eligibility requirement. However, unlike a layoff period, a furlough period may count for purposes of the 12-month FMLA eligibility requirement, depending on all of the circumstances of the case (see section 3.04[4] above).

(xi) Employer Acts of Interference with "Hours Worked"

Employees have sought to excuse their failure to satisfy the 1,250-hour FMLA eligibility requirement by alleging that some action by the employer (e.g., failure to schedule work) precluded them from reaching the requisite 1,250 hours of service. In *Brown v. Daimler-Chrysler*

Corp., the court rejected the employee's claim that but for the employer's denial of her request for light duty, she would have worked the requisite 1,250 hours for FMLA eligibility.[98] The court reasoned that Congress imposed clear statutory prerequisites for FMLA eligibility and did not provide a waiver of the minimum eligibility requirements when an employer has taken some action that allegedly precluded the employee from meeting the statutory eligibility requirements.

(xii) Joint Employment and Successors in Interest

As with the 12-month eligibility requirement, the hours worked by an individual in a joint employment relationship count toward the 1,250-hour FMLA eligibility requirement.[99] For example, a school contracts with a temporary-help agency for clerical work. The temporary-help agency sends Margaret. Margaret works full-time at the school for 2 months. The school then hires Margaret for a full-time position. Margaret works 4 months in that job and then asks for FMLA leave. For purposes of meeting the 1,250-hours-worked eligibility requirement, both the hours that Margaret worked during the 2 months she was employed through the temporary-help agency and the hours she worked during her 4 months of full-time employment with the school count toward the 1,250-hours-worked FMLA eligibility requirement.

(xiii) Employees Stationed outside the United States

It is clear that the federal FMLA applies only to employees of a covered employer who are employed within the United States or any territory or possession of the United States.[100] Accordingly, an employee who is employed outside these areas is not counted for purposes of FMLA coverage or employee eligibility;[101] nor are such employees entitled to FMLA benefits.[102] What is unclear, however, is whether hours worked by an employee of a covered employer who is employed outside the territorial jurisdiction of the United States count for purposes of FMLA eligibility. The issue becomes relevant where an employee who has worked more than 1,250 hours in the 12-month period before leave commencement returns to employment within the United States or its territories or possessions. The courts have not yet addressed the issue, but the answer will likely depend on whether hours worked outside the United States count as "hours worked" for purposes of section 7 of the FLSA.

(xiv) Proof Employee Worked 1,250 Hours

The 1,250-hour FMLA eligibility determination is based on the hours an employee actually worked within the meaning of the FLSA. Compensation agreements or methods of record keeping that do not accurately reflect the actual number of FLSA hours an employee has worked or has been in service for an employer are not controlling.[103] As addressed more fully in Chapter 12, *Record-Keeping Requirements*, the federal FMLA does not mandate any particular form of records be kept to determine FMLA eligibility. Any accurate accounting of actual hours worked under FLSA principles may be used.[104]

An employee may be deemed to have met the 1,250-hour FMLA eligibility requirement where the employer does not maintain an accurate record of hours worked by an employee.[105] For example, employers rarely keep accurate records of the hours actually worked by employees exempt from the FLSA's overtime record-keeping requirements (e.g., bona fide executive, administrative, and professional employees as defined in 29 C.F.R. pt. 541).[106] The presumption that an employee has met the 1,250-hour eligibility requirement that arises due to inaccurate records, however, may be rebutted. An employer has the burden of showing that the employee has not worked the requisite hours. If the employer is unable to meet this burden, the employee is deemed to have met the 1,250-hour FMLA eligibility requirement.[107]

(xv) Presumption of Teacher FMLA Eligibility

Full-time teachers in an elementary or secondary school system or at an institution of higher education or other educational establishment or institution are deemed to have met the 1,250-hour test.[108] The DOL regulations define a "teacher" as an employee employed principally in an instructional capacity by an educational agency or school whose principal function is to teach and instruct students in a class, a small group, or an individual setting, and includes athletic coaches, driving instructors, and special educational assistants such as signers for the hearing impaired. The term does not include teacher assistants or aides who do not have as their principal function actual teaching or instructing, or auxiliary personnel such as counselors, psychologists, curriculum specialists, cafeteria workers, maintenance workers, bus drivers, or other primarily noninstructional employees.[109] The presumption that a teacher has worked the requisite 1,250 hours, however, is rebuttable. An employer must be able to clearly demonstrate that a covered teacher did not work 1,250 hours during the previous 12 months in order to claim that the employee is not "eligible" for FMLA leave.[110] Note that the burden on school administrators to rebut the presumption of eligibility for teachers is higher than the similar burden to rebut the presumption of eligibility created as a result of inaccurate employee time records.

[3] 12-Month Period prior to Leave Commencement

For an employee to be eligible for FMLA leave, the 1,250 hours must have been worked by the employee during the 12-month period prior to leave commencement. Like the 12-month eligibility requirement, the determination as to whether an employee has worked for the covered employer for at least 1,250 hours in the past 12 months is made as of the date leave commences.[111] As addressed in section 3.04[2] above, neither the statute nor the DOL implementing regulations define what constitutes "leave." Because FMLA leave may be taken in a single block of time or multiple times for the same covered condition, whether "leave" is synonymous with each and every "absence" or may cover multiple related absences is important for purposes of determining FMLA eligibility.

The court in *Barron v. Runyon* was the first to address what "leave" means for purposes of the 1,250-hour eligibility requirement.[112] In that case, the Postal Service (the employer) argued that "leave" was synonymous with "absence" and that, as a result, it was correct in determining hours worked to confirm that the employee met the 1,250-hour eligibility requirement for every FMLA absence. The employee argued that where all of his intermittent absences were related to the same covered condition (his need to provide care for his ill wife), for purposes of the 1,250 hour eligibility requirement, leave commenced as of the start of the first absence for that single covered condition. The court agreed with the employee. The court reasoned, essentially, that the

Postal Service's interpretation of "leave" as being synonymous with every FMLA absence was contrary to the statute's recognition that leave could be taken all at once or on an intermittent or reduced leave schedule basis. The DOL agreed with *Barron* and subsequently adopted the decision.[113]

The net result of the *Barron* decision, as adopted by the DOL, is that FMLA eligibility is determined as of the first absence for each covered condition during a given 12-month FMLA leave year. For a further discussion of the four types of FMLA leave years, see Chapter 8, *Leave Amount and Scheduling*.

FMLA Illustrated: 1,250-Hour Eligibility Example

Sharon has been a full-time schoolteacher in the Pierce, Nebraska, school system for many years. Sharon is injured in an automobile accident at the beginning of the school year. As part of her treatment, she must go to physical therapy twice a week for the next 6 months. Sharon requests FMLA leave to attend physical therapy twice a week for the next 6 months.

Because she did not work for the school system during the summer, Sharon just satisfied the 1,250-hour eligibility requirement at the time of her first physical therapy session. Thereafter, due to absences for physical therapy and to receive other medical treatment, Sharon falls below the 1,250-hour eligibility threshold. Sharon's husband, Karl, subsequently is admitted into the hospital for chest pains. Sharon asks for 2 days of FMLA leave to visit him.

Sharon's absences from school are costly and causing major disruptions. School administrators want to deny Sharon any further FMLA leave. They notice that as of the time she requested FMLA leave to visit her husband in the hospital, Sharon no longer meets the 1,250-hour eligibility requirement.

Question: Can school administrators deny Sharon FMLA leave?

Answer: The school would violate the FMLA if it denied her request for intermittent FMLA leave to attend physical therapy based on eligibility. Because she met the 1,250-hour eligibility requirement as of the first absence for physical therapy, Sharon has met the 1,250-hour eligibility requirement for that purpose for the remainder of the FMLA leave year, even if along the way she were to drop below the 1,250-hour threshold. Sharon would not, however, be eligible for FMLA leave to care for her hospitalized husband, a separate covered condition. At the time she sought to take leave to care for her hospitalized husband, Sharon had not worked 1,250 hours in the preceding 12-month period. As such, Sharon is not eligible for FMLA leave for that purpose.

3.06 EMPLOYS 50 OR MORE EMPLOYEES WITHIN 75 MILES OF THE EMPLOYEE'S WORKSITE

[1] General Rule

The third eligibility requirement that an employee of an FMLA-covered employer must meet in order to be entitled to the benefits and protections of the federal FMLA is that the employee work at a worksite where, within 75 miles of that worksite, there are at least 50 other employees of the employer.[114] The so-called 50/75 eligibility test applies to all employees of covered school employers, including employees of local educational agencies.[115] A school employee who does not meet the 50/75 eligibility test is not eligible for the benefits and protections of the FMLA.

For example, employees of a rural elementary school would not be eligible for FMLA leave if the school has fewer than 50 employees and there are no other schools under the jurisdiction of the same employer (usually a school board) within 75 miles.[116] Similarly, an employee of a large school employer that employs hundreds or even thousands of employers nationally would not be eligible if that employer does not employ at least 50 other employees within 75 miles of the worksite of the employee requesting FMLA leave.

The 50/75 eligibility requirement has four major components: (1) when eligibility is determined, (2) how the employee's worksite is determined, (3) how the 75-mile distance is measured, and (4) how the number of employees is calculated. These elements are reviewed below.

[2] When Satisfaction of 50/75 Eligibility Test Is Determined

(i) General Rule

Whether a covered employer employs 50 or more employees within 75 miles of the employee's worksite is determined at the time the employee gives notice of the need for FMLA leave.[117] Note that the 50/75 requirement differs from the previously discussed 12-month and 1,250-hour eligibility requirements, satisfaction of which are determined as of leave commencement. The DOL explained that it tied the 50/75 eligibility test to the employee's request for leave rather than to leave commencement to avoid the situation where the number of employees falls below 50 between the employee's request and the actual commencement of leave, rendering the employee ineligible for FMLA leave.[118]

(ii) Changes in Number of Employees within 75 Miles of Worksite

Once an employee is determined to be eligible, the employee's eligibility (for leave related to the covered condition for which the employee gave notice) is not affected by any subsequent change in the number of employees employed at or within 75 miles of the employee's worksite.[119] Similarly, an employer may not terminate an employee's leave that has already started if the number of employees at or within 75 miles of the worksite drops below 50.

For example, if in May a school has 60 employees but expects that the number of employees will drop to 20 in July, the school must grant FMLA benefits to an otherwise eligible employee who gives notice in May of the need for leave for a period of leave to begin in July.[120] If the employee begins leave in July and, as expected, the number of employees at the school drops below 50, the school could not at that point terminate the employee's leave because the 50/75 eligibility test is performed, and was satisfied, at the time the employee requested FMLA leave.

[3] Determining the Employee's Worksite

Fixing the worksite of the employee requesting FMLA leave is the essential first step in determining whether the 50/75 eligibility test has been met. The "worksite" marks the point from which it must be determined whether the employer has at least 50 employees within 75 miles. Ironically, neither the Act nor the DOL regulations specifically define the term "worksite." The legislative and regulatory history, however, indicate that it was Congress's express intention that "worksite" be construed in the same manner as "single site of employment" for purposes of the Worker Adjustment and Retraining Notification Act (WARN Act).[121]

(i) General Rule: Worksite Location

An employee's "worksite" for purposes of the FMLA is ordinarily the site where the employee reports to work. Some employees, however, do not have a fixed worksite. For example, in large school districts there may be employees who float from one school to another performing work. For employees with no fixed place of work, the "worksite" is the site to which they are assigned as a home base, from which their work is assigned, or to which they report.[122] Under the WARN Act, the source of work assignments is the location where the employee receives day-to-day instructions, notwithstanding centralized management, payroll, and other personnel functions.[123]

Not all employees at a given worksite count for purposes of the 50/75 FMLA eligibility test. For example, if a trade school headquartered in Phoenix, Arizona, set up a school in Boston, the facility where the Boston school was located would be the worksite for employees hired locally who report to the school daily for work assignments. If the Phoenix school also sent personnel from Phoenix to Boston to help get the school up and running, those employees sent from Phoenix continue to have the headquarters in Phoenix as their "worksite." The employees who have Boston as their worksite would not be counted in determining FMLA eligibility of employees whose home base is Phoenix. The Phoenix employees working in Boston to get the school up and running would, however, be counted for purposes of the 50/75 test to determine eligibility of employees whose worksite is Boston.[124]

(ii) Single or Multiple Locations

Generally, a worksite can be either a single location or a group of contiguous locations.[125] For example, a school composed of a single building may be a worksite for all employees who work at that school. On the other hand, a school or college may be composed of a group of separate buildings or facilities that form a campus or that are otherwise in reasonably close proximity to one another, and these buildings and facilities may together be considered a single "worksite" for purposes of the FMLA.[126] For example, if a school has three geographically separate facilities in a metropolitan area but regularly shifts or rotates the same employees from one building to another, the multiple facilities would be a single worksite.[127] Conversely, separate facilities of the same employer that are not within close proximity to each other and do not share the same staff or operational purposes are considered separate worksites. Geographically separate schools (e.g., grammar school, middle school, high school) managed by the same school district are separate worksites if they employ different teachers and staff.[128]

A single building may also be the site of several separate worksites. For example, a school located in a large city may be only one of fifty other tenants housed in the same office building. Assuming that the tenants are unrelated, the offices of each building tenant may be considered separate "worksites" for purposes of the FMLA.

The personal residence of an employee is not the employee's "worksite" for purposes of the FMLA.[129] Rather, the "worksite" is the office to which the employee reports and from which the employee's assignments are made.[130] This issue arises with employees who telecommute or who travel a lot, leaving from and returning to their homes rather than another worksite.[131]

(iii) Worksite of Joint Employees

The worksite of a joint employee of two or more employers is the primary employer's office from which the employee is assigned or to which the employee reports.[132] For employees of temporary-help or leasing agencies, the placement office of the temporary agency is the worksite of the primary employer.[133] As addressed more fully in subsection [5] below, for purposes of the 50/75 FMLA eligibility test, joint employees count as employees of all joint employers.

[4] 75-Mile Distance

The 75-mile distance from the worksite is measured by the shortest route from the worksite of the employee in need of FMLA leave, using available surface transportation over public streets, roads, highways, and waterways.[134] It is not measured in terms of a 75-mile radius.[135] Where surface transportation between worksites is not available, the distance is measured by using the most frequently utilized mode of transportation (e.g., airline miles).[136]

Note that when multiple means of surface transportation are available, the rules require calculation based on the shortest route between destinations, which may not be the most frequently used method. For example, an employee of a private New York school commutes from New Jersey by train. There is, however, a public ferry service that shaves 20 miles off the commute. Because it costs 10 times the amount of a monthly train ticket, ridership on the ferry is significantly lower than on the commuter trains. Nevertheless, for purposes of the 50/75 FMLA eligibility test, if the private school has employees in New Jersey, the 75-mile distance must be measured by incorporating the shorter, albeit far less used, ferry service. School employers with employees at different facilities within a few hundred miles of each other should use creative combinations of public roads, rail, and ferry service before finding that an employee is not eligible because the 50/75 test has not been met.

[5] Calculating the Number of Employees

(i) General Rule

The determination of how many employees are employed within 75 miles of a worksite is based on the number of employees maintained on the payroll.[137] Maintenance on the payroll is used as a proxy for establishing the existence of a continuing employment relationship between the school employer and the employee.[138] Employees of educational institutions who are employed permanently or who are under contract are considered to be "maintained on the payroll" during any portion of the year when school is not in session.[139] The rule counts these employees because the employer has a reasonable expectation that the employees will return to active employment the following academic year.[140] The calculation of whether the employer has 50 employees within 75 miles is similar to the calculation of the number of employees for employer FMLA coverage.[141]

For purposes of the 50/75 eligibility test, the employee head count includes all employees who are maintained on the payroll as of the date FMLA leave is requested, including part-time, full-time, eligible, and noneligible employees.[142] For this purpose, the employee head count also includes employees on paid or unpaid leaves of absence.[143]

However, employees who have been laid off, whether the layoff is temporary, indefinite, or long term, are not included.[144] While the treatment of suspended workers is not specifically addressed in the 50/75 test regulations, by analogy to the regulations governing calculation of the employee head count for purposes of employer coverage, employees who have been suspended from employment will generally count provided the employer has a reasonable belief that the employees will return to work after the suspension.[145] In the absence of a reasonable expectation by the employer that they will return to work, employees who have been terminated or have been put on long-term or permanent disability leave with no apparent ability to return to work may be excluded from the 50/75 employee count.[146] One court found that an educational employee who abandoned her job after receiving her last paycheck was not an employee that counted for purposes of the 50/75 FMLA eligibility test, even though the employee was still carried on the payroll.[147]

(ii) Military Duty

The DOL regulations do not address whether school employees on military leave are counted for purposes of the 50/75 eligibility test. Nor is the issue addressed in the DOL's recent memorandum entitled *Protection of Uniformed Service Members' Rights on Family and Medical Leave* (July 22, 2002).[148] Absent other guidance, school administrators should apply the general rule governing the counting of employees for purposes of the 50/75 FMLA eligibility test: if an employee on military leave remains on the school's payroll, the employee should be counted for purposes of the 50/75 eligibility test; if, however, the employee is no longer on the payroll, the employee should not count toward the 50/75 eligibility.

(iii) Joint Employment

As discussed previously, joint employment occurs where two or more employers exercise some control over the work of an employee.[149] Employees jointly employed by two or more employers must be counted by all of the employers, whether or not maintained on the payroll of each of the employers, for purposes of the 50/75 FMLA eligibility test.[150]

FMLA Illustrated: 50/75 Test—Joint Employment Example

Sarah is a clerical employee with Speedy Clerical, a temporary-employment agency. Central School contracts with Speedy Clerical for temporary clerical help when the need arises. Central contracted with Speedy Clerical for temporary clerical help due to the maternity leave of an employee. Speedy Clerical sent Sarah to perform work at Central School. Central School employs 49 full- and part-time employees within 75 miles of the school, not including temporaries. John, a full-time teacher who has worked at Central for 10 years, requests FMLA leave. John will have worked 1,250 hours by the time leave commences.

Question: Is John eligible for FMLA leave?

Answer: Yes. At the time leave commences, John will have met the 12-month and 1,250-hour eligibility requirements. At the time John requests FMLA leave, John satisfies the 50/75 test as Central has 50 employees within 75 miles of the school, including Sarah.

(iv) Proof of Employees Maintained on Payroll

Proof of employee eligibility for FMLA leave is determined based on all of the facts and employment records.[151] Courts have looked for proof that employees were retained on the payroll from payroll records, tax records, 1099 forms, and benefits records. For example, in *Gazda v. Pioneer Chlor Alkali Co.*, the court approved the employer's compilation of a list of all company employees who worked in the state at any time during the year of the FMLA leave request in dispute.[152] The list was prepared from payroll records, tax records, 1099 forms, and benefits records, as attested to by the human resources manager. School employers should similarly rely on such records (and expect to turn those records over to opposing counsel if the matter goes to litigation) in order to establish that the 50/75 eligibility test was not met.

3.07 INDIVIDUAL IS "DEEMED" TO HAVE MET THE FMLA ELIGIBILITY REQUIREMENTS

[1] General Rule

The DOL FMLA regulations recognize four situations in which an employee who may not technically meet all three eligibility requirements is nevertheless legally treated as if he or she has met the eligibility requirements. First, as discussed earlier in this chapter, the DOL regulations provide that all full-time schoolteachers are deemed to have met the 1,250-hour requirement.[153] A school employer has the burden of clearly demonstrating that the schoolteacher did not work the requisite 1,250 hours in the 12-month period preceding leave commencement.[154] If the school employer fails to clearly demonstrate that an employee does not meet the 1,250-hour requirement, the employee is deemed to have met that requirement, whether the employee actually worked the requisite hours or not.

Second, any employee (not just a teacher) will be deemed to have met the 1,250-hour eligibility test if the employer does not maintain accurate records of actual hours worked and is unable to prove that the employee did not work the minimum requisite hours.[155] FMLA recordkeeping requirements are addressed in Chapter 12.

Third, an employee will be deemed to have met the FMLA eligibility requirements if an employer fails to timely notify an employee that the employee is eligible for FMLA leave.[156]

Fourth, the DOL regulations prohibit an employer from challenging an employee's eligibility for FMLA leave if the employer previously confirmed that the employee met the eligibility requirements.[157]

This section will address the third and fourth situations in which an employee has been determined to have met the FMLA eligibility requirements. These situations involve employer notice obligations, which are addressed in detail in Chapter 6, *Notice Requirements*. This section will also address equitable principles that courts have applied to prevent employers from asserting that an employee failed to meet the FMLA eligibility requirements.

[2] Deemed Eligible as a Penalty for an Employer's Notification Failure

(i) General Rule

The federal FMLA imposes a number of employee-notification requirements on covered employers regarding FMLA benefits and obligations, including notice that the employee meets the eligibility requirements for FMLA leave. An employer may satisfy its employee eligibility notice obligation at three points in time.

First, if an employee notifies the employer of the need for FMLA leave before the employee meets the eligibility requirements, the employer must either (1) confirm the employee's eligibility based on a projection that the employee will be eligible on the date leave would commence or (2) advise the employee when the eligibility requirement is met.[158] If the employer confirms that the employee is eligible, the employer may not subsequently dispute the employee's eligibility.[159]

Second, if the employer does not initially confirm eligibility based on projections, the employer can wait until the employee satisfies the eligibility requirements before notifying the employee. In that case, the employer must notify the employee of FMLA eligibility as soon as practicable after the date eligibility is determined.[160] "As soon as practicable" requires employee notice of FMLA eligibility within two business days.[161] Extenuating circumstances can increase the "as soon as practicable" time period beyond two business days.[162] If the employer fails to advise the employee whether the employee is eligible prior to the date the requested leave is to commence, the employee will be deemed eligible for FMLA leave.[163] The employer may not then deny the leave.[164]

Third, if the employee does not give notice of the need for FMLA leave more than two business days prior to the date the leave is to commence, the employer must advise the employee that he or she is not eligible for FMLA leave within two business days of receiving the employee's request for leave.[165] If the employer does not notify the employee of FMLA eligibility within two business days, the employee will be deemed eligible.[166] Note that in this case extenuating circumstances will not extend the time period for an employer to advise an employee of FMLA eligibility. Note also that unlike in the previous situations discussed above, in this situation the DOL regulations do not specifically prohibit an employer from challenging the employee's eligibility or from denying the employee FMLA leave.

(ii) Court Treatment of "Deemed Eligible" Penalty Provision

The courts have been uniformly hostile to the "deemed eligible" penalty provision contained in 29 C.F.R. § 825.110(d) for an employer's failure to timely notify an employee of FMLA eligibility. The overwhelming majority of courts that have addressed this issue have found the penalty provision invalid. These courts reasoned that the DOL exceeded its rule-making powers by imposing a penalty that could make eligible for FMLA leave employees who did not meet the statutory eligibility requirements mandated by Congress.[167] The one judge of the sole court decision[168] sustaining the validity of the "deemed eligible" penalty provision in § 825.110(d) later reversed himself.[169]

The decision of the U.S. Supreme Court in *Ragsdale v. Wolverine World Wide, Inc.*,[170] likely has sealed the fate of the "deemed eligible" penalty provision in 29 C.F.R. § 825.110(d). The issue in *Ragsdale* was the validity of the FMLA penalty provision in 29 C.F.R. § 825.700(a) for an employer's failure to timely notify an employee that it had designated leave as FMLA qualifying. The DOL regulations provide, as a penalty, that FMLA leave already taken does not count against the employee's yearly 12-workweek entitlement. In this case, the effect of the penalty was to grant an employee more than the 12 workweeks of leave provided by the statute. The Supreme Court found the penalty provision invalid as it extended more leave to employees than permitted by the statute. At least one court has cited *Ragsdale* as support for its determination that the "deemed eligible" penalty provision in 29 C.F.R. § 825.110(d) is invalid.[171]

Employers must continue to notify employees whether they meet the FMLA eligibility requirements in accordance with 29 C.F.R. § 825.110(d). The courts invalidated only the *penalty* imposed by the DOL regulations for an employer's failure to timely notify an employee whether the employee meets the FMLA eligibility requirements for leave. The requirement in 29 C.F.R. § 825.110(d) that employers timely notify employees that they meet the FMLA eligibility requirements remains valid.[172] And an employer's violation of the notice provisions is not without consequence. While the courts have invalidated the "deemed eligible" penalty provision of 29 C.F.R. § 825.110(d), they have imposed equitable doctrines (discussed below) that preclude an employer from challenging an employee's FMLA eligibility.

[3] Estoppel from Challenging Eligibility

Courts have applied general equitable principles to prevent an employer from challenging the FMLA eligibility of an employee. Courts have applied these equitable principles even where it results in an otherwise ineligible employee's being afforded the benefits and protections of the FMLA. Similarly, at least one court applied an interference theory to reach a similar result. These areas are discussed further below.

(i) Equitable Estoppel

Equitable estoppel is a doctrine of equity (e.g., fairness) created by the courts that operates apart from statutory law.[173] Equitable estoppel arises where the enforcement of the rights of one party would work an injustice upon another party due to the latter's justifiable reliance on the former's words or conduct.[174] While courts use various factors to determine whether the doctrine of equitable estoppel applies, fundamentally the doctrine requires that (1) the party to be estopped make a material misrepresentation to the other party with reason to believe the other party will rely upon it and (2) the other party reasonably rely upon it (3) to his or her detriment.[175] Equitable estoppel applies even where the employer believes in good faith that what it told the employee is true.[176] An employer's silence regarding an employee's FMLA eligibility has been found by some courts to constitute misrepresentation justifying application of the doctrine of equitable estoppel.[177] As a result of an employer's defective notice of FMLA eligibility, where all of the elements of equitable estoppel are met, an employer may be estopped or prevented from challenging an employee's eligibility. Of course, in the absence of detrimental reliance on the part of the employee, courts have declined to estop an employer from challenging an employee's FMLA eligibility.[178]

The majority of courts that have addressed the issue have applied the doctrine of equitable estoppel to disputes regarding FMLA eligibility. Again, by preventing an employer from challenging an employee's eligibility, these courts necessarily treat otherwise ineligible employees as being eligible for purposes of receiving FMLA benefits and protections. At least one court, however, has declined to apply equitable estoppel that would have resulted in an employee's being treated as if she were eligible notwithstanding the fact that the employer did not employ 50 or more employees within 75 miles of her worksite.[179]

Equitable estoppel is often asserted in two instances: (1) where the employer fails to notify an employee whether he or she is eligible for

FMLA leave as required by § 825.110(d) and (2) where the employer initially confirms that the employee is eligible for FMLA leave and later challenges that determination. With respect to the former, the potential that equitable estoppel will prevent any challenge to an employee's FMLA eligibility should be sufficient incentive for school employers to abide by the eligibility notice provisions of § 825.110(d). Regarding the latter, the DOL regulations and equitable estoppel prohibit an employer from subsequently challenging an employee's FMLA eligibility after the employer notifies the employee that he or she meets the eligibility requirements.

Courts have equitably estopped employers from challenging an employee's FMLA eligibility after the employer initially confirmed that the employee met the eligibility requirements. For example, in one case an employer erroneously confirmed that an employee was eligible for FMLA leave even though the employee had not worked for the employer for at least 12 months. The employer subsequently challenged the employee's eligibility for FMLA leave. The court found that the employer was equitably estopped from challenging FMLA eligibility because the employer notified the employee prior to leave commencement that the employee was eligible and the employee relied on those representations before deciding to take leave.

Because an employee would have taken leave anyway, one court declined to apply equitable estoppel to prevent an employer from challenging eligibility where the employer had previously confirmed the FMLA eligibility.[180] The court reasoned that the employee did not detrimentally rely on the employer's confirmation of eligibility because the employee would have taken leave in any event.

(ii) Defective Eligibility Notice as Interference with FMLA Rights

The DOL regulations and the courts have indicated that an employer's failure to notify an employee of eligibility may constitute actionable interference with FMLA rights. The DOL regulations provide: "Any violations of the Act or of these regulations constitute interfering with, restraining, or denying the exercise of rights provided by the Act."[181]

The Supreme Court in *Ragsdale v. Wolverine World Wide, Inc.* certainly left open the door for actions based on employer violation of

FMLA notice requirements, at least where the employee can show detrimental reliance and prejudice resulting in actual harm to the employee.[182] Note that while similar, the test for finding an FMLA notice violation in *Ragsdale* is not the same as equitable estoppel.

Before *Ragsdale*, one district court suggested that as a result of employer interference with FMLA rights, eligibility could be extended to an employee who is otherwise not eligible under the FMLA.[183] In that case, the employee fell just short of the 1,250 hours of work required before taking the disputed leave. The court opined that if the employee's failure to meet the FMLA eligibility requirements was caused by the employer's failure to fulfill its FMLA notice requirements, such employer interference could be considered to excuse the employee's ineligibility.

(iii) Collateral Estoppel

Collateral estoppel is a doctrine that seeks to give preclusive effect to matters that have already been adjudicated. The issue typically arises where an FMLA dispute is initially addressed by an arbitrator pursuant to a collective bargaining agreement or an individual employment contract. The FMLA dispute subsequently blossoms into civil litigation, and one of the parties seeks to estop or prevent the other party from raising or challenging issues that were allegedly previously resolved by the finding of the arbitrator. Most federal courts have refused to apply collateral estoppel to give preclusive effect to arbitration decisions involving employee statutory rights such as the FMLA.[184] Courts refusing to give preclusive effect to arbitration note that "arbitral fact-finding is not equivalent to judicial fact-finding, the arbitrator's expertise is the law of the shop, not the law of the land, and the arbitrator's authority derives solely from contract so that he has no general authority to invoke public laws that conflict with the collective bargaining agreement."[185]

In *Thoele v. U.S. Postal Service*, the employee argued that the court was bound by an arbitrator's determination that the employee should be deemed eligible as a result of the employer's failure to notify the employee otherwise.[186] Collateral estoppel, the court noted, applies if (1) the issue sought to be precluded is the same as that involved in a prior action, (2) the issue was actually litigated, (3) the determination of the issue was essential to the final judgment, and (4) the party against whom estoppel is to be applied was fully represented in the prior case. The court concluded that the doctrine of collateral estoppel did not apply based on the facts of the case because the determination of the issue was not essential to the arbitrator's final decision.

3.08 EFFECT OF MORE LENIENT EMPLOYEE ELIGIBILITY REQUIREMENTS VOLUNTARILY ADOPTED BY EMPLOYERS

The FMLA encourages employers to provide more generous leave benefits than the minimum required by the FMLA.[187] An employer must observe any employment benefit program or plan that provides greater family or medical leave rights to employees than the rights established by the federal FMLA.[188] One of the ways that employers may provide more generous family and medical leave benefits than are required by the FMLA is to reduce the eligibility requirements for such leave by company policy or pursuant to the terms of a collective bargaining agreement. For example, school policy may allow employees to take family and medical leave after working only 6 months, not the 12 months required by the FMLA. The question is, what effect does the lowering of eligibility requirements by more generous school policy have on an employee's right to take job-protected FMLA leave?

Courts that have addressed this issue have held that, while an employer is permitted to offer more generous family and medical leave policies, leave taken under the more generous provisions of those policies is not protected by the federal FMLA. Rather, what protections exist are governed by the employer's policies or contract. For example, in *Thomas v. Pearle Vision, Inc.*, company policy permitted an employee with 12 months of employment and 1,250 hours of work to take FMLA leave.[189] The policy left out the 50/75 FMLA eligibility test. The court held that, notwithstanding Pearle Vision's policy, the employee was not an eligible employee under the Act because he was employed at a worksite where there were not 50 employees within 75 miles. The court opined that the employee might have a claim for breach of contract based on the more generous company family and medical leave policy.[190]

Other courts have held that the language in 29 U.S.C. § 2652 requiring an employer to abide by more generous family and medical leave policies than the minimum required by the FMLA is "merely a truism which emphasizes that employers are legally bound by valid contractual agreements made with their employees regarding employment benefits. An employer's contractual obligations are distinct, however, from . . . the FMLA itself."[191]

In *Rich v. Delta Airlines, Inc.*, company policy provided family and medical leave to employees who worked a minimum of 540 hours, rather than the 1,250 hours required by the FMLA.[192] Relying on 29 C.F.R. § 825.700(a), the employee argued that 540 hours should be used to compute her eligibility for the benefits and protections of the FMLA. The court disagreed. The court held that the FMLA expressly and unequivocally provides that for an employee to be eligible for protections under the Act, the employee must have worked 1,250 hours in the previous 12-month period. The employee cannot use the employer's internal policy to amend the explicit coverage provision adopted by Congress. Regarding the employee's reliance on 29 C.F.R. § 825.700(a), which requires employers to observe any employment benefit plan or program that provides more generous family or medical leave benefits, the court observed:

> Section 825.700 does not, and could not, however, create a federal cause of action under the FMLA to enforce the voluntary employer policies of providing benefits that exceed those required by the FMLA. The Department of Labor has no regulatory power to rewrite, and clearly did not rewrite, the FMLA in such a manner.
>
> The purpose of this regulation is to ensure that the FMLA is not interpreted to abrogate any currently existing employee-benefit plan. Therefore, if an employer has a plan or program more generous than the FMLA, then the FMLA will not supersede or reduce those more generous benefits which the employer has chosen to provide.[193]

Schools should proceed with caution when agreeing to more generous family or medical leave benefits in the form of reduced eligibility. Any leave taken before an employee reaches the eligibility requirements mandated by the federal FMLA would not count against the employee's 12-week entitlement. For example, a school agrees to a collective bargaining agreement that permits an employee to take family or medical leave for the same reasons as the federal FMLA, but the employee has to work only 600 hours to be eligible for leave. Any family or medical leave taken by the employee before the employee reaches 1,250 hours would, by definition, be covered only by school policy. Such leave would not be covered by the federal FMLA and, therefore, could not be deducted from the employee's 12-week federal FMLA leave entitlement. The end result is that a school that provides more generous benefits than the minimum required by the federal FMLA will necessarily need to administer the program carefully to avoid violation of the federal FMLA. A school will violate the federal FMLA by charging leave against the employee's 12-week federal FMLA account where such charge is not warranted because, for example, the employee does not meet the eligibility requirements for federal FMLA leave.

3.09 ELIGIBILITY REQUIREMENTS UNDER STATE FAMILY AND MEDICAL LEAVE LAWS

Eligibility requirements vary greatly under state family and medical leave laws. State eligibility requirements may be less than, the same as, or greater than (and in some cases, much greater than) those of the federal FMLA. For example, under Alaska's family and medical leave law, employees of covered public employers are eligible for leave if they have been employed by the covered employer for at least 35 hours a week for at least 6 consecutive months or for at least 17.5 hours a week for at least 12 consecutive months during the period immediately preceding leave commencement.[194] Eligibility under Connecticut's private sector family leave law requires an employee, at leave commencement, to have been employed for a total of at least 12 months and to have worked for at least 1,000 hours.[195] Note that eligibility under Alaskan and Connecticut law does not include a minimum employee–head count requirement comparable to the federal FMLA's 50/75 test.

School administrators must carefully weigh the requirements of any applicable state family or medical leave laws to determine whether the employee meets the eligibility requirements of state law.

3.10 INTERACTION OF THE FEDERAL FMLA WITH STATE FAMILY AND MEDICAL LEAVE LAWS: EMPLOYEE ELIGIBILITY

The interaction of the federal FMLA with state and local family and medical leave laws is an area fraught with confusion. The confusion flows from the general rule that the federal FMLA does not supersede any state or local law that provides greater family or medical leave rights than those provided by the FMLA.[196] Neither the statute nor the DOL regulations define what constitutes "greater" or more generous family and medical leave laws. In comments accompanying the final regulations, the DOL indicates that the determination of which law applies (e.g., state versus federal) in any given situation and which law is more generous is examined on a provision-by-provision basis.[197] The DOL regulations also provide some examples as a guide for employers to address the intersection of federal, state, and local family and medical leave laws.[198] We will be referring back to these DOL comments throughout this book.

In terms of eligibility, where there is a state or local family and medical leave law in addition to the federal FMLA, an employee must meet the basic eligibility requirements of each applicable law. An employee eligible under only one law would receive benefits in accordance only with that law.[199] For example, to be eligible for family and medical leave under Alaska's law, the employee must have been employed by the employer for at least 35 hours a week for 6 consecutive months or 17.5 hours a week for at least 12 consecutive months preceding leave commencement.[200] Eligibility for family medical leave under Alaska law is clearly more generous than under the federal FMLA. An employee who meets the minimum eligibility requirements under Alaska's law may not satisfy the higher requirements under the federal FMLA. In that case, the employee's family and medical leave would be governed solely by Alaska's law. A covered employee who met the lower eligibility requirements under Alaska's family and medical leave law would not automatically be eligible for purposes of the federal FMLA.

Of course, an employee could simultaneously meet the eligibility requirements of both the federal FMLA and an applicable state family and medical leave law. In our example, the federal FMLA would apply only where a covered Alaska employee met all three eligibility requirements under federal law. Where a covered Alaska employee meets the requirements of the family and medical leave law of Alaska and the federal FMLA, both laws apply. The determination of whether the benefits and protections of the federal FMLA or of Alaska's law apply is thereafter made on a provision-by-provision basis. Whichever law, state law or the federal FMLA, provides the more generous benefits to employees is what governs.

NOTES

1. 29 U.S.C. § 2611(2); 29 C.F.R. §§ 825.110(a)(1)–(3), 825.600(b) (providing that the usual requirements for employees to be eligible apply to local educational agencies); accord *Washington v. Cooper Hospital/University Medical Center*, No. 03-5791 (RBK), 2005 U.S. Dist. LEXIS 31062, at *12 (D.N.J. Dec. 2, 2005); *Tornberg v. Business Interlink Services, Inc.*, 237 F. Supp. 2d 778, 784 (E.D. Mich. 2002).

2. *Lackey v. Jackson County, Tennessee*, No. 2:01-0058, 2003 U.S. Dist. LEXIS 25686 (M.D. Tenn. Jan. 6, 2003), *aff'd*, No. 03-5193, 2004 App. LEXIS 13708 (6th Cir. Tenn. June 22, 2004).

3. 29 U.S.C. § 2612(a)(1); 29 C.F.R. § 825.100(a).

4. 29 U.S.C. § 2614(a)(1).

5. 29 U.S.C. § 2617(a)(1).

6. 29 U.S.C. § 2611(3); 29 C.F.R. § 825.800 ("employee" defined); see also *Figueira v. Black Entertainment Television*, 944 F. Supp. 299, 308 n.2 (S.D.N.Y. 1996).

7. 29 U.S.C. § 203(e).

8. 29 U.S.C. § 2611(3); 29 C.F.R. § 825.800 ("employee" defined).

9. 29 U.S.C. § 203(e).

10. See, e.g., 29 C.F.R. § 825.105(b) (employee whose name appears on employer's payroll considered employed by employer).

11. DOL WH FMLA Advisory Opinion No. 7 (Oct. 8, 1993).

12. Comments on Regulations Implementing the Family and Medical Leave Act of 1993 (§ 825.800), 60 Fed. Reg. at 2233.

13. *Id.*

14. DOL WH FMLA Advisory Opinion No. 9 (Oct. 18, 1993).

15. 29 C.F.R. § 825.800 ("employee" defined).

16. *Id.*

17. 29 U.S.C. § 2611(2)(B) (excluding from definition of "eligible employee" any federal officer or employee covered by subchapter 63 of Title 5). The FMLA rights of most federal employees are governed by Title II of the FMLA, 5 U.S.C. §§ 6381–6387.

18. Discussion of the differences between Title I and II of the federal FMLA is beyond the scope of this book. For additional information on the FMLA rights of federal employees, see Carl C. Bosland, *A Federal Sector Guide to the Family and Medical Leave Act & Related Litigation* (Dewey Publications 2003).

19. 29 C.F.R. § 825.800 ("employee" defined).

20. *Id.*

21. 29 C.F.R. § 825.105(a); see also *Gazda v. Pioneer Chlor Alkali Co.*, 10 F. Supp. 2d 656, 675 (S.D. Tex. 1997).

22. See *Astudillo v. U.S. News & World Report*, No. 02-Civ. 7902 (WHP), 2004 U.S. Dist. LEXIS 18685 (S.D.N.Y. Sept. 17, 2004), at *10–12; *Sousa v. Orient Arts Inc.*, No. 97 Civ. 0819 (BSJ), 1999 U.S. Dist. LEXIS 2934 (S.D.N.Y. Mar. 16, 1999); *Bonnetts v. Arctic Express, Inc.*, 7 F. Supp. 2d 977, 982 n.2 (S.D. Ohio 1998).

23. See *Holliday v. Vacationland Federal Credit Union*, No. 3:03 CV 7493, 2004 U.S. Dist. LEXIS 5655 (N.D. Ohio Apr. 5, 2004).

24. *Id.* at *8 n.1.

25. See *id.*; *Astudillo*, 2004 U.S. Dist. LEXIS 18685, at *10–11; *Bonnetts*, 7 F. Supp. 2d 977.

26. *Astudillo*, 2004 U.S. Dist. LEXIS 18685, at *10–11; *Bonnetts*, 7 F. Supp. 2d 977.

27. 29 U.S.C. § 2618; 29 C.F.R. § 825.600(a).

28. 29 C.F.R. § 825.600(b).

29. *Brohm v. JH Properties, Inc.*, 149 F.3d 517, 523 (6th Cir. 1998) (holding that denial of request for FMLA leave did not violate the Act where request was made after individual had been terminated and was no longer an employee); *Klaus v. Builders Concrete Co.*, No. 00 C 7757, 2002 U.S. Dist. LEXIS 1919, at *14–*15 (N.D. Ill. Feb. 7, 2002); *Hammon v. DHL Airways, Inc.*, 980 F. Supp. 919, 927 (S.D. Ohio 1997) (holding that former employee was not an eligible employee entitled to benefits and protections of the FMLA), *aff'd*, 165 F.3d 441 (6th Cir. 1999).

30. 29 U.S.C. § 2611(2)(A)(i); 29 C.F.R. § 825.110(a)(1).

31. *Dolse v. Office Depot, Inc.*, 231 F.3d 202, 203 (5th Cir. 2000); *McEachern v. Prime Hospitality Corp.*, No. 02-536 ADM/AJB, 2003 U.S. Dist. LEXIS 7997, at *9 (D. Minn. May 8, 2003); *Sewall v. Chicago Transit Authority*, No.

99-C-8372, 2001 U.S. Dist. LEXIS 330, at *10–*11 (N.D. Ill. Jan. 16, 2001); *Stewart v. Intern, Inc.*, No. 00-314-HA, 2000 U.S. Dist. LEXIS 12980, at *13–*15 (D. Or. June 19, 2000); *Scheidecker v. Arvig Enterprises, Inc.*, 122 F. Supp. 2d 1031, 1045 (D. Minn. 2000).

32. 29 C.F.R. § 825.110(b).

33. *Id.*

34. *Id.*

35. *Id.*; see also *Ruder v. Maine General Medical Center*, 204 F. Supp. 2d 16, 18–20 (D. Me. 2002) (holding that 2 weeks of paid vacation at end of first year counted toward 12-month eligibility requirement).

36. 29 C.F.R. § 825.110(d).

37. *Id.*

38. The manner in which FMLA leave may be taken is addressed in Chapter 8, *Leave Amount and Scheduling*.

39. See *Barron v. Runyon*, 11 F. Supp. 2d 676, 679–83 (E.D. Va. 1998); DOL WH FMLA Advisory Opinion No. 112 (Sept. 11, 2000).

40. See *Walker v. Elmore County Board of Education*, 223 F. Supp. 2d 1255, 1257–58 (M.D. Ala. 2002), *aff'd*, 369 F.3d 1249 (11th Cir. 2004); *Sewall v. Chicago Transit Authority*, No. 99-C-8372, 2001 U.S. Dist. LEXIS 330, at *13–*15 (N.D. Ill. Jan. 16, 2001); *Broidy v. American General Finance Co.*, No. 98-2728, 1999 U.S. Dist. LEXIS 8405, at *21 (E.D. Pa. May 27, 1999).

41. *Ruder v. Maine General Medical Center*, 204 F. Supp. 2d 16, 18–20 (D. Me. 2002).

42. The USERRA is codified at 38 U.S.C. § 4301–4333.

43. See U.S. Department of Labor, USERRA-FMLA Questions and Answers: The Effect of the Uniformed Services Employment and Reemployment Rights Act on Leave Eligibility Under the Family and Medical Leave Act, question 4 (July 25, 2002), available at http://www.dol.gov/vets/media/fmlaq-a.pdf.

44. *Id.* question 5.

45. *Id.*

46. 29 C.F.R. § 825.112(f); see also 29 C.F.R. § 825.105(c) (addressing which employees count for purposes of employer FMLA coverage).

47. 29 C.F.R. § 825.112(f).

48. See 29 C.F.R. § 825.110(b); see also 29 C.F.R. § 825.105(c) (counting employees on disciplinary suspension or leave for purposes of employer FMLA coverage because employer has a reasonable expectation that the employee will later return to active employment).

49. 29 C.F.R. § 825.110(b).

50. Comments on Regulations Implementing the Family and Medical Leave Act of 1993 (§ 825.105), 60 Fed. Reg. 2180, 2181 (Jan. 6, 1995).

51. 29 C.F.R. § 825.105(c).

52. Comments on Regulations Implementing the Family and Medical Leave Act of 1993 (§ 825.105), 60 Fed. Reg. at 2182.

53. *Id.*

54. 29 C.F.R. § 825.105(c).

55. *Id.* (emphasis added).

56. *Id.*

57. Comments on Regulations Implementing the Family and Medical Leave Act of 1993 (§ 825.105), 60 Fed. Reg. at 2181.

58. See *Ricco v. Potter*, 377 F.3d 599, 603–06 (6th Cir. 2004); *Moore v. U.S. Postal Service*, 83 M.S.P.R. 533 (1999), *petition dismissed*, 85 M.S.P.R. 249 (1999).

59. See *Plumley v. Southern Container, Inc.*, 303 F.3d 364, 367 (1st Cir. 2002).

60. 29 C.F.R. § 825.106(d).

61. DOL WH FMLA Advisory Opinion No. 37 (July 7, 1994); see also *Miller v. Defiance Metal Products, Inc.*, 989 F. Supp. 945, 946–48 (N.D. Ohio 1997).

62. 29 C.F.R. § 825.107(c); accord *Vanderhoof v. Life Extension Institute,* 988 F. Supp. 507, 514 (D.N.J. 1997); *Rhoads v. FDIC*, 956 F. Supp. 1239, 1252 (D. Md. 1997), *aff'd in part, vacated and remanded in part on other grounds*, 257 F.3d 373 (4th cir. 2001).

63. 29 C.F.R. § 825.107(c).

64. *Id.*

65. 29 U.S.C. § 2611(2)(A)(ii); 29 C.F.R. §§ 825.110(a)(2), 825.800 ("eligible employee" defined).

66. See *Woodford v. Community Action of Greene County, Inc.*, 268 F.3d 51, 54–58 (2nd Cir. 2001); *Plumley v. Southern Container, Inc.*, No. 00-140-P-C, 2001 U.S. Dist. LEXIS 16040, at *18–*21 (D. Me. Oct. 9, 2001), *aff'd*, 303 F.3d 364, 372 (1st Cir. 2002); *Nelson v. City of Cranston*, 116 F. Supp. 2d 260, 267 (D.R.I. 2000); *Thoele v. U.S. Postal Service*, 996 F. Supp. 818, 822 (N.D. Ill. Mar. 11, 1998).

67. *Ricco v. Potter*, 377 F.3d 599, 604 (6th Cir. 2004).

68. 29 U.S.C. § 2611(2)(C); 29 C.F.R. § 825.110(c).

69. *Ricco*, 377 F.3d at 604.

70. *Id.*

71. 29 C.F.R. § 825.110(c); accord *Ricco*, 377 F.3d at 604; *Kosakow v. New Rochelle Radiology Associates*, 274 F.3d 706, 715–22 (2nd Cir. 2001); *Robinson-Scott v. Delta Airlines, Inc.*, 4 F. Supp. 2d 1183 (N.D. Ga. 1998).

72. *Plumley v. Southern Container, Inc.*, 303 F.3d 364, 372 (1st Cir. 2002) (rejecting argument that status as a full-time employee supplanted FMLA eligibility requirements); *Lacoparra v. Pergament Home Centers, Inc.*, 982 F. Supp. 213, 219 (S.D.N.Y. 1997) (asserting that employee's status as a full-time employee was not probative of the hours actually worked for purposes of the FMLA 1,250-hour eligibility requirement).

73. 29 C.F.R. § 785.7; see also *Armour & Co. v. Wantock*, 323 U.S. 126 (1944); *Skidmore v. Swift & Co.*, 323 U.S. 134 (1944).

74. 29 C.F.R. §§ 785.15, 785.16.

75. 29 C.F.R. §§ 785.11–785.13.

76. 29 C.F.R. § 785.16(a).

77. 29 C.F.R. § 785.16.

78. 29 C.F.R. §§ 785.18, 785.19(a).

79. 29 C.F.R. § 785.18.

80. 29 U.S.C. §§ 251–262; 29 C.F.R. § 785.9.

81. *Kosakow v. New Rochell Radiology Associates, P.C.*, 274 F.3d 706, 717–18 (2d Cir. 2001).

82. *Rich v. Delta Airlines, Inc.*, 921 F. Supp. 767, 774 (N.D. Ga. 1996); see also *Robinson-Scott v. Delta Air Lines*, 4 F. Supp. 2d 1183, 1185–86 (N.D. Ga. 1998).

83. Comments on Regulations Implementing the Family and Medical Leave Act of 1993 (§ 825.110), 60 Fed. Reg. 2180, 2186 (Jan. 6, 1995); DOL WH FMLA Advisory Opinion No. 18 (Nov. 15, 1993).

84. DOL WH FMLA Advisory Opinion No. 70 (Aug. 23, 1995).

85. Comments on Regulations Implementing the Family and Medical Leave Act of 1993 (§ 825.110), 60 Fed. Reg. at 2186; DOL WH FMLA Advisory Opinion No. 70 (Aug. 23, 1995) (explaining that "hours worked" does not include time paid but not "worked" (paid vacation, personal or sick leave, holidays); nor does it include unpaid leave (of any kind) or periods of layoff); DOL WH FMLA Advisory Opinion No. 46 (Oct. 14, 1994) (asserting that paid or unpaid leave, sick days, and sabbatical leave are not counted toward FMLA eligibility, even if the employee continues to receive some compensation); DOL WH FMLA Advisory Opinion No. 18 (Nov. 15, 1993) (asserting that paid or unpaid leave does not count toward 1,250-hour FMLA eligibility requirement).

86. See *Sepe v. McDonnell Douglas Corp.*, 176 F.3d 1113, 1115 (8th Cir. 1999) (holding that time on medical leave does not count toward FMLA "hours worked"), *cert. denied*, 528 U.S. 1062 (1999); *Aldrich v. Greg*, 200 F. Supp. 2d 784, 788 (N.D. Ohio 2002) (holding that paid vacations and holidays

do not count toward 1,250-hour requirement); *Walters v. AP Supermarket Service*, No. 3:98-CV-1222, 2001 U.S. Dist. LEXIS 2696, at *10–*11 (M.D. Pa. Jan. 31, 2001) (holding that time spent on FMLA leave does not count toward 1,250-hour eligibility requirement); *Nelson v. City of Cranston*, 116 F. Supp. 2d 260, 266–67 (D.R.I. 2000) (holding that time spent on paid leave and LWOP not counted toward FMLA eligibility); *Veal v. AT& T*, No. 99-0370 "K"(2), 2000 U.S. Dist. LEXIS 3863, at *23 (E.D. La. Mar. 22, 2000) (disability leave); *Rockwell v. Mack Trucks, Inc.*, 8 F. Supp. 2d 499, 502 (D. Md. 1998) (employee absences); *Clark v. Allegheny University Hospital*, No. 97-6113, 1998 U.S. Dist. LEXIS 2305, at *13–*14 (E.D. Pa. 1998) (paid and unpaid leave); *Caruthers v. Proctor & Gamble Manufacturing*, 961 F. Supp. 1484, 1490 (D. Kan. 1997) (holding that leave time does not count toward 1,250-hour eligibility requirement); *Robbins v. Bureau of National Affairs*, 896 F. Supp. 18, 20–21 (D.D.C. 1995) (maternity leave).

87. 29 C.F.R. § 785.42.

88. *Id.*; see also *Koontz v. USX Corp.*, No. 99-3191, 2001 U.S. Dist. LEXIS 9319, at *25–*26 (E.D. Pa. July 2, 2001) (holding that time spent by union official processing grievances was not "hours worked" for purposes of FMLA where employer neither tracked nor compensated the hours employees spent performing union business and where the union paid the employee for this time).

89. U.S. Department of Labor, USERRA-FMLA Questions and Answers: The Effect of the Uniformed Services Employment and Reemployment Rights Act on Leave Eligibility under the Family and Medical Leave Act (July 25, 2002), available at http://www.dol.gov/vets/media/fmlaq-a.pdf.

90. *Id.*

91. 921 F. Supp. 767, 774 (N.D. Ga. 1996).

92. *Kosakow v. New Rochelle Radiology Associates, P.C.*, 274 F.3d 706, 720–22 (2d Cir. 2001).

93. *Id.*; see also *Rich v. Delta Airlines, Inc.*, 921 F. Supp. 767, 774 (N.D. Ga. 1996) (holding that because it was predominately for the benefit of employer, time spent by employee in jet recurrent training constituted "hours worked" under FLSA and counted toward 1,250-hour eligibility requirement).

94. See *Nelson v. City of Cranston,* 116 F. Supp. 2d 260, 266–67 (D.R.I. 2000) (holding that 20-day suspension period not included in 1,250 hours of work for FMLA eligibility); *Thoele v. U.S. Postal Service,* 996 F. Supp. 818, 821–22 (N.D. Ill. 1998) (holding that period of suspension not counted toward FMLA 1,250-hour eligibility requirement).

95. 303 F.3d 364, 369–72 (1st Cir. 2002).

96. 377 F.3d 599, 603–05 (6th Cir. 2004).

97. Comments on Regulations Implementing the Family and Medical Leave Act of 1993 (§ 825.110), 60 Fed. Reg. 2180, 2186 (Jan. 6, 1995) (explaining that "hours worked" does not include unpaid leave (of any kind) or periods of layoff).

98. No. 3:99-CV-1286-D, 1999 U.S. Dist. LEXIS 15189, at *5–*6 (N.D. Tex. Sept. 24, 1998).

99. 29 C.F.R. § 825.106(d); DOL WH FMLA Advisory Opinion No. 37 (July 7, 1994); see also *Miller v. Defiance Metal Products, Inc.*, 989 F. Supp. 945, 946–48 (N.D. Ohio 1997).

100. 29 C.F.R. § 825.105(b); DOL WH FMLA Advisory Opinion No. 9 (Oct. 18, 1993).

101. 29 C.F.R. § 825.105(b).

102. DOL WH FMLA Advisory Opinion No. 9 (Oct. 18, 1993).

103. 29 C.F.R. § 825.110(c).

104. *Id.*

105. *Id.*

106. *Id.*

107. *Id.*

108. *Id.*

109. 29 C.F.R. § 825.800 ("teacher" defined).

110. 29 C.F.R. § 825.110(c).

111. 29 C.F.R. § 825.110(d).

112. 11 F. Supp. 2d 676, 680–81 (E.D. Va. 1998).

113. DOL WH FMLA Advisory Opinion No. 112 (Sept. 11, 2000).

114. 29 U.S.C. § 2611(2)(B)(ii); 29 C.F.R. § 825.110(a)(3), (f).

115. 29 C.F.R. § 825.600(b).

116. *Id.*

117. 29 C.F.R. § 825.110(f).

118. Comments on Regulations Implementing the Family and Medical Leave Act of 1993 (§ 825.110), 60 Fed. Reg. 2180, 2186 (Jan. 6, 1995).

119. 29 C.F.R. § 825.110(f).

120. *Id.* Note that employees of educational institutions who are employed permanently or who are under contract are "maintained on the payroll" during any portion of the year when school is not in session. 29 C.F.R. § 825.111(c).

121. S. Rep. No. 103-3, at 23 (1993), as reprinted in 1993 U.S.C.C.A.N. 3, 25; H.R. Rep. No. 103-8(I), at 35 (1993), as reprinted in 1993 U.S.C.C.A.N. 3, 23; Comments on Regulations Implementing the Family and Medical Leave Act of 1993 (§ 825.111), 60 Fed. Reg. 2180, 2187 (Jan. 6, 1995); accord *Cialini v. Nilfisk-Advance American, Inc.*, No. 99-3954, 2000 U.S. Dist. LEXIS 2042, at *10–*12 (E.D. Pa. Feb. 28, 2000) (looking to

WARN Act regulations and case law to determine location of employee worksite for purposes of FMLA). The DOL regulations governing the 50/75 FMLA test are codified at 29 C.F.R. § 825.111. Regulations implementing the WARN Act may be found at 20 C.F.R. pt. 639. The WARN Act regulations defining a "single site of employment" are set forth in 20 C.F.R. § 639.3(i).

122. 29 C.F.R. § 825.111(a)(1), (2).

123. *Cialini*, 2000 U.S. Dist. LEXIS 2042, at *11–*12 (asserting that the true source of instructions, not mere conduits through which instructions flow, is the worksite of a sales employee without a fixed worksite).

124. 29 C.F.R. § 825.111(a)(2).

125. 29 C.F.R. § 825.111(a)(1).

126. *Id.*

127. *Id.*

128. See 20 C.F.R. § 639.3(i)(3).

129. 29 C.F.R. § 825.111(a)(2).

130. 29 C.F.R. § 825.111(a)(1), (2); 20 C.F.R. § 639.3(i)(6).

131. 29 C.F.R. § 825.111(a)(2); see also *Cialini v. Nilfisk-Advance American, Inc.*, No. 99-3954, 2000 U.S. Dist. LEXIS 2042, at *16–*17 (E.D. Pa. Feb. 28, 2000) (holding that worksite of sales representative was not personal residence but office to which plaintiff reported and received assignments).

132. 29 C.F.R. § 825.111(a)(3).

133. 29 C.F.R. § 825.106(c).

134. 29 C.F.R. § 825.111(b).

135. Comments on Regulations Implementing the Family and Medical Leave Act of 1993 (§ 825.111), 60 Fed. Reg. 2180, 2187 (Jan. 6, 1995); accord *Hackworth v. Progressive Casualty Insurance Co.*, No. 05-6198, 2006 U.S. App. LEXIS 28179, at *10–*23 (10th Cir. Nov. 14, 2006) (75-mile rule measured by surface miles, not linear or "as the crow flies" miles).

136. 29 C.F.R. § 825.111(b).

137. 29 C.F.R. § 825.111(c).

138. Comments on Regulations Implementing the Family and Medical Leave Act of 1993 (§ 825.111), 60 Fed. Reg. at 2188.

139. 29 C.F.R. § 825.111(c).

140. *Id.* (citing 29 C.F.R. § 825.105(c)).

141. 29 C.F.R. § 825.105(b)–(c).

142. See Comments on Regulations Implementing the Family and Medical Leave Act of 1993 (§ 825.111), 60 Fed. Reg. at 2189.

143. See *id.*

144. See *id.* (referring to the discussion under 29 C.F.R. § 825.105 for employer coverage).

145. 29 C.F.R. § 825.105(c).

146. Comments on Regulations Implementing the Family and Medical Leave Act of 1993 (§ 825.105), 60 Fed. Reg. at 2181–82.

147. *Grimsley v. Fiesta Salons, Inc.*, No. 01-10376-BC, 2003 U.S. Dist. LEXIS 298 (E.D. Mich. Jan. 7, 2000).

148. The memo is available at http://www.dol.gov/vets/media/fmlarights.pdf.

149. 29 C.F.R. § 825.106(a).

150. 29 C.F.R. § 825.106(d).

151. *Figueria v. Black Entertainment Television, Inc.*, 944 F. Supp. 299, 308 (S.D.N.Y. 1996).

152. 10 F. Supp. 2d 656, 674–75 (S.D. Tex. 1997).

153. 29 C.F.R. § 825.110(c).

154. *Id.*

155. *Id.*

156. 29 C.F.R. § 825.110(d).

157. *Id.*

158. *Id.*

159. *Id.*

160. *Id.*

161. *Id.*

162. *Id.*

163. *Id.*

164. *Id.*

165. *Id.*

166. *Id.*

167. *Evanoff v. Minneapolis Public Schools*, No. 00-2479, 2001 U.S. App. LEXIS 6469, at *4–*5 (8th Cir. Apr. 17, 2001); *Woodford v. Community Action of Green County, Inc.*, 268 F.3d 51, 57 (1st Cir. 2001); *Brungart v. BellSouth Telecommunications, Inc.*, 231 F.3d 791, 795–97 (11th Cir. 2000), *cert. denied*, 532 U.S. 1037 (2002); *Dormeyer v. Comerica Bank-Illinois*, 223 F.3d 579, 581–83 (7th Cir. 2000).

168. *Miller v. Defiance Metal Products, Inc.*, 989 F. Supp. 945, 948–49 (N.D. Ohio 1997).

169. *Rocha v. Sauder Woodworking Co.*, 221 F. Supp. 2d 818, 819–20 (N.D. Ohio 2002).

170. 535 U.S. 81 (2002).

171. *Gurley v. Ameriwood Industries, Inc.*, 232 F. Supp. 2d 969, 974 (E.D. Mo. 2002).

172. *Kosakow v. New Rochelle Radiology Associates, P.C.*, 274 F.3d 706, 726 n.6 (2nd Cir. 2001).

173. *Kosakow*, 274 F.3d at 724; *Nordquist v. City Finance Co.*, 173 F. Supp. 2d 537, 540 (N.D. Miss. 2001).

174. *Kosakow*, 274 F.3d at 724; *Woodford v. Community Action of Greene County, Inc.*, 268 F.3d 51, 57 (2d Cir. 2001); *Dormeyer v. Comerica Bank-Illinois*, 223 F.3d 579, 582 (7th Cir. 2000).

175. *Kosakow*, 274 F.3d at 724; see also *Farina v. Compuware Corp.*, 256 F. Supp. 2d 1033, 1057–58 (D. Ariz. 2003); *Rocha*, 221 F. Supp. 2d at 820–21; *Restatement (Second) of Torts* § 894(1)(a) (1979).

176. *Rocha*, 221 F. Supp. 2d at 821; *Restatement (Second) of Torts* § 894(1) (1979).

177. *Kosakow*, 274 F.3d at 724; *Dormeyer*, 223 F.3d at 582–83; *Rocha*, 221 F. Supp. 2d at 821 (noting that in the Sixth Circuit, estoppel requires more than a showing of mere silence; plaintiff must show it was mislead though actual misrepresentation).

178. *Brungart v. Bellsouth Telecommunications, Inc.*, 231 F.3d 791, 797 n.4 (11th Cir. 2000), *cert. denied*, 532 U.S. 1037 (2002); *Nordquist*, 173 F. Supp. 2d at 540 (concluding that there was no detrimental reliance where employee testified she would have taken leave anyway).

179. *Coen v. Sybron Dental Specialties*, No. 99-1932, 2001 U.S. App. LEXIS 531, at *5–*6 (6th Cir. 2001) (declining to apply estoppel to extend eligibility where there were not 50 employees within 75 miles of worksite).

180. *Nordquist*, 173 F. Supp. 2d at 540.

181. 29 C.F.R. § 825.220(b).

182. 535 U.S. 81 (2002).

183. *Lacoparra v. Pergament Home Center, Inc.*, 982 F. Supp. 213, 220 (S.D.N.Y. 1997).

184. *Plumley v. Southern Container, Inc.*, 303 F.3d 364, 373–74 (1st Cir. 2002); *Dillaway v. Ferrante*, No. 02-715 (JRT/JSM), 2003 U.S. Dist. LEXIS 23468, at *16–*20 (D. Minn. Dec. 9, 2003).

185. *Dillaway*, 2003 U.S. Dist. LEXIS 23468, at *19.

186. 996 F. Supp. 818, 821 (N.D. Ill. 1998).

187. 29 U.S.C. § 2653; 29 C.F.R. § 825.700(b).

188. 29 U.S.C. § 2952(a); 29 C.F.R. § 825.700(b)

189. 251 F.3d 1132, 1136–37 (7th Cir. 2001).

190. See also *Douglas v. E.G. Baldwin Associates*, 150 F.3d 604 (6th Cir. 1998) (holding that company policy adopting FMLA but without 50/75 eligibility requirement did not bring employees within the FMLA and therefore that employee may have enhanced contractual rights but no rights under the FMLA); *Haywood v. Schwan's Sales Enterprise, Inc.*, No. 96-1439, 1997 U.S. App. LEXIS 7719 (6th Cir. Apr. 16, 10997) (same).

191. *Pert v. Value RX*, No. 96-CV-73153-DT, 1996 U.S. Dist. LEXIS 17748, at *7 (E.D. Mich. Oct. 9, 1996) (quoting *Rich v. Delta Airlines, Inc.*, 921 F. Supp. 767, 773 (N.D. Ga. 1996)).

192. 921 F. Supp. 767, 772–73 (N.D. Ga. 1996).

193. 921 F. Supp. at 773

194. Alaska Stat. § 39.20.500(b).

195. Conn. Agencies Regs. § 31-51qq-1(f) ("eligible employee" defined).

196. 29 U.S.C. § 2651(b); 29 C.F.R. § 825.701(a).

197. Comments on Regulations Implementing the Family and Medical Leave Act of 1993 (§ 825.701), 60 Fed. Reg. 2180, 2230 (Jan. 6, 1995).

198. 29 C.F.R. § 825.701(a).

199. *Id.*

200. Alaska Stat. §§ 39.20.305–39.20.330, 39.20.500, 39.20.550.

CHAPTER 4

Covered Family Members

4.01 OVERVIEW

If the school is a covered employer and the employee meets the eligibility requirements, the third question a school administrator must ask is whether the leave involves a covered individual. Generally, FMLA leave is available for the eligible employee's own covered condition or the covered condition of certain family members. However, not all family members are covered by the federal FMLA. Federal and state family medical leave laws, moreover, differ on which family members are covered for purposes of an employee's entitlement to take job-protected family medical leave. Under the federal FMLA, a spouse, a son or daughter, and a parent are covered family members. An employee is not entitled to family medical leave for a family member with a covered condition unless that family member is a covered individual within the meaning of the applicable federal or state family and medical leave law. Of course, the employee may be entitled to non-FMLA leave to care for a family member who is not covered by federal or state family medical leave laws pursuant to other federal, state, or local laws, school policies, or the terms of a collective bargaining agreement.

This chapter addresses which family members are covered for purposes of an eligible employee's right to take job-protected leave under federal and state family and medical leave laws, with particular emphasis on the federal FMLA.[1] It addresses the federal FMLA's definitions of "spouse," "son or daughter," and "parent." It also addresses which family members are generally not covered by the federal FMLA, covered family members under state family and medical leave laws, the effect of more generous employer policies on family member coverage, and the interaction of the federal FMLA with state family and medical leave laws.

4.02 SPOUSE

Under the federal FMLA, an eligible employee may be entitled to FMLA leave to care for his or her spouse with a covered condition.[2] A "spouse" is defined by the FMLA regulations as "a husband or wife as defined or recognized under State law for purposes of marriage in the State where the employee resides, including common law marriage in States where it is recognized."[3] Note that the individual must *currently* be the spouse of the eligible employee at the time of FMLA leave. FMLA leave is not available for a former spouse. The federal FMLA does not define what constitutes "marriage" but looks to state law. The terms "marriage" and "spouse" were modified by the Defense of Marriage Act of 1996,[4] and, as set forth below, that modification impacts the federal FMLA.

[1] Marriage

The federal FMLA defines marriage by reference to the state law of the residence of the employee. Each state has its own laws governing marriage. Two forms of marriage are generally recognized by state law: (1) statutory marriage and (2) common law marriage. A third, civil unions, has been recognized in a half dozen states and the District of Columbia.

(i) Statutory Marriage

Statutory marriage encompasses the form of matrimony most commonly associated with marriage: marriage pursuant to a religious or civil ceremony. States often impose restrictions on statutory marriage. Generally, individuals must meet a minimum age requirement. Many states prohibit marriage between close family relatives. Some states impose a waiting period between the time a marriage license is secured and the effective date of the marriage. In all states, an individual may be married to only one spouse at a time. Under the Full Faith and Credit Clause of the U.S. Constitution, a valid marriage or divorce in one state is generally recognized as valid in all other states.[5] As set forth in subsection [2] below, the Defense of Marriage Act of 1996 may have changed that practice.

(ii) Common Law Marriage

Some states recognize marriages that arise outside of a religious or civil ceremony. So-called common law marriages are treated as contracts created by the consent of the parties.[6] Common law marriages are currently recognized in eleven states (Alabama, Colorado, Iowa, Kansas, Montana, Oklahoma, Pennsylvania, Rhode Island, South Carolina, Texas, and Utah) and the District of Columbia.[7] Here again, pursuant to the Full Faith and Credit Clause of the U.S. Constitution, a common law marriage arising under Colorado law will be recognized as valid in states that do not themselves recognize the validity of common law marriages. For example, a husband and wife with a common law marriage from Colorado move to Virginia. Virginia does not recognize common law marriages. However, pursuant to the Full Faith and Credit Clause, because the couple's common law marriage arose out of Colorado where it was valid, Virginia must recognize the marriage as valid.

The laws of the jurisdictions that recognize common law marriages differ and should be consulted to determine whether a claimed common law marriage exists. Generally, however, to be valid common law marriages must meet the following requirements: (1) legal capacity to marry, (2) present agreement to enter into a marriage relationship, and (3) consummation of the marriage.[8] Like statutory marriage, a common law marriage may only be between individuals with the capacity to marry, including being of sound mind, of a minimum age, and not currently married. A present agreement to marry can be established by words or conduct. Finally, the marriage must be consummated to create a common law marriage. A marriage is consummated where individuals with legal capacity to marry presently agree to become husband

and wife and live in a way that presents themselves as married.[9] Factors evidencing that a marriage has been consummated have been described as follows:

> A sexual relationship between the parties is not an indispensable element of cohabitation, and consummation is not established by mere proof that the parties lived, ate, and slept together. Consummation can be proved by evidence that, among other things, the parties considered themselves married, shared household duties and expenses, maintained joint accounts, filed joint tax returns, used the same surname, referred to or introduced each other as a spouse, listed themselves as "married" on legal and other documents, or reared children together. Perhaps the most crucial requirement is proving that the parties gained public recognition of their status as husband and wife.[10]

A common misconception is that there is some simple formula for determining whether a common law marriage has been created based on the number of years the parties have lived together. That is simply not true. While the number of years that individuals live together as husband and wife is an important factor in determining whether a common law marriage exists, it is only one of several factors to take into consideration. There is no stated minimum period of time that individuals must live together in order to create a common law marriage.

(iii) Same-Sex Marriage

Marriage is generally defined by state law as a union of one man and one woman. Eighteen states have constitutional provisions that define marriage as a union of one man and one woman, while twenty-four other states have laws containing similar definitions. However, on November 18, 2003, the Massachusetts Supreme Court in *Goodridge v. Department of Public Health* ruled that the state's ban on same-sex marriage was unconstitutional and gave the state legislature 180 days to change the law.[11]

In an attempt to overturn the Massachusetts Supreme Court's decision, the Commonwealth of Massachusetts convened a constitutional convention beginning February 11, 2004. After 6 weeks of debate, an amendment to the Constitution of the Commonwealth of Massachusetts that would ban same-sex marriage but allow civil unions was passed. To take effect, the amendment must be approved by the legislature and pass a popular vote.[12]

On July 12, 2006, the Massachusetts legislature, meeting at a state constitutional convention, voted to adjourn without considering an amendment to ban same-sex marriages in the state.[13] As of May 17, 2004, the Massachusetts Supreme Court's *Goodridge* ruling went into effect, making the Commonwealth of Massachusetts the first and only state to recognize same-sex marriage.

Same-sex marriage in Massachusetts is limited to Massachusetts residents. Governor Mitt Romney has been enforcing a 1913 Massachusetts law that bans "evasive" marriages—marriages where couples who could not marry in their own state travel to another that will permit their marriage.[14] The validity of the marriage evasion law is currently before the Massachusetts Supreme Court.[15] The effect on the FMLA of the recognition of same-sex marriage by the Commonwealth of Massachusetts is manifest. As enacted, the FMLA looks to state law to determine what constitutes a valid marriage for purposes of determining who is a covered "spouse" of an eligible employee. Were it not for the Defense of Marriage Act of 1996, a "spouse" in Massachusetts would include an individual in a same-sex marriage for purposes of FMLA leave. However, as set forth more fully below, the Defense of Marriage Act of 1996 effectively amends the federal FMLA by adding a definition of marriage and spouse that excludes same sex marriages.

(iv) Civil Unions and Domestic Partnerships

Vermont, Connecticut, California, Maine, Hawaii, New Jersey, and the District of Columbia offer benefits similar to marriage to same-sex partners through the recognition of civil unions, reciprocal benefits, or domestic partner laws.[16] New Jersey joined Vermont and Connecticut with the December 2006 enactment of a law recognizing same-sex civil unions.[17] While similar to marriage, these state-sanctioned relationships are not marriages.[18] Accordingly, an eligible school employee would not be entitled to take federal FMLA leave for a same-sex partner pursuant to a valid same-sex civil union or domestic partnership.

[2] The Defense of Marriage Act of 1996

The Defense of Marriage Act of 1996 (DOMA)[19] established a federal definition of "marriage" and "spouse." Specifically, the DOMA provides the following:

> In determining the meaning of any Act of Congress, or of any ruling, regulation, or interpretation of the various administrative bureaus and agencies of the United States, the word "marriage" means only a legal union between one man and one woman as husband and wife, and the word "spouse" refers only to a person of the opposite sex who is a husband or wife.[20]

For federal FMLA purposes, the definitions of "marriage" and "spouse" by the DOMA effectively limits job-protected leave to legally married heterosexual couples. The DOMA prohibits eligible employees in legally recognized civil unions and domestic partnerships, as well as in same-sex marriages in the Commonwealth of Massachusetts, from taking federal FMLA leave to care for a same-sex spouse or partner with a covered condition. Of course, state family and medical leave laws, school policy, or the terms of a collective bargaining agreement may permit or require a school administrator to permit such leave with equal or similar benefits to those of the federal FMLA.

In addition to the federal DOMA, states have enacted so-called mini-DOMAs. Currently, thirty-nine states have passed legislation prohibiting the recognition of same-sex marriages,[21] and eighteen states have amended their constitutions to define marriage as being between one man and one woman.[22]

[3] Divorce

The dissolution of a legal marriage is governed by state law. Under state law there are only two ways to dissolve a legal marriage: death or divorce.[23] There is no such thing as a common law divorce by mutual agreement of the parties without a state-sanctioned decree of divorce that formally ends the marriage.[24] Accordingly, absent death or divorce, parties to a legal marriage are husband and wife for FMLA purposes, regardless of the practical state of their marriage.

FMLA Illustrated: Divorce Examples

Example 1

John is a teacher at East Public High School and an eligible employee for federal FMLA leave. He has been separated from his wife, Janet, for 3 years. Their 2 children live with Janet. They have never formally divorced. For the past 2 years John has been living with Mary and her 2 children from her pervious marriage. Mary is diagnosed with cancer, undergoes surgery, and is in the hospital recuperating. John asks for federal FMLA leave to care for Mary in the hospital.

Question: Is he entitled?

Answer: No. Because John and Janet never divorced, Janet, not Mary, is John's spouse for purposes of the federal FMLA. Of course, the school may permit John to visit Mary using some other type of leave.

Example 2

Laura works in administration at County College and is an FMLA-eligible employee. She asks for 2 weeks of federal FMLA leave to care for Mike, who she says is her former husband. Mike is in the hospital and is not expected to live long. For the 10 years you have known her, Laura has presented Hank, with whom she has 2 children, as her husband. Laura reveals that she married Mike, her high school sweetheart, during a weekend in Las Vegas 20 years ago. Their relationship ended shortly thereafter, but they never bothered to get divorced. She and Hank are not formally married. The state in which Laura resides recognizes common law marriage.

Question: Do you grant Laura federal FMLA leave to care for Mike?

Answer: Yes. Because they never divorced, Mike is still Laura's spouse. A common law marriage between Laura and Hank does not exist because Laura is already married. Assuming that Mike has an FMLA-covered condition, and all other things being equal, Laura is entitled to leave to care for her spouse, Mike.

Example 3

Connie and Jerry have 3 young children. Their marriage of 10 years ended in divorce. Devoted parents, Jerry and Connie live a few doors down from each other. The kids live with Connie. Connie and Jerry are in serious relationships with others. Connie and Jerry share parenting duties and count on each other to help out. Jerry frequently watches the kids, drives them to their activities, and attends their events. Jerry sees the kids almost every day. Jerry has a heart attack and is hospitalized. Connie, a public elementary school employee, requests intermittent federal FMLA leave to care for Jerry while he recuperates at home. Connie meets the federal FMLA eligibility requirements.

Question: Is Connie entitled to leave?

Answer: No. Because they are divorced, Jerry is currently not Connie's spouse.

As a practical matter, the identity of an eligible employee's spouse will not be in dispute. Such identity will have been disclosed at the beginning of the employment relationship in insurance documents and emergency-contact-information disclosures. However, as set forth later in this chapter, school administrators have the right to require the employee seeking federal FMLA leave to provide documentation establishing their familial relationship, including a legal marriage. This may be useful to establish the existence of a common law marriage.

4.03 SON OR DAUGHTER

A "son or daughter" is the second category of covered family members within the meaning of the federal FMLA. A "son or daughter" is broadly defined by the federal FMLA:

> The term "son or daughter" means a biological, adopted, or foster child, a stepchild, a legal ward, or a child of a person standing in loco parentis, who is—
>
> (A) under 18 years of age; or
>
> (B) 18 years of age or older and incapable of self-care because of a mental or physical disability.[25]

The federal FMLA definition of "son or daughter" has two requirements: (1) a current relationship with the eligible employee requesting leave and (2) an age requirement.

[1] Current Relationship Requirement

The federal FMLA's definition of "son or daughter" goes beyond the traditional biological parent-child relationship arising out of a traditional nuclear family. It broadly defines "son or daughter" to cover virtually every possible parent-child relationship an eligible employee may have. The DOL explained the rationale for this expansive definition as follows:

> The terms "parent" and "son or daughter" . . . reflect the reality that many children in the United States today do not live in traditional "nuclear"

> families with their biological father and mother. Increasingly, those who find themselves in need of workplace accommodation of their child care responsibilities are not the biological parents of the children they care for, but their adoptive, step, or foster parents, their guardians, or sometimes simply their grandparents or other relatives or adults. This legislation deals with such families by tying the availability of "parental" leave to the birth, adoption, or serious health condition of a "son or daughter" and then defining the term "son or daughter" to mean "a biological, adopted, or foster child, a stepchild, a legal ward, or a child of a person standing in loco parentis."[26]

The federal FMLA defines some of these relationships but not others. Although undefined, a biological relationship would appear to simply require paternity. The terms "stepchild," "legal ward," "adopted," and "foster child" are similarly undefined. A stepchild is generally considered to be the child of a husband or wife by a former marriage. A legal ward is generally a person who by reason of incapacity (due to minority or mental disability) is under the protection of a court either directly or, more typically, through a guardian appointed by a court. Presumably, for purposes of FMLA leave, the eligible employee would be serving as the court-appointed guardian of the "son or daughter."

The absence of a definition for "adopted" and "foster care" relationships is curious because the FMLA permits an eligible employee to take leave due to the placement of a "son or daughter" with the employee for adoption or foster care.[27] The DOL regulations do provide, however, that the source of the adopted child (e.g., licensed adoption agency or otherwise) is not relevant.[28] In contrast, the source of a foster child is relevant. A foster child is one that is placed pursuant to an agreement between the state and the foster parent or guardian subsequent to the removal of the son or daughter from his or her home, either by voluntary agreement or judicial decree.[29] A legal ward and a foster child would appear to be very similar.

The federal FMLA does define "in loco parentis." Persons who stand in loco parentis are those with day-to-day responsibility to care for and financially support a child. A biological or legal relationship is not required to establish that a person stands in loco parentis to a

FMLA Illustrated: In Loco Parentis Examples

Example 1

Wendy is a single mother of Henry, who is 6 years old. Wendy's National Guard unit is called to active duty. Wendy's parents, Richard and Terri, agree to care for Ben while she is gone. Richard and Terri take Ben into their home and provide for him. Wendy's National Guard pay barely covers the mortgage on her condo. Ben is injured in an automobile accident and is required to spend a week in the hospital. Terri requests FMLA leave to care for Ben.

Question: Is she entitled?

Answer: Yes, assuming that she is eligible and all other FMLA requirements are met. Richard and Terri have assumed responsibility to care for and financially support Ben during Wendy's absence. While as a grandparent Terri would normally not be entitled to FMLA leave to care for her grandchild Ben, because she stands in loco parentis to Ben at the time she requested FMLA leave, Terri meets the relationship requirement.

Example 2

Lee and Sue are proud, albeit exhausted, new parents of 1-year-old Natalie. For surviving a difficult pregnancy and endless months of colic, Lee and Sue are surprised by a 2-week Hawaii vacation as a wedding anniversary present from Lee's parents. Lee's parents, Walt and Jean, also agree to take care of Natalie during their vacation. When the time comes, Walt and Jean move into Lee and Sue's home to care for Natalie. During the vacation, Natalie gets sick and is rushed to the hospital. Walt, principal of the local middle school, requests FMLA leave to comfort Natalie in the hospital.

Question: Assuming that Walt is an eligible employee and all other FMLA conditions are met, does Walt get the leave?

Answer: Probably not. It will all depend on whether Walt is considered to have assumed day-to-day financial responsibility for Natalie during the 2-week vacation. Walt and Jean certainly are caring for Natalie at the time of the request for FMLA leave. Whether Walt is considered to have assumed day-to-day financial responsibility for Natalie will depend on how literally that requirement is interpreted. Here, Walt and Jean are living in Lee and Sue's home. If Lee and Sue paid the mortgage and the the bills and filled the refrigerator before they left, the day-to-day financial responsibilities assumed by Walt and Jean would, as a practical matter, be little or nothing. Of course, one could argue that Walt and Jean assumed day-to-day care and financial responsibilities for Natalie when they agreed to care for her because something could have come up (and did).

child.[30] Note that the term "child" is undefined. Presumably, the term "child" in the definition of "in loco parentis" has the same meaning as "son or daughter."

Note also that the definition does not set a minimum period of time that an eligible employee must have provided day-to-day care and financial support to a son or daughter in order to be considered in loco parentis. All that is required for an eligible employee to stand in loco parentis with the son or daughter is that at the time of FMLA leave, the employee have day-to-day responsibility to care for and financially support the son or daughter. This could conceivably cover relatively short periods of time.

The broad definition of a "son or daughter" is limited by the requirement that the individual be a "son or daughter" of the eligible employee during the period for which FMLA leave is requested. This is demonstrated by the use of the present tense to describe the relationship between the eligible employee requesting leave and the "son or daughter." For example, an in loco parentis relationship is defined as "a child of a person standing in loco parentis."[31] Similarly, the requirement of a current relationship at the time of FMLA leave is demonstrated by the provision that an employee is entitled to take FMLA leave "to care for the employee's spouse, son, daughter, or parent with a serious health condition."[32]

Whether an individual is a "son or daughter" of an eligible employee during the period of FMLA leave depends on the permanency of the relationship. As set forth above, relationships that fall within the definition of a "son or daughter" for purposes of the federal FLMA range from temporary to indelible. For example, a legal ward "son or daughter" relationship may last only days or weeks. A biological relationship with a son or daughter, on the other hand, is forever. In order for the individual to be a "son or daughter" within the meaning of the federal FMLA, the individual must be in that relationship throughout the period of FMLA leave.

Temporary relationships can, of course, turn into permanent relationships. For example, an eligible employee can formally adopt a stepchild or foster child. Once adopted, the individual is the "son or daughter" of the adoptive parent unless and until that relationship is legally severed.

FMLA Illustrated: Current "Son or Daughter" Examples

Stepchild

Lisa and Brian married. Lisa's 6-year-old son, Mark, served as best man. Lisa and Brian got divorced 8 years later. In the interim, Brian had become very close with Mark. Brian continues to take Mark on camping and fishing trips and otherwise remains active in Mark's life. Mark was injured playing baseball and was hospitalized for several days. Brian requests FMLA leave to comfort Mark while he recuperates at home.

Question: Assuming that Brian is an eligible employee and all other FMLA conditions are met, is Brian entitled to FMLA leave?

Answer: No. Although Mark was Brian's stepchild while Brian and Lisa were married, that parent-child relationship ended when Lisa and Brian divorced. As Brian did not otherwise have a "son or daughter" relationship with Mark at the time Brian requested FMLA leave, Brian is not entitled to FMLA leave to comfort Mark.

Foster Child

Pete and Vickie take in minor foster children who have been removed from their homes by the state due to abuse or neglect. They are paid for this service. Most placements last less than 6 months, after which the child is either returned home or placed with relatives. Pete and Vickie figure they have been foster parents to nearly 50 children over the years. They have remained in close contact with all of their foster children. Vickie requests FMLA leave to provide care and comfort for a 12-year-old child who passed through their home a few years ago. The child is being treated for cancer.

Question: Assuming she is eligible and otherwise meets the other FMLA requirements, is Vickie entitled to the leave?

Answer: No. Because the foster care relationship ended a few years before the need for FMLA leave, the child does not currently stand as a "son or daughter" to Vickie.

[2] Age Requirement

To fit within the federal FMLA definition of a "son or daughter," in addition to meeting the relationship requirement at leave commencement, the child must also satisfy an age requirement. There are two age categories: (1) children under 18 years of age and (2) certain adult children 18 years of age and older.[33] A child that does not meet the age requirement is not a "son or daughter" within the meaning of the federal

FMLA and, therefore, cannot support an eligible employee's request for federal FMLA leave for that child.

(i) Children under 18 Years of Age

All children under 18 years of age who meet the relationship requirement fall within the federal FMLA definition of a covered "son or daughter." As set forth later in this chapter, school administrators may require an eligible employee to document proof of the child's age by, for example, furnishing a birth certificate.

(ii) Children 18 Years of Age and Above

Adult children (children over the age of 18) fall within the federal FMLA definition of "son or daughter" only if they are "incapable of self-care because of a mental or physical disability."[34] "Incapable of self-care" means that the adult child requires active assistance or supervision to provide daily self-care in three or more of the "activities of daily living" (ADLs) or "instrumental activities of daily living" (IADLs).[35] The DOL regulations implementing the federal FMLA provide the following nonexclusive list of these activities:[36]

ADLs	*IADLs*
• grooming	• cooking
• hygiene	• cleaning
• bathing	• shopping
• dressing	• taking public transportation
• eating	• paying bills
	• maintaining a residence
	• using telephones and directories
	• using a post office

Note that an adult child can meet the activities requirement with proof that he or she cannot perform three or more ADLs *or* IADLs; examples from both categories are not required. Proof that an adult child meets the activities requirement falls within the scope of the medical documentation that a school employer may require to establish that the son or daughter has a covered serious health condition.[37] Courts have declined to find that an adult child meets the activities requirement absent medical evidence.[38]

The adult child's inability to perform self-care activities must be because of a "mental or physical disability." The DOL regulations implementing the federal FMLA define "physical or mental disability" to mean "a physical or mental impairment that substantially limits one or more of the major life activities of an individual."[39] The DOL defines the terms contained in the preceding sentence by reference to regulations issued by the Equal Employment Opportunity Commission (EEOC) implementing the Americans with Disabilities Act of 1990.[40] *Warning*: this area is hopelessly complicated. School administrators evaluating whether an adult child's "incapability of self-care" is due to a mental or physical disability should exercise their right to require the eligible employee to provide medical documentation of the adult child's condition and should consult legal counsel. With that warning, a brief overview of the incorporated EEOC ADA regulations follows.

A "physical or mental impairment" is broadly defined in the EEOC regulations as

> (1) [a]ny physiological disorder, or condition, cosmetic disfigurement, or anatomical loss affecting one or more of the following body systems: neurological, musculoskeletal, specials sense organs, respiratory (including speech organs), cardiovascular, reproductive, digestive, genito-urinary, hemic and lymphatic, skin, and endocrine; or
> (2) [a]ny mental or psychological disorder, such as mental retardation, organic brain syndrome, emotional or mental illness, and specific learning disabilities.[41]

"Major life activities" are defined in the EEOC ADA regulations as "functions such as caring for oneself, performing manual tasks, walking, seeing, hearing, speaking, breathing, learning, and working."[42]

"Substantially limited" is defined by the EEOC ADA regulations to mean

> (i) [u]nable to perform a major life activity that the average person in the general population can perform; or

(ii) [s]ignificantly restricted as to the condition, manner, or duration under which an individual can perform a particular life activity as compared to the condition, manner, or duration under which the average person in the general population can perform that same major life activity.[43]

With respect to the major life activity of working, the EEOC ADA regulations define "substantially limits" to mean "significantly restricted in the ability to perform either a class of jobs or a broad range of jobs in various classes are compared to the average person having comparable training, skills, and abilities."[44]

The EEOC ADA regulations identify three factors to judge whether an individual is substantially limited in a major life activity:[45]

- The nature and severity of the impairment
- The duration or expected duration of the impairment
- The permanent or long-term impact, or the expected permanent or long-term impact, of or resulting from the impairment

Additional factors to consider in determining whether an individual is substantially limited in the major life activity of "working" include

- the geographic area to which the individual has reasonable access;
- the job from which the individual has been disqualified because of an impairment, and the number and types of jobs utilizing similar training, knowledge, skills, or abilities, within that geographic area, from which the individual is also disqualified because of the impairment (class of jobs); and
- the job from which the individual has been disqualified because of an impairment, and the number and types of jobs not utilizing similar training, knowledge, skills or abilities, within the geographic area, from which the individual is also disqualified because of the impairment (broad range of jobs in various classes).[46]

The onset of the adult child's physical or mental disability can have occurred before or after the child has reached 18 years of age.[47]

4.04 PARENT

"Parents" are the third category of family members that an eligible employee may take federal FMLA leave to care for. "Parent" is defined as a biological parent or an individual who stands or stood in loco parentis to an employee when the employee was an FMLA-covered "son or daughter."[48]

The relationship requirement of the federal FMLA definition of "parent" does not simply mimic the forms of parental relationships contained in the definition of "son or daughter." Arguably, a parent by adoption or foster care placement, a legal guardian, and a stepparent will fall within the broader definition of in loco parentis. Persons who are in loco parentis include those with day-to-day responsibilities to care for and financially support a child or in the case of an employee, who had such responsibility for the employee when the employee was a child. A biological or legal relationship is not necessary.[49]

FMLA Illustrated: Parent Example

Jeff is a fifth-grade schoolteacher at Washington Elementary, a public school. Jeff is the product of an abusive childhood. He was removed from his home by Social Services and, for a period of 2 years, lived in several foster homes. He initially lived with foster parents Hal and Daryl for 6 months. He was subsequently placed with David and Caroline for nearly a year and a half. Jeff was returned home again without incident. Jeff has stayed in contact with David and Caroline over the years by sending holiday cards and through the occasional telephone call. Jeff recently learned that David is recovering from a heart attack and triple bypass surgery. He requests FMLA leave to provide comfort and care for David.

Question: Assuming that Jeff is eligible and that all other FMLA conditions are met, is Jeff entitled to FMLA leave?

Answer: Yes. David is a "parent" for purposes of the federal FMLA, as he had responsibility to care for and financially support Jeff when Jeff was a child.

Same facts, except that on his return to work, Jeff's biological father is hospitalized with a life-threatening illness. Jeff requests FMLA leave.

Question: Do you grant it?

Answer: Yes. An employee may have more than two parents under the federal FMLA.

The parental relationship covered by the federal FMLA encompasses both current and past parental relationships. In contrast, only a current "son or daughter" relationship is covered by the federal FMLA. As a result, an individual can meet the federal FMLA definition of "parent" even though that individual has ceased serving as that eligible employee's parent. Moreover, the period of time an individual had to serve as a parent when the employee was a child is, at best, minimal (day-to-day responsibility). Finally, the term "child" is undefined. Presumably it means below the age of majority.

4.05 INDIVIDUALS WHO ARE NOT USUALLY COVERED BY THE FEDERAL FMLA

The federal FMLA does not cover an eligible employee's need for job-protected leave for covered conditions involving anyone other than a spouse, son or daughter, or parent—brothers and sisters,[50] grandparents,[51] in-laws,[52] aunts, uncles, cousins, and anyone else who may be or have been dependent on the eligible employee are not covered. Of course, if the employee or any of these individuals stands or stood in loco parentis they may satisfy the definition of an FMLA-covered "parent" or "son or daughter."

FMLA Illustrated: In Loco Parentis Exception

Jane works in school administration at Public Middle School. When Jane was 9 years old she was removed from her abusive home by Social Services and placed with her grandparents. Jane was returned to her home 6 months later. Jane remains close with her grandparents. Now, 10 years later, Jane's grandmother is hospitalized. Jane asks for FMLA leave.

Question: Assuming Jane is eligible and otherwise meets all FMLA requirements, is Jane entitled to FMLA leave to provide comfort and care to her grandmother?

Answer: Yes. Although a grandparent is normally not a covered family member within the meaning of the FMLA, because her grandmother was in loco parentis to Jane while Jane was a child, Jane's grandmother is considered a parent for purposes of FMLA leave.

4.06 CONFIRMATION OF FAMILIAL RELATIONSHIP

School administrators may require eligible employees requesting federal FMLA leave for a covered family member to provide documentation confirming that the individual is an FMLA-covered spouse, son, daughter, or parent.[53] The subject is addressed more fully in Chapter 7, *Documentation Requirements*.

4.07 EFFECT OF MORE GENEROUS EMPLOYER POLICIES

What would the legal effect be if a school were to adopt a policy that extended family and medical leave benefits to family members other than a spouse, son, daughter, or parent? The federal FMLA sets forth minimum, not maximum, requirements. Covered employers are encouraged to adopt leave policies that are more generous than what is required by the FMLA.[54] If a school were to adopt a more generous family and medical leave policy, the federal FMLA requires that the school observe any employment benefit program or plan that provides greater family or medical leave rights to employees than the rights established by the federal FMLA.[55] Notwithstanding the implications of the DOL regulations, courts have generally held that an employer's violation of the provisions of a more generous family and medical leave policy may not constitute an actionable violation of the federal FMLA. Rather, such violations are generally enforced pursuant to whatever process is available to the employee for violation of school policies, including the grievance process. This topic is addressed more fully in Chapter 13, *Coordination of the FMLA with Other Employee Rights and Benefits*.

4.08 STATE FAMILY AND MEDICAL LEAVE LAWS

State family and medical leave laws generally permit an eligible employee to take leave for the same covered individuals as does the federal FMLA (the employee and the employee's spouse, son, daughter, or parent). A few states, however, define a covered family member more expansively by including grandparents, grandchildren, brothers, sisters,

sisters-in-law, brothers-in-law, sons-in-law, daughters-in-law, mothers-in-law, fathers-in-law, aunts, uncles, nephews, or nieces. For example, Hawaii's family leave law allows an eligible employee to take leave for the employee's own serious health condition or to care for the employee's child, spouse or reciprocal beneficiary, or parent with a serious health condition.[56] A "reciprocal beneficiary" includes same-sex partners.[57] A "parent" is defined to include in-laws, grandparents, and grandparents-in-law.[58] In-laws are also covered by the family leave laws of New Jersey, North Dakota, Oregon, Rhode Island, Vermont, and Wisconsin.[59]

States with and without a general family and medical leave law may have other forms of leave available to employees that could qualify as family or medical leave as defined by the federal FMLA. For example, many states have laws mandating maternity leave and leave for adoption or foster care, catastrophic leave, and bone marrow or organ donation leave. If the law allows an employee to use such leave for the employee or the employee's spouse, son or daughter, or parent, the law may constitute family and medical leave for purposes of the federal FMLA.

4.09 INTERACTION OF THE FEDERAL FMLA WITH STATE FAMILY AND MEDICAL LEAVE LAWS: COVERED FAMILY MEMBERS

Some schools are covered by both the federal FMLA and state family and medical leave laws. As we have seen, the requirements of state family and medical leave laws often differ from the requirements of the federal FMLA. Generally, the federal FMLA requires schools to abide by the applicable requirements of both laws.[60] The federal FMLA does not supersede any provision of state or local law that provides greater family or medical leave rights than those provided by the FMLA.[61] The DOL does not, however, enforce state family or medical leave laws, and states may not enforce the federal FMLA.[62] An employer covered by one law and not the other has to comply only with the law under which it is covered. Similarly, an employee eligible under one law must receive benefits in accordance with that law.[63] If leave qualifies for both federal FMLA leave and leave under state law, the leave used counts against the employee's entitlement under both laws.[64]

With respect to the interaction between the federal FMLA and state family and medical leave laws, the DOL regulations provide the following example regarding covered family members:

> If state law provides six weeks of leave, which may include leave to care for a seriously ill grandparent or a "spouse equivalent," and leave was used for that purpose, the employee is still entitled to 12 weeks of FMLA leave, as the leave used was provided for a purpose not covered by the FMLA. If FMLA leave is used first for a purpose also provided under State law, and State leave has thereby been exhausted, the employer would not be required to provide additional leave to care for the grandparent or "spouse equivalent."[65]

This issue is addressed more fully in Chapter 13, *Coordination of the FMLA with Other Employee Rights and Benefits*.

NOTES

1. For a discussion of who is an "employee" for purposes of federal and state family and medical leave laws, see section 3.02 of Chapter 3, *Employee Eligibility*.
2. When an employee may be "needed to care for" a covered family member is separately addressed in Chapter 5, *Covered Conditions*. The focus here is under what circumstances an individual is considered to be the spouse of the eligible employee for purposes of FMLA coverage.
3. 29 C.F.R. § 825.113(a).
4. Pub. L. No. 104-199, 110 Stat 2419 (1996) (codified at 1 U.S.C. § 7 and 28 U.S.C. § 1738V).
5. Lisa Milot, Note, *Restitching the American Marital Quilt: Untangling Marriage from the Nuclear Family*, 87 Va. L. Rev. 701, 707 & n.34 (2001).
6. John B. Crawley, *Is the Honeymoon Over for Common-Law Marriage: A Consideration of the Continued Viability of the Common Law Marriage Doctrine*, 29 Cumb. L. Rev. 399, 401 n.7 (1998–1999).
7. Milot, *supra* note 5, at 707 & n.32.
8. Crawley, *supra* note 6, at 404.
9. Milot, *supra* note 5, at 704 n.32.
10. Crawley, *supra* note 6, at 409.

11. *Goodrich v. Department of Public Health*, 798 N.E.2d 941 (Mass. 2003).

12. Rick Klein, *Vote Ties Civil Unions to Gay-Marriage Ban; Romney to Seek Stay of SJS Order*, Boston Globe, Mar. 30, 2004, available at http://www.boston.com/news/specials/gay_marriage/articles/2004/03/30/vote_ties_civil_unions_to_gay_marriage_ban/.

13. Andrea Estes and Russell Nichols, *Lawmakers Delay Vote on Gay Marriage Measure*, Boston Globe, July 13, 2006, available at http://www.boston.com/news/specials/gay_marriage/articles/2006/07/13/lawmakers_delay_vote_on_gay_marriage_measure/.

14. Joanna Grossman, *Will Non-resident Same-Sex Couples Be Able to Marry in Massachusetts? The State's Highest Court Considers the Marriage Evasion Law*, FindLaw: Legal News and Commentary, Mar. 1, 2005, available at http://writ.news.findlaw.com/grossman/20050301.html.

15. *Id.*

16. Toni Lester, *Adam and Steve vs. Adam and Eve: Will the New Supreme Court Grant Gays the Right to Marry?*, 14 Am U.J. Gender Soc. Pol'y & L. 253, 263 & nn.59–65 (2006).

17. Tom Baldwin, *Same-Sex Unions in New Jersey Legal, with Limits*, USA Today, Dec. 22, 2006, available at http://www.usatoday.com/news/nation/2006-12-21-gay_x.htm?csp=34.

18. See *Rosengarten v. Downes*, 71 Conn. App. 372, 376–77 (2002) (holding that civil union under Vermont law is not the same as marriage).

19. 1 U.S.C. § 7.

20. *Id.*

21. Jackie Gardina, *The Perfect Storm: Bankruptcy, Choice of Law, and Same-Sex Marriage*, 86 B.U. L. Rev. 881, 894–95 & n.84 (2006) (Alabama, Alaska, Arizona, Arkansas, California, Colorado, Delaware, Florida, Georgia, Hawaii, Idaho, Illinois, Indiana, Iowa, Kansas, Kentucky, Louisiana, Maine, Maryland, Michigan, Minnesota, Mississippi, Missouri, Montana, New Hampshire, North Carolina, Ohio, Oklahoma, Pennsylvania, South Carolina, South Dakota, Tennessee, Texas, Utah, Virginia, Washington, West Virginia, and Wyoming).

22. *Id.* at 894–95 & n.85 (Alaska, Arkansas, Georgia, Hawaii, Kansas, Kentucky, Louisiana, Michigan, Mississippi, Missouri, Montana, Nebraska, Nevada, North Dakota, Ohio, Oklahoma, Oregon, and Utah). But see *Citizens for Equal Protections, Inc. v. Bruning*, 368 F. Supp. 2d 980 (D. Neb. 2005) (striking down Nebraska's constitutional amendment because it deprived plaintiffs of the associational rights protected by the First Amendment and Due Process Clause of the U.S. Constitution).

23. Milot, *supra* note 5, at 704 & n.14 (2001).

24. *Id.* at 708; Crawley, *supra* note 6, at 405, 410.

25. 29 U.S.C. § 2611(12); see also 29 C.F.R. § 825.113(c).

26. Comments on Regulations Implementing the Family and Medical Leave Act of 1993 (§ 825.112), 60 Fed. Reg. 2180, 2190 (Jan. 6, 1995).

27. 29 U.S.C. § 2612(a)(1)(B). For further discussion, see Chapter 5, *Covered Conditions*.

28. 29 C.F.R. § 825.112(d).

29. 29 C.F.R. § 825.112(e).

30. 29 C.F.R. § 825.113(c).

31. *Id.*

32. 29 C.F.R. § 825.112(a)(3).

33. 29 U.S.C. § 2611(12); 29 C.F.R. § 825.113(c).

34. 29 U.S.C. § 2611(12)(B); see also 29 C.F.R. § 825.113(c).

35. 29 C.F.R. § 825.113(c)(1).

36. *Id.*

37. Medical certification requirements are addressed in Chapter 7, *Documentation Requirements*.

38. See *Sakellarion v. Judge & Dolph, Ltd.*, 893 F. Supp. 800, 807 (N.D. Ill. 1995) (holding that absent supporting medical evidence, employee-parent's assertion that daughter was incapable of self-care was insufficient).

39. 29 C.F.R. § 825.113(c)(2).

40. Americans with Disabilities Act of 1990, 42 U.S.C. §§ 12111–12117; 29 C.F.R. § 825.113(c)(2) (citing 29 C.F.R. § 1630.2(h)–(j).

41. 29 C.F.R. § 1630.2(h).

42. 29 C.F.R. § 1630.2(i).

43. 29 C.F.R. § 1630.2(j)(1).

44. 29 C.F.R. § 1630.2(j)(3).

45. 29 C.F.R. § 1630.2(j)(2).

46. 29 C.F.R. § 1630.2(j)(3)(ii).

47. DOL WH FMLA Advisory Opinion No. 51 (Nov. 28, 1994); see also *Navarro v. Pfizer Corp.*, 261 F.3d 90, 104 (1st Cir. 2001) (addressing disability due to adult child's current pregnancy).

48. 29 U.S.C. § 2611(7); 29 C.F.R.§ 825.113(b).

49. 29 C.F.R. § 825.113(c)(3).

50. DOL WH FMLA Advisory Opinion No. 73 (Oct. 23, 1995).

51. *Krohn v. Forsting*, 11 F. Supp. 2d 1082, 1091–92 (E.D. Mo. 1998); DOL WH FMLA Advisory Opinion No. 21 (Dec. 7, 1993).

52. 29 C.F.R. § 825.113(b).

53. 29 C.F.R. § 825.113(d).

54. 29 U.S.C.§ 2653; 29 C.F.R. § 825.700(b).

55. 29 C.F.R. § 825.700(a).

56. Haw. Code R. § 12-27-6.

57. Haw. Code R. § 12-27-1 ("reciprocal beneficiary" defined).

58. *Id.* ("parent" defined).

59. N.J. Stat. Ann. § 34:11B-3(h); N.D. Cent. Code §§ 54-52.4-01(7) ("parent" defined); Or. Rev. Stat. Ann. § 659A.150(4) ("family member" defined); R.I. Gen. Laws § 28-48-1(5) ("family member" defined); Vt. Stat. Ann. tit. 21, § 472(a)(1)–(2); Wis. Stat. Ann. § 103.10(f).

60. 29 C.F.R. § 825.701(a).

61. *Id.*

62. *Id.*

63. *Id.*

64. *Id.*

65. 29 C.F.R.§ 825.701(a)(5).

CHAPTER 5

Covered Conditions

5.01 OVERVIEW

The fourth question a school administrator should ask is whether the eligible employee's need for FMLA leave is due to a covered condition. To qualify for the benefits and legal protections afforded by both federal and state family medical leave laws, the need for leave, whether due to the employee's own condition or that of a covered family member, must be covered by the applicable federal or state family medical leave laws. If the need for leave is not covered by applicable family medical leave laws, the leave may still be governed by other federal or state laws or by the school's normal leave policies. The school's standard leave policies may be more or less generous than the federal or state family medical leave laws. Therefore, it is critical for a school administrator to determine whether the employee's need for leave is due to a condition covered by applicable federal or state family medical leave laws.

The federal FMLA identifies four circumstances that justify an eligible employee's use of job-protected FMLA leave:[1]

- The birth of a son or daughter of the employee and the need to care for such son or daughter
- The placement of a son or daughter with the employee for adoption or foster care
- The need to care for the employee's spouse son, daughter, or parent with a serious health condition

- A serious health condition that makes the employee unable to perform the functions of his or her position

The DOL regulations implementing the federal FMLA clarify and greatly expand the scope of the conditions covered by the FMLA.[2]

This chapter addresses which conditions are covered by federal and state family and medical leave laws, with particular focus on the federal FMLA. It addresses job-protected FMLA leave for the birth, adoption, or foster care placement of a child. It also addresses FMLA leave due to the employee's own serious health condition, as well as the serious health condition of a spouse, son, daughter, or parent. This chapter also reviews which conditions are covered by the various state family and medical leave laws and how that coverage compares with that of the federal FMLA.

5.02 BIRTH, ADOPTION, AND FOSTER CARE PLACEMENT

Under the federal FMLA, an eligible employee may take job-protected leave because of the birth, adoption, or foster care placement of a son or daughter, and to care for the newborn.[3] Fathers and mothers are equally entitled to take FMLA leave for this purpose.[4] FMLA leave is available to an eligible employee for this purpose even though neither the mother nor the child is sick.

[1] Birth

The federal FMLA fails to define what "because of" and "birth" means. The failure of the DOL to define these core terms is complicated, because incapacity due to pregnancy, including prenatal care, is an FMLA-covered serious health condition. Presumably, for purposes of "birth," FMLA-covered leave is available provided the need for leave is causally related to the birth of a son or daughter. Arguably, this could cover leave for prenatal care, leave to deliver the baby, and post-delivery leave. Again, such leave is available even though neither the mother nor the baby has a serious health condition within the meaning of the federal FMLA. The conflict with prenatal care is addressed more fully in subsection (i) below.

The DOL regulations also fail to explain the meaning of the phrase "and to care for the newborn." Presumably, this means both physical and psychological care. The similar term "needed to care for" is defined for purposes of FMLA leave for a serious health condition to include both physical and psychological care.[5] The legislative history of the FMLA and DOL comments accompanying adoption of the final implementing regulations indicate that the federal FMLA covers leave for infant-parent bonding.[6] Here again, the infant does not have to be sick in order for an eligible employee, mother or father, to be entitled to job-protected FMLA leave.

(i) Prenatal Care

It is clear that FMLA leave is available for prenatal care. It is unclear, however, whether the expectant mother must be incapacitated because of pregnancy in order to take FMLA leave for prenatal care.[7] The lack of clarity results from the interplay of subsections (a) and (c) of 29 C.F.R. § 825.212. As set forth above, § 825.212(a) permits an eligible employee to take federal FMLA leave "because of the birth" of a son or daughter. The critical phrase "because of the birth" is not defined and, arguably, could cover prenatal leave that is causally related to birth. On the other hand, § 825.212(c) provides that an expectant mother may take FMLA leave for prenatal care or if her condition makes her unable to work, pursuant to subsection (a)(4).[8] Subsection (a)(4) of § 825.112, in turn, provides that FMLA leave is available because of a serious health condition that makes the employee unable to perform the functions of the employee's job.[9]

The language of § 825.112(c) suggests that federal FMLA leave is available for prenatal care only where the mother has a serious health condition due to pregnancy. A counterargument would be that § 825.112(c) does not preclude leave for prenatal care pursuant to § 825.112(a) because of the birth of a child, but merely clarifies that prenatal care is also available where the expectant mother has a serious health condition due to pregnancy. School administrators should check with legal counsel before denying federal FMLA leave to an eligible employee for prenatal care where the expectant mother does not have a serious health condition.

Note that § 825.112(c) limits federal FMLA leave to an expectant mother for prenatal care or if her condition renders her unable to work.[10] Fathers are apparently precluded from taking federal FMLA leave for these reasons. This would appear to conflict with the legislative intent that the right to take FMLA leave "appl[y] equally to male and female employees. A father, as well as a mother, can take family leave because of the birth or serious health condition of his child."[11] The statute and the DOL regulations require covered school employers to grant federal FMLA leave to eligible employees for the birth or serious health condition of a son or daughter.[12]

Finally, I note that the term "prenatal care" is undefined. Presumably it means medical care prior to the birth. Because it is undefined, however, arguments could be made that prenatal care may include something other than medical care.

(ii) Availability of Child Care

An eligible employee is entitled to federal FMLA leave "to care for" a newborn son or daughter regardless of whether others are available to provide child care during the leave period. As observed in the legislative history:

> When both the father and mother, or more than one sibling, are involved in the care of a child . . . they can take leave at the same time, on an overlapping basis, or sequentially, as long as leave is taken "because of" one of the circumstances specified in Section 102(a). Section 102 makes it possible, among other things, for a father to take leave during his wife's childbirth and recovery, an especially crucial time, even if his wife is herself an employee who is also on leave.[13]

Because FMLA leave "to care for" a newborn includes bonding time, an eligible employee could take federal FMLA leave to bond with his or her newborn son or daughter even though the infant's physical needs are concurrently being met by a nanny or some other form of day care. Although undefined, presumably "bonding time" requires the actual physical presence of the eligible employee with the newborn child in order to qualify for federal FMLA leave.

(iii) Multiple Births

No matter how many births occur within an eligible employee's family during the leave year, the employee is not entitled to more than 12 workweeks of federal FMLA leave during the leave year.[14] An employee is not entitled to 12 workweeks of leave for each birth during the leave year. Of course, multiple births would afford an eligible employee more opportunities to use the 12 workweeks of FMLA leave during the leave year. For further discussion of the selection of the leave year and the amount of FMLA leave available to an eligible employee during that leave year, see Chapter 8, *Leave Amount and Scheduling*.

(iv) Physical Ability to Return to Work Earlier

School administrators may not require an eligible employee to return to work from FMLA leave following the birth of a son or daughter simply because the employee is physically capable of returning to work earlier. Because FMLA leave is available for the birth and *care of* a newborn, the DOL has opined that an employee who is medically cleared to return to work after, for example, 4 weeks of recovery following the birth may nevertheless stay out on FMLA leave *to care for* the newborn until that employee exhausts her 12 workweeks of federal FMLA leave.[15]

(v) Intermittent and Reduced Leave Schedule Leave

School administrators may legally deny an eligible employee's request for FMLA leave following the birth of a son or daughter where the leave is taken intermittently or on a reduced leave schedule. This is because an employer must agree to an employee's request for intermittent or reduced leave schedule FMLA leave.[16] As discussed more fully in Chapter 8, *Leave Amount and Scheduling*, federal FMLA leave may be taken in one of three ways: (1) in a block, (2) intermittently, or (3) on a so-called reduced leave schedule. A "block" of FMLA leave is one continuous absence for the same covered condition. "Intermittent" leave is more than one absence for the same covered condition.[17] A reduced leave schedule is a form of intermittent leave involving multiple absences for the same covered condition, such as where an eligible employee's schedule is reduced from full-time to part-time.[18] Employers do not have the right to deny FMLA leave following the birth of a son or daughter where the leave is taken in a single block of time.

It is unclear whether an employer may deny an eligible employee's request for intermittent leave or a reduced leave schedule prior to or on the actual birth date. The DOL implementing regulations limit application of the employer's right to deny the eligible employee's request for leave where the need for intermittent leave or a reduced leave schedule is taken *after* the birth. The statute, on the other hand, does not distinguish between *before* the birth and *after* the birth where leave is taken on an intermittent or reduced leave schedule.[19] Assuming the DOL regulations on this point are valid, an employer would not have the right to deny an eligible employee's request for leave to be taken intermittently or on a reduced leave schedule *before* the birth of a child but could do so for any such leave taken *after* the child's birth. Schools wishing to take a more aggressive legal stance might consider, after consultation with counsel, exercising their statutory right to deny an eligible employee intermittent or reduced leave schedule leave both before and after the birth of a son or daughter.

(vi) Paid Leave Substitution

FMLA leave is unpaid leave.[20] The federal FMLA, however, allows for the substitution of accrued and available paid leave for unpaid FMLA leave.[21] When an employee has earned or accrued paid vacation, personal, sick, or family leave, that paid leave may be substituted for all or part of any otherwise unpaid FMLA leave relating to the birth or care of a newborn son or daughter.[22] An employer is not, however, required to substitute accrued paid leave for unpaid FMLA leave where the paid leave is not available under school policies for the intended FMLA use. For example, school policy may limit the use of paid sick leave to the school employee's own illness and not that of any family member. In that situation, if the eligible employee requested FMLA leave to take his wife to the doctor for prenatal care, the school would not be required to substitute any of the employee's accrued paid sick leave for that purpose. All things being equal, the school might be required to grant the employee FMLA leave for that purpose.

The rules governing the interaction of paid leave and FMLA leave are addressed in Chapter 9, *Paid Leave Substitution*.

(vii) Documentation of Need for FMLA Leave

The federal FMLA gives employers the right to request reasonable documentation or a statement of familial relationship.[23] This documentation may take the form of a simple statement from the employee, a child's birth certificate, or other document.[24] Employers have the right to examine such documents, but the employee is entitled to the return of any official documentation like a birth certificate.[25] Documentation of the need for FMLA leave prior to the birth of a son or daughter could be in the form of medical documentation. Such documentation, however, would not need to establish the existence of a serious health condition, as prebirth leave is available even though no one is sick. Rather, such documentation could establish pregnancy, paternity, and the expected birth date.

It is unclear at what point in time an employer can request documentation of familial relationship. The DOL regulations suggest that an employer's request should occur within a reasonable period of time after the employee gives notice of the need for leave.[26] The regulations fail to identify the time frame an employee has to provide such documentation. School employers would be well advised to give the employee a reasonable period of time under the circumstances to produce such documentation. Nor do the DOL regulations state what happens if an employee fails to provide such family documentation. Arguably, an eligible employee who fails to provide such documentation has not perfected his or her right to FMLA leave, and as a result, an employer could delay or deny that employee the benefits and protections of the FMLA for the absence at issue. School employers may look by analogy to the consequences of an employee's failure to provide medical certification where the need for leave is due to an FMLA-covered serious health condition.

FMLA documentation requirements are discussed more fully in Chapter 7, *Documentation Requirements*.

(viii) Leave Conclusion

An eligible employee's entitlement to federal FMLA leave for the birth of or to care for a newborn son or daughter expires at the end of the 12-month period following the birth date.[27] The 12-month period beginning on the birth date is not extended because an employee begins FMLA leave during that period.[28] This is a "use it or lose it" regulation. An eligible employee who fails to take FMLA leave to care for a newborn son or daughter before the expiration of the 12-month period following the birth loses this as a reason to take job-protected FMLA leave for that child. Of course, the employee could take available FMLA leave for other covered conditions.

Note that the 12-month period is calculated as of the birth date. The taking of FMLA leave prior to the birth date does not start the running of the 12-month period.[29]

The DOL regulations recognize that the 12-month period may be extended as permitted by state law or as permitted by the employer.[30] However, if state law or a school employer were to extend the 12-month period for an eligible employee to take leave because of the birth of or to care for a newborn, any leave taken after the expiration of the 12-month period would fall outside the benefits and protections of the federal FMLA and would not count against the eligible employee's 12-workweek FMLA leave entitlement.[31]

[2] Adoption

An eligible employee is entitled take job-protected federal FMLA leave because of the placement of a son or daughter with the employee for adoption.[32] The terms "adoption" and "because of the placement" are undefined. Leave that is causally related to the adoption of a son or daughter, presumably, is "because of the placement" and, therefore, would qualify.

Leave is available "to care for" a newly adopted son or daughter, although the DOL implementing regulations are not a model of clarity on this point. Section 825.112(a)(2) fails to include "to care for" the newly adopted son or daughter within the permissible scope of leave. In contrast, as discussed above, § 825.112(a)(1), addressing leave for the birth of a new son or daughter, specifically adds "and to care for the newborn child" within the permissible scope of leave. Leave for "bonding time" with the newly adopted son or daughter is, however, inexplicably included in § 825.200(a)(2) and § 825.202(a)(2).[33] The scope of leave "because of the placement" of a newly adopted son or daughter with the eligible employee is not the primary focus of these sections; rather, the primary focus of § 825.200 is the method for calculating the FMLA leave year, and the focus of § 825.202 is the amount of leave available to an eligible employee where both the husband and wife work for the same covered employer. Nevertheless, the DOL has opined that the inclusion of bonding time within the scope of federal FMLA leave is consistent with the legislative history of the Act.[34] An eligible employee may take leave to bond with a newly adopted son or daughter; illness is not required.

What constitutes "bonding" is not defined by the Act or implementing regulations. In comments accompanying publication of the final implementing regulations, the DOL suggests that the "act of providing care" to a newly adopted son or daughter is not a qualifying reason for FMLA leave.[35] If staying at home to watch the newly adopted child, cooking, and engaging in similar activities does not count as "bonding" time between the parent and child, one wonders exactly what activities would count.

(i) Son or Daughter

To fall within the scope of the federal FMLA, the eligible employee must adopt a person who fits the definition of an FMLA-covered "son or daughter." As set forth in the preceding chapter, a "son or daughter" is defined by the federal FMLA as a biological, adopted, or foster child, a stepchild, a legal ward, or a child of a person standing in loco parentis, who is either under 18 years of age or 18 years of age or older and incapable of self-care because of a mental or physical disability.[36] In an unusual case, a court found that an eligible employee was entitled to FMLA leave to attend a custody hearing to adopt a biological child.[37] By its terms, the adoption of children over the age of 18 by an eligible employee falls outside of the scope of the FMLA, unless the son or daughter is incapable of self-care due to a mental or physical disability.

Similarly, absent adoption, an eligible employee is not entitled to federal FMLA leave to bond with a stepchild. The eligible employee would, however, be entitled to federal FMLA leave if the employee were needed to care for a stepchild with a serious health condition, provided the child met the age and other definitional requirements of an FMLA-covered "son or daughter." FMLA leave for serious health conditions is addressed in section 5.03 below.

(ii) Source of Adoption

The source of an adopted child, whether a licensed placement agency or otherwise, is not a factor in determining whether to grant an eligible employee FMLA leave.[38] An eligible employee would be equally entitled to federal FMLA leave to adopt a son or daughter whether the son or daughter was secured through a state-licensed placement agency or through the black market. No rationale is provided for this curious provision.

(iii) Leave prior to Adoption

School employers must grant FMLA leave for the placement of a son or daughter with the eligible employee for adoption if an absence from work is required for the placement or adoption to proceed.[39] For example, the employee may be required to attend counseling sessions, appear in court, consult with his or her attorney or the doctor(s) representing the birth parent, or submit to a physical examination.[40]

Note that in order for leave prior to adoption to be granted, the need for such leave must be "required" for the placement or adoption to proceed. In contrast, the DOL regulations regarding leave prior to birth do not mandate that such leave be "required."[41] If leave prior to adoption were permitted rather than required, the leave would not fall within the protections of the federal FMLA. Presumably, a school employer may determine whether leave prior to adoption is required by requiring the employee to provide appropriate documentation substantiating that the employee is engaged in the adoption process.[42]

(iv) Multiple Adoptions

An eligible employee may take FMLA leave for multiple adoptions during the 12-month leave year. Each son or daughter placed with the employee is treated as a separate qualifying event for purposes of federal FMLA leave. If all other FMLA conditions are met, an employer is required to grant an eligible employee federal FMLA leave for each adoption of a son or daughter with the employee, up to the total of 12 workweeks of FMLA leave available for all FMLA-covered conditions during the leave year. An eligible employee is entitled to a total of 12 workweeks of leave each leave year, not 12 workweeks of leave for each adopted child.

(v) Intermittent or Reduced Leave Schedule Leave

As in the case of leave related to the birth of a child, an eligible employee needs the approval of his or her employer in order to take federal FMLA leave related to adoption on an intermittent or reduced leave schedule basis.[43] The statute and the DOL implementing regulations differ regarding the circumstances requiring an employer's consent for an employee to take leave on an intermittent or reduced leave schedule basis due to adoption. The statute provides that all leave for adoption placement taken on an intermittent or reduced leave schedule basis requires approval by the eligible employee's employer.[44] The DOL regulations, on the other hand, provide that employer consent is required only where the intermittent or reduced leave schedule leave is sought *after* the placement of a covered child for adoption.[45] The difference is significant in terms of leave prior to adoption placement. Under the DOL regulations, a school employer could not simply deny an eligible employee's request for FMLA leave on an intermittent or reduced leave schedule basis prior to adoption. Under the statute, however, a school employer arguably could deny such leave prior to adoption. Schools administrators should check with legal counsel before electing to follow the statute and not the DOL regulations on this issue.

Each placement of a child for adoption with an eligible employee is a separate FMLA-qualifying event for purposes of federal FMLA leave.[46] A school employer would not, therefore, have the right to treat multiple adoptions as a single qualifying event for purposes of exercising the right to deny an eligible employee's request for federal FMLA leave on an intermittent or reduced leave schedule basis. Rather, the adoption of each child is viewed as a discrete event separate and apart from the adoption of other children, even though the adoptions may, in fact, take place at the same time. In order for a school employer to have the right to deny an eligible employee's request to take FMLA leave for adoption on an intermittent or reduced leave schedule basis, multiple leave requests must involve the same adopted son or daughter.

FMLA Illustrated: Multiple Adoption/Intermittent Leave Example

Mary is a school teacher at Public Elementary and is eligible for federal FMLA leave. Mary and her husband decided to adopt 2 Russian children, Sasha and Dimitri, ages 4 and 6, respectively. Sasha and Dimitri are biological brother and sister. Mary asks for federal FMLA leave on 5 dates to facilitate both adoptions. Of those 5 dates, 4 are for Sasha, who has physical problems that complicate the adoption, and 1 is for Dimitri.

Question: Assuming that all of the dates are required to facilitate the adoptions, can you deny Mary's request for federal FMLA intermittent leave?

Answer: You could not deny all of Mary's requested FMLA leave because not all of it is intermittent. Mary asks for only 1 absence for Dimitri, which is a block of leave. Leave for Dimitri and Sasha are separate FMLA events. As such, leave for Dimitri is not intermittent because it cannot be combined with leave for Sasha. You could deny Mary's request for federal FMLA leave for Sasha, as that leave is intermittent.

(vi) Paid Leave Substitution

FMLA leave is unpaid.[47] Accrued and available paid leave may, however, be substituted for unpaid federal FMLA leave.[48] Where, for example, an eligible employee has earned or accrued paid vacation, personal, or family leave, that paid leave may be substituted for all or part of any otherwise unpaid federal FMLA leave involving the adoption of a son or daughter.[49] An employer is not required to provide substituted paid leave to an eligible employee because of an FMLA-covered adoption where, pursuant to policy, the accrued paid leave does not cover leave incident to an adoption. For example, school policy may limit an employee's use of accrued paid sick leave to situations where the employee or a family member is sick. In that instance, accrued paid sick leave would not be available to substitute for unpaid federal FMLA leave because of an adoption if the adopted child is not sick. In these situations, an eligible employee's accrued vacation or personal leave would be a more likely source of available paid leave for substitution.[50]

Paid leave substitution is addressed more fully in Chapter 9, *Paid Leave Substitution*.

(vii) Documentation of Need for FMLA Leave

As noted regarding leave because of birth, the federal FMLA permits an employer to require an eligible employee to provide documentation establishing family relationship.[51] The documentation may take the form of a simple statement from the employee, a court document, or other similar documentation.[52] The employer is entitled to examine family documentation provided by the employee, but the employee is entitled to the return of official documents.[53] The adoption process generally involves an extraordinary amount of paperwork, so documentation of the family relationship between the eligible employee and the adoptive child should be a relatively straightforward exercise.

The DOL implementing regulations fail to specify when an employer may request such documentation, how long the employee has to provide it, and what happens if the employer determines that the documentation provided by the employee is inadequate or if the employee fails to provide any documentation. A school employer might consider applying by analogy at least some of the procedural requirements for handling requests for medical certification.

Documentation issues are addressed more fully in Chapter 7, *Documentation Requirements*.

(viii) Leave Conclusion

As in the case of leave because of birth, an eligible employee's entitlement to federal FMLA leave because of the adoption of a son or daughter expires at the end of the 12-month period beginning on the date of placement.[54] The DOL has rejected the position that such leave need only commence during the 12-month period in order for an eligible employee to preserve the right to take up to 12 workweeks of leave. "The leave must be concluded (i.e., completed) within the statutory entitlement period."[55] The 12-month period is measured beginning on the placement date. The taking of leave prior to adoption does not initiate the running of the 12-month period.[56]

An employee who fails to take federal FMLA leave because of the adoption of a son or daughter within 12 months of the placement date loses the right to take FMLA leave to bond with the child. For example, in one case an employee adopted his brother's children who lived in the Philippines. Three years after the adoption, he requested federal FMLA leave to travel to the Philippines to pick up the children and, upon their return to the United States, to spend some time bonding with them. The court found that the employer's denial of leave to the employee did not violate the federal FMLA, observing: "While we recognize the importance of child-parent bonding and of a parent's presence in early child rearing, we cannot read the Act to extend 'placement for adoption' to encompass [the employee's] situation."[57]

As in the case of birth, the DOL regulations recognize that the 12-month period may be extended as permitted by state law or as permitted by the employer.[58] However, if state law or a school employer were to extend the 12-month period for an eligible employee to take leave because of the adoption of a son or daughter, any leave taken after the expiration of the 12-month period would fall outside the benefits and protections of the federal FMLA and would not count against the eligible employee's 12-workweek FMLA leave entitlement.[59]

[3] Foster Care Placement

An eligible employee is entitled to federal FMLA leave because of the placement of a son or daughter with the employee for foster care.[60] "Foster care" means "24-hour care for children in substitution for, and away from, their parents or guardian."[61] "Care" is not defined, but presumably it includes physical, financial, and psychological care. There is no minimum period of time that a foster child must be with the eligible employee before the employee is entitled to FMLA leave because of the foster care placement of the child with the employee.[62]

Federal FMLA leave for foster care placement includes leave to permit the eligible employee to care for the newly placed foster son or daughter, including time to bond with the foster child.[63] For a further discussion of this issue, see subsection [2] above regarding adoption. The DOL regulations on bonding that apply regarding adoption also apply to foster care placement.

Finally, the fact that the employee receives compensation or other consideration for his or her services as a foster parent is not material for purposes of the employee's entitlement to FMLA leave.[64]

(i) Son or Daughter

To fall within the scope of the federal FMLA, the foster care placement must be of a "son or daughter." As addressed in the preceding chapter, the term "son or daughter" is defined by the federal FMLA to mean a biological, adopted, or foster child, a stepchild, a legal ward, or a child of a person standing in loco parentis, who is either under 18 years of age or age 18 or older and incapable of self-care because of a mental or physical disability.[65] If the foster child to be placed with the eligible employee does not fit the definition of a "son or daughter," the leave is not covered by the federal FMLA. Of course, the leave may be covered by state family leave laws or school policies.

(ii) Source of Placement Relevant

The source of a foster care placement, unlike the source of an adoption, is relevant for federal FMLA coverage. Foster care placements must be made by or with the agreement of the state as a result of a voluntary agreement between the state and the parent or guardian that the child must be removed from the home, or pursuant to a judicial determination of the necessity for foster care, and involves agreement between the state and foster family that the foster family will take care of the child.[66] Foster care placements made through a state-approved agency fall within these requirements.[67]

Absent a state-approved or judicially approved placement, the act of providing "foster care" alone is not a qualifying reason for leave.[68] For example, an eligible employee who assumes the responsibility as primary caretaker for his grandchildren while his son or daughter undergoes drug treatment is not "foster care" within the meaning of the FMLA absent formal state action placing the grandchildren with the eligible employee.[69] As such, the employee would not be entitled to federal FMLA leave to bond with each child. If, however, the child has a serious health condition, an eligible employee would be entitled to federal FMLA leave as an in loco parentis parent.

(iii) Leave prior to Foster Care Placement

As with adoption, federal FMLA leave is available to an eligible employee before the actual foster care placement date if the absence from work is required for the placement to proceed.[70] For example, an eligible employee may be required to attend counseling sessions, appear in court, consult with his or her attorney or doctors, or submit to a physical examination in furtherance of the foster care placement.[71] Note that entitlement to leave prior to foster care placement is conditioned on that leave being "required" for the foster care placement to proceed. If the leave is not required in order for the foster care placement to proceed, the leave is not covered by the benefits and protections of the FMLA. The DOL does not explain what circumstances are "required" in order for a foster care placement to "proceed." Given the requirement of state or court action for this type of leave, presumably leave is "required" where it is a mandatory rather than a permitted part of the foster care placement process.

For example, if an eligible employee requests federal FMLA leave to attend a court proceeding that will order the foster care placement and the employee's attendance is required for the court to finalize that placement, the leave would fall within the benefits and protections of the FMLA. On the other hand, if the employee requests leave to visit with the prospective foster child and such visitation is not required by a state-approved placement agency or a court as part of the placement process, the leave is merely permissible and would not fall within the benefits and protections of the federal FMLA.

(iv) Multiple Foster Care Placements

Multiple foster care placements with an eligible employee do not affect the employee's entitlement to FMLA leave. Each son or daughter placed with the employee is treated as a separate qualifying event for purposes of federal FMLA leave.[72] If all other FMLA conditions are met, a school employer would be required to grant an eligible employee federal FMLA leave for each foster care placement of a son or daughter with the employee, up to the total of 12 workweeks of FMLA leave available for all FMLA-covered conditions during the leave year. An eligible employee is entitled to a total of 12 workweeks of leave each leave year, not 12 workweeks of leave for each foster child placement.[73]

(v) Intermittent or Reduced Leave Schedule Leave

An employer must agree to permit an eligible employee to take federal FMLA leave on an intermittent or reduced leave schedule basis.[74] As previously discussed regarding FMLA leave for the birth or adoption of a son or daughter, the statute and regulations differ regarding the circumstances under which employer consent is required for intermittent or reduced leave schedule FMLA leave for foster care placement. The difference between the statute and DOL regulations involves leave prior to foster care placement. The statute requires employer approval for foster care placement leave taken on an intermittent or reduced leave schedule basis—whether that leave is to be taken before or after the foster care placement.[75] The DOL regulations, on the other hand, require employer consent only where the intermittent or reduced leave schedule leave is sought *after* the foster care placement.[76] Under the DOL regulations, an employee would not need the separate agreement of an employer to take preplacement federal FMLA leave on an intermittent or reduced leave schedule basis. The pros and cons to school employers of following the language of the statute over the language of the DOL regulations on this point is addressed more fully in subsection [2](iv) above.

Because each foster care child placement is treated separately, the rules governing FMLA leave taken on an intermittent or reduced leave schedule basis apply only with respect to leave for each foster child. Leaves of absence taken for two or more foster children may not be combined for purposes of meeting the intermittent or reduced leave schedule leave federal FMLA requirements. The example given in subsection [2](iv) above regarding multiple adoptions and intermittent or reduced leave schedule FMLA leave would similarly apply to foster care placement.

(vi) Paid Leave Substitution

FMLA leave is unpaid.[77] Accrued and available paid leave may, however, be substituted for unpaid federal FMLA leave.[78] Where, for example, an eligible employee has earned or accrued paid vacation, personal, sick, or family leave, that paid leave may be substituted for all or part of any otherwise unpaid federal FMLA leave involving the foster care placement of a son or daughter.[79] An employer is not required to provide substituted paid leave to an eligible employee because of an FMLA-covered foster care placement where, pursuant to policy, the accrued paid leave does not cover leave incident to foster care placement. For example, school policy may limit an employee's use of accrued paid sick leave to situations where the employee or a family member is sick. In that instance, accrued paid sick leave would not be available to substitute for unpaid federal FMLA leave because of the foster care placement of a son or daughter if the foster child is not sick. In these situations, an eligible employee's accrued vacation or personal leave would be a more likely source of available paid leave for substitution.[80]

Paid leave substitution is addressed more fully in Chapter 9, *Paid Leave Substitution*.

(vii) Documentation of Need for FMLA Leave

As with leave because of birth or adoption, the federal FMLA permits an employer to require an eligible employee to provide documentation establishing family relationship.[81] The documentation may take the form of a simple statement from the employee, a court document, or other similar documentation.[82] Presumably, documentation of family relationship would include evidence that the leave requested by the employee is "required" in order for the foster care placement process to proceed. The employer is entitled to examine family documentation provided by the employee, but the employee is entitled to the return of official documents.[83] The foster care placement process generally involves a lot of paperwork, so documentation of the family relationship between the eligible employee and the foster child should be a relatively straightforward exercise.

The DOL implementing regulations fail to specify when an employer may request such documentation, how long the employee has to provide it, and what happens if the employer determines that the documentation provided by the employee is inadequate or if the employee fails to provide any documentation. A school employer might consider applying by analogy at least some of the procedural requirements for handling requests for medical certification.

Documentation issues are addressed more fully in Chapter 7, *Documentation Requirements*.

(viii) Leave Conclusion

As with leave because of birth and adoption, an eligible employee's entitlement to leave because of the foster care placement of a son or daughter expires at the end of the 12-month period beginning on the date of placement.[84] The DOL has rejected the position that such leave need only commence during the 12-month period in order for an eligible employee to preserve the right to take up to 12 workweeks of leave. "The leave must be concluded (i.e., completed) within the statutory entitlement period."[85] The 12-month period is measured beginning on the placement date. The taking of leave prior to placement does not initiate the running of the 12-month period.[86]

As in the case of birth and adoption, the DOL regulations recognize that the 12-month period may be extended as permitted by state law or as permitted by the employer.[87] However, if state law or a school employer were to extend the 12-month period for an eligible employee to take leave because of the foster care placement of a son or daughter, any leave taken after the expiration of the 12-month period would fall outside the benefits and protections of the federal FMLA and would not count against the eligible employee's 12-workweek FMLA leave entitlement.[88]

5.03 SERIOUS HEALTH CONDITIONS

[1] Overview

Federal FMLA leave is available to eligible employees for "serious health conditions."[89] An eligible employee may be entitled to federal FMLA leave if the employee is incapacitated due to his or her own serious health condition or if the employee is needed to care for a spouse, son, daughter, or parent with a serious health condition. The federal FMLA broadly defines a serious health condition as "an illness, injury, impairment, or physical or mental condition that involves . . . inpatient care in a hospital, hospice, or residential medical care facility" or "continuing treatment by a health care provider."[90] The legislative history and DOL implementing regulations add substantially to our understanding of what constitutes "inpatient care" and "continuing treatment" within the meaning of the federal FMLA. Although the definition is broad, the circumstances that fall within the definition of an FMLA-covered serious health condition are not limitless. For an employee to secure the benefits and protections of the federal FMLA, leave due to the illness of the eligible employee or the employee's spouse, son, daughter, or parent must meet at least one of the definitions of a serious health condition. If the illness does not meet all of the requirements of at least one serious health condition, leave for that condition will not be covered by the federal FMLA—no matter how severe the illness.[91]

To determine whether an eligible employee has a serious health condition within the meaning of the federal FMLA, school employers must answer two questions:

1. Who has the serious health condition?
2. Does the condition meet at least one of the definitions of a federal FMLA-covered serious health condition?

Regarding the first question, the requirements for federal FMLA coverage differ depending on whether the eligible employee or a covered family member has the serious health condition. Whether the condition meets at least one of the definitions of a serious health condition is one of the most complex questions that school employers must address in order to avoid substantial liability for violating the law.

School employers bear the considerable burden of determining whether an employee's request for leave is covered by the federal FMLA. As we will see in subsequent chapters, they are assisted in this responsibility by the employee's duty to timely and adequately notify employers of their need for leave. Employers may also require medical documentation in support of a request for FMLA leave due to a serious health condition. At the end of the day, however, whether to grant or deny an employee's request for federal FMLA leave rests with school administrators. Employers that get this wrong can be sued for substantial civil damages. The federal FMLA allows aggrieved employees to sue individual supervisors and managers for violations of the FMLA, even where those violations were unintended. The rules governing covered "serious health conditions" are complex and require that administration of the federal FMLA be accomplished with great care.

This section begins with a review of the rules governing who has the serious health condition. It will then address the various types of serious health conditions recognized by the federal FMLA. Along the way we will discuss important definitions, such as who is a health care provider for purposes of the federal FMLA.

[2] Whose Serious Health Condition? Employee, Spouse, Son, Daughter, or Parent

An eligible employee must meet two requirements in order to be entitled to federal FMLA leave for his or her own serious health condition or the serious health condition of a spouse, son, daughter, or parent. The first requirement is that the illness satisfy at least one of the federal FMLA definitions of a serious health condition. We will discuss this requirement in more detail in the next section. Our concern in this section is with the second requirement, which differs depending on who has the serious health condition. If it is the eligible employee's own serious health condition, that condition must incapacitate the employee such that the employee is unable to perform the functions of his or her position. Where the spouse, son, daughter, or parent has the serious health condition, the leave must be "in order to care for" that person. If the eligible employee does not meet either the incapacity (for his or her own serious health condition) or the "needed to care for" (for the serious health condition of a spouse, son, daughter, or parent) requirement, the employee is not entitled to federal FMLA leave—even if a serious health condition is involved and the employee meets all other requirements.

(i) Incapacity Due to Employee's Own Serious Health Condition

An eligible employee is entitled to federal FMLA leave because of a serious health condition that makes the employee unable to perform the functions of his or her job.[92] The federal FMLA recognizes two circumstances in which an eligible employee is unable to perform the functions of his or her position: (1) if the employee must be absent from work to receive treatment for a serious health condition[93] or (2) if a health care provider has found that the employee is unable to work at all or is unable to perform one or more of the essential functions of the employee's position.[94] Regarding the first situation, one court explained that "'unable to perform' does not necessarily mean that an employee's physical condition itself 'actually incapacitates' him and prevents him from working. The statute could also be read to protect absences from work for whatever time the employee needs in order to be diagnosed and treated for a serious health condition."[95] The inability of the employee to perform the functions of his or her position must last during the absence for treatment.[96] To satisfy this requirement, the eligible employee need only establish that a medical appointment conflicts with his or her work schedule.[97]

The term "medical treatment" is not defined in the statute or DOL implementing regulations. "Treatment" is defined for purposes of a "serious health condition" to include (but is not limited to) examinations to determine if a serious health condition exists and evaluations of the condition.[98] Treatment does not include routine physical examinations, eye examinations, or dental examinations.[99] Receipt of treatment requires an inpatient visit with a health care provider; telephone conversations with health care providers are not considered treatment.[100]

The second circumstance permitting an eligible employee to take federal FMLA leave due to his or her own serious health condition arises where a health care provider has found that the employee is unable to work at all or is unable to perform one or more of the essential functions of the employee's position. The determination as to whether something is considered to be an essential function of the employee's position is made in accordance with the Americans with Disabilities Act of 1990 (ADA) and the regulations at 29 C.F.R. § 1630.2(n).[101] The ADA regulations define essential job functions as follows:

> (n) Essential functions—(1) In general. The term essential functions means the fundamental job duties of the employment position the individual with a disability holds or desires. The terms "essential functions" does not include the marginal functions of the position.
>
> (2) A job function may be considered essential for any of several reasons, including but not limited to the following:
>
> (i) The function may be essential because the reason the position exists is to perform that function;
>
> (ii) The function may be essential because of the limited number of employees available among whom the performance of that job function can be distributed; and/or
>
> (iii) The function may be highly specialized in that the incumbent in the position is hired for his or her expertise or ability to perform the particular function.
>
> (3) Evidence of whether a particular function is essential includes, but is not limited to:
>
> (i) The employer's judgment as to which functions are essential;
>
> (ii) Written job descriptions prepared before advertising or interviewing applicants for the job;
>
> (iii) The amount of time spent on the job performing the function;
>
> (iv) The consequences of not requiring the incumbent to perform the function;
>
> (v) The terms of a collective bargaining agreement;
>
> (vi) The work experience of past incumbents in the job; and/or
>
> (vii) The current work experience of incumbents in similar jobs.[102]

The essential functions of the employee's position are determined in reference to the position the eligible employee holds at the time the employee gives notice of the need for FMLA leave or at the time leave commences, whichever is earlier.[103] If the eligible employee is away from his or her permanent position on a temporary assignment at the time the employee gives notice of the need for leave or at the time leave commences, whichever is earlier, the determination of whether the employee can perform the job's essential functions is based on the temporary assignment and not the employee's permanent position. The essential functions are determined based on the job the employee holds for a particular employer. The fact that the employee works another job for another employer during the leave period does not disprove that the employee could not perform one or more essential job functions for his or her employer.[104]

> The federal FMLA does not require that an eligible employee be completely unable to work before that employee is entitled to FMLA leave for his or her own serious health condition.

Note that the federal FMLA does not require that the eligible employee be totally incapacitated from working.[105] A common misconception held by school employers is that to be entitled to leave under the federal FMLA the employee must be completely unable to perform work of any kind. That is simply not true. An eligible employee is "unable to perform work" within the meaning of the federal FMLA if the employee cannot perform *any one or more* of the essential functions of the job held by the employee at the time the need for FMLA leave arises.[106] Of course, if the employee is unable to work at all due to a serious health condition, the employee would also be "unable to work" within the meaning of the federal FMLA.

A school employer may not deprive an eligible employee who is unable to perform one or more essential job functions of the right to take federal FMLA leave by modifying the job or requiring the employee to take another job as a reasonable accommodation.[107] In some cases, an employee's FMLA-covered serious health condition also constitutes a disability within the meaning of the Americans with Disabilities Act of

FMLA Illustrated: Essential Job Functions Example

John is a chemistry teacher at Public High School. His job has four essential functions: (1) the ability to communicate verbally for 6 hours a day, (2) the ability to lead a class, (3) the ability to work with chemicals in a classroom setting, and (4) the ability to grade papers in a timely manner. John develops an allergic reaction to chemicals.

Question: Assuming John meets the eligibility requirements, would he be entitled to federal FMLA leave?

Answer: Probably yes. Even though John could verbally communicate for 6 hours a day, lead a classroom, grade papers in a timely manner, and perform all other essential job functions of a chemistry teacher, because he was unable to work with chemicals, he could not perform an essential function of his job. The remaining question is whether John's allergic reaction to chemicals constitutes a serious health condition within the meaning of the FMLA. For our purposes here, however, John is unable to work because he is unable to perform one of several essential job functions. John is not required to be totally disabled from working in order to be considered "unable to work."

1990.[108] The ADA, as well as similar state laws, requires covered employers to offer disabled employees reasonable accommodation in order to do their jobs. While a school employer may be required to offer a disabled employee a modified position as a reasonable accommodation, if the eligible employee is also considered to have an FMLA-covered serious health condition, the school may not change the essential functions of the job in order to deny FMLA leave. The leave provisions of the FMLA are wholly distinct from the reasonable accommodation obligations of employers covered by the ADA and similar state laws.[109] School employers faced with an eligible employee whose serious health condition also constitutes a disability under the ADA or similar state laws must observe the requirements of both laws and apply those laws in a manner that ensures the most beneficial rights and protections.[110]

The interaction of the FMLA with the ADA is addressed more fully in Chapter 13, *Coordination of the FMLA with Other Employee Rights and Benefits*.

(ii) In Order to Care for a Covered Family Member

An eligible employee is entitled to a total of 12 workweeks of leave during a 12-month leave year *in order to care for* a spouse, son, daughter, or parent of the employee who has a serious health condition.[111] The legislative history indicates that Congress intended that "to care for" be read broadly to include both physical and psychological care.[112] The DOL regulations implementing the federal FMLA uses the phrase "needed to care for" rather than the statutory language of "in order to care for."[113] In accordance with the legislative history, "needed to care for" encompasses both physical and psychological care.[114] It includes situations where, for example, because of a serious health condition

- the covered family member is unable to care for his or her own basic medical, hygienic, or nutritional needs, or safety;
- the covered family member is unable to transport himself or herself to the doctor;
- the eligible employee may be needed to fill in for others who are caring for the family member; or
- the eligible employee may be needed to make arrangements for changes in care, such as transfer to a nursing home.[115]

The term also includes situations in which the eligible employee provides psychological comfort and reassurance that is beneficial to a spouse, son, daughter, or parent with a serious health condition who is receiving inpatient or home care.[116] With respect to an eligible employee's need for intermittent leave or a reduced leave schedule to care for a family member, covered leave includes not only situations in which the family member's condition itself is intermittent but also situations in which the employee is needed only intermittently—such as where other care is normally available or care responsibilities are shared with another member of the family or a third party.[117]

Attendance at a care conference, where the eligible employee meets with the covered family member, doctors, nurses, dieticians, physical therapists, activity directors, and others taking part in the family member's care to discuss the family member's condition, immediate needs, and general well-being has been found to fall within FMLA-protected physical and psychological care because it aids the employee's ability to care for the covered family member.[118] Similarly, a court found that an employee was needed to provide physical and psychological care within the meaning of the FMLA based on evidence that the employee's spouse required basic medical assistance, assistance with his personal needs, and assistance to ensure his safety because he could not walk, prepare meals, go to the bathroom, or feed himself.[119] An employee who took leave to talk with his 73-year-old father with a serious health condition (grieving for a murdered sister), perform various household chores (shovel snow, chop wood, clean the garage), and drive his father to counseling sessions was providing physical and psychological care within the meaning of the federal FMLA.[120] Leave was available for an eligible employee to assist in making medical decisions for a badly burned parent.[121] Conversely, an employee did not establish that she was needed to care for her husband with an FMLA-covered serious health condition when the need for leave was to assist her husband with his lawsuit against his former employer and union, not to provide physical or psychological care.[122]

An eligible employee is "needed to care for" the physical and psychological needs only of the living, not of the recently deceased.[123] The deceased do not have basic medical, nutritional, or psychological needs to be cared for.[124] Similarly, federal FMLA leave is not available to allow the employee to wrap up the affairs of the deceased family member.[125] Bereavement leave is generally not covered by the federal FMLA.[126] Of course, if the eligible employee or another covered family member were to have a serious health condition as a result of grieving for the deceased, the employee might be entitled to federal FMLA leave to provide physical or psychological care to the grieving family member.

The level of physical or psychological care that an eligible employee must provide to a covered family member with a serious health condition appears to be minimal. For example, the testimony of a hospitalized father that the time his son spent with him was comforting and reassuring met the threshold of psychological care.[127] Although the level of care an eligible employee must provide is modest, it is not nonexistent. An eligible employee must establish that he or she did something to care for the covered family member in order to secure the protections of the federal FMLA. The federal FMLA's "to care for" provision does not automatically protect mere visitation.[128] In one case the court found that the employee had failed to establish that he was entitled to federal FMLA leave to care for his hospitalized mother. While the employee did go to the hospital, there was no evidence that he saw his mother or that his mother was aware that he was at the hospital. The court found that while the Act is broad, the federal FMLA "cannot be read so broadly that the concept of providing care is read out of the statute."[129]

It is unclear whether an eligible employee is entitled to federal FMLA leave to travel with a covered family member with a serious health condition in order "to care for" that family member while traveling. Several courts have held that absent evidence that the travel was needed in order for the covered family member to secure medical or psychological treatment, the federal FMLA does not cover an eligible employee's request for federal FMLA leave to "care for" a covered family member while traveling.[130] This result does not appear to be mandated by the language of the statute or the DOL implementing regulations. Neither the statute nor the regulations prohibit an eligible employee from providing physical or psychological care to a covered family member while that family member travels for whatever reason.

Finally, the availability of other caregivers is generally considered to have no bearing on an eligible employee's entitlement to FMLA leave "to care for" a covered family member with a serious health condition. According to the DOL, whether care is being provided by health care services or other family members is not relevant to the "to care for" determination.[131] Most courts have agreed with the DOL that the availability of other caregivers has no effect on an eligible employee's entitlement to FMLA leave "to care for" the covered family member.[132] One court, however, held that an employer properly denied an eligible employee's request for FMLA leave, finding that the employee was not "needed to care for" a covered family member because a sister was performing those duties.[133]

[3] Types of Serious Health Conditions

An eligible employee is entitled to federal FMLA leave for "serious health conditions." The statute defines a "serious health condition" as an illness, injury, impairment, or physical or mental condition that involves inpatient care in a hospital, hospice, or residential medical care facility or continuing treatment by a health care provider.[134] The statutory definition is intended to be broad.[135] The broad language of the statute, however, is of limited utility in determining whether a particular illness constitutes a "serious health condition" within the meaning of the federal FMLA. But the legislative history of the Act and the DOL implementing regulations provide additional insight and detail into the types of conditions that fall within the meaning of a "serious health condition."

Congress intended that only more serious illnesses fall within the protections of the federal FMLA. This is demonstrated by the following examples given by Congress of what it considered to be serious health conditions:

> Examples of serious health conditions include but are not limited to heart attacks, heart conditions requiring heart bypass or valve operations, most cancers, back conditions requiring extensive therapy or surgical procedures, strokes, severe respiratory conditions, spinal injuries, appendicitis, pneumonia, emphysema, severe arthritis, severe nervous disorders, injuries caused by serious accidents on or off the job, ongoing pregnancy, miscarriages, [or] complications or illnesses related to pregnancy, such as severe morning sickness, the need for prenatal care, childbirth and recovery from childbirth. All of these conditions meet the general test that either the underlying health condition or the treatment for it requires that the employee be absent from work on a recurring basis or for more than a few days for treatment or recovery. They also involve either inpatient care or continuing treatment or supervision by a health care provider, and frequently involve both.[136]

Congress did not intend to include relatively minor illnesses of short duration within the coverage of the federal FMLA.[137] Congress expected that minor illnesses would fall within "even the most modest sick leave policies."[138]

The DOL regulations implementing the federal FMLA add a substantial amount of detail to the definition of a "serious health condition.[139] The DOL regulations, like the statute, divide "serious health conditions" into two categories: (1) inpatient care and (2) continuing treatment by a health care provider.[140] The DOL regulations identify five situations that constitute "continuing treatment by a health care provider" within the meaning of the federal FMLA.[141] The remainder of this section addresses the requirements of the DOL regulations governing "serious health conditions." Whether the DOL regulations properly reflect Congress's intent to cover only "serious" medical conditions and exclude minor illnesses of short duration has been the subject of considerable and continuing debate in the courts, by academics, and in Congress.

> If the illness does not satisfy at least one of the definitions of a "serious health condition" in the DOL regulations, the eligible employee is not entitled to federal FMLA leave—no matter how serious the illness may in fact be.

In order for an employee to be entitled to federal FMLA leave, the illness giving rise to the request, whether it is the eligible employee's own illness or that of a covered family member, must fit within one or more of the DOL regulatory definitions of a "serious health condition." If the illness does not satisfy at least one of the definitions of a "serious health condition" in the DOL regulations, the eligible employee is not entitled to federal FMLA leave—no matter how serious the illness may in fact be. While broad, the DOL's definition of a "serious health condition" is not limitless.

(i) Inpatient Care

An FMLA-covered "serious health condition" includes an illness, injury, impairment, or physical or mental condition that involves inpatient care in a hospital, hospice, or residential medical care facility.[142] To qualify, inpatient care must involve an "overnight stay" in a hospital, hospice, or residential medical care facility.[143] The regulations do not define what "inpatient" means or what constitutes an "overnight stay." Also undefined are the terms "hospital, hospice, or residential medical care facility." Presumably, these terms have their normally understood meaning.

Federal FMLA leave is available for an overnight stay in a hospital, hospice, or residential medical care facility, as well as for any period of incapacity or any subsequent treatment in connection with inpatient care.[144] "Incapacity" is defined by example to mean "inability to work, attend school, or perform other regular daily activities due to the serious health condition, treatment therefor, or recovery therefrom."[145] "Treatment" includes, but is not limited to, examinations to determine if a serious health condition exists and evaluations of the condition.[146] "Treatment" does not include routine physical examinations, eye examinations, or dental examinations.[147]

Other than the requirement of an overnight stay, there is no minimum period of incapacity that is required before federal FMLA leave protections apply. For example, an eligible employee is hospitalized for three days for an FMLA-covered serious health condition. Several months after his release, the employee returns to the hospital and spends two hours receiving postoperative treatment related to the FMLA-covered serious health condition for which he was originally hospitalized. The two hours would be covered by the FMLA. Many people erroneously believe that to be an FMLA-covered serious health condition the employee or covered family member must be incapacitated for more than three consecutive days. Generally speaking, this is simply not the case.

School employers need to look at an eligible employee's absences both before and after an overnight stay in the hospital. This may be easier said than done. So long as the leave is due to inpatient care, periods of incapacity and leave for subsequent treatment are covered by the federal FMLA. The absence of a temporal limitation on an employee's use of inpatient care leave may greatly complicate a school employer's ability to properly identify the leave request as being covered by the FMLA.

Note that so long as an eligible employee stays in a hospital or other covered medical facility overnight, the employee would be entitled to federal FMLA leave even if the employee is ultimately found not to have a serious health condition. For example, an employee is admitted to the hospital with complaints of chest pains and shortness of breath. The hospital runs a series of tests for a heart attack, which come up negative, but decides to keep the employee overnight as a precaution. The employee received treatment within the meaning of the federal FMLA. Treatment includes examinations to determine if a serious health condition exists. Moreover, that treatment was in connection with an overnight stay in a hospital. The eligible employee's hospital stay would be covered by the federal FMLA.

FMLA Illustrated: Inpatient Care

Brenda is a coach at Public High School and is eligible for federal FMLA leave. She injures herself at work while coaching. She is taken to the hospital for X-rays. Brenda subsequently undergoes surgery. She is released from the hospital 3 days after the surgery. She receives treatment once a month for the next 6 months. Three years after the last postoperative treatment, Brenda aggravates her injury, requiring resumption of her postoperative treatment regimen. Assume Brenda needs leave from work for her absences.

Question: Which of Brenda's absences from work are covered by the federal FMLA?

Answer: Potentially all of them. Brenda stayed in a hospital overnight. Any leave she needed prior to her hospital admittance due to her incapacity would be covered, as would her treatment with an X-ray. The time Brenda spent in the hospital would be covered as she was both incapacitated and receiving treatment due to, and in connection with, her inpatient care. Similarly, because all of her postoperative treatments are in connection with her inpatient care, leave to receive such treatments would also be covered. The fact that some of that leave occurred years later is of no consequence.

(ii) Continuing Treatment by a Health Care Provider

The second category of FMLA-covered "serious health conditions" involves an illness, injury, impairment, or physical or mental condition that involves continuing treatment by a health care provider.[148] The phrase "continuing treatment by a health care provider" is defined in the DOL implementing regulations, not the statute.[149] The statute and DOL regulations define who is a "health care provider" for purposes of the federal FMLA.[150] They also identify five broad situations that fall within the definition of a serious health condition involving "continuing treatment by a health care provider.[151]

FMLA-covered "health care providers" include the usual suspects: doctors, dentists, psychologists, and nurses, as well as some you might not suspect, such as midwives, clinical social workers, and registered Christian Science practitioners.

Whether an individual is an FMLA-covered "health care provider" is important for two reasons. First, in order for an individual's condition to fit within the definition of a serious health condition involving "continuing treatment," that individual must be receiving continuing treatment by *a health care provider*. If the ill individual is not receiving continuing treatment from an FMLA-covered "health care provider," the illness is not a "serious health condition" within the meaning of the federal FMLA—no matter how ill the individual. Second, an employer may require medical documentation to confirm that the illness is an FMLA-covered "serious health condition.[152] To be valid, that documentation must be from an FMLA-covered "health care provider."

For federal FMLA purposes, a "health care provider" is

- a doctor of medicine or osteopathy who is authorized to practice medicine or surgery by the state in which he or she practices;
- a podiatrist, dentist, clinical psychologist, optometrist, or chiropractor (limited to treatment consisting of manual manipulation of the spine to correct a subluxation as demonstrated by X-ray to exist) authorized to practice under state law and performing within the scope of that practice as defined under state law;
- a nurse-practitioner, nurse-midwife, or clinical social worker who is authorized to practice under state law and who is performing within the scope of that practice as defined under state law;
- a Christian Science practitioner listed with the First Church of Christ, Scientist, in Boston, Massachusetts;
- any health care provider from whom an employer or the benefits manager of a group health plan will accept certification of the existence of a serious health condition to substantiate a claim for benefits; or
- a health care provider as defined above who practices in a country other than the United States and who is licensed to practice in accordance with the laws and regulations of that country.[153]

To be "authorized to practice in the state," the provider must be authorized to diagnose and treat physical or mental health conditions without supervision by a doctor or other health care provider.[154]

Note that all health care providers are treated equally for purposes of the federal FMLA. As long as the health care providers are licensed and performing within the scope of their practice, it makes no difference whether the eligible employee or covered family member with a serious health condition is receiving continuing treatment from a doctor, a nurse, a clinical social worker, or any of the other FMLA-covered health care providers.

Assuming that you have determined that an FMLA-covered "health care provider" is in the picture, you must next determine whether the illness falls within the definition of "continuing treatment" for purposes of the federal FMLA. To do that, the illness must fit within one or more of the five broad categories of "continuing treatment" identified by the DOL and described below.

(A) Incapacity of More Than Three Consecutive Calendar Days Plus Health Care Provider Treatments

A "serious health condition" within the meaning of the federal FMLA means an illness, injury, impairment, or physical or mental condition that involves continuing treatment by a health care provider. "Continuing treatment by a health care provider" includes a period of incapacity of more than three consecutive calendar days and any subsequent treatment or period of incapacity relating to the same condition that also involves (1) treatment two or more times by a health care provider, by a nurse or physician's assistant under the direct supervision of a health care provider, or by a provider of health care services (e.g., physical therapist) under orders of, or on referral by, a health care provider or (2) treatment by a health care provider on at least one occasion that results in a regimen of continuing treatment under the supervision of a health care provider.[155]

A "period of incapacity" means inability to work, attend school, or perform other regular daily activities due to the serious health condition, treatment for the serious health condition, or recovery from that condition. "Other regular daily activities" are undefined. Eating, drinking, learning, taking care of oneself, and engaging in marital relations have been found to be a partial list of "other regular daily activities."[156] For an infant, another court considered whether the illness disrupted the child's ability to participate in his or her normal routine, whether the illness made the child more difficult to care for, and whether the illness would have prevented the child from attending day care.[157] Note that the regulations require only that the activities be regular and daily. The regulations do not place a value on the activities, so long as they are regular and daily.

The three consecutive calendar days of incapacity may occur wholly or partially over the weekend or other nonwork time. One court has found that more than three consecutive *whole* days of incapacity are required. Partial days count only at the beginning and end of the three-consecutive-day period in order to meet the "more than" requirement.[158]

Treatment is defined in the same manner for all serious health conditions. It includes, but is not limited to, examinations to determine if a serious health condition exists and evaluations of the condition.[159] Where multiple treatments are involved, treatments may be provided by different health care providers; it is not required that all treatments be provided by the same health care provider.[160] Phone calls to a health care provider are not "treatment" within the meaning of the federal FMLA.[161] Routine physical exams, dental exams, and eye exams are also not considered "treatment" within the meaning of the federal FMLA.[162]

A "regimen of continuing treatment" includes, for example, a course of prescription medication (e.g., antibiotics) or therapy requiring special equipment to resolve or alleviate health conditions (e.g., oxygen).[163] The taking of over-the-counter medications such as aspirin, antihistamines, or salves; bed rest; drinking fluids; exercise; and other similar activities that can be initiated without a visit to a health care provider do not, by themselves, constitute a regimen of continuing treatment for purposes of federal FMLA leave.[164]

(B) Pregnancy or Prenatal Care

Any period of incapacity due to pregnancy or for prenatal care is the second form of "continuing treatment" covered by the federal FMLA.[165] "Incapacity" is not separately defined by the DOL in this regulation. Presumably it means inability to work, attend school, or perform other regular daily activities due to the serious health condition, treatment therefor, or recovery therefrom.[166] Incapacity due to pregnancy includes miscarriages and complications or illnesses related to pregnancy, such as severe morning sickness, the need for prenatal care, childbirth, and recovery from childbirth.[167] Depression, however, is not a pregnancy-related serious health condition.[168] Absent evidence of his wife's incapacity due to pregnancy, a court held that an eligible employee did not have the right to federal FMLA leave to be with his pregnant wife.[169]

There is no minimum period of time that an employee or covered family member must be incapacitated due to pregnancy in order to meet this definition of a serious health condition. Many employers erroneously believe that federal FMLA leave is available only where the period of incapacity exceeds three consecutive calendar days. That is simply not the case with incapacity due to pregnancy or for prenatal care. As explained by the DOL, "Pregnancy is similar to a chronic condition in that the patient is periodically visiting a health care provider for prenatal care, but may be subject to episodes of severe morning sickness, for example, which may not require an absence from work for more than three days."[170] "Any period" of incapacity would cover absences of a few hours due to pregnancy-related incapacity.

An eligible employee is entitled to federal FMLA leave for incapacity due to pregnancy even though the pregnant individual (employee or covered family member) does not receive treatment during the absence.[171] For example, an eligible employee is entitled to federal FMLA leave to care for his pregnant wife who is suffering from severe morning sickness. The wife does not have to be treated by a health care provider during the employee's absence in order for the employee to perfect his right to federal FMLA leave. The employee can attend to his wife while she rests at home. Of course, to remain within the requirements of a pregnancy-related serious health condition, the wife, in this example, must generally be under the continuing treatment of a health care provider. In this context, "continuing treatment" requires at least periodic visits with a health care provider for treatment.

A common situation regarding FMLA leave due to pregnancy involves an eligible employee's request for leave to care for a pregnant daughter who is 18 years of age or older. As we discussed in Chapter 4, *Covered Family Members*, a parent is entitled to federal FMLA to care for an adult child (a child who is 18 years of age or older) with a serious health condition only if the child has a physical or mental disability and is incapable of self-care. A physical or mental disability is defined by incorporation of the requirements of the ADA. Generally, absent complications, pregnancy is not considered an ADA disability.[172] Notwithstanding the general rule, one court has found that an employee-mother was entitled to take federal FMLA leave to care for her seriously ill adult child with pregnancy-related high blood pressure.[173] Significantly, the court rejected long-standing EEOC guidance excluding short-term, nonchronic impairments as ADA-covered "disabilities." The court opined that such guidance does not apply in the FMLA context.

Schools would be well advised to consult with counsel regarding an employee request for FMLA leave to care for an adult daughter suffering from a pregnancy-related illness.

(C) Chronic Serious Health Conditions

The third type of "continuing treatment" covered by the FMLA is any period of incapacity or treatment for such incapacity due to a chronic serious health condition.[174] A "chronic serious health condition" is one that

- requires periodic visits for treatment by a health care provider, or by a nurse or physician's assistant under direct supervision of a health care provider;
- continues over an extended period of time (including recurring episodes of a single underlying condition); and
- may cause episodic rather than a continuing period of incapacity.[175]

Comments accompanying the final rules shed additional light on the conditions that the DOL had in mind for "chronic serious health conditions":

> The Department recognizes that certain conditions, such as asthma and diabetes, continue over an extended period of time (i.e., from several months to several years), often without affecting day-to-day ability to work or perform other activities but may cause episodic periods of incapacity of less than three days. Although persons with such underlying conditions generally visit a health care provider periodically, when subject to a flare-up or

> other incapacitating episode, staying home and self-treatment are often more effective than visiting the health care provider (e.g., the asthma-sufferer who is advised to stay home and inside due to the pollen count being too high). The definition has, therefore, been revised to include such conditions as serious health conditions, even if individual episodes of incapacity are not for more than three days duration.[176]

As in the case of pregnancy, absences for chronic serious health conditions qualify for FMLA protection even if the ill individual does not receive health care provider treatment during the absence and even if the absence does not last more than three consecutive days.[177] "Incapacity" is not defined for purposes of a chronic serious health condition, but presumably means inability to work, attend school, or perform other regular daily activities due to the chronic serious health condition, treatment therefor, or recovery therefrom.[178] "Treatment" for a chronic serious health condition includes examinations to determine if a serious health condition exists and evaluations of the condition, but not routine physical, dental, or eye examinations.[179]

Key terms of a chronic serious health condition are undefined. For example, it is unclear how many health care provider visits in a given period of time are needed to constitute "periodic visits." Absent a definition, arguably days, weeks, months, or years could pass between health care provider visits and the visits could be viewed as periodic. Periodic health care provider visits do not have to be with the same health care provider.[180]

The second requirement of an FMLA-qualifying chronic serious health condition is that the condition continue over "an extended period of time." In comments accompanying the final rule, the DOL opined that "an extended period of time" means from several months to several years.[181] For example, in one case an employee's receipt of multiple health care provider treatments for a chipped tooth and dry socket over a 1-month period failed to establish that the condition continued over "an extended period of time" within the meaning of a serious health condition.[182] In contrast, another court found that a peptic ulcer that continued over a 3-year period continued over an extended period of time within the meaning of the FMLA.[183]

The DOL regulations provide that a serious chronic condition may manifest itself in episodic rather than continuing periods of incapacity. Again, no time frame is given to judge whether episodic periods of incapacity are caused by the serious chronic condition. Arguably, an employee who was absent for a day 10 years ago due to a chronic condition and is again absent for 15 minutes for the same condition has demonstrated "episodic" periods of incapacity. Courts have been less than enthusiastic about finding "episodic" incapacity where, although multiple absences are involved, the underlying condition is not of a similar severity as asthma, diabetes, or epilepsy.[184]

(D) Permanent or Long-Term Incapacity Due to a Condition for Which Treatment May Not Be Effective

The fourth type of "continuing treatment" covered by the FMLA is a period of incapacity that is permanent or long-term due to a condition for which treatment may not be effective.[185] Examples in this category include Alzheimer's, a severe stroke, or the terminal stages of a disease.[186]

The regulations are hopelessly vague and fail to define key terms, including "periodic," "permanent," "long-term," and "incapacity." Presumably, "incapacity" means an inability to work, attend school, or perform other regular daily activities due to the serious health condition, treatment therefor, or recovery therefrom.[187] Note that the "period of incapacity" must be permanent or long-term. By its terms, FMLA leave for this category of serious health condition is not available for short-term absences due, for example, to an employee's inability to work, the need to receive treatment, or the need to recover from treatment for a condition for which treatment may not be effective. Given that an eligible employee is entitled to only 12 workweeks of federal FMLA leave a year, a period of permanent or long-term incapacity would appear to equate with the need to use all or a substantial part of the employee's annual 12-week FMLA entitlement. While this result logically flows from the language of the DOL regulations, I don't believe that this was the intention of the DOL. I believe instead that the DOL intended this regulation to cover *any* period of incapacity due to a condition for which treatment may not be effective; that is, I think that the reference to "permanent or long-term" refers to the duration of the condition and not the period of incapacity.

A period of incapacity includes absences for treatment. To satisfy the requirement that the employee or covered family member is under the "continuing treatment" of a health care provider, the individual need only be under the continuing supervision of a health care provider; the individual does not have to be receiving active treatment from a health care provider.[188]

(E) Multiple Treatments

The final category of "continuing treatment by a health care provider" covered by the FMLA is any period of absence to receive multiple treatments (including any period of recovery therefrom) by a health care provider or provider of health care serves under orders of, or on referral by, a health care provider for either (1) restorative surgery after an accident or other injury or (2) a condition that would likely result in a period of incapacity of more than three consecutive calendar days in the absence of medical intervention or treatment.[189] Examples of the latter category include cancer (treatments such as chemotherapy and radiation), severe arthritis (physical therapy), and kidney disease (dialysis).[190]

FMLA leave for this type of condition is available only to receive or recover from treatments. Unlike other serious health conditions, it is not available where the employee or covered family member is unable to go to work or school or perform other regular daily activities due to a serious health condition (except to receive treatment). This serious health condition does not use the term "incapacity." Rather, it refers to absences to receive or recover from treatments only. It is not clear which "absences" for treatment are covered. Certainly, it would cover absences from work, school, day care, or other activities where attendance is normally expected or required. The concept of being "absent" raises questions when it is applied to other regular daily activities. For example, an eligible employee wants FMLA leave to take his infant daughter to the hospital for a follow-up visit following treatment for an injury. The infant is at home asleep with the employee's wife. To say that the infant needs to be "absent" from napping or playing at the house for treatment appears strained.

This provision of the DOL regulations is not a model of clarity. For example, one can read the "multiple treatments" requirement at least two ways. As written, the regulations appear to require that the individual receive multiple treatments during each period of absence. Alternatively, "any period of absence" could be read to mean "any absence" to receive or recover from multiple health care provider treatments. The examples given by the DOL suggest that the latter interpretation is what the DOL intended, so that multiple treatments may occur over a period of separate absences.

Under this provision, the treatments an individual receives must be for restorative surgery after an accident or other injury or for a condition that would likely result in a period of incapacity of more than three consecutive days in the absence of medical intervention or treatment. The first category of treatment, "restorative surgery," is not defined. By requiring that treatment be due to restorative surgery, the regulations exclude absences not connected with restorative surgery (unless the treatment falls under the second category provided for). Restorative surgery would also appear to be a smaller subset of all surgeries. The terms "accident" and "other injury" are also undefined. Presumably, they are given their normal meaning.

The second category of treatment is treatment for a condition that would likely result in incapacity of more than three consecutive days in the absence of medical treatment. Let's be clear that the employee or covered family member does not have to actually incur a period of incapacity of more than three consecutive days to fall within the scope of this provision. Rather, this condition requires school employers, with the assistance of medical documentation, to make an educated guess that in the absence of receipt of multiple medical treatments, the individual would incur a period of incapacity of more than three consecutive calendar days.

The regulations do not address how strong a likelihood there must be that incapacity of more than three consecutive days would result in the absence of medical intervention or treatment. This is an area where school employers would be well advised to request medical documentation of the condition. Courts have held that the likelihood of future incapacity must be determined based on the actual facts of the situation and not based on a hypothetical "reasonable patient."[191]

[4] Special Issues Concerning Serious Health Conditions

This section addresses which conditions are normally not considered to be serious health conditions and special rules governing cosmetic treatments, substance abuse, mental illness, and combination conditions.

(i) Minor Illnesses

The federal FMLA was not intended to cover minor illnesses. As explained by Congress in the legislative history:

> The term "serious health condition" was not intended to cover short-term conditions for which treatment and recovery are very brief. It is expected that such conditions will fall within even the most modest sick leave policies. Conditions or medical procedures that would not normally be covered by the legislation include minor illnesses that last only a few days, and surgical procedures that typically do not involve hospitalization and require only a brief recovery period. Complications arising out of such procedures that develop into "serious health conditions" will be covered by the Act.[192]

One court offered its own colorful gloss on Congress's intention to exclude minor illnesses from FMLA coverage:

> The slings and arrows of everyday life, in Congress's view, should not be the stuff of a federal statute nor federal litigation based on it. Rather, Congress believed that quotidian afflictions like the common cold or flu should be covered by even the most modest of employer sick leave policies and chose not to legislate in that area.[193]

The DOL codified Congress's intention to exclude minor illnesses from the definition of a serious health condition covered by the federal FMLA.[194] Ordinarily, unless complications arise, the following conditions do not meet the definition of an FMLA-qualifying serious health condition:

- the common cold
- the flu

- earaches
- upset stomach
- minor ulcers
- headaches other than migraines
- routine dental or orthodontia problems
- periodontal disease

Note that minor illnesses such as the common cold and flu can, with complications, become FMLA-covered serious health conditions. Ordinarily, however, they are not. Just as there is no "magic list" of illnesses that are always FMLA-qualifying serious health conditions, there is no "blacklist" of minor illnesses that may never be serious health conditions within the meaning of the FMLA. School employers must evaluate each employee request for leave due to illness on its merits.

Just as there is no "magic list" of illnesses that are always FMLA-qualifying serious health conditions, there is no "blacklist" of minor illnesses that may never be serious health conditions within the meaning of the FMLA. School employers must evaluate each employee request for leave due to illness on its merits.

According to the legislative history and the DOL regulations, minor illnesses may constitute FMLA-covered serious health conditions as a result of complications. Unfortunately, "complications" is not defined by the statute or the DOL regulations. The DOL has since abandoned "complications" as a necessary component for converting otherwise minor illnesses into FMLA-covered serious health conditions. This was not always the case. Originally, the DOL opined that absent complications, minor illnesses did not constitute FMLA-covered serious health conditions simply because they met the regulatory requirements of one of the definitions of a serious health condition.[195] Twenty months later the DOL reversed its position.[196] Now, so long as the minor illness meets the requirements of at least one of the definitions of a serious health condition, the illness is covered by the federal FMLA. "Complications, per se, need not be present to qualify as a serious health condition."[197]

The DOL has not, however, completely forsaken "complications" as a means to convert an otherwise ordinary minor illness into an FMLA-covered serious health condition.[198] The DOL cited bronchitis turning into bronchial pneumonia as an example. Significantly, the DOL opinion did not indicate that the bronchial pneumonia must meet all of the definitional requirements of an FMLA-covered serious health condition. School employers will almost certainly want to argue that the DOL meant that the criteria of at least one FMLA serious health condition had to be met and that the DOL did not mean otherwise.

The court decisions are mixed regarding minor illnesses as serious health conditions. Some courts have followed the lead of the DOL and found that minor illnesses that meet all of the regulatory requirements are FMLA-covered serious health conditions.[199] Other courts have found that absent complications, minor conditions are not serious health conditions within the meaning of the federal FMLA even if they satisfy the definitional requirements of a serious health condition.[200] School employers would be well advised to consult with counsel before denying an eligible employee FMLA leave due to a minor illness that meets the definitional requirements of a serious health condition but does not involve complications.

School employers would be well advised to consult with counsel before denying an eligible employee FMLA leave due to a minor illness that meets the definitional requirements of a serious health condition but does not involve complications.

(ii) Cosmetic Treatments

Conditions for which cosmetic treatments are administered (such as most treatments for acne or plastic surgery) are not FMLA-covered serious health conditions unless inpatient hospital care is required or unless complications arise.[201] The term "cosmetic treatments" is not formally defined but is illustrated with two examples: most treatments for acne and plastic surgery.[202] "Complications" remains undefined. Note that conditions for which cosmetic treatments are administered may be recognized as serious health conditions if inpatient hospital care is required. As discussed earlier in this chapter, inpatient care is a defined term under the federal FMLA that involves an overnight stay in a hospital, hospice, or residential medical care facility.[203] However, even though a hospital is only one of three facilities recognized as being able to provide inpatient care, the regulations provide that cosmetic treatments are not FMLA-covered serious health conditions unless inpatient *hospital* care is required; conditions for which cosmetic treatments are administered in a hospice or residential medical facility do not count as serious health conditions. No explanation is provided for this result.

(iii) Substance Abuse

Substance abuse is not, standing alone, its own form of an FMLA-covered serious health condition. For substance abuse to be an FMLA-covered serious health condition, it must meet the requirements of at least one of the definitions of a serious health condition.[204] If the substance abuse does meet the definition of a serious health condition, FMLA leave is available only to receive treatment by a health care provider or a provider of health care services on referral by a health care provider,[205] or to care for a covered family member who is receiving treatment for substance abuse.[206] Absences because of the employee's or covered family member's substance abuse, rather than for treatment, do not qualify for FMLA leave.[207]

Note, however, that absences because of the employee's substance abuse count for purposes of determining whether the employee meets the definitional requirements of one of the FMLA-covered serious health conditions.[208] However, only absences for substance abuse treatment are covered by the federal FMLA. For example, an eligible employee goes on an alcoholic binge and is absent from work for more than three consecutive calendar days. At the end of the binge, the employee sees a health care provider on one occasion. His physician prescribes medication that will lower his alcoholic cravings and make him ill if he drinks alcohol. Subsequently, the employee is admitted into an inpatient treatment program. The employee's initial absence (because of his binge) meets the requirements of an FMLA-covered serious health condition. However, the FMLA does not cover the greater-than-three-day period during which the employee was abusing alcohol and absent from work. FMLA leave would, however, cover the employee's outpatient treatment by his physician. It would also cover his attendance in the inpatient treatment program.

FMLA leave is available for treatment for substance abuse provided the conditions of 29 C.F.R. § 825.114 have been met. However, treatment for substance abuse does not prevent an employer from taking disciplinary action against an employee.[209] Of course, an employer may not take disciplinary action against the employee because the employee has exercised his or her right to take FMLA leave for treatment.[210] However, an employer may take disciplinary action against an employee for substance abuse if the school has an established policy that has been communicated to all employees and that provides that under certain circumstances an employee may be terminated for substance abuse and if the policy is applied in a nondiscriminatory way.[211] If those conditions are met, an employee may be terminated whether or not the employee is presently taking FMLA leave.[212]

An employer may not take action against an employee who is providing care for a covered family member receiving treatment for substance abuse.[213] By omission, it appears that a school employer would be entitled to discipline an employee for taking leave to care for a covered family because of that family member's substance abuse, rather than because of that family member's treatment. Here again, the FMLA covers an employee's need for leave to care for a covered family member who is receiving treatment, not leave for the family member's substance abuse itself.[214]

In an advisory opinion released on April 28, 1995, the DOL provided a series of questions and answers to illustrate the rules regarding FMLA leave and substance abuse.[215] A modified version of those questions and answers follows.

Question 1: An employee is randomly selected for drug testing and tests positive for illegal narcotics. The employee has never requested FMLA leave. Under the employer's policy this employee is subject to immediate termination. Is the employer obligated to provide FMLA leave to this employee?

Answer 1: No. The FMLA does not require the employer to allow the employee the opportunity to seek treatment and reinstatement. Of course, an employer could allow the employee to seek treatment and reinstatement. Moreover, the terms of an applicable collective bargaining agreement may also govern the employee's rights and the employer's responsibilities in this situation.

Question 2: The employer receives information that an employee is using illegal narcotics. As a result, the employee is requested to submit to a drug test under the "for cause" provisions of the testing policy. The employee tests positive for illegal narcotics. The employee has never requested FMLA leave. Under the provisions of the testing policy, the employee is subject to immediate termination. Does the FMLA require the employer to permit the employee to seek treatment in lieu of termination?

Answer 2: No. The FMLA does not require the employer to allow the employee to seek treatment and reinstatement.

Question 3: An employee comes forward and admits to the employer that he is addicted to drugs and indicates that a doctor is placing him in rehabilitative treatment. Again, the employer's policy requires immediate termination in this instance. Does the FMLA require the employer to permit this employee to seek treatment?

Answer 3: No. Where the employee admits to illegal drug use and the employer's policy requires immediate termination, the FMLA does not require that the employee seek treatment or be reinstated.

Question 4: An employee who tests positive for illegal narcotics is granted FMLA leave, and the terms and conditions of reinstatement include a requirement that the employee submit to weekly drug testing. If the employee tests positive a second time, does the FMLA require that the employer allow the employee the opportunity to seek treatment and be reinstated for a second time? Does the answer depend on whether the employee has used all of his or her allotted FMLA leave?

Answer 4: No to both questions. The employer's policy could provide for termination of employment regardless of whether the employee has exhausted his or her FMLA leave allotment in the applicable 12-month leave year period.

The questions and answers above are a good illustration of the general rule that the FMLA does not provide employees with greater rights than they would have had if they had not taken FMLA leave.

(iv) Mental Illness

Mental illness is not a separate category of FMLA-covered serious health conditions. To be covered under the FMLA, the mental illness of the eligible employee or covered family member must meet at least one of the definitions of a serious health condition.[216] The DOL regulations, moreover, are worded in a way that suggests that only mental illness resulting from stress or allergies may be a serious health condition, provided the requirements of one of the other serious health conditions are met. It is doubtful that the DOL intended to exclude from coverage mental illness not caused by allergies or stress. Rather, mental illness, whatever the cause, that satisfies at least one of the definitions of a serious health condition should be treated as falling within the coverage of the federal FMLA.

(v) Combination Conditions

An illness caused by the combination of many seemingly unrelated illnesses may be considered together for purposes of determining whether the condition as a whole qualifies as an FMLA-covered serious health condition.[217] In *Price v. City of Fort Wayne*, the employee simultaneously suffered from "an assemblage of [conditions] including elevated blood pressure, hyperthyroidism, back pain, severe headaches, sinusitis, infected cyst, sore throat, swollen throat, coughing, and feelings of stress and depression."[218] It was undisputed that the employee was incapacitated by the combination of these conditions and that she received treatment from a health care provider. The court rejected the argument that each of the conditions had to be analyzed separately for purposes of determining whether the employee had a serious health condition within the meaning of the FMLA. The court concluded that conditions that combine to incapacitate a person and require continuing treatment can, together, constitute a serious health condition.

Where, however, separate illnesses are too disparate, courts will not combine them for purposes of finding a serious health condition.[219] In *Marchischeck v. San Mateo County*, the employee argued that her son suffered from a combination of physical and psychological conditions that rose to the level of a serious health condition. There, the employee asked for 5 weeks of FMLA leave to move her son to the Philippines for his safety after he was assaulted. The employee argued that the combination of multiple counseling sessions her son had received for mild depression, several substance abuse sessions, and minor physical injuries suffered in the assault constituted an FMLA-covered serious health condition.[220] The court disagreed. The court found that

> there is no competent evidence in the record to suggest that Shaun suffered from combined conditions that incapacitated him. Shaun received sporadic counseling beginning in 1991 and was assaulted in 1995, but there is nothing to suggest that Shaun ever was treated for a combination of physical and psychological symptoms, or that he was incapacitated by a combined condition.[221]

Absent evidence that the son suffered from, and was treated for, combined conditions that incapacitated him, the court asserted that "[t]here is simply no basis in this record to conclude that Shaun's various behavioral and emotional problems ever 'combined' with the passing physical effects of the assault to create a "serious health condition."[222]

5.04 COVERED CONDITIONS UNDER STATE FAMILY AND MEDICAL LEAVE LAWS

State family and medical leave laws generally permit covered employees to take leave for the same covered conditions as does the federal FMLA. Eligible employees are entitled to family and medical leave pursuant to state law because of the birth, adoption, or foster care placement of child; due to the incapacitating serious health condition of the employee; or to care for a covered family member with a serious health condition. There are, however, some noteworthy differences.

For example, the Alaska Family Leave Act covers leave for adoption but not if the employee is adopting a stepchild.[223] Alaska's law does not cover leave for foster care placement. Connecticut's private sector family leave law generally tracks the federal FMLA but includes leave in order for an employee to serve as an organ or bone marrow donor.[224] Hawaii's family leave law is less generous than the federal FMLA. For example, Hawaii's law does not cover leave for foster care placement of a child with the employee or due to the employee's own serious health condition.[225] Minnesota's Parenting Leave Act allows an employee to take leave in conjunction with the birth or adoption of a child, but the employee must take the leave within 6 weeks after the birth or adoption unless the child is hospitalized.[226] The federal FMLA, in contrast, provides that the right to take leave after the birth or adoption of a child expires 12 months after the birth or placement date.

States with and without general family and medical leave laws may have other forms of leave available to employees that could qualify as family or medical leave as defined by the federal FMLA. For example, many states have laws mandating maternity leave and leave for adoption or foster care, catastrophic leave, and bone marrow or organ donation leave. If the law allows an employee to use such leave for the employee or the employee's spouse, son or daughter, or parent, the law may constitute family and medical leave for purposes of the federal FMLA. As set forth below, whether the leave is covered by both state law and the FMLA is an important determination, as the state family and medical leave law may affect the requirements of the federal FMLA.

5.05 INTERACTION OF THE FEDERAL FMLA WITH STATE FAMILY AND MEDICAL LEAVE LAWS: COVERED CONDITIONS

The federal FMLA does not supersede any provision of state or local law that provides greater family or medical leave rights than those provided by the FMLA.[227] If applicable, the more generous provisions of state or local family and medical leave laws may reduce or eliminate some procedural requirements of the federal FMLA. For example, the federal FMLA requires an eligible employee to timely notify his or her employer of the need for FMLA leave. However, an employer may not require compliance with stricter FMLA notice requirements where, among other reasons, the provisions of state law allow less advance notice to the employer.[228] It is therefore important for school administrators to determine whether leave is covered by either the federal FMLA or applicable state family and medical leave laws, or both.

To be covered by the federal FMLA, leave must fall within the covered conditions of the federal FMLA. An employee covered by one law and not the other has to comply only with the law under which that employee is covered.[229] For example, we have seen several state family and medical leave laws that do not cover leave for foster care placement. Leave by an eligible employee for foster care placement would be covered by the federal FMLA only. Conversely, if the state law allows leave for a "serious illness" that does not rise to the level of a federal FMLA "serious health condition," the leave is covered only by the state family and medical leave law, not the federal FMLA. If leave qualifies for both FMLA leave and leave under state law, the leave used counts against the employee's entitlement under both laws.[230]

School administrators must carefully review each employee request for leave to determine whether it falls within the coverage of either the federal FMLA or applicable state or local family and medical leave laws, or both. As addressed in later chapters, if the leave is covered by both the federal FMLA and state or local family and medical leave laws, school administrators will need to determine if the state or local laws provide greater family and medical leave procedural rights than does the federal FMLA. Where both the federal FMLA and state family and medical leave laws apply, whichever law provides the greater procedural rights will apply.

NOTES

1. 29 U.S.C. § 2612(a).
2. 29 C.F.R. §§ 825.112, 825.114–825.18.
3. 29 U.S.C. § 2612(a)(1)(A); 29 C.F.R. § 825.112(a)(1).
4. 29 C.F.R. § 825.112(b).
5. 29 C.F.R. § 825.116(a).
6. See S. Rep. No. 103-3, at 9 (1993), as reprinted in 1993 U.S.C.C.A.N. 3, 11; Comments on Regulations Implementing the Family and Medical Leave Act of 1993 (§ 825.112), 60 Fed. Reg. 2180, 2190 (Jan. 6, 1995).
7. See *Dormeyer v. Comerica Bank-Illinois*, No. 96-C-4805, 1997 U.S. Dist. LEXIS 10260, at *10 n.2 (N.D. Ill. July 15, 1997) (acknowledging that it is unclear whether prenatal care needs to result in incapacitation in order to be covered by the FMLA).
8. 29 C.F.R. § 825.112(c).
9. 29 C.F.R. § 825.112(a)(4).

10. 29 C.F.R. § 825.112(c)

11. S. Rep. No. 103-3, at 24, as reprinted in 1993 U.S.C.C.A.N.3, 26.

12. 29 U.S.C. § 2612(a)(1)(A), (C); 29 C.F.R. § 825.112(a)(1), (3).

13. S. Rep. No. 103-3, at 24, as reprinted in 1993 U.S.C.C.A.N.3, 26.

14. DOL WH FMLA Advisory Opinion No. 45 (Oct. 14, 1994).

15. Comments on Regulations Implementing the Family and Medical Leave Act of 1993 (§ 825.112), 60 Fed. Reg. 2180, 2189–90 (Jan. 6, 1995).

16. 29 U.S.C. § 2612(b)(1); 29 C.F.R. § 825.203(b).

17. 29 C.F.R. § 825.203(a).

18. *Id.*

19. 29 U.S.C. § 2612(b)(1).

20. 29 U.S.C. § 2612(c); 29 C.F.R. § 825.207(a).

21. 29 U.S.C. § 2612(d); 29 C.F.R. § 825.207.

22. 29 C.F.R. § 825.207(b).

23. 29 C.F.R. § 825.113(d).

24. *Id.*

25. *Id.*

26. *Id.* ("For purposes of confirmation of family relationship, the employer may require the *employee giving notice* of the need for leave to provide reasonable documentation or statement of family relationship." (emphasis added)).

27. 29 U.S.C. § 2612(a)(2); 29 C.F.R. § 825.201.

28. Comments on Regulations Implementing the Family and Medical Leave Act of 1993 (§ 825.201), 60 Fed. Reg. 2180, 2200–01 (Jan. 6, 1995).

29. *Id.*

30. 29 C.F.R. § 825.201.

31. Comments on Regulations Implementing the Family and Medical Leave Act of 1993 (§825.201), 60 Fed. Reg. at 2200.

32. 29 U.S.C.§ 2612(a)(1)(B); 29 C.F.R. § 825.112(a)(2).

33. 29 C.F.R.§§ 825.200(a)(2), 825.202(a)(2).

34. See Comments on Regulations Implementing the Family and Medical Leave Act of 1993 (§825.112), 60 Fed. Reg. at 2190.

35. *Id.*

36. 29 U.S.C. § 2611(12); 29 C.F.R. § 825.113(c).

37. *Kelley v. Crossfield Catalysts*, 135 F.3d 1202, 1205 (7th Cir. 1998).

38. 29 C.F.R.§ 825.112(d).

39. *Id.*

40. *Id.*

41. 29 C.F.R. § 825.112(c).

42. 29 C.F.R. § 825.113(d).

43. 29 U.S.C. § 2612(b)(1); 29 C.F.R. § 825.203(b).

44. 29 U.S.C. § 2612(b)(1).

45. 29 C.F.R. § 825.203(b).

46. DOL WH FMLA Advisory Opinion No. 84 (Oct. 25, 1996).

47. 29 U.S.C. § 2612(c); 29 C.F.R. § 825.207(a).

48. 29 U.S.C. § 2612(d)(2); 29 C.F.R. § 825.207.

49. 29 C.F.R. § 825.207(b).

50. See DOL WH FMLA Advisory Opinion No. 85 (Nov. 18, 1996).

51. 29 C.F.R. § 825.113(d).

52. *Id.*

53. *Id.*

54. 29 U.S.C. § 2612(a)(2); 29 C.F.R. § 825.201.

55. Comments on Regulations Implementing the Family and Medical Leave Act of 1993 (§ 825.201), 60 Fed. Reg. 2180, 2200 (Jan. 6, 1995).

56. *Id.* at 2200–01.

57. *Bocalbos v. National Western Life Insurance Company*, 162 F.3d 379, 384 (5th Cir. 1998), *cert. denied*, 528 U.S. 872 (1999).

58. 29 C.F.R. § 825.201.

59. Comments on Regulations Implementing the Family and Medical Leave Act of 1993 (§ 825.201), 60 Fed. Reg. at 2200.

60. 29 U.S.C. § 2612(a)(1)(B); 29 C.F.R. § 825.112(a)(2).

61. 29 C.F.R. § 825.112(e); see also DOL WH FMLA Advisory Opinion No. 84 (Oct. 25, 1996).

62. DOL WH FMLA Advisory Opinion No. 84 (Oct. 25, 1996).

63. 29 C.F.R. §§ 825.200(a)(2), 825.202(a)(2).

64. DOL WH FMLA Advisory Opinion No. 84 (Oct. 25, 1996).

65. 29 U.S.C. § 2611(12); 29 C.F.R. § 825.113(c).

66. 29 C.F.R. § 825.112(e).

67. DOL WH FMLA Advisory Opinion No. 84 (Oct. 25, 1996) (addressing placements by Vermont Children's Aid Society, a state-approved agency).

68. Comments on Regulations Implementing the Family and Medical Leave Act of 1993 (§ 825.112), 60 Fed. Reg. 2180, 2190 (Jan. 6, 1995).

69. *Id.*

70. 29 C.F.R. § 825.112(d).

71. *Id.*

72. DOL WH FMLA Advisory Opinion No. 84 (Oct. 25, 1996).

73. *Id.*

74. 29 U.S.C. § 2612(b)(1); 29 C.F.R. § 825.203(b).

75. 29 U.S.C. § 2612(b)(1).

76. 29 C.F.R. § 825.203(b).

77. 29 U.S.C. § 2612(c); 29 C.F.R. § 825.207(a).

78. 29 U.S.C. § 2612(d)(2); 29 C.F.R. § 825.207.

79. 29 C.F.R. § 825.207(b).

80. See DOL WH FMLA Advisory Opinion No. 85 (Nov. 18, 1996).

81. 29 C.F.R. § 825.113(d).

82. *Id.*

83. *Id.*

84. 29 U.S.C. § 2612(a)(2); 29 C.F.R. § 825.201.

85. Comments on Regulations Implementing the Family and Medical Leave Act of 1993 (§ 825.201), 60 Fed. Reg. 2180, 2200 (Jan. 6, 1995).

86. *Id.* at 2200–01.

87. 29 C.F.R. § 825.201.

88. Comments on Regulations Implementing the Family and Medical Leave Act of 1993 (§825.201), 60 Fed. Reg. at 2200.

89. 29 U.S.C. § 2612(a)(1)(C)–(D); 29 C.F.R. § 825.112(a)(3)–(4).

90. 29 U.S.C. § 2611(11).

91. DOL WH FMLA Advisory Opinion No. 77 (Jan. 30, 1996) (asserting that an employee whose illness does not meet the statutory and regulatory definitions of a serious health condition will not be entitled to take FMLA leave even if the employee cannot perform any of the essential functions of his or her job).

92. 29 U.S.C. § 2612(a)(1)(D); 29 C.F.R. § 825.115.

93. 29 C.F.R. § 825.115.

94. *Id.*

95. *Hodgens v. General Dynamics Corp.*, 144 F.3d 151, 164 (1st Cir. 1998).

96. 29 C.F.R. § 825.115.

97. *Lukacinsky v. Panasonic Service Co.*, No. 03-40141-FDS, 2004 U.S. Dist. LEXIS 25846, at *29 n.11 (D. Mass. Nov. 29, 2004).

98. 29 C.F.R. § 825.114(b).

99. *Id.*

100. DOL WH FMLA Advisory Opinion No. 87, question 1B (Dec. 12, 1996).

101. 29 C.F.R. § 825.115.

102. 29 C.F.R. § 1630.2(n)(3); see also 42 U.S.C. §12111(8).

103. 29 C.F.R. § 825.115.

104. *Wheeler v. Pioneer Development Services, Inc.*, 349 F. Supp. 2d 158, 168 (D. Mass. 2004).

105. *Id.*

106. Comments on Regulations Implementing the Family and Medical Leave Act of 1993 (§ 825.115), 60 Fed. Reg. 2180, 2196 (Jan. 6, 1995).

107. 29 C.F.R. § 825.702(d)(1); DOL WH FMLA Advisory Opinion No. 17 (Nov. 15, 1993).

108. 42 U.S.C. § 12111–12117.

109. DOL WH FMLA Advisory Opinion No. 55 (Mar. 10, 1995).

110. *Id.*

111. 29 U.S.C. § 2612(a)(1)(C); 29 C.F.R. §§ 825.100(a), 825.101(a), 825.112(a)(3), 825.200(a)(3).

112. S. Rep. No. 103-3, at 24 (1993), as reprinted in 1993 U.S.C.C.A.N. 3, 26; see also *Fioto v. Manhattan Woods Golf Enterprises, LLC*, 270 F. Supp. 2d 401 (S.D.N.Y. 2003).

113. 29 C.F.R. § 825.116.

114. 29 C.F.R. § 825.116(a).

115. 29 C.F.R. § 825.116(a)–(b).

116. 29 C.F.R. § 825.116(a).

117. 29 C.F.R. § 825.116(c).

118. DOL WH FMLA Advisory Opinion No. 94 (Feb. 27, 1998).

119. *Bradley v. Mary Rutan Hospital Associates*, 322 F. Supp. 2d 926, 941–42 (S.D. Ohio 2004).

120. *Scamihorn v. General Truck Drivers, Local 952*, 282 F.3d 1078, 1082 (9th Cir. 2002).

121. *Brunell v. Cytec Plastics, Inc.*, 225 F. Supp. 2d 67 (D. Me. 2002).

122. *Gilbert v. Star Building Systems*, No. CIV-95-1932-L, 1996 U.S. Dist. LEXIS 22435, at *7–8 (W.D. Okla. Nov. 15, 1996).

123. *Barone v. Leukemia Society of America*, 42 F. Supp. 2d 452, 460 (D.N.J. 1998); *Sharpe v. MCI Telecommunications Corp.*, 19 F. Supp. 2d 483, 489 (E.D.N.C. 1998); *Lange v. Showbiz Pizza Time, Inc.*, 12 F. Supp. 2d 1150, 1153–54 (D. Kan. 1998).

124. *Beal v. Rubbermaid Commercial Products, Inc.*, 972 F. Supp. 1216, 1226 (S.D. Iowa 1997), *aff'd*, 1998 U.S. App. LEXIS 9295 (8th Cir. 1998).

125. *Brown v. J.C. Penney Corp.*, 924 F. Supp. 1158, 1163 (S.D. Fla. 1996).

126. *Barone*, 42 F. Supp. 2d at 460; *Lange*, 12 F. Supp. 2d at 1153–54; *Beal*, 972 F. Supp. at 1226.

127. *Plumley v. Southern Container, Inc.*, 2001 U.S. Dist. LEXIS 16040 (D. Me. Oct. 9, 2001), *aff'd*, 303 F.3d 364 (1st Cir. 2002).

128. *Fioto v. Manhattan Woods Golf Enterprises, LLC,* 270 F. Supp. 2d 401, 405–06 (S.D.N.Y. 2003).

129. *Id.* at 406.

130. *Gradillia v. Ruskin Manufacturing*, 320 F.3d 951, 958 (9th Cir. 2003); *Marchischeck v. San Mateo County*, 199 F.3d 1068, 1076 (9th Cir. 1999), *cert. denied*, 530 U.S. 1214 (2000).

131. Comments on the Regulations Implementing the Family and Medical Leave Act of 1993 (§ 825.116), 60 Fed. Reg. 2180, 2197 (Jan. 6, 1995).

132. See *Mora v. Chem-Tronics, Inc.*, 16 F. Supp. 2d 1192 (S.D. Cal. 1998).

133. *Cianci v. Pettibone Corp.*, 1997 U.S. Dist. LEXIS 4482 (N.D. Ill. Apr. 7, 1997), *aff'd*, 152 F.3d 723 (7th Cir. 1998).

134. 29 U.S.C. § 2611(11).

135. S. Rep. No. 103-3, at 28 (1993), as reprinted in 1993 U.S.C.C.A.N. 3, 30.

136. *Id.* at 29, as reprinted in 1993 U.S.C.C.A.N. 3, 31

137. *Id.* at 28, as reprinted in 1993 U.S.C.C.A.N. 3, 30.

138. *Id.*

139. 29 C.F.R. § 825.114.

140. *Id.*

141. 29 C.F.R. § 825.114(a)(2).

142. 29 U.S.C. § 2611(11).

143. 29 C.F.R. § 825.114(a)(1).

144. *Id.*

145. *Id.*

146. 29 C.F.R. § 825.114(b); see also *Miller v. AT&T Corp.*, 250 F.3d 820, 831 (4th Cir. 2001).

147. 29 C.F.R. § 825.114(b).

148. 29 U.S.C. § 2611(11).

149. *Russell v. North Broward Hospital*, 346 F.3d 1335, 1338 (11th Cir. 2003).

150. 29 U.S.C. § 2611(6); 29 C.F.R. § 825.118.

151. 29 C.F.R. § 825.114(a)(2).

152. See Chapter 7, *Documentation Requirements*.

153. 29 C.F.R. § 825.118(a)(1), (b).

154. 29 C.F.R. § 825.118(c).

155. 29 C.F.R. § 825.114(a)(2)(i).

156. *Haefling v. UPS, Inc.*, 169 F.3d 494, 500 (7th Cir. 1999), *cert. denied*, 528 U.S. 820 (1999).

157. *Caldwell v. Holland of Texas, Inc.*, 208 F.3d 671, 674–76 (8th Cir. 2000).

158. *Russell v. North Broward Hospital*, 346 F.3d 1335, 1338 (11th Cir. 2003).

159. 29 C.F.R. § 825.114(b).

160. *Sims v. Alameda-Contra Costa Transit District*, 2 F. Supp. 2d 1253, 1264–65 (N.D. Cal. 1998).

161. *Dowell v. Indiana Heart Physicians, Inc.*, No. 1:03-cv-1410-DFH-TAB, 2004 U.S. Dist. LEXIS 26431, at *23 (S.D. Ind. Dec. 22, 2004).

162. 29 C.F.R. § 825.114(b).

163. *Id.*

164. *Id.*

165. 29 U.S.C. § 2611(11); 29 C.F.R. § 825.114(a)(2)(ii).

166. See 29 C.F.R. §§ 825.114(a)(1)–(2)(i).

167. S. Rep. No. 103-3, at 29 (1993), as reprinted in 1993 U.S.C.C.A.N. 3, 31; see also *Aubuchon v. Knauf Fiberglass, GMBH*, 240 F. Supp. 2d 859, 865 (S.D. Ind. 2003), *aff'd*, 359 F.3d 950 (7th Cir. 2004).

168. *Dowell v. Indiana Heart Physicians, Inc.*, No. 1:03-cv-1410-DFH-TAB, 2004 U.S. Dist. LEXIS 26431, at *18 (S.D. Ind. Dec. 22, 2004).

169. *Aubuchon v. Knauf Fiberglass, GMBH*, 359 F.3d 950, 952 (7th Cir. 2004).

170. Comments on Regulations Implementing the Family and Medical Leave Act of 1993 (§ 825.114), 60 Fed. Reg. 2180, 2195 (Jan. 6, 1995).

171. 29 C.F.R. § 825.114(e).

172. DOL WH FMLA Advisory Opinion No. 51 (Nov. 28, 1994); see also *Patterson v. Xerox Corp.*, 901 F. Supp. 274 (N.D. Ill. 1995); *EEOC Compliance Manual* § 902 (1998), available at http://www.eeoc.gov/policy/docs/retal.html. Amendments to the manual are available at http://www.eeoc.gov/policy/compliance.html.

173. *Navarro v. Pfizer Corp.*, 261 F.3d 90 (1st Cir. 2001).

174. 29 C.F.R. § 825.114(a)(2)(iii).

175. *Id.*; *Hoffman v. Professional Med Team*, 394 F.3d 414, 418 (6th Cir. 2005).

176. Comments on Regulations Implementing the Family and Medical Leave Act of 1993 (§ 825.114), 60 Fed. Reg. 2180, 2195 (Jan. 6, 1995).

177. 29 C.F.R. § 825.114(e); see also *Perry v. Jaguar of Troy*, 353 F.3d 510, 514 (6th Cir. 2003).

178. 29 C.F.R. § 825.114(a)(1)–(2)(i).

179. 29 C.F.R. § 825.114(b).

180. *Brock v. United Grinding Technologies, Inc.*, 257 F. Supp. 2d 1089, 1098–99 (S.D. Ohio 2003).

181. Comments on Regulations Implementing the Family and Medical Leave Act of 1993 (§ 825.114), 60 Fed. Reg. at 2195.

182. *Flanagan v. Keller Products, Inc.*, No. 00-542-M, 2002 U.S. Dist. LEXIS 3663, at *20 (D.N.H. Feb. 25, 2002) (looking to definition of a chronic condition used by the U.S. National Center for Health Statistics as a condition lasting three months or longer).

183. *Victorelli v. Shadyside Hospital*, 128 F.3d 184, 189 (3d Cir. 1997).

184. See *Beal v. Rubbermaid Commercial Products, Inc.*, 972 F. Supp. 1216, 1224–25 (S.D. Iowa 1997), *aff'd*, 1998 U.S. App. LEXIS 9295 (8th Cir.

1998); *Bauer v. Dayton-Walther Corp.*, 910 F. Supp. 306, 310 (E.D. Ky. 1996), *aff'd*, 118 F.3d 1109 (6th Cir. 1997).

185. 29 C.F.R. § 825.114(a)(2)(iv).

186. *Id.*

187. 29 C.F.R. § 825.114(a)(1)–(2)(i).

188. 29 C.F.R. § 825.114(a)(2)(iv).

189. 29 C.F.R. § 825.114(a)(2)(v); see also *Merritt v. E.F. Transit, Inc.*, No. IP02-0393-C-H/K, 2004 U.S. Dist. LEXIS 4310, at *16 (S.D. Ind. Mar. 11, 2004).

190. 29 C.F.R. § 825.114(a)(2)(v).

191. See *Bauer v. Dayton-Walther Corp.*, 910 F. Supp. 306, 310 (E.D. Ky. 1996), *aff'd*, 118 F.3d 1109 (6th Cir. 1997); *Seidle v. Provident Mutual Life Insurance Co.*, 871 F. Supp. 238, 246 (E.D. Pa. 1994).

192. S. Rep. No. 103-3, at 28 (1993), as reprinted in 1993 U.S.C.C.A.N. 3, 30; see also *Thorson v. Gemini, Inc.*, 205 F.3d 370, 379–80 (8th Cir. 2000), *cert. denied*, 531 U.S. 871 (2000).

193. *Bradley v. Mary Rutan Hospital Associates*, 322 F. Supp. 2d 926, 941–42 (S.D. Ohio 2004).

194. 29 C.F.R. §§ 825.114(b); 825.800 ("serious health condition" defined); see also *Miller v. AT&T Corp.*, 250 F.3d 820, 831 (4th Cir. 2001).

195. DOL WH FMLA Advisory Opinion No. 57 (Apr. 7, 1995).

196. DOL WH FMLA Advisory Opinion No. 87 (Dec. 12, 1996).

197. *Id.*

198. *Id.* question 3B.

199. See *Miller*, 250 F.3d at 830–31 (4th Cir. 2001); *Thorson v. Gemini, Inc.*, 205 F.3d 370, 380 (8th Cir. 2000), *cert. denied*, 531 U.S. 871 (2000).

200. See *Brown v. Seven Seventeen HB Philadelphia Corp., No. 2*, No. 01-1741, 2002 U.S. Dist. LEXIS 15066, at *14 (E.D. Pa. Aug. 8, 2002); *DuCharme v. Cape Industries, Inc.*, No. 01-74503, 2002 U.S. Dist. LEXIS 21926 (E.D. Mich. Oct. 8, 2002).

201. 29 C.F.R. §§ 825.114(c), 826.800 ("serious health condition" defined).

202. 29 C.F.R. § 825.114(c).

203. 29 U.S.C. § 2611(11); 29 C.F.R. § 825.114(a)(1).

204. 29 C.F.R. §§ 825.114(c), 825.800 ("serious health condition" defined).

205. 29 C.F.R. §§ 825.114(c), 825.800 ("serious health condition" defined). A "provider of health care services" is undefined. The regulations cite a physical therapist as an example.

206. 29 C.F.R. § 825.112(g).

207. 29 C.F.R. §§ 825.114(c), 825.800 ("serious health condition" defined); see also *Darst v. Interstate Brands Corp.*, No. IP01-0788-C-T/K, 2003 U.S. Dist. LEXIS 22200, at *12–16 (S.D. Ind. Sept. 30, 2003).

208. See *Dominick v. Ver Halen, Inc.*, No. 02-C-375-X, 2003 U.S. Dist. LEXIS 11694 (W.D. Wis. Mar. 10, 2003) (holding that physical symptoms and inpatient care resulting from employee's abuse of alcohol covered by the FMLA).

209. 29 C.F.R. § 825.112(g).

210. *Id.*

211. *Id.*

212. *Id.*

213. *Id.*

214. *Id.*

215. DOL WH FMLA Advisory Opinion No. 59 (Apr. 28, 1995).

216. 29 C.F.R. §§ 825.114(c); 825.800 ("serious health condition" defined); see also *Jones v. Willow Gardens Care Center*, No. C98-0007 MJM, 2000 U.S. Dist. LEXIS 3559, at *38 (N.D. Iowa Jan. 28, 2000).

217. *Price v. City of Fort Wayne*, 117 F.3d 1022 (7th Cir. 1997).

218. *Id.* at 1023.

219. *Marchischeck v. San Mateo County*, 199 F.3d 1068 (9th Cir. 1999), *cert. denied*, 530 U.S. 1214 (2000).

220. 199 F.3d at 1075.

221. *Id.* at 1076.

222. *Id.*

223. Alaska Stat. § 39.20.305(a)(1).

224. Conn. Gen. Stat. § 31-51ll(a)(2)(A)–(E).

225. Haw. Code R. § 12-27-1 (defining "serious health condition" to exclude the employee's own serious health condition).

226. Minn. Stat. Ann. § 181.941(2).

227. 29 C.F.R. § 825.701(a).

228. 29 C.F.R. § 825.302(g).

229. 29 C.F.R. § 825.700(a).

230. *Id.*

CHAPTER 6

Notice Requirements

6.01 OVERVIEW

The federal FMLA imposes notification requirements on both employers and employees. Penalties exist for an employer's or an employee's failure to meet their respective federal FMLA notice requirements. To perfect the right to federal FMLA leave, an eligible employee must provide timely and adequate notice of the need for FMLA leave. Employees who fail to provide school administration with proper notice may see their FMLA leave requests delayed or denied. Employers that fail to satisfy their notice obligations may have to grant FMLA leave in circumstances where they would otherwise be able to deny leave. It should be noted, however, that the courts have invalidated a number of the penalty provisions imposed on employers for failure to meet their notice obligations.

Section 6.02 of this chapter addresses employer notice obligations. Section 6.03 addresses employee notice obligations. Section 6.04 reviews employer and employee notice obligations under state family and medical leave laws. Section 6.05 discusses the interaction of federal and state family medical leave notice requirements.

6.02 EMPLOYER NOTICE REQUIREMENTS

The federal FMLA imposes ten separate notice requirements on employers. The content and timing of employer notice is specified in some of these notice requirements but not in others. Similarly, penalties for an employer's notice failures are imposed for some notice requirements but not others. All employer notice failures, however, constitute FMLA violations. Given the sheer number of notice requirements and the availability of penalties, this is an area in which school employers should exercise great caution to ensure compliance.

[1] FMLA Poster

The federal FMLA provides that covered employers must

> post and keep posted, in conspicuous places on the premises of the employer where notice to employees and applicants for employment are customarily posted, a notice, to be prepared by or approved by the Secretary [of Labor], setting forth excerpts from, or summaries of, the pertinent provisions of this Title and information pertaining to the filing of a charge.[1]

The notice requirement is designed to ensure that employees have sufficient information to make an educated decision regarding the availability of FMLA leave.[2] The posting requirement is the only employer notice provision required by the Act.[3]

The DOL implementing regulations provide additional detail to the posting requirement.[4] A covered employer must post and keep posted the approved federal FMLA notice whether or not it has any eligible employees.[5] The notice must be posted prominently where it can be readily seen by employees and applicants for employment.[6] The poster and the text must be large enough to be easily read and contain fully legible text.[7] The DOL suggests that the poster be at least the size of an 8½ × 11 inch piece of paper.[8] The DOL appears to prefer that the posted FMLA notice be freestanding and not part of a larger, commercially available poster designed to address multiple legal posting requirements.[9] Schools with websites containing applications for employment should seriously consider how they will satisfy their FMLA and other employment law notice obligations.

Where an employer's workforce is composed of a significant portion of workers who are not literate in English, the employer is responsible for providing notice in a language in which the employees are literate.[10]

The DOL does not give guidance on what it means by a "significant portion of workers" and when an employee is "not literate in English." Schools should play this one safe and set those standards relatively low in terms of numbers of employees whose primary language is other than English to determine whether the school needs to post notice of FMLA rights in another language in addition to posting such a notice in English.

The DOL has created and made available an approved FMLA poster (see Appendix A). Note that employers are not mandated to use the DOL-approved poster.[11] Employers may satisfy the requirement to post notice of FMLA rights with a commercially available poster. It is strongly recommended, however, that schools use the DOL-approved FMLA poster. The poster is readily available by download from the DOL website.[12] Employers that use a poster that is not identical to the DOL-approved poster run the risk that the posting may be found by a court not to comply with the posting requirement.

Employers face two penalties for failure to post the required federal FMLA notice. An employer that willfully violates the posting requirement may be assessed a civil penalty by the DOL Wage and Hour Division not to exceed $100 for each separate offense.[13] It is not clear what would constitute a "willful" failure to post the required FMLA notice. As set forth in Chapter 14, *Prohibited Acts, Enforcement, and Remedies*, "willful" has been interpreted for purposes of damages to include an employer's willful ignorance of its FMLA responsibilities. To cite an oft-quoted phrase, ignorance of the law is no excuse.

The DOL regulations do not explain what it means by "each separate offense." If "each separate offense" is calculated on a daily basis for every posting failure, a school district with many schools each requiring an FMLA poster could face considerable civil penalties for a systemic failure to post the required FMLA notice. To avoid large civil penalties, schools should periodically check to ensure that the required FMLA posters are posted as required.

The second penalty imposed by the federal FMLA for an employer's failure to post the FMLA notice restricts the employer's options when an eligible employee has failed to give timely advance notice of the need for FMLA leave. Specifically, an employer that fails to post the required FMLA notice is prohibited from taking any adverse action against an employee, including denying leave, where the employee fails to give the school advance notice of the need for FMLA leave.[14] An employer's failure to post the required FMLA notice does not impede the employer's options when the employee's need for leave was not foreseeable. Section 6.03 below addresses employee notice requirements.

Courts have dismissed lawsuits filed by employees seeking monetary damages based solely on an employer's failure to post the required FMLA notice.[15] In order to have an actionable claim, an employee must establish that an employer's failure to post notice of FMLA rights caused the employee to forfeit FMLA protections.[16]

[2] Handbooks, Manuals, and Other Written Guidance

If an FMLA-covered employer has any eligible employees and has any written guidance for employees concerning employment benefits or leave rights, such as in an employee handbook or manual, information concerning federal FMLA rights must be included in that handbook or other document.[17] For example, if a covered school provides all employees with an employee handbook that describes the employer's policies regarding leave, wages, attendance, and similar matters, the handbook must incorporate information on FMLA rights and responsibilities and the employer's policies regarding the FMLA.[18] The DOL suggests that employers may satisfy this requirement by incorporating DOL informational publications describing the Act's provisions in employer handbooks and similar written guidance.[19]

Note that to be subject to this requirement, a covered employer must satisfy two conditions: (1) the employer must have eligible employees, and (2) the employer must have an employee handbook or other written guidance addressing employment benefits or leave rights. A covered employer that does not have any eligible employees does not have to include information on FMLA rights in an employee handbook. Similarly, a covered employer with eligible employees that does not have any written guidance regarding employment benefits or leave rights does not have to create a handbook in order to insert information on FMLA rights. As set forth in the next subsection, however, an employer is not relieved of the obligation to provide written notice of FMLA rights in the unlikely event that it does not have an employee handbook or other written guidance on employment benefits or leave rights.

The DOL regulations do not specify the FMLA language that an employer must incorporate in existing employee handbooks or other written guidance. The DOL has, however, opined that a covered employer is not required to include information on how an employee may file a complaint with the DOL or file a civil suit in the employee handbook or other written guidance.[20] School employers would be well advised to rely heavily on the FMLA informational pamphlets from the DOL to develop the FMLA information included in employee handbooks. Courts have held that the FMLA information contained in an employee handbook must be clear and accurate.[21] In *Fry v. First Fidelity Bancorp.*, the employer's written policy provided 16 weeks of family and medical leave, 4 more weeks than the minimum required by the FMLA. The employer's policy failed to explain that an employee's right to return to work from family and medical leave expired after 12 weeks, not the full 16 weeks. An employee who was denied the right to return to work from family and medical leave after 16 weeks sued. The court found that the notice contained in the employee handbook was misleading, as it failed to clearly provide that an employee lost the right to return to work after 12 weeks of leave. The court therefore found that the employer had violated the FMLA by refusing to reinstate the employee.

The DOL regulations fail to identify what constitutes written policies regarding employment benefits and leave rights. In one case, a court held that an employer's attendance control policy was not a "written policy" regarding employment benefits or leave rights.[22] There, the employee argued that the attendance control policy constituted "written guidance" regarding leave rights and, therefore, the employer was in violation of the FMLA because it did not incorporate notice of FMLA rights as part of that written guidance. The court disagreed. The court found that the attendance control policy

> did not function as, nor was it intended to provide, written guidance to employees concerning their general benefits and leave rights. The sole purpose of Abbott's attendance control program was to provide a system of progressive discipline for unexcused absences. By the express terms

of 825.301(a)(1), information concerning FMLA entitlements and employee obligations was not required to be included in the program.[23]

The DOL regulations do not specify any penalty for a covered employer's violation of the FMLA employee handbook/written guidance notice requirement. However, an employer's failure to abide by the requirement technically constitutes interference with an employee's FMLA rights. As in *Fry*, courts generally require that an employee suffer a loss of FMLA rights as a result of relying on inadequate employer notice of FMLA rights in a handbook or other written guidance in order to maintain a lawsuit against the employer for violation of the FMLA.[24]

[3] No Written FMLA Guidance

The DOL regulations address employer FMLA notice obligations in the unlikely event that the employer does not have any written guidance regarding employment benefits or leave rights. In that case, covered employers must provide written guidance to an employee concerning all of the employee's rights and obligations under the FMLA each time an employer is required to give specific written notice to employees.[25] (Specific written notice as required under § 825.301(b) of the DOL regulations is addressed in the next subsection.) Employers can satisfy the written guidance requirement by providing the employee with a copy of the DOL-developed FMLA Fact Sheet.[26] A copy of the FMLA Fact Sheet is contained in Appendix C. This means that a school employer without written guidance on employment benefits or leave rights must provide the employee with both a copy of the FMLA Fact Sheet and specific written notice of FMLA rights at the same time. Finally, the DOL regulations do not impose a separate penalty on employers who fail to satisfy this notice requirement. But here again, an employer's failure to provide such notice constitutes a violation of the anti-interference provisions of the federal FMLA.

[4] Specific Written Notice of Employee FMLA Rights and Obligations

In addition to posting the FMLA notice and including notice of FMLA rights and obligations in an employee handbook or other written guidance, covered employers must also provide an employee with written notice detailing the specific expectations and obligations of the employee and explaining any consequences of a failure to meet these obligations.[27] Unlike the posting and employee handbook notice requirements, an employer's obligation to provide specific written notice of FMLA rights and obligations is conditioned on the employee's providing adequate notice of the need for FMLA leave.[28]

(i) Content of Specific Written Notice

The DOL regulations specify the content of the specific written notice that a covered employer must provide an eligible employee requesting FMLA leave. Specific written notice must explain, as applicable,

- that the leave will be counted against the employee's annual FMLA leave entitlement;
- any requirements for the employee to furnish medical certification of a serious health condition and the consequences of failing to do so;
- the employee's right to substitute paid leave and whether the employer will require the substitution of paid leave, and the conditions related to any substitution;
- any requirement for the employee to make any premium payments to maintain health benefits, the arrangements for making such payments, and the possible consequences of failure to make such payments on a timely basis (i.e., the circumstances under which coverage may lapse);
- any requirement for the employee to present a fitness-for-duty certificate to be restored to employment;
- the employee's status as a "key employee" and the potential consequence that restoration may be denied following FMLA leave, explaining the conditions required for such denial;
- the employee's right to restoration to the same or an equivalent job upon return from leave; and
- the employee's potential liability for payment of health insurance premiums by the employer during the employee's unpaid FMLA leave if the employee fails to return to work after taking FMLA leave.[29]

An employer may include additional information in the specific written notice, such as whether the employer will require periodic reports of the employee's status and intent to return to work.[30] The DOL regulations prohibit a covered employer from providing an employee with less information in the specific written notice of FMLA rights and obligations, not more information. A covered employer is not, however, required to include information on periodic reports or any other information in the specific written notice of FMLA rights and obligations.

The DOL has developed a prototype notice for use by covered employers that satisfies the content requirement for specific written notice.[31] Note that the prototype notice requires employers to add information unique to each employee requesting FMLA leave. Employers that elect to create their own version of specific written notice of FMLA rights and obligations must avoid using a static form for all occasions. A static form of specific written notice that requires no individualized input would likely fail to satisfy the content requirements of the FMLA.[32] To avoid unnecessary litigation, schools would be well advised to use the DOL-approved prototype forms (see Appendix E).

(ii) Manner, Timing, and Frequency of Providing Specific Written Notice

Employers must provide the employee with specific written notice in a language in which the employee is literate.[33] Pursuant to this requirement, employers are required to determine on a case-by-case basis whether each employee requesting federal FMLA leave is literate in the language of the employer's specific written FMLA notice. Similarly, an employer is required to post notice of FMLA rights in languages other than English where a "significant portion" of the workforce is not literate in English. Unfortunately, the DOL regulations fail to define what "literate" means for purposes of this requirement. Presumably, an employer may use any reasonable means of determining employee literacy in the language, presumably English, of the FMLA specific written notice. Where an employee is multilingual (e.g., literate in more than one language), an employer satisfies its obligation by providing the specific written FMLA notice in any language in which the employee is literate. The employer is not required to provide specific written notice to a multilingual employee in the language that the employee prefers or is more comfortable with.[34] Schools may nevertheless wish to play this safe and offer the specific written notice in both English and the employee's preferred or primary language where the literacy of the employee is in question.

Employers furnishing FMLA-required notices to sensory-impaired employees must also comply with all applicable requirements under federal and state law.[35] The DOL regulations do not elaborate on what this means for FMLA notice purposes. Presumably it means that employers with hearing- and sight-impaired employees must satisfy all school FMLA notice obligations in a manner that is designed to inform employees of their rights and obligations, such as providing notices in Braille or sign language, as warranted. Note that this requirement applies to all forms of employer FMLA notice to employees, not just specific written notice.

The frequency with which an employer must provide specific written notice of an employee's FMLA rights and obligations depends on several factors. Generally, a covered employer must provide the employee requesting FMLA-qualifying leave with specific written notice of that employee's FMLA rights and obligations no less often than the first time in each 6-month period that an employee gives notice of the need for FMLA leave, if FMLA leave is taken during the 6-month period.[36] An employer does not satisfy this requirement by simply sending all employees a copy of the employer's version of the FMLA specific written notice every 6 months. This is because the provision of specific written notice is tied to an employee's request and use of FMLA leave during 6-month intervals. An employer could, of course, provide employees with more notice of FMLA leave rights and obligations; it simply cannot provide less. To avoid confusion regarding this rule, schools are encouraged to provide specific written notice every time an employee requests FMLA leave. Specific written notice must be given within a reasonable time after the employee provides notice of the need for FMLA leave.[37] Generally, a reasonable period of time means one or two business days, if feasible.[38] If leave has already begun, the specific written notice should be mailed to the employee's address of record.[39]

There are two exceptions to the general rule above. If an employer requires an employee to furnish medical certification or submit a fitness-for-duty report, that employer must provide specific written notice of FMLA rights and obligations *every time* an employee provides notice of the need for FMLA leave.[40] Once this specific written notice has been given to an employee requesting FMLA leave, an employer that requires medical certification or a fitness-for-duty report can avoid the requirement to provide *subsequent* written notification of FMLA rights and obligations to that employee if several conditions are met. As described below, however, it is difficult to envision the circumstances that would render this Rube Goldberg exemption from the written notice requirement worth the effort.

> It is difficult to envision the circumstances that would make this Rube Goldberg exemption from the written notice requirement worth the effort simply to avoid giving the employee an additional piece of paper.

To fall within the scope of this exemption to the specific written notice requirement, an employer must first provide the employee with specific written notice of FMLA rights and obligations the first time that the employee notifies the employer of the need for FMLA leave and the leave is taken within six months of that notice. Second, that notice must clearly state that medical certification or a fitness-for-duty report is required.[41] Third, the employee handbook or other written documents, if any, describing the employer's leave policies must also clearly provide that medical certification or a fitness-for-duty report is required.[42] For example, specific written notice and the handbook or other leave-related documents would satisfy this exemption if they stated certification would be required in all cases in which leave of more than a specified number of days is taken, or by stating that a "fitness-for-duty" report would be required in all cases for back injuries for employees in certain occupations.[43] Where all of these conditions are met, subsequent written notice is not required. However, employers that require medical certification or a fitness-for-duty report must still orally notify the employee requesting leave of his or her FMLA rights and obligations *every time* the employee requests FMLA leave.[44]

Schools would be better advised to ignore this exemption and provide the employee with specific written notice of his or her rights and obligations every time the employee gives notice of the need for FMLA leave. Even with leave-tracking software, the administrative burden of keeping track of this information in order to orally inform an employee of his or her rights rather than giving that employee a piece of paper containing those rights is, in my opinion, simply not worth the time and effort.

The second exception to the general rule regarding specific written notice arises when there has been a change in circumstances regarding the employee's leave. An employer will be required to provide specific written notice to an employee more than once in a given six-month period if specific information included in the initial notice given to an employee changes with respect to a subsequent period of FMLA leave during the 6-month period. In that case, the employer must, within one or two business days of receipt of the employee's notice of need for leave, provide written notice referencing the prior notice and setting forth any of the information that has changed.[45] For example, if the initial leave period was paid leave and the subsequent leave period would be unpaid leave, an employer may need to give notice of the arrangements for the employee to make health care premium payments during the period of unpaid leave (since there would no longer be paychecks from which to deduct the premium payments).[46]

(iii) Failure of Employer to Provide Specific Written Notice

The DOL regulations impose penalties for an employer's failure to provide an employee with specific written notice of FMLA rights and obligations as required. An employer that fails to provide specific written notice is prohibited from taking action against an employee for failure to comply with any provision required to be set forth in the notice.[47] Given the broad scope of the employer notice requirements set forth in § 825.301 of the DOL regulations, this is not an insignificant penalty. An employer who fails to provide an employee with specific written notice of a medical certification requirement violates the FMLA.[48]

Courts have found employers to be in violation of this rule where the employer gave misleading, inaccurate, or otherwise erroneous information regarding FMLA rights and obligations to an employee requesting leave.[49] Other courts, however, have found that in order for a notice violation to be actionable (i.e., in order for an employee to maintain a civil action against an employer), the employee must establish both that the employer failed to provide notice as required and that the employee was prejudiced as a result.[50] At least one court has found the penalty provision of § 825.301(f) to be constitutionally invalid.[51]

[5] Notice of Employee Eligibility

Covered employers are required to notify employees whether they meet the eligibility requirements for FMLA leave.[52] When the employer must provide such notification depends on when the employee gives notice of the need for leave.

(i) Employee Is Not Yet Eligible

If an employee notifies his or her employer of the need for FMLA leave before the employee meets the eligibility requirements, the employer must either confirm the employee's eligibility based on a projection that the employee will be eligible on the date leave would commence or advise the employee when the eligibility requirements are met.[53] If the employer confirms eligibility at the time the notice for leave is received, the employer may not subsequently challenge the employee's eligibility.[54]

If instead the employer elects to advise the employee when the eligibility requirements are met, the employer must do so as soon as practicable (i.e., within two business days absent extenuating circumstances) after the date employee eligibility is determined.[55] If the employer fails to timely inform the employee that he or she is eligible as soon as practicable, the employee will be considered to have satisfied the notice requirements until the employer does advise the employee.[56] If the employer fails to advise the employee whether the employee is eligible prior to the date the requested leave is to commence, the employee will be deemed eligible. The employer may not then deny the leave.[57] Presumably, the regulations should be read as meaning that an employer could not deny the employee's request for FMLA leave because the employee is ineligible, as opposed to meaning that an employer could not deny leave for other reasons such as the fact that the leave does not involve a covered condition.

(ii) Employee Notice of Need for Leave of Less Than Two Business Days

Where an employee does not give notice of the need for leave more than two business days prior to commencing leave, the employee will be deemed to be eligible if the employer fails to advise the employee that the employee is not eligible within two business days of receiving the employee's notice.[58] If the employee is "deemed eligible" an employer would violate the Act by denying FMLA leave because the employee was not eligible.

(iii) Deemed Eligible

As set forth more fully in section 3.07[2] of Chapter 3, many courts have found the "deemed eligible" penalty provision of 29 C.F.R. § 825.110(d) invalid. Essentially, courts have found that the DOL exceeded its authority by requiring employers, as a penalty for failing to meet a DOL-created deadline for informing an employee of eligibility, to recognize an employee as meeting the eligibility requirements for FMLA leave even though, in fact, the employee does not satisfy the statutory eligibility requirement. These courts reason that the DOL cannot by regulation waive statutory eligibility requirements as a penalty for failing to meet regulatory timelines. To do so would allow employees who did not meet the eligibility requirements created by Congress to take FMLA leave. The courts determined that by doing so, the DOL exceeded its rule-making authority.

Note that simply because the penalty provisions have been invalidated does not mean that employers are free to ignore their responsibility to notify employees whether they meet the eligibility requirements for federal FMLA leave. Employers are still required to notify employees whether they meet the eligibility requirements. If an employer fails to abide by the eligibility notification requirements, an employee denied FMLA leave may file suit alleging that the employer interfered with his or her FMLA rights. As discussed previously, if the employee can establish that the employer's failure to notify the employee violated 29 C.F.R. § 825.110 and prejudiced the employee, the employee may have a viable claim for damages against the employer for interference with the employee's FMLA rights.

[6] Designation of Leave as FMLA-Qualifying

Covered employers must notify employees that their leave has been designated by the employer as FMLA leave and will count against the employee's annual FMLA leave entitlement. In all circumstances, it is the employer's responsibility to designate leave, whether paid or unpaid, as FMLA-qualifying and to give notice of the designation to the employee.[59] An employer may designate leave as FMLA-qualifying over the objection of the employee.[60] An employee may not bar a covered employer from designating any qualifying absence as FMLA leave.[61] An employer may make FMLA leave mandatory for eligible employees who are taking leave for qualifying events, but it is not required to do so by the federal FMLA.[62] If the leave is FMLA-qualifying, an employer cannot ignore FMLA coverage and designate the leave as unprotected by the Act.[63] One court has held that a covered employer is not required to inform an employee that leave has not been designated as FMLA-qualifying.[64] This would appear to run counter to the requirement in § 825.208(e)(2) that employers notify employees in writing where a preliminary designation that leave is FMLA-qualifying is being withdrawn based on the receipt of medical documentation that fails to confirm that the leave is for an FMLA-covered condition.[65]

An employer's designation decision must be based only on information received from the employee or the employee's spokesperson.[66] For example, if the employee is incapacitated, the employee's spouse, adult child, parent, doctor, or others may provide notice to the employer of the employee's need to take FMLA leave.[67] Notwithstanding the language of the DOL regulations, one court has found that an employer did not violate the FMLA when it based its decision to deny FMLA leave on information other than what was initially provided by the employee at the time leave was requested.[68] In that case, the employer denied FMLA leave based on a prior medical certification from the employee's physician indicating that the condition was not a serious health condition within the meaning of the FMLA.

If the employer does not have sufficient information regarding the reason for an employee's use of paid leave, the employer should inquire further of the employee or spokesperson to ascertain whether the paid leave is potentially FMLA-qualifying.[69] It is expected that the employer will obtain any additional required information through informal means.[70] For example, in one case a court found that two telephone messages the employer left at the employee's home satisfied its obligation to inquire further by informal means to ascertain whether the leave was FMLA-qualifying.[71]

(i) Timing of Employer Notice of FMLA Designation

The DOL regulations identify three points in time when an employer may be required to notify the employee that the leave has been designated as FMLA-qualifying: (1) before FMLA leave commences, (2) during leave, and (3) after the employee returns to work. When such notice must be given depends on the circumstances, including whether the leave is paid or unpaid.[72] According to the DOL, the regulations are designed to resolve the question of FMLA designation as early as possible in the leave request process to eliminate protracted "after the fact" disputes.[73] Designation of leave as FMLA-qualifying is expected to take place "up front" whenever possible.[74] The DOL regulations in this area are unnecessarily convoluted.

(A) Before FMLA Leave Commences

Whether an employer must notify an employee—before leave commences—that it has designated leave as FMLA-qualifying depends on whether the leave is paid or unpaid. If the leave is paid, an employer must provide notice of the FMLA designation before the employee's leave starts unless the employer does not have sufficient information about the employee's reason for taking the leave until after the leave has commenced.[75] Once an employer acquires knowledge that the leave is being taken for an FMLA-covered condition, the employer must promptly (within two business days absent extenuating circumstances) notify the employee that the paid leave is designated as FMLA leave and will be counted against the employee's FMLA leave entitlement.[76]

The DOL designation regulations do not specifically require notification before leave commences in the case of unpaid leave. In the absence of direction by the DOL regulations, many employers apply the two-business-day rule for notification of paid leave and notify employees within two business days of the determination that the leave is FMLA-qualifying. Such a practice would appear to satisfy the DOL's intent that designation decisions occur as far "up front" as possible. I recommend that schools follow the practice of applying the two-business-day rule to inform employees whether unpaid leave has been designated as FMLA qualifying even though schools are not technically required to apply this rule by the DOL regulations.

I recommend that schools follow the practice of applying the two-business-day rule to inform employees whether unpaid leave has been designated as FMLA-qualifying even though schools are not technically required to apply this rule by the DOL regulations.

If there is a dispute between a school and an employee as to whether paid leave qualifies as FMLA leave, it should be resolved through discussions between the employee and the school. Such discussions and the decision must be documented.[77] By their terms, the regulations do not apply to disputes regarding an employer's designation of unpaid leave as FMLA-qualifying. No explanation is given for this disparity. In any event, an ongoing dispute would presumably result in the employer's having insufficient information to make a designation determination and thereby extend the time the employer has to designate the leave as FMLA-qualifying until the dispute has been resolved, or within two business days thereafter.

The DOL regulations impose a penalty for an employer's failure to timely designate paid leave as FMLA-qualifying. If at the time the employee either gives notice of the need for leave or commences leave an employer has the requisite knowledge to make a determination that paid leave is for an FMLA-covered reason and the employer fails to designate the leave as FMLA leave (and so notify the employee as required), the employer may not retroactively designate the leave as FMLA leave and may designate only prospectively as of the date of notification to the employee of the designation. In such circumstances, the employee is subject to the full protections of the Act, but no portion of the employee's leave that preceded the employer's designation notice may be counted against the employee's 12-week FMLA leave entitlement.[78] By its terms, the penalty provision applies only when paid leave is designated as FMLA-qualifying, not when unpaid leave is so designated.

Many courts have held that the penalty provision of § 825.208(c) is invalid.[79] Following the reasoning of the Supreme Court in *Ragsdale v. Wolverine World Wide, Inc.*,[80] these courts have opined that the penalty provision of § 825.208(c) would result in an employee's getting more than the 12 workweeks of FMLA leave permitted by the statute. These courts have found that the DOL exceeded its authority in providing more FMLA leave to employees than is permitted by the statute as a penalty for an employer's designation-notice failure.

While many courts have invalidated the penalty provision of § 825.208(c), they have not invalidated the underlying pre-leave-commencement notice requirement. Employers still must comply with the designation-notice requirements of § 825.208(c). If an employer fails to notify an employee that it has designated paid leave as FMLA-qualifying pursuant to § 825.208(c), the employer has illegally interfered with the employee's FMLA rights. An employee who can establish both that the school employer violated § 825.208(c) by failing to notify the employee that paid leave was being counted against his or her FMLA leave entitlement *and* that the employee was prejudiced by such failure could potentially maintain a costly lawsuit against the school and individual managers or supervisors who were directly involved in the failure to notify the employee of the FMLA leave designation.[81]

(B) Notice During Leave

Under certain circumstances, employers may designate leave as FMLA-qualifying after the leave has commenced. If the employer learns that leave is for an FMLA-covered purpose after leave has begun, such as where an employee gives notice of the need for an extension of paid leave with unpaid FMLA leave, all or a portion of the paid leave period may be retroactively designated as FMLA leave to the extent that such leave qualifies as FMLA leave.[82] For example, an employee is granted 2 weeks' paid vacation leave for a ski trip. In the middle of the second week, the employee contacts the employer for an extension of the leave with unpaid FMLA leave. The employee explains that at the beginning of the second week of paid vacation leave, he suffered a severe accident requiring hospitalization. The employer may notify the employee that both the extension and the second week of paid vacation leave (from the date of the injury) is designated as FMLA leave.[83] Similarly, if an employee takes sick leave for a minor condition that subsequently turns into an FMLA-covered serious health condition (e.g., the flu turns into bronchial pneumonia) and the employee gives notice of the need for an extension of leave, the entire period during which the employee suffered from the serious health condition (including time originally designated as sick leave) may be counted as FMLA leave.[84]

It is unclear how much time an employer has to notify an employee that some or all leave has been retroactively designated as FMLA-qualifying. Section 825.208(d) does not separately establish a time period for an employer to notify the employee. Absent a separate time period, it would appear that in the case of paid leave, an employer must notify the employee that some or all of the paid leave has been retroactively designated as FMLA-qualifying within two business days of the time the employer acquired knowledge that the leave is being taken for an FMLA-covered condition.[85] As discussed earlier, the DOL regulations fail to set a standard for the timing of an employer's notice to the employee that unpaid leave has been designated as FMLA-qualifying. In these circumstances, school employers would be well advised to apply the same two-business-day rule (absent extenuating circumstances) to unpaid FMLA leave.

Note that the penalty provisions of § 825.208(c) do not apply in the event an employer fails to timely notify the employee that it has designated leave as FMLA-qualifying. By its terms, the penalty provision applies only where an employer has the requisite information at the time the employee either gives notice of the need for leave or commences leave and the employer fails to timely designate the leave as FMLA-qualifying.[86] In a post-leave-commencement situation, the employer does not have the requisite knowledge that the leave is FMLA-qualifying until after the leave has begun. Accordingly, the penalty provision does not apply in this situation.

(C) Designation of FMLA Leave after an Employee Returns to Work from Leave

As a general rule, employers may not designate leave as FMLA-qualifying after the employee has returned to work.[87] There are two exceptions, however, pursuant to which employers may be permitted to retroactively designate leave as FMLA-qualifying after the conclusion of such leave.

First, if the employee was absent for an FMLA-covered reason and the employer did not learn of the reason for the absence until the employee's return (e.g., where the employee was absent for only a brief period of time), the employer may, upon the employee's return to work, promptly (within two business days of the employee's return to work) retroactively designate the leave as FMLA leave with appropriate notice to the employee.[88] Note that the use of the permissive term "may" suggests that employers are not required to designate the leave as FMLA-qualifying in these situations. To secure the protections of the FMLA, the employee must notify the employer within two business days of returning to work of the FMLA-qualifying reason for the leave. If the employee does not so timely notify the school, the employee may not subsequently assert FMLA protections for the absence.[89] Note also the absence of "extenuating circumstances" that might extend the two-day period for an employer to notify the employee that the leave has been retroactively designated as FMLA-qualifying.

Second, even if the employer knew the reason for the leave before leave began, the employer may be able to retroactively designate the leave as FMLA-qualifying after the employee returns to work if, when the leave began,

- the employer had been unable to confirm that the leave qualifies under the FMLA;
- the employer had not received requested medical certification; or
- the parties were in the process of obtaining a second or third medical opinion.[90]

Under such circumstances, a school employer should make a preliminary designation and so notify the employee at the time leave begins or as soon as the reason for the leave becomes known.[91] Upon receipt of the requisite information from the employee or of the medical certification that confirms the leave is for an FMLA-covered reason, the preliminary designation becomes final.[92]

While an employer is required to notify an employee of the preliminary designation, the regulations do not identify a time period in which the employer is required to do so. Presumably, a school should notify an employee of the preliminary designation of leave as FMLA-qualifying within two business days of when the leave begins or as soon as the reason for the leave becomes known. Oddly, by its terms, § 825.208(e)(2) does not require an employer to notify the employee that the preliminary designation of FMLA leave has become final. It does, however, require an employer to notify the employee in writing in the event the employer withdraws the preliminary FMLA leave designation because the medical certification fails to confirm that the absence is for an FMLA-covered serious health condition, although the regulations fail to specify a time period for such notification.[93] School employers would be well advised to apply the two-business-day rule in this situation. The regulations do not require that an employer notify the employee in the event that a preliminary designation of leave is withdrawn because the employer is unable to confirm that the leave qualifies under the FMLA or in the event that a second or third medical opinion fails to confirm that the leave is for a reason recognized by the FMLA. Presumably, schools should provide written notice to the employee of the withdrawal of the preliminary designation in these circumstances as well.

(ii) Manner and Frequency of Designation Notice

Notice that leave has been designated as FMLA-qualifying may be provided to the employee in writing or orally.[94] If the notice is oral, it must be confirmed in writing no later than the following payday.[95] But if that payday is less than a week after the oral notice, written confirmation must be made no later than the subsequent payday.[96] The written notice may be in any form, including a notation on the employee's pay stub.[97] For a pay-stub notation to meet this standard, it must explicitly inform the employee that leave was FMLA-qualifying.[98] The employee bears the burden of proof that the employer failed to follow up oral notice with timely written confirmation.[99] Written notice is required when an employer withdraws a preliminary designation of leave as FMLA-qualifying because the medical certification fails to confirm that the reason for the absence is covered by the FMLA.[100]

Generally, employers need only notify an employee once that leave has been designated as FMLA-qualifying. This is true whether the leave is taken in a single block of time, intermittently, or on a reduced leave schedule.[101] Leave is taken intermittently where more than one absence is taken during a 12-month leave year for the same underlying covered condition. A reduced leave schedule is a schedule that reduces the usual number of hours per workweek or hours per workday of an employee (e.g., full-time to part-time status). An employer is required to provide designation notice more than once, however, if circumstances regarding the leave have changed.[102] For example, a school employee initially requests FMLA leave due to the flu. The leave does not qualify for FMLA leave, and the school so notifies the employee. The school, however, grants the employee sick leave pursuant to school policy. The employee's condition develops into pneumonia. If the condition otherwise meets the requirements for an FMLA-covered serious health condition, the school would be obligated to notify the employee that continued leave is FMLA-qualifying.

[7] Method of Calculating 12-Month Leave Year

Under the federal FMLA, eligible employees are entitled to 12 workweeks of FMLA leave during a 12-month leave year. Employers that are covered by the federal FMLA and that have eligible employees must select the method for calculating the 12-month leave year from four options.[103] This section addresses the rules governing a school's obligation to notify employees of the method the school has selected.

The DOL regulations do not explicitly require that employees be informed of the 12-month FMLA leave year initially selected by the employer. However, there is some evidence that employers should include the method for calculating the FMLA leave year in any employee handbook or other written materials addressing employment benefits or leave rights. In comments accompanying the publication of the final FMLA implementing regulations, the DOL opined that "[e]mployers must inform employees of the applicable method for determining FMLA leave entitlement when informing employees of their FMLA rights."[104] Several courts have agreed.[105]

Schools should identify the method they have selected to calculate the FMLA leave year in employee handbooks or other written material regarding employment benefits and leave rights. Notice of the calculation method is not required in the FMLA poster or specific written notice given to employees.

> Schools should identify the method they have selected to calculate the FMLA leave year in employee handbooks or other written materials regarding employment benefits and leave rights.

Covered employers are required to notify employees if they change the method for calculating the FMLA leave year. The notice obligation arises in two circumstances: (1) where the employer has initially failed to select from one of the four leave year options and (2) where the employer wishes to change the method for calculating the FMLA leave year to an alternative method.

Where an employer initially fails to select one of the four available options for measuring the 12-month FMLA leave year, the DOL regulations require application of the option that provides the most beneficial outcome for the employee.[106] To subsequently select one of the four options in this circumstance, the employer must provide at least 60 days' notice to all employees of the option it intends to implement.[107] During the 60-day period, other employees who need FMLA leave may use the option providing the most beneficial outcome to those employees.[108]

Similarly, an employer that has selected one of the four methods for calculating the FMLA leave year may change to one of the other methods but must give at least 60 days' notice to all employees.[109] Additionally, the transition must take place in such a way that employees retain the full benefit of 12 weeks of leave under whichever method affords the greatest benefit to the employee.[110] Under no circumstances may a new method be implemented in order to avoid the Act's leave requirements.[111]

The DOL regulations do not specify the manner in which an employer must notify employees regarding a change in the method for calculating the FMLA leave year. Presumably, any reasonable manner of notification to all employees would suffice. The manner of notice elected should be reasonably calculated to actually notify all employees of the change in the method of calculating the FMLA leave year. Conspicuously posting such notice in appropriate places, including the notice in an employee's paycheck envelope, or distributing written notice or modified employee handbooks that prominently disclose the change would be possible methods. Changing the disclosure regarding the calculation method in an employee handbook without a mass distribution of the revised handbooks to employees would likely fail to be viewed as a reasonable means of apprising all employees of the change in the method for calculating the FMLA leave year. Schools with employee handbooks or other written employment benefit or leave policies would be well advised to revise their handbooks and other written materials to incorporate the change and to distribute or otherwise make the revised versions reasonably available to all employees. Schools with unions may be required to bargain before implementing such a change.

[8] Employment Benefits

Covered employers are required to notify employees of FMLA entitlements and obligations regarding employment benefits. Maintenance of benefits during FMLA leave is discussed in Chapter 10, *Maintenance of Employment Benefits*. This section addresses an employer's notice obligations regarding benefits under the federal FMLA.

Information regarding employment benefits during FMLA leave and after an employee's return to work from FMLA leave must be included in an employee handbook or other written guidance of employment benefits or leave rights maintained by the school.[112] The specific written notice of FMLA rights and obligations schools are required to provide employees includes information on maintenance of employment benefits during FMLA leave.[113] The specific written notice must inform employees of any requirements for employees to make premium payments to maintain group health benefits, the arrangements for making such payments, and the consequences for an employee's failure to make such payments.[114]

During FMLA leave, employers must notify employees of any changes to existing health plans or benefits and afford employees the opportunity to make any elections regarding the changes to the same extent as if the employees were not on FMLA leave.[115] An employer is similarly required to notify an employee if it plans to terminate an employee's group health coverage during FMLA leave because the employee failed to make required premium payments. In order to terminate group health plan coverage because of an employee's nonpayment of premiums, an employer must first provide written notice to the employee that payment has not been received.[116] Such notice must also advise the employee that coverage will be dropped on an identified date at least 15 days after the date of written notice unless payment is received by that date.[117] Written notice must be mailed at least 15 days before health coverage is scheduled to end.[118] The regulations do not identify a penalty in the event the employer fails to notify the employee of changes to benefits plans or cancellation of health coverage for employee nonpayment of premiums. If the employee can establish prejudice as a result of the employer's notice failure, it would appear the employee would have a viable claim of interference with FMLA rights against the employer.

[9] "Key Employees"

The federal FMLA generally provides that at the conclusion of leave, eligible employees have the right to return to their same or an equivalent position.[119] Covered employers may, however, deny job restoration to certain highly compensated "key employees." Key employees may be denied job restoration to avoid substantial and grievous economic injury if the employee were permitted to return to work. Job-restoration rights are addressed in Chapter 11, *Return to Work from Family and Medical Leave*. This section will address school employer notice requirements regarding key employees.

The DOL regulations impose three notice requirements on a covered employer in order for the employer to perfect its right to deny job restoration to a key employee. First, an employer that believes that reinstatement may be denied to a key employee must notify the individual in writing that he or she qualifies as a key employee.[120] At the same time, an employer must also fully inform the employee of the potential consequences with respect to reinstatement and maintenance of health benefits if the employer should determine that substantial and grievous economic injury to its operations will result if the key employee is reinstated from FMLA leave.[121] Generally, such notice must be given either at the time the key employee notifies the employer of the need for FMLA leave or at leave commencement, whichever is earlier.[122] If notice cannot be given immediately because of the need to determine whether the employee is a key employee, it must be given as soon as practicable after the employee gives notice of the need for leave (or the commencement of leave, if earlier).[123] Written notice to an employee within two to three days of request for leave has been found to be "as soon as practicable."[124] It is expected that in most circumstances there will be no desire that a key employee be denied restoration after FMLA leave and, therefore, no need to provide such notice. However, an employer that fails to provide such timely notice will lose its right to deny restoration even if substantial and grievous economic injury would result from reinstatement.[125]

Second, as soon as an employer makes a good faith determination based on the available facts that substantial and grievous economic injury to its operations will result if a key employee who has given notice of the need for FMLA leave or is using FMLA leave is reinstated, the employer must notify the employee in writing of its determination, that it cannot deny FMLA leave, and that it intends to deny restoration to employment upon completion of the FMLA leave.[126] It is anticipated that an employer will ordinarily be able to give such notice before the key employee goes on leave.[127] An employer must serve this notice either in person or by certified mail.[128] This notice must explain the basis for the employer's finding that substantial and grievous economic injury will result and if leave has commenced, must provide the employee a reasonable time in which to return to work, taking into account the circumstances, such as the length of the leave and the urgency of the need for the employee to return to work.[129] Schools may combine the first and second notices.

Third, an employer may be required to provide notice to a key employee after the conclusion of FMLA leave. After the key employee has received the first and second notices, the employee is still entitled to request reinstatement at the end of the leave period if the employee did not return to work in response to the employer's prior notices.[130] If such a request for reinstatement is received, an employer must again determine whether there will be substantial and grievous economic injury if the key employee is reinstated, based on the facts at that time.[131] If it is confirmed that substantial and grievous economic injury will result from job restoration, the employer must notify the employee that it is denying the employee's request for job restoration.[132] Such notice may be in writing and delivered either in person or by certified mail.[133]

Note the absence of a penalty provision should an employer violate the second and third notice requirements. If, however, a school employee could establish both a violation of these notice requirements by the school employer and prejudice, the employee would likely have a viable claim against the school and individual school administrators involved with the notification failure.

[10] Joint Employment

Covered employers within the meaning of the federal FMLA include so-called joint employers.[134] Joint employment occurs when two or more entities exercise some control over the work or working conditions of the employee.[135] For example, a joint employment relationship would arise where a school hires temporary secretarial help through a temporary-help agency. Both the school and the temporary-help agency would be the joint employers of the individual performing temporary secretarial help.[136]

In joint employment relationships, only the primary employer is responsible for giving required notices to its employees.[137] The primary employer generally has the authority to hire and fire, to assign and place the employee, to maintain payroll, and to provide employment benefits.[138] Typically, the temporary-help agency is the primary employer of the temporary employee supplied to the school.

[11] Record Keeping

The federal FMLA requires covered employers to keep and preserve certain records regarding the FMLA.[139] Employers with eligible employees must retain copies of all general and specific written notices given to employees as required by the FMLA.[140] Record keeping is addressed more fully in Chapter 12, *Record-Keeping Requirements*.

6.03 EMPLOYEE NOTICE OBLIGATIONS

Employees, like employers, have multiple notice obligations under the federal FMLA. Employees must provide timely and adequate notice of their need for FMLA leave. This section will address employee federal FMLA notice obligations.

[1] Need for FMLA Leave

To enjoy the benefits and protections of the federal FMLA, an eligible employee must notify the employer of the need for FMLA leave. The DOL regulations establish rules governing the timing, adequacy, and manner of employee notice of the need for FMLA leave. An employee who fails to provide timely and adequate notice of the need for FMLA leave will likely fall outside the protections of the federal FMLA. As a result, this area has been the subject of considerable litigation.

(i) When Notice Must Be Given

Whether an eligible employee has provided timely notice of the need for FMLA leave depends on whether the need for the leave is foreseeable or not foreseeable.[141] Where the need for leave is foreseeable based on an expected birth or placement for adoption or foster care or based on a planned medical treatment for a serious health condition of the employee or a covered family member, the employee must provide the employer with at least 30 days' advance notice before leave begins.[142] For example, an eligible employee is adopting a child. The employee is advised 90 days in advance of the placement date. The employee needs to take a day off to attend a hearing and bring the child home. To provide timely notice, the eligible employee must notify his or her employer no less than 30 days prior to when the leave is to begin. Of course, the employee could give more notice than the minimum 30 days; to comply with the FMLA notice provisions, the employee simply can't give less than 30 days' advance notice.

If 30 days' notice is not practicable, such as because of a lack of knowledge of approximately when leave will be required to begin, a change in circumstances, or a medical emergency, the employee must notify his or her employer "as soon as practicable."[143] "As soon as practicable" means as soon as both possible and practical taking into account all of the facts and circumstances in the individual case.[144] For foreseeable leave where it is not possible to give as much as 30 days' notice, "as soon as practicable" ordinarily would at a minimum mean verbal notification to the employer within one or two business days after the need for leave becomes known to the employee.[145] For example, an employee knows that he will need leave to be with his wife while she gives birth. The child is due in August. Due to complications with the pregnancy, the employee needs to take leave to be with his wife in July. In this case, the leave is foreseeable, but its exact timing was not. The employee is required to give notice of the need for FMLA leave as soon as practicable, generally within one or two business days after the need for leave becomes known to the employee.

Note that the employee's notice requirement in these circumstances is "as soon as practicable." It is not automatically one or two business days. Where the facts suggest that the employee knew of the need for leave and it was both possible and practical for the employee to give the employer notice in a shorter period of time than one or two business days, an employee who waits one or two business days before giving notice may be untimely. It is also possible that an employee can provide timely notice of a need for leave after the employee goes on leave or returns to work from that leave. The issue will depend on whether, under the circumstances, the need for leave is foreseeable but the approximate timing of the need for leave is not and whether the employee provides notice of the need for leave as soon as both possible and practical.

Where the approximate timing of the need for leave is not foreseeable, an employee should give notice to the employer of the need for FMLA leave as soon as practical under the facts and circumstances of the particular case.[146] It is expected that an employee will give notice to the employer within no more than one or two working days of learning of the need for leave, except in extraordinary circumstances where such notice is not feasible.[147] Here again, an employee's notice of the need for leave that is not foreseeable may be timely even if it is provided after the leave commences or the employee returns to work.

> School leave policies may extend the time frame that employees have to provide notice of the need for FMLA leave. School leave notice policies may not, however, impose shorter notice requirements than those imposed by the FMLA.

Employer policies may extend the time frame that employees have to provide notice of the need for FMLA leave. However, an employer may not require employee compliance with notice requirements shorter than the minimum permitted by the federal FMLA. This is true whether the shorter notice requirements are required by the terms of a collective bargaining agreement or applicable leave plan.[148]

An employer's policies regarding paid and unpaid leave may also impact the timing of an employee's notice of the need for FMLA leave. Here again, an employer may not require more stringent notice requirements for paid or unpaid leave than those imposed by the FMLA. If, however, paid leave is substituted for unpaid FMLA leave and the procedural requirements for requesting paid leave are less stringent than are the requirements of the FMLA, only the less stringent requirements may be imposed.[149] For example, if an employee (or employer) elects to substitute paid vacation leave for unpaid FMLA leave and the school's paid vacation leave plan imposes no prior notification requirements for taking such vacation leave, the school may not require advance notice for the FMLA leave taken in these circumstances. Similarly, where FMLA leave is unpaid, the notice requirements of the federal FMLA apply unless school policy imposes lesser notice requirements on employees taking unpaid leave. In that case, only the school's lesser notice requirements apply.[150]

(ii) Adequacy of Employee Notice

In addition to being timely, the leave notice provided by the employee must include sufficient information to alert the school employer that the leave may be FMLA-qualifying.[151] An employee is not, however, required to invoke the FMLA by name.[152] An employee giving notice of the need for leave, whether paid or unpaid, must explain the reasons for the needed leave to allow the employer to determine if the leave qualifies under the Act.[153] The "critical question is whether the information imparted to the employer is sufficient to reasonably apprise it of the employee's request to take time off" for an FMLA-covered condition.[154] As observed by one court:

> So that the scope of our holding is clear, we emphasize that the employee's duty is merely to place the employer on notice of a probable basis for FMLA leave. He doesn't have to write a brief demonstrating legal entitlement. He just has to give the employer enough information to establish probable cause, as it were, to believe that he is entitled to FMLA leave.[155]

An employee can request FMLA leave even though the employee is unaware of his or her rights under the FMLA.[156] Whether notice is sufficient will depend on the facts and circumstances of each individual case.[157]

> **An employee is not required to invoke the FMLA by name.**

Generally, to fall within the protections of the FMLA, an eligible employee must request leave.[158] An employee need not, however, use the words "leave" or "leave of absence" in order to be found to have requested leave. A request for leave may be found based on the circumstances. For example, an employee who called in stating he would not be at work as he had just been released from the hospital after a motorcycle accident was found to have requested FMLA-covered leave even though the employee never formally asked for "leave."[159] An employee's request for a reduced work schedule may qualify as a request for FMLA leave.[160] Courts have found that an employee requested

FMLA leave by engaging in unusual behavior.[161] Similarly, an employee was excused from requesting leave where, after the employee suffered a work-related injury, the employee was advised by his attorneys not to have contact with anyone at work and the employer knew the employee was injured at work and that the employee might need leave.[162] However, an employee's notice of a potential need for FMLA leave at some unspecified time in the future is not a request for leave within the meaning of the FMLA.[163]

For notice to be adequate, the FMLA requires that an employee disclose certain information when FMLA leave is taken on an intermittent or reduced leave schedule basis. In addition to providing notice that is sufficient to apprise the employer that the employee seeks FMLA-qualifying leave, the employee must also notify the employer of the anticipated timing and duration of the leave.[164] Where the need for intermittent or reduced leave schedule leave is due to medical necessity, an employee must also notify the employer, upon request, of the reasons why the intermittent or reduced leave schedule leave is necessary and of the schedule for treatment.[165]

When it comes to the adequacy of employee notice, the DOL regulations impose a burden-shifting scheme. Initially, to implicate the benefits and protections of the FMLA, an employee is supposed to provide notice of an FMLA-qualifying reason for leave. If an employer feels it does not have sufficient information to determine whether the employee's reasons for requesting leave are encompassed by the FMLA, the employer should inquire further of the employee to ascertain whether the leave is potentially FMLA-qualifying.[166] Courts have interpreted the regulations as requiring employers to investigate further where an employee provides notice of a probable basis for FMLA leave.[167] As a practical matter, the burden on employees to adequately inform their employers that leave may potentially be FMLA-qualifying is relatively low. School employers should inquire further if the leave notice provided by the employee could arguably implicate the FMLA, even if the actual notice provided does not initially satisfy all of the elements of an FMLA-covered condition.

The courts are split on whether an employee has provided adequate notice of the need for FMLA leave when the employee indicates that he or she is sick, ill, not feeling well, or going to see the doctor, or makes

As a practical matter, the burden on employees to adequately inform their employers that leave may potentially be FMLA-qualifying is relatively low. School employers should inquire further if the leave notice provided by the employee could arguably implicate the FMLA, even if the actual notice provided does not initially satisfy all of the elements of an FMLA-covered condition.

similar statements. A majority of the courts have found that such notice fails to adequately inform an employer that the employee's request for leave may be FMLA-qualifying.[168] A minority of courts have held either that notice that an eligible employee or covered family member is "sick" or "ill" is itself adequate or that such notice is sufficient to shift the burden to the employer to investigate further.[169]

Employees who offer reasons for leave that are not covered conditions within the meaning of the federal FMLA, of course, fail to provide adequate notice that the leave may be FMLA-qualifying. For example, an employee's request for time off for a European vacation did not give the employer adequate notice that the leave may be covered by the FMLA.[170] An employee's request for leave to attend to personal problems and child care issues was also found insufficient to implicate the protections of the FMLA.[171]

School employers are entitled to truthful information in order to determine whether an employee's request for leave is FMLA-qualifying.

False or misleading information provided by an employee as the basis for a request for leave is insufficient to invoke the protections of the FMLA. This is true even if the real reason for leave is FMLA-qualifying.[172] Employers are entitled to truthful information in order to determine whether an employee's request for leave is FMLA-qualifying. This issue frequently arises where the employee needs FMLA leave to address psychological problems. Given the continuing societal stigma that unfortunately attaches to such treatment, employees sometimes give evasive or even false information as the reason for the leave. An employee who does so runs the considerable risk that the leave will be found to be outside the protections of the

FMLA, even if the real reason for leave would have otherwise been covered. Under the DOL regulations, an employee who fraudulently obtains FMLA leave from an employer is not protected by the FMLA's job-restoration provisions.[173]

The adequacy of the information an employee must impart to an employer in order to alert the employer that the leave request may be FMLA-qualifying may also be impacted by an employer's prior knowledge of an employee's need for leave due to an FMLA-covered condition. The courts are divided on the impact of an employer's prior knowledge on the adequacy of an employee's notice of the need for FMLA leave. Where an employee's marginal notice of a need for FMLA leave is linked to a previously known FMLA-covered condition, courts have found the present notice sufficient to invoke FMLA protections. For example, an employee's notice that she was suffering "depression again" was held sufficient where the employer knew that the employee suffered from depression and had used FMLA leave in the past for such depression.[174] Where the linkage with a known FMLA-covered condition is not made in the employee's current request for leave, the better-reasoned decisions have found that the employee failed to provide adequate notice of the need for FMLA leave.[175] A minority of courts have found marginal employee notice of the need for leave sufficient even absent linkage with a known condition based on the employer's duty to investigate where the employer is aware that the employee has been eligible for FMLA leave in the past.[176]

FMLA Illustrated: Examples of Adequate Notice of Employee Need for FMLA Leave

- An employee stated that he was injured in a motorcycle accident and had just left the hospital.
- An employee informed her supervisor that she was having a mental breakdown, that she was seen by a doctor who excused her from work for four days, and that she was prescribed medication.
- An employee cited a "medical need" for leave and attached a doctor's note stating the employee could not work.
- An employee gave notice of swelling and tightness in his legs.
- An employee stated that she could not work. (This notice was found to be sufficient to trigger the employer's duty to investigate further.)

FMLA Illustrated: Examples of Inadequate Notice of Employee Need for FMLA Leave

- An employee requested leave for personal business and because he was sick.
- An employee provided notice that his arm had gone numb.
- An employee provided notice that he was sick and unable to work. (Courts are split on whether this amount of information is sufficient to place the employer on notice that the employee may be requesting FMLA leave. Other courts under very similar circumstances have found such employee notice insufficient.)
- An employee called in sick to an automated absence-reporting line. (Here, too, courts are split on the issue.)
- An employee stated that he had been in a motorcycle accident and would not be able to work that evening, but would be back the following day.

(iii) Frequency and Manner of Providing Employee Notice

Generally, employee notice of the need for FMLA-qualifying leave must only be given once.[177] This is true whether the employee takes leave in one continuous block of time, intermittently, or on a reduced leave schedule. For example, an employee needs to take a half day of leave once a week for 6 weeks to receive physical therapy as a result of an inpatient stay in a hospital. The FMLA considers the hospital stay and the 6 absences to constitute one intermittent-leave period. Assuming the employee knew the physical therapy schedule at the time of hospitalization, the employee need only inform the school once of the need for intermittent leave covering all future absences. Of course, the employee would have to provide timely notice pursuant to the requirements of the FMLA. An employee is required to notify a school employer as soon as practicable if dates of scheduled intermittent or reduced schedule leave change, are extended, or were initially unknown.[178] As soon as practicable means as soon as both possible and practical under the particular circumstances and generally means within one or two business days.[179]

Notice of an employee's need for FMLA leave may be provided by the employee or the employee's spokesperson, such as an employee's spouse, adult child, parent, or doctor if the employee is unable to do so personally.[180] The FMLA permits an employee to provide notice of the need for FMLA leave to the employer either in person or by telephone, telegraph, facsimile machine, or other electronic means.[181]

The FMLA does not prohibit an employer from requiring written notice by an employee to take or request leave if this is the employer's "usual or customary" procedure. For example, a school may require that written notice set forth the reasons for the requested leave, the anticipated duration of the leave, and the anticipated start of the leave.[182] The school employer, however, may not deny or delay FMLA-qualifying leave when the employee provides verbal notice as soon as practicable.[183] According to the DOL:

> Having a hard and fast rule that the employee must give written notice or confirm the verbal notification within one or two working days would work an unnecessary hardship on many employees who have taken leave for a medical emergency and are not in a position to provide written notice either due to their own serious health condition or that of an immediate family member.[184]

An employee is required to provide notice of his or her need to take FMLA leave to the same person that the employee ordinarily contacts to request other forms of leave—usually the employee's supervisor. It is the responsibility of the supervisor either to refer the employee who needs FMLA leave to the appropriate person or to alert that person to the employee's notice. Once the employee has provided notice to the supervisor or other appropriate person in the usual manner, the employee's obligation to provide notice of the need for FMLA leave has been fulfilled.[185]

(iv) Failure of Employee to Provide Notice

An employer has several options to address an employee's failure to provide timely or adequate notice of the need for FMLA leave. An employer may waive any employee notice deficiencies.[186] On the other hand, if the employee fails to give adequate notice of the need for FMLA-qualifying leave, the employer may delay or deny the employee's request for FMLA leave.[187]

Where the employee fails to give at least 30 days' advance notice of the need for leave that is foreseeable and does not have a reasonable excuse for delaying notice, the employer may delay the taking of FMLA leave until at least 30 days after the date the employee first gives notice of the need for FMLA leave.[188] Note that an employer may only delay the commencement of leave, not deny leave, where the employee fails to timely provide notice of the need for foreseeable leave.

For an employer to delay an employee's FMLA leave for failure to provide timely notice, two requirements must be met: (1) it must be clear that the employee had actual notice of the FMLA notice requirements, and (2) the need for leave and the approximate start date for such leave must have been clearly foreseeable to the employee 30 days in advance of the leave.[189] Actual notice of employee notice requirements may be satisfied by the employer's proper posting of the required FMLA poster at the worksite where the employee is employed.[190] Regarding the foreseeability of the need for leave, notice that an employee would receive a telephone call about the availability of a child for adoption at some unknown point in the future, for example, would not be sufficient employee notice.[191]

An employer may not require compliance with stricter FMLA notice requirements where the provisions of a collective bargaining agreement, state law, or applicable leave plan allow less advance notice by the employee to the school.[192] For example, if the need for leave was foreseeable more than 30 days in advance but the school employee failed, without a reasonable excuse, to timely notify the school, the FMLA regulations permit the school to delay the employee's commencement of leave. If, however, the school's leave policy or applicable state family and medical leave laws do not impose a penalty for an employee's failure to timely notify the school of foreseeable leave, the school would be prohibited from delaying the start of the employee's leave.

An employer may require an employee to comply with its "usual and customary" notice and procedural requirements for requesting leave.[193] An employer is not, however, permitted to disallow or delay the taking of FMLA leave as a penalty for an employee's failure to meet those "usual and customary" notice requirements if the employee gives timely verbal or other notice.[194]

The DOL regulations do not provide a penalty where an employee fails to timely provide notice as soon as practicable where the need for leave is not foreseeable. Courts that have addressed this situation, however, have found that an employee who fails to notify an employer of the need for FMLA leave as soon as practicable is not entitled to the benefits and protections of the FMLA. A school employer may deny FMLA leave to an employee who fails to provide notice of the need for unforeseen FMLA leave as soon as practicable.[195]

[2] Additional Employee Notice Requirements

The federal FMLA imposes nine other notice requirements on employees. While these requirements are discussed in more detail in other chapters of this book, an overview of these requirements is provided below.

(i) Changed Circumstances

Employees must notify their employers when circumstances have changed necessitating the need for more or less FMLA leave. In both situations, an employer may require that the employee provide reasonable notice (i.e., within two business days) of the changed circumstances where foreseeable.[196] Employers may also obtain information on such changed circumstances through requested status reports.[197]

Note that this employee notice requirement is not self-executing. To be entitled to receive this information from an employee, an employer must make this a requirement. It is recommended that schools include such a requirement as part of their leave policies in order to maximize the information they have regarding an employee's FMLA leave status.

It is recommended that schools include such a requirement as part of their leave policies in order to maximize the information they have regarding an employee's FMLA leave status.

(ii) Consultation with Employer on Medical Treatment Schedule

When planning medical treatment, an employee must consult with the employer and make a reasonable effort to schedule the leave so as not to unduly disrupt the employer's operations, subject to the approval of the health care provider.[198] Employees are ordinarily expected to consult with employers prior to scheduling treatment in order to work out a treatment schedule that best suits the needs of both the employer and the employee.[199]

If an employee who provides notice of the need to take FMLA leave on an intermittent basis for planned medical treatment neglects to consult with the employer to make a reasonable attempt to arrange the schedule of treatments so as not to unduly disrupt the employer's operations, the employer may initiate discussions with the employee and require the employee to attempt to make such arrangements, subject to the approval of the health care provider.[200] The DOL regulations do not impose a penalty in the event an employee fails to reasonably engage in the consultation process. But courts have held that employees who fail to make reasonable attempts to schedule their leave so as not to unduly disrupt the employer's operations are not protected by the FMLA.

(iii) Consultation with Employer on Intermittent or Reduced Leave Schedule Leave

The federal FMLA imposes an obligation on both the employee and an employer to attempt to work out a schedule that meets the employee's needs without unduly disrupting the employer's operations, subject to the approval of the employee's health care provider.[201] This requirement differs from the requirement in 29 C.F.R. § 825.302(e) discussed in subsection (ii) above in two respects. First, the consultation duty imposed by § 825.302(e) is imposed on the employee. Here, the consultation duty is imposed on both the employee and the employer. Second, the consultation duty in § 825.302(e) is limited to medical treatment schedules. Section 825.302(f), in contrast, involves intermittent and reduced leave schedule leave, which could be for medical treatment or incapacity.

The DOL regulations do not impose a penalty for the failure of an employee to engage in the scheduling process. But again, courts have held that employees who fail to make reasonable attempts to schedule their leave so as not to unduly disrupt the employer's operations are not protected by the FMLA. A school employer's failure to engage in the consultation process would constitute unlawful interference with the employee's FMLA rights.

(iv) Paid Leave Substitution

An employee may elect, or an employer may require the employee, to substitute any accrued paid leave for unpaid FMLA leave.[202] Neither the statute nor the DOL regulations specify the manner in which an employee should communicate his or her election. Presumably, notice of an employee's election to substitute paid leave for unpaid FMLA leave may be provided verbally, consistent with the general employee notice requirements.

Substitution of paid leave is addressed more fully in Chapter 9, *Paid Leave Substitution.*

(v) Notice during and after FMLA Leave

Certain notice obligations are imposed on employees after leave has begun. In order to fall within the protections of the federal FMLA, an employee must timely notify the employer of the need for FMLA leave. As we have previously discussed, such notice is normally provided before FMLA leave begins. An employee may, however, provide notice of the need for FMLA-qualifying leave during the employee's absence or even after the employee has returned to work from an absence. For example, an employee takes 2 weeks of vacation to go skiing. At the end of the first week, the employee is injured. The injury constitutes a serious health condition. Under the DOL regulations, some or all of the leave may be FMLA-qualifying. Of course, to perfect his or her right to FMLA leave, the employee must provide timely and adequate notice of the need for FMLA leave. Generally, the need for this leave will not be foreseeable. Therefore, the employee is required to notify the employer as soon as practicable after learning of the need for leave.[203]

An employee may also retroactively notify an employer of the need for FMLA leave after the employee has returned to work. If leave is taken for an FMLA reason but the employer was not aware of the reason and the employee desires that the leave be counted as FMLA leave, the employee must notify the employer within two business days of returning to work of the reason for the leave.[204] The regulation is intended to cover those limited situations where an employee is absent for only a brief period of time before returning to work and the employee was unable, despite making reasonable efforts, to provide notice before or during FMLA leave.[205] The regulation is not a catchall that excuses employees who have otherwise failed to provide timely notice of the need for FMLA leave.

(vi) Maintenance of Benefits

The employer's obligation to maintain group health benefits during FMLA leave can change based on information provided by the employee. An employee on FMLA leave must inform the employer whether he or she wants to receive any changes in health benefits that may occur during the course of the leave.[206] An employee may also inform an employer that he or she has decided not to maintain group health coverage during FMLA leave.[207] Presumably, the employee must communicate this election to the employer. Finally, the employer's obligation to continue group health coverage ceases when the employee informs the employer of his or her intention to not return to work from FMLA leave.[208] Note that the rules do not provide time frames or penalties for an employee's failure to provide the required notices regarding maintenance of benefits during FMLA leave.

Maintenance of health benefits during FMLA leave is addressed in Chapter 10, *Maintenance of Employment Benefits*.

(vii) Return to Work from FMLA Leave

Employers may require employees to report periodically about their status and intent to return to work.[209] Where an employee gives unequivocal notice of intent not to return to work, the employer's obligations under the FMLA to maintain health benefits and to restore the employee cease.[210] An employee who fails to provide notice of his or her intent to return to work (when asked by the employer) is not entitled to the protections of the FMLA.[211]

Return to work issues are addressed more fully in Chapter 11, *Return to Work from Family and Medical Leave*.

(viii) School Employees

Special FMLA rules apply to employees of local educational agencies and private elementary and secondary schools.[212] Generally, these rules regulate an employee's return to work from FMLA leave at certain points of the academic year. The usual rules governing an employee's need to provide timely and adequate notice of the need for FMLA leave apply to employees of local educational agencies. In one instance, however, the penalty for an employee's failure to notify a school employer of the need for foreseeable FMLA leave is modified.

If an instructional employee needs intermittent leave or leave on a reduced leave schedule due to his or her own serious health condition or the serious health condition of a covered family member, such leave is foreseeable based on planned medical treatment, and the employee would be on leave for more than 20 percent of the total working days over the leave period, then the employee must provide notice of the need for the leave in accordance with 29 C.F.R. § 825.301.[213] If an instructional employee fails to give such notice, the school may require the employee to take "leave of a particular duration" or to transfer temporarily to a different position.[214] Alternatively, the school may require the employee to delay the taking of leave until the notice provision is met.[215]

"Leave of a particular duration" means a block or blocks of time beginning no earlier than the first day for which leave is needed and ending no later than the last day on which leave is needed and may include one uninterrupted period of leave.[216]

Return to work issues are addressed more fully in Chapter 11, *Return to Work from Family and Medical Leave*.

(ix) "Key Employees"

Employers may deny job restoration to highly compensated "key employees" at the conclusion of FMLA leave if the return of the employee would cause substantial and grievous economic injury to the operations of the employer.[217] While a key employee is on FMLA leave, his or her rights under the FMLA continue unless and until either the employee gives notice that he or she no longer wishes to return to work or the employer actually denies reinstatement at the conclusion of the leave period.[218]

6.04 NOTICE OBLIGATIONS UNDER STATE FAMILY AND MEDICAL LEAVE LAWS

Notice requirements under state family and medical leave laws vary greatly. Some states do not address employee or employer notice requirements at all. Others have detailed notice requirements. In some instances these state notice requirements are nearly identical to the requirements of the federal FMLA. In other instances, the state notice requirements are markedly different from those of the federal FMLA. For example, the Alaska Family Leave Act imposes notice requirements on employees but not on employers. Moreover, the notice requirements imposed on employees (e.g., that they provide prior notice of the expected need for leave in a manner that is reasonable and practicable where the need for leave is foreseeable) appears more generous than the comparable employee notice requirements under the federal FMLA.[219] Minnesota's Parental Leave Act imposes notice obligations on both employers and employees. Covered Minnesota employers must post a notice setting forth employee leave rights.[220] Minnesota law permits employers to adopt reasonable policies governing the timing requirements for employee notice of the need for leave.[221] Rhode Island law requires employers to post a notice of employee leave rights.[222] Employees must give at least 30 days' notice of the intended date that parental or family leave will commence and terminate unless prevented by medical emergency.[223]

There are a wealth of state laws requiring employers to provide leave to employees for pregnancy, maternity, adoption, and organ or bone marrow donation, to name just a few circumstances that could also be covered by the federal FMLA. School administrators must carefully review all applicable state and local laws to determine if the leave at issue is covered by state or local law as well as the federal

FMLA. If so, as discussed in section 6.05, school administrators will have to sort out how the state or local leave law interacts with the federal FMLA, in this case in terms of notice.

6.05 INTERACTION OF THE FEDERAL FMLA WITH STATE FAMILY AND MEDICAL LEAVE LAWS: NOTICE REQUIREMENTS

Leave may qualify for coverage under either the federal FMLA or state family and medical leave laws, or both. As addressed in earlier chapters, where an employer is covered by one law and not the other, the employer has to comply only with the law under which it is covered.[224] Similarly, an employee eligible under one law (e.g., state law) must receive benefits in accordance with that law only.[225] The same is true for covered conditions. If state law provides leave for a condition that is not covered by the federal FMLA, the employer must comply only with the state law and not the federal FMLA.[226] It gets interesting, however, where the leave at issue falls under the coverage of both applicable state law and the federal FMLA (i.e., the employer is considered a covered employer, the employee meets the eligibility requirements, and the leave is a covered condition under both a state family and medical leave law and the federal FMLA).

The federal FMLA does not supersede any provision of state or local law that provides greater family or medical leave rights than those provided by the federal FMLA.[227] Because of this statutory "nonpreemption" language, employers must determine which law applies (state or federal) in a particular situation on a provision-by-provision basis.[228] The DOL explained:

> Where the requisite coverage or applicability standards of both laws are met and the laws contain differing provisions, an analysis must be made of both laws, provision-by-provision, to determine which standard(s) from each law will apply to the particular situation. The standard providing the greater right or more generous benefit to the employee from each law (provision-by-provision) will apply.[229]

In terms of notice, the federal FMLA provides that an employer may not require compliance with stricter FMLA notice requirements where the provisions of state law allow less advance notice to the employer.[230] Where an employee's leave is covered by both the federal FMLA and a state family or medical leave law, school administrators must determine which law, the federal FMLA or state law, is more or less generous in terms of employee notice requirements. This may not be an easy task. For example, a shorter notice period under state law must be allowed by the employer unless an employer has already provided, or the employee is requesting, more leave than required under state law.[231]

> Where an employee's leave is covered by both the federal FMLA and a state family or medical leave law, school administrators will have to determine which law, the federal FMLA or the state law, is more or less generous in terms of employee notice requirements. This may not be an easy task, yet it must be done in order to be in compliance with the federal FMLA.

The DOL has also addressed how employers should handle situations in which state or local law is silent on a provision contained in the federal FMLA. In comments accompanying publication of the final DOL regulations implementing the federal FMLA, the DOL agreed with the following:

> The Equal Rights Advocates suggested additional examples where a State law is silent on an issue addressed by FMLA. If an employee is "eligible" under both FMLA and a State or local law, and the State or local law is silent on a provision contained in FMLA, and if the FMLA provision is restrictive (as to employee rights and benefits), then the State or local law would govern as to that provision. If the FMLA provision is not restrictive (or extends a right, benefit, or privilege to employees), then the FMLA would govern as to that provision. For example, a State law that grants employers the right to deny the taking of leave to high-level executives could not be applied to any FMLA-eligible employees, because FMLA extends to all eligible employees the entitlement to leave for qualifying reasons. If the same State law contained a provision mandating all employees who take leave be restored to employment when the leave ends, then FMLA's "key" employee exemption could not be applied to deny an employee reinstatement (i.e., the Federal law would not apply at the time of reinstatement).[232]

In terms of notice, if an applicable state law is silent regarding the time frame in which an employee must notify the employer to be entitled to leave, because the minimum time frames established in the federal FMLA restrict an employee's rights and benefits, that state law would govern employee notice.

NOTES

1. 29 U.S.C. § 2619(a).

2. *Tornberg v. Business Interlink Services, Inc.*, 237 F. Supp. 2d 778, 785 (E.D. Mich. 2002).

3. *Ragsdale v. Wolverine World Wide, Inc.*, 535 U.S. 81, 88 (2002); *Sarno v. Douglas Elliman-Gibbons & Ives, Inc.*, 183 F.3d 155, 161 (2d Cir. 1999).

4. 29 C.F.R. § 825.300.

5. 29 C.F.R. § 825.300(a).

6. *Id.*

7. *Id.*

8. Comments on Regulations Implementing the Family and Medical Leave Act of 1993 (§ 825.300), 60 Fed. Reg. 2180, 2219 (Jan. 6, 1995).

9. *Id.* (criticizing commercially available multipurpose posters as confusing to employees).

10. 29 C.F.R. § 825.300(a).

11. *Id.* (explaining that "employers *may* duplicate the text of the notice" prepared by the DOL (emphasis added)).

12. http://www.dol.gov/esa/regs/compliance/posters/fmla.htm.

13. 29 C.F.R. § 825.300(b).

14. *Id.*

15. See *Mullin v. Rochester Manpower, Inc.*, 204 F. Supp. 2d 556, 563 (W.D.N.Y. 2002); *Kidwell v. Board of County Commissioners*, 40 F. Supp. 2d 1201, 1224 (D. Kan. 1998), *aff'd*, 1999 U.S. App. LEXIS 15690 (10th Cir. 1999).

16. *Goodwin-Haulmark v. Menninger Clinic, Inc.*, 76 F. Supp. 2d 1235, 1242 (D. Kan. 1999).

17. 29 C.F.R. § 825.301(a)(1).

18. *Id.*

19. *Id.*

20. Comments on Regulations Implementing the Family and Medical Leave Act of 1993 (§ 825.301), 60 Fed. Reg. 2180, 2219 (Jan. 6, 1995).

21. *Fry v. First Fidelity Bancorp.*, No. 95-6019, 1996 U.S. Dist. LEXIS 875 (E.D. Pa. Jan. 31, 1996).

22. *Bond v. Abbott Laboratories*, No. 98-3923, 1999 U.S. App. LEXIS 22242 (6th Cir. Sept. 9, 1999).

23. *Id.* at *13–*14.

24. See also *Hunt v. Rapides Healthcare System, LLC*, 277 F.3d 757, 768 (5th Cir. 2001); *Dodgens v. Kent Manufacturing Co.*, 955 F. Supp. 560, 564–65 (D.S.C. 1997).

25. 29 C.F.R. § 825.301(a)(2).

26. *Id.*

27. 29 C.F.R. § 825.301(b)(1).

28. *Levine v. The Children's Museum of Indianapolis, Inc.*, No. 02-3013, 2003 U.S. App. LEXIS 5755 (7th Cir. Mar. 24, 2003).

29. 29 C.F.R. § 825.301(b)(1).

30. 29 C.F.R. § 825.301(b)(2).

31. *Id.*

32. Comments on Regulations Implementing the Family and Medical Leave Act of 1993 (§ 825.301), 60 Fed. Reg. 2180, 2220 (Jan. 6, 1995) (asserting that it would be inappropriate to use a generic notice, as much of the information may be employee specific, particularly the arrangements for payment of insurance co-payments).

33. 29 C.F.R. § 825.301(b)(1).

34. *Chan v. Loyola University Medical Center*, No. 97-C-3170, 1999 U.S. Dist. LEXIS 2790 (N.D. Ill. Mar. 3, 1999).

35. 29 C.F.R. § 825.301(e).

36. 29 C.F.R. § 825.301(c).

37. *Id.*

38. *Id.*

39. *Id.*

40. 29 C.F.R. § 825.301(c)(2)(i).

41. 29 C.F.R. § 825.301(c)(2)(ii).

42. *Id.*

43. *Id.*

44. *Id.*

45. 29 C.F.R. § 825.301(c)(2)(i).

46. *Id.*

47. 29 C.F.R. § 825.301(f).

48. *Bitney v. Fed Meyer Jewelers, Inc.*, No. 02-1226-JE, 2004 U.S. Dist. LEXIS 19283, at *24 (D. Or. Sept. 17, 2004).

49. See *Mora v. Chem-Tronics, Inc.*, 16 F. Supp. 2d 1192, 1226–27 (S.D. Cal. 1998).

50. *Conoshenti v. Public Service Electric & Gas Co.*, 364 F.3d 135, 142–45 (3d Cir. 2004).

51. *Felder v. Winn-Dixie Louisiana, Inc.*, No. 03-1438 Section "N," 2003 U.S. Dist. LEXIS 22535, at *5 (E.D. La. Dec. 16, 2003).

52. 29 C.F.R. § 825.110(d).

53. *Id.*

54. *Id.*

55. *Id.*

56. *Id.*

57. *Id.*

58. *Id.*

59. 29 C.F.R. § 825.208(a).

60. DOL WH FMLA Advisory Opinion No. 42, question 9 (Aug. 23, 2004).

61. DOL WH FMLA Advisory Opinion No. 83 (Aug. 7, 1996).

62. DOL WH FMLA Advisory Opinion No. 49 (Oct. 27, 1994).

63. *Williamson v. Mississippi Department of Human Services*, No. 3:96CV160-D-D, 1997 U.S. Dist. LEXIS 9968 (N.D. Miss. May 1, 1997).

64. See *Thornton v. BASF*, No. 99-2243, 2000 U.S. App. LEXIS 15909, at *5 (4th Cir. July 11, 2000).

65. 29 C.F.R. § 825.208(e)(2).

66. 29 C.F.R. § 825.208(a).

67. *Id.*

68. *Stoops v. One Call Communications, Inc.*, 141 F.3d 309, 312 (7th Cir. 1998).

69. 29 C.F.R. § 825.208(a).

70. 29 C.F.R. § 825.303(b).

71. *McCarron v. British Telecom*, No. 00-CV-6123, 2002 U.S. Dist. LEXIS 15151 (E.D. Pa. Aug. 7, 2002), *appeal dismissed*, 2003 U.S. App. LEXIS 16239 (3d Cir. 2003), *cert. denied*, 540 U.S. 1202 (2004).

72. Paid leave substitution is addressed in Chapter 9.

73. Comments on Regulations Implementing the Family and Medical Leave Act of 1993 (§ 825.208), 60 Fed. Reg. 2180, 2207 (Jan. 6, 1995).

74. *Id.*

75. 29 C.F.R. § 825.208(c).

76. 29 C.F.R. § 825.208(b)(1).

77. *Id.*

78. 29 C.F.R. § 825.208(c).

79. See *Katekovich v. Team Rent-A-Car of Pittsburgh, Inc.*, No. 00-2389, 2002 U.S. App. LEXIS 8853 (3d Cir. Apr. 19, 2002); *Sisturn v. Time-Warner Cable*, No. 02-CV-8023, 2004 U.S. Dist. LEXIS 16681 (E.D. Pa. Aug. 19, 2004); *Sims v. Schultz*, 305 F. Supp. 2d 838, 845 (N.D. Ill. 2004); *Donahoo v. Master Data Center*, 282 F. Supp. 2d 540, 554 (E.D. Mich. 2003).

80. 535 U.S. 81 (2002) (invalidating a similar penalty provision in § 825.700(a)).

81. See *Consoshenti v. Public Service Electric & Gas Co.*, 364 F.3d 135, 142 (3d Cir. 2004); *Smith v. Blue Dot Services Co.*, 283 F. Supp. 2d 1200, 1204 (D. Kan. 2003).

82. 29 C.F.R. § 825.208(d).

83. *Id.*

84. *Id.*

85. 29 C.F.R. § 825.208(b)(1).

86. 29 C.F.R. § 825.208(c).

87. 29 C.F.R. § 825.208(e).

88. *Id.*

89. 29 C.F.R. § 825.208(e)(1).

90. 29 C.F.R. § 825.208(e)(2).

91. *Id.*

92. *Id.*

93. *Id.*

94. 29 C.F.R. § 825.208(b)(2).

95. *Id.*

96. *Id.*

97. *Id.*

98. *Chan v. Loyola University Medical Center*, No. 97-C-3170, 1999 U.S. Dist. LEXIS 2790, at *31 (N.D. Ill. Mar. 3, 1999) (holding that pay stub that only showed that paid leave balances were decreasing during period at issue was insufficient, absent explicit notice, to demonstrate that leave had been designated as FMLA-qualifying).

99. *Chan*, 1999 U.S. Dist. LEXIS 2790.

100. 29 C.F.R. § 825.208(e)(2).

101. 29 C.F.R. § 825.208(a). How FMLA leave may be taken is addressed in Chapter 8, *Leave Amount and Scheduling*.

102. 29 C.F.R. § 825.208(a).

103. The four options for calculating the FMLA leave year are discussed more fully in Chapter 8, *Leave Amount and Scheduling*.

104. Comments on Regulations Implementing the Family and Medical Leave Act of 1993 (§ 825.200), 60 Fed. Reg. 2180, 2200 (Jan. 6, 1995).

105. See *Bachelder v. America West Airlines, Inc.*, 259 F.3d 1112, 1128 (9th Cir. 2001); *Dodaro v. Village of Glendale Heights*, No. 01-C-6396, 2003 U.S. Dist. LEXIS 5056, at *23–*24 (N.D. Ill. Mar. 31, 2003). But see *Phillips v. Leroy-Somer North America*, No. 01-1046-T, 2003 U.S. Dist. LEXIS 5349, at *14–*15 (W.D. Tenn. Mar. 28, 2003).

106. 29 C.F.R. § 825.200(e).

107. *Id.*

108. *Id.*

109. 29 C.F.R. § 825.200(d)(1).

110. *Id.*

111. *Id.*

112. 29 C.F.R. § 825.301(a).

113. 29 C.F.R. § 825.301(b).

114. 29 C.F.R. §§ 825.210(d), 825.301(b)(1)(iv).

115. 29 C.F.R. § 825.209(c)–(d).

116. 29 C.F.R. § 825.212(a).

117. 29 C.F.R. § 825.212(a)(1).

118. *Id.*

119. 29 U.S.C. § 2614(a)(1).

120. 29 C.F.R. § 825.219(a).

121. *Id.*

122. *Id.*

123. *Id.*

124. *Woodford v. Community Action of Greene County, Inc.*, 103 F. Supp. 2d 97, 100–101 (N.D.N.Y. 2000).

125. 29 C.F.R. § 825.219(a).

126. 29 C.F.R. § 825.219(b).

127. *Id.*

128. *Id.*

129. *Id.*

130. 29 C.F.R. § 825.219(d).

131. *Id.*

132. *Id.*

133. *Id.*

134. 29 U.S.C. § 2611(4). Joint employment is addressed more fully in Chapter 2, *Schools as FMLA-Covered Employers*.

135. 29 C.F.R. § 825.106.

136. 29 C.F.R. § 825.106(b).

137. 29 C.F.R. § 825.106(c).

138. *Id.*

139. FMLA recordkeeping is addressed more fully in Chapter 12, *Record-Keeping Requirements*.

140. 29 C.F.R. § 825.500(c)(4).

141. 29 U.S.C. § 2612(e); 29 C.F.R. §§ 825.302, 825.303.

142. 29 C.F.R. § 825.302(a).

143. *Id.*

144. 29 C.F.R. § 825.302(b).

145. *Id.*

146. 29 C.F.R. § 825.303(a).

147. *Id.*

148. 29 C.F.R. § 825.302(g).

149. 29 C.F.R. §§ 825.207(h), 825.302(g).

150. 29 C.F.R. § 825.302(g).

151. *Peeples v. Coastal Office Products, Inc.*, No. 02-1848, 2003 U.S. App. LEXIS 8644 (4th Cir. May 7, 2003); *Levine v. The Children's Museum of Indianapolis, Inc.*, No. 02-3013, 2003 U.S. App. LEXIS 5755, at *7 (7th Cir. Mar. 24, 2003).

152. 29 C.F.R. § 825.208(a); see also *Hoffman v. Professional Med Team*, 394 F.3d 414, 418 (6th Cir. 2005).

153. 29 C.F.R. § 825.208(a).

154. *Moorer v. Baptist Memorial Health Care System*, 398 F.3d 469, 488 (6th Cir. 2005); *Hoffman*, 394 F.3d at 418 (6th Cir. Jan. 7, 2005).

155. *Aubuchon v. Knauf Fiberglass, GMBH*, 359 F.3d 950, 951–52 (7th Cir. 2004).

156. *Wheeler v. Pioneer Development Services, Inc.*, 349 F. Supp. 2d 158, 166 (D. Mass. 2004).

157. *Cavin v. Honda of America Manufacturing, Inc.*, 346 F.3d 713, 720 (6th Cir. 2003).

158. *Brenneman v. MidCentral Health Systems*, 366 F.3d 412, 421 (6th Cir. 2004), *cert denied*, 125 S. Ct. 1300 (2005); *Bailey v. Southwest Gas Co.*, 275 F.3d 1181, 1185 (9th Cir. 2002).

159. *Cavin*, 346 F.3d at 720.

160. *Daoud v. Avamere Staffing & Home Care, LLC*, 336 F. Supp. 2d 1129, 1139 (D. Or. 2004).

161. *Byrne v. Avon Products, Inc.*, 328 F.3d 379, 381 (7th Cir. 2003) (holding that an employer's awareness of dramatic change in employee's behavior provided sufficient notice of an employee's need for FMLA leave), *cert. denied*, 540 U.S. 881 (2003).

162. *McNeela v. United Airlines, Inc.*, No. 98-C-1433, 1999 U.S. Dist. LEXIS 20042 (N.D. Ill. May 13, 1999).

163. *Artis v. Palos Community Hospital*, No. 02-C-8855, 2004 U.S. Dist. LEXIS 20150 (N.D. Ill. Sept. 23, 2004); *Mullin v. Rochester Manpower, Inc.*, 204 F. Supp. 2d 556, 562–63 (W.D.N.Y. 2002).

164. 29 C.F.R. § 825.302(c).

165. 29 C.F.R. § 825.302(f).

166. 29 C.F.R. § 825.208(a).

167. *Aubuchon v. Knauf Fiberglass, GMBH*, 359 F.3d 950, 951–52 (7th Cir. 2004).

168. *Brenneman v. MidCentral Health System*, 366 F.3d 412, 421 (6th Cir. 2004), *cert. denied*, 125 S. Ct. 1300 (2005) (finding employee call that "he was not doing well and wouldn't be in today" insufficient notice of a need for FMLA-qualifying leave); *Henegar v. DaimlerChrysler Corp.*, 280 F. Supp. 2d 680, 686 (E.D. Mich. 2003) (electing "ill" option on employer automated telephone attendance system insufficient notice of need for FMLA leave).

169. See *Price v. City of Fort Wayne, Indiana*, 117 F.3d 1022, 1025 (7th Cir. 1997) (finding insufficient "medical need" for leave); *Sims v. Alameda-Contra Costa Transit District*, 2 F. Supp. 2d 1253, 1267–68 (N.D. Cal. 1998) (finding employee request to be placed on "sick book" sufficient notice).

170. *Daoud v. Avamere Staffing & Home Care, LLC*, 336 F. Supp. 2d 1129, 1140 (D. Or. 2004).

171. *Niese v. General Electric Co.*, No. IP99-1457-C-T/G, 2001 U.S. Dist. LEXIS 5352 (S.D. Ind. Jan. 31, 2001).

172. *Gay v. Gilman Paper Co.*, 125 F.3d 1432, 1434 (11th Cir. 1997).

173. 29 C.F.R. § 825.312(g).

174. *Spangler v. Federal Home Loan Bank of Des Moines*, 278 F.3d 847, 852 (8th Cir. 2002).

175. *Brenneman v. MidCentral Health System*, 366 F.3d 412, 421 n.9 (6th Cir. 2004) (known diabetic employee call that he wasn't doing well and wouldn't be in found insufficient notice of need for FMLA leave where employee did not link present need with known diabetic condition), *cert denied*, 125 S. Ct. 1300 (2005).

176. *Rhoades v. FDIC*, 956 F. Supp. 1239 (D. Md. 1997), *aff'd in part, vacated and remanded in part on other grounds*, 257 F.3d 373 (4th Cir. 2001), *cert. denied*, 535 U.S. 933 (2002).

177. 29 C.F.R. § 825.302(a).

178. 29 C.F.R. § 825.302(a).

179. 29 C.F.R. § 825.302(b).

180. 29 C.F.R. §§ 825.208(a); 29 C.F.R. 825.302(b).

181. 29 C.F.R. § 825.302(b).

182. 29 C.F.R. § 825.302(d).

183. Comments on Regulations Implementing the Family and Medical Leave Act of 1993 (§ 825.303), 60 Fed. Reg. 2180, 2221 (Jan. 6, 1995).

184. *Id.*

185. Comments on Regulations Implementing the Family and Medical Leave Act of 1993 (§ 825.302), 60 Fed. Reg. 2180, 2220 (Jan. 6, 1995).

186. 29 C.F.R. § 825.302(g).
187. 29 C.F.R. § 825.208(a)(1)-(2).
188. 29 C.F.R. § 825.304(b).
189. 29 C.F.R. § 825.304(c).
190. *Id.*
191. *Id.*
192. 29 C.F.R. § 825.302(g).
193. 29 C.F.R. § 825.302(d).
194. *Id.*
195. *Aubuchon v. Knauf Fiberglass, GMBH*, 359 F.3d 950, 951–52 (7th Cir. 2004); *Russell v. First Health Services* No 01-1149, 2001 U.S. App. LEXIS 10774 (4th Cir. May 23, 2001).
196. 29 C.F.R. § 825.309(c).
197. *Id.*
198. 29 C.F.R. § 825.302(e).
199. *Id.*
200. *Id.*
201. 29 C.F.R. § 825.302(f).
202. 29 U.S.C. § 2612(d)(2)(A); 29 C.F.R. § 825.207(a).
203. 29 C.F.R. § 825.303(a).
204. 29 C.F.R. § 825.208(e).
205. 29 C.F.R. § 825.208(e)(1).
206. 29 C.F.R. § 825.209(c).
207. 29 C.F.R. § 825.209(e).
208. 29 C.F.R. §§ 825.209(f); 825.211(e)(3).
209. 29 C.F.R. §§ 825.309(a); 825.312(e); 825.209(f).
210. 29 C.F.R. §§ 825.312(e); 825.309(a).
211. *Peeples v. Coastal Office Products, Inc.*, No. 02-1848, 2003 U.S. App. LEXIS 8644 (4th Cir. May 7, 2003).
212. 29 U.S.C. § 2618; 29 C.F.R. § 825.500(a).
213. 29 C.F.R. § 825.601(b).
214. *Id.*
215. 29 C.F.R. § 825.601(a)(2).
216. *Id.*
217. 29 C.F.R. § 825.218(a).
218. 29 C.F.R. § 825.219(c).
219. Alaska Stat. § 39.20.510.
220. Minn. Stat § 181.9436.
221. Minn. Stat § 181.941(2).
222. R.I. Gen. Laws § 28-48-10(a).

223. R.I. Gen. Laws § 28-48-2(a).

224. 29 C.F.R. § 825.701(a).

225. *Id.*

226. 29 C.F.R. § 825.701(a)(5).

227. 29 U.S.C. § 2651(b); 29 C.F.R. § 825.701(1).

228. Comments on Regulations Implementing the Family and Medical Leave Act of 1993 (§ 825.701), 60 Fed. Reg. 2180, 2230 (Jan. 6, 1995).

229. *Id.*

230. 29 C.F.R. § 825.302(g).

231. 29 C.F.R. § 825.701(a)(3).

232. Comments on Regulations Implementing the Family and Medical Leave Act of 1993 (§ 825.701), 60 Fed. Reg. at 2230–31.

CHAPTER 7

Documentation Requirements

7.01 OVERVIEW

The federal FMLA permits employers to require employees to provide documentation in support of their request for FMLA-qualifying leave and confirming their ability to return from FMLA leave. Employees may be required to provide medical and nonmedical documentation to support their request for leave. Four forms of medical documentation may be required: certifications, recertifications, periodic status reports, and certifications of fitness to return to duty. The form, timing, and circumstances for requesting certification, the employee's duty to respond, the certification challenge process, and the consequences for an employee's failure to respond are governed by the DOL regulations.

Section 7.02 of this chapter addresses the rules governing medical certifications. Section 7.03 discusses the process for challenging a medical certification. Section 7.04 addresses an employee's failure to satisfy the medical certification process. Section 7.05 addresses the recertification of an established FMLA-qualifying serious health condition. Section 7.06 discusses periodic status reports. Section 7.07 addresses medical documentation requirements regarding an employee's fitness to return to duty from FMLA leave. Section 7.08 discusses documentation requirements to confirm the familial relationship of the claimed covered family member to the employee requesting FMLA leave. Section 7.09 addresses the documentation requirements of state family and medical leave laws. Finally, section 7.10 covers the interaction of the documentation requirements of the federal FMLA with state family and medical leave laws.

7.02 MEDICAL CERTIFICATION

[1] Introduction

Employers *may* require an employee to support his or her request for FMLA-qualifying leave with a medical certification from a health care provider for the employee's own serious health condition or the serious health condition of a covered spouse, son, daughter, or parent.[1] Congress described the purpose for permitting employers to require medical documentation as a "check against employee abuse of leave."[2] Requiring medical certification is permissible, not mandatory. Employers are not required to ask employees for medical certification to support a request for FMLA leave.[3] Absent a request, employees are not required to provide medical certification to support their FMLA leave request.[4] Indeed, the FMLA suggests that employers are expected to obtain the necessary information through informal means, such as asking the employee questions when the employee gives notice of the need for leave.[5] The federal FMLA does not authorize an employer to require an employee to provide medical certification to support a request for FMLA leave where the leave is not due to a serious health condition (e.g., for birth, adoption, or foster care placement).

The medical certification must be from the "health care provider" of the employee or of the employee's son, daughter, spouse, or parent, as the case may be.[6] Chapter 5, *Covered Conditions*, addresses which health care providers fall within the provisions of the federal FMLA.[7] For the most part, health care providers must be licensed to practice by the state and must be performing within the scope of their practice.[8] To be authorized to practice in the state, a health care provider must be authorized to diagnose and treat physical or mental conditions without supervision by a doctor or other health care provider.[9] Affidavits or notes from the employee, or from the employee's spouse, parent, or friends are not from a health care provider and, therefore, are not effective.[10]

An employer may not rely on the medical opinion of its own physician in lieu of the certification provided by the health care provider initially selected by the employee.[11] Similarly, an employer may not insist that an employee provide certification from the employee's primary care physician.[12] The federal FMLA does not require that the employee provide medical certification from a specialist. All that is required is that the medical certification be from a health care provider as defined by the federal FMLA. Employers violate the FMLA if they reject certification from a covered health care provider and demand that the employee seek certification from a specialist.[13] Certifications need not be submitted from the same health care provider.[14]

[2] Notice of Certification Requirement

As addressed in Chapter 6, *Notice Requirements*, employers must notify employees in writing that medical certification is going to be required. Specifically, employers must give written notice of the requirement for medical certification each time the employer requires certification.[15] The written notice must detail the specific expectations and obligations of the employee and explain the consequences if an employee fails to satisfy those requirements.[16] An employer that fails to provide notice of the requirement that an employee provide medical certification in accordance with the DOL regulations is precluded from taking action against the employee for failure to timely provide medical certification.[17]

[3] Time Limits for an Employer to Request Medical Certification

There are four points in time when an employer may request that an employee support the need for FMLA leave with medical documentation. In most cases, an employer should request that an employee furnish medical certification at the time the employee gives notice of the need for FMLA leave, or within two business days thereafter.[18] Where the need for leave is unforeseen, an employer should request that the employee furnish medical certification within two business days after FMLA leave has commenced.[19] An employer may also request medical certification at some later date if the employer has reason to question the appropriateness of the leave or its duration.[20] An employer that fails to timely request medical certification may have interfered with the employee's FMLA rights.[21] Such untimely request by an employer may excuse an employee's failure to provide medical certification.

[4] Time Limits for an Employee to Provide Certification

The time limits for an employee to provide medical certification depend on whether the need for leave was foreseeable. Where the need for leave is foreseeable and at least 30 days' notice has been provided, the employee should provide medical certification before the leave begins.[22] When this is not possible, the employee must provide the requested certification to the employer within the time frame requested by the employer (which must allow at least 15 calendar days after the employer's request) unless it is not practicable to do so under the particular circumstances and despite the employee's diligent, good faith efforts.[23] An employer may, of course, provide a more generous deadline or dispense with the certification requirement in its entirety.[24]

Note that where the need for leave is foreseeable and 30 days' advance notice has been given, it must be *impossible* for the employee to provide medical certification before leave commences in order for the employee to be entitled to provide the certification after leave has commenced. "Impossibility" is a very difficult standard to overcome. Of course, schools may excuse an employee's failure to provide certification before leave commences. They are not, however, required to do so.

Courts have addressed the circumstances under which it was "not practicable to do so under the particular circumstances and despite the employee's diligent, good faith efforts" to meet the 15-day deadline. For one court, "good faith" required the employee to at least "contact his employer by telephone and make [the employer] aware that he [was] unable to return his certification before the deadline."[25] Courts have split on whether a doctor's failure to timely return the medical certification forms made it "impracticable" for the employee to timely provide medical certification.[26] Courts have found that the physical inability of the employee rendered it "impracticable" for the employee to timely provide a medical certification to the employer.[27] An employer that afforded an employee more than one opportunity to provide a medical certification was not required to apply the 15-day rule to the subsequent attempts.[28]

Employers that fail to give the employee the required period of time to provide medical certification violate the FMLA.[29] On the other hand, employers do not have to wait the full 15 days for a medical certification to deny FMLA leave if the employee provides medical certification sooner and the certification does not support the employee's request for FMLA leave.[30]

[5] Effect of Employer Policies on Certification Procedural Requirements

If the employer's sick or medical leave plan imposes medical certification requirements that are less stringent than the certification requirements of the DOL regulations and the employee or employer elects to substitute paid sick, vacation, personal, or family leave for unpaid FMLA leave where authorized, only the employer's less stringent sick leave certification requirements may be imposed.[31] An employee who complies with the employer's less stringent requirements may not have leave for an FMLA-covered purpose delayed or denied on the grounds that the employee has not complied with the stricter certification requirements of the FMLA.[32] School employers should take care in crafting more generous policies to ensure that they are, in fact, more generous. For example, a school policy that permits employees 20 days to provide medical certification, without more, may actually be more restrictive than the FMLA. The FMLA, remember, includes an exception to the 15-day rule where it is not practicable under the circumstances for the employee to provide the certification. A 20-day rule without such an exception may be more restrictive under certain circumstances than the FMLA.

Note that the regulations do not prohibit an employer from having more stringent paid leave policies than those required by the FMLA. The regulations simply provide that if the employee substitutes paid leave for unpaid FMLA leave, the employer must apply the less stringent certification policy, whether that is the employer's policy or the FMLA. If the employer's paid leave certification requirements are more stringent than those of the FMLA, an employee who does not satisfy the paid leave certification requirements but does satisfy the FMLA certification requirements is entitled to unpaid FMLA leave.

FMLA rights may not be diminished by any collective bargaining agreements or any employment benefit programs or plans.[33] Where an employer's internal policies conflict with the FMLA, an employee will gain the protections of the FMLA if he or she meets the requirements of the Act. For example, where the terms of a collective bargaining agreement require employees to provide a doctor's note for absences exceeding 5 consecutive days in order to return to work, if the absence is covered by the FMLA, the employee generally will have 15 or more days to provide the certification.[34] The employer's less generous leave provisions are effectively supplanted by the FMLA.

[6] Form of Medical Certification

The FMLA does not mandate that medical certification be provided in any particular written form.[35] The permissible scope of information that an employer may require an employee to provide as medical certification, however, is strictly prescribed.[36] No additional information may be required.[37] The medical information collected in the certification must relate only to the serious health condition for which the current need for leave exists.[38]

The DOL has created an optional preapproved form for use by employers to obtain medical certification.[39] A copy of the form, WH-380, is included in Appendix D. Absent a compelling reason not to, schools should use this preapproved medical certification form to ensure compliance with the FMLA.

> Absent a compelling reason not to, schools should use the preapproved DOL WH-380 medical certification form to ensure compliance with the FMLA.

Three categories of information may be obtained as part of the employee's FMLA medical certification: (1) basic identifying information, (2) information where the employee's need for FMLA leave is due to his or her own serious health condition, and (3) information where the employee is needed to care for a covered family member with a serious health condition. These categories are addressed below.

(i) Basic Identifying Information

Basic identifying information addresses the identity of the health care provider and the serious health condition. The information includes

- the identity of the health care provider and the type of medical practice (including specialization, if any);
- certification as to which part of the definition of a "serious health condition," if any, applies to the patient's condition and the medical facts that support the certification, including a brief statement as to how the medical facts meet the criteria of the definition;
- the approximate date the serious health condition commenced and its probable duration, including the probable duration of the patient's present incapacity;
- whether it will be necessary for the employee to take leave intermittently or to work on a reduced leave schedule basis as a result of the serious health condition and if so, the probable duration of such schedule;
- if the serious health condition is pregnancy or a chronic condition, whether the patient is presently incapacitated and the likely duration and frequency of episodes of incapacity;
- if additional treatments will be required for the condition, an estimate of the probable number of such treatments; and
- if a regimen of continuing treatment by the patient is required under the supervision of the health care provider, a general description of the regimen.[40]

(ii) Employee's Own Serious Health Condition

In addition to requiring basic identifying information, where the need for FMLA leave is due to the employee's own serious health condition, an employer may require an employee to provide additional information in the medical certification, including

- whether the employee is unable to perform work of any kind;
- whether the employee is unable to perform any one or more of the essential functions of the employee's position, including a statement of the essential functions the employee is unable to perform, based on either information provided in a statement from the employer of the essential functions of the position or if such a statement is not provided, discussion with the employee about the employee's job functions; and
- whether the employee must be absent from work for treatment.[41]

Note that an employer may provide the certifying health care provider with a statement identifying the essential functions of the employee's job in order for the health care provider to assess whether the employee is unable to perform any one or more of his or her essential job functions. School employers should always prepare and provide such a statement for the health care provider's use to ensure that the health care provider is accurately assessing the employee's abilities in light of his or her condition.

The DOL has also opined that employers may include a record of an employee's absences along with the medical certification form (or recertification form) for the health care provider's consideration in determining the employee's likely period of future absences.[42] The disclosure of such information may be governed by the Health Insurance Portability and Accountability Act (HIPPA).[43] Schools should consult with counsel before releasing any employee medical information. The interaction of the FMLA and the HIPPA is addressed later in this chapter. To the extent that schools may permissibly provide a health care provider evidence of the employee's attendance, it is recommended that they do so.

(iii) Serious Health Condition of a Covered Family Member

Where the need for leave is due to the serious health condition of a covered family member, employers may require, in addition to the basic identifying information, that the employee's certification address

- whether the patient requires assistance for basic medical or personal needs, for safety, or for transportation;
- whether the employee's presence to provide psychological comfort would be beneficial to the patient or assist in the patient's recovery; and
- if the employee's family member will need care only intermittently or on a reduced leave schedule basis, the probable duration of the need.[44]

The employee is also required to indicate on the certification the type of care that he or she will provide and an estimate of the time period for providing such care.[45]

(iv) Effect of Employer Leave Policies on Certification Content

The amount of information that an employer may require an employee to provide in a certification may be diminished by school leave policies. The FMLA permits employers to adopt employment benefit programs or plans that provide greater FMLA rights to employees than the rights established by the FMLA.[46] A school employer, therefore, could agree in a collective bargaining agreement or as a matter of policy to accept less information in a medical certification than what is permitted by the FMLA. This situation often arises where paid leave is substituted for unpaid FMLA leave. If the school's sick or medical leave plan requires less information to be furnished in medical certifications than what is permitted by the FMLA and the employee or employer elects to substitute paid sick, vacation, personal, or family leave for unpaid FMLA leave where authorized, only the school's lesser sick leave certification requirements may be imposed.[47] To the extent the school's sick or medical leave plan requires more information, however, a school could not require an employee to provide more information in a medical certification than is permitted by the FMLA if the need for leave is FMLA-qualifying.

Because of the importance of obtaining as much medical information as possible when considering an employee's request for FMLA leave, school employers should review their paid and unpaid leave policies to ensure that they have not inadvertently relieved employees of the obligation to provide all permissible medical certification information.

> School employers should review their paid and unpaid leave policies to ensure that they have not inadvertently relieved employees of the obligation to provide all permissible medical certification information.

[7] Common Certification Problems

Problems with FMLA medical certification forms are common, time consuming, and frustrating for employers, employees, and health care providers. A common problem is incomplete, terse, or vague certifications. To ensure that they are making correct FMLA determinations, employers want all of the medical information to which they are entitled. Health care providers, on the other hand, frequently view the forms as a bother. Many times health care providers are not compensated for filling out the FMLA medical certification forms. As a result, the certification forms are frequently given short shrift by health care providers. When a school returns the form to an employee because it is incomplete, that employee begins to feel that the school is simply hassling him or her.

What follows is a discussion of several of the most common medical certification problems and what school administrators may do to preempt or redress such problems.

(i) Medical Facts

One of the most common certification problems is the failure of health care providers to provide a meaningful description of how the facts of the employee's or covered family member's medical condition fit within the requirements of the claimed serious health condition. On the DOL WH-380 certification form, this information is requested in question 4. More often than not, the information either is not provided at all or is a terse restatement of the cited serious health condition definition without any medical facts or a description of how those facts meet the serious health condition definition. Courts that have addressed this issue have found such perfunctory, nondescriptive statements of fact to be insufficient.

For example, in one case involving a claim of incapacity of more than three consecutive days plus health care provider treatments, the court found insufficient the health care provider's factual statement that the patient "required counseling for adjustment reaction to childhood." The court noted that the statement failed to identify a period of incapacity.[48] Similarly, in another case, the court found the health care provider's statement "Patient phoned the office on 9/5/02 with complaints of emotional state & depression. Wants to take 12 weeks FMLA" insufficient because it failed to provide any medical facts and did not describe how those facts satisfied the claimed serious health condition.[49]

Unfortunately, the DOL WH-380 certification form contributes to the problem by providing an inadequate amount of space for the health care provider to respond to question 4, among other questions. The resolution of this problem would appear to be communication to the health care provider of the employer's reasonable expectations regarding the amount and specificity of information needed to satisfy this requirement and that this might require more information than can fit in the space provided on the form. The DOL regulations, however, generally frown on an employer's making direct contact with the health care provider absent the prior voluntary approval by the employee.[50] Arguably, the prohibition on direct contact applies after the employer receives the certification, not beforehand. At least one court has found that an employer did not violate the FMLA by providing the certification form directly to the health care provider rather than through the employee.[51]

The safer practice is for school employers to instruct the employee to relay to the health care provider that detailed, responsive factual information is required to fully answer question 4 and that the form will be returned if answers are incomplete.

(ii) Estimates of Probable Number of Absences and Leave Duration

Employers are entitled to receive estimates of the probable number and intervals of absences, actual or estimated treatment dates, and estimates of the probable duration of incapacity.[52] The conflict here is between the employer's need for as accurate information as possible in order to be able to plan ahead to get the work done and the reality that some medical conditions are not predictable with a high degree of certainty. The issue often arises where the health care provider gives the employee a blank check for absences—for example, the health care provider states "indeterminate" or "0–30 days a month for the foreseeable future." Of course, in some situations such an assessment may be medically accurate. In many situations, however, such an assessment is not medically accurate but designed to relieve the health care provider of a paperwork burden.

Schools faced with a blank-check certification should consider treating the certification as incomplete. As discussed later in this chapter, the school should return the certification to the employee and identify it as incomplete because it does not set forth a reasonable estimate of the probable number, frequency, and duration of FMLA absences. The employee should be told to tell the health care provider that estimates can frequently be made based on the history of the patient or the experience of the health care provider with other patients. Many health care providers, if pressed, will provide such estimates. Many won't. I wouldn't recommend going back more than once on this issue. If a health care provider refuses to provide more specific estimates, it is time for the school to decide whether to challenge the validity of the certification. The challenge process is addressed more fully later in this chapter.

(iii) Essential Job Functions

Health care providers often fail to identify the essential job functions that an employee is unable to perform. The issue is addressed in question 7b of the DOL WH-380 certification form. Frequently, the reason the health care provider fails to provide this information is because the employer fails to provide the health care provider with the essential job functions of the employee's job. As discussed previously, employers have the right to provide the health care provider with documentation establishing the essential functions of the employee's job.[53] School employers should exercise this right every time certification is requested due to an employee's own serious health condition. If the school does not provide this information, it is at the mercy of the employee's explanation to the health care provider of what the essential job functions are and why the employee cannot perform one or more of them. Given that the employee is asking for leave, it should come as no surprise to school employers that the health care provider finds that the employee is unable to perform essential job functions as described by the employee.

(iv) Basis for Employee's Care for Covered Family Member

Employees frequently fail to state the type of care that they will provide to covered family members with serious health conditions. They also frequently fail to provide an estimate of the time period during which care will be provided and a schedule if leave is to be taken intermittently or on a reduced leave schedule basis. The issue is addressed on the bottom of the third page of the DOL WH-380 form. If any information is provided at all, it is erroneously provided by the health care provider not the employee. School employers can insist that the employee provide responsive information addressing what he or she will be doing for the covered family member during leave. Here again, the small space provided to answer this question on the form encourages insufficient answers. Knowing that this is a problem area, a school employer should advise employees that it expects a reasonably specific explanation responsive to the question.

[8] Clarification of Complete Certifications

Employers have limited rights to question the adequacy of an otherwise complete medical certification short of the challenge process. If an employee submits a complete certification signed by the health care provider, employers may not request additional information from the employee's health care provider.[54] A health care provider representing the employer may contact the employee's health care provider, with the employee's permission, for purposes of clarification and confirmation of the authenticity of the medical certification.[55]

The DOL regulations do not define or otherwise explain what "clarification" means. Presumably, it means that an employer may clarify information in the certification that the employer is entitled to receive. "Additional information" would appear to refer to information beyond what is permitted by the FMLA.

Note that employers are prohibited from confirming the authenticity of the medical certification provided by the employee without the employee's permission. If an employer suspects that the employee provided a fraudulent or altered certification, the employer must first seek the permission of the employee before the employer's health care provider can contact the patient's health care provider to confirm the authenticity of the employee's certification. The employee has the right to deny the employer such permission. In the event the employee denies the employer permission to contact the patient's health care provider, the employer, according to the DOL, should invoke the certification challenge process.[56] The challenge process is at the expense of the employer. A second or third medical opinion can cost the employer thousands of dollars. The irony here is that the DOL regulations provide that an employee who fraudulently obtains FMLA leave is not protected by the FMLA,[57] but the DOL regulations certainly don't make it easy for an employer to prove fraud.

The DOL regulations create a workers' compensation exception to the rule prohibiting employers from seeking clarification from the employee's health care provider without first obtaining the permission of the employee. The exception applies where the employee's FMLA leave is concurrent with workers' compensation leave, a fairly common occurrence. Where the provisions of the applicable workers' compensation statute permit an employer or the employer's representative to have direct contact with the employee's health care provider, the employer may follow the workers' compensation provisions.[58] Generally, state workers' compensation laws do not require an employer to obtain the consent of the employee before the employer is permitted to directly contact the employee's health care provider. Schools should confirm that applicable workers' compensation laws do in fact permit direct health care provider contact before attempting to make such contact.

[9] Incomplete Certifications

Employers have two options when presented with an incomplete certification. The first option is for the employer to waive any deficiency and accept the certification. Since requiring a medical certification is optional, an employer can accept an otherwise deficient medial certification. By doing so, the employer is providing greater family or medical leave benefits than the minimum required by the FMLA, which is permissible.[59] The second option available to an employer arises where the employer is unwilling to accept an incomplete certification. The DOL regulations provide: "The employer shall advise an employee whenever the employee finds a certification incomplete, and provide the employee a reasonable opportunity to cure any such deficiency."[60] In explaining the rationale for the rule, one court opined that "in the real world, it is not to be supposed that doctors will always answer in full compliance with the statute on the first inquiry; as such, the statute and the regulations contemplate follow-up requests by the employer for more information until a 'complete certification' has been supplied."[61] The duty imposed on an employer to inform the employee of any deficiency and permit a reasonable opportunity to cure it is affirmative rather than permissive.[62] Once an employee submits a complete certification, the employee is entitled to the benefits and protections of the FMLA unless and until there is contrary medical evidence.[63] Termination is not an appropriate initial response for an incomplete certification.[64]

The DOL regulations do not define when a certification is "incomplete." One court has equated "incomplete" with "inadequate."[65] This has resulted in some interesting case law. There is no controversy that a certification is incomplete if it is physically missing required information.[66] If, however, the information is not relevant to the leave request at issue, the absence of the information from the certification does not make the certification incomplete.[67]

Courts are split on whether a certification that is physically complete may nevertheless be considered "incomplete" because it does not support the employee's request for FMLA leave. A number of courts have held that an employer may rely on a complete certification that fails to support the employee's FMLA leave request. These employers, the courts found, were not required to inform the employee that the certification did not support the employee's leave request or provide the employee a reasonable opportunity to cure any deficiency because they were not incomplete.[68] Other courts have held that physically complete certifications are "incomplete" where they fail to support the employee's request for FMLA leave. As such, these courts have found employers to have violated the federal FMLA where they did not inform the employee that the certification did not support the request for FMLA leave and provide the employee with a reasonable opportunity to cure such deficiency.[69]

Courts have rejected arguments that an employee's total failure to provide a medical certification rendered the certification "incomplete" thereby implicating an employer's duty to both inform the employee of the deficiency and permit the employee a reasonable opportunity to cure the deficiency.[70] That is, "incomplete" is not synonymous with "nonexistent."[71] For example, an employee asks her doctor to fill out the medical certification form and send it in to her employer to support her request for FMLA leave. The doctor says she will but unbeknownst to the employee, never does. The employer denies the employee's request for FMLA leave for failure to provide medical certification. The employee argues that the employer should have told her that it never received the medical certification from her doctor. The employee cites the DOL regulation that an employer must inform an employee when her medical certification is incomplete and argues that the provision applies where the doctor failed to submit medical certification supporting her request for FMLA leave. Most courts do not accept this argument.

A few courts have addressed the adequacy of an employer's notice to the employee that the certification was incomplete. One court found that the employer's notice must "clearly apprise the [employee] of the information necessary to meet the certification requirement." The court found the employer's notice defective because it failed to accurately inform the employee of the time period for providing medical certification. Because of that deficiency, the court found that the employee did not lose FMLA protections.[72] School employers should be as specific as possible when notifying employees in writing how the certification is deficient.[73]

The DOL regulations also fail to provide guidance on what might constitute a reasonable opportunity to cure an incomplete certification. Courts have held that what constitutes a reasonable opportunity is determined on a case-by-case basis.[74] Arguably, that might require employers to permit employees more than one opportunity to attempt to cure an incomplete certification. Schools should avoid setting a standard period of time to cure a certification deficiency that applies to all employees regardless of the circumstances. Such a requirement would likely be found to violate the FMLA. An employer's obligation to afford an employee a reasonable opportunity to cure an incomplete certification ceases when the employer informs the employee of the deficiency and the employee refuses to provide the missing information.[75]

7.03 CHALLENGING THE EMPLOYEE'S MEDICAL CERTIFICATION: THE CERTIFICATION REVIEW PROCESS

[1] Introduction

If an employee provides a complete certification from a health care provider, the employer has three choices: (1) accept the certification as is, (2) challenge the validity of the certification through the certification review process, or (3) deny FMLA leave based on the initial certification. This section focuses on the second and third options.

The FMLA sets up an appellate process whereby an employer may require the employee or covered family member with the serious health condition to submit to a second certification by a health care provider selected by the employer. If the second health care provider certification differs from the first certification, the FMLA affords the parties the opportunity to obtain a third health care provider certification. This certification is the tiebreaker and is final and binding on all parties.

[2] Second Health Care Provider Opinion

An employer who has reason to doubt the validity of a medical certification may require the employee to obtain a second medical opinion.[76] The employer may designate the health care provider to furnish the second opinion, but the selected health care provider may not be employed on a regular basis by the employer (except as provided in the next sentence).[77] An employer may designate a health care provider that it employs on a regular basis only if the employer is located in an area where access to health care is extremely limited (e.g., rural areas where no more than one or two doctors practice in the relevant specialty in the vicinity).[78] Employers may require an employee or covered family member who is receiving treatment from a registered Christian Science practitioner to submit to an examination (but not treatment) by a second or third health care provider other than a Christian Science practitioner, except as otherwise provided under applicable state or local law or a collective bargaining agreement.[79]

A limitation on an employer's right to designate the second health care provider exists where the employee or covered family member is out of the country. If the employee or a family member is visiting another country, or a family member resides in another country, and a serious health condition develops, the employer must accept a medical certification as well as second and third opinions from a health care provider who practices in that country.[80] The employer may still select the second health care provider, but the selection is limited to health care providers in the country where the employee or covered family member is located.

The ability to select the second health care provider is of great advantage to school employers. It allows school employers to have the employee or covered family member assessed by a specialist in the area of the claimed serious health condition. School employers should seriously consider requiring the employee or family member to submit to an examination by a second health care provider where the original certification is from a generalist or other health care provider who is operating on the outer fringes of his or her area of practice. For example, a psychiatric diagnosis from a general family medicine practitioner should raise a red flag for the need for a second opinion by a psychiatrist.

> Schools must have a valid reason for questioning the validity of the initial certification provided by the employee before demanding that the employee or family member submit to an examination by a second health care provider.

What circumstances would give rise to an employer's "reason to doubt the validity" of the initial certification is not addressed by the DOL regulations.[81] What is clear is that an employer does not have an automatic right to require the employee or family member to submit to an examination by a second health care provider.[82] Rather, an employer needs a specific reason to doubt the validity of the employee's certification in order to demand a second examination.[83] That reason must have motivated the employer at the time it required the second opinion, not years later at the onset of litigation.[84] According to one court, the second opinion process "does not contemplate an adversarial investigation into a patient's symptoms and complaints."[85] The court continued:

> At times, the [employer] writes as if it needs sufficient information to independently assess [the employee's] condition or to evaluate Dr. Smith's diagnosis. However, an employer is not entitled to require information beyond that alleged by 29 U.S.C. § 2613, in order to make its own assessment. See 29 C.F.R. § 825.306(b) ("[n]o additional information may be required"). Moreover, the limited information that the FMLA permits an employer to demand shows that the statute does not authorize an em-

> ployer to make an independent assessment of the employee's medical condition. Instead, the employer should determine whether the provided information demonstrates that the diagnosed condition is a serious health condition within the meaning of the FMLA.[86]

In rejecting the employer's argument that it had the right to send the employee for a second health care provider opinion, the court in *Albert v. Runyon* noted that the employer had failed to identify any deficiency with the certification provided by the employee. It also rejected the employer's allegation that it questioned the objectivity of the employee's health care provider, noting that there was no evidence that this rationale was the motivation for the employer's demand that the employee submit to a second opinion. Absent evidence that the health care provider did not follow generally accepted treating practices, the *Albert* court rejected the employer's vague "objectivity" claim as insufficient evidence of "a reason to doubt the validity" of the original certification.[87]

The disparity between medical opinions rendered by an employee's two physicians has been cited as grounds for an employer to doubt the validity of the certification offered by the employee.[88] In another case, a physician's failure to investigate the underlying facts of an employee's claimed serious health condition by contacting the employee's supervisor did not justify the employer's rejection of the initial medical certification.[89]

Employers are responsible for the cost of the second opinion.[90] The employer must also reimburse the employee or covered family member for any reasonable out-of-pocket expenses incurred to obtain the second opinion.[91] An employer may not require the employee or family member to travel more than a normal commuting distance for purposes of obtaining the second medical opinion except in very unusual circumstances.[92] Unfortunately, the regulations do not illustrate what the DOL considers to be "normal commuting distance" or "very unusual circumstances." Schools should proceed with caution. A practical rule of thumb may be that absent very unusual circumstances, schools should select a second health care opinion provider approximately the same distance from the employee's home as the employee commutes to work. The mileage distance from the employee's home to work can be easily ascertained on Internet websites that calculate driving distances, such as MapQuest or Yahoo! Maps.

The FMLA does not require that an employee be paid for the time spent acquiring the second opinion. The DOL explained: "The Department [of Labor] has . . . concluded that Congress did not intend that employees on unpaid FMLA leave be paid for the time spent obtaining second and third opinions."[93] A school employer may, however, have a more generous leave policy that pays the employee wages for the time they spend obtaining second and third opinions. School employers should closely scrutinize their existing paid leave policies and collective bargaining agreements to determine whether they are required to pay an employee wages for the time they spend obtaining second or third health care provider opinions. Other than paying expenses, employers are not required to pay wages to covered family members for the time they spend obtaining second or third opinions. The fact that obtaining a second or third opinion may be onerous or unduly burdensome is not a recognized excuse for failure to obtain the certification.[94]

The DOL regulations do not address the timing of the second opinion or the method of notice an employer must use to start the second-opinion process. One court has applied a reasonable notice and timing standard.[95] In that case, the court found that the employer's notice that the second opinion would take place in eight days was reasonable. The court rejected the employee's argument that he did not receive timely notice of the need to submit to an examination by a second health care provider because he was in Mexico. The employer had sent notice by letter to the employee's address in Indiana. Because the governing collective bargaining agreement required that all notices be served at the employee's home address, the court found the employer's method of notice reasonable. The court noted that it was incumbent on the employee to either notify the employer of a new mailing address or arrange to have his mail opened while he was away.

> Schools should consider adopting a policy that specifies the manner of notice to employees, such as at the employee's address of record. The policy would also place the burden on employees to timely notify identified school administrators of changes to that address.

Pending receipt of the second opinion, the employee is provisionally entitled to the benefits of the Act, including maintenance of group health benefits.[96] If the second or third health care provider certifications do not ultimately establish the employee's entitlement to FMLA leave, the leave "shall not be designated as FMLA leave and may be treated as paid or unpaid leave under the employer's established leave policies."[97] If the leave is not covered by the FMLA, employers may use the leave as a basis for discipline, subject of course to the employer's usual leave and discipline policies. Employers are required, upon request, to provide the employee with a copy of the second certification.[98] The employer must provide the requested copies within two business days unless extenuating circumstances prevent such action.[99] Ironically, the FMLA does not require an employer to provide the employee with a copy of the original certification.[100] Here again, school leave policies, state law, or the terms of a collective bargaining agreement may permit the employee to access and copy his or her medical files.

[3] Third Health Care Provider Opinion

The certification challenge process provides a tiebreaker where the medical opinions of the employee's and employer's health care providers differ. If the opinion of the second health care provider differs from the initial certification provided by the employee, the employer *may* require the employee to obtain certification from a third health care provider.[101] Unless an employer's policy or state law permits otherwise, the federal FMLA does not permit an employee to request a third opinion if the employer does not. The selection process for the third health care provider differs from that for the second health care provider.

The third health care provider must be designated or approved jointly by the employer and the employee.[102] The employer and the employee must each act in good faith to attempt to reach agreement on the selection of the third health care provider.[103] If the employer does not attempt in good faith to reach agreement, the employer will be bound by the first certification.[104] If the employee does not attempt in good faith to reach agreement, the employee will be bound by the second certification.[105] For example, an employee who refuses to agree to see a doctor in the specialty in question may be failing to act in good faith. On the other hand, an employer that refuses to agree to any doctor on a list of specialists in the appropriate field provided by the employee and with whom the employee has not previously consulted may be failing to act in good faith.[106] Note the absence of any limitation that the employer not regularly employ the third health care provider. While it is doubtful that an employee would agree to use such a health care provider, it is not prohibited.

An employer's ability to negotiate a third health care provider is somewhat circumscribed where the employee or family member is out of the country. As with second opinions, where the employee or a family member is visiting another country, or a family member resides in another country, and a serious health condition develops, the employer must accept a medical certification as well as second and third opinions from a health care provider who practices in that country.[107]

The employer bears the expense of the third health care provider.[108] Employers must also reimburse an employee or family member for any reasonable out-of-pocket travel expenses incurred to obtain the third medical opinion.[109] Employers may not require the employee or family member to travel more than a normal commuting distance for purposes of obtaining the third opinion except in very unusual circumstances.[110] Upon request, the employer must provide a copy of the third health care provider opinion to the employee.[111] The employer must provide the requested copies within two business days unless extenuating circumstances prevent such action.[112]

The third health care opinion is final and binding on the parties.[113] Pending receipt of the third medical opinion, the employee is provisionally entitled to the benefits and protections of the Act.[114] If the third health care provider certification does not establish the employee's entitlement to FMLA leave, the leave cannot be designated as FMLA leave but may be treated as paid or unpaid leave under the employer's established leave policies.[115]

[4] Exclusivity of Certification Review Process

There is a split in the courts as to whether the certification review process outlined above is the exclusive means available to employers to challenge whether an employee or covered family member has an FMLA-qualifying serious health condition. The split is based on the use of the term "may" in the statute and DOL regulations regarding an employer's use of the certification review process. A majority of courts have held that an employer is not precluded from challenging at trial the existence of a serious health condition even though the employer did not request that an employee obtain a second opinion.[116] These courts reason that the use of the term "may" in the statute and DOL regulations makes obtaining a second opinion permissible, not mandatory. A minority of courts have held that an employer who elects not to challenge the existence of a serious health condition through the certification review process is thereafter precluded from challenging the existence of an FMLA-qualifying serious health condition, typically at trial.[117]

School employers should consult with counsel before electing to forgo a challenge to the validity of an employee's serious health condition through the certification review process. The failure to require an employee to obtain a second (or third) opinion can place schools in a precarious evidentiary situation. Courts have frowned on employer attempts to establish that an employee did not have a serious health condition based on health care provider review of available medical records years after the leave request at issue.[118] In many ways, it is to the school's advantage to settle whether the employee or covered family member has a serious health condition within the meaning of the FMLA as early in the process as possible so that the school can concentrate on managing the leave, if any.

[5] Employee Failure to Cooperate in the Certification Review Process

An employee who fails to cooperate in the certification review process may lose the benefits and protections of the FMLA. The DOL regulations do not impose a penalty for an employee's failure to obtain a second or third opinion as requested by the employer. Courts, however, have found that an employee's lack of cooperation in the certification challenge process rendered the employee outside the protections of the FMLA.[119]

7.04 EMPLOYEE FAILURE TO SATISFY MEDICAL CERTIFICATION REQUIREMENTS

What actions an employer may take in the event an employee fails to satisfy the medical certification requirements depends on whether the need for leave was or was not foreseeable. In the case of foreseeable leave, an employer may delay the taking of FMLA leave if an employee fails to provide timely certification after being requested to furnish such certification (i.e., within 15 calendar days if practicable), until the required certification is provided.[120] If the employee never produces the certification, the leave is not protected by the FMLA.[121] An employee's (or a covered family member's) failure to complete the second and third opinion provider process constitutes a failure to provide medical certification rendering the leave outside the protections of the FMLA.

Where the need for leave is not foreseeable, an employee must provide certification within the time frame requested by the employer (which must allow at least 15 days after the employer's request) or as soon as practicable under the particular facts and circumstances.[122] In the case of a medical emergency, it may not be practicable for an employee to provide the required medical certification within 15 calendar days.[123] If an employee fails to provide a medical certification within a reasonable time under the pertinent circumstances, the employer may delay the employee's continuation of FMLA leave.[124] If the employee never produces the certification, the leave is not FMLA leave.[125]

Employers must refrain from denying FMLA leave or taking disciplinary action against an employee if an employee fails to timely provide medical certification. The DOL regulations initially require employers to delay the commencement or continuation of FMLA leave. The regulations require an employer to wait an unspecified period of time until the certification is provided. Only when the certification is "never" provided may a school deny FMLA leave. "Never" is theoretically an infinite period of time. Fortunately, courts have rejected a literal reading of "never" in favor of "a reasonable period of time."[126] According to one court:

> The requirement that an employee return his FMLA certification within a reasonable time or else lose his entitlement to FMLA fulfills Con-

> gress's desire to balance the demands of the workplace with the needs of families. The FMLA protects an employee from losing his leave when his certification is reasonably delayed and protects an employer from the unreasonable burden of indefinitely maintaining records of potentially eligible but unclaimed FMLA leave. See S. Rep. No. 103-3, at 2 (1993), 1993 U.S.C.C.A.N. 3. Accordingly, the Court concludes that an employer may deny FMLA leave where the employee failed to timely submit the required certification unless timely submission was not reasonably possible under the employee's particular facts and circumstances.[127]

Another court observed that "although the regulations *permit* the employer to extend the established deadline, they cannot be read to *require* an employer to wait indefinitely for medical certification of a need for leave."[128] The determination of whether a school has permitted an employee a reasonable period of time under the circumstances must be determined on a case-by-case basis.

7.05 RECERTIFICATION OF MEDICAL OPINIONS

The FMLA allows employers to require employees to subsequently recertify a serious health condition.[129] Neither the statute nor the DOL regulations define what constitutes "recertification." In the comments accompanying publication of the final FMLA regulations, the DOL observed that recertification addresses the "appropriate length of time that a medical certification should be valid."[130] In the FMLA context, recertification would appear to mean a renewal of a certification that has grown stale over time.

The regulations also fail to identify the content or form of recertification. Presumably, use of the prefix "re" means that recertification is governed by the same regulations as certifications.

[1] Circumstances Permitting Recertification

Under the statute, employers are permitted to require an eligible employee to obtain subsequent recertification on a reasonable basis.[131] The DOL implementing regulations have added considerable detail to the recertification requirements. The regulations identify recertification rules in four circumstances.

(i) Pregnancy, Chronic Conditions, or Permanent/Long-Term Conditions

Where the serious health condition of the employee or covered family member involves pregnancy, a chronic condition, or a permanent/long-term condition under the continuing treatment of a health care provider, an employer may request recertification no more often than every 30 days and only in connection with an absence by the employee.[132] Pursuant to the regulations, an employer may not simply require an employee to provide medical recertification every 30 days where the need for leave is due to pregnancy, a chronic condition, or a permanent/long-term condition. An employer must wait for the first absence on or after the passage of 30 days before it can require a subsequent recertification. Note that the rule does not require that this first employee absence be FMLA leave.

Employers may require an employee to provide recertification of a serious health condition involving pregnancy, a chronic condition, or a permanent/long-term condition more often than every 30 days and even though the leave is not connected with an absence where

- circumstances described by the previous certification have changed significantly (e.g., the duration or frequency of absences, the severity of the condition, complications); or
- the employer receives information that casts doubt on the employee's stated reason for the absence.[133]

For example, the certification originally accepted by the school indicates that an employee will be out between 3 and 6 times a month for the foreseeable future due to asthma attacks. The school notices that the employee is actually out 10 times in each of the next 2 consecutive months. The increase in the frequency of absences appears significant. As a result, a school could require the employee to recertify his or her medical condition immediately, even if less than 30 days have passed and the employee has not been absent since the last recertification.

The above example illustrates one reason why it is important for school employers to obtain information in the original certification that is as specific as possible regarding the duration and frequency of absences constituting FMLA leave. Those numbers will serve as a baseline for determining whether and when a school may require an employee to submit subsequent recertification.

The DOL has indicated that a pattern of Friday/Monday absences may cast doubt on the employee's stated reason for the absence, thus justifying a school employer to request recertification more frequently than every 30 days.[134] The DOL cautioned that if there was a medical reason for the Friday/Monday timing of such absences, the exception would not apply.

(ii) Minimum Duration of Incapacity Exceeds 30 Days

Where the minimum period of incapacity specified on a certification furnished by the health care provider is more than 30 days, an employer may not request recertification until after the expiration of that minimum period.[135] "Incapacity" means inability to attend work, attend school, or perform other regular daily activities due to the serious health condition.[136] Note that this provision focuses on the period of incapacity, which may be different from the period of time the employee may have the serious health condition.

For example, the employee requests FMLA leave for 40 days to recover from surgery. The request is supported by a medical certification. Here, a school would not be permitted to require the employee to submit a recertification until the day after the passage of the 40-day recovery period.

Notwithstanding this rule, an employer may request recertification before the expiration of the period of incapacity specified in the prior certification if

- the employee requests an extension of leave;
- circumstances described in the previous certification have changed significantly (e.g., the duration of the illness, the nature of the illness, complications); or
- the employer receives information that casts doubt on the continuing validity of the certification.[137]

For example, a school employee is originally scheduled to be out on 40 days of FMLA leave due to incapacity. If during that leave the employee informed the school that he or she was unable to return to work and needed an additional 10 days of FMLA leave, the school could require the employee to submit a recertification at that time.

(iii) Intermittent or Reduced Leave Schedule Leave

For FMLA leave taken intermittently or on a reduced leave schedule basis, an employer may not request recertification in less than the minimum period specified on the certification as necessary for such leave (including treatment).[138] Absent an exception, the regulation would prohibit a school employer from requiring recertification during a period of leave on an intermittent or reduced leave schedule basis, which could, for certain serious health conditions, be years or a lifetime.

However, an employer may require an employee to submit subsequent recertification during a period of leave on an intermittent or reduced leave schedule basis if

- the employee requests an extension of leave;
- circumstances described in the previous certification have changed significantly (e.g., the duration of the illness, the nature of the illness, complications); or
- the employer receives information that casts doubt on the continuing validity of the certification.[139]

For example, a school employee with a chronic condition is originally certified to require intermittent leave 4 to 6 times a month for the next 5 years. Generally, a school would not be permitted to require the employee to submit a subsequent recertification during that 5-year period. If, however, during the 5-year period the employee is absent due to the chronic condition 8 times a month for several months in a row, the school could require the employee to recertify the serious health condition.

The regulations do not explain how the rules regarding recertification of intermittent or reduced leave schedule leave interact with the recertification rules governing pregnancy, chronic conditions, or permanent/long-term conditions. That is, if an employee is on intermittent FMLA leave due to pregnancy, which rules govern an employer's request for subsequent recertification? Presumably, the intermittent/reduced leave schedule rules would govern. As a matter of regulatory construction, because the intermittent/reduced leave schedule rules come after the recertification rules governing pregnancy, chronic conditions, and permanent/long-term conditions, they are assumed to take into consideration all prior rules. Schools should consult with counsel in this area before requiring recertification where more than one set of recertification rules applies to any given situation.

(iv) All Other Circumstances

The DOL regulations contain recertification rules governing "all other circumstances."[140] Excluding leave for the previously identified serious health conditions, the following serious health conditions are covered by this rule:

- Inpatient care
- Continuing treatment by a health care provider involving a period of incapacity of more than three consecutive calendar days, plus one or more health care provider treatments
- Any period of absence to receive multiple treatments by a health care provider either for restorative surgery after an accident or other injury or for a condition that would likely result in a period of incapacity of more than three consecutive calendar days in the absence of medical intervention

For the above serious health conditions, employers may request subsequent recertification at any reasonable interval, but not more often than every 30 days.[141] The inclusion of a "reasonable interval" requirement suggests that employers must take into consideration all of the facts and circumstances of each case, rather than mandate a standard period regardless of the facts.

An employer may, however, require an employee with one of the identified serious health conditions above to provide subsequent recertification more often than every 30 days if

- the employee requests an extension of leave;
- circumstances described in the previous certification have changed significantly (e.g., the duration of the illness, the nature of the illness, complications); or
- the employer receives information that casts doubt on the continuing validity of the certification.[142]

[2] Notice Requirement for Recertification

The DOL regulations do not specifically require an employer to notify an employee of the requirement for recertification or the consequences of an employee's failure to comply with an employer's recertification request. Arguably, the recertification requirement should be included as part of any written guidance the employer has regarding leave or employment benefits, such as an employee handbook.[143] Although they are not mandated to do so, school employers would be well advised, for purposes of notice, to treat a request for recertification in the same manner as a request for an initial certification. Schools should provide specific written notice to the employee each time the school requires the employee to provide recertification. Schools can't get into trouble by providing more notice than is required by the FMLA.

The rules regarding notice and certification are set forth more fully in Chapter 6, *Notice Requirements*.

[3] Form and Content of Recertification

The DOL regulations fail to address the permissible content of recertification or to provide an optional form for use by employers. Schools would be well advised, however, to abide by the content requirements governing certifications. As addressed earlier in this section, the prefix "re" implies that the recertification is merely an updated version of the original certification. As such, the content requirements governing the original medical certification would appear to apply to recertification. For the same reason, schools should use the DOL-approved WH-380 certification form for recertification.

The rules governing the permissible content of FMLA certifications are addressed earlier in this chapter.

[4] Payment for Recertification

Recertification is at the employee's expense, unless the employer voluntarily provides otherwise.[144] Schools should review their paid leave policies and collective bargaining agreements to determine whether they have voluntarily agreed to pay the expense of recertification.

[5] Selection of Recertification Provider

The DOL regulations do not specify who, the employee or the employer, has the right to select the recertification health care provider. The strong implication, however, is that the recertification is provided by the employee's or the covered family member's health care provider, depending on who has the serious health condition. Unlike second opinions, neither the statute nor the DOL regulations provide for an employer to select the recertification health care provider. Moreover, a recertification is an updated certification. The original certification is obtained from the health care provider of the patient, whether the eligible employee or the covered family member.

[6] Time Limits for Employee to Provide Recertification

An employee must provide the requested medical recertification to the employer within the time frame requested by the employer (which must allow at least 15 calendar days after the employer' request) unless it is not practicable under the particular circumstances to do so despite the employee's diligent, good faith efforts.[145] This is the same time frame an employee has to submit the original certification. An employer that requires an employee to submit a recertification in less time, absent application of an exception, is in violation of the FMLA.[146]

[7] Second and Third Opinions on Recertification

The certification challenge process does not apply to recertification. That is, second and third health care provider opinions are not permitted on medical recertification.[147] Because recertification cannot be challenged through the certification review process, schools should carefully consider their documentation needs before exercising their right to require recertification. Schools that exercise the right to demand recertification may forever preclude themselves from using the certification challenge process for FMLA leave for that covered condition.

For example, a school does not challenge an employee's request for FMLA leave that is supported by medical certification. Time goes by and the school notices that circumstances have changed regarding the frequency of the employee's use of FMLA leave. The school demands that the employee recertify the serious health condition. Because recertification updates the now-stale certification that preceded it, the original certification falls by the wayside, having been replaced by the updated recertification. Because recertification cannot be challenged by a second (or third) opinion, arguably the school will be barred from ever challenging the original certification.

There is no formal DOL guidance on this issue. I have heard DOL investigators agree with the above analysis. I have heard others maintain that the certification review process remains available to challenge the original certification even though an employer requests recertification of the condition in the interim. Schools should exercise caution in this area and consult with counsel before recertifying a serious health condition that has not been challenged through the certification challenge process.

[8] Employee Failure to Provide Recertification

The DOL regulations are murky regarding the consequences of an employee's failure to timely provide recertification. The lack of clarity stems from the inclusion of "recertification" in the title of the regulation governing the consequences if an employee fails to satisfy the certification and recertification requirements, but the near absence of any reference to "recertification" in the text of the regulation.

The relevant regulation, 29 C.F.R. § 825.311, is entitled "What happens if an employee fails to satisfy the medical certification and/or recertification requirements?" However, the text of that regulation specifically refers to "recertification" only once and only regarding the time period an employee has to provide the recertification.[148] When it comes to addressing the consequences of an employee's failure to meet those requirements, the regulation refers only to a "medical certification."[149] Recertification is not mentioned at all.

Similarly, § 825.312 addresses the circumstances under which a covered employer may refuse to provide FMLA leave or reinstatement to eligible employees. Here again, the relevant regulation addresses the consequences to an employee if he or she fail to timely provide a "requested medical certification," but the consequences of an employee's failure to provide recertification are not specifically addressed.[150]

Because recertification is an updated medical certification, it is likely that the rules that govern an employee's failure to provide a medical certification would also apply to recertification. Those rules were addressed earlier in this chapter.

7.06 PERIODIC STATUS REPORTS

The FMLA allows employers to require employees on FMLA leave to report periodically on their status and intent to return to work.[151] The regulations do not address whether such reports must be in writing, the permissible content of such reports, or the form of such reports. Periodic status reports are addressed in Chapter 11, *Return to Work from Family and Medical Leave*.

7.07 CERTIFICATION OF FITNESS TO RETURN TO DUTY FROM FMLA LEAVE

In the case of FMLA leave for an employee's own serious health condition, the FMLA permits employers under certain circumstances to condition the employee's return to work on the presentation of a certification from the employee's health care provider that the employee is able to resume work.[152] Return-to-work certifications are addressed in Chapter 11, *Return to Work from Family and Medical Leave*.

7.08 CERTIFICATION OF EMPLOYEE'S INABILITY TO RETURN TO WORK FROM FMLA LEAVE

Employers may require an employee to provide medical certification to substantiate a claim that the employee is unable to return to work because of the continuation, recurrence, or onset of the employee's serious health condition or a covered family member's serious health condition.[153] Employers are precluded from recovering their share of health plan premium payments made during a period of unpaid FMLA leave if the employee fails to returns to work after the employee's FMLA leave entitlement has been exhausted or expired if the failure to return to work is due to the continuation, recurrence, or onset of a serous health condition of the employee or the employee's covered family member.[154] The certification requirement is designed to provide employers with some medical substantiation that the employee's claimed inability to return to work is medically justified before the employer loses the right to recoup health plan premiums from the employee.

Unless requested to do so, an employee is not required to provide this medical certification.[155] The employee has 30 days from the time of the employer's request to provide the medical certification.[156] School employers may use the DOL-approved WH-380 form for this purpose.[157] The cost of the certification is borne by the employee, and the employee is not entitled to be paid for the time spent in acquiring the certification or reimbursed for any travel expenses associated with such certification.[158]

If the employer requests medical certification and the employee does not provide such certification in a timely manner (within 30 days), the employer may recover 100 percent of the health benefit premiums it paid during the period of unpaid FMLA leave.[159]

The regulations do not address whether the certification of an employee's inability to return to work due to the continuation, recurrence, or onset of a serious health condition is subject to the certification challenge process. It does not appear that the challenge process would apply. In the statute, the challenge process refers to an employee's request for leave due to a serious health condition.[160] The medical certification requirement to substantiate an employee's inability to return to work does not involve an employee's request for leave. As such, the second or third health care provider challenge process would not apply.

Issues regarding the maintenance of health benefits are addressed in Chapter 10, *Maintenance of Employment Benefits*.

7.09 DOCUMENTATION ESTABLISHING FAMILIAL RELATIONSHIPS

Eligible employees are entitled to FMLA leave if they are needed to care for a spouse, son, daughter, or parent. The FMLA allows employers to confirm that the individual is the spouse, son, daughter, or parent of the employee as claimed. An employer may require an employee giving notice of the need for leave to provide reasonable documentation or a statement of family relationship.[161] The documentation may take the form of a simple statement from the employee or a child's birth certificate, a court document, or other official document. The regulations do not limit the type of documents that may be requested to establish the familial relationship. Other documents that school employers might wish to consider requesting to establish the claimed familial relationship would include a marriage license, divorce decree, tax records, or school records. Schools may wish to accept a statement from the employee of a common law marriage in lieu of requiring other records. They may, however, request documents that tend to indicate a common law marriage, such as jointly filed tax returns, evidence of joint bank accounts, and joint mortgage records. Employers have the right to examine such documents, but the employee is entitled to the return of the official document submitted for this purpose.[162]

7.10 STATE FAMILY AND MEDICAL LEAVE LAWS

The ability of employers to require medical or other documentation to support an employee's request for leave varies under state family and medical leave laws. As in other areas, the range runs from state laws that fail to mention a documentation requirement to those that virtually copy some or all of the detailed documentation requirements of the federal FMLA. For example, Vermont's family and parental leave law permits covered employers to require certification from a physician to verify the serious illness as well as the necessity of the leave and the amount of leave requested.[163] Vermont law does not impose a time frame for an employee to provide such certification or any penalty for an employee's failure to provide the certification. The law does not address documentation of familial relationships, medical recertification, a challenge process for questionable medical certifications, or a fitness-for-duty certification on return from leave.

West Virginia's Parental Leave Act permits employers to require an employee who asks for leave for a family member with a serious health condition to provide certification from a health care provider of the health condition. The certification is sufficient if it contains the following: (1) that the child, dependent, or parent of the employee has a serious health condition; (2) the date the serious health condition commenced and its probable duration; and (3) the medical facts regarding the serious health condition.[164] West Virginia law does include time frames for an employee to provide the medical certification. Nor does it impose penalties in the event the employee fails to provide such certification. The law does not address an employer's right to request documentation to establish familial relationship, medical recertification, or a fitness-for-duty certification on return from leave. It also does not provide a process to challenge the validity of a medical certification provided by an employee.

As with other areas, school administrators must carefully review applicable state family and medical leave laws to determine appropriate documentation procedures.

7.11 INTERACTION OF THE FEDERAL FMLA WITH STATE FAMILY AND MEDICAL LEAVE LAWS: DOCUMENTATION REQUIREMENTS

The federal FMLA interacts with state or local family and medical leave laws only where both laws apply to the same leave situation. For both laws to apply, the employer must be covered under the applicable state or local law as well as the federal FMLA, the employee must meet the eligibility requirements of both laws, and the reason for the leave at issue must be covered by both the applicable state or local law and the federal FMLA. Where that is not the case, the only law—whether the state or local law or the federal FMLA—that will apply to the leave situation at issue is the one for which all of those criteria are met.

Where both state or local family and medical leave laws and the federal FMLA apply to the same leave situation, the federal FMLA mandates that employers apply the provision that provides the greater family and medical leave rights to employees. The federal FMLA does not supersede any provision of state or local law that provides greater family or medical leave rights than those provided by the federal FMLA.[165] Because of this statutory "nonpreemption" language, schools must determine which law applies (state or federal) in a particular situation on a provision-by-provision basis.[166] The DOL explained:

> Where the requisite coverage or applicability standards of both laws are met and the laws contain differing provisions, an analysis must be made of both laws, provision-by-provision, to determine which standard(s) from each law will apply to the particular situation. The standard providing the greater right or more generous benefit to the employee from each law (provision-by-provision) will apply.[167]

In terms of documentation, the federal FMLA provides that an employer may not require compliance with stricter FMLA documentation requirements where the provisions of an applicable state or local law are less demanding in terms of documentation. School administrators must therefore determine which law, the federal FMLA or state law, is more or less generous to employees in terms of documentation requirements. This may not be an easy task, yet it must be done in order for school employers to be in compliance with the federal FMLA. For example, if state law provides for only one medical certification, no additional certifications may be required by the employer unless the employer has already provided, or the employee is requesting, more leave than required under state law.[168] The DOL further illustrated this issue in the comments accompanying publication of the final FMLA regulations as follows:

> The University of California observed that, under California law, employers may not obtain second or third opinions except in the case of an employee's own serious health condition. Thus, because FMLA was

> intended to permit Christian Science practitioner certification, employers would not be able to obtain second or third medical opinions in connection with the serious health condition of a spouse, child, or parent. Under applicable statutes, this would be true.[169]

The burden on school employers to properly determine whether the documentation requirements of the federal FMLA or applicable state or local family and medical leave laws provide the greater benefit to employees is further complicated where state or local law is silent on a provision contained in the federal FMLA. In comments accompanying publication of the final DOL regulations implementing the federal FMLA, the DOL agreed with the following discussion of how such matters should be addressed:

> The Equal Rights Advocates suggested additional examples where a State law is silent on an issue addressed by FMLA. If an employee is "eligible" under both FMLA and a State or local law, and the State or local law is silent on a provision contained in FMLA, and if the FMLA provision is restrictive (as to employee rights and benefits), then the State or local law would govern as to that provision. If the FMLA provision is not restrictive (or extends a right, benefit, or privilege to employees), then the FMLA would govern as to that provision. For example, a State law that grants employers the right to deny the taking of leave to high-level executives could not be applied to any FMLA-eligible employees, because FMLA extends to all eligible employees the entitlement to leave for qualifying reasons. If the same State law contained a provision mandating all employees who take leave be restored to employment when the leave ends, the FMLA's "key employee" exemption could not be applied to deny an employee reinstatement (i.e., the Federal law would not apply at the time of reinstatement).[170]

In terms of documentation, if an applicable state or local law is silent regarding the time frame an employee has to provide documentation, because the minimum time frames established by the federal FMLA are more restrictive of an employee's rights and benefits, that state or local law would govern the timing of an employee's obligation to provide documentation. That is, the absence of a time limit provides a greater benefit to employees than a provision of the federal FMLA that imposes a time limit, no matter how generous. Similarly, if an applicable state law did not permit a school employer to condition an employee's return to work on submission of a fitness-for-duty report, a school employer covered by both that state law and the federal FMLA could not condition an employee's return to work on submission of such a report even though it could do so if only the federal FMLA applied.

NOTES

1. 29 U.S.C. § 2613(a); 29 C.F.R. § 825.305(a).

2. S. Rep. No. 103-3, at 25–26 (1993), as reprinted in 1993 U.S.C.C.A.N. 3, 27–28.

3. *Levine v. Children's Museum of Indianapolis, Inc.*, No. 02-3013, 2003 U.S. App. LEXIS 5755 (7th Cir. March 24, 2003); *Carmen v. Unison Behavioral Health Group, Inc.*, 295 F. Supp. 2d 809, 813 (N.D. Ohio 2003).

4. *Thorson v. Gemini, Inc.*, 205 F.3d 370, 381 (8th Cir. 2000), *cert. denied*, 531 U.S. 871 (2000); *Marrero v. Camden County Board of Social Services*, 164 F. Supp. 2d 455, 463–64 (D.N.J. 2001).

5. 29 C.F.R. § 825.303(b); see also *Peeples v. Coastal Office Products, Inc.*, 203 F. Supp. 2d 432, 449 (D. Md. 2001), *aff'd*, 2003 U.S. App. LEXIS 8644 (4th Cir. 2003).

6. 29 U.S.C. § 2613(a).

7. See section 5.03[3](ii) of Chapter 5, *Covered Conditions*.

8. This requirement does not apply to Christian Science practitioners, individuals recognized as health care providers by the employer or the benefits manager of the employer's group health plan, or a health care provider who practices in a country other than the United States.

9. 29 C.F.R. § 825.118(c).

10. *Gulan v. Federal Reserve Bank of Cleveland*, No. 1:01-CV-1784, 2003 U.S. Dist. LEXIS 15749, at *15–*16 (N.D. Ohio July 31, 2003).

11. *Krohn v. Forsting* 11 F. Supp. 2d 1082, 1090 (E.D. Mo. 1998).

12. *Schober v. SMC Pneumatics, Inc.*, No. IP99-1285-C T/G, 2000 U.S. Dist. LEXIS 12478, at *35 (S.D. Ind. Dec. 4, 2000).

13. *Giuliani v. Minnesota Vikings Football Club, LLC*, No. 99-CV-1811 DDA/FLN, 2001 U.S. Dist. LEXIS 20207, at *8 (D. Minn. June 11, 2001).

14. *Sims v. Alameda-Contra Costa Transit District*, 2 F. Supp. 2d 1253, 1264–65 (N.D. Cal. 1998).

15. 29 U.S.C. § 2613(a); 29 C.F.R. §§ 825.301(c)(2)(ii), 825.305(a).

16. 29 C.F.R. § 825.301(b)(1).

17. 29 C.F.R. § 825.301(f).

18. 29 C.F.R. § 825.305(c).

19. *Id.*

20. *Id.*

21. *Schober v. SMC Pneumatics, Inc.*, No. IP99-1285-C-T/G, 2000 U.S. Dist. LEXIS 12478, at *31–*32 (S.D. Ind. Aug. 21, 2000).

22. 29 C.F.R. § 825.305(b).

23. *Id.*

24. See *Electrolux Home Products, Inc. v. The United Automobile, Aerospace and Agricultural Implement Workers of America,* 343 F. Supp. 2d 747 (N.D. Iowa 2004), *aff'd*, 416 F.3d 848 (8th Cir. 2005).

25. *Peter v. Lincoln Technical Institute*, 255 F. Supp. 2d 417, 441–42 (E.D. Pa. 2002).

26. Compare *id.* (excusing employee failure to timely provide medical certification due to physician delay), *Toro v. Mastex Industries*, 32 F. Supp. 2d 25, 29 (D. Mass. 1998) (same), *Uema v. Nippon Export Hawaii, Inc.*, 26 F. Supp. 2d 1241, 1248 (D. Haw. 1998) (same), with *Muriekes v. Boeing Co.*, No. 03-35265, 2004 U.S. App. LEXIS 20350, at **3 (9th Cir. Sept. 24, 2004) (holding that clerical error on part of employee's physician did not render it "impracticable" so as to excuse employee's untimely submission of medical certification).

27. *Muriekes*, 2004 U.S. App. LEXIS 20350, at **3; *Konipol v. Restaurant Associates*, No. 01-Civ. 7857 (GEL), 2002 U.S. Dist. LEXIS 22439, at *16 (S.D.N.Y. Nov. 20, 2002).

28. *Baldwin-Love v. Electronic Data Systems Corp.*, 307 F. Supp. 2d 1222, 1230 (M.D. Ala. 2004).

29. *Chenoweth v. Wal-Mart Stores, Inc.*, 159 F. Supp. 2d 1032, 1037 (S.D. Ohio 2001); *Giuliani v. Minnesota Vikings Football Club, LLC.*, No. 99-CV-1811 DDA/FLN, 2001 U.S. Dist. LEXIS 20207, at *8 (D. Minn. June 11, 2001); *Schober v. SMC Pneumatics, Inc.*, No. IP99-1285-C-T/G, 2000 U.S. Dist. LEXIS 12478 (S.D. Ind. Aug. 21, 2000).

30. *Boyd v. State Farm Insurance Companies*, 158 F.3d 326, 332 (5th Cir. 1998), *cert. denied*, 526 U.S. 1051 (1999).

31. 29 C.F.R. §§ 825.305(e); 825.207(h).

32. 29 C.F.R. § 825.207(h).

33. 29 U.S.C. § 2652(b); 29 C.F.R. § 825.700(a).

34. *Marrero v. Camden County Board of Social Services*, 164 F. Supp. 2d 455, 463–64 (D.N.J. 2001).

35. 29 C.F.R. § 825.306(b).

36. 29 U.S.C. § 2613(b); 29 C.F.R. § 825.306.

37. 29 C.F.R. § 825.306(b).

38. *Id.*

39. 29 C.F.R. § 825.306(a)–(b).

40. 29 C.F.R. § 825.306(b)(1)–(3).

41. 29 C.F.R. § 825.306(b)(4).

42. DOL WH FMLA Advisory Opinion, 2004 DOL FMLA LEXIS 2 (May 25, 2004).

43. Health Insurance Portability and Accountability Act, Pub. L. No. 104-191, 110 Stat. 1936 (1996) (codified as amended in scattered sections of 42 U.S.C. and 29 U.S.C.).

44. 29 C.F.R. § 825.306(b)(5).

45. 29 C.F.R. § 825.306(b)(5)(i).

46. 29 U.S.C. § 2652(a); 29 C.F.R. § 825.700(a)–(b).

47. 29 C.F.R. § 825.306(c).

48. *Cool v. BorgWarner Diversified Transmission Products, Inc.*, No. IP 02-960-C-B/S, 2004 U.S. Dist. LEXIS 570, at *25–*26 (S.D. Ind. Jan. 12, 2004).

49. *Dowell v. Indiana Heart Physicians, Inc.*, No. 1:03-cv-1410-DFH-TAB, 2004 U.S. Dist. LEXIS 26431, at *24 (S.D. Ind. Dec. 22, 2004).

50. See 29 C.F.R. § 825.307(a).

51. *White v. Interstate Brake Products, Inc.*, No. 3:96-CV5-S-A, 1997 U.S. Dist. LEXIS 10921, at *9 (N.D. Miss. June 2, 1997).

52. DOL WH-380, questions 5–6.

53. 29 C.F.R. § 825.306(b)(4)(ii).

54. 29 C.F.R. § 825.307(a).

55. *Id.*

56. Comments on Regulations Implementing the Family and Medical Leave Act of 1993 (§ 825.307), 60 Fed. Reg. 2180, 2224 (Jan. 6, 1995).

57. 29 C.F.R. § 825.312(g).

58. 29 C.F.R. § 825.307(a)(1).

59. 29 C.F.R. § 825.700(a)–(b).

60. 29 C.F.R. § 825.305(d).

61. *Morris v. VCW, Inc.*, No. 95-0737-CV-W-3-6, 1996 U.S. Dist. LEXIS 11124, at *4 (W.D. Mo. July 24, 1996).

62. *Sorrell v. Rinker Materials Corp.*, 395 F.3d 332, 337 (6th Cir. 2005).

63. *Wheeler v. Pioneer Development Services, Inc.*, 349 F. Supp. 2d 158, 168 (D. Mass. 2004).

64. *Jiminez v. Velcro USA, Inc.*, No. 01-001-JD, 2002 U.S. Dist. LEXIS 3900, at *9 (D.N.H. Mar. 4, 2002); *Shtab v. The Greate Bay Hotel and Casino, Inc.*, 173 F. Supp. 2d 255, 264 (D.N.J. 2001).

65. *Sorrell*, 395 F.3d at 338.

66. See *Bailey v. Southwest Gas Co.*, 275 F.3d 1181, 1185–86 (9th Cir. 2002).

67. *Miller v. AT&T*, 250 F.3d 820, 836 (4th Cir. 2001).

68. *Cash v. Smith*, 231 F.3d 1301, 1307 (11th Cir. 2000); *Stoops v. One Call Communications, Inc.*, 141 F.3d 309, 313–14 (7th Cir. 1998).

69. See *Jiminez*, 2002 U.S. Dist. LEXIS 3900, at *10–*11; *Washington v. Fort James Operating Co.*, 110 F. Supp. 2d 1325, 1333 (D. Or. 2000).

70. *Urban v. Dolgencorp of Texas, Inc.*, 393 F.3d 572, 574 (5th Cir. 2004); *Baldwin-Love v. Electronic Data Systems Corp.*, 307 F. Supp. 2d 1222, 1230 (M.D. Ala. 2004).

71. *Neppl v. Signature Flight Support Corp.*, 234 F. Supp. 2d 1016, 1027 (D. Minn. 2002).

72. *LeGrand v. Village of McCook*, No. 96-C-5951, 1998 U.S. Dist. LEXIS 5230, at *7 (N.D. Ill. Apr. 15, 1998).

73. See *Porter v. NYU School of Law*, No. 99 Civ. 4693 (TPG), 2003 U.S. Dist. LEXIS 14674, at *17–*18 (S.D.N.Y. Aug. 25, 2003), *aff'd*, 392 F.3d 530 (2d Cir. 2004).

74. *Cavin v. Honda of America Manufacturing, Inc.*, No. C2-00-400, 2002 U.S. Dist. LEXIS 19601, at *72 (S.D. Ohio Feb. 22, 2002), *aff'd in part, rev'd in part on other grounds*, 346 F.3d 713 (6th Cir. 2003).

75. *Bailey v. Southwest Gas Co.*, 275 F.3d 1181, 1185–86 (9th Cir. 2002).

76. 29 U.S.C. § 2613(c)(1); 29 C.F.R. § 825.307(a)(2).

77. 29 U.S.C. § 2613(c)(2); 29 C.F.R. § 825.307(a)(2), (b).

78. 29 C.F.R. § 825.307(b).

79. 29 C.F.R. § 825.118(b)(3).

80. 29 C.F.R. § 825.307(f).

81. See *Albert v. Runyon*, 6 F. Supp. 2d 57, 63–65 (D. Mass. 1998) (noting that what constitutes a "reason to doubt the validity" of a medical certification is not well established).

82. *Id.*

83. *Id.*

84. *Id.*

85. *Id.*

86. *Id.*

87. *Id.* at 65.

88. *Diaz v. Fort Wayne Foundry Corp.*, 131 F.3d 711, 713 (7th Cir. 1997).

89. *Patterson v. Department of the Air Force*, 74 M.S.P.R. 648 (1997).

90. 29 U.S.C. § 2613(c)(1); 29 C.F.R. § 825.307(a)(2).

91. 29 C.F.R. § 825.307(e).

92. *Id.*

93. Comments on Regulations Implementing the Family and Medical Leave Act of 1993 (§ 825.307), 60 Fed. Reg. 2180, 2223 (Jan. 6, 1995).

94. *Id.* (rejecting proposed exemption to second/third opinion process where securing same would be onerous or unduly burdensome).

95. *Diaz v. Fort Wayne Foundry Corp.*, 131 F.3d 711, 714 (7th Cir. 1997).

96. 29 C.F.R. § 825.307(a)(2).

97. *Id.*

98. 29 C.F.R. § 825.307(d).

99. *Id.*

100. Comments on Regulations Implementing the Family and Medical Leave Act of 1993 (§ 825.305), 60 Fed. Reg. 2180, 2221 (Jan. 6, 1995) ("As the employee is providing the certification to the employer, if the employee wishes to have a copy he/she may make a copy before submission to the employer.")

101. 29 U.S.C. § 2613(d)(1); 29 C.F.R. § 825.307(c).

102. 29 U.S.C. § 2613(d)(1); 29 C.F.R. § 825.307(c).

103. 29 C.F.R. § 825.307(c).

104. *Id.*

105. *Id.*

106. *Id.*

107. 29 C.F.R. § 825.307(f).

108. 29 U.S.C. § 2613(d)(1); 29 C.F.R. § 825.307(c).

109. 29 C.F.R. § 825.307(e).

110. *Id.*

111. 29 C.F.R. § 825.307(d).

112. *Id.*

113. 29 U.S.C. § 2613(d)(2); 29 C.F.R. § 825.307(c).

114. 29 C.F.R. § 825.307(a)(2).

115. *Id.*

116. *Levine v. The Children's Museum of Indianapolis, Inc.*, No. 02-3013, 2003 U.S. App. LEXIS 5755 (7th Cir. Mar. 24, 2003); *Rhoades v. FDIC*, 257 F.3d 373, 386 (4th Cir. 2001), *cert denied*, 535 U.S. 933 (2002); *Stekloff v. St. John's Mercy Health System*, 218 F.3d 858, 860 (8th Cir. 2000); *Porter v. NYU School of Law*, No. 99 Civ. 4693 (TPG), 2003 U.S. Dist. LEXIS 14674 (S.D.N.Y. Aug. 25, 2005), *aff'd*, 392 F.3d 530 (2d Cir. 2004).

117. *Wheeler v. Pioneer Development Services, Inc.*, 349 F. Supp. 2d 158, 168 (D. Mass. 2004); *Miller v. AT&T*, 60 F. Supp. 2d 574, 580 (S.D. W.Va. 1999), *aff'd*, 250 F.3d 820 (4th Cir. 2001).

118. *Thorson v. Gemini, Inc.*, 205 F.3d 370, 381–82 (8th Cir.), *cert. denied*, 531 U.S. 871 (2000).

119. *Diaz v. Fort Wayne Foundry Corp.*, 131 F.3d 711, 713 (7th Cir. 1997).

120. 29 C.F.R. §§ 825.311(a), 825.312(b).

121. 29 C.F.R. § 825.312(b).

122. 29 C.F.R. § 825.311(b).

123. *Id.*

124. 29 C.F.R. §§ 825.311(b), 825.312(b).

125. 29 C.F.R. §§ 825.311(b), 825.312(b).

126. *Cavin v. Honda of America Manufacturing, Inc.*, No. C2-00-400, 2002 U.S. Dist. LEXIS 19601, at *76 (S.D. Ohio Feb. 22, 2002), *aff'd in part, rev'd in part on other grounds*, 346 F.3d 713 (6th Cir. 2003); *Washington v. Fort James Operating Co.*, 110 F. Supp. 2d 1325, 1331–32 (D. Or. 2000).

127. *Washington*, 110 F. Supp. 2d at 1331–32.

128. *Cavin*, 2002 U.S. Dist. LEXIS 19601, at *76–*77.

129. 29 U.S.C. § 2613(e); 29 C.F.R. § 825.308.

130. Comments on Regulations Implementing the Family and Medical Leave Act of 1993 (§ 825.308), 60 Fed. Reg. 2180, 2224–25 (Jan. 6, 1995).

131. 29 U.S.C. § 2613(e).

132. 29 C.F.R. § 825.308(a).

133. *Id.*

134. DOL WH FMLA Advisory Opinion, 2004 DOL FMLA LEXIS 2, question 2 (May 25, 2004).

135. 29 C.F.R. § 825.308(b)(1).

136. 29 C.F.R. § 825.306(b)(2)(i).

137. 29 C.F.R. § 825.308(b)(1).

138. 29 C.F.R. § 825.308(b)(2).

139. 29 C.F.R. § 825.308(b)(2), (c).

140. 29 C.F.R. § 825.308(c).

141. *Id.*

142. *Id.*

143. 29 C.F.R. § 825.301(a)(1).

144. 29 C.F.R. § 825.308(e).

145. 29 C.F.R. § 825.308(d).

146. *LeGrand v. Village of McCook*, No. 96-C-5951, 1998 U.S. Dist. LEXIS 5230, at *15–*16 (N.D. Ill. Apr. 15, 1998).

147. 29 C.F.R. § 825.308(e).

148. 29 C.F.R. § 825.311(b).

149. *Id.*

150. 29 C.F.R. § 825.312(b).

151. 29 C.F.R. § 825.309(a).

152. 29 U.S.C. § 2614(a)(4); 29 C.F.R. § 825.310(a).

153. 29 U.S.C. § 2614(c)(3); 29 C.F.R. § 825.310(h).

154. 29 C.F.R. § 825.213(a)(1).

155. 29 C.F.R. § 825.213(a)(3).

156. *Id.*

157. *Id.*

158. 29 C.F.R. § 825.310(h).

159. 29 C.F.R. § 825.213(a)(3).

160. 29 U.S.C. § 2613(a), (c).

161. 29 C.F.R. § 825.113(d).

162. *Id.*

163. Vt. Stat. Ann. tit. 26, § 472(e).

164. W.Va. Code § 21-5D-5.

165. 29 U.S.C. § 2651(b); 29 C.F.R. § 825.701(1).

166. Comments on Regulations Implementing the Family and Medical Leave Act of 1993 (§ 825.701), 60 Fed. Reg. 2180, 2230 (Jan. 6, 1995).

167. *Id.*

168. 29 C.F.R. § 825.701(a)(4).

169. Comments on Regulations Implementing the Family and Medical Leave Act of 1993 (§ 825.701), 60 Fed. Reg. at 2231.

170. *Id.* at 2230.

CHAPTER 8

Leave Amount and Scheduling

8.01 OVERVIEW

Employees are entitled to a maximum of 12 workweeks of job-protected leave over the course of a 12-month leave year under the federal FMLA. Employees may take FMLA leave in a single block of time, intermittently, or on a so-called reduced leave schedule basis. These rules are important as they instruct employers how they must count FMLA leave for purposes of the employee's 12-workweek entitlement.

Section 8.02 of this chapter addresses the leave year options available to employers. Section 8.03 discusses the manner in which employers calculate the 12 workweeks of FMLA leave an eligible employee is entitled to receive during the leave year. Section 8.04 examines the rules governing how FMLA leave may be scheduled. Section 8.05 examines the effect of more generous employer leave policies on the amount and scheduling of FMLA leave. Section 8.06 discusses state family and medical leave laws. Finally, section 8.07 addresses the interaction of federal and state family medical leave laws on the amount of leave and leave scheduling requirements.

8.02 ELECTION OF THE 12-MONTH FMLA LEAVE YEAR

Employers may choose from one of the following four options for calculating the 12-month FMLA leave year:[1]

- The calendar year
- Any fixed 12-month "leave year," such as a fiscal year, a year required by state law, or a year starting on the employee's "anniversary" date
- The 12-month period measured forward from the date an employee commences any FMLA leave
- A "rolling" 12-month period measured backward from the date an employee uses any FMLA leave

Employers may choose any of the leave years described above, provided that the method for determining the leave year is applied consistently and uniformly to all employees.[2] An exception to this required uniformity applies in the case of a multistate employer who has eligible employees in a state that has a family and medical leave statute. The state may require that a single method for determining the leave year be used. This method may conflict with the method chosen by the employer for purposes of the federal FMLA. In that case, the employer may comply with the applicable state provisions for all employees employed within that state and uniformly use another method provided by the federal FMLA for all other employees.[3]

[1] Fixed Leave Year Method

Under a calendar or other fixed 12-month leave year, an employee would be entitled to take up to 12 weeks of FMLA leave at any time in the fixed 12-month period.[4] An employer can elect any fixed 12-month period under this category. For example, a school may elect a fixed 12-month year beginning at the start of the academic year or on the employee's anniversary date, a calendar year, or a fiscal year. Again, whatever fixed leave year period is selected, it must be consistently and uniformly applied to all employees.[5]

The advantage to school administrators of using a fixed leave year is ease of administration compared with other methods for calculating the leave year. Use of the calendar year or other fixed leave year, however, provides the maximum FMLA benefits to employees. An employee would be entitled to up to 12 weeks of FMLA leave at any time during the fixed 12-month period selected.[6] This would allow employees to combine FMLA leave at the end of one leave year and at the beginning of the next leave year, resulting in up to 24 weeks of continuous FMLA leave. This "stacking" of FMLA leave by straddling the end of one leave year and the beginning of the next leave year is specifically permitted by the FMLA.[7] Some schools may find that the ability of eligible school employees to stack FMLA leave outweighs the administrative ease of using a calendar year or other fixed leave year,

[2] Measuring Forward Method

If an employer uses a "forward leave year," the 12-month FMLA leave year begins on the first date FMLA leave is taken by an eligible employee.[8] The next leave year begins on the first day following the completion of the current leave year that the employee takes FMLA leave. As a result, this next leave year may start more than 12 months after the first leave year. For example, Nancy is an eligible school employee. On May 15, 2005, she takes her first FMLA leave. Under the "measuring forward" method, her FMLA leave year beings on My 15, 2005, and will run until May 14, 2006. Her next leave year begins on the first day after May 14, 2006, that Nancy takes FMLA leave. If the first day she takes FMLA leave is August 12, 2006, her FMLA leave year would begin that day and go until August 11, 2006.

Under the measuring forward method, an employee cannot stack 24 weeks of FMLA leave in a row but can come pretty close. In our example with Nancy, if she took all 12 weeks of FMLA leave in a row beginning on May 15, 2005, Nancy would have no FMLA leave to stack if she were take FMLA leave at the beginning of the next leave year in 2006. However, Nancy could take a day of FMLA leave on May 15, 2005. That would start her FMLA leave year. Nancy could then take her remaining 11 weeks and 4 days of FMLA leave during the period immediately preceding May 14, 2006, the end of her leave year. If she were eligible and the leave qualified, she could take 12 weeks of FMLA leave beginning on May 15, 2006, which would begin the start of her next leave year.

Because the forward leave year must be calculated separately for each eligible employee, the measuring forward method is more difficult to administer than the fixed leave year method. On the plus side, the measuring forward method makes it more difficult, although not impossible, for employees to stack FMLA leave in a way that creates very long absences from work and gives rise to the inherent administrative problems associated with lengthy absences.

[3] Rolling Back Method

Under the "rolling" method, each time the employee takes FMLA leave, the remaining leave entitlement is any balance of the 12-week entitlement that has not been used during the immediately preceding 12 months.[9] For example, if an employee has taken 8 weeks of FMLA leave during the past 12 months, an additional 4 weeks of leave could be taken. If an employee used 4 weeks beginning April 1, 2005, 4 weeks beginning June 1, 2005, and 4 weeks beginning October 1, 2005, the employee would not be entitled to any additional leave until April 1, 2006. Beginning on April 1, 2006, the employee would be entitled to 4 weeks of FMLA leave, on June 1, 2006, the employee would be entitled to an additional 4 weeks of leave, and so on.[10]

The DOL has described the "rolling back" method as "a snapshot of the 12-month period that changes daily (i.e., as each new day is added to the 12-month period, one day from 12 months ago is eliminated)."[11] The DOL further observed that "[w]hile many comments were received opposing this method, it has been retained as one of the available options because it is the one method that most literally tracks the statutory language."[12]

The rolling back method is the most difficult method to administer. It is, however, the only method available that prevents employees from stacking FMLA leave. Schools that are interested in controlling long periods of FMLA absences should seriously consider the "rolling" method for calculating the FMLA leave year. Attendance-tracking software has greatly alleviated the administrative burdens of both the "rolling" and "measuring forward" methods for calculating the 12-month FMLA leave year.

[4] Failure to Select One of the Four Leave Year Methods

If an employer fails to select one of the four methods for determining the 12-month FMLA leave year, it must apply the method that provides the most beneficial outcome for an employee seeking FMLA leave.[13] An employer that initially failed to select one of the four leave year methods may, however, subsequently select a method, provided it gives 60 days' notice to all employees of the method the it intends to use.[14] During the 60-day notice period, any employee who needs FMLA leave may use the method for determining the leave year that provides the most beneficial outcome to the employee.[15] At the conclusion of the 60-day notice period, the employer may begin using the method it selected.[16] One court has opined that the failure of an employer to select one of the four methods for determining the FMLA leave year was not actionable absent a showing of harm by the employee.[17]

[5] Changing the Method for Determining the Leave Year

Employers may change the method they are using to calculate the FMLA leave year.[18] However, a new method may not be implemented in order to avoid the Act's leave requirements.[19] An employer wishing to change methods must give at least 60 days' notice to all employees, and the transition must take place in such a way that employees retain the full benefit of 12 weeks of leave under whichever method affords the greatest benefit to employees.[20]

[6] Notifying Employees of Method Chosen

The extent of an employer's duty to notify employees of the method it has chosen to calculate the 12-month FMLA leave year is unclear. The lack of clarity results from gaps in DOL guidance on the intersection of employer notice requirements and the election of the method for calculating the FMLA leave year. This section examines employer notice obligations at three points in time: (1) when the employer initially selects the method for calculating the FMLA leave year, (2) when an employee requests FMLA leave, and (3) when the employer changes the method for calculating the leave year. School FMLA notice obligations are addressed more fully in Chapter 6, *Notice Requirements*.

(i) Initial Selection of FMLA Leave Year

The DOL regulations do not specifically require employers to notify employees of the method initially selected for calculating the 12-month FMLA leave year.[21] Notwithstanding the absence of a regulatory directive mandating employers to notify employees of the method for calculating the FMLA leave year, some courts have read that requirement into the DOL regulations. The Ninth Circuit held that pursuant to 29 C.F.R. § 825.301(a)(1), an employer is required to include information in the employee handbook about the method it uses to calculate the FMLA leave year.[22] In pertinent part, 29 C.F.R. § 825.301(a)(1) provides:

> If an FMLA-covered employer has any eligible employees and has any written guidance regarding employee benefits or leave rights, such as an employee handbook, information concerning FMLA entitlements and employee obligations under the FMLA must be included in the handbook or other document.[23]

The court found that requiring employers to notify employees of the method selected by the employer to calculate the FMLA leave year was in keeping with the purpose of the general notice provision to "provide employees the opportunity to learn from their employers of the manner in which the employer intends to implement the FMLA and what company policies and procedures are applicable so that employees may make FMLA plans fully aware of their rights and obligations."[24] The court concluded that "the initial selection of a method for calculating the FMLA leave year must be an open—not a secret—one before it can be applied to an employee's disadvantage."[25]

Similarly, another court found that an employer's failure to notify employees in the handbook of the method used by the employer to calculate the FMLA leave year amounted to a defective election.[26] The fact that the employer had provided the employee with a separate written notice clearly identifying that it had elected the rolling method was unpersuasive because, the court opined, the notice was not provided in the handbook as required.[27]

Finding that § 825.301(a)(1) "does not go as far as to require the specific notice to which the Ninth Circuit refers," one court found that an employer was not required to notify the employee of the method it used to calculate the FMLA leave year.[28]

Given the developing case law, school employers would be well advised to identify the method used for calculating the FMLA leave year in an employee handbook or other written guidance regarding employee benefits or leave rights.

(ii) Specific Written Notice at the Time FMLA Leave Is Requested

It is unclear whether employers must identify the method used to calculate the FMLA leave year as part of the specific written notice employers must provide employees. The lack of clarify results from the fact that although language in the preamble to § 825.301strongly suggests that such information must be provided, there is no specific language in the DOL regulations requiring that such information be provided.

In the preamble to the final regulations, the DOL states: "Employers must inform employees of the applicable method for determining FMLA leave entitlement when informing employees of the FMLA rights."[29] Of course, that statement may be directed to other employer notice obligations contained in § 825.301, such as the inclusion of FMLA rights and responsibilities in an employee handbook or other written guidance involving employee benefits or leave rights.

As discussed in Chapter 6, *Notice Requirements*, employers are required to give notice to employees detailing the specific expectations and obligations of the employee and explaining any consequences in the event the employee fails to meet those obligations.[30] In contrast to the preamble statement of the DOL, § 825.301(b)(1), which details what information must be included in notice to employees, does not specifically identify the method an employer has selected for calculating the FMLA leave year as a mandatory part of that notice. Similarly,

WH-381, the optional prototype notice prepared by the DOL to satisfy the employer specific written notice requirement, does not include the method for calculating the FMLA leave year. This suggests that the DOL's statement in the preamble to the regulations does not require notice of the method for calculating the leave year as part of the specific written notice under § 825.301(b)(1).

School employers that want to play it safe can include in the specific written notice of FMLA rights and obligations that they are required to provide employees pursuant to § 825.301(b)(1) information identifying the method used to calculate the FMLA leave year.

(iii) Change of Methodology

As addressed earlier in this chapter, employers are required to notify employees when they are changing the method used to calculate the FMLA leave year. The notice requirement applies both where the employer initially failed to select one of the four methods and where the employer is changing from one approved method to another.

[7] Expiration of 12-Month Period for Birth or Placement for Adoption/Foster Care

The need for FMLA leave due to the birth or placement of a son or daughter for adoption or foster care expires at the end of the 12-month period beginning on the birth or placement date unless state law allows, or the employer permits, leave to be taken after such date.[31] All FMLA leave for these purposes must be concluded within this 12-month period.[32] This is a "use it or lose it" requirement. An employee does not preserve his or her right to use up to the full 12 weeks of FMLA leave for these purposes by commencing leave before expiration of the 12-month period following the birth or placement date. Once the 12-month period starting on the birth or placement date expires, the employee may not use FMLA leave for the birth or placement of that son or daughter. Of course, if the employee has any unused FMLA leave, the employee could use that leave for the birth or placement of another child, for his or her own serious health condition, or for the serious health condition of a covered son, daughter, spouse, or parent.

[8] More Generous Employer Leave Policies and the Calculation of the FMLA Leave Year

Employers may provide greater family and medical leave benefits to employees than are required by the federal FMLA.[33] Presumably, this would apply to the method of calculating the 12-month leave year. For example, the FMLA requires an employer to give employees 60 days' notice of any change to the method used to calculate the FMLA leave year. A school could adopt a policy requiring that it provide 90 days' notice to all employees of a change in the method for calculating the 12-month FMLA leave year. By giving the employees more notice than is required by the FMLA, the school would be providing greater family and medical leave benefits than the minimum required by the FMLA.

It is decidedly unclear whether an employer could elect to use a method for calculating the leave year other than one of the four methods prescribed in the regulations if that alternate method provides greater leave benefits to employees. Arguably, this would be permissible under the FMLA. Schools, however, would want to consult with counsel before implementing a method for calculating the 12-month FMLA leave year other than one of the four approved methods—even if that method would be more beneficial to employees.

8.03 CALCULATING THE 12 WORKWEEKS OF FMLA LEAVE

[1] General Rule

Eligible employees are entitled to a maximum of 12 workweeks of leave each 12-month FMLA leave year for covered conditions.[34] Eligible employees are not entitled to 12 workweeks of leave for *each* covered condition they experience during the FMLA leave year. Rather, the employee is entitled to 12 workweeks of FMLA leave each leave year for *all* covered conditions. The FMLA is a "use it or lose it" statute. If an employee does not use all of the available 12 workweeks of FMLA leave in any given leave year, the leave is lost. Unused FMLA leave is not carried over for the employee's use during the next leave year.

While all eligible employees are entitled to 12 workweeks of FMLA leave each leave year, each employee's 12-workweek entitlement may differ. This is because the amount of FMLA leave that each eligible employee is entitled to take each leave year is calculated based on the number of hours in that employee's workweek prior to the start of FMLA leave.[35] Ironically, the term "workweek" is not defined in the statute or the DOL regulations. The DOL has, however, opined that "[u]nder the FMLA, the term "workweek" is the employee's usual or normal schedule (hours/days per week) prior to the start of FMLA leave."[36] Because each employee's usual or normal work schedule may differ, the amount of available FMLA leave may vary from employee to employee, including employees who work in the same work group.

If an employee works in excess of 40 hours a week as part of his or her usual or normal work schedule, then such overtime hours form part of the usual and normal workweek schedule of the employee and must be used in determining the maximum amount of leave available to the employee under the FMLA.[37] For example, if a school employee normally works overtime in 3 of every 4 weeks, then such overtime hours are part of the usual and normal workweek schedule of the employee and would be included in calculating the amount of FMLA leave available to the employee.[38] This would be the case even where the school may not know in advance of the workweek when overtime will be scheduled or how much overtime the employee will have to work that week, as overtime hours may be based upon business demand that varies from week to week.[39] On the other hand, if overtime hours are on an "as needed basis" and are not part of the employee's usual or normal workweek, or if overtime is voluntary, such hours would neither be counted in calculating the amount of the employee's FMLA leave entitlement nor be charged against the employee's FMLA leave entitlement.[40] Where overtime hours are not part of the employee's usual or normal workweek, an employer may not take disciplinary action against an employee for being unable to work overtime as a result of limitations contained in a medical certification obtained for overtime purposes.[41]

The amount of FMLA leave available to an employee exempt from the overtime pay requirements of the wage and hour laws is not capped at 480 hours. According to the DOL:

> Nothing in the Act or its legislative history suggests that the maximum amount of leave available to an [exempt] employee is 480 hours. If an

employee's normal workweek exceeds 40 hours, the calculation of total FMLA leave available for pro rata reduction of total leave entitlement during intermittent leave or reduced leave schedules should be based on the employee's normal workweek—even if it exceeds 40 hours.[42]

Where an employee normally works a part-time schedule or variable hours, the amount of leave to which an employee is entitled is determined on a pro rata or proportional basis by comparing the new schedule with the employee's normal schedule.[43] For example, if an employee who normally works 30 hours per week works only 20 hours a week under a reduced leave schedule, the employee's 10 hours of leave would constitute one-third of a week of FMLA leave for each week the employee works the reduced leave schedule.[44] In this example, it would take the employee 24 weeks to exhaust his or her FMLA leave entitlement if no other FMLA leave were taken during the 12-month leave year period.[45]

The calculation of the amount of federal FMLA leave available to an employee whose work schedule varies from week to week is based on the employee's average workweek over the 12-week period prior to the beginning of the FMLA leave period.[46]

FMLA Illustrated: Work Schedule Varies From Week to Week

An eligible employee whose work schedule varies form week to week worked the following hours in the 12 weeks preceding the beginning of FMLA leave:

Week 1	*Week 2*	*Week 3*	*Week 4*	*Week 5*	*Week 6*
33	36	44	45	29	50
Week 7	*Week 8*	*Week 9*	*Week 10*	*Week 11*	*Week 12*
50	41	36	32	30	42

The employee's FMLA entitlement for the leave year is the average hours worked during the 12-week period, or 39 hours (468 total hours divided by 12).

Where an employer has made a permanent or long-term change in an employee's schedule (for reasons other than the FMLA and prior to the notice of the need for FMLA leave), the hours worked under the new schedule are to be used for calculating the amount of FMLA leave entitlement.[47] For example, if an employee with a disability has already switched to a permanently reduced work schedule for reasons other than the FMLA and needs leave on an intermittent basis, the hours worked under the current schedule would be used for making the calculation.[48]

[2] The Marriage Penalty: Husbands and Wives Who Work for the Same Employer

The FMLA imposes a "marriage penalty" on spouses who work for the same employer by reducing the total amount of FMLA leave available to both spouses in three situations:[49]

(1) For the birth of the employee's son or daughter or to care for the child after birth
(2) For placement of a son or daughter with the employee for adoption or foster care, or to care for the child after placement
(3) To care for the employee's parent with a serious health condition

Under the so-called marriage penalty provision, an eligible husband and wife are limited to a combined total of 12 weeks of FMLA leave during the 12-month leave year for the birth, adoption, or foster care placement of a son or daughter, or where the employee is needed to care for a parent with a serious health condition.[50] The provision does not apply to the serious health condition of the employee or the employee's spouse, son, or daughter. The provision does not apply to other combinations of relatives who happen to work for the same employer, such as siblings.[51] If the leave is not within the scope of this marriage penalty provision, employees, even if husband and wife, are treated separately for purposes of entitlement to federal FMLA leave. According to the legislative history, the marriage penalty was intended to eliminate any employer incentive to refuse to hire married couples.[52]

For the so-called marriage penalty to apply, the employees must currently be husband and wife pursuant to a valid marriage. The provision does not apply to unmarried parents employed by the same employer.[53] Similarly, it would not apply to employees who have been legally divorced. The penalty provision would, however, apply to employees who have been separated but have not been legally divorced. A divorce decree requires legal action by the government; there is no such thing as a common law divorce. Pursuant to the Defense of Marriage Act, the FMLA does not recognize same-sex marriages.[54] The marriage penalty provision, therefore, would not apply to same-sex married couples working for the same employer.

For the marriage penalty provision to apply, the husband and wife must work for the same employer. The provision would apply where the husband and wife worked for the same employer, even if they worked in geographically separate locations or in different operating divisions.[55] Determining who is a covered employer for purposes of the FMLA is addressed in Chapter 2, *Schools as FMLA-Covered Employers*.

The following examples illustrate the operation of the marriage penalty.

FMLA Illustrated: Marriage Penalty Examples

Scenario 1

Ken and Wendy work for the Block Island public school system. They are both eligible for FMLA leave. The Block Island school system uses a fixed academic year for the FMLA leave year. During the leave year, Wendy takes 8 weeks of FMLA leave to bond with the couple's newborn son, Henry. Ken has not taken any FMLA leave during the leave year.

The FMLA leave taken by Wendy is subject to the marriage penalty. As such, for the remainder of the leave year, Ken is limited to 4 weeks of FMLA leave for conditions covered by the marriage penalty provision (e.g., birth, adoption, or foster care placement of a son or daughter or to care for a parent with a serious health condition). Ken could take up to 4 weeks of FMLA leave to bond with Henry or to care for Ken's parents with a serious health condition.

Ken also has 12 weeks of FMLA leave available during the leave year for conditions not within the scope the marriage penalty. Ken could use his 12 weeks of leave for his own serious health condition or to care for his daughters Julie and Ellen, his son Henry, or Wendy if any of them were to suffer from a serious health condition.

Scenario 2

During the leave year, Ken and Wendy take 12 weeks combined (Wendy took 10 weeks, Ken took 2 weeks) for the birth and care of a newborn child. Wendy would have 2 workweeks of FMLA leave to care for their own serious health condition or that of her children or spouse. Ken would have 10 weeks of leave remaining to care for his own serious health condition or that of Wendy or his children. Since Ken and Wendy used 12 workweeks of FMLA leave for the birth and care of the newborn child, no additional FMLA leave may be taken by either to care for a parent with a serious health condition for the remainder of the 12-month leave year.

Scenario 3

In this scenario, Ken is an eligible employee and Wendy is not. During the leave year, Wendy wants to take 2 weeks of FMLA leave to bond with their newly adopted 3-year old son. Ken plans on taking 8 weeks of FMLA leave at the same time to bond with their son.

Wendy is not eligible for FMLA leave. As such, the marriage penalty provision does not apply. Wendy would not be entitled to any FMLA leave. Ken could take up to 12 workweeks of FMLA leave during the leave year to bond with his son.

Scenario 4

Ken and Wendy are both eligible employees. In addition to teaching, Ken coaches. Ken's usual or normal work schedule is 60 hours in a 6-day workweek. Wendy normally works 40 hours a week in school administration. During the fixed 12-month leave year, Wendy took 60 hours of FMLA leave for her own serious health condition, 20 hours to care for Ken who was laid up with a serious health condition, and 20 hours to care for Ellen, their 8-year-old daughter who had a serious health condition.

During the same leave year, Ken took 32 hours of FMLA leave for his own serious health condition and 20 hours to care for Wendy, who was laid up with a serious health condition. Ken also took 120 hours of FMLA leave to care for his mother, who has a long-term serious health condition.

Wendy has requested 100 hours of FMLA leave to care for her father, who is incapacitated with a serious health condition. Ken also needs 100 hours of FMLA leave to care for his mother.

Because of the marriage penalty, an eligible husband and wife are limited to a combined total of 12 weeks of leave during the 12-month FMLA leave year for any conditions within the scope of the marriage penalty. In this example, Wendy is entitled to 480 hours of FMLA leave during the 12-month leave year. She has already used 100 hours, leaving her with 380 hours. However, that amount is further reduced for the 120 hours of

(*continued*)

FMLA Illustrated: Marriage Penalty Examples (*continued*)

FMLA leave taken by Ken to care for his seriously ill mother. That leave is subject to the marriage penalty. Subtracting the marriage penalty leave used by Ken from the 380 hours of FMLA leave available to Wendy leaves 260 hours for future use. Subtracting the 100 hours Wendy plans to use and the 100 hours Ken plans to use, both of which are subject to the marriage penalty, leaves Wendy with 60 additional FMLA hours she could use during the remainder of the FMLA leave year.

Ken's total FMLA leave entitlement for the year is 720 hours (60 hours per week multiplied by 12 workweeks). He has used 172 hours of FMLA leave so far, leaving him with 548 hours. None of the 100 hours of leave Wendy has taken so far involves the marriage penalty. Subtracting the 100 hours of leave Wendy plans on taking to care for her father, which is covered by the marriage penalty, leaves Ken with 448 hours of FMLA leave remaining. Subtracting the 100 hours Ken plans on using to care for his mother (which is subject to the marriage penalty) leaves Ken with 328 hours of FMLA leave for future use.

Note that many state pregnancy-disability laws specify a period of disability either before or after the birth of a child; such periods would also be considered FMLA leave for a serious health condition of the mother, but would not be subject to the marriage penalty.[56] The FMLA does not prohibit a husband and wife from taking FMLA leave simultaneously. Some state family and medical leave laws, however, do prohibit husbands and wives who work for the same employer from simultaneously taking FMLA leave.[57]

[3] Determining the Amount of FMLA Leave Used by an Employee

The DOL regulations establish rules for determining the amount of FMLA leave an employee has used and whether absences for an FMLA-covered condition must be charged against the employee's 12-week FMLA leave entitlement. If an employee performs work for the employer while on FMLA leave, the time the employee spent working does not count against the employee's annual 12-workweek FMLA leave entitlement.[58] The amount of time that the employee is "suffered and permitted" to work for the employer, whether requested or not by the employer, must be counted as "hours worked" pursuant to the Fair

Labor Standards Act.[59] For example, if while recuperating from surgery at home, a teacher graded papers or prepared a test or course work, the time the teacher spent performing such activities while on FMLA leave could not be charged against his or her 12-workweek FMLA leave entitlement.

For purposes of determining the amount of leave used by an employee, the fact that a holiday may occur within the week taken as FMLA leave has no effect; the week is counted as a week of FMLA leave.[60] If, however, for some reason the employer's activities have temporarily ceased and employees generally are not expected to report for work for one or more weeks, the days the employer's activities have ceased do not count against the employee's FMLA leave entitlement.[61] For example, the time an employee spent on FMLA leave would not count against the employee's FMLA leave entitlement during a school's winter break (or summer vacation, or if the school closed for lengthy repairs).[62]

8.04 LEAVE SCHEDULING

FMLA leave may be taken by an eligible employee in a single block of time, intermittently, or on a reduced leave schedule. There are rules governing the manner in which an employee takes FMLA leave. Special rules for schools govern leave taken by certain school employees near the end of an academic term. Whether an employee takes FMLA leave in a single block of time, intermittently, or on a reduced leave schedule may impact other employee and school FMLA requirements.

[1] Intermittent and Reduced Leave Schedule Leave

FMLA leave may be taken on an intermittent or reduced leave schedule basis.[63] Intermittent leave is leave taken in separate periods of time due to the same FMLA covered condition rather than as one continuous period of time.[64] Examples of intermittent leave would include leave taken on an occasional basis for medical appointments or leave taken several days at a time spread over a period of six months, such as for chemotherapy.[65] Leave on a reduced leave schedule means a leave schedule that reduces the usual number of hours per workweek, or hours per workday, of an employee.[66] For example, an employee who went from full-time to part-time work as a result of taking FMLA leave would be said to be on a reduced leave schedule.[67] In that sense, a reduced leave schedule is simply a more systematic form of intermittent leave. Although the statute uses the term "reduced leave schedule," it might be better understood as meaning a reduced work schedule. School administrators don't need to know whether leave is intermittent or on a reduced leave schedule, as they are treated the same way for purposes of the FMLA regulations. To determine which FMLA rules apply, school administrators must identify whether leave is being taken in a single block of time or whether more than one absence is being taken for the same covered condition.

School administrators don't need to know whether leave is intermittent or on a reduced leave schedule, as they are treated the same way for purposes of the FMLA regulations.

There is no limit on the duration of an increment of leave when an employee takes intermittent leave or leave on a reduced leave schedule.[68] However, school employers may (and should) limit leave increments to the shortest period of time that the school employer's payroll system uses to account for absences or use of leave, provided it is one hour or less.[69] For example, if the school's payroll system records absences or leave usage down to the minute, an eligible employee who met all other requirements could take a minute of FMLA leave on an intermittent or reduced leave schedule basis. Generally, employers may not require employees to take more FMLA leave than necessary to address the circumstances that precipitated the need for leave, though there are some exceptions for certain school employees as discussed in subsection (v) below.[70]

(i) Birth, Adoption, and Foster Care Placement

An employee does not have an absolute right to FMLA leave on an intermittent or reduced leave schedule basis for the birth, adoption, or foster care placement of a son or daughter, or to care for the newly born or newly placed child.[71] The employee must secure the permission of the employer.[72] Remember, in this situation the employee is entitled to FMLA leave even though the newly born or placed child does not have an FMLA-covered serious health condition.

Schools need to exercise caution to ensure that the FMLA leave request is truly intermittent or on a reduced leave schedule for a single covered condition before denying the employee permission to take such leave. Particularly where the need for leave is due to birth, employees often mix their use of FMLA leave so that all leave is not based on the same covered condition. For example, an employee may take FMLA leave to care for his wife who is pregnant, which is a serious health condition. After the child is born, the employee may ask for FMLA leave to bond with the newborn child. This is not intermittent FMLA leave. The absence to care for the pregnant wife is due to a serious health condition. The absence to bond with the newborn child is not due to a serious health condition. Therefore, because the two absences are based on different covered conditions, the second leave request to bond with the child is not intermittent FMLA leave. An employer would not be able to deny the employee permission for the second absence on the grounds that it was intermittent FMLA leave.

A school employer should carefully consider its interests before exercising its right to deny the employee permission to take intermittent leave due to birth, adoption, or foster care placement. This is because an employee in this situation who has been denied FMLA leave on an intermittent or reduced leave schedule basis may turn around and request FMLA leave for a continuous block of time. Employees do not need the school employer's permission to take one continuous block of FMLA leave due to birth, adoption, or foster care placement. A school employer must weigh whether it is better to allow the employee to go out on the requested intermittent or reduced leave schedule or whether a single continuous absence of up to 12 full workweeks is better in terms of school operations.

For example, to bond with a newborn child, a school employee asks to take 6 weeks of FMLA leave after the birth and to work half days for the next 6 weeks thereafter. Feeling that the employee's request is overly burdensome, the school exercises its rights and denies permission to take the requested intermittent leave. The employee subsequently requests 12 continuous weeks of FMLA leave to bond with the newborn child. All other things being equal, the school cannot deny the employee permission to take FMLA leave, because this leave is not on an intermittent or reduced leave schedule. The question for the school is whether it is better off allowing the employee to take leave on an intermittent basis or on a continuous basis. Schools would be well advised to work with employees in this situation to minimize the impact of the employee's FMLA leave on school operations.

(ii) Serious Health Conditions

FMLA leave is available to eligible employees on an intermittent or reduced leave schedule basis if the employee or covered family member has an FMLA-covered serious health condition. The right, however, is not absolute.[73] In order to be entitled to FMLA leave on an intermittent or reduced leave schedule basis for a serious health condition, "an employee must pass through a series of substantive requirements and procedural hoops as provided by the statute."[74] There are four procedural requirements that an eligible employee must meet: (1) intermittent leave or a reduced leave schedule due to a serious health condition must be "medically necessary," (2) the employee must make a reasonable effort to schedule treatment so as not to unduly disrupt the employer's operations, (3) the employee must give timely and adequate notice of the need for FMLA leave on an intermittent or reduced leave schedule basis, and (4) if requested, the employee must timely provide medical certification in support of the medical necessity of intermittent leave or a reduced leave schedule.[75] An employee who fails to meet all of these requirements is not entitled to FMLA leave on an intermittent or reduced leave schedule basis due to a serious health condition.[76]

For leave to be medically necessary, there must be a medical need for leave that is best accommodated through intermittent leave or a reduced leave schedule.[77] Whether leave on an intermittent or reduced leave schedule basis is "medically necessary" is determined exclusively by the health care provider for the employee or covered family member with the serious health condition.[78] Voluntary treatments and procedures, however, generally are not "medically necessary."[79] Several courts have interpreted "medically necessary" to require both necessity and urgency. Routine medical examinations or appointments are not medically necessary.[80] Similarly, an employee's election to reschedule a medical appointment has been cited as evidence that the leave was not "medically necessary."[81] On the other hand, leave was "medically necessary" where it was necessary for a diabetic employee to eat something in order for the employee to control his blood sugar.[82] On the extreme end of the spectrum, one court found that an employee's absence from work while drinking at a local bar after caring for his seriously ill father was "medically necessary."[83]

To perfect the right to federal FMLA leave on an intermittent or reduced leave schedule basis, employees must make a reasonable effort to schedule leave so as not to unduly disrupt employer operations.[84] When planning medical treatment, the employee must consult with the employer and make a reasonable effort to schedule leave so as not to unduly disrupt the employer's operations, subject to the approval of the health care provider.[85] Ordinarily, employees are expected to consult with their employers prior to scheduling treatment in order to work out a treatment schedule that best suits the needs of both the employer and the employee.[86] Where an employee fails to consult with the employer to make a reasonable attempt to arrange a schedule of treatments so as not to unduly disrupt the employer's operations, the employer may initiate discussions with the employee and require the employee to attempt to make such arrangements, subject to the approval of the health care provider.[87] Courts have upheld the denial of FMLA leave and disciplinary action where an employee fails to make reasonable efforts to consult with the employer or reschedule intermittent leave.[88]

To be entitled to FMLA leave, an eligible employee must give timely and adequate notice of the need for leave.[89] Where the need is for leave on an intermittent or reduced leave schedule basis, the FMLA requires that certain additional information be included as part of the employee's notice of the need for FMLA leave.[90] In addition to providing notice to apprise the employer that the request may fall within the protections of the FMLA, an employee requesting leave on an intermittent or reduced leave schedule basis due to a serious health condition must also advise the employer, upon request, of the reasons the intermittent leave or reduced leave schedule is necessary and of the treatment schedule, if applicable.[91]

An employee need only give the employer notice of the need for leave on an intermittent or reduced leave schedule basis one time, but the employee must notify the employer as soon as practicable if dates of scheduled leave change, are extended, or were initially unknown.[92] Because a period of intermittent leave or a reduced leave schedule may take place over a long period of time, schools need to be alert to the fact that technically, once the employee properly gives notice of the need for intermittent leave or a reduced leave schedule, the FMLA does not require any additional notice unless circumstances change. This gives rise to the absurd but very real prospect that employees may simply come and go as they please for subsequent related FMLA absences without giving the school notice that they are taking FMLA leave. Schools need to initiate paid and unpaid leave policies that require employees to give notice every time they are going to be absent.

Employers may require an employee requesting leave due to a serious health condition to support that leave with a medical certification.[93] If the need for leave is on an intermittent or reduced leave schedule basis, employers may require additional information in the medical certification. Employers may require that the certification identify whether it is medically necessary for the employee to take leave intermittently or to work on a reduced leave schedule basis as a result of a serious health condition.[94] If so, the employer may require that the certification include an estimate of the probable duration of such schedule, an estimate of the probable number of treatments and the interval between treatments, actual or estimated dates of treatment, if known, and the period required for recovery, if any.[95]

Employers may not require medical certification for each and every absence on an intermittent or reduced leave schedule basis. Employers are supposed to request that the employee furnish medical certification at the time the employee gives notice of the need for leave or within two business days thereafter.[96] For leave on an intermittent or reduced leave schedule basis, absent a change in circumstances, employers are only permitted to request certification on or about the first absence in the series of intermittent or reduced leave schedule FMLA absences.[97]

Where intermittent leave or a reduced leave schedule is involved, employers may not require an employee to medically recertify the serious health condition in less than the minimum period specified on the certification as necessary for such leave (including treatment) unless one of three exceptions apply.[98] Finally, employers may not require an employee to submit medical certification that the employee is fit to return to duty from intermittent FMLA-covered leave due to a serious health condition.[99]

(iii) Transfer to an Alternative Position

The FMLA permits covered employers to transfer employees who need FMLA leave on an intermittent or reduced leave schedule basis to an equivalent alternative position that better accommodates recurring periods of leave than the employee's regular position.[100] The DOL explained the rationale for this rule as follows:

> [T]his provision was intended to give greater staffing flexibility to employers by enabling them temporarily to transfer employees who need intermittent leave or leave on a reduced leave schedule to positions more suitable for recurring periods of leave. At the same time it ensures that employees will not be penalized for their need for leave by requiring that they receive equivalent pay and benefits during the temporary transfer. Congress anticipated that a reduced leave schedule would often be perceived as desirable by employers who would prefer to retain a trained and experienced employee part-time for the weeks that the employee is on leave rather than hire a full-time temporary replacement.[101]

If an employee needs intermittent leave or leave on a reduced leave schedule that is foreseeable based on planned medical treatment for the employee or a family member, including during a period of recovery from a serious health condition, or if the employer agrees to permit intermittent or reduced schedule leave for the birth of a child or placement of a child for adoption or foster care, an employer may require the employee to transfer temporarily to an available alternative position for which the employee is qualified and which better accommodates recurring periods of leave than does the employee's regular position.[102] Transfer to an alternative position may include altering an existing job to better accommodate the employee's need for intermittent or reduced leave.[103]

Transfer to an alternative position may require compliance with any applicable collective bargaining agreement, other federal law (such as the Americans with Disabilities Act), and state law.[104] The conditions of a temporary transfer may not violate any applicable collective bargaining agreement containing higher standards or more generous provisions for employees than those of the FMLA.[105] For example, if a collective bargaining agreement requires a school employer to maintain full vacation benefits during a period of paid leave regardless of the number of hours worked, including during FMLA leave, the school could not proportionately reduce vacation benefits to reflect the reduced number of hours the employee has worked in the alternative position.

The alternative position must have equivalent pay and benefits but need not have equivalent duties.[106] An employer may increase the pay and benefits of an existing alternative position so as to make them equivalent to the pay and benefits of the employee's regular job.[107] An employer may also transfer the employee to a part-time job with the same hourly rate of pay and benefits, provided the employee is not required to take more leave than is necessary.[108] For example, an employee desiring to take leave in increments of 4 hours per day could be transferred to a half-time job, or could remain in the employee's same job on a part-time schedule, receiving the same hourly rate as in his or her previous job and enjoying the same benefits.[109] While the employee is in the alternative position, an employer may not eliminate benefits that otherwise would not be provided to part-time employees; however, an employer may proportionately reduce benefits such as vacation leave if an employer's normal procedure is to base such benefits on the number of hours worked.[110]

For example, if a full-time employee switches to a part-time or reduced leave schedule under the FMLA, the employee must continue to receive the same (full) level of benefits that the employee enjoyed before starting FMLA leave and may not be required to pay more to maintain that same level of benefits enjoyed prior to the start of the FMLA leave, regardless of any employer policy applicable to part-time employees that would suggest a different result.[111] To permit otherwise would result in the employee not receiving equivalent pay and benefits as required by the FMLA. An employer, may, however, proportionately reduce the benefits that are computed based on the number of hours worked during the period—for example, vacation and sick leave, insurance, or other benefits that are determined by the amount of earnings.[112]

Employers may not transfer an employee to an alternative position in order to discourage the employee from taking FMLA leave or otherwise impose a hardship on the employee.[113] For example, a white-collar employee may not be assigned to perform laborer's work; an employee working the day shift may not be reassigned to the graveyard shift; an employee working in the headquarters facility may not be reassigned to a branch a significant distance away from the employee's normal job location. Any such attempt on the part of an employer to make such a transfer will be held to constitute a prohibited act in violation of the FMLA.[114] Generally, school employers who want to transfer the employee to an alternative equivalent position will want to demonstrate how the position better accommodates the employee's need for leave on an intermittent or reduced leave schedule basis.[115]

When an employee who is taking leave intermittently or on a reduced leave schedule and who has been transferred to an alternative position no longer needs to continue on leave and is able to return to full-time work, the employee must be placed in the same or equivalent job as the job he or she left when the leave commenced.[116] An employee may not be required to take more leave than necessary to address the circumstances that precipitated the need for leave.[117]

(iv) Determining the Amount of Leave Taken on an Intermittent or Reduced Leave Schedule

Generally, employers may count only the actual amount of FMLA leave taken against the employee's annual 12-workweek FMLA entitlement. The DOL regulations provide that there is no limit on the duration of an increment of leave when an employee takes intermittent leave or reduced schedule leave.[118] The FMLA, however, recognizes that the attendance systems used by employers may not be capable of recording very small increments of leave. As a practical matter, the smallest increment of intermittent or reduced schedule FMLA leave that an employee may take, and an employer must record, is the lesser of an hour or the smallest increment of time the employer's payroll system uses to account for absences or use of leave.[119]

> To comply with the FMLA schools must have a payroll system that accounts for absences or use of leave in increments of one hour or less.

Generally, employers may not require employees to take more FMLA leave than is necessary to address the circumstances that precipitated the need for leave.[120] For example, an eligible school employee who wants to take 3 hours and 25 minutes of leave every day can't be required to take 4 hours leave so that the employee can easily be placed into a part-time position pursuant to the school's existing policies. As noted in the next subsection, an exception to the general prohibition against requiring an employee to take more FMLA leave than is necessary exists for certain employees of local educational agencies.

(v) Special School Rules

The FMLA has special rules for certain educational employees who take FMLA leave on an intermittent or reduced leave schedule basis or who take leave near the end of an academic term.[121] The special rules apply to employees of "local educational agencies." Local educational agencies include public school boards and elementary and second schools under their jurisdiction.[122] The special rules also apply to private elementary and secondary schools.[123] The special rules do not apply to other kinds of educational institutions such as colleges and universities, trade schools, and preschools.[124]

The special rules affect the taking of intermittent or reduced schedule leave and leave near the end of an academic term (semester) by *instructional employees*.[125] "Instructional employees" are those whose principal function is to teach and instruct students in a class, a small group, or an individual setting.[126] Included within this category are athletic coaches, driving instructors, and special education assistants such as signers for the hearing impaired.[127] The special rules do not apply to teacher assistants or aides who do not have as their principal job function actual teaching or instructing, nor does it include auxiliary personnel such as counselors, psychologists, curriculum specialists, cafeteria workers, maintenance workers, or bus drivers.[128]

The FMLA places limitations on the use of leave on an intermittent or reduced leave schedule basis by instructional employees of local educational agencies and private elementary and secondary schools (1) if the employee would be on leave for more than 20 percent of the working days over the leave period or (2) if the employee seeks to take FMLA leave near the end of an academic term.

In the first case, if an eligible instructional employee needs FMLA leave on an intermittent or reduced leave schedule that is foreseeable based on planned medical treatment for a serious health condition and the employee would be on leave for more than 20 percent of the total number of working days over the period the leave would extend, the school employer may require the employee to choose from the following two alternatives:[129]

- The employee may take leave for a period or periods of a particular duration, not greater than the duration of the planned treatment.
- The employee may transfer temporarily to an available alternative position for which the employee is qualified and which has equivalent pay and benefits and better accommodates recurring periods of leave than does the employee's regular position.

A "period of particular duration" means a block, or blocks, of time beginning no earlier than the first day for which leave is needed and ending no later than the last day on which leave is needed, and may include an uninterrupted period of leave.[130] Essentially, the special rules allow schools to require instructional employees to take FMLA leave in up to one large block of time for planned medical treatment, even though the treatment may only involve intermittent or partial days. If the employee elects to take leave for a "particular duration," the entire period of leave taken counts against the employee's annual 12-week FMLA leave entitlement.[131]

For example, if an instructional employee who normally works 5 days a week needs to take 2 days of FMLA leave per week over a period of several weeks, the special rules would apply. Employees taking leave that constitutes 20 percent or less of the working days during the leave period would not be subject to transfer to an alternative position.[132] A school is not required to exercise this option; it is permissible, not mandatory.

Generally, a local educational agency or private elementary or secondary school may require the instructional employee to choose between the two alternatives, but the choice of which alternative remains with the employee. An exception to that general rule applies if the instructional employee fails to provide notice of the need for FMLA leave and the need was foreseeable. In that case, if an instructional employee does not give the required notice, the school may require the employee to

- take leave of a particular duration;
- transfer temporarily to an alternative position; or
- delay the taking of FMLA leave until the notice provision is met.[133]

Special rules apply to instructional employees of local educational agencies and private elementary or secondary schools who begin leave near the end of an academic term. These special rules apply whether FMLA leave is taken intermittently, on a reduced leave schedule, or in a single continuous block of time. The rules differ, however, depending on whether leave begins more than 5 weeks before the end of the term, less than 5 weeks before the end of a term, or less than 3 weeks before the end of a term.[134] For FMLA purposes a school may not have more than two academic terms or semesters each year.[135]

If an instructional employee begins FMLA leave more than 5 weeks before the end of the academic term, the school employer may require the employee to continue taking leave until the end of the term if (1) the leave will last at least 3 weeks and (2) the employee would otherwise return to work during the 3-week period before the end of the term.[136] For example, an instructional employee begins FMLA leave 8 weeks before the end of the academic term. The FMLA leave is taken in a block of time and will continue for 6 weeks. Because the employee began leave more than 5 weeks from the end of the academic term and is scheduled to return from FMLA leave within the 3-week period before the academic term ends, the school employer would be within its rights to require the employee to continue taking leave until the end of the academic term.

If an instructional employee begins FMLA leave for purposes other than the employee's own serious health condition *during* the 5-week period before the end of the academic term, the school employer may require the employee to continue taking leave until the end of the term if (1) the leave will last more than 2 weeks and (2) the employee would otherwise return to work during the 2-week period before the end of the term.[137] For example, an instructional employee takes FMLA leave on a reduced leave schedule beginning 4 weeks before the end of the academic term to care for a spouse with a serious health condition. The leave is to last 3 weeks. Because the leave is not for the employee's own serious health condition, it began within 5 weeks before the end of the academic term, and the employee is set to return within the 2-week period before the end of the academic term, the school could require the employee to remain on leave until the end of the academic term.

If an instructional employee begins FMLA leave for a purposes other than the employee's own serious health condition during the 3-week period before the end of the academic term and the leave will last more than 5 working days, the school employer may require the employee to remain on leave until the end of the academic term.[138] For example, an instructional employee begins FMLA leave for 10 working days within the 3-week period prior to the end of the academic term to care for a parent with a serious health condition. Because the leave began within the 3-week period at the end of the academic term and would last more than 5 working days, the school employer could require the employee to remain on leave until the end of the academic term.

The special rules limit the leave that counts against the instructional employee's 12-workweek FMLA leave entitlement. If an instructional employee chooses to take leave for "periods of a particular duration" in the case of intermittent or reduced schedule leave, the entire period of leave taken counts as FMLA leave.[139] Where an instructional employee is required to take leave until the end of an academic term, however, only the period of leave until the employee is ready and able to return to work "shall be charged against the employee's FMLA leave entitlement."[140] The DOL explained the rationale for the rule as follows:

> The legislative history provides the following guidance: Whenever a teacher is required to extend his or her leave under section 108(c) or (d), such leave would be treated as other leave under the act, with the same rights to employment and benefits protection contained in section 104. . . . However, the Department agrees that because the employer had the option of not requiring the employee to take leave until the end of the term, the leave should not count against the 12-week entitlement.[141]

If an instructional employee is required to take leave until the end of the academic term, school employers must maintain the employee's group health insurance and restore the employee to the same or equivalent job, with the same benefits the employee had prior to leave, at the conclusion of the leave.[142]

(vi) FLSA-Exempt Employees

The FMLA allows employees to take FMLA leave intermittently or on a reduced leave schedule without losing their exemption from the overtime requirements of the Fair Labor Standards Act (FLSA). The FMLA provides that when an employee is otherwise exempt from the FLSA requirements for payment of minimum wage and overtime compensation for hours worked in excess of 40 per week (the exemption for "executive, administrative, and professional" employees), compliance by an employer with the FMLA's requirement to provide unpaid leave will not affect the exempt status of the employee under the FLSA exemption and its implementing regulations.[143] Employers can legally dock the pay of otherwise exempt, salaried employees for FMLA leave taken for partial day absences.[144]

This means that under the regulations currently in effect, if an employee is an executive, administrative, or professional employee , is paid on a salary basis, and is paid a salary of at least the amount specified in the regulations, the employer may reduce the employee's salary for any hours taken as intermittent or reduced FMLA leave within a workweek, without affecting the exempt status of the employee.[145] For example, an employee is a salaried supervisor exempt from the overtime requirements of the FLSA. Due to a serious health condition the employee takes FMLA leave on a reduced leave schedule, effectively going from full-time to part-time status. While she works part-time, the employee is paid an hourly figure prorated from her full-time salary. The employee would not have a viable claim for overtime wages based on the argument that receipt of hourly wages took the employee out of the FLSA exemption from overtime for salaried professional employees. The FMLA provides a limited exception to the FLSA overtime requirements that preserves the employee's FLSA-exempt status during FMLA leave.[146]

For an employee paid in accordance with the "fluctuating workweek" method of payment for overtime,[147] the employer, during the period in which intermittent or reduced schedule FMLA leave is scheduled to be taken, may compensate an employee on an hourly basis and pay the employee only for the hours the employee works, including time and a half for overtime.[148] A "fluctuating workweek" method of payment is used for employees who are salaried but who fall into a gray area in terms of whether they qualify under the executive, administrative, or professional employee exemption. Employers can pay these employees a salary for all hours worked under a fluctuating workweek payment plan. Essentially, the employee is paid a base salary covering straight-time wages for all hours worked in a workweek.[149] The change to payment on an hourly basis would be in effect for the entire period during which the employee is taking intermittent leave, including weeks in which no leave is taken.[150] The hourly rate is determined by dividing the employee's weekly salary by the employee's normal or average schedule of hours worked during weeks in which FMLA leave is not being taken.[151]

If an employer elects to follow this exception from the fluctuating workweek method of payment, the employer must do so uniformly with respect to all employees paid on a fluctuating workweek basis who take FMLA leave on an intermittent or reduced leave schedule basis.[152] If an employer does not elect to convert the employee's compensation to hourly pay, the employer may not reduce the employee's salary for FMLA leave absences.[153] Once the need for FMLA leave on an intermittent or reduced leave schedule is over, the employee may be restored to payment on the fluctuating workweek basis.[154]

This special exception to the "salary basis" requirements of the FLSA exemption and the fluctuating workweek payment requirements applies only to employees of covered employers who are eligible for FMLA leave and whose leave qualifies as FMLA leave.[155]

[2] Block Leave

An eligible employee may take FMLA leave in a single continuous block of time due to the same FMLA covered condition. That single block of time does not have to be an employee's entire annual entitlement of 12 workweeks of leave. So long as the continuous absence is due to the same covered condition, the absence may be any length of time up to the employee's entire annual entitlement of 12 workweeks of leave. For example, an employee's request for 2 hours of FMLA leave to drive a parent with a covered condition to the doctor for treatment, without more, is one continuous absence for the same covered condition. Of course, if the employee requests leave to drive his or her parent to the doctor on more than one occasion for the same covered condition, the leave is no longer one continuous absence for the same covered condition. As addressed earlier in this chapter, multiple absences for the same covered condition fall within the requirements for leave on an intermittent or reduced leave schedule basis. School administrators must be aware that a single short period of absence falls within the requirements for a block of FMLA leave, not intermittent or reduced schedule leave. Applying the intermittent/reduced leave schedule rules to a block of leave may result in a violation of the employee's FMLA rights and school liability.

The rules governing an employee's use of FMLA leave in a single block of time are not formally laid out in the statute or the DOL regu-

School administrators must be aware that a single short period of absence falls within the requirements for a block of FMLA leave, not intermittent or reduced schedule leave. Applying the intermittent/reduced leave schedule rules to a block of leave may result in a violation of the employee's FMLA rights and school liability.

lations. Rather, the rules governing a single block of time are generally derived from what they are not: the rights and responsibilities that attach to employees or employers because the leave is intermittent or on a reduced leave schedule. For example, as discussed earlier in this chapter, employers may deny an eligible employee permission to take FMLA leave to bond with a newborn or newly adopted child if the leave is to be taken intermittently or on a reduced leave schedule. If the same leave is to be taken in a single continuous block of time (e.g., 6 continuous weeks), the employer does not enjoy the same right to deny the employee permission to take FMLA leave. Where leave is taken in a single continuous block of time for the same covered condition, school employers may not require employees to abide by the added requirements for intermittent leave or a reduced leave schedule. On the positive side, schools are not required to abide by the added requirements imposed on employers where intermittent or reduced schedule leave is involved.

The absence of formal rules governing FMLA leave taken in a single block of time sometimes creates unnecessary confusion. For example, from our earlier discussion we know that the smallest amount of time for recording intermittent or reduced schedule leave is the shortest period of time that an employer's payroll system uses to account for absences or use of leave, provided it is one hour or less. The DOL regulations do not provide a similar rule for leave taken in a single continuous block of time. School employers would, however, be well advised to use the same increment of time to record block leave as they use to record intermittent or reduced schedule leave.

8.05 EFFECT OF MORE GENEROUS EMPLOYER LEAVE POLICIES

Employers must observe any employment benefit program or plan that provides greater family or medical leave rights to employees than the rights established by the FMLA.[156] Conversely, the rights established by the Act may not be diminished by any employment benefit program or plan.[157] For example, school policy or a collective bargaining agreement may eliminate or soften the marriage penalty imposed by the

FMLA on spouses who work for the same employer. Such a policy would be more beneficial to employees, and therefore, the school would have to abide by that more generous policy rather than the more restrictive provisions of the FMLA. Schools will have to look at their existing policies to determine whether they are more generous to employees than the FMLA is.

The FMLA permits employers to amend existing leave and employee benefit programs provided that, as amended, they comply with the FMLA.[158] Schools with more generous family and medical leave benefits could, therefore, amend those policies so that they provide the minimum rights and benefits required by the FMLA. Of course, any amendment to family and medical leave policies must be done in accordance with school policies. Schools with collective bargaining agreements may have to bargain over such changes. Schools should not attempt to amend existing family and medical leave policies in order to thwart an employee's attempt to secure leave benefits under the more generous existing policy. Any such attempt would likely be viewed as retaliatory or discriminatory and in violation of the FMLA. Amendments that reduce more generous school family and medical leave benefits to the minimum required by the FMLA should be implemented prospectively.

8.06 STATE FAMILY AND MEDICAL LEAVE LAWS

State family and medical leave laws are not uniform regarding the amount of leave available to eligible employees or the scheduling of that leave. The amount of family and medical leave available and the time period of availability varies under state law, in many cases depending on the reason for leave. Many state laws do not address the calculation of the leave year at all. In contrast, most states allow employees to take leave intermittently, on a reduced leave schedule basis, or in a block of time. A few states include a marriage penalty for spouses who work for the same covered employers, while others do away with the penalty.

Colorado's family and medical leave regulations provide that if the employee has worked full-time, up to 520 hours per fiscal year will be granted as family medical leave.[159] Part-time employees receive a prorated amount of leave based on their regular appointment schedule. If a part-time employee works an irregular, variable schedule, the amount of leave is prorated based on the average number of hours worked in the 12 weeks prior to the beginning of leave.[160] In the case of a serious health condition and when medically necessary, family medical leave can be used on an intermittent basis or with a reduced work schedule.[161] Requests for intermittent leave or a reduced leave schedule in other circumstances may be granted at the sole discretion of the employing state agency.[162] To accommodate such requests, the employer may temporarily transfer the employee to another position.[163] All other types of leave available to state employees run concurrently with FMLA leave, and taking paid leave concurrent with FMLA leave does not extend an employee's 12-workweek FMLA entitlement.[164] Compensatory time is not leave and is not counted against the employee's FMLA entitlement.[165]

The District of Columbia Family and Medical Leave Act of 1990 provides a total of 16 workweeks of family leave during any 24-month period. Like the federal FMLA, leave due to the birth, adoption, or foster care placement of a child expires 12 months after the birth or placement. An employee may take medical leave for his or her own serious health condition on an intermittent basis when medically necessary.[166] Leave on an intermittent basis is available to an employee in the case of a family member with a serious health condition when medically necessary.[167] Upon the agreement of the employer and the employee, family leave may be taken on a reduced leave schedule, during which the 16 workweeks of allowable family leave may be taken over a period not to exceed 24 consecutive workweeks.[168] If two family members are employees of the same employer, (1) the employer may limit to 16 workweeks during a 24-month period the aggregate number of family leave workweeks to which the family members are entitled and (2) the employer may limit to 4 workweeks during a 24-month period the aggregate number of family leave workweeks to which the family members are entitled to take simultaneously.[169]

Maine's Family and Medical Leave Act provides every eligible employee with up to 10 consecutive workweeks of family medical leave in any 2 years.[170] The Maine statute does not address many issues covered by the federal FMLA regarding the amount and scheduling of family and medical leave. For example, Maine's law does not address whether leave may be taken intermittently or on a reduced leave schedule basis. Nor does it address the marriage penalty.

8.07 INTERACTION OF THE FEDERAL FMLA WITH STATE FAMILY AND MEDICAL LEAVE LAWS: LEAVE AMOUNT AND SCHEDULING

The interaction of the federal FMLA and state or local family and medical leave laws in this area is complex. Which law, the federal FMLA or state law, governs appears to depend on the issue. Generally, nothing in the FMLA supersedes any provision of state or local law that provides greater family or medical leave rights than those provided by the FMLA.[171] Employees are not required to designate whether the leave they are taking is FMLA leave or leave under an applicable state law, and an employer must comply with the appropriate (applicable) provisions of both.[172] An employer covered by one law and not the other has to comply only with the law under which it is covered.[173] The DOL has rejected arguments that the requirement that an employer apply the provisions of whichever law, federal or state, provides the greater leave rights to employees applies only to procedural provisions (e.g., eligibility, certification, notice) and not to substantive provisions.[174]

The federal FMLA allows employers to choose one of four methods for calculating the 12-month leave year. In contrast, state family and medical leave laws may mandate a particular method for calculating the leave year. The DOL concluded that multistate employers with eligible employees in a state with a family and medical leave statute that mandates a particular method for calculating the 12-month leave year "may comply with the State provision for all employees employed within that State, and uniformly use another method provided by this regulation for all other employees."[175] Note that the regulations do not require employers to determine and apply whichever law, the federal FMLA or applicable state law, provides the greater leave benefits to employees in terms of the calculation of the leave year. By its terms, the deference of the federal FMLA to state law on the calculation of the leave year applies only to multistate employers. The DOL does not explain whether the rule also applies to an employer who does not have employees outside the state. The use of the permissive word "may" is also confusing as it suggests that multistate employers may or may not defer to the state method of calculating the FMLA leave year, which does not appear to be what was intended.

Generally, leave taken for a reason specified under both the federal FMLA and state law may be simultaneously counted against the employee's entitlement under both laws.[176] However, because of differences between the federal FMLA and state family and medical leave laws, employees may be entitled to more than 12 workweeks of leave each 12-month leave year. For example, if state law provides 16 weeks of leave entitlement over two years, an employee would be entitled to take 16 weeks one year under state law and 12 weeks the next year under the federal FMLA. If the employee took 12 weeks the first year, the employee would be entitled to a maximum of 12 weeks the second year under the federal FMLA (not 16 weeks). An employee would not be entitled to 28 weeks in one year.[177]

The DOL further illustrated this issue in its comments accompanying publication of the final FMLA regulations. In pertinent part, the DOL observed:

> The Association of Washington Cities commented that an employee could take 12 weeks of FMLA-qualifying leave for a purpose other than the birth or adoption of a child and still be eligible under applicable State law to another (subsequent) 12 weeks of "parenting" leave, which could enable an employee to take 24 weeks of leave in a single year. Under the terms of the applicable statutes, this is true.
>
> The State of Oregon's Bureau of Labor and Industries noted that Oregon's parental leave law provides a 12-week window following the birth of a child for the use of parental leave, and asked if an employee's use of 12 weeks of parental leave within the first 12 weeks following the birth exhausts the parent's Federal right to take parental leave within the first year. An employee "eligible" under both the Federal and State law would exhaust both entitlements simultaneously within that 12-week period. Note, however, that if the employee used fewer than 12 weeks during the initial 12-week period following the birth, the employee could use the remainder of his or her Federal leave entitlement under FMLA within one year after the birth.

> Hill & Barlow pointed out that the Massachusetts maternity leave statute entitles an eligible employee to up to eight weeks of leave for the purpose of giving birth or for adopting a child. They asked if an employee had used 12 weeks of FMLA leave earlier in the year for a purpose other than giving birth or adopting a child, would the employee still be eligible to the State leave entitlement? The answer is "Yes."[178]

Finally, addressing differences between the federal FMLA and state law regarding the marriage penalty, in some states a parent may have to share entitlement to family and medical leave with his or her spouse regardless of whether they work for separate employers. Under the federal FMLA, each FMLA-eligible spouse would retain a federal entitlement equal to 12 weeks minus their portion of the state leave taken.[179] In this case, the federal FMLA provides the greater leave benefits to the employee than state law.

If leave is covered by both the federal FMLA and state law, school employers must take great care to determine, on a provision-by-provision basis, which law, federal or state, provides the greater leave benefits to an eligible employee and must apply that provision for purposes of the federal FMLA. Absent a similar provision under state law, school employers are not required to apply the more generous provisions of the federal FMLA to family and medical leave under applicable state law.

NOTES

1. 29 C.F.R. § 825.200(b).
2. 29 C.F.R. § 825.200(d)(1).
3. 29 C.F.R. § 825.200(d)(2).
4. 29 C.F.R. § 825.200(c).
5. 29 C.F.R. § 825.200(d)–(e).
6. 29 C.F.R. § 825.200(c).
7. *Id.*; see also *Bachelder v. America West Airlines, Inc.*, 259 F.3d 1112, 1126 (9th Cir. 2001).
8. 29 C.F.R. § 825.200(c).
9. *Id.*
10. *Id.*
11. Comments on Regulations Implementing the Family and Medical Leave Act of 1993 (§ 825.200), 60 Fed. Reg. 2180, 2200 (Jan. 6, 1995).

12. *Id.*

13. 29 C.F.R. § 825.200(e).

14. *Id.*

15. *Id.*

16. *Id.*

17. *Krohn v. Forsting*, 11 F. Supp. 2d 1082, 1092 (E.D. Mo. 1998).

18. 29 C.F.R. § 825.200(d)(1).

19. *Id.*

20. *Id.*

21. See *Bachelder v. America West Airlines, Inc.*, 259 F.3d 1112, 1127 (9th Cir. 2001) ("The regulations allow employers to choose among four methods for calculating their employees' eligibility for FMLA leave, but they do not specifically state how an employer indicates its choice.")

22. *Id.*

23. 29 C.F.R. § 825.301(a)(1).

24. *Bachelder*, 259 F.3d at 1127.

25. *Id.*

26. *Dodaro v. Village of Glendale Heights*, No. 01-CC-6396, 2003 U.S. Dist. LEXIS 5056 (N.D. Ill. March 31, 2003).

27. *Id.*

28. *Phillips v. Leroy-Somer North America*, No. 01-1046-T, 2003 U.S. Dist LEXIS 5349, at *14 (W.D. Tenn. March 28, 2003).

29. Comments on Regulations Implementing the Family and Medical Leave Act of 1993 (§ 825.200), 60 Fed. Reg. 2180, 2200 (Jan. 6, 1995).

30. 29 C.F.R. § 825.301(b)(1).

31. 29 U.S.C. § 2612(a)(2); 29 C.F.R. § 825.201.

32. 29 C.F.R. § 825.201.

33. 29 U.S.C. § 2653; 29 C.F.R. § 825.700(a)–(b).

34. 29 U.S.C. § 2612(a)(1); 29 C.F.R. § 825.200(a).

35. Comments on Regulations Implementing the Family and Medical Leave Act of 1993 (§ 825.205), 60 Fed. Reg. 2180, 2103 (Jan. 6, 1995).

36. *Id.*; DOL WH FMLA Advisory Opinion No. 107 (July 19, 1999).

37. DOL WH FMLA Advisory Opinion No. 107 (July 19, 1999).

38. *Id.*

39. *Id.*

40. *Id.*

41. *Id.*

42. Comments on Regulations Implementing the Family and Medical Leave Act of 1993 (§ 825.205), 60 Fed. Reg. 2180, 2203 (Jan. 6, 1995).

43. 29 C.F.R. § 825.205(b).

44. *Id.*

45. Comments on Regulations Implementing the Family and Medical Leave Act of 1993 (§ 825.205), 60 Fed. Reg. at 2203.

46. 29 C.F.R. § 825.205(d); DOL WH FMLA Advisory Opinion No. 107 (July 19, 1999).

47. 29 C.F.R. § 825.205(c).

48. Comments on Regulations Implementing the Family and Medical Leave Act of 1993 (§ 825.205), 60 Fed. Reg. at 2203.

49. 29 C.F.R. § 825.202(a)(1)–(3).

50. 29 C.F.R. § 825.202(a); DOL WH FMLA Advisory Opinion No. 66 (July 19, 1995).

51. Comments on Regulations Implementing the Family and Medical Leave Act of 1993 (§ 825.202), 60 Fed. Reg. at 2201; DOL WH FMLA Advisory Opinion No. 99 (Jan. 12, 1999).

52. Comments on Regulations Implementing the Family and Medical Leave Act of 1993 (§ 825.202), 60 Fed. Reg. at 2201; DOL WH FMLA Advisory Opinion No. 99 (Jan. 12, 1999).

53. Comments on Regulations Implementing the Family and Medical Leave Act of 1993 (§ 825.202), 60 Fed. Reg. at 2201; DOL FMLA Advisory Opinion No. 66 (July 19, 1995).

54. The Defense of Marriage Act is discussed more fully in Chapter 4, *Covered Family Members*.

55. 29 C.F.R. § 825.202(b).

56. 29 C.F.R. § 825.202(c).

57. See Alaska Stat. § 23.10.500.

58. DOL WH FMLA Advisory Opinion No. 67 (July 21, 1995).

59. *Id.*

60. 29 C.F.R. § 825.200(f).

61. *Id.*

62. *Id.*

63. 29 U.S.C. § 2612(b); 29 C.F.R. § 825.203(a).

64. 29 C.F.R. §§ 825.203(a), 825.800 ("intermittent leave" defined).

65. 29 C.F.R. § 825.800 ("intermittent leave" defined).

66. 29 U.S.C. § 2611(9); 29 C.F.R. §§ 825.203(a), 825.800 ("reduced leave schedule" defined).

67. 29 C.F.R. § 825.203(a).

68. 29 C.F.R. § 825.203(d).

69. *Id.*

70. *Id.*

71. See Chapter 5, *Covered Conditions*.

72. 29 C.F.R. § 825.203(b).

73. *Palazzolo v. Galen Hospitals of Texas, Inc.*, No. 1: 96-CV-2550-TWT, 1997 U.S. Dist LEXIS 21915 (N.D. Ga. Nov. 25, 1997).

74. *Kaylor v. Fannin Regional Hospital, Inc.*, 946 F. Supp. 988, 997 (N.D. Ga. 1996).

75. 29 U.S.C. § 2612(b)(1).

76. *Kaylor*, 946 F. Supp. at 997.

77. 29 C.F.R. § 825.117.

78. Comments on Regulations Implementing the Family and Medical Leave Act of 1993 (§ 825.117), 60 Fed. Reg. 2180, 2197 (Jan. 6, 1995).

79. 29 C.F.R. § 825.117.

80. See *Palazzolo v. Galen Hospitals of Texas, Inc.*, No. 1: 96-CV-2550-TWT, 1997 U.S. Dist LEXIS 21915, at *15 (N.D. Ga. Nov. 25, 1997); *Kaylor*, 946 F. Supp. at 997.

81. *Palazzolo*, No. 1: 96-CV-2550-TWT, 1997 U.S. Dist LEXIS 21915 (N.D. Ga. Nov. 25, 1997).

82. *Sabrrese v. Lowe's Home Centers, Inc.*, 320 F. Supp. 2d 311, 321 (W.D. Pa. 2004).

83. *Brunelle v. Cyro Industries, Inc.*, 225 F. Supp. 2d 67, 77 (D. Me. 2002).

84. 29 C.F.R. §§ 825.117, 825.302(e)–(f); DOL WH FMLA Advisory Opinion No. 101 (Jan. 15, 1999); DOL WH FMLA Advisory Opinion No. 60 (May 2, 1995).

85. 29 C.F.R. § 825.302(e).

86. *Id.*

87. *Id.*

88. See *Palazzolo v. Galen Hospitals of Texas, Inc.*, No. 1: 96-CV-2550-TWT, 1997 U.S. Dist LEXIS 21915 (N.D. Ga. Nov. 25, 1997); *Kaylor v. Fannin Regional Hospital, Inc.*, 946 F. Supp. 988, 997 (N.D. Ga. 1996).

89. 29 U.S.C. § 2612(e)(2)(B); 29 C.F.R. § 825.303(a). Employee notice obligations are addressed more fully in Chapter 6, *Notice Requirements*.

90. Employee notice requirements are addressed more fully in Chapter 6, *Notice Requirements*.

91. See 29 C.F.R. § 825.302(c), (f).

92. 29 C.F.R. § 825.302(a).

93. Medical certification requirements are discussed more fully in Chapter 7, *Documentation Requirements*.

94. 29 C.F.R. § 825.306(b)(2)(ii).

95. 29 C.F.R. § 825.306(b)(3)(i)(B).

96. 29 C.F.R. § 825.305(c).

97. *Id.*

98. 29 C.F.R. § 825.308(b)(2); see Chapter 7, *Documentation Requirements*.

99. 29 C.F.R. § 825.306(b)(2)(ii).

100. 29 U.S.C. § 2612(b)(2); 29 C.F.R. § 825.204.

101. Comments on Regulations Implementing the Family and Medical Leave Act of 1993 (§ 825.204), 60 Fed. Reg. 2180, 2202 (Jan. 6, 1995).

102. 29 C.F.R. § 825.204(a).

103. 29 C.F.R. § 825.204(b).

104. *Id.*

105. Comments on Regulations Implementing the Family and Medical Leave Act of 1993 (§ 825.204), 60 Fed. Reg. at 2202.

106. 29 C.F.R. § 825.204(c).

107. *Id.*

108. *Id.*

109. *Id.*

110. *Id.*

111. Comments on Regulations Implementing the Family and Medical Leave Act of 1993 (§ 825.204), 60 Fed. Reg. 2180, 2203 (Jan. 6, 1995).

112. *Id.*

113. 29 C.F.R. § 825.204(d).

114. *Id.*

115. See *Summerville v. ESCO Co. Ltd. Partnership*, 52 F. Supp. 2d 804, 816 (W.D. Mich. 1999) (In finding that transfer to alternative position was not intended to discourage employee from taking FMLA leave, court cited benefit to employer of moving employee to alternative position that was less sensitive to attendance than employee's regular position).

116. 29 C.F.R. § 825.204(e).

117. *Id.*

118. 29 C.F.R. § 825.203(d).

119. *Id.*

120. 29 C.F.R. § 825.209(d).

121. 29 U.S.C. § 2618; 29 C.F.R. § 825.600.

122. 29 U.S.C. § 2618(a)(1)(A); 29 C.F.R. § 825.600(a).

123. 29 U.S.C. § 2618(a)(1)(A); 29 C.F.R. § 825.600(a).

124. 29 C.F.R. § 825.600(a).

125. 29 U.S.C. § 2618(c); 29 C.F.R. § 825.600(c).

126. 29 C.F.R. §§ 825.600(c), 825.800 ("teacher" defined).

127. 29 C.F.R. §§ 825.600(c), 825.800 ("teacher" defined).

128. 29 C.F.R. §§ 825.600(c), 825.800 ("teacher" defined).

129. 29 U.S.C. § 2618(c)(1); 29 C.F.R. § 825.601(a)(1).

130. 29 C.F.R. § 825.601(a)(2).

131. 29 C.F.R. § 825.601(a).

132. 29 C.F.R. § 825.601(a)(2).

133. 29 C.F.R. § 825.601(b).

134. 29 C.F.R. § 825.602(a).

135. 29 C.F.R. § 825.602(b).

136. *Id.*

137. 29 C.F.R. § 825.602(a)(2).

138. 29 C.F.R. § 825.602(a)(3).

139. 29 C.F.R. § 825.603(a).

140. 29 C.F.R. § 825.603(b).

141. Comments on Regulations Implementing the Family and Medical Leave Act of 1993 (§ 825.603), 60 Fed. Reg. 2180, 2229 (Jan. 6, 1995); see also 29 C.F.R. 825.603(b).

142. 29 C.F.R. § 825.603(b).

143. 29 U.S.C. § 2612(c).

144. Comments on Regulations Implementing the Family and Medical Leave Act of 1993 (§ 825.206), 60 Fed. Reg. at 2204.

145. 29 C.F.R. § 825.206(a); DOL WH FMLA Advisory Opinion No. 89 (July 3, 1997).

146. See *Rowe v. Laidlaw Transit, Inc.*, 244 F.3d 1115, 1118 (9th Cir. 2001).

147. See 29 C.F.R. § 778.114.

148. 29 C.F.R. § 825.206(b).

149. Tony B. Griffin & Youndy C. Cook, *Wage and Hour Answer Book* question 9:13 (Aspen Publishers 2000).

150. 29 C.F.R. § 825.206(b).

151. *Id.*

152. *Id.*

153. *Id.*

154. *Id.*

155. 29 C.F.R. § 825.206(c).

156. 29 U.S.C. § 2652; 29 C.F.R. § 825.700(a).

157. 29 C.F.R. § 825.700(a).

158. 29 C.F.R. § 825.700(b).

159. 4 Colo. Code Regs. § 801-5-25.

160. *Id.*

161. 4 Colo. Code Regs. § 801-5-26.

162. *Id.*

163. *Id.*

164. 4 Colo. Code Regs. § 801-5-27.

165. *Id.*

166. D.C. Code Ann. § 32-503(a).

167. D.C. Code Ann. § 32-502(c).

168. D.C. Code Ann. § 32-502(d).

169. D.C. Code Ann. § 32-502(h)(1)(A)–(B).

170. Me. Rev. Stat. Ann. tit. 26, § 844(1).

171. 29 C.F.R. § 825.701(a).

172. *Id.*

173. *Id.*

174. Comments on Regulations Implementing the Family and Medical Leave Act of 1993 (§ 825.701), 60 Fed. Reg. 2180, 2231 (Jan. 6, 1995).

175. 29 C.F.R. § 825.200(d)(2).

176. 29 C.F.R. § 825.700(a).

177. 29 C.F.R. § 825.701(a)(1).

178. Comments on Regulations Implementing the Family and Medical Leave Act of 1993 (§ 825.701), 60 Fed. Reg. at 2231.

179. *Id.* at 2231–32.

CHAPTER 9

Paid Leave Substitution

9.01 OVERVIEW

Federal FMLA leave is unpaid. However, the FMLA allows for the substitution of accrued paid leave for unpaid FMLA leave. This chapter addresses the rules governing the substitution of paid leave for unpaid FMLA leave.

Section 9.02 discusses paid leave substitution, including what accrued paid leave may be used; the treatment of workers' compensation, unemployment compensation, and temporary disability plans; who has the right to elect to substitute paid leave; and the effect of paid leave substitution on other FMLA procedural requirements. Section 9.03 addresses the effect of more generous employer paid leave programs on the federal FMLA. Section 9.04 addresses paid leave substitution under state family and medical leave laws. Section 9.05 concludes the chapter by addressing the interaction of the federal FMLA with state family and medical leave laws.

9.02 SUBSTITUTION OF ACCRUED PAID LEAVE

[1] Introduction

All leave under the federal FMLA is unpaid.[1] Technically, there is no such thing as "paid" federal FMLA leave. Congress did not provide for or mandate employers to provide paid FMLA leave. When people, including yours truly, refer to paid FMLA leave, what they generally mean is an election to take available and accrued paid leave concurrently with unpaid FMLA leave. Under certain circumstances, the FMLA permits the substitution of accrued paid leave for unpaid FMLA leave.[2] Specifically, the FMLA permits an eligible employee to elect, or an employer to require, the substitution of accrued paid leave for unpaid FMLA leave. Accrued paid vacation, personal, sick or medical, or family leave of the employee may be substituted for all or part of any otherwise unpaid FMLA leave relating to birth, placement of a child for adoption or foster care, the employee's own serious health condition, or care for a spouse, son or daughter, or parent with a serious health condition.[3] The rationale behind paid leave substitution is to "mitigate the financial impact of wage loss due to family and temporary medical leave."[4] Where the circumstances allowing paid leave substitution do not exist or an election is not made, FMLA leave is unpaid.

Note that the FMLA does not require an employer to have paid leave programs for FMLA purposes. School employers are, therefore, free to amend or eliminate existing paid leave programs without violating the FMLA.[5] If, as is likely the case, a school employer does provide paid leave programs, the FMLA substitution provisions "assure that an employee is entitled to the benefits of applicable paid leave, plus any remaining leave time made available by [the] FMLA on an unpaid basis."[6]

[2] Substitution Undefined

The FMLA does not define the key term "substitute." This is unfortunate because the term is susceptible to at least two interpretations. One court has characterized the term "substitute" as "inartful and [an] unfortunate use of language."[7] Some courts have narrowly interpreted "substitute" as focusing solely on the payment of wages. For these courts, "substitute" allows an employee to concurrently take job-protected FMLA leave with accrued and available paid leave.[8] This would appear to be the interpretation of "substitute" preferred by the DOL.

Other courts have interpreted "substitute" literally. The Eleventh Circuit in one case held that an employee who "substitutes" paid leave for unpaid FMLA leave loses all FMLA leave protections for that leave. Once the substitution has been made, the leave is governed solely by the employer's paid leave policies and not the FMLA.[9] Other courts have taken a middle ground, indicating that an employee who elects to substitute paid leave for unpaid leave loses FMLA leave protections unless at the time of the election the employee advises the employer that he or she wants the paid leave to run concurrently with unpaid FMLA leave.[10]

School employers would be well advised to consult with counsel regarding the effects of paid leave substitution for purposes of the federal FMLA. I believe that the proper interpretation of "substitute" is that FMLA leave runs concurrently with paid leave.

[3] Who Elects Paid Leave

An eligible employee has the initial right to elect to substitute paid leave for unpaid FMLA leave.[11] An employee always has the right to request, in the first instance, that appropriate paid leave be substituted.[12] An employer may not override an employee's initial election to substitute appropriate paid leave for FMLA leave nor place any other limitations on its use. For example, a school employer could not require that an employee who has elected to substitute available paid leave use that paid leave only in full-day increments.[13] At the same time, in the absence of other limiting factors (e.g., more generous leave terms pursuant to school policy or a collective bargaining agreement), if an employee does not initially elect to substitute available paid leave, the employee must accept the employer's decision to require substitution, even if the employee opposes such substitution.[14] If the eligible employee does not choose to substitute accrued paid leave, the employer may require the employee to substitute paid leave for unpaid FMLA leave.[15] If neither the employee nor the employer elects to substitute paid leave for unpaid FMLA leave, the leave is covered as unpaid leave only, and the employee retains the use of the accrued paid leave.[16] Unpaid FMLA leave is the default where neither the employee nor the employer elects paid leave substitution.

Note that an employee does not have the option to forgo the benefits of the FMLA by electing paid leave only. This is because the FMLA empowers employers to determine whether the leave is FMLA-qualifying. The employee does not have the authority to decline

FMLA leave protection. Leave designation is addressed more fully in Chapter 6, *Notice Requirements*.

The FMLA does not address whether the right to substitute accrued paid leave for unpaid FMLA leave includes the right to select a specific paid leave balance over others that may be available. School employers need to be careful in this area to avoid violating the FMLA. Where the employee initially decides to forgo paid leave, the employer can compel substitution. In this situation there does not appear to be any restriction on an employer's ability to select from any accrued and available paid leave balance, even if the employee prefers the use of one paid leave balance over another. For example, an employee may prefer to exhaust available paid sick leave rather than vacation leave. Even if the leave at issue is for a serious health condition (thereby suggesting that sick leave would be more appropriate), there is nothing in the DOL regulations that would prohibit a school from selecting paid vacation leave. Of course, school employers should not make such a selection in order to discriminate or retaliate against an employee's use of FMLA leave. Schools should closely scrutinize their policies and past practices to ensure that their paid leave selection does not discriminate against employees who use FMLA leave.

It is less clear that an employer may require an employee to exhaust a particular paid leave balance (e.g., vacation) if an employee initially elects to substitute another paid leave balance (e.g., sick leave). The DOL has observed: "An employer may not override an employee's initial election to substitute appropriate paid leave for FMLA leave or place any other limitations on its use (e.g., minimum of full days or weeks at a time, etc)."[17]

This language suggests that an employee's initial selection of a specific available paid leave balance cannot be overridden by employers who would prefer to exhaust a different available paid leave balance. One court, however, has found that an employer may override an employee's paid leave election in order to substitute a different paid leave balance.[18]

Generally, it is in the interest of school employers to elect to substitute available paid leave for unpaid FMLA leave where possible. By so doing, the school reduces the amount of leave available to an employee, thereby reducing absenteeism. The unwanted depletion of an employee's paid leave balance for FMLA leave may also deter or limit marginal requests for leave. Employees generally dislike depleting their paid vacation leave, especially when they are required to do so against their wishes.

The timing and manner of employee and employer notice of an election to substitute paid leave for unpaid leave are addressed more fully in Chapter 6, *Notice Requirements*.

[4] Permissible Sources of Paid Leave for Substitution

There are three sources of accrued paid leave available for substitution of unpaid FMLA leave: (1) vacation leave, (2) personal or family leave, and (3) sick or medical leave.[19]

A review of the requirements for each category follows.

(i) Family Leave

"Family leave" refers to paid leave provided by the employer for the birth of a child and to care for such child, for the placement of a child for adoption or foster care, or to care for a spouse, son or daughter, or parent with a serious health condition.[20] Employers are not required to have a paid family leave plan. However, if they do, to the extent the paid family leave plan applies to the situation faced by the eligible employee and the leave is also covered by the FMLA, accrued family leave would be available to substitute for unpaid FMLA leave. For example, if the school employer's leave plan allows the use of family leave to care for a child but not for a parent, the school employer is not required to allow accrued paid family leave to be substituted for FMLA leave used to care for a parent.[21] In that case, the employee would be entitled to unpaid FMLA leave only.

(ii) Medical or Sick Leave

Substitution of accrued paid medical or sick leave may be made for any otherwise unpaid FMLA leave needed for the employee's own serious health condition or to care for a family member with a serious health condition.[22] Substitution of paid sick or medial leave may be elected to the extent the circumstances meet the employer's usual requirements for the use of sick or medical leave.[23] An employer is not required to allow substitution of paid sick or medical leave for unpaid FMLA leave in any situation where the employer's uniform policy would not normally allow such paid leave. For example, an eligible employee or employer has the right to substitute paid sick or medical leave to care for a covered family member with a serious health condition if the employer's leave plan allows sick or medical leave to be used for that purpose.[24] Similarly, an employee does not have a right to substitute paid sick or medical leave for a serious health condition that is not covered by the employer's leave plan.[25] Of course, in the event that the employee's leave is not covered by the school's leave plan, if the need for leave constitutes a serious health condition within the meaning of the federal FMLA, the school should grant unpaid FMLA leave. Conversely, if an employee uses paid leave under circumstances that do not qualify as FMLA leave, the leave will not count against the employee's annual 12-workweek FMLA leave entitlement.[26]

(iii) Vacation or Personal Leave

Substitution of accrued paid vacation or personal leave is permitted for unpaid FMLA leave for all or part of any FMLA leave related to birth, placement of a child for adoption or foster care, or a serious health condition.[27] Paid vacation or personal leave, including leave earned or accrued under plans allowing "paid time off," may be substituted, at either the employee's or the employer's option, for any qualified FMLA leave.[28] No limitations may be placed by the employer on the substitution of paid vacation or personal leave for these purposes.[29] For example, a school employer may not limit the time of year in which paid vacation or personal leave may be substituted for FMLA-qualifying absences or impose other limitations.[30]

[5] Compensatory Overtime

Compensatory time off or "comp time" is a limited exception recognized by the Fair Labor Standards Act that allows certain employees to earn and accrue hours toward paid time off in lieu of cash compensation for overtime hours worked.[31] It is not, however, a form of accrued paid leave that an employer may compel substitution for unpaid FMLA leave.[32] According to the DOL, paid leave substitution is limited to paid leave provided by the employer.[33] Comp time, on the other hand, is an alternative form of paying employees for overtime hours worked.[34]

The FLSA compensatory-time exception applies to employees of a public agency, defined as a state, a political subdivision of a state, or an interstate governmental agency.[35] FLSA public agency employers may pay an employee compensatory time off accrued at the rate of one and a half hours for each overtime hour worked in lieu of monetary compensation for the employee's overtime hours.[36] There are limitations in the number of comp-time hours an employee may accrue depending on the position of employee. Public school employees would appear entitled to accumulate up to 240 hours of comp time.[37]

Public agency employees covered by the FLSA comp-time exception may request to use accrued compensatory time for an FMLA reason.[38] If the public school employer permits the accrual to be used in compliance with the FLSA regulations (29 C.F.R. 553.25), the absence that is paid from the employee's accrued compensatory-time "account" may not be counted against the employee's FMLA leave entitlement.[39] Because it is not a recognized form of employer paid leave, an FLSA-covered public school employer may not compel an employee to use comp time in substitution for unpaid FMLA leave.

[6] Workers' Compensation

Workers' compensation is not a form of accrued paid leave within the meaning of the federal FMLA.[40] Rather, workers' compensation is a statutory entitlement, and workers' compensation payments are drawn from funds provided by employers but administered by states. Leave under a workers' compensation law is also not considered "unpaid leave" within the meaning of the FMLA. Workers' compensation leave is paid leave. Because, however, it is not a form of paid leave provided by employers but is a program administered by states, and because it is not unpaid, the FMLA provisions governing paid leave substitution do not apply to employees receiving workers' compensation.[41] Employers may not, therefore, compel an employee to substitute paid workers' compensation leave for unpaid FMLA leave.[42] In addition, when an employee is receiving payments from the state workers' compensation fund, the employee may not elect, and the school employer may not require, the employee to exhaust any form of paid leave provided by the employer during any portion of the absence covered by the workers' compensation payments.[43]

An employee who is injured at work and whose injury constitutes a serious health condition within the meaning of the FMLA may concurrently take FMLA leave with a workers' compensation absence.[44] Employers may count workers' compensation leave against the employee's annual 12-workweek FMLA leave entitlement, provided the on-the-job illness or injury constitutes an FMLA-covered serious health condition and all other conditions are met.[45]

[7] Temporary Disability Leave

Payments provided under school employer plans covering temporary disabilities, whether such payments are provided voluntarily through insurance or under a self-insured plan or such payments are required to meet legally mandated disability provisions (e.g., pregnancy disability laws), are treated the same as workers' compensation payments.[46] Assuming that the temporary disability is an FMLA-qualifying serious health condition and that all other FMLA requirements are met, the time an employee spends on temporary disability leave may be counted against the employee's annual 12-workweek FMLA entitlement.[47] Because temporary disability leave is paid leave, an employee may not elect, and an employer may not require, substitution of any form of accrued paid leave for any part of the absence covered by temporary disability payments.[48] If the requirements to qualify for payments pursuant to the employer's temporary disability plan are more stringent than those of the FMLA, the employee must meet the more stringent requirements of the plan to receive pay for the leave. Alternatively, the employee may choose not to meet the requirements of the temporary disability plan and instead receive no payment from the plan and use unpaid FMLA leave or substitute available accrued paid leave.[49]

[8] Unemployment Compensation

Between August 14, 2000, and November 10, 2003, states were permitted, although not required, as part of a voluntary experiment to amend their state unemployment compensation laws to provide partial wage replacement for parents taking approved leave, or otherwise leaving employment, following the birth or placement for adoption of a child. The experiment was initiated by President Clinton to address the financial barrier preventing parents from taking advantage of unpaid leave after the birth or adoption of a child.[50] The DOL issued final Birth and Adoption Unemployment Compensation (BAA-UC) regulations, codified at 20 C.F.R. pt. 604, implementing the experimental initiative on June 13, 2000.[51] Ultimately, no state elected to participate in the BAA-UC experiment. On December 4, 2002, the DOL published a notice proposing to remove the BAA-UC regulations.[52] The DOL proposed to remove the regulations because the BAA-UC experiment was "poor policy and a misapplication of federal UC law relating to" the "able and available" requirements for entitlement to unemployment compensation.[53] On October 9, 2003, the Bush administration finalized repeal of the BAA-UC regulations, and the repeal became effective on November 10, 2003.[54]

[9] When Has Paid Leave Accrued?

In order for an employee (or employer) to substitute paid vacation, personal, family, sick, or medical leave for unpaid FMLA leave, the paid leave must have accrued to the employee. The DOL explained what accrued means as follows:

> The legislative history indicates that the purpose of this section was "to provide that specified paid leave which was accrued but has not yet been taken, may be substituted for the unpaid leave under this act in order to mitigate the financial impact of wage loss due to family and temporary medical leaves." (House Report 103-8, Feb. 2, 1993, p. 38)[55]

In order to be *accrued* within the meaning of the FMLA, the employee must have earned the leave and must be able to use that leave during the FMLA leave period.[56] An employee could not elect and an employer could not require, paid leave substitution where accrued paid leave was not available to an employee during FMLA leave. For example, under a school's family leave policy, an employee who has worked 800 hours in the current year earns paid family leave that may not be used until the next year. An employee could not elect and the school could not require the substitution of paid family leave for FMLA leave during the current year, because the leave is not available to the employee until the following year.[57] Of course, the FMLA would not prohibit the school from having a more generous policy that voluntarily advances paid family or vacation leave to the employee for use with unpaid FMLA leave.[58]

9.03 EFFECT OF PAID LEAVE SUBSTITUTION ON FMLA PROCEDURAL REQUIREMENTS

The substitution of paid leave for unpaid FMLA leave may lessen the burden of meeting FMLA procedural requirements regarding notice and certification. The substitution of paid leave will never increase the burden placed on employees to meet the FMLA's notice, certification, and other procedural requirements.

If an eligible employee elects, or an employer requires, substitution of accrued and available paid leave for unpaid FMLA leave and the employer's procedural requirements (e.g., notice or certification requirements) are less stringent than the requirements of the FMLA, only the less stringent requirements may be imposed.[59] An employee who complies with an employer's less stringent leave plan requirements in such cases may not have leave for an FMLA purpose delayed or denied on the grounds that the employee has not complied with the stricter requirements of the FMLA.[60] However, where accrued paid vacation or personal leave is substituted for unpaid FMLA leave for a serious health condition, an employee may be required to comply with any less stringent medical certification requirements of the employer's sick leave program.[61] An employer may make revisions to its leave program to require notice or certification requirements that correspond to the requirements of the federal FMLA or may treat paid and unpaid leave differently, provided the program is not amended in a discriminatory manner that treats employees on FMLA leave differently from other similarly situated employees.[62]

The FMLA does not prohibit employers from imposing more stringent notice and procedural requirements on paid leave programs than are required by the FMLA. In that case, if the employee meets the notice and certification requirements of the FMLA but not the more stringent procedural requirements of the employer's paid leave program, the employee would be entitled to FMLA leave, but not paid leave. Employers with more stringent notice and certification requirements for paid leave than are required by the FMLA may not deny FMLA leave because the employee does not meet the more stringent paid leave procedural requirements. Again, in that case, the employee is not entitled to take paid leave concurrently with unpaid FMLA leave. The employee would, however, still be entitled to unpaid FMLA leave if he or she meets the notice and certification requirements of the FMLA.

One recent federal case has, however, found that an employer's enforcement of more stringent paid leave notice requirements violated the FMLA as they interfered with the employee's right to take paid leave.[63] In that case, the collective bargaining agreement required an employee to give 2 weeks' notice to use paid vacation time for leave. The employee was granted leave to attend to her father who had unexpectedly fallen critically ill. The employee wanted to use paid vacation leave for some of her absence. Relying on the 2-week notice provision, the employer denied the employee's request to substitute paid vacation leave. The employee was, however, granted unpaid leave for the absence. Citing 29 U.S.C. § 2612(d)(2)(A) and 29 C.F.R. § 825.207(e), the court concluded that the FMLA expressly granted the employee the right to use her accrued vacation time without the restriction of the 2-week notice policy. The decision would appear to negate an employer's ability to deny paid leave substitution where an employee fails to meet the more stringent procedural requirements for paid leave, at least where the employee meets the minimum procedural requirements of the federal FMLA.

School employers would be well advised to review their existing paid and unpaid leave policies to make sure that they have preserved their right to require appropriate notice and certification in the event that the employee elects paid leave substitution. To avoid discrimination claims, the school's paid leave notice and certification policies should apply uniformly to all employees, not just employees who seek to substitute paid leave for unpaid FMLA leave. Employee notice requirements are addressed in Chapter 6, *Notice Requirements*. Medical certification requirements are addressed in Chapter 7, *Documentation Requirements*.

9.04 EFFECT OF MORE GENEROUS EMPLOYER PAID LEAVE POLICIES

Employers may adopt leave policies that are more generous than the minimum required by the federal FMLA.[64] Employers may not, however, adopt leave policies that diminish FMLA rights.[65] If an employer adopts more generous leave benefits than the minimum required by the FMLA, the employer must abide by those more generous requirements.[66] For example, a school's collective bargaining agreement could provide that an employee has the exclusive right to elect to substitute paid leave for unpaid FMLA leave. Similarly, a school employer could adopt paid leave notice or certification requirements that are less stringent than the minimum required by the FMLA, and those more generous procedural requirements would apply where paid leave substitution has been elected.

9.05 STATE FAMILY AND MEDICAL LEAVE LAWS

Like the federal FMLA, state family and medical leave laws generally, although not universally, provide that family and medical leave is unpaid. California provides paid family leave. In the majority of states where unpaid family leave is the norm, some or all accrued and available paid leave generally may be substituted for unpaid family and medical leave. For example, the Massachusetts family and medical leave regulations provide state employees with up to 26 weeks of state family or medical leave a year, but no more than 10 days may be paid, with the remainder unpaid, except that if the employee has accumulated sick leave, vacation leave, or other personal leave credits, the employee may use such credits for which he or she may be eligible under the applicable rules.[67] During family leave taken in conjunction with the birth, adoption, or foster care placement of a child, an employee must receive his or her regular salary for 10 days of such leave, at a time requested by the employee. The 30 days of paid parental sick leave an employee may take for the birth or adoption of a child is in addition to these 10 days of family leave.[68]

Ohio's parental leave law provides that employees granted leave cannot receive paid leave for the first 14 days they are on parental leave.[69] Employees may choose to work during the waiting period. During the remaining 4 weeks of the leave period, employees receive paid leave equal to 70 percent of their base rate of pay.[70] In lieu of receiving this paid leave benefit for parental leave, employees may elect to receive $2,000 for adoption expenses.[71] Employees receiving parental leave may use sick leave, personal leave, vacation leave, or compensatory time balances in order to be paid during the 14-day waiting period and to supplement the 70 percent of their base rate of pay received during the remaining part of their parental leave period, in an amount sufficient to give them up to 100 percent of their pay for time on parental leave.[72] Parental leave runs concurrently with federal FMLA leave[73] Disability leave benefits may also be available.[74]

Finally, West Virginia's Parental Leave Act provides unpaid family leave following the exhaustion of all of the employee's annual and personal leave.[75]

9.06 INTERACTION OF THE FEDERAL FMLA WITH STATE FAMILY AND MEDICAL LEAVE LAWS: PAID LEAVE SUBSTITUTION

In some instances, the federal FMLA will incorporate the paid and unpaid leave provisions of applicable state family and medical leave laws. This is because the FMLA does not supersede any provision of state or local law that provides greater family or medical leave rights than the rights under the federal FMLA.[76] Because of this statutory nonpreemption language, the determination of which law applies (state versus federal) in a particular situation must be examined on a provision-by-provision basis.[77] The DOL further explained:

> Where the requisite coverage or applicability standards of both laws are met and the laws contain differing provisions, an analysis must be made

> of both laws, provision-by-provision, to determine which standard(s) from each law will apply to the particular situation. The standard providing the greater right or more generous benefit to the employee from each law (provision-by-provision) will apply. Note, however, that leave taken for a reason specified in both the Federal and State law may be simultaneously counted against the employee's entitlement under both laws.[78]

The mandatory "provision-by-provision" analysis to determine which applicable law, the federal FMLA or state law, extends greater rights to employees in any given situation does not distinguish between procedural and substantive provisions.[79] Where leave is covered by both the federal FMLA and state family and medical leave laws, school administrators will have to determine whether the paid and unpaid leave provisions of the federal FMLA or state law provide greater rights to employees and, for purposes of the federal FMLA, apply those provisions. For example, if an applicable state law provides half pay for up to 6 weeks for employees temporarily disabled because of pregnancy, the employee would be entitled to an additional 6 weeks of unpaid FMLA leave (or accrued paid leave).[80] In this case, the federal FMLA extends greater leave benefits to the employee in terms of leave substitution and the length of the allowable leave period.[81] In terms of paid leave substitution, the federal FMLA allows an employee to substitute any applicable accrued paid leave for FMLA leave, whereas the applicable state law caps that amount at 6 weeks.

Unless the state law has a similar provision, there is no requirement that employers apply the provisions of the federal FMLA that extend greater rights to employees than the applicable state law. As addressed in Chapter 13, the laws of a number of state family and medical leave laws include language that could be construed to require employers to apply the greater benefits of any other law, which would include the federal FMLA.

NOTES

1. 29 U.S.C. § 2612(c); 29 C.F.R. § 825.207(a).
2. 29 U.S.C. § 2612(d); 29 C.F.R. § 825.207(a).
3. 29 U.S.C. § 2612(d)(2)(A); 29 C.F.R. § 825.207(b)–(c).

4. Comments on Regulations Implementing the Family and Medical Leave Act of 1993 (§ 825.207), 60 Fed. Reg. 2180, 2205 (Jan. 6, 1995).

5. *Funkhouser v. Wells Fargo Bank, N.A.*, 289 F.3d 1137 (9th Cir. 2002).

6. Comments on Regulations Implementing the Family and Medical Leave Act of 1993 (§ 825.207), 60 Fed. Reg. at 2205.

7. *Strickland v. Water Works and Sewer Board*, 239 F.3d 1199, 1204 (11th Cir. 2001).

8. See *id.*; *Miller v. Personal-Touch of Virginia, Inc.*, 342 F. Supp. 2d 499, 512 (E.D. Va. 2004), *aff'd*, 2005 U.S. App. LEXIS 24240 (4th Cir. Nov. 9, 2005).

9. See *Thorton v. BASF*, No. 99-2243, 2000 U.S. App. LEXIS 15909 (4th Cir. July 11, 2000).

10. *Solis v. Phillips Puerto Rico Core, Inc.*, No. 98-1879 (CCC), 2000 U.S. Dist. LEXIS 1763 (D.P.R. Jan. 13, 2000); *Walthall v. Fulton County School District*, 18 F. Supp. 2d 1378, 1383–84 (N.D. Ga. 1998), *aff'd*, 192 F.3d 131 (11th Cir. 1999).

11. 29 U.S.C. § 2612(d)(2)(A); 29 C.F.R. § 825.207(a).

12. Comments on Regulations Implementing the Family and Medical Leave Act of 1993 (§ 825.207), 60 Fed. Reg. 2180, 2205 (Jan. 6, 1995).

13. *Id.*

14. *Id.*

15. 29 U.S.C. § 2612(d)(2)(A); 29 C.F.R. § 825.207(a).

16. 29 C.F.R. § 825.207(a), (f).

17. Comments on Regulations Implementing the Family and Medical Leave Act of 1993 (§ 825.207), 60 Fed. Reg. at 2205.

18. *Haggard v. Farmers Insurance Exchange*, 1996 U.S. Dist. LEXIS 4078 (D. Or. Mar. 26, 1996) (holding that employer did not violate FMLA by substituting unpaid FMLA leave with paid leave from accrued vacation time rather than from paid sick leave as requested by employee).

19. 29 U.S.C. § 2612(d); 29 C.F.R. § 825.207(b)–(c).

20. 29 C.F.R. § 825.207(b).

21. *Id.*

22. 29 C.F.R. § 825.207(c).

23. *Id.*

24. *Id.*

25. *Id.*

26. 29 C.F.R. § 825.207(g).

27. 29 C.F.R. § 825.207(b)–(c).

28. 29 C.F.R. § 825.207(e).

29. *Id.*

30. Comments on Regulations Implementing the Family and Medical Leave Act of 1993 (§ 825.207), 60 Fed. Reg. 2180, 2205 (Jan. 6, 1995).

31. 29 U.S.C. § 207(o); 29 C.F.R. § 825.207(i).

32. 29 C.F.R. § 825.207(i).

33. DOL WH FMLA Advisory Opinion No. 34 (April 12, 1994).

34. *Id.*

35. 29 U.S.C. § 207(o).

36. 29 C.F.R. § 825.207(i); 29 C.F.R. § 553.21.

37. 29 C.F.R. § 825.207(i); 29 C.F.R. § 553.21.

38. 29 C.F.R. § 825.207(i).

39. *Id.*; DOL WH FMLA Advisory Opinion No. 34 (Apr. 12, 1994).

40. Comments on Regulations Implementing the Family and Medical Leave Act of 1993 (§ 825.207), 60 Fed. Reg. 2180, 2205–06 (Jan. 6, 1995).

41. 29 C.F.R. § 825.207(d)(2); DOL WH FMLA Advisory Opinion No. 92 (Dec. 12, 1997).

42. Comments on Regulations Implementing the Family and Medical Leave Act of 1993 (§ 825.207), 60 Fed. Reg. at 2205–06; DOL WH FMLA Advisory Opinion No. 92 (Dec. 12, 1997).

43. Comments on Regulations Implementing the Family and Medical Leave Act of 1993 (§ 825.207), 60 Fed. Reg. at 2205–06.

44. 29 C.F.R. § 825.207(d)(2).

45. *Id.*; DOL WH FMLA Advisory Opinion No. 92 (Dec. 12, 1997); DOL WH FMLA Advisory Opinion No. 43 (Aug. 24, 1994); DOL WH FMLA Advisory Opinion No. 42 (Aug. 23, 1994).

46. Comments on Regulations Implementing the Family and Medical Leave Act of 1993 (§ 825.207), 60 Fed. Reg. at 2206.

47. 29 C.F.R. § 825.207(d)(1).

48. Comments on Regulations Implementing the Family and Medical Leave Act of 1993 (§ 825.207), 60 Fed. Reg. at 2206.

49. 29 C.F.R. § 825.207(d)(1).

50. See Steven K. Wisensale, *Family Leave Policy: The Political Economy of Work and Family in America* 187–94 (Sharpe 2001).

51. 65 Fed. Reg. 37209 (June 13, 2000) (codified at 20 C.F.R. pt. 604).

52. 67 Fed. Reg. 72122 (Dec. 4, 2002).

53. 68 Fed. Reg. 58539, 58540 (Oct. 9, 2003).

54. 68 Fed. Reg. 58539 (Oct. 9, 2003).

55. DOL WH FMLA Advisory Opinion No. 61 (May 12, 1995).

56. DOL WH FMLA Advisory Opinion No. 81 (June 18, 1996); DOL WH FMLA Advisory Opinion No. 61 (May 12, 1995).

57. DOL WH FMLA Advisory Opinion No. 81 (June 18, 1996); DOL WH FMLA Advisory Opinion No. 61 (May 12, 1995).

58. DOL WH FMLA Advisory Opinion No. 81 (June 18, 1996); DOL WH FMLA Advisory Opinion No. 61 (May 12, 1995).

59. 29 C.F.R. § 825.207(h).

60. *Id.*

61. *Id.*

62. Comments on Regulations Implementing the Family and Medical Leave Act of 1993 (§ 825.207), 60 Fed. Reg. 2180, 2206 (Jan. 6, 1995).

63. *Solovey v. Wyoming Valley Health Care System-Hospital*, No. 3:04-CV-2683, 2005 U.S. Dist. LEXIS 24519 (M.D. Pa. Oct. 13, 2005).

64. 29 U.S.C. § 2652; 29 C.F.R. § 825.700(a).

65. 29 C.F.R. § 825.700(a).

66. *Id.*

67. Mass. Gen. Laws ch. 7, § 28; Massachusetts Human Resources Division, *Rules Governing Paid Leave and Other Benefits for Managers and Confidential Employees* § 5.08 (2005) [hereinafter Massachusetts Human Resources Division, *Red Book*], available at http://www.mass.gov/?pageID=hrdsubtopic&L=4&L0=Home&L1=Policies+%26+Benefits&L2=Types+of+Leave&L3=Red+Book&sid=Ehrd.

68. Mass. Gen. Laws § 28; Massachusetts Human Resources Division, *Red Book*, *supra* note 67, § 5.02.

69. Ohio Rev. Code Ann. § 124.136(B).

70. *Id.*

71. Ohio Rev. Code Ann. § 124.136(A)(2).

72. Ohio Rev. Code Ann. § 124.136(C).

73. *Id.*

74. Ohio Rev. Code Ann. § 124.136(D).

75. W.Va. Code § 21-5D-4(a).

76. 29 U.S.C. § 2651(b); 29 C.F.R. § 825.701(a).

77. Comments on Regulations Implementing the Family and Medical Leave Act of 1993 (§ 825.701), 60 Fed. Reg. 2180, 2230 (Jan. 6, 1995).

78. *Id.* at 2231.

79. *Id.*

80. 29 C.F.R. § 825.701(a)(2).

81. Comments on Regulations Implementing the Family and Medical Leave Act of 1993 (§ 825.701), 60 Fed. Reg. at 2231.

CHAPTER 10

Maintenance of Employment Benefits

10.01 OVERVIEW

The FMLA protects employment benefits during an employee's use of FMLA leave in two ways: (1) employees retain any benefits accrued prior to the commencement of FMLA leave, and (2) employers must maintain certain health benefits during FMLA leave. Additionally, there are rules governing the accrual of employment benefits during FMLA leave and an employee's payment of health benefit premiums during leave.

Section 10.02 of this chapter addresses the rules governing the retention of accrued employment benefits. Section 10.03 discusses the rules governing the accrual of employment benefits during FMLA leave. Section 10.04 discusses the maintenance of health benefits during FMLA leave. Section 10.05 addresses the effect of more generous employer benefit programs on the maintenance of employment benefits during FMLA leave. Section 10.06 addresses the maintenance of employment benefits under state family and medical leave laws. Section 10.07 addresses the interaction of federal and state family and medical leave laws regarding the maintenance of employment benefits.

10.02 RETENTION OF ACCRUED EMPLOYMENT BENEFITS

The taking of FMLA leave "shall not result in the loss of any employment benefit accrued prior to the date on which FMLA leave commenced."[1] "Employment benefits" means all benefits provided or made available to employees by an employer, including

- group life insurance;
- health insurance;
- disability insurance;
- sick leave;
- annual leave;
- educational benefits; and
- pensions.

In addition, the DOL broadly interprets "employment benefits" to include any attendance, safety, or production bonuses to which the employee would be entitled.[2] The benefits listed above are "employment benefits" within the meaning of the FMLA regardless of whether they are provided by a practice or written policy of an employer or through an employee benefit plan as defined in section 3(3) of the Employee Retirement Income Security Act of 1974 (ERISA) (29 U.S.C. § 1002(3)).[3] "Employment benefits," however, do not include non-employment-related obligations paid by employees through voluntary deductions, such as supplemental insurance.[4]

10.03 ACCRUAL OF EMPLOYMENT BENEFITS

The FMLA does not require that all employment benefits accrue during FMLA leave. Although the FMLA permits employees to accrue additional employment benefits or seniority during unpaid FMLA leave,[5] absent more generous policies, employers are not mandated to allow employees to accrue vacation time, sick leave, or seniority or longevity benefits during FMLA leave.[6] Time spent on FMLA leave generally does not count toward pension plan credit.[7] Employers are not required to continue to pay a cash benefit in lieu of health and welfare benefits during any period of unpaid FMLA leave.[8]

Where, however, employees on paid or unpaid leave are entitled to accrue seniority or employment benefits as a matter of employer policy, employees on FMLA leave would also be so entitled.[9] To do otherwise, the DOL has opined, would be considered a discriminatory act on the part of the employer.[10] That is, an employee's entitlement to accrue seniority and employment benefits during FMLA leave is entirely dependent on the employer's established leave policies.[11]

The following examples illustrate the DOL's rules governing the accrual of employment benefits and seniority during FMLA leave:[12]

- If the employer's established leave policies do not permit the accrual of seniority during an unpaid leave of absence, this same policy would apply to unpaid leave covered by the FMLA. The employer in the same example would be in compliance so long as the returning employee is restored to the same level of seniority that the employee accrued prior to the commencement of FMLA leave.
- If the employer's established policies provide for the accrual of seniority during an absence where paid leave benefits have been applied, then the employer must permit, consistent with its policies, the accrual of seniority during the portion of FMLA leave for which paid leave benefits (i.e., vacation, personal, sick or medical, or family leave) are substituted for unpaid FMLA leave.
- If the employer's established policies do not permit the accrual of seniority during an absence covered by a state workers' compensation plan, nothing in the FMLA will require the employer to modify its policies to permit the accrual of seniority during the workers' compensation absence that also qualifies for and is designated as FMLA leave. This position would also apply where an employee on FMLA leave receives paid disability leave benefits and the accrual of seniority under the employer's established policies is not permitted.

To avoid costly FMLA violations, schools need to closely examine their existing policies and practices governing the accrual of employment benefits and seniority during paid or unpaid FMLA leave before denying benefit accrual during periods of FMLA leave. Schools can change existing polices that permit accrual of employment benefits or seniority during FMLA leave so that the policy reflects the minimum entitlement required by the FMLA. Of course, such changes must be accomplished in accordance with school policies, state and federal law, and any collective bargaining agreements.

10.04 MAINTENANCE OF HEALTH BENEFITS

[1] General Rule

An employer must maintain the employee's coverage under any "group health plan" during FMLA leave on the same conditions as coverage would have been provided if the employee had not taken FMLA leave.[13] The same is true for group health coverage under a multiemployer plan.[14] A "group health plan" is any plan of, or contributed to by, an employer, including self-insured plans, to provide health care (directly or otherwise) to the employer's employees, former employees, or families of employees and former employees.[15] "Group health plans" do not include insurance programs providing health coverage purchased solely by employees on a voluntary basis without contributions by the employer.[16] "Group health plans" do not include non-employment-related health benefits paid for directly by employees through voluntary deductions—for example, individual life insurance or disability insurance. An employer is not responsible for maintaining or restoring these non-group-health benefits for employees who take FMLA leave.[17] A "multiemployer health plan" is a plan to which more than one employer is required to contribute and which is maintained pursuant to one or more collective bargaining agreements between employee organizations and employers.[18]

An employer must provide the same level of group health benefits during FMLA leave as the employee enjoyed prior to taking such leave.[19] For example, if family member coverage is provided to an employee, family member coverage must be maintained during FMLA leave. Similarly, if included in the employer's group health plan, benefit coverage for medical care, surgical care, hospital care, dental care, eye care, mental health counseling, substance abuse treatment, and the like must be maintained during the FMLA leave period.[20] Employers in multiemployer group health plans must also provide the same type and level of group health benefits to employees during FMLA leave as the employee enjoyed prior to taking FMLA leave.[21]

[2] Changes to Group Benefit Plans

If the employer provides a new health plan or benefits or changes health benefits or plans while an employee is on FMLA leave, the employee is entitled to the new or changed benefits to the same extent as if the employee were not on leave.[22] For example, if a school employer changes a group health plan so that dental care becomes covered under the plan, an employee on FMLA leave must be given the same opportunity as other employees to receive (or obtain) the dental care coverage. Any other plan changes (e.g., in coverage, premiums, deductibles) that apply to all employees of the workforce would also apply to an employee on FMLA leave.[23] Presumably, the same rules apply to coverage changes for group health benefits in multiemployer plans. However, it should be noted that the multiemployer regulations do not specifically address changes to group health plans.

Employers must notify employees on FMLA leave of the opportunity to change plans or benefits.[24] For example, if the group health plan permits an employee to change from single to family coverage upon the birth of a child or otherwise add new family members, such a change in benefits must be made available while an employee is on FMLA leave.[25] The employer must grant the change in coverage requested by the employee on FMLA leave.[26] Here again, the multiemployer health plan regulations do not specifically require employers to notify employees on FMLA leave of opportunities to change group health plans or benefits, but presumably the same rules apply.

[3] Payment of Group Health Plan Premiums

Employees may be required to continue to pay their share of any group health plan premiums during FMLA leave.[27] If premium rates are raised or lowered, the employee would be required to pay the new premium rates.[28] "Any changes to premium rates and levels of coverage or other conditions of the plan that apply to the employer's active workforce also apply to eligible employees on FMLA leave."[29]

Employers must provide employees with advance written notice of the terms and conditions governing employee payment of their share of group health plan premiums during FMLA leave.[30] Employees on

FMLA leave may not be required to meet more stringent premium-payment requirements than required of employees on other forms of leave.[31] If the employee is using substituted paid leave, the employee's share of premiums must be paid under the payment method normally used during any paid leave, presumably payroll deductions.[32] If FMLA leave is unpaid, employers may require employees to make premium payments to the employer or to the insurance carrier in any of the following ways:[33]

- The employee makes periodic premium payments that are due at the same time as payroll deductions would otherwise be made.
- The employee makes premium payments based on the schedule for COBRA payments.
- The employee prepays the premiums pursuant to a cafeteria plan at the employee's option.
- The employee follows the employer's existing rules for payment by employees on "leave without pay," provided that such rules do not require prepayment (i.e., payment prior to the commencement of the leave) of the premiums that will become due during a period of unpaid FMLA leave or payment of higher premiums than if the employee had continued to work instead of taking leave.
- The employee follows any other system voluntarily agreed to by both the employer and the employee, which may include prepayment of premiums (e.g., through increased payroll deductions when the need for the FMLA leave is foreseeable).

The employer may not, however, add any additional charges to the employee's premium payment for administrative expenses.[34] An employee who is receiving payments as a result of a workers' compensation injury must make arrangements with the employer for payment of group health plan benefits when simultaneously taking FMLA leave.[35]

Employers must continue to pay their share of the employee's group health plan premiums during the employee's FMLA leave as if the employee had not gone on FMLA leave. Of course, if prior to FMLA leave the employer did not make any contributions toward the employee's health care insurance, the employer would not have to pay any premiums during an employee's FMLA leave.[36] As discussed above, if an employer does not contribute to an employee's health coverage, such coverage is not group health coverage, and the employer is not responsible for ensuring continuity of such coverage unless it has agreed to do otherwise as a matter of policy. An employee's entitlement to benefits other than group health benefits during a period of FMLA leave is determined by the employer's established paid and unpaid leave policies.[37]

Under a multiemployer group health plan, an employer must continue to make contributions on behalf of an employee on FMLA leave as though the employee had been continuously employed unless the plan contains an explicit FMLA provision for maintaining coverage such as through pooled contributions by all employers who are a party to the plan.[38] An employee using FMLA leave cannot be required to use "banked" hours or pay a greater premium than the employee would have been required to pay if the employee had been continuously employed.[39]

[4] Employee Election to Drop Group Health Plan Coverage

An employee may elect not to retain group health plan coverage during FMLA leave.[40] But even if the employee chooses not to retain group health coverage during FMLA leave, upon his or her return from leave the employee is entitled to be reinstated on the same terms as prior to taking the leave, including coverage under the group health plan without being required to wait for the commencement of an open-enrollment period and without any qualifying period, physical examination, or exclusion of preexisting conditions.[41]

[5] Consequences of Employee Failure to Make Timely Health Plan Premium Payments

The FMLA relieves employers of the obligation to continue group health plan coverage if an employee's premium payment is more than 30 days late.[42] To drop coverage for an employee's failure to make timely premium payments, the employer must provide written notice to the employee that the payment has not been received.[43] This written notice must be sent to the employee at least 15 days before coverage is to cease.[44] The letter must inform the employee that group health plan coverage will cease on a specified date at least 15 days after the date of the letter unless the payment has been received by that date.[45] Provided the 15-day notice was given, an employer may drop an employee from coverage retroactively to the date the unpaid premium payment was due if the employer's established unpaid leave policies provide for such retroactive termination of coverage.[46] In the absence of a policy allowing retroactive cessation, group health plan coverage for the employee may be terminated only at the end of the 30-day grace period, again on condition that the required 15-day notice was provided.[47]

Note that all other employer FMLA obligations continue even though group health plan benefits have been terminated.[48] For example, the school employer is still required to reinstate an employee upon return from FMLA leave. Similarly, if group health benefits lapse because of employee nonpayment of premiums, upon return to work from leave the employee is entitled to be reinstated on the same terms as prior to taking leave, including coverage under the group health plan without being required to wait for the commencement of an open-enrollment period and without any qualifying period, physical examination, or exclusion of preexisting conditions.[49]

Of course, an employer may elect to pay the employee's share of missed group health benefit premiums.[50] School employers often elect to pay an employee's missed premium payments to ensure an orderly resumption of the same level of benefits upon the employee's return to work. For the same reason, school employers will often elect to pick up the costs during FMLA leave of other employment benefits such as life and disability insurance. An employer does not have to secure the permission of the employee before deciding to pay the employee's share of group health plan premium payments.[51] To the extent an employer does maintain the employee's health coverage by paying the employee's share of any missed premium payments during the FMLA leave period, the employer is entitled to recover such amounts.[52]

[6] Termination of Group Health Plan Coverage

The obligation of an employer to maintain group health plan coverage during an employee's FMLA leave ceases if the employee fails to make timely premium payments as well as in three other situations.

First, if the employment relationship would have terminated if the employee had not taken FMLA leave, the employer is not required to continue to pay for group health plan benefits.[53] This is because an employee on FMLA leave has no greater right to employment than if the employee had not taken FMLA leave.[54] If the job of the employee would have been eliminated, such as through a department-wide downsizing or layoff, or for another nondiscriminatory reason (including discipline for performance or conduct) not related to the employee's use of FMLA leave, the employer's obligation to continue group health benefits ceases along with the employee's job.[55]

Second, if an employee informs the employer that he or she does not intend to return to work from FMLA leave, the employer is released from the obligation to maintain the employee's group health care benefits. Specifically, an employer who has been advised by the employee before or during FMLA leave that the employee does not intend to return to work may terminate group health benefits.[56] If the employee notifies the employer before FMLA leave starts that he or she does not intend to return to work from leave, the employer may terminate the employee's group health benefits before FMLA leave begins.[57] The notice given by the employee of his or her intention not to return to work from FMLA leave must be unequivocal.[58] An employee who states that he or she "does not think," "does not believe," or "does not expect" to return to work has not given unequivocal notice of the intent not to return to work from FMLA leave. School employers who receive equivocal notice would be well advised to seek further clarification from the employee to determine whether the employee knows for certain whether he or she intends to return. It is also recommended that the school obtain written confirmation of an employee's unequivocal notice of intent not to return to work from FMLA leave before terminating the employee's group health benefits.

Third, an employer's FMLA obligation to continue an employee's group health plan coverage ends if the employee fails to return from FMLA leave or continues on leave after exhausting his or her 12-work-week FMLA leave entitlement during the 12-month FMLA leave year.[59]

Group health coverage under a multiemployer health plan may be terminated by a school employer during an employee's FMLA leave in the same three situations as under group health plans.[60]

Of course, the employer may be required to continue group health benefits under the Consolidated Omnibus Budget Reconciliation Act of 1986 (COBRA),[61] other federal or state laws, or school policy, including the terms of a collective bargaining agreement.

Different rules govern an employer's obligation to continue group health coverage for certain key employees.[62] Presumably, these exceptions also apply to group health benefits in a multiemployer health plan.[63] If a highly compensated or "key" employee does not return from FMLA leave when notified by the employer that substantial and grievous economic injury will result from his or her reinstatement, the employee's entitlement to group health benefits continues unless and until

- the employee advises the employer that he or she does not desire restoration to employment at the conclusion of FMLA leave;
- the employee exhausts his or her annual 12-workweek entitlement to FMLA leave; or
- reinstatement is denied by the employer.[64]

The rights and obligations of "key" employees are addressed more fully in Chapter 11, *Return to Work from Family and Medical Leave*.

[7] Recovery of Employer Group Health Plan Costs

The FMLA allows employers in certain cases to recapture the premiums paid for maintaining an employee's group health plan coverage. To the extent an employer maintains an employee's health coverage by paying the employee's share of any missed premium payments during an FMLA leave period, the employer is always entitled to recover such payments.[65] An employer can recoup these payments whether or not the employee returns to work. Whether an employer may also recover *its* share of premium payments made for group health benefits during an employee's FMLA leave absence if the employee does not return to work depends on whether the leave is paid or unpaid and the reason the employee is unable to return to work from FMLA leave.

An employer may not recover its share of health insurance or other non-health-benefit premiums for any period of FMLA leave covered by substituted paid leave.[66] If an employee receives workers' compensation or payments pursuant to a temporary disability plan while on FMLA leave, even though such leave is not unpaid, an employer is nevertheless precluded from recovering its share of group health premium payments.[67]

An employer may recover its share of health plan premiums during a period of unpaid FMLA leave if the employee fails to return to work after the employee's FMLA leave entitlement has either been exhausted or expires, subject to two exceptions.[68] Under the first exception, the employer may not recover its share of premium payments if the employee is unable to return to work from FMLA leave due to the continuation, recurrence, or onset of a serious health condition of the employee or a covered family member that would otherwise entitle the employee to leave under the FMLA.[69] An employee who returns to work for at least 30 calendar days is considered to have "returned to work" for purposes of this provision.[70] Additionally, an employee who retires immediately after FMLA leave is considered to have "returned to work."[71]

Employers may verify an employee's claim that he or she cannot return to work from FMLA leave due to the continuation, recurrence, or onset of a serious health condition by requiring the employee to provide medical certification of the serious health condition.[72] Unless requested, however, medical certification is not required.[73] The employee must provide the certification within 30 days from the date of the employer's request.[74] An employee may use the medical certification form developed by the DOL (the WH-380 medical certification form) for this purpose.[75] The DOL regulations do not set forth a penalty for an employee's failure to timely provide medical certification verifying the existence of a serious health condition that prevents the employee from returning to work. Presumably, the penalty would be that the employer could recoup its group health plan premium payments made during the employee's unpaid FMLA leave absence.

Under the second exception, the employer is prohibited from collecting group health premiums made during an employee's unpaid FMLA absence if the employee's failure to return to work is due to "other circumstances beyond the employee's control." "Other circumstances beyond the employee's control" is broadly construed; for example:[76]

- A parent chooses to stay home with a newborn child who has a serious health condition.
- An employee's spouse is unexpectedly transferred to a job location more than 75 miles from the employee's worksite.
- A relative or individual other than an immediate family member has a serious health condition and the employee is needed to provide care.
- The employee is laid off while on leave.
- The employee is a "key employee" who decides not to return to work upon being notified of the employer's intention to deny job restoration because of substantial and grievous economic injury to the employer's operations and is not reinstated by the employer.

"Other circumstances" beyond the employee's control would not include a situation where an employee desires to remain with a parent in a distant city even though the parent no longer requires the employee's care or where a parent chooses not to return to work to stay home with a healthy newborn child.[77]

FMLA Illustrated: Recouping Group Health Benefits

- An employee who returns to work for 20 days but resigns to take care of a parent with a serious health condition has not returned to work for purposes of this section. Nonetheless, an employer would not be entitled to recoup its share of group health plan premium payments.
- An employee returns to work for 15 days following unpaid FMLA leave for the birth of her daughter. The employee subsequently quits to spend more time with the child. The employer would be able to recoup group health care premium costs. The employee failed to return to work, but it does not appear that such failure was due to a serious health condition or other circumstances outside of the employee's control.

The DOL has opined that an employer would be unable to collect its share of group health insurance premium payments made during an employee's unpaid FMLA leave if the employee elects retirement and the retirement date is retroactive to a date before the employee commenced FMLA leave and exhausted his or her 12-week entitlement. According to the DOL, a decision subsequent to the granting of an FMLA leave request approving disability retirement with a retroactive effective date for purposes of receiving pension benefits does not preempt or extinguish in anyway the employee's statutory rights under the FMLA, including the right to have group health benefits maintained under the same terms for the duration of the protected leave period. If an employee cannot return to work at the end of the leave period due to the continuation of a serious health condition, the employer cannot recover premium payments.[78]

When an employee does return to work, the employer and employee should discuss the amount owed and agree to a method of repayment that does not unduly impact the employee's financial condition, such as periodic payroll deduction.[79] In the event the employee and the employer cannot reach agreement on the amount proposed by the employer to be deducted from the employee's wages, the DOL has opined that the arrangements for repayment should be reasonable and should not impose unreasonable hardships or difficulties on either party.[80] For example, an employer should not attempt to recover payments all at once by having the entire amount due deducted from the employee's first paycheck. On the other hand, the employee should not attempt to stretch payments out over an unreasonably long time. The DOL has opined that additional deductions equal to the amount deducted for a regular group health plan premium payment would be reasonable.[81]

The employer may recover the costs through deduction from any sums due to the employee (e.g., unpaid wages, vacation pay, profit sharing), provided such deductions do not otherwise violate applicable federal wage payment or other laws.[82] Alternatively, an employer may initiate legal action against the employee to recover such costs.[83]

The DOL regulations do not provide for the recovery by an employer of group health plan premium payments made by the employer pursuant to a multiemployer health plan. Self-insured employers may only recoup the employer's share of allowable premiums as would be calculated under COBRA, excluding the 2 percent fee for administrative costs.[84]

When an employee fails to return to work, any premiums that an employer is permitted to recover are considered to be a debt owed by the nonreturning employee to the employer.[85] The existence of a debt owed by the employee to the employer for premium payments caused by the employee's failure to return to work does not alter the employer's responsibilities for health benefit coverage and under a self-insurance plan, payment of claims incurred during the period of FMLA leave.[86]

10.05 EFFECT OF MORE GENEROUS EMPLOYER BENEFIT PROGRAMS ON THE MAINTENANCE OF EMPLOYMENT BENEFITS DURING FMLA LEAVE

The FMLA sets the minimum requirements that covered employers must meet. Employers are free to adopt more generous family and medical leave benefits than those required by the FMLA.[87] Employers simply can't provide less generous family and medical leave benefits than the minimum required by the federal FMLA.[88] If an employer adopts a more generous employment benefit program or plan that provides greater family or medical leave rights to employees than the rights established by the FMLA, the employer must observe those greater benefits.[89]

With respect to the maintenance of group or other health benefits, a greater employment benefit plan, for example, could take the form of an employer's agreeing to pay both the employer's and the employee's share of the premium payments during FMLA leave and waiving any obligations of the employee to repay such amounts paid by the employer. Indeed, a school employer's decision to forgo collecting premium payments made on behalf of the employee or the school's own premium payments where the employee is not going to return to work would be a form of more generous employment benefit. School employers should review their exiting policies to determine whether they are currently providing more generous benefits regarding the maintenance of employment benefits during leave than the minimum required by the FMLA. Schools may amend overly generous existing policies to comply with the minimum requirements established by the FMLA.[90] Of course, before doing so schools may have to negotiate with unions or satisfy state law or school policy requirements regarding notice before such changes may take effect.

10.06 MAINTENANCE OF BENEFITS UNDER STATE FAMILY AND MEDICAL LEAVE LAWS

The rights and responsibilities of employers and employees to maintain employment benefits during an employee's use of family and medical leave vary widely under state law. States that have family and medical leave laws generally include language that echoes the federal FMLA's benefit maintenance requirements. States that have narrower laws regarding only very specific and limited types of leave, however, often do not include language in those laws addressing the maintenance of benefits during leave. For example, organ and bone marrow donation leave laws in most states do not address the maintenance of benefits during leave.

Under Alaska's Family Leave Act, employers must maintain an employee's group health plan coverage during the time an employee is on leave.[91] An employer must maintain such group health coverage at the level and under the conditions that coverage would have been provided if the employee had been employed continuously from the date the leave began to the date the employee returns from leave. The employer may require that the employee pay all or part of the costs for maintaining health insurance coverage during a period of unpaid leave.[92]

Massachusetts's family and medical leave regulations for state employees similarly provide that employees are entitled to the same group health insurance coverage and benefits that they received at the start of unpaid leave for the entire 26 weeks of unpaid leave unless prohibited by law.[93] Employees taking unpaid leave accumulate sick and vacation leave benefits only for the first 8 weeks of such unpaid leave.

Rhode Island's Parental and Family Medical Leave Act requires covered employers to maintain any existing health benefits of the employee as if the employee had continued in employment continuously from the date he or she commenced leave until the date he or she returns to employment.[94] Prior to the commencement of parental or family leave, the employee must pay the employer a sum equal to the premium required to maintain the employee's health benefits in force during the period of leave. The employer must return the payment to the employee within 10 days following the employee's return to work.[95]

School administrators must carefully review the requirements of the any applicable state leave laws regarding the maintenance of employment benefits.

10.07 INTERACTION OF THE FEDERAL FMLA WITH STATE FAMILY AND MEDICAL LEAVE LAWS: MAINTENANCE OF BENEFITS

Where a leave of absence is covered by only one law, either the federal FMLA or an applicable state family and medical leave law, the leave is governed only by the one law that applies.[96] Where a leave of absence is covered by both the federal FMLA and a state family and medical leave law, school administrators must determine, on a provision-by-provision basis, which law applies, state or federal. The federal FMLA does not supersede any provision of state or local law that provides greater family or medical leave rights than the rights under the federal FMLA.[97] The standard providing the greater right or more generous benefit to the employee from each law will apply.[98] This determination applies to both procedural and substantive rights.[99]

The determination whether the provisions of the federal FMLA or applicable state or local law provide greater right or more generous benefits to the employee is complicated where the state or local law is silent on an issue addressed in the federal FMLA. In this situation, the DOL indicates that if the federal FMLA provision is restrictive as to employee rights or benefits, then the state or local law would govern that provision. If the federal FMLA provision is not restrictive or extends a right, benefit, or privilege to employees, then the federal FMLA would govern as to that provision.[100] The DOL provides the following example to illustrate the point:

> For example, a State law that grants employers the right to deny the taking of leave to high-level executives could not be applied to any FMLA-eligible employees, because FMLA extends to all eligible employees the entitlement to leave for qualifying reasons. If the same State law contained a provision mandating that all employees who take leave be restored to employment when the leave ends, then FMLA's "key" employee exemption could not be applied to deny an employee reinstatement (i.e., the Federal law would not apply at the time of reinstatement).[101]

In comments accompanying publication of the final regulations implementing the federal FMLA, the DOL addressed the following query regarding the maintenance of benefits and the interaction of the federal FMLA and state law:

> The Women's Legal Defense Fund recommended the regulation address the interaction between FMLA and State workers' compensation laws. The State of Oregon's Bureau of Labor and Industries asked if State workers' compensation laws qualify under FMLA as a "State . . . law that provides greater . . . medical leave rights"

> If a State workers' compensation law provides a job guarantee to workers out of work temporarily due to occupational injuries that is more generous than FMLA's job restoration provisions, such law is a "State . . . law that provides greater . . . medical leave rights" and would govern an employee's reinstatement. On the other hand, where such occupational injuries also meet FMLA's definition of a "serious health condition that makes the employee unable to perform the functions of the position," the employer would have to maintain the injured employee's group health benefits under the same terms and conditions as if the employee had continued to work during the workers' compensation leave of absence (at least for the duration of the employee's remaining FMLA leave entitlement in the 12-month period.[102]

To comply with the federal FMLA and any applicable state or local laws, school administrators will have to determine, on a provision-by-provision basis, whether the federal FMLA or applicable state or local family and medical leave laws provide the greater rights or benefits to employees. Given the plethora of state and local family and medical leave laws, this is not an easy task. School administrators would be well advised to make this determination with the assistance of counsel.

NOTES

1. 29 U.S.C. § 2614(a)(2); see also 29 C.F.R. § 825.215(d)(2).
2. DOL WH FMLA Advisory Opinion No. 93 (Feb. 6, 1998) (asserting that paid administrative leave for physical fitness is an employment benefit); DOL WH FMLA Advisory Opinion No. 79 (Feb. 23, 1996) (discussing safety incentive bonus); DOL WH FMLA Advisory Opinion No. 31 (Mar. 21, 1994) (discussing perfect attendance bonus).
3. 29 U.S.C. § 2611(5); 29 C.F.R. §§ 825.215(d); 825.800 (defining "employment benefits").
4. 29 C.F.R. §§ 825.215(d) (defining "benefits"); 825.800 (defining "employment benefits").
5. 29 U.S.C. § 2614(a)(3); 29 C.F.R. § 825.215(d)(2); DOL WH FMLA Advisory Opinion No. 56 (Mar. 28, 1995); DOL WH FMLA Advisory Opinion No. 54 (Feb. 22, 1995); DOL WH FMLA Advisory Opinion No. 24 (Jan. 6, 1994).
6. DOL WH FMLA Advisory Opinion No. 109 (Sept. 8, 2000); DOL WH FMLA Advisory Opinion No. 102 (March 26, 1999); DOL WH FMLA Advi-

sory Opinion No. 42 (Aug. 23, 1994); DOL WH FMLA Advisory Opinion No. 24 (Jan. 6, 1994).

7. DOL WH FMLA Advisory Opinion No. 54 (Feb. 22, 1995).

8. DOL WH FMLA Advisory Opinion No. 1 (June 15, 1993).

9. 29 C.F.R. § 825.825.700(a), (c).

10. 29 C.F.R. § 825.220(c); DOL WH FMLA Advisory Opinion No. 42 (Aug. 23, 1994); DOL WH FMLA Advisory Opinion No. 24 (Jan. 6, 1994) .

11. DOL WH FMLA Advisory Opinion No. 109 (Sept. 8, 2000).

12. DOL WH FMLA Advisory Opinion No. 109 (Sept. 8, 2000).

13. 29 U.S.C. § 2614(c); 29 C.F.R. § 825.209(a).

14. 29 C.F.R. § 825.211(c).

15. 29 C.F.R. §§ 825.209(a), 825.800 ("group health plan" defined).

16. 29 C.F.R. § 825.800 ("group health plan" defined).

17. 29 C.F.R. §§ 825.210(a), 825.212(a)(2); see also DOL WH FMLA Advisory Opinion No. 19 (Dec. 6, 1993) (concluding that an employer plan allowing employees covered by insurance from another source to receive weekly cash supplement in lieu of insurance is not a group health plan that must be maintained during FMLA leave).

18. 29 C.F.R. § 825.211(a).

19. 29 C.F.R. § 825.209(b).

20. *Id.*

21. 29 C.F.R. § 825.211(c).

22. 29 C.F.R. § 825.209(c).

23. 29 C.F.R. § 825.209(d).

24. *Id.*

25. *Id.*

26. *Id.*

27. 29 C.F.R. § 825.210(a).

28. *Id.*

29. Comments on Regulations Implementing the Family and Medical Leave Act of 1993 (§ 825.210), 60 Fed. Reg. 2180, 2209 (Jan. 6, 1995).

30. 29 C.F.R. §§ 825.210(d), 825.301(b)(iv).

31. Comments on Regulations Implementing the Family and Medical Leave Act of 1993 (§ 825.210), 60 Fed. Reg. at 2209.

32. 29 C.F.R. § 825.210(b).

33. 29 C.F.R. § 825.210(c).

34. *Id.*

35. 29 C.F.R. § 825.210(f).

36. *LaCoparra v. Pergament Home Centers, Inc.*, 982 F. Supp. 213, 221 (S.D.N.Y. 1997).

37. 29 C.F.R. § 825.209(h).
38. 29 C.F.R. § 825.211(b).
39. 29 C.F.R. § 825.211(d).
40. 29 C.F.R. § 825.209(e).
41. *Id.*
42. 29 C.F.R. § 825.212(a)(1).
43. *Id.*
44. *Id.*
45. *Id.*
46. *Id.*
47. *Id.*
48. 29 C.F.R. § 825.212(a)(3).
49. 29 C.F.R. § 825.212(c); DOL WH FMLA Advisory Opinion No. 64 (June 21, 1995); DOL WH FMLA Advisory Opinion No. 42 (Aug. 23, 1994).
50. 29 C.F.R. § 825.212(b).
51. DOL WH FMLA Advisory Opinion No. 11 (Nov. 2, 1993).
52. 29 C.F.R. § 825.212(b).
53. 29 C.F.R. § 825.209(f).
54. 29 C.F.R. § 825.312(d).
55. Comments on Regulations Implementing the Family and Medical Leave Act of 1993 (§§ 825.209, 825.312), 60 Fed. Reg. 2180, 2208, 2226–27 (Jan. 6, 1995).
56. 29 C.F.R. § 825.209(f).
57. *Id.*; DOL WH FMLA Advisory No. 1 (June 15, 1993).
58. 29 C.F.R. § 825.209(f).
59. *Id.*
60. 29 C.F.R. § 825.211(e).
61. 29 C.F.R. § 825.210(c)(2).
62. 29 C.F.R. § 825.209(f).
63. 29 C.F.R. § 825.211(e) (cross-referencing § 825.209(f)).
64. 29 C.F.R. § 825.209(g).
65. 29 C.F.R. §§ 825.212(b), 825.213(a).
66. 29 C.F.R. § 825.213(d).
67. *Id.*
68. 29 U.S.C. § 2614(c)(2); 29 C.F.R. § 825.213(a).
69. 29 U.S.C. § 2614(c)(2)(B)(i); 29 C.F.R. § 825.213(a)(1).
70. 29 C.F.R. § 825.213(c).
71. *Id.*
72. 29 C.F.R. § 825.213(a)(3).
73. *Id.*

74. *Id.*

75. *Id.*

76. 29 C.F.R. § 825.213(a)(2).

77. *Id.*

78. See DOL WH FMLA Advisory Opinion No. 26 (Jan. 14, 1994).

79. DOL WH FMLA Advisory Opinion No. 11 (Nov. 2, 1993).

80. DOL WH FMLA Advisory Opinion No. 65 (July 13, 1995).

81. *Id.*

82. 29 C.F.R. § 825.213(f).

83. *Id.*

84. 29 C.F.R. § 825.213(e).

85. 29 C.F.R. § 825.213(f).

86. 29 C.F.R. § 825.213(f).

87. 29 U.S.C. §§ 2652(a), 2653; 29 C.F.R. § 825.700(a), (b).

88. 29 U.S.C. § 2652(b); 29 C.F.R. § 825.700(a).

89. 29 C.F.R. § 825.700(a).

90. 29 C.F.R. § 825.700(b).

91. Alaska Stat. § 39.20.500(d).

92. *Id.*

93. Mass. Gen. Laws ch. 7, § 28; Massachusetts Human Resources Division, *Rules Governing Paid Leave and Other Benefits for Managers and Confidential Employee* § 5.10 (2005) [hereinafter Massachusetts Human Resources Division *Red Book*], available at http://www.mass.gov/?pageID=hrdsubtopic&L=4&L0=Home&L1=Policies+%26+Benefits&L2=Types+of+Leave&L3=Red+Book&sid=Ehrd.

94. R.I. Gen. Laws § 28-48-3(b).

95. R.I. Gen. Laws § 28-48-3(c).

96. 29 § C.F.R. 825.701(a).

97. 29 U.S.C. § 2651(b); 29 C.F.R. § 825.701(a).

98. Comments on Regulations Implementing the Family and Medical Leave Act of 1993 (§ 825.701), 60 Fed. Reg. 2180, 2230 (Jan. 6, 1995).

99. *Id.* at 2231.

100. *Id.*

101. *Id.*

102. *Id.*

CHAPTER 11

Return to Work from Family and Medical Leave

11.01 OVERVIEW

Eligible employees who take federal FMLA leave have the right to return to their same or an equivalent position at the conclusion of their leave. The right to take FMLA leave wouldn't be worth much without the right to return to one's job. The right to return to work from FMLA leave is not, however, absolute. To perfect that right, returning employees must satisfy several conditions. Employers too must meet stringent requirements in order to return an employee to work from leave within the meaning of the FMLA. As with other areas of the federal FMLA, there are many pitfalls that wary school employers must avoid in order to successfully return an employee to work from FMLA leave. There are also helpful special rules for certain school employers.

Section 11.02 addresses the basic rules governing an employee's return to work from FMLA leave. Section 11.03 discusses the conditions that an employee must meet in order to perfect the right to return to work. Section 11.04 examines the employer's right to request a fitness-for-duty medical certification as a condition of an employee's return to work. Section 11.05 considers situations in which employers are not required to reinstate an employee. Section 11.06 discusses special rules governing the return-to-work rights of "key employees." Section 11.07 addresses the effect of more generous employer return-to-work policies on the FMLA right to return to work. Section 11.08 reviews the job-restoration requirements of state family and medical leave laws. Section 11.09 considers the interaction of the return-to-work requirements of the federal FMLA and state family medical leave laws.

11.02 EMPLOYEE'S RIGHT TO RETURN TO WORK FROM FMLA LEAVE

[1] Right to Return to Work

The rights and responsibilities governing an employee's return to work from FMLA leave initially depend on the status of the employer. In addition to the general job-restoration rules, there are special rules governing certain school employees and highly compensated "key employees."

(i) General Job-Restoration Requirements

An eligible employee who takes FMLA-qualifying leave is entitled, upon return from such leave, to be restored by the employer to the same position the employee held when the leave commenced or to an equivalent position with equivalent benefits, pay, and other terms and conditions of employment.[1] An employee is entitled to reinstatement even if the employee has been replaced or if his or her position has been restructured to accommodate the employee's absence.[2] For example, a school employer redistributes the functions of the employee's position to other employees during the employee's FMLA leave. If the redistribution of work was solely due to the employee's absence on FMLA leave, the employee would be entitled to be restored to the same or an equivalent position upon return from FMLA leave. As discussed in section 11.05, a different result would occur if the redistribution of work would have happened even if the employee had not taken FMLA leave.[3] An employer that fails to restore an eligible employee to the same or an equivalent position upon return from FMLA leave violates the FMLA.[4]

(A) Eligibility

By its terms, the statute provides that only eligible employees enjoy the right to return to work from FMLA leave.[5] Interestingly, the DOL regulations do not refer to the eligibility requirement.[6] The question arises whether an employee who meets the eligibility requirements at the commencement of FMLA leave but not at the conclusion of that leave has the FMLA right to return to work. The statute strongly implies that the employee need only meet the eligibility requirements at the commencement of FMLA leave to qualify for the right to return to work.[7]

(B) Return from FMLA Leave

An eligible employee's right to job restoration is from FMLA leave. If the employee remains absent pursuant to an employer's more generous leave policy after exhausting his or her annual 12-workweek federal FMLA leave entitlement, the employee is not entitled to job restoration pursuant to the FMLA. For example, in addition to 12 weeks of FMLA leave, a school employer provides 1 week of job-protected leave for every year of service. Pursuant to that policy, Jane, a 6-year employee, has 18 weeks of job-protected leave available. Jane takes leave due to the serious health condition of her husband. The leave is properly designated as FMLA leave, and Jane is so notified in writing. She remains out on leave past the 12 weeks of FMLA leave. All entitlements and rights under the federal FMLA cease after 12 weeks. Jane is no longer entitled to any job-restoration rights under the FMLA and may be terminated without violating the FMLA.[8]

An employer, however, must observe any employment benefit program or plan or collective bargaining agreement that provides greater family or medical leave rights to employees than the rights established by the FMLA.[9] Thus in the above example, a school employer would have an obligation under its own leave of absence policies to extend leave benefits and job-restoration rights for up to 18 weeks, but not beyond.

(C) Employee's Return

Neither the statute nor the DOL regulations clearly define when an employee is considered to have returned from FMLA leave, triggering the employer's obligation to restore the employee to the same or an equivalent position.[10] Ordinarily, this is not an issue because the employer and the employee will communicate and establish a return date for an employee taking FMLA leave. In such cases, the timing of the employee's "return" will not be at issue, and the restoration entitlement will arise when the employee returns in a timely manner and in a physical condition to perform the essential functions of the job he or she left (confirmed by a fitness-for-duty medical certification, if required).[11] If the parties have not settled on the employee's return date, it appears that an employee is considered to have "returned" to work from FMLA leave when the employee no longer needs FMLA leave and the employee has notified the employer of his or her desire to return to work.[12]

The employee's physical presence at the worksite qualifies as having "returned" to work from FMLA leave.[13] A telephone call from the employee on or before the expiration of FMLA leave that the employee is ready to return to work has been found to be sufficient "return" to implicate the employer's job-restoration responsibilities.[14]

If the employee's return date is uncertain or changes, the FMLA requires that the employee provide reasonable notice of the employee's anticipated return-to-work date. The DOL regulations provide:

> It may be necessary for an employee to take more leave than originally anticipated. Conversely, an employee may discover after beginning leave that the circumstances have changed and the amount of leave originally anticipated is no longer necessary. An employee may not be required to take more FMLA leave than necessary to resolve the circumstances that precipitated the need for leave. In both of these situations, the employer may require that the employee provide the employer with reasonable notice (i.e., within two business days) of the changed circumstances where foreseeable. The employer may also obtain information on such changed circumstances through requested status reports.[15]

Section 825.312(e) of the DOL regulations similarly provides: "If the employee is able to return to work earlier than anticipated, the employee shall provide the employer two business days notice where feasible; the employer is required to restore the employee once such notice is given."[16]

(D) Timing of an Employee's Return to Work

Employers generally must immediately return an employee to the same or an equivalent position from FMLA leave.[17] Employers do not have a reasonable period of time within which to return an employee from FMLA leave.[18] Conversely, employers do not violate the FMLA by directing an employee to immediately report to work at the conclusion of FMLA leave.[19] An employee who delays returning to work from FMLA leave loses FMLA protections, including the right to job restoration.[20]

There are three exceptions to the general rule requiring that an employee be immediately returned to the same or an equivalent position; an employer may delay the return of an employee from FMLA leave if (1) the employer is waiting to receive requested medical certification that the employee is fit to return to duty,[21] (2) the employee failed to give the employer reasonable notice of the employee's return to work,[22] or (3) the employee is an "instructional employee" and takes FMLA leave near the end of an academic term.[23] Delays while waiting for fitness-for-duty certification are addressed separately in section 11.04.

As discussed in subsection (C) above, the DOL regulations require an employee who is able to return to work earlier than anticipated to provide the employer at least two business days' notice, where feasible, of his or her intention to return. In *Hoge v. Honda of America Manufacturing, Inc.*, the employee showed up for work from FMLA leave unexpectedly.[24] The court ruled that the employee's showing up for work fulfilled the notice requirement of § 825.309(c) and § 825.312(e). If the employer did not have reasonable notice of the employee's return date as a result of her simply showing up at work, the court ruled that the employer could delay the employee's return to work for two business days. If, however, the employer had reasonable notice of the employee's earlier return date, it would have to return her to work immediately.

(ii) Special School Rules

The FMLA provides that the restoration of eligible employees of local educational agencies or private elementary or secondary schools to an equivalent position must be made on the basis of established school board policies and practices, private school policies and practices, and collective bargaining agreements, as applicable.[25] "Local educational agencies" include public school boards and elementary and secondary schools under their jurisdiction.[26] The special rules do not apply to other kinds of educational institutions, such as colleges and universities, trade schools, and preschools.[27] Covered school employers that are not within the scope the special school rules must comply with the general return-to-work requirements of the FMLA (discussed above). Note that the special school rules governing return to work apply to all employees of these schools, not just instructional employees.

The "established policies" and collective bargaining agreements used as a basis for restoration must

- be in writing;
- be made known to the employee prior to the taking of FMLA leave; and
- clearly explain the employee's job-restoration rights upon return from leave.[28]

Any established policy that is used as the basis for restoration of an employee to "an equivalent position" must provide substantially the same protections as provided by the federal FMLA for reinstated employees.[29] In other words, the policy or collective bargaining agreement must provide for restoration to an "equivalent position" with equivalent employment benefits, pay, and other terms and conditions of employment.[30] An employee may not, for example, be restored to a position requiring additional licenses or certification.[31] The DOL has similarly opined that a collective bargaining agreement that mandates that a first-year probationary employee who takes FMLA leave must repeat the first-year probationary period provides less protection than is otherwise provided by the FMLA to returning employees and, therefore, fails to provide substantially the same protections as provided by the Act.[32]

School employers covered by the special school rules would be well advised to adopt school policies and collective bargaining agreements that comply with the general return-to-work requirements set forth in § 825.215 of the regulations, as modified by the special school rules in 29 C.F.R. §§ 825.600–825.604. While "substantially the same protections" is certainly different from "the same or identical protections," schools covered by the special school rules should seek advice from counsel before enacting return-to-work policies that differ from the requirements of 29 C.F.R. § 825.215.

Schools covered by the special school rules also may delay the return from FMLA leave of some employees. The special rules affect the taking of intermittent leave or leave on a reduced leave schedule, as well as leave near the end of an academic term, by "instructional employees."[33] "Instructional employees" are those whose principal job function is to teach and instruct students in a class, a small group, or an individual setting.[34] The term includes not only teachers but also athletic coaches, driving instructors, and special education assistants such as signers for the hearing impaired.[35] It does not include, and the special rules do not apply to, teacher assistants or aides who do not have as their principal job actual teaching or instructing; nor does it include auxiliary personnel such as counselors, psychologists, curriculum specialists, cafeteria workers, maintenance workers, or bus drivers.[36]

The special rules allow local educational agencies and private elementary and secondary school employers to delay the return of an employee from FMLA leave in two situations. First, if an instructional employee requests leave on an intermittent or reduced leave schedule basis that is foreseeable based on planned medical treatment for a serious health condition and the employee will be on leave for more than 20 percent of the working days during the leave period, the school employer may require the employee to either temporarily transfer to an alternative position that better accommodates the employee's leave schedule or take leave for a period or periods of a particular duration that is not greater than the duration of the planned treatment.[37] A "period of a particular duration" means "a block, or blocks, of time beginning no earlier than the first day for which leave is needed and ending no later than the last day on which leave is needed and may include one uninterrupted period of leave."[38] By compelling the employee to take leave for a "period of a particular duration" the school employer may permissibly delay the employee's return to work from intermittent or reduced schedule leave until the expiration of the "period of a particular duration."

Second, a school employer may delay an employee's return to work from FMLA leave if an instructional employee takes leave near the end of the academic term. "Academic term" means the school semester, which typically ends near the end of the calendar year and the end of the spring each school year.[39] The rules allowing a school employer to delay the employee's return to work differ depending on whether the employee begins FMLA leave more than 5 weeks before the end of a term, less than 5 weeks before the end of a term, or less than 3 weeks before the end of a term.[40] If an instructional employee begins leave more than 5 weeks before the end of an academic term, the school employer may require the employee to continue taking leave until the end of the term if (1) the leave will last at least 3 weeks and (2) the employee would otherwise return to work during the 3-week period before the end of the term.[41]

If the leave is for a purpose other than the employee's serious health condition, and the leave begins during the 5-week period before the end of the term, the school employer may require the instructional employee to continue taking leave until the end of the term if (1) the leave will last more than 2 weeks and (2) the employee would otherwise return to work during the 2-week period before the end of the term.[42]

Finally, if the instructional employee beings leave for a purpose other than the employee's own serious health condition during the 3-week period before the end of an academic term and the leave will last more than 5 working days, the school employer may require the employee to stay out on leave (i.e., the employer could refuse reinstatement) until the end of the term.[43] Absent application of the special rules, the normal rules governing an employee's return to work apply.[44]

[2] Same or Equivalent Position

The FMLA guarantees an employee the right to be restored by the employer to the same position the employee held when FMLA leave commenced or to an equivalent position with equivalent employment benefits, pay, and other terms and conditions of employment.[45] The statute does not require that an employer first attempt to restore the employee to his or her original position before offering an equivalent position.[46] An employer satisfies the FMLA by offering to restore a returning employee to either his or her pre–FMLA leave position or an equivalent position.[47]

(i) Same Position

Upon return from FMLA leave, an employee is entitled to be restored by the employer to the position of employment held by the employee when leave commenced.[48] An employee remains entitled to the same pre-leave-commencement position even if the employee has been replaced or that position has been restructured to accommodate the employee's absence.[49] An employer does not, however, violate the Act by permanently filling the employee's former position. In that case, the employer would be required to offer the employee an equivalent position.[50]

To be returned to the same preleave position, the employee must enjoy the same pay, benefits, and other terms and conditions of employment he or she had at the time FMLA leave commenced. If greater benefits have been added during the period of FMLA leave, the employee must receive the enhanced benefits as well. Placement of an employee in the same position but with reduced or adversely altered pay, benefits, or other terms and conditions of employment may violate the federal FMLA. An employee who has been returned to the same position with the same title, pay, and benefits, however, is not restored to the same position within the meaning of the FMLA if the job duties and essential functions of the position are materially different from those of the employee's preleave position.[51]

Absent a nondiscriminatory policy providing for such action, an employee serving a probationary period at the commencement of FMLA leave may not be required, upon returning to work, to begin the probationary period again.[52] Nor could the employer simply extend the probationary period.[53] If, however, school policy were to premise successful completion of the probationary period on the accumulation of a certain number of hours or days of work, the school could legitimately delay completion of the probationary period by an amount reflecting the amount of unpaid FMLA leave.[54]

Courts are divided on whether a permanent employee can be required to serve a probationary period upon return to work.[55] Schools would be well advised to have a legitimate, nondiscriminatory reason independent of the taking of FMLA leave before imposing a probationary period on a permanent employee upon return from FMLA leave.

An employee does not have the right to refuse to be returned to the same position, and the FMLA does not obligate the employer to accede to the employee's request to be returned to a different position.[56] Of course, schools may be required to place an employee in an alternative position pursuant to school policy or to satisfy the requirements of other federal or state laws such as the ADA.

FMLA Illustrated: Same Position

State law provides that a teacher who has been employed in any district as a full-time teacher for a probationary period of 2 consecutive school terms will become a full-time regular career employee unless given written notice stating the specific reasons for dismissal. The collective bargaining agreement provides that should a teacher experience a "break in service" during this probationary period before being recommended for reemployment for the second year, the teacher will return to work the following year as a first-year probationary teacher and be required to complete 2 terms of uninterrupted service. A break in service for this purpose would include any period of unpaid leave.

Question: May a probationary teacher that takes FMLA-qualifying leave that would be considered a break in service be returned to work as a first-year probationary teacher without violating the FMLA's provisions for restoration to an equivalent position with equivalent employment benefits, pay, and other terms and conditions of employment?

Answer: Where continued service is calculated based on an anniversary date, no. A probationary teacher who takes a period of unpaid leave subject to the FMLA may not be required, upon returning to work, to begin the probationary period again. To do so would result in the employee's losing an earned benefit that accrued prior to when the leave began, contrary to the FMLA. A position as a first-year probationary employee is not equivalent to a position as a second-year probationary employee because additional time must be served before being granted tenure and any associated privileges. Prior to taking leave the employee had accrued at least 1 year of service toward the completion of the 2-term probationary period. Returning to a position as a first-year probationary employee constitutes a loss of this benefit.

A school could not simply extend the probationary period for 1 additional school term. Where attaining full-time regular career status is based on an employee's anniversary date, not the accumulation of a certain number of hours or days of work, because the collective bargaining agreement permits an employee who takes unpaid leave to attain full-time regular career status after the second year, it must do the same where the employees takes unpaid FMLA leave.

If, however, the collective bargaining agreement based completion of the probationary period for full-time regular career status on a certain number of hours or days worked rather than on an anniversary date, the school could delay the granting of full-time regular career status by an amount of time reflecting the amount of unpaid FMLA leave taken.

(ii) Equivalent Position

The FMLA guarantees an employee the right to be restored by the employer to an equivalent position. An equivalent position is one that is virtually identical to the employee's former position in terms of pay, benefits, working conditions, privileges, perquisites, and status. It must involve the same or substantially similar duties and responsibilities, which must entail substantially equivalent skill, effort, responsibility, and authority.[57] The legislative history describes the standard for determining "equivalence" as a stringent one.[58] According to the DOL:

> As described in the legislative history . . . the standard for evaluating job "equivalence" under FMLA parallels [the workplace antidiscrimination provisions of Title VII of the Civil Rights Act of 1964, as amended[59]], and is intended to be interpreted in a similar manner. "Equivalence" necessarily requires a correspondence to the duties and other terms, conditions and privileges of an employee's previous position, which is more than mere "comparability" or "similarity." Moreover, the intended standard encompasses all "terms and conditions" of employment, not just those specified.[60]

Equivalence does not necessarily require that the positions be identical or exactly the same. Rather, equivalence means substantially equal or similar.[61]

(A) Equivalent Pay and Bonuses

An employee returning to work from FMLA leave is entitled to have the same or an equivalent opportunity for pay, bonuses, profit sharing, and other similar discretionary and nondiscretionary payments.[62] Equivalent pay includes entitlement to any unconditional pay increases enacted during an employee's FMLA leave, such as cost of living increases.[63] Absent the requirements of state law or a more generous employer policy, an equivalent position would not entitle an employee to pay increases conditioned on seniority, length of service, or work performed (e.g., piece work).[64] In these cases, absent a more generous leave policy, the employee would be entitled to a pay increase prorated for the time the employee did work, excluding the unpaid FMLA leave period.[65] By prorating the pay increase, the employee retains all benefits the employee accrued up to the commencement of FMLA leave.

Equivalent pay includes entitlement to a position with the same or equivalent pay premiums, such as shift differentials.[66] For example, if the employee's preleave position averaged 10 hours of overtime a week, the equivalent position upon return from FMLA leave must afford the employee an equivalent opportunity to work overtime and receive the corresponding overtime pay.[67]

Employers must consider the opportunity to earn bonuses in determining whether an employee has been returned to an equivalent position.[68] As in the case of pay, whether the employee is entitled to a bonus after returning from FMLA leave depends on how the bonus is calculated. Essentially, there are two forms of bonuses that most employers pay: bonuses for the absence of certain occurrences and performance-based bonuses.[69] Bonuses for the absence of occurrences generally recognize employees for what they have not done. Bonuses premised on "perfect attendance" or "perfect safety" are rewards not for work or production but for compliance with rules; that is, they are the opposite of penalties for infractions of attendance or safety rules.[70] An employee who takes FMLA leave and met all of the qualifications to receive this type of bonus (e.g., attendance, safety) at the time he or she commenced FMLA leave remains entitled to the bonus upon return from FMLA leave.[71] This can lead to some strange results. For example, school policy rewards employees with a bonus for perfect attendance during the school year. An employee who during the school year took all 12 weeks of FMLA leave, but who otherwise had perfect attendance, would be entitled to the full perfect-attendance bonus.[72]

Employers can create an attendance policy that does not penalize those who take unpaid FMLA but provides only a prorated share of such a bonus. For example, a school might have a policy under which employees accrue a weekly bonus if they work each day in the workweek. Failure to work the entire workweek for any reason causes forfeiture of the weekly bonus, unless an employee is on vacation or absent due to FMLA-qualifying conditions or events. Employees on vacation or absent for FMLA-qualifying conditions or events are entitled to a pro rata share of the bonuses based on the number of days worked. For example, if an employee missed one day of the week for an FMLA-qualifying condition, the employee would receive the amount of the bonuses otherwise accrued for the workweek—four-fifths of the weekly amount. An employee who misses one or more days for a reason other than vacation or an FMLA-qualifying event would not receive any bonus for that week.[73]

A second common type of bonus is a performance- or production-based bonus. This type of bonus requires some positive effort on the employee's part at the workplace.[74] For example, a monthly production bonus based on the measurement of some quantity of work output requires positive effort on the part of an employee. If the employee is on FMLA leave during any part of the period used to calculate the performance bonus, the employee is entitled to the same consideration for the bonus as other employees on paid or unpaid leave.[75] Depending on the terms and conditions governing the production award program, an employee may be awarded a reduced bonus or be deemed ineligible as a result of having been on FMLA leave and not having had the opportunity to continue to produce during the award period.[76]

Schools should review their bonus programs to ensure that they meet the minimum requirements of the FMLA.

(B) Equivalent Benefits

An equivalent position must provide equivalent benefits to the employee returning from FMLA leave. "Equivalent benefits" means all benefits provided or made available to employees by an employer, including group life insurance, health insurance, disability insurance, sick leave, annual leave, educational benefits, and pensions.[77] An employee returning from FMLA leave cannot be required to requalify for any benefits that the employee enjoyed before FMLA leave began.[78] For example, if an employee was covered by a life insurance policy before taking leave but coverage lapsed during the period of unpaid FMLA leave (perhaps because the employee neglected to pay his share of the premiums), the employee cannot be required to meet any qualifications, such as taking a physical examination, in order to requalify for life insurance upon return from leave.[79] Because of this rule, most school employers would be well advised to consider paying the employee's share of all benefit premiums during FMLA leave, subject to recovery upon the employee's return.

Upon return from FMLA leave, an employee is entitled to all benefits accrued prior to taking FMLA leave.[80] An employee is not automatically entitled to accrue benefits or seniority during unpaid FMLA leave, unless the employer's policies provide for such accrual.[81] Employees are generally entitled to changes in benefit plans that took effect or were available during unpaid FMLA leave.[82] Employees would not, however, be entitled to benefit plan changes that are premised on seniority or hours worked if because of the employee's use of unpaid FMLA leave, the employee did not meet those new requirements.[83]

Unpaid FMLA leave is not treated as a break in service for purposes of vesting and eligibility to participate in any pension or retirement plan.[84] For example, if a plan requires an employee to be employed on a specific date in order to be credited with a year of service for vesting, contributions, or participation purposes, an employee on unpaid FMLA leave on that date is deemed to have been employed on that date.[85] Unpaid FMLA leave, however, need not be treated as credited service for purposes of benefit accrual, vesting, and eligibility to participate.[86]

(C) Equivalent Terms and Conditions of Employment

An equivalent position must have substantially similar duties, conditions, responsibilities, privileges, and status as the employee's original position.[87] For an alternative position to be considered equivalent, an employee must be reinstated to the same or a geographically proximate worksite (i.e., one that does not involve a significant increase in commuting time or distance).[88] An employee must be returned to the same shift or the same or an equivalent work schedule.[89] Restoration to a job slated for layoff when the employee's original position is not would not meet the requirements of an equivalent position.[90]

Given the stringent nature of equivalency mandated by the federal FMLA, placing an employee in a position upon return from FMLA leave other than the position the employee held when FMLA leave began with increased, decreased, or substantially different work requirements than the preleave position will likely result in the position being found to be not equivalent. For example, the loss of supervisor responsibilities and a private office has been held to render a post–FMLA leave position not equivalent.[91] An employee who worked as a computer analyst prior to FMLA leave and was returned to a data entry job was not returned to a position of equal status, even though the employee received the same pay and benefits.[92] In another case, increased typing requirements in the postleave position rendered it not equivalent to the employee's preleave secretary position.[93] Finally, a court found sufficient evidence of a change in working conditions to preclude awarding summary judgment to the employer where, after the employee's return to work, business calls the employee would have normally handled prior to taking leave were routinely being routed to another employee who temporarily covered the position during leave.[94]

(D) De Minimis, Intangible, or Immeasurable Aspects of the Job

The requirement that an employee be restored to the same or an equivalent position with the same or equivalent pay, benefits, and terms and conditions of employment does not extend to de minimis or intangible aspects of the job.[95] The DOL regulations do not explain what might qualify as de minimis or intangible aspects of a job. Courts have filled the void. In one case, a warm greeting upon an employee's return to work was a de minimis or intangible aspect of the job that is not required by the FMLA.[96] Being kept "out of the loop" after returning from FMLA leave regarding a company decision made by the CEO was found in another case to be a de minimis aspect of the job. The court noted that the CEO did not report to the employee and otherwise had no obligation to consult with her prior to making the decision without the employee's input.[97] Where an employee retains the same grade, pay, and job duties, the mere fact that the postleave job is in a different salary category was found by another court to be de minimis.[98] A postleave change in job title and reassignment to a different chain of command has also been found to be de minimis.[99]

The postleave assignment of new tasks for a limited period of time each day was found to be the type of de minimis changes permitted by the FMLA in an equivalent position.[100] Similarly, one court has found that the fact that an employee must receive additional training in order to perform the duties of the postleave position does not establish that the position is not equivalent.[101] In that case, the employee had held the position of food and beverage manager before taking FMLA leave. Upon her return, she was offered the position of food and beverage manager at her same salary, benefits, and terms and conditions of employment, albeit with some changes to her job duties. The court found de minimis the employee's argument that the positions were not the same because she would have to be trained to perform in her new position. The court noted that both positions involved supervisor duties and both had the same goal: customer service and maintenance of the Baton Rouge Marriott in a managerial capacity.

A reduction in the complexity of administrative tasks and the sharing of a workspace was found in another case to fall within the excluded de minimis category. In that case, the employee claimed that in her former position her duties were "truly administrative," but upon her return to work, they "are the simplest, most menial of clerical functions: answering the phone, taking messages, typing simple correspondence, and the like."[102] In finding that such changes fell within the de minimis exception, the court opined: "The difference between 'truly administrative tasks' and 'answering the phone, taking messages, typing simple correspondence' is not of sufficient magnitude, especially given the equivalent pay, grade, increment level, and administrative classification, to constitute an FMLA violation."[103]

Schools need to exercise great caution when placing an employee returning from FMLA leave in an equivalent position. The employee must receive the same pay, benefits, and other terms and conditions of employment. There is a bit of flexibility when it comes to the location and duties of the position. A different location must be within the same commuting area. The duties do not have to be exactly the same, but they should be very close to the duties of the employee's preleave position.

(E) Lapsed Qualifications for the Job

If, because of FMLA leave, the employee is no longer qualified for the same or an equivalent position—for example, because of the employee's inability to attend a necessary course, renew a license, fly a minimum number of hours—employers must give the employee a reasonable opportunity to fulfill any training or other requirements of the job upon return to work.[104] Note that by its terms, the regulation does not permit an employer to delay or deny an employee's return to work until the employee requalifies for the same or an equivalent position. Rather, employers are supposed to reinstate the employee and then allow the employee a reasonable opportunity to requalify.

At least one court has disagreed with this requirement where the employee did not have the required nursing license to perform 75 percent of her preleave job.[105] The court found that under those circumstances, the employee was not entitled to reinstatement.[106]

What constitutes a reasonable opportunity to requalify for the position will depend on the facts of each case.[107] Clearly, however, a reasonable opportunity is not an endless opportunity. In one case, a court held that it was not reasonable to require an employer to wait 3 months for a delivery employee to renew his driver's license.[108]

The regulations are less than clear regarding what the employer is supposed to do with the employee during this requalification period. The regulations do not explicitly relieve employers of their obligation to return an employee to the same or an equivalent position during this period. Of course, if the employee has lost a necessary license that may be difficult or impossible. Schools wishing to avoid costly litigation should seriously consider resuming the employee's pay, benefits, and other terms and conditions of employment. As for duties, the school should provide the employee with as many equivalent duties as the employee had prior to taking FMLA leave. If that is not possible, the school should assign the employee whatever duties are appropriate, provided that the duties assigned are not so different from the preleave duties that it appears that the school is penalizing or discriminating against the employee for taking FMLA leave. For example, a teacher who needs 2 months to regain a required license should not be assigned to the maintenance department during that time.

For an employee to be protected by the FMLA in this situation, the employee's loss of a required license or similar qualification must be due to the use of FMLA leave. If the employee's loss of a required license was for reasons other than the use of FMLA leave, the exception does not apply and the federal FMLA would not require the employer to reinstate the employee. In one case, a delivery driver lost a required driver's license for a 5-month period under state law because he had a defibrillator implanted in his chest following two heart attacks. The employee's doctor cleared him to return to work. At the time, his license was still suspended by operation of state law. The employer refused to reinstate the employee because of the suspension of his license. The employee sued, alleging violations of the FMLA. The court disagreed, finding that 29 C.F.R. § 825.215(b) applies only where the license was lost as a result of FMLA leave. Here, the employee lost his license by operation of state law due to the underlying illness, not the employee's use of FMLA leave.

(F) Employee Election to Take Alternative Position; Light Duty

Employers may accommodate an employee's request to be restored to a different shift, schedule, or position that better suits the employee's personal needs upon return from leave.[109] However, an employee cannot be induced by the employer to accept a different position against the employee's wishes.[110] Employers are not, however, required by the FMLA to offer to accommodate an employee with a different position or promotion upon return from FMLA leave.

Schools may have a program under which an employee could voluntarily accept a "light duty" assignment and return to work before he or she is able to perform all the essential functions of his or her original job. In that case, because the employee cannot waive his or her FMLA rights, the employee's right to be restored to his or her original or an equivalent position would continue until the expiration of the yearly 12-workweek FMLA entitlement, with all FMLA leave and the "light duty" period (during which the employee would otherwise have been on leave) counting against the FMLA leave entitlement.[111] Generally, an employee who is unable to perform all essential job functions upon return from FMLA leave does not have the FMLA right to return to work. The issue is addressed in section 11.03.

(G) Reasonable Accommodation Distinguished

Unlike the Americans with Disabilities Act (ADA) or similar state antidiscrimination laws, the federal FMLA does not require an employer to reasonably accommodate an employee's serious health condition.[112] The leave provisions of the FMLA are wholly distinct from the "reasonable accommodation" obligations of employers covered under the ADA.[113] An employer cannot require an employee on FMLA leave to take a light-duty position in lieu of remaining on FMLA leave.[114] Nor is an employer required by the FMLA to reasonably accommodate an employee with a light-duty position in order to facilitate an employee's return to work from FMLA leave.[115] As set forth in section 11.03, if an employee is not able to perform all of the essential functions of his or her former position at the time of return from FMLA leave, the employee does not have an FMLA right to return to work. Of course, school employers may have an obligation pursuant to the ADA, state antidiscrimination laws, or school policy to accommodate the returning employee in a position other than the employee's preleave (or equivalent) position.

The interaction of the FMLA with the Americans with Disabilities Act and similar state antidiscrimination laws is addressed in Chapter 13.

[3] The Return-to-Work Obligations of Joint Employers

Employers have return-to-work responsibilities with respect to joint employees. Joint employment occurs where two ore more entities exercise some control over the work or working conditions of the same employee.[116] The classic example of a joint employment relationship is where a temporary-help or leasing agency supplies an employee to a school.[117] In that situation, the temporary-help or leasing agency is the primary employer and the school is the secondary employer.[118] As the primary employer, the temporary-help or leasing agency has the authority to hire and fire, assign or place the employee, maintain the payroll, and provide employment benefits.

Job restoration upon the conclusion of FMLA leave is the responsibility of the primary employer.[119] The secondary employer is responsible for accepting the employee returning from FMLA leave.[120] The responsibility of the school to accept the return of the temporary or leased employee is conditional. A school employer must accept the return of a joint employee only where (1) the school continues to use a replacement employee from the temporary-help or leasing agency and (2) the temporary-help or leasing agency elects to place the employee back with the school.[121] If both of those conditions are not met, the school is not required to accept the return of joint employee from a temporary-help or leasing agency from FMLA leave.

11.03 EMPLOYEE PERFECTION OF RIGHT TO RETURN TO WORK

The FMLA right of an employee to job restoration at the conclusion of FMLA leave is not absolute.[122] Employers may insist that a returning employee satisfy three conditions in order to perfect his or her right to return to work: (1) that the employee return to work before the expiration of the employee's annual 12-workweek leave entitlement, (2) that upon return the employee is able to perform all essential job functions of the former position, and (3) that if requested, the employee provide documentation from a health care provider certifying that the employee is fit to return to duty. A returning employee who fails to meet these conditions has not perfected the FMLA right to return to work. Of course, the employee may be entitled to work due to a more generous employer policy, including the terms of a collective bargaining agreement, or federal or state law.

This section will explore the first two FMLA requirements: the requirement that the employee return to work before the expiration of the annual 12-workweek FMLA leave entitlement and the requirement that an employee return to work able to perform all essential job functions. Section 11.04 addresses the third requirement and the rules governing fitness-for-duty reports. Additional limitations on an employer's FMLA obligation to reinstate an employee are addressed in section 11.05.

[1] Return to Work before Expiration of Annual FMLA Leave Entitlement

To perfect the FMLA right to job restoration, the employee must return to work before he or she exhausts the annual 12-workweek leave entitlement.[123] Addressing this matter in the comments accompanying the final FMLA regulations, the DOL observed:

> Three commentators requested clarification regarding the employee's status when the employee fails to return at the conclusion of the leave or after 12 weeks of absence.
>
> If the employee is unable to or does not return to work at the end of 12 weeks of FMLA leave, all entitlements and rights under FMLA cease at that time; the employee is no longer entitled to any further restoration

rights under the FMLA, and the employer is no longer required to maintain group health benefits pursuant to the FMLA.[124]

Some courts have excused an employee's failure to request reinstatement before the expiration of the employee's annual 12-workweek leave entitlement for an employer's failure to notify the employee that it had designated the leave as FMLA-qualifying and that the employee, therefore, had to return to work before exhausting all FMLA leave.[125] Other courts have suggested that if the employee can establish that he or she could have and would have returned to work before exhausting the 12-week FMLA leave entitlement had the employer properly notified the employee that the leave was designated as FMLA-qualifying, the employee may still be entitled to job restoration.[126]

Employer notice obligations are addressed more fully in Chapter 6, *Notice Requirements*.

[2] Employee Is Able to Perform All Essential Job Functions

The second condition that an employee must satisfy to perfect the FMLA right to return to work is that the employee be able to perform all essential job functions of the employee's preleave position. An employee who is unable to perform all essential job functions of the position because of a physical or mental condition, including the continuation of the serious health condition prompting the need for FMLA leave, does not have the FMLA right to job restoration.[127] An employer is not required under the FMLA to create an equivalent position that does not exist for an employee who is unable to perform the functions of his or her former position at the end of FMLA leave.[128] If, at the end of 12 weeks of FMLA leave, an employee is unable to perform the essential functions of the position that the employee held when leave commenced, the employee has exhausted his or her job-protected leave entitlement under the FMLA and would not be entitled, under the federal FMLA, to be restored to employment in a different job.[129] A school employer may nevertheless be required to restore the employee pursuant to school policy or other federal or state statutes (e.g., the ADA).[130]

An employee is "unable to perform the essential functions of the position of the employee" where (1) a health care provider finds that the employee is unable to work at all or (2) the employee is unable to perform any one of the essential functions of the employee's position within the meaning of the ADA.[131] It also includes situations where the employee must be absent from work to receive medial treatment for a serious health condition.[132] In keeping with the DOL regulations, most courts apply ADA concepts when determining a job's essential functions. One court, however, has applied a modified ADA inquiry limited to whether the employee can perform the essential functions of his or her former job.[133]

FMLA claims have been precluded where the employee was no longer able to perform a wide variety of essential job functions upon return to work from FMLA leave. Lifting restrictions for jobs requiring the ability to lift certain amounts of weight have caused employees to lose their right to job restoration under the FMLA.[134] Employees have lost the FMLA right to job restoration where, upon return to work, they were restricted as to the number of hours they could work during the work day[135] or the number of days they could work in a week.[136] An employee whose work environment was characterized by dust and fumes did not have the FMLA right to return to work because of restrictions that prohibited him from working in dust and fumes.[137] Of course, if an employee is able to perform all essential job functions upon return from FMLA leave, an employer would be liable for failing to restore the employee to the same or an equivalent position.[138]

11.04 FITNESS-FOR-DUTY MEDICAL CERTIFICATION

[1] General Rule

As a condition of job restoration, employers may require employees on FMLA leave for their own serious health condition to submit a certification from the employee's health care provider that the employee is able to return to work.[139] To exercise that authority, employers must have a "uniformly applied practice or policy" requiring employees to provide medical certification of their ability to return to work.[140] Such a practice or policy is "uniformly applied" where the employer requires all similarly situated employees (i.e., same occupation, same serious health condition) who take leave for such conditions to provide medical certification attesting to their ability to return to work.[141] For example, a policy or practice that requires all employees absent from work for a certain number of days due to their own serious health condition to submit a health care provider certification in order to return to work is such a uniform policy or practice.[142] If the employee has been properly notified of the fitness-for-duty certification requirement (discussed below), an employer may delay the employee's job restoration pending receipt of the certification.[143] If the employee fails to provide a fitness-for-duty certification or a new medical certification for a serious health condition at the time FMLA leave is concluded, the employee may be terminated.[144]

The DOL regulations do not specify a time frame that an employee has to provide a return-to-work certification. Absent a time frame, an employer is only empowered by the FMLA to delay the employee's return to work from leave up to some unspecified point where it is determined that the employee has failed to provide such certification. Absent a more definite cutoff, school employers run the considerable risk of being accused of prematurely concluding that the employee has failed to provide a fitness-for-duty certification and improperly terminating the employee instead of further delaying job restoration. Employers have two time frames to consider applying as a cutoff point for return-to-work certification.

Section 825.213(a)(3) of the regulations allows employees 30 days from the date of an employer's request to provide certification establishing that the employee is unable to return to work due to the onset, recurrence, or continuation of a serious health condition, thereby precluding the employer from recovering its share of health benefit premiums paid on the employee's behalf during a period of unpaid FMLA leave. It should be noted that § 825.213(a)(3) is specifically referenced in § 825.311(c) as support for the proposition that an employee who fails to provide a return-to-work certification may be terminated. A second time frame school employers might consider is the minimum of 15 calendar days, absent unusual circumstances, that an employee has to provide medical certification to support the employee's request for FMLA leave due to a serious health condition.[145] A third option, of course, would be for school employers to wait a reasonable period of time based on the circumstances of each case.

Absent further guidance by the DOL regarding the time frame an employee has to provide a return-to-work certification, school employers should consult with counsel before concluding that an employee has failed to timely provide such certification, particularly where the school will be making that conclusion within 30 calendar days of the employer's request for a fitness-for-duty certification.

[2] Intermittent Leave Exception

An employer may not condition an employee's return to work from intermittent leave on the submission of a fitness-for-duty certification.[146] Note that the prohibition is absolute. As written, the regulations prohibit employers from requiring an employee who has taken intermittent leave to submit a fitness-for-duty certification during a course of intermittent absences or upon return from the last absence. By its terms, the exception to an employer's right to require a fitness-for-duty certification applies only if an employee has taken intermittent leave. The prohibition does not appear to apply to leave on a reduced leave schedule basis. That makes little sense, and school employers should proceed with caution (and consult with counsel) before requiring employees on a reduced leave schedule to submit a health care certification in order to return to work after each reduced leave schedule absence (which could be daily).

[3] Contents of Certification

The certification need only be a simple statement of an employee's ability to work and must relate only to the particular health condition that caused the employee's need for leave.[147] For example, a school employer could not require that the certification address the returning employee's general state of health. As such, the return-to-work certification is much narrower than the certification permitted to establish the existence of an FMLA-qualifying serious health condition. Pursuant to this requirement, a health care provider statement that "pt. may return back to work" has been approved by the courts.[148] Employers may require that the certification be in writing.[149] Notwithstanding the DOL regulatory requirements, courts have approved of employer requirements that the certification specifically state that the employee was "fully able to resume performing the essential functions of the employee's position."[150]

[4] Employee's Health Care Provider

The return-to-work certification is from the employee's health care provider.[151] "Health care providers" recognized by the FMLA are defined in 29 C.F.R. § 825.118.[152] Employers generally may not insist that an employee submit to a health care provider of the employer's choosing before returning to work from FMLA leave.[153] Employers may not insist that the fitness-for-duty certification be from a specialist.[154]

[5] Cost of Return-to-Work Certification

The cost of a return-to-work certification is borne by the employee.[155] The FMLA does not require a school employer to pay the employee for the time spent or travel costs incurred by the employee to acquire the return-to-work certification.[156] School policy, state or local law, or the terms of a collective bargaining agreement, of course, could require that school employers bear some or all of the costs associated with an employee's acquisition of a return-to-work medical certification.

[6] Clarification

An employer may, with the permission of the employee, seek clarification regarding the return-to-work certification submitted by the employee. After gaining the employee's permission, a health care provider employed by the employer may contact the employee's health care provider for purposes of clarifying the employee's fitness to return to work certification.[157] No additional information may be requested, and clarification may be requested only for the serious health condition for which FMLA leave was taken.[158] If the employer invokes this right and directs a health care provider it employs to contact the employee's health care provider, the employer may not delay the employee's return to work while such contact is being made.[159]

Clarification would appear to be of very limited utility. Given the brevity of return-to-work certification, clarification would appear to be little more than a means to decipher poor handwriting.

[7] Challenges to the Return-to-Work Certification

The FMLA does not permit employers to challenge the adequacy of the fitness-for-duty certification.[160]

[8] Effect of State or Local Law and Collective Bargaining Agreements

The FMLA provisions regarding fitness-for-duty certification do not supersede any valid state or local laws or collective bargaining agreements that govern return to work for covered employees.[161] If state or local law or the terms of a collective bargaining agreement govern an employee's return to work, those provisions shall apply.[162] If the terms of a collective bargaining agreement require a fitness-for-duty examination in addition to a return-to-work certification, then those terms apply—with two conditions.[163]

The first condition is that the fitness-for-duty examination must be related to the employee's job and consistent with business necessity as required by the ADA.[164] For example, even if such an examination were permitted by state or local law or the terms of a collective bargaining agreement, the FMLA would not permit a school to condition a math teacher's job restoration on successful completion of a medical examination because he had a leg amputated. The essential functions of the math teacher's job do not require use of both legs; therefore, the inquiry would not be job related. On the other hand, a school could require a maintenance employee whose back impairment affects his ability to lift objects to be examined by an orthopedist as a condition of job restoration, as required by the terms of an applicable collective bargaining agreement. The school could not, however, require the same employee to submit to an HIV test where the test is not related to either the essential functions of the employee's job or the employee's impairment.[165]

The second condition, which is discussed more fully in subsection [11] below, requires the employer to notify an employee of the return-to-work certification requirements. The FMLA notification procedures establish the minimum notice due when a collective bargaining agreement establishes the return-to-work certification requirements.[166] An employer that fails to meet the FMLA notice requirements violates the FMLA.

In order for the collective bargaining agreement exception to apply, the employee must be covered by the collective bargaining agreement. The collective bargaining agreement exception applies to bargaining unit employees, not members of management.[167] Presumably, the same is true for the state and local law exceptions. If the state or local law and collective bargaining agreement exceptions don't apply, absent more generous employer leave policies, the general FMLA requirements apply.[168]

The DOL has opined that where required by state law, employers could condition an employee's return to work on execution of a return-to-work agreement that requires the employee to submit to mandatory drug testing for a period of time following treatment and return to work.[169] Such a program was authorized by the ADA and the applicable state workers' compensation law. The DOL noted that the FMLA return-to-work certification provisions do not supersede the requirements of a valid state law and that the practice was therefore permissible.

Courts have split on whether employers may impose more stringent return-to-work certification requirements pursuant to a collective bargaining agreement. Some courts have held that an employer's requirement that an employee submit to a return-to-work fitness-for-duty examination as permitted by the terms of a collective bargaining agreement did not violate the FMLA.[170] Other courts have held that employers may not impose requirements on employees that are more burdensome than what is required by the return-to-work provisions of the FMLA.[171] For these courts, the proscription in 29 U.S.C. § 2652(b) that the rights established for employees under the FMLA cannot "be diminished by the terms of any collective bargaining agreement" negates an interpretation of 29 U.S.C. § 2614(a)(4) and 29 C.F.R. § 825.310(b) that would allow an employer to impose more stringent return-to-work certification requirements pursuant to a collective bargaining agreement.

Schools would be well advised to consult with counsel before imposing more stringent return-to-work requirements pursuant to a collective bargaining agreement than are generally permitted by the federal FMLA. The court decisions opposed to such a practice are highly persuasive.

[9] DOT Requirements

The U.S. Department of Transportation (DOT) has issued regulations entitling employers to require an employee to submit to a medical examination where the physical qualification of the employee to operate a commercial vehicle is in question.[172] The interaction of the DOT regulations and the return-to-work provisions of the FMLA were addressed by the district court in *Matthews v. Fairview Health Services*.[173] The court found that while the employer (Fairview) could condition Matthews's return to work on his passing a DOT physical, it violated the FMLA by requiring him to submit to a second DOT physical with a cardiac specialist for issues unrelated to his ability to drive a commercial vehicle (e.g., lifting restrictions).

In that case, Mr. Matthews was a part-time commercial truck driver and materials handler. His job entailed driving, loading, unloading, pushing, pulling, and lifting. Mr. Matthews was granted FMLA leave to receive a pacemaker. Pursuant to company policy, he submitted a return-to-work certification from his physician indicating that he could return to work but could not work more than 40 hours during the first 2-week period. Upon receipt of that certification, Fairview required Mr. Matthews to undergo a DOT physical before returning to work, which he did. Mr. Matthews passed his DOT physical. In response to an inquiry by Fairview, the physician indicated that Mr. Matthews should refrain from lifting heavy objects. Fairview refused to allow Matthews to return to work until he was cleared by a cardiac specialist. Matthews sued, alleging violation of the FMLA.

The court found that Fairview did not have the right under the DOT regulations or the FMLA to delay Matthews's return to work because of reservations involving non-driving-related issues (lifting). Since he was cleared to drive, the court found that Matthews should have been returned to work. Interestingly, the court did not find that Fairview violated the FMLA by delaying Mr. Matthews's return-to-work while he submitted to the first permissible DOT-required examination.

This is a tricky area, and schools would be well advised to consult with counsel to ensure compliance with both the DOT commercial-driving requirements and the return-to-work provisions of the FMLA.

[10] Interaction with ADA-Approved Medical Examinations

As we have seen, the FMLA permits an employer, pursuant to a uniform policy or practice, to require a return-to-work certification from the employee's health care provider attesting to the employee's ability to return to work. The ADA also allows employers in certain circumstances to require an employee to undergo a more comprehensive medical examination as a condition of job restoration. This section addresses how these two laws, the FMLA and the ADA, interact. Basically, there is a split in the courts regarding the appropriate interplay of the ADA and the FMLA regarding return-to-work fitness-for-duty requirements.

The FMLA provides that nothing "in this Act or any amendment made by this Act shall be construed to modify or affect any Federal or State law prohibiting discrimination on the basis of . . . disability."[174] According to the DOL, "the FMLA was not intended to modify or affect the ADA or any regulations issued under that Act."[175]

The ADA permits employers to make inquiries and require fitness-for-duty medical examinations where there is a need to determine whether an employee is able to perform the essential functions of his or her job.[176] The examination must be related to the employee's job and consistent with business necessity.[177] Employers may require employees who suffered on-the-job injuries that appear to affect their ability to perform essential job functions to submit to a medical examination or inquiry, consistent with business necessity.[178]

The issue is whether an employer may, consistent with the ADA, require an employee who suffered an on-the-job injury to submit to a medical examination as a condition of job restoration where the employee is out on FMLA leave. In *Porter v. United States Alumoweld Co.*, the Fourth Circuit held that the employer could, consistent with the ADA, require the employee to submit to a return-to-work physical examination as a condition of job restoration.[179] In so holding, the court rejected the employee's argument that his employer violated the FMLA by refusing to reinstate him based on his submission of a simple statement from his doctor that he was able to return to work. The court reasoned that the ADA and FMLA requirements were distinct and that the employee may be required to meet both in order to perfect the right to job restoration.

The district court in *Underhill v. Willamina Lumber Co.*, rejected the reasoning of the Fourth Circuit in *Porter*.[180] The court, relying extensively on the decision in *Albert v. Runyon*,[181] found that an employer could require an employee to submit to a medical examination as a condition of returning the employee to work in compliance with the ADA but nevertheless violate the return-to-work provisions of the FMLA. As observed by the court in *Albert*, "There, of course, is no logical reason that an examination which does not violate the ADA cannot violate the FMLA—indeed, it would not be surprising to find that the prohibitions of these different statutes were not co-extensive."[182] The court in *Albert* continued,

> The ADA and the FMLA do not conflict if the ADA's business necessity requirement requires more than employee's having taken FMLA leave. In sum, an employer may not order an employee returning from FMLA leave to submit to a fitness-for-duty examination because of that leave, or because of an underlying condition that the employee's health care provider has certified will not interfere with the employee's ability to work, or because the employer views the certification as inadequate for its own purposes. An employer only has a sufficient "business need" to examine a returning employee where the employee's ongoing limitations may interfere with her ability to work.[183]

The practical effect of the *Albert* decision is to preclude employers from conditioning an employee's return to work on submission to an ADA-approved medical examination where the employee has provided a simple statement from the employee's own health care provider that the employee is able to return to work.

Given the split in the courts, school employers should consult with counsel before requiring an employee to submit to a medical examination consistent with the ADA as a condition of job restoration, particularly where the employee has provided a return-to-work certification that conforms to the requirements of the FMLA. As set forth later in this section, school employers can require employees to submit to an ADA-approved medical examination the moment they return to work.

[11] Employer Notice Requirements

In order to require an employee to submit a return-to-work medical certification pursuant to a uniform policy or practice, the employer must notify the employee of this obligation. School employers with employee handbooks describing employment policies and benefits should include a statement explaining the employer's general policy regarding any requirements for fitness-for-duty certification to return to work.[184] Employers must also provide specific notice to any employee from whom the employer requires fitness-for-duty certification.[185] If reinstatement under the employer's leave policies differs from federal FMLA reinstatement rights, the employer's required FMLA notice to the employee must explain the difference between reinstatement under the employer's leave policy and reinstatement under the FMLA.[186] The employer must provide such specific notice of the fitness-for-duty requirement either at the time the employee provides notice of the need for FMLA leave or immediately after leave commences and the employer is advised of the medical circumstances requiring the leave unless the employee's condition changes from one that did not previously require certification pursuant to the employer's practice or policy.[187]

Employee notice requirements are addressed more fully in Chapter 6, *Notice Requirements*.

[12] Unfit to Return to Duty

If the return-to-work certification indicates that the employee is not fit to return to work, the employee has no FMLA right to return to work from FMLA leave.[188] Remember, to be fit to return to work within the meaning of the FMLA, the employee must be able perform all of the essential job functions of his or her former position.

If the employee is unfit to return to duty from FMLA leave due to the onset, recurrence, or continuation of a serious health condition, an employer would be prevented from recovering its share of health benefit premiums paid on the employee's behalf during a period of unpaid FMLA leave.[189] In that case, the employer may require an employee to provide medical certification in a timely manner (e.g., within 30 days of the employer's request) substantiating the onset, recurrence, or continuation of the serious health condition.[190] If the employer requests medical certification and the employee does not provide such certification in a timely manner, or the reason for not returning to work does not meet the test of "other circumstances beyond the employee's control," the employer may recover 100 percent of the health benefit premiums it paid during the period of unpaid FMLA leave.[191]

Health benefit premium issues are addressed more fully in Chapter 10, *Maintenance of Employment Benefits*.

[13] Postreturn Fitness-for-Duty Examinations

The FMLA does not prohibit employers from requiring an employee to submit to more stringent fitness-for-duty examinations after the employee has returned to work from FMLA leave, including on the first day the employee returns to work.[192] Of course, to avoid an ADA violation, a postreturn fitness-for-duty examination would have to be job related and consistent with business necessity.[193] Please remember that several courts have held that the mere taking of FMLA leave, or the condition giving rise to the need for FMLA leave, alone fails to establish the requisite job-related business necessity to require an employee to submit to a postreturn fitness-for-duty examination as permitted by the ADA.[194] Basically, absent additional information, employers must allow these returned employees to demonstrate that they cannot adequately perform an essential job function in order for the employer to have the requisite job-related business necessity to require a postreturn fitness-for-duty examination.

11.05 LIMITATIONS ON OBLIGATION TO REINSTATE EMPLOYEES

[1] General Rule

The employee's general right to return to work from FMLA leave is not absolute.[195] An employee has no greater right to job restoration or to other benefits and conditions of employment than if the employee had been continuously employed during the FMLA leave period.[196] This provision has been described as the "omnibus exception" to the general requirement of job restoration at the conclusion of federal FMLA leave.[197] In order to deny job restoration, an employer must be able to show that the employee would not otherwise have been employed at the time reinstatement is requested, even if leave had not been taken.[198] This broad exception to the benefits and protections of the FMLA, including the right to job restoration, has been successfully invoked by employers in a wide variety of factual settings. What follows is a review of the more common of these circumstances.

(i) Discipline and Termination

The taking of FMLA leave does not immunize an employee from discipline, including termination, for conduct or performance problems unrelated to the exercise of FMLA rights. As a result, an employee who has been terminated for a reason not related to the FMLA—even where the employee is on FMLA leave at the time of the termination—is not entitled to job restoration pursuant to the FMLA.[199]

Similarly, an employer who terminated an employee for performance problems after the employee requested and was approved to take FMLA leave, but before she began FMLA leave, did not violate the FMLA.[200] The fact that the poor performance or conduct was caused by the same illness that gave rise to the need for FMLA leave does not protect the employee from dismissal or give the employee the right to return to work and demonstrate improved performance when not ill.[201] For example, an alcoholic employee who took FMLA leave to receive treatment for his substance abuse could still be terminated for violation of employer policies prohibiting the use of alcohol on the job.[202] The fact that the conduct or performance deficiencies that resulted in discipline or termination were discovered because the employee took FMLA leave does not protect the employee or bar the employer from taking appropriate disciplinary action.[203]

Of course, employers who use the taking of FMLA leave as a factor in support of discipline or termination violate the Act.[204] However, one court held that the employer did not violate the FMLA where it terminated an employee for violation of a "last chance" attendance agreement that included periods of FMLA leave, because the employee had incurred other non-FMLA-leave absences that violated the last-chance agreement. The last chance agreement provided that "any" violation thereof was grounds for termination.[205]

(ii) Layoff/Reductions-in-Force

Where an employee is laid off during the course of taking FMLA leave and his or her employment is terminated, the employer is no longer obligated to (1) continue the employee's FMLA leave, (2) maintain group health plan benefits, or (3) restore the employee to the same or equivalent position.[206] Of course, if school policies, the terms of a collective bargaining agreement, or state law provides more generous benefits (i.e., requires employers to allow the employee to finish out FMLA leave, maintain group health benefits, or restore the employee), the school employer must abide by those more generous requirements.[207] An employer has the burden of proving that an employee would have been laid off during the FMLA leave period even if the employee had not taken leave and, therefore, that the employee is not entitled to job restoration.[208] An employer is not obligated to transfer an employee, simply because the employee has requested FMLA leave, where the employee's position has been eliminated in a restructuring.[209] If the employee is recalled from layoff or otherwise reemployed, an eligible employee is immediately entitled to further FMLA leave for an FMLA-qualifying reason.[210]

Schools need to exercise great care when claiming that the employee's position has been eliminated during the employee's FMLA leave. What often happens is that the employer redistributes the employee's job functions to others during leave. The employer learns that it can do without the employee and restructures to eliminate the employee's (and, frequently, only the employee's) position. Under the federal FMLA, an employee is entitled to reinstatement even if the employee has been replaced or his or her position has been restructured to accommodate the employee's absence.[211] Courts have declined to apply the omnibus exception where there is evidence that the employee's position was not eliminated but merely redistributed to accommodate the employee's absence and that the employer learned that the performance of other employees could substitute for that employee's performance.[212]

The FMLA does not necessarily prohibit an employer from eliminating only the job held by an employee on FMLA leave as part of a reorganization. What is required, however, is evidence of a legitimate non-FMLA reason for the restructuring. For example, evidence that the employee's position was slated for elimination before the employee requested FMLA leave has been found sufficiently independent of the use of FMLA leave to apply the omnibus exception and deny the employee job restoration under the FMLA.[213] Evidence that the employee's job performance had been deteriorating for some time before her request and use of FMLA leave combined with other company changes supported another court's finding that the elimination of the employee's job while she was on leave did not violate the FMLA.[214]

(iii) Shift Eliminated/Overtime Reduced

If a shift has been eliminated, or overtime has been reduced, an employee would not be entitled to return to work that shift or the original amount of overtime.[215] However, if a position on, for example, the night shift has been filled by another employee during the FMLA leave period, the employee returning to work from leave is entitled to return to the night shift where he or she was employed before taking FMLA leave, either in the same or an equivalent position.[216]

(iv) Employee Hired for Specific Term or Project

Employers may deny job restoration to employees hired for a specific term or to perform work on a discrete project if the employment term or project is finished and the employer would not otherwise have continued to employ the employee.[217] If, however, an employee was hired to perform work under a contract and after the contract period the contract was awarded to another contractor, the successor contractor may be required to restore the employee if it is a successor employer within the meaning of the FMLA.[218]

The FMLA obligations of successor and joint employers are addressed more fully in Chapter 2, *Schools as FMLA-Covered Employers*.

(v) Workers' Compensation

If an employee on both workers' compensation leave and FMLA leave for his or her own serious health condition (due to an on-the-job injury) is unable, before the expiration of 12 workweeks of leave, to return to work at all or to perform all essential job functions of his or her former position, the employee no longer has the FMLA right to job restoration.[219] The employee's right to return to work would be governed by workers' compensation law, the ADA, or a more generous school policy, if any.[220]

(vi) Probationary Periods; Retraining

The omnibus exception applies to employees who take FMLA leave during their probationary period. They are not entitled to greater FMLA rights and protections, including job restoration, than if they had not taken FMLA leave. They simply cannot receive fewer employment rights and benefits because they took FMLA leave. For example, if a school employer's policy permits the extension of a probationary period for unpaid or paid leave, the probationary period would be extended where the employee is on paid or unpaid FMLA leave during the probationary period. If, however, school policy does not allow for the extension of a probationary period for paid or unpaid leave, the FMLA would not permit an employer to extend the probationary period because an employee took FMLA leave. An employer would violate the FMLA by extending the probationary period only where employees took FMLA leave.

Employers may impose a probationary period on an employee's return to work from leave if the employer, because of the employee's conduct or performance, would have placed the employee on probation even if the employee had not taken FMLA leave. For example, an employee is injured in a motor vehicle accident incident to the employee's job. The employee takes FMLA leave. The employer investigates the accident and determines that it was avoidable. Pursuant to the employer's uniform policy, upon return from FMLA leave the employee is placed on probation for violating company policy regarding safety. The placement of the employee on probation pursuant to a uniformly applied policy for safety violations does not violate the FMLA.[221]

One court has held that an employer did not violate the FMLA when it required an employee to go through new employee orientation and computer training upon her return from FMLA leave. The employee had just returned from a 25-week leave of absence, 12 weeks of which were covered by the FMLA. The employee had been employed by the employer for several years before the request for FMLA leave. The court found that the employer did not violate the FMLA by requiring the employee to go through new employee orientation upon her return to work. The court opined that the requirement of retraining was reasonable after such a lengthy absence and noted that the employee had not established that she was singled out for this requirement.[222]

(vii) Outside Employment

The FMLA recognizes that employers may have policies governing whether and the extent to which its employees may engage in outside or supplemental employment. Where an employer has a uniformly applied policy governing outside or supplemental employment, such a policy may continue to apply to an employee while on FMLA leave.[223] An employee who violates that uniformly applied policy against working on FMLA leave is not entitled to reinstatement if the employee would have lost his or her job for violating that work rule if the employee had not taken FMLA leave.[224]

(viii) Fraud

An employee is entitled to job restoration only where he or she takes FMLA leave "for the intended purpose of the leave."[225] An employee who fraudulently obtains FMLA leave from an employer is not protected by the FMLA's job-restoration or maintenance-of-health-benefits provisions.[226] An employer need only have an honestly held suspicion that an employee is not using medical leave for its intended purpose to defeat an employee claim that discipline or termination while the employee was on leave violated the FMLA.[227] Pursuant to that standard, an employer could be wrong in its belief that an employee secured FMLA leave by fraud and still defeat an FMLA claim so long as it reasonably believed that the employee wrongfully obtained FMLA leave.[228]

[2] Undue Hardship or Compelling Business Interest

Generally, "undue hardship" or a "compelling business need" is not an exception to an employer's obligation to restore an employee to the same or an equivalent position at the conclusion of FMLA leave.[229] As addressed in section 11.07, there is an exception to the job-restoration requirement that applies to certain highly compensated "key employees." That exception does not, however, apply to other employees. There are also special rules that allow certain local educational agencies and private elementary and secondary school employers to delay the return of instructional employees from FMLA leave. Those rules are addressed above in section 11.02[1](ii).

An employer may redistribute the employee's work, restructure the position, or take other actions during the employee's absence on FMLA leave as required for the continued operation of the employer's business.[230] Regardless of the action taken, the employer is required to restore the employee taking FMLA leave to the same or an equivalent position at the end of the leave. With the exception of the special school rules permitting certain schools to delay the return of instructional employees who take leave near the end of an academic term, there simply is no exception that would allow a school employer to refuse to reinstate an employee from FMLA leave because it would impose an undue hardship on the school.

11.06 EMPLOYEE RETURN-TO-WORK NOTICE REQUIREMENTS

Employees have three notice obligations regarding return to work from FMLA leave:

[1] Periodic Status Reports

An employer may require an employee on FMLA leave to report periodically on the employee's status and intent to return to work.[231] The employer's policy regarding such reports may not be discriminatory and must take into account all of the relevant facts and circumstances related to the individual employee's leave situation.[232] The DOL explained that the regulation intended that such requests be reasonable under the circumstances and that an employer who misuses or abuses this provision may be found to have engaged in prohibited acts under the FMLA.[233]

The regulations do not address what constitutes a periodic status report, whether such a report must be in writing, how long an employee has to provide such a report, or what happens if the employee fails to provide periodic status reports. Presumably, school employers may have reasonable policies requiring periodic status reports, provided that such policies take into account the facts and circumstances of each case. A set policy that requires an employee to provide periodic status reports regardless of the facts will likely violate the Act.

Notice of a requirement that employees must provide periodic status reports during FMLA leave should be included in any employee handbook, manual, or other written materials regarding leave and benefits.[234] Employers may, but are not required to, include notice of the requirement to provide periodic status reports as part of the specific notice of FMLA rights and obligations that must be given to employees.[235] School employers who wish to require periodic status reports would be well advised to include notice of that requirement in the specific employee FMLA notice.

[2] Notice of Intent to Return to Work Earlier Than Anticipated

An employee may discover after beginning leave that the circumstances have changed and the amount of leave originally anticipated is no longer necessary. In that case, an employer may require that the employee provide reasonable notice (i.e., within two business days) of the changed circumstances where foreseeable.[236] The employer may also obtain information on such changed circumstances by requesting periodic status reports.[237]

The consequences of an employee's failure to provide timely notice of an intent to return to work earlier than anticipated are addressed above in section 11.02[1](i).

[3] Unequivocal Notice of Intent Not to Return to Work

If an employee gives unequivocal notice of intent not to return to work from FMLA leave, the employer is no longer obligated by the FMLA to maintain health benefits or to restore the employee.[238]

The termination of health benefits is addressed more fully in section 10.04[6] of Chapter 10, *Maintenance of Employment Benefits*.

11.07 "KEY EMPLOYEE" EXCEPTION TO REINSTATEMENT

The FMLA permits employers to deny job restoration to certain highly compensated "key employees." Interestingly, the exception applies because the return of the employee from FMLA leave, not the loss of the employee for taking FMLA leave, would cause the employer "substantial and grievous economic injury." As discussed more fully below, the requirements to meet this exception are both numerous and stringent.

[1] General Rule

An employer is not required by the FMLA to return certainly highly compensated or key employees to work from FMLA leave:[239]

- The exemption is limited to a salaried eligible employee who is among the highest paid 10 percent of the employer's workforce within 75 miles of the facility where employed.
- The denial of job restoration (but not the taking of the leave) must be necessary to prevent "substantial and grievous economic injury" to the employer's operations.

- The employer must notify the employee of its intent to deny restoration under this exemption at the time the employer determines that such grievous economic injury would occur.
- The employer must allow the employee an opportunity to elect to return to work after receiving that notice from the employer.

The factors are addressed more fully below.

[2] "Key Employee" Defined

A "key employee" is a salaried, FMLA-eligible employee who is among the highest paid 10 percent of all employees employed by the employer within 75 miles of the worksite at which the employee is employed.[240] A "salaried employee" is one who is paid on a salary basis and is exempt from the FLSA minimum wage and overtime requirements.[241]

In determining whether a "key employee" is within the top 10 percent of employees in terms of compensation, the earnings of all employees—whether salaried or nonsalaried and whether eligible for FMLA leave or not—must be taken into account.[242] The determination of which employees at the worksite are among the highest paid 10 percent is made based on year-to-date earnings divided by weeks worked by the employee (including weeks in which paid leave was taken).[243] Earnings include wages, premium pay (including overtime and shift differential premium pay), incentive pay (e.g., commissions), and nondiscretionary and discretionary bonuses.[244] For purposes of the "key employee" determination, "earnings" do not include incentives whose value is determined at some future date, for example, stock options, benefits, or perquisites.[245] The "key employee" determination is made at the time the employee gives notice of the need for FMLA leave.[246]

[3] Substantial and Grievous Economic Injury

To deny restoration to a "key employee," the employer must establish that restoring the employee would cause "substantial and grievous economic injury" to the employer's operations.[247] Note that it is the *return* of the key employee from FMLA leave, not the loss of the employee due to the taking of FMLA leave, that must cause "substantial and grievous economic injury" to the employer's operations.[248]

An employer must make a good faith determination based on the available facts at the time the employee gives notice of the need for FMLA leave or when FMLA leave commences, whichever is earlier, that the employee qualifies as a "key employee."[249] If the determination cannot be made at this time, employers must make the determination as soon as practicable after being notified of a need for leave or leave commencement, if earlier.[250] Employers must also determine that substantial and grievous economic injury would result from the return of the key employee at the end of the employee's leave period where the employee elects to take or stay on FMLA leave rather than immediately return to work.[251]

Due to the fact-specific nature of the determination, "a precise test cannot be set for the level of hardship or injury to the employer that must be sustained."[252] The level of hardship, however, appears very high. If the reinstatement of a "key employee" threatens the economic viability of the employer, that would constitute substantial and grievous economic injury.[253] A lesser injury that causes long-term economic injury would also be sufficient.[254] Minor inconveniences and costs that an employer would experience in the normal course of doing business would not constitute substantial and grievous economic injury.[255] An employer may take into account its ability to replace on a temporary basis (or temporarily do without) the employee on FMLA leave; if permanent replacement is unavoidable, the cost of reinstating the employee in an equivalent position can be considered in evaluating whether substantial and grievous economic injury will occur from restoration.[256]

[4] Notice to Key Employees

Employers potentially have three notice obligations that must be satisfied to deny job restoration to a "key employee."

(i) Initial Notice

Under the key employee regulations, employers have three opportunities to provide the initial notice of "key employee" determination. An employer who believes that reinstatement may be denied to a "key employee" must give written notice to the employee at the time the employee gives notice of the need for FMLA leave or when leave commences, if earlier, that he or she qualifies as a "key employee."[257] If the employer cannot give such notice immediately because of the need to determine whether the employee is a key employee, the notice must be given as soon as practicable after being notified of a need for leave or leave commencement, if earlier.[258] A delay of two or three days between the employee's notice of the need for FMLA leave and the employer's written notice of the key employee designation was "not so great as to place [the employer] in violation of the [regulations'] requirement that the employer give written notice 'as soon as practicable' after the request for leave."[259]

In addition to informing the employee of the key employee designation, the employer must at the same time fully inform the employee of the potential consequences with respect to reinstatement and maintenance of health benefits if the employer should determine that substantial and grievous economic injury to the employer's operations would occur if the employee were reinstated from FMLA leave.[260]

The initial notice must be in writing.[261] If the initial notice includes the determination that substantial and grievous economic injury would result from the employee's reinstatement, such notice must be provided to the employee by personal service or by certified mail.[262] Otherwise, the regulations do not specify a required method of delivery for the initial notice. School employers would be well advised to provide such notice in writing and either in person, by certified mail, or by some other method that documents that the employee timely received the notice.

An employer that fails to timely provide the initial "key employee" notice loses the right to deny job restoration to the key employee, even if substantial and grievous economic injury to the employer's operations would result from reinstatement.[263]

I do not believe that the penalty provision for failure to timely provide the initial notice to the key employee would survive a challenge. In the wake of the Supreme Court's decision in *Ragsdale v. Wolverine World-Wide, Inc.* striking down less egregious penalty provisions created by the DOL for employer notice violations,[264] it is simply inconceivable that a court would allow an employer to suffer crippling or even fatal economic injury to its operations because it was a day late in notifying the employee that it had designated him or her as a "key employee." As in *Ragsdale*, the penalty provision at issue here automatically presumes an impairment of FMLA rights as a result of a violation and, arguably, does not bear a substantial relation to the harm suffered by the employee—contrary to the Act's remedial scheme.[265]

(ii) Notice of Substantial and Grievous Economic Injury

The DOL regulations afford an employer the opportunity to make the determination that job restoration would result in substantial and grievous economic injury to its operations either at the same time as the initial notice or afterward. As soon as an employer makes a good faith determination, based on the facts available, that substantial and grievous economic injury to its operations will result if a key employee who has given notice of the need for FMLA leave or who is using FMLA leave is reinstated, the employer must notify the employee in writing that

- it has determined that the employee is a key employee;
- the employer cannot deny the employee FMLA leave; and
- it intends to deny restoration to employment upon completion of the employee's FMLA leave.[266]

Again, it is anticipated that an employer will ordinarily be able to give such notice prior to leave commencement.[267] The employer must serve this notice either in person or by certified mail.[268] The notice must explain the basis for the employer's finding that the substantial and grievous injury will result and if leave has commenced, must provide the employee a reasonable time in which to return to work, taking into account the circumstances, such as the length of the leave and the urgency of the need for the employee to return.[269]

The regulations governing the notice of substantial and grievous economic injury do not include a penalty provision in the event the employer fails to timely provide such notice. Presumably, the penalty set forth for the failure to provide timely initial notice also applies to this notice—namely, the employer cannot deny job restoration.[270]

If the "key employee" on leave elects not to return to work in response to the employer's notification of intent to deny restoration, the employee remains entitled to the maintenance of health benefits.[271] An employer also would not be entitled to recover its share of the cost of health benefit premiums.[272] A key employee's rights under the FMLA continue unless and until the employee either gives notice that he or she no longer wishes to return to work or the employer actually denies reinstatement at the conclusion of the leave period.[273]

(iii) Notice of Denial of Job Restoration

After notice to an employee has been given that substantial and grievous economic injury will result if the employee is reinstated to employment, an employee is still entitled to request reinstatement at the end of the leave period.[274] An employee may make this request even if he or she did not return to work in response to the employer's notice.[275]

If the employee asks for reinstatement, the employer must again determine whether there will be substantial and grievous economic injury if the employee is reinstated, based on the facts at that time.[276] If it is determined that substantial and grievous economic injury will result, the employer must notify the employee in writing that job restoration is denied.[277] The employer must deliver this final written notice to the employee in person or by certified mail.[278]

Presumably, if the employee does not ask for reinstatement, the employer is not obligated to reevaluate whether job restoration would result in substantial and grievous economic injury and notify the employee of those results. Here again, the DOL regulations do not impose a penalty for an employer's failure to notify the employee in writing of the result of its reevaluation and denial of job restoration. Certainly, the employer's failure to so notify the employee would constitute a technical violation of the FMLA.[279] Many courts have held that absent proof of actual damages, technical violations of the FMLA notice provisions generally will not support a viable FMLA claim.

11.08 RETURN-TO-WORK REQUIREMENTS UNDER STATE FAMILY MEDICAL LEAVE LAWS

As in the case of other issues covered in this book, job restoration rights and responsibilities under state family medical leave laws vary greatly. Some states do not impose any special return-to-work requirements on employees or employers. Others virtually copy the job-restoration provisions of the federal FMLA. Many states do not have special return-to-work rules governing school employees, although some do. For example, under Arizona's parental leave regulations, an employee returning to work from covered leave without pay must be returned to the position occupied at the start of the parental leave. If the position no longer exists, the agency must conduct a reduction in force.[280] The provisions of the federal FMLA, not section R2-5-412(H) of the Arizona Administrative Code, govern an employee's return to work from family leave or leave due to the employee's own serious health condition leave.[281]

Florida's parental or family medical leave law provides that upon returning at the end of parental or family medical leave, the employee must be reinstated to the same job or to an equivalent position with equivalent pay and with seniority, retirement, fringe benefits, and other service credits accumulated prior to the leave period. If any portion of the parental or family medical leave is paid leave, the employee is entitled to accumulate all benefits granted under paid leave status.[282]

Vermont's Parental and Family Leave Act requires that employees, upon return from leave, be offered the same or a comparable job at the same level of compensation, employment benefits, seniority, and any other term or condition of employment existing on the day leave began.[283] This right does not apply if prior to requesting leave, the employee had been given notice or had given notice that the employment would terminate.[284] The job-restoration right also does not apply if the employer can demonstrate by clear and convincing evidence that (1) during the period of leave the employee would have been terminated or laid off for reasons unrelated to the leave or the condition for which the leave was granted or (2) the employee performed unique services and hiring a permanent replacement during the leave, after giving reasonable notice to the employee of intent to do so, was the only alternative available to the employer to prevent substantial and grievous economic injury to the employer's operation.[285] An employee may return from leave earlier than estimated with the approval of the employer.[286] Vermont law does not contain special school rules.

11.09 INTERACTION OF THE FEDERAL FMLA WITH STATE FAMILY AND MEDICAL LEAVE LAWS: RETURN-TO-WORK REQUIREMENTS

If a leave of absence is covered by only one law, the federal FMLA or a state family and medical leave law, the leave is governed only by the one law that applies.[287] Where a leave of absence is covered by both the federal FMLA and a state family medical leave law, school administrators must determine, on a provision-by-provision basis, which law applies, state or federal. The federal FMLA does not supersede any provision of state or local law that provides greater family and medical leave rights than the rights under the federal FMLA.[288] The standard providing the greater right or more generous benefit to the employee from each law will apply.[289] This determination applies to both procedural and substantive rights, including rights and benefits associated with job restoration at the conclusion of the need for leave.[290] Regarding job-restoration rights, the DOL illustrated the operation of the rule as follows:

> If State law prohibits mandatory leave beyond the actual period of pregnancy disability, an instructional employee of an educational agency subject to special FMLA rules may not be required to remain on leave until the end of the academic term, as permitted by FMLA under certain circumstances.[291]

In comments accompanying publication of the final FMLA regulations, the DOL provided two additional examples of note in response to comments it received regarding the regulations. Addressing the interaction of the federal FMLA and state workers' compensation laws, the DOL observed:

> If a State workers' compensation law provides a job guarantee to workers out of work temporarily due to occupational injuries that is more gen-

> erous than the FMLA's job restoration provisions, such law is a "State . . . law that provides greater . . . medical leave rights" and would govern an employee's reinstatement.[292]

The example also serves to remind us that the source of state family and medical leave laws that may interact with the federal FMLA is broad. Essentially, any state or local law that covers an employee's need for leave for the birth, adoption, or foster care placement of a child, or due to the serious health condition of the employee or the employee's spouse, son, daughter, or parent may meet that requirement.

The second DOL example illustrates how school employers should compare employee rights and benefits where state law is silent on an issue addressed by the federal FMLA. According to the DOL, in cases where an employee is eligible under both the FMLA and state or local law, the state or local law is silent on a provision contained in the federal FMLA, and the federal FMLA provision is restrictive as to employee rights or benefits, then the state or local law would govern as to that provision. If the FMLA provision is not restrictive or expands a right, benefit, or privilege to employees, then the FMLA would govern as to that provision.[293] The DOL illustrated the operation of this rule with the following example:

> For example, a State law that grants employers the right to deny the taking of leave to high-level executives could not be applied to any FMLA-eligible employees, because FMLA extends to all eligible employees the entitlement to leave for qualifying reasons. If the same State law contained a provision mandating that all employees who take leave be restored to employment when the leave ends, then FMLA's "key" employee exemption could not be applied to deny an employee reinstatement (i.e., the Federal law would not apply at the time of reinstatement).[294]

In the above example, state law governed because it provided greater rights and benefits to employees by not treating "key employees" differently from other employees in terms of the right to return to work from covered leave.

Where leave is covered by both federal and state family or medical leave laws, school administrators must carefully review the job-restoration provisions of both laws and determine, on a provision-by-provision basis, which law, the federal FMLA or applicable state law, provides greater rights and benefits to employees and must restore the employee in accordance with that law.

NOTES

1. 29 U.S.C. § 2614(a); 29 C.F.R. § 825.214(a).
2. 29 C.F.R. § 825.214(a).
3. See DOL WH FMLA Advisory Opinion No. 95, question 3 (June 3, 1998).
4. See *Hillstrom v. Best Western TLC Hotel*, 265 F. Supp. 2d 117, 126 (D. Mass. 2003), *affd*, 354 F.3d 27 (1st Cir. 2003).
5. 29 U.S.C. § 2614(a)(1).
6. 29 C.F.R. § 825.214(a).
7. See, e.g., *Welty v. Honda of America Manufacturing, Inc.*, 411 F. Supp. 2d 824, 827–28 (S.D. Ohio 2005). In *Welty*, the court rejected summary judgment where the employee claimed that, in violation of the FMLA, he was transferred to a nonequivalent position upon his return to work from FMLA leave and eventually discharged at a time when he did not meet eligibility requirements. The court opined that because the employee met the eligibility requirements at the time leave began, he could maintain a subsequent FMLA interference claim at a time he did not meet the eligibility requirements.
8. DOL WH FMLA Advisory Opinion No. 91, question 3 (Dec. 9, 1997).
9. 29 C.F.R. § 825.700(a)–(b); DOL WH FMLA Advisory Opinion No. 91, question 3 (Dec. 9, 1997).
10. *Hoge v. Honda of America Manufacturing, Inc.*, 384 F.3d 238, 247 (6th Cir. 2004).
11. *Id.*
12. See 29 U.S.C. § 2614(c)(2)(A) (discussing case where employee fails to return to work from leave after the period of leave to which the employee is entitled has expired); 29 C.F.R. § 825.203(d) (providing that employee may not be required to take more FMLA leave than necessary to address the circumstances that precipitated the need for the leave); 29 C.F.R. § 825.309(c).
13. *Hoge*, 384 F.3d at 248.
14. *Duty v. Norton-Aloca Proppants*, 293 F.3d 481, 494 (8th Cir. 2002); *Watkins v. J&S Oil Co., Inc.*, 164 F.3d 55, 59 (1st Cir. 1998); *Barry v. Wing Memorial Hospital*, 142 F. Supp. 2d 161, 165–66 (D. Mass. 2001).

15. 29 C.F.R. § 825.309(c).

16. 29 C.F.R. § 825.312(e); see also *Hoge*, 384 F.3d 238.

17. *Hoge*, 384 F.3d at 248.

18. *Id.* (rejecting argument that employer should have reasonable period of time to return employee from FMLA leave in order to give the employer time to evaluate whether the employee is disabled and, therefore, entitled to reasonable accommodation).

19. See *Warrant v. Aetna Life Insurance Co.*, No. 3:97-CV-1030-R, 1999 U.S. Dist. LEXIS 12849 (N.D. Tex. Aug. 13, 1999) (holding that Aetna did not violate the FMLA when it ordered employee to immediately return to work upon receipt of medical release indicating employee could return to work immediately).

20. *Brown v. J.C. Penney Corp.*, 924 F. Supp. 1158, 1163 (S.D. Fla. 1996).

21. 29 C.F.R. § 825.310(f).

22. 29 C.F.R. §§ 825.309(c), 825.312(e).

23. 29 C.F.R. § 825.602.

24. *Hoge v. Honda of America Manufacturing, Inc.*, 384 F.3d 238, 248–49 (6th Cir. Sept. 16, 2004).

25. 29 U.S.C. § 2618(e); 29 C.F.R. § 825.604.

26. 29 C.F.R. § 825.600(a).

27. *Id.*

28. 29 C.F.R. § 825.604.

29. *Id.*

30. *Id.*

31. *Id.*

32. DOL WH FMLA Advisory Opinion No. 80 (Apr. 24, 1996).

33. 29 U.S.C. § 2618(c), (d); 29 C.F.R. § 825.600(c).

34. 29 C.F.R. § 825.6000(c).

35. *Id.*

36. *Id.*

37. 29 C.F.R. § 825.601(a)(1).

38. 29 C.F.R. § 825.601(a)(2).

39. 29 C.F.R. § 825.602(b).

40. 29 C.F.R. § 825.602(a).

41. 29 C.F.R. § 825.602(a)(1).

42. 29 C.F.R. § 825.602(a)(2).

43. 29 C.F.R. § 825.602(b).

44. 29 C.F.R. § 825.602(a).

45. 29 U.S.C. § 2614(a)(1).

46. Comments on Regulations Implementing the Family and Medical Leave Act of 1993 (§ 825.214), 60 Fed. Reg. 2180, 2213 (Jan. 6, 1995); see also *Watkins v. J&S Oil Co., Inc.*, 164 F.3d 55 (1st Cir. 1998).

47. See *LaFortune v. Fiber Materials, Inc.*, No. 03-275-P-H, 2004 U.S. Dist. LEXIS 21405, at *10–*11 (D. Me. Oct. 25, 2004) (asserting that statute expresses no preference for restoration to the original position; all an employer need do is provide an equivalent position).

48. 29 U.S.C. § 2614(a)(1); 29 C.F.R. § 825.214(a).

49. 29 C.F.R. § 825.214(a).

50. *Brown v. J.C. Penney Corp.*, 924 F. Supp. 1158, 1163 (S.D. Fla. 1996).

51. See *Cooper v. Olin Corp., Winchester Div.*, 246 F.3d 1083, 1090 (8th Cir. 2001).

52. DOL WH FMLA Advisory Opinion No. 80 (Apr. 24, 1996).

53. *Id.*

54. *Id.*

55. Compare *Robinson v. Overnite Transportation Co.*, No. 95-3067, 1997 U.S. App. LEXIS 6574 (4th Cir. Apr. 9, 1997) (holding that return to same position with probationary period following workplace accident did not fundamentally alter nature of position), with *Blackwell v. Harris Chemical North America, Inc.*, 11 F. Supp. 2d 1302 (D. Kan. 1998) (holding that permanent employee may not be placed on probationary period on return from FMLA leave).

56. *Williams v. SAAD's Healthcare*, No. 99-1070-BH-S, 2000 U.S. Dist. LEXIS 4180 (S.D. Ala. Mar. 16, 2000).

57. 29 C.F.R. § 825.215(a).

58. S. Rep. No. 103-3, at 29–30 (1993), as reprinted in 1993 U.S.C.C.A.N. 3, 31–32.

59. 42 U.S.C. §§ 2000e–2000e-17.

60. Comments on Regulations Implementing the Family and Medical Leave Act of 1993 (§ 825.215), 60 Fed. Reg. 2180, 2214 (Jan. 6, 1995).

61. *Watkins v. J&S Oil Inc.*, 164 F.3d 55, 59 (1st Cir. 1998).

62. 29 C.F.R. § 825.215(e)(3).

63. 29 C.F.R. § 825.215(c)(1).

64. *Id.*

65. *Id.*

66. *Id.*

67. *Id.*

68. 29 C.F.R. § 825.215(c)(2).

69. 29 C.F.R. § 825.215(c)(1); DOL WH FMLA Advisory Opinion No. 31 (Mar. 21, 1994).

70. DOL WH FMLA Advisory Opinion No. 79 (Feb. 23, 1996); DOL WH FMLA Advisory Opinion No. 31 (Mar. 21, 1994).

71. 29 C.F.R. § 825.215(c)(2); DOL WH FMLA Advisory Opinion No. 79 (Feb. 23, 1996); DOL WH FMLA Advisory Opinion No. 31 (Mar. 21, 1994).

72. 29 C.F.R. § 825.215(c)(2); DOL WH FMLA Advisory Opinion No. 110 (Sept. 11, 2000); DOL WH FMLA Advisory Opinion No. 79 (Feb. 23, 1996); DOL WH FMLA Advisory Opinion No. 57 (April 7, 1995).

73. DOL WH FMLA Advisory Opinion No. 56 (Mar. 28, 1995).

74. 29 C.F.R. § 825.215(c)(1); DOL WH FMLA Advisory Opinion No. 31 (Mar. 21, 1994).

75. 29 C.F.R. § 825.215(c)(2).

76. DOL WH FMLA Advisory Opinion No. 79 (Feb. 23, 1996).

77. 29 C.F.R. § 825.215(d).

78. 29 C.F.R. § 825.215(d)(1).

79. *Id.*

80. *Id.*

81. *Id.*

82. 29 C.F.R. § 825.215(d)(5).

83. *Id.*

84. 29 C.F.R. § 825.215(d)(4).

85. *Id.*

86. *Id.*

87. 29 C.F.R. § 825.215(e); see also *Hangar v. Lake County*, 390 F.3d 579 (8th Cir. 2004).

88. 29 C.F.R. § 825.215(e)(1).

89. 29 C.F.R. § 825.215(e)(2); DOL WH FMLA Advisory Opinion No. 3 (Sept. 9, 1993).

90. 29 C.F.R. § 825.215(f).

91. *LaFortune v. Fiber Materials, Inc.*, No. 03-275-P-H, 2004 U.S. Dist. LEXIS 21405 (D. Me. Oct. 25, 2004).

92. *Donahoo v. Master Data Center*, 282 F. Supp. 2d 540, 551 (E.D. Mich. 2003).

93. *Peterson v. Slidell Memorial Hospital and Medical Center*, No. 96-2487 "G," 1996 U.S. Dist. LEXIS 18944 (E.D. La. Dec. 16, 1996).

94. *Martin v. Inhabitants of the City of Biddeford*, No. 02-122-P-H, 2003 U.S. Dist. LEXIS 5375 (D. Me. Apr. 1, 2003), *adopted*, 261 F. Supp. 2d 34 (D. Me. 2003).

95. 29 C.F.R. § 825.215(f).

96. *Borner v. Zale Lipsky University Hospital*, No. CA-3:01-CV-227-R, 2002 U.S. Dist. LEXIS 4787 (N.D. Tex. Mar. 20, 2002).

97. *Noyer v. Viacom, Inc.*, 22 F. Supp. 2d 301 (S.D.N.Y. 1998).

98. *Oby v. Baton Rouge Marriott*, 329 F. Supp. 2d 772 (M.D. La. 2004).

99. *Hillstrom v. Best Western TLC Hotel*, 265 F. Supp. 2d 117, 126–27 (D. Mass. 2003), *affd*, 354 F.3d 27 (1st Cir. 2003).

100. *Mitchell v. Dutchmen Manufacturing, Inc.*, 389 F.3d 746, 748 (7th Cir. 2004).

101. *Oby*, 329 F. Supp. 2d 772 (M.D. La. 2004).

102. *Montgomery v. Maryland*, 266 F.3d 334, 341 (4th Cir. 2001), *vacated and remanded on other grounds*, 535 U.S. 1075 (2002).

103. *Id.* at 342.

104. 29 C.F.R. § 825.215(b).

105. *Geromanous v. Columbia University*, 322 F. Supp. 2d 420, 427 (S.D.N.Y. 2004).

106. *Id.*

107. See *Fejes v. Gilpin Ventures, Inc.*, 960 F. Supp. 1487 (D. Colo. 1997).

108. *Jewell v. Reid's Confectionary Co.*, 172 F. Supp. 2d 212 (D. Me. 2001).

109. 29 C.F.R. § 825.215(e)(4).

110. *Id.*; DOL WH FMLA Advisory Opinion No. 17 (Nov. 15, 1993).

111. 29 C.F.R. § 825.220(d); DOL WH FMLA Advisory Opinion No. 55 (Mar. 10, 1995).

112. 29 C.F.R. §§ 825.214(b), 825.702(a).

113. DOL WH FMLA Advisory Opinion No. 55 (Mar. 10, 1995).

114. *Id.*

115. See *Fogelman v. Greater Hazelton Health Alliance*, No. 03-4413, 2004 U.S. App. LEXIS 26861 (3d Cir. Dec. 23, 2004); *Passauer v. Quest Diagnostics, Inc.*, No. CCB-03-159, 2004 U.S. Dist. LEXIS 6966 (D. Md. April 22, 2004).

116. 29 C.F.R. § 825.106(a).

117. *Id.*

118. *Id.*

119. *Id.*

120. *Id.*

121. *Id.*

122. *Pharakhone v. Nissan North America, Inc.*, 324 F. 3d 405 (6th Cir. 2003).

123. *Hicks v. Leroy's Jewelers, Inc.*, No. 98-6596, 2000 U.S. App. LEXIS 17568 (6th Cir. July 17, 2000) (holding that employee on FMLA leave has no right to job restoration if she fails to return to work within 12 weeks of when

leave began), *cert. denied*, 531 U.S. 1146 (2001); *McGregor v. AutoZone, Inc.*, 180 F.3d 1305, 1308 (11th Cir. 1999)(same).

124. Comments on Regulations Implementing the Family and Medical Leave Act of 1993 (§ 825.309), 60 Fed. Reg. 2180, 2225 (Jan. 6, 1995).

125. See *Duty v. Norton-Alcoa Proppants*, 293 F.3d 481, 493–94 (8th Cir. 2002).

126. See *Ragsdale v. Wolverine Worldwide, Inc.*, 535 U.S. 81 (2002).

127. 29 C.F.R. § 825.214(a); see also *Hoge v. Honda of America Manufacturing, Inc.*, 384 F.3d 238, 249 (6th Cir. 2004); *Tardie v. Rehabilitation Hospital of Rhode Island*, 168 F.3d 538, 543 (1st Cir. 1999).

128. 29 C.F.R. § 825.214(b); DOL WH FMLA Advisory Opinion No. 47 (Oct. 17, 1994).

129. DOL WH FMLA Advisory Opinion No. 47 (Oct. 17, 1994).

130. 29 C.F.R. § 825.214(b); DOL WH FMLA Advisory Opinion No. 47 (Oct. 17, 1994).

131. 29 C.F.R. § 825.115; see also *St. Kilaire v. Minco Products, Inc.*, 288 F. Supp. 2d 999 1098 (D. Minn. 2003).

132. 29 C.F.R. § 825.115.

133. *Duty v. Norton-Alcoa Proppants*, 293 F.3d 481, 495 (8th Cir. 2002).

134. *Reynolds v. Phillips & Temro Industries, Inc.*, 195 F.3d 411, 414 (8th Cir. 1999); *Passauer v. Quest Diagnostics, Inc.*, No. CCB-03-159, 2004 U.S. Dist. LEXIS 6966 (D. Md. Apr. 22, 2004); *Strykowski v. Rush North Shore Medical Center*, No. 02 C 0778, 2003 U.S. Dist. LEXIS 13206 (N.D. Ill. July 30, 2003).

135. See *Tardie v. Rehabilitation Hospital of Rhode Island*, 168 F.3d 538, 543 (1st Cir. 1999) (inability to work overtime); *Voskuil v. Environmental Health Center-Dallas* No. 3:96-CV-0683-D, 1997 U.S. Dist. LEXIS 23565 (N.D. Tex. Aug. 19, 1997).

136. *Routes v. Henderson*, 58 F. Supp. 2d 959, 977 (S.D. Ind. 1999).

137. *Rinehimer v. Cemocolift, Inc.*, 292 F.3d 375, 384 (3d Cir. 2002).

138. See *Holmes v. E. Spire Communications, Inc.*, 135 F. Supp. 2d 657, 664 (D. Md. Mar.15, 2001).

139. 29 U.S.C. § 2614(a)(4); 29 C.F.R. § 825.310(a); DOL WH FMLA Advisory Opinion No. 113 (Sept. 11, 2000).

140. 29 U.S.C. § 2614(a)(4); 29 C.F.R. § 825.310(a); DOL WH FMLA Advisory Opinion No. 113 (Sept. 11, 2000).

141. 29 C.F.R. § 825.310(a); DOL WH FMLA Advisory Opinion No. 113 (Sept. 11, 2000).

142. See *Routes v. Henderson*, 58 F. Supp. 2d 959, 977 (S.D. Ind. 1999).

143. 29 C.F.R. § 825.310(f); DOL WH FMLA Advisory Opinion No. 113 (Sept. 11, 2000).

144. 29 C.F.R. § 825.311(c); see also *Burton v. Neumann*, No. 97-8061-CIV-HURLEY, 1999 U.S. Dist. LEXIS 16122 (S.D. Fla. Apr. 8, 1999).

145. 29 C.F.R. § 825.305(b).

146. 29 C.F.R. § 825.310(g).

147. 20 U.S.C. § 2614(a)(4); 29 C.F.R. 825.310(c); DOL WH FMLA Advisory Opinion No. 113 (Sept. 11, 2000); DOL WH FMLA Advisory Opinion No. 58 (Apr. 28, 1995).

148. See *Underhill v. Willamina Lumber Co.*, No. 98-630-AS, 1999 U.S. Dist. LEXIS 9722 (D. Or. June 17, 1999).

149. *Rogers v. New York University*, 250 F. Supp. 2d 310 (S.D.N.Y. 2002).

150. *Burton v. Neumann*, No. 97-8061-CIV-HURLEY, 1999 U.S. Dist. LEXIS 16122 (S.D. Fla. Apr. 8, 1999).

151. 29 U.S.C. § 2614(a)(4); 29 C.F.R. § 825.310(a).

152. 29 C.F.R. § 825.118. Who is a health care provider within the meaning of the FMLA is addressed more fully in Chapter 5, *Covered Conditions*.

153. *Albert v. Runyon*, 6 F. Supp. 2d 57 (D. Mass. 1998).

154. *Matthews v. Fairview Health Services*, No. 01-2151-ADM/AJB, 2003 U.S. Dist. LEXIS 5901 (D. Minn. Apr. 7, 2003).

155. 29 C.F.R. § 825.310(d).

156. *Id.*

157. 29 C.F.R. § 825.310(c); DOL WH FMLA Advisory Opinion No. 58 (Apr. 28, 1995).

158. 29 C.F.R. § 825.310(c); DOL WH FMLA Advisory Opinion No. 58 (Apr. 28, 1995).

159. 29 C.F.R. § 825.310(c); DOL WH FMLA Advisory Opinion No. 58 (Apr. 28, 1995).

160. 29 C.F.R. § 825.310(e).

161. DOL WH FMLA Advisory Opinion No. 113 (Sept. 11, 2000); DOL WH FMLA Advisory Opinion No. 58 (Apr. 28, 1995).

162. 29 U.S.C. § 2614(a)(4); 29 C.F.R. § 825.310(b); DOL WH FMLA Advisory Opinion No. 113 (Sept. 11, 2000); DOL WH FMLA Advisory Opinion No. 58 (Apr. 28, 1995).

163. DOL WH FMLA Advisory Opinion No. 113 (Sept. 11, 2000).

164. 29 C.F.R. § 825.310(b); DOL WH FMLA Advisory Opinion No. 113 (Sept. 11, 2000).

165. 29 C.F.R. § 825.310(b).

166. DOL WH FMLA Advisory Opinion No. 113 (Sept. 11, 2000).

167. *Albert v. Runyon*, 6 F. Supp. 2d 57 (D. Mass. 1998).

168. DOL WH FMLA Advisory Opinion No. 113 (Sept. 11, 2000).

169. DOL WH FMLA Advisory Opinion No. 27 (Jan. 31, 1994).

170. See *Harris v. Emergency Providers, Inc.*, No. 02-1056, 2002 U.S. App. LEXIS 17861 (8th Cir. Aug. 28, 2002).

171. See *Harrell v. U.S. Postal Service*, 415 F.3d 700 (7th Cir. 2005); *Routes v. Henderson*, 58 F. Supp. 2d 959, 994–95 (S.D. Ind. 1999).

172. 49 C.F.R. § 391.45.

173. No. 01-2151-ADM/AJB, 2003 U.S. Dist. LEXIS 5901 (D. Minn. Apr. 7, 2003).

174. 29 U.S.C. § 2651(a); 29 C.F.R. § 825.702(a); DOL WH FMLA Advisory Opinion No. 27 (Jan. 31, 1994).

175. DOL WH FMLA Advisory Opinion No. 27 (Jan. 31, 1994).

176. 42 U.S.C. § 12112(d)(4); 29 C.F.R. § 1630.14(c).

177. 42 U.S.C. § 12112(d)(4).

178. *EEOC Technical Assistance Manual on the Employment Provisions of the ADA* § 9.4 (1992), available at http://www.jan.wvu.edu/links/ADAtam1 .html.

179. 125 F.3d 243, 247 (4th Cir. 1997).

180. No. 98-630-AS, 1999 U.S. Dist. LEXIS 9722 (D. Or. June 17, 1999).

181. 6 F. Supp. 2d 57, 67–69 (D. Mass. 1998).

182. *Id.* at 67–68.

183. *Id.* at 69.

184. 29 C.F.R. § 825.310(e).

185. 29 C.F.R. §§ 825.310(e), 825.301(b)(1)(v).

186. *Conoshenti v. Public Service Electric & Gas Co.*, 364 F.3d 135 (3d Cir. 2004); *Reid-Falcone v. Luzerne County Community College*, 3:CV-02-1818, 2005 U.S. Dist. LEXIS 12713 (M.D. Pa. June 28, 2005).

187. 29 C.F.R. § 825.310(e).

188. 29 C.F.R. § 825.214(b).

189. 29 C.F.R. §§ 825.310(h), 825.213(a)(3).

190. 29 C.F.R. § 825.213(a)(3).

191. *Id.*

192. Comments on Regulations Implementing the Family and Medical Leave Act of 1993 (§ 825.310), 60 Fed. Reg. 2180, 2226 (Jan. 6, 1995); see also *Harrell v. U.S. Postal Service*, 415 F.3d 700 (7th Cir. 2005).

193. Comments on Regulations Implementing the Family and Medical Leave Act of 1993 (§ 825.310), 60 Fed. Reg. at 2226; see also *Harrell*, 415 F.3d 700.

194. See *Underhill v. Willamina Lumber Co.*, No. 98-630-AS, 1999 U.S. Dist. LEXIS 9722 (D. Or. June 17, 1999); *Routes v. Henderson*, 58 F. Supp. 2d

959, 995–96 (S.D. Ind. 1999); *Albert v. Runyon*, 6 F. Supp. 2d 57 (D. Mass. 1998).

195. *Taylor v. The Union Institute*, Nos. 99-4443, 00-4026, 2002 U.S. App. LEXIS 2787 (6th Cir. Feb. 19, 2002).

196. 29 U.S.C. § 2614(a)(3); 29 C.F.R. §§ 825.216(a), 825.312(d); see also *Hoge v. Honda of America Manufacturing, Inc.*, 384 F.3d 238 (6th Cir. 2004).

197. *Gerking v. Wabash Ford/Sterling Truck Sales, Inc.*, No. IP-IPOO-0495-C-B/K, 2002 U.S. Dist. LEXIS 17365, at *30 (S.D. Ind. Sept. 6, 2002).

198. 29 C.F.R. §§ 825.216(a), 825.312(d).

199. *Hoge*, 384 F.3d at 245; *Conoshenti v. Public Service Electric & Gas Co.*, 364 F.3d 135, 141 (3d Cir. 2004); *Spangler v. Federal Home Loan Bank of Des Moines*, 278 F.3d 847, 853 (8th Cir. 2002).

200. *Maldonado v. Frio County, Texas*, No. SA-02-CA-1046-XR, 2004 U.S. Dist. LEXIS 10723 (W.D. Tex. June 1, 2004).

201. *McBride v. Citgo Petroleum Corp.*, 281 F.3d 1099, 1108 (10th Cir. 2002).

202. *Renaud v. Wyoming Department of Family Services*, 203 F.3d 723, 732 (10th Cir. 2000).

203. *Kohls v. Beverly Enterprises Wisconsin, Inc.*, 259 F.3d 799, 806 (7th Cir. 2001).

204. *Smith v. Diffee Ford-Lincoln-Mercury, Inc.*, 298 F.3d 955, 961 (10th Cir. 2002); *Kohls*, 259 F.3d at 806.

205. *Conoshenti v. Public Service Electric & Gas Co.*, 364 F.3d 135, 141 (3d Cir. 2004).

206. 29 C.F.R. §§ 825.216(a)(1), 825.312(d).

207. 29 U.S.C. § 2652(a); 29 C.F.R. §§ 825.216(a)(1), 825.700(a)–(b).

208. 29 C.F.R. §§ 825.216(a)(1), 825.312(d).

209. *Skrjanc v. Great Lakes Power Service Co.*, 272 F.3d 309, 314 (6th Cir. 2001).

210. 29 C.F.R. § 825.312(d).

211. 29 C.F.R. § 825.214(a).

212. *Parker v. Hahnemann University Hospital*, 234 F. Supp. 2d 478 n.13 (D.N.J. 2002).

213. See *Parris v. The Miami Herald Publishing Co.*, 216 F.3d 1298, 1302–1303 (11th Cir. 2000).

214. *Dressler v. Community Service Communications, Inc.*, No. 03-2260, 2004 U.S. App. LEXIS 24190 (1st Cir. Nov. 19, 2004).

215. 29 C.F.R. § 825.216(a)(2).

216. *Id.*

217. 29 C.F.R. § 825.216(b).

218. *Id.*

219. 29 C.F.R. § 825.216(d).

220. *Id.*

221. *Robinson v. Overnite Transportation Co.*, No. 95-3067, 1997 U.S. App. LEXIS 6574 (4th Cir. Apr. 9, 1997).

222. *Ynoa v. New York-Presbyterian, the University Hospitals of Columbia and Cornell*, No. 03-Civ. 3721 (DC), 2005 U.S. Dist. LEXIS 14086 (S.D.N.Y. July 14, 2005).

223. 29 C.F.R. § 825.312(h).

224. *Gray v. U.S. Postal Service*, No. 05-3074, 2005 U.S. App. LEXIS 10961 (Fed. Cir. June 9, 2005); *Pharakhone v. Nissan North America, Inc.*, 324 F.3d 405 (6th Cir. 2003); *Geromanos v. Columbia University*, 322 F. Supp. 2d 420, 432–33 (S.D.N.Y. 2004) (sustaining termination of employee for working job during FMLA leave in violation of company policy).

225. 29 U.S.C. § 2614(a)(1); 29 C.F.R. § 825.312(g).

226. 29 C.F.R. § 825.312(g); *Kariotis v. Navistar International Transportation Corp.*, 131 F.3d 672, 681 (7th Cir. 1997); *Chalimoniuk v. Interstate Brands Corp.*, 172 F. Supp. 2d 1055, 1058 (S.D. Ind. 2001).

227. *Kariotis*, 131 F.3d at 681; *Crouch v. Whirlpool Corp.*, 3:04-cv-010RLY-WGH, 2005 U.S. Dist. LEXIS 12807 (S.D. Ind. June 20, 2005).

228. See *O'Reilly v. Consolidated Edison Co. of New York, Inc.*, 374 F. Supp. 2d 278 (E.D.N.Y. 2005).

229. DOL WH FMLA Advisory Opinion No. 95 (June 3, 1998).

230. *Id.* question 1.

231. 29 C.F.R. § 825.309(a); see also *Woods v. Daimler-Chrysler Corp.*, 409 F.3d 984, 991 (8th Cir. 2005).

232. 29 C.F.R. § 825.309(a).

233. Comments on Regulations Implementing the Family and Medical Leave Act of 1993 (§ 825.309), 60 Fed. Reg. 2180, 2225 (Jan. 6, 1995).

234. 29 C.F.R. § 825.301(a)(1).

235. 29 C.F.R. § 825.301(b)(2).

236. 29 C.F.R. § 825.309(c).

237. *Id.*

238. 29 C.F.R. § 825.309(b).

239. 29 U.S.C. § 2614(b); 29 C.F.R. § 825.216(c).

240. 29 U.S.C. § 2614(b)(2); 29 C.F.R. § 825.217(a).

241. 29 C.F.R. § 825.217(b) (defining "salaried employee" by cross-reference to 29 C.F.R. § 541.118, the DOL regulations defining employees who may qualify for exemption from the minimum wage and overtime requirements of the FLSA).

242. 29 U.S.C. § 2614(b)(2); 29 C.F.R. § 825.217(c).

243. 29 C.F.R. § 825.217(c).

244. 29 C.F.R. § 825.217(c)(1).

245. *Id.*

246. 29 U.S.C. § 2614(b)(1)(B); 29 C.F.R. § 825.217(c)(2).

247. 29 U.S.C. § 2614(b)(1)(A); 29 C.F.R. § 825.218(a).

248. 29 C.F.R. § 825.218(a); *Kephart v. Cherokee County, North Carolina*, No. 99-1789, 2000 U.S. App. LEXIS 18924 (4th Cir. Aug. 4, 2000); *Oby v. Baton Rouge Marriott*, 329 F. Supp. 2d 772 (M.D. La. 2004).

249. 29 C.F.R. § 825.219(a).

250. *Id.*

251. 29 C.F.R. § 825.219(d).

252. 29 C.F.R. § 825.218(c); see also Oby, 329 F. Supp. 2d 772.

253. 29 C.F.R. § 825.218(c); see also Oby, 329 F. Supp. 2d 772.

254. 29 C.F.R. § 825.218(c); see also Oby, 329 F. Supp. 2d 772.

255. 29 C.F.R. § 825.218(c); see also Oby, 329 F. Supp. 2d 772.

256. 29 C.F.R. § 825.218(b).

257. 29 C.F.R. §§ 825.219(a), 825.301(b)(1)(iv).

258. 29 C.F.R. § 825.219(a).

259. *Woodford v. Community Action of Greene County, Inc.*, 103 F. Supp. 2d 97, 100–01 (N.D.N.Y. 2000).

260. 29 C.F.R. §§ 825.219(a), 825.301(b)(1)(iv).

261. 29 C.F.R. § 825.219(a).

262. 29 C.F.R. § 825.219(b).

263. 29 C.F.R. § 825.219(a).

264. 535 U.S. 81 (2002).

265. The Supreme Court's decision in *Ragsdale* is discussed more fully in Chapter 6, *Notice Requirements*.

266. 29 C.F.R. § 825.219(b).

267. *Id.*

268. *Id.*

269. *Id.*

270. 29 C.F.R. § 825.219(a).

271. 29 C.F.R. § 825.219(c).

272. *Id.*

273. *Id.*

274. 29 C.F.R. § 825.219(d).

275. *Id.*

276. *Id.*

277. *Id.*

278. *Id.*

279. 29 C.F.R. § 825.220(b).

280. Ariz. Admin. Code § R2-5-411(6).

281. Ariz. Admin. Code § R2-5-412(A)(4), (B)(4).

282. Fla. Stat. § 110.221(3).

283. Vt. Stat. Ann. tit. 21, § 472(f).

284. *Id.*

285. Vt. Stat. Ann. tit. 21, § 472(f)(1)–(2).

286. Vt. Stat. Ann. tit. 21, § 472(e).

287. 29 C.F.R. § 825.701(a).

288. 29 U.S.C. § 2651(b); 29 C.F.R. § 825.701(a).

289. Comments on Regulations Implementing the Family and Medical Leave Act of 1993 (§ 825.701), 60 Fed. Reg. 2180, 2230 (Jan. 6, 1995).

290. *Id.* at 2231.

291. 29 C.F.R. § 825.701(a)(6).

292. Comments on Regulations Implementing the Family and Medical Leave Act of 1993 (§ 825.701), 60 Fed. Reg. at 2231.

293. *Id.* at 2230.

294. *Id.* at 2230–31.

CHAPTER 12

Record-Keeping Requirements

12.01 OVERVIEW

The FMLA requires covered employers to maintain certain FMLA-related records. The regulations identify which records must be maintained, describe how the records must be kept, and specify a time period for keeping such records. The regulations also address DOL access to FMLA-related records.

Section 12.02 of this chapter addresses the employment records that employers are required to keep pursuant to the Fair Labor Standards Act of 1938 (FLSA). Section 12.03 identifies the FMLA-related records that employers are required to maintain. Section 12.04 addresses the prescribed method of record retention. Section 12.05 discusses the disclosure of FMLA records. Section 12.06 examines the rules governing document destruction. Section 12.07 reviews record keeping under state family and medical leave laws. Section 12.08 addresses the interaction of federal and state family and medical leave record-keeping requirements.

12.02 REQUIRED RECORDS UNDER THE FLSA

To better understand the record-keeping requirements of the FMLA, it is important to understand the employment records that employers must maintain pursuant to the Fair Labor Standards Act (FLSA).[1] While a detailed analysis of the FLSA is beyond the scope of this work, the provisions of the FLSA set forth, among other things, the requirements for minimum wages, overtime pay, equal pay, and record keeping. As in the case of the FMLA, the Wage and Hour Division of the DOL is responsible for issuing rules and regulations, conducting investigations, and enforcing the FLSA.

As a practical matter, the FLSA applies to all private sector employers regardless of size. It also applies to most, although not all, public sector employers, including schools.[2] Elected public officials and their staff are excluded.[3] The FLSA record-keeping regulations require all covered employers to keep records for all employees, exempt and nonexempt, covered by the FLSA.

The records an FLSA-covered employer must keep depend on whether the employee is exempt from the FLSA's minimum wage and overtime provisions. It is well established that teachers are exempt from the FLSA's minimum wage and overtime requirements pursuant to the professional employee exemption. For employees exempt from the FLSA's overtime and minimum wage requirements, employers must maintain the following records:[4]

- Name in full, including, on the same record, any identifying symbol or number used for that employee on any time, work, or payroll records
- Home address, including zip code
- Date of birth, if the employee is under 19 years of age
- Sex
- Occupation in which the employee is employed
- The day of the week on which the employee's workweek begins
- Basic pay, plus fringe benefits
- Total pay per pay period, including the date each employee was paid, the pay period covered by the payment, and the total payment

For employees subject to the minimum wage or overtime requirements of the FLSA, covered employers must maintain the following information:[5]

- Name in full, including, on the same record, any identifying symbol or number used for the employee on any time, work, or payroll records

- Home address, including zip code
- Date of birth, if the employee is under 19 years of age
- Sex
- Occupation in which the employee is employed
- The time of day and day of the week on which the employee's workweek begins
- Total daily or weekly straight-time earnings or wages due for hours worked during the workday or workweek, exclusive of premium overtime compensation
- Total premium pay for overtime hours
- Total additions to or deductions from wages paid each pay period, including employee purchase orders or wage assignments, and in individual employee records, the dates, amounts, and nature of the items that make up the total additions and deductions
- Total wages paid each pay period
- The date of payment and the pay period covered by payment

The FLSA also requires covered employers to maintain the following records for 3 years:[6]

- Payroll records
- Collective bargaining agreements
- Plans, trusts, and employment contracts
- Individual contracts (if not written, must be reduced to a written memorandum summarizing the terms)
- Sales and purchase records providing the total dollar volume of sales or business and the total volume of goods received during such periods in such form as the employer maintains in the regular course of business

The FLSA requires employers to maintain the following records for 2 years:[7]

- Time sheets
- Documentation on start and end work time
- Documentation on hours worked

- Wage rate tables and like documents
- Documentation on additions or deductions from wages
- Order, shipping, and billing records
- All records used by the employer in determining the original cost, operating and maintenance costs, and depreciation and interest charges, if such costs and charges are involved in the additions to or deductions from wages paid

12.03 REQUIRED RECORDS UNDER THE FMLA

The FMLA requires covered employers to "make, keep, and preserve" records pertaining to compliance with the FMLA in accordance with § 11(c) of the Fair Labor Standards Act, 29 U.S.C. 211(c)."[8] Employers must "create, maintain, and preserve" two types of FMLA-related records: (1) nonmedical records and (2) medical records.

[1] Nonmedical FMLA Records

The type of nonmedical records that an employer is required to maintain depends on whether the employer has eligible employees.

(i) Employers without Eligible Employees

The FMLA record-keeping requirements apply to covered employers without any eligible employees. Covered employers who do not have any eligible employees must maintain basic payroll and identifying employee data, including

- name;
- address;
- occupation;
- rate of pay or basis of pay and terms of compensation;
- daily and weekly hours worked per pay period;
- additions to or deductions from wages; and
- total compensation paid.[9]

The DOL has opined that this information is required to enable a covered employer to determine employee eligibility.[10] The information listed above is some of the same information that the FLSA requires employers to keep.

(ii) Employers with Eligible Employees

Covered employers with eligible employees have added FMLA nonmedical record-keeping responsibilities. In addition to the basic payroll and identifying employee data discussed above, employers must also maintain the following information:[11]

- Dates FMLA leave is taken by FMLA-eligible employees (leave must be designated in records as FMLA leave; leave so designated may not include leave required under state law or an employer plan that is not also covered by the FMLA)
- The hours of FMLA leave, if leave is taken by eligible employees in increments of less than one full day
- Copies of employee notices of leave furnished to the employer under the FMLA, if in writing
- Copies of all general and specific notice given to employees as required under the FMLA and the regulations (copies may be maintained in employee personnel files)
- Any documents (including written and electronic documents) describing employee benefits or employer policies and practices regarding the taking of paid and unpaid leave
- Premium payments of employee benefits
- Records of any dispute between the employer and an eligible employee regarding the designation of leave as FMLA leave, including any written statement from the employer or employee of the reasons for the designation and for the disagreement

A covered employer that fails to keep these required records is in violation of the FMLA.[12] An employee challenging the accuracy of basic payroll records maintained by an employer pursuant to the FMLA (e.g., challenging the employer's determination that the employee did not meet the 1,250-hour eligibility requirement) must go beyond summary assertion that the records are inaccurate. To create a triable issue of fact, an employee must offer concrete evidence from which a reasonable juror could return a verdict in the employee's favor that the time records offered by the employer to establish that the employee did not meet the 1,250-hour eligibility requirement were, in fact, inaccurate.[13]

(iii) FLSA-Exempt-Employee Exception

Employers are not required to keep a record of actual hours worked for FMLA-eligible employees who are not subject to the FLSA's record-keeping regulations for purposes of minimum wages or overtime compliance (i.e., not covered by or excepted from the FLSA) *provided*

- eligibility for FMLA leave is presumed for any employee who has been employed for at least 12 months; and
- with respect to employees who take FMLA leave intermittently or on a reduced leave schedule, the employer and employee agree on the employee's normal schedule or average hours worked each week and reduce their agreement to a written record maintained in a personnel record in accordance with the DOL regulations.[14]

By implication, if written agreement is not reached on the employee's work schedule or average hours worked each week, covered employers are required to keep a record of the actual hours worked for FMLA-eligible FLSA-exempt employees! To avoid this record-keeping nightmare, covered school employers are strongly encouraged to secure written agreements with FLSA-exempt employees. It is unclear what happens if an employee unreasonably refuses to enter into such an agreement.

The presumption of FMLA eligibility of FLSA-exempt employees who have worked at least 12 months for a covered employer appears to be rebuttable. That is, a covered employer may still challenge the eligibility of an FLSA-exempt employee on the grounds that the employee did not work the requisite 1,250 hours.[15] The DOL regulations fail to explain why an employee's status as exempt under the FLSA presumes satisfaction of the 50/75 test (i.e., that there are 50 employees within 75 miles of the worksite). Presumably, a covered employer can challenge eligibility for failure to meet the 50/75 eligibility test, although that is less than clear in the DOL regulations. Since, however, the eligibility requirements are statutory, a very good argument could be made that the DOL regulations cannot do away with the 50/75 eligibility requirement simply because the employee is exempt under the FLSA and meets the 12-month requirement.

[2] Medical Records

The FMLA pays special attention to the maintenance of medical records. An employer must maintain—as confidential medical records—records and documents relating to medical certification, recertification, and medical histories of employees or employee family members created for purposes of the FMLA. FMLA medical records must be maintained separately from an employee's usual personnel records.[16]

Medical records created for purposes of the FMLA and the Americans with Disabilities Act (ADA) must be maintained in conformance with the ADA's confidentially requirements.[17] The ADA requires that medical records be kept confidential. To that end, like the FMLA, the ADA requires that employee medical records be kept separate from other personnel records.[18]

The FMLA incorporates exceptions permitting limited access to employee and employee family member medical records:[19]

- Supervisors and managers may be informed regarding necessary restrictions on the work or duties of an employee and necessary accommodations.
- First aid and safety personnel may be informed (when appropriate) if the employee's physical or medical condition might require emergency treatment.
- Government officials investigating compliance with the FMLA (or other pertinent law) must be provided relevant information on request.

These same limited exceptions are contained in the ADA.[20] A court held, pursuant to those exceptions, that an employer that allowed supervisors to review an employee's confidential FMLA medical file did not violate the FMLA where the supervisor needed the information to investigate the employee's refusal to work mandatory overtime.[21] Disclosure of confidential FMLA medical information for reasons other than legitimate business reasons may, however, violate the confidentiality provisions of the FMLA, the ADA, or other applicable confidentiality laws. For example, a supervisor who, after reviewing the employee's confidential FMLA medical records, broadcast throughout the workforce that an employee had been diagnosed with AIDS may have caused the employer to violate the FMLA, the ADA, and the Privacy Act of 1974.[22]

Note that the FMLA regulations governing the maintenance of medical records apply regardless of whether a covered employer has any employees who meet the FMLA eligibility requirements.

[3] Record-Keeping Obligations of Joint Employers

In a joint employment relationship the FMLA records that an employer must maintain depend on the primary or secondary status of the employee. Generally, a joint employment relationship is characterized by two employers who exercise some control over the work or working conditions of the same employee.[23] Joint employment is typically found to exist where a temporary-help or leasing agency supplies employees to a second employer.[24] The primary employer has the authority to hire and fire, assign and place the employee, maintain payroll, and provide employment benefits.[25] The secondary employer generally is the immediate employer of the joint employee. For employees of temporary-help or leasing agencies, the placement agency most commonly would be the primary employer, and the school would be the secondary employer.[26]

With respect to primary employees, employers in a joint employment relationship must maintain all of the same nonmedical records that employers with eligible employees must maintain (see above).[27] Taken literally, employers are required to maintain this information even where the primary employee is not eligible for FMLA leave. Regarding secondary employees, employers need only keep the same basic nonmedical payroll and identifying employee data that employees without eligible employees are required to maintain.[28] Presumably, because only the primary employer is responsible for providing FMLA leave, only the primary employer (e.g., the temporary-help or leasing agency) is responsible for maintaining medical records regarding joint employees.

12.04 FORM AND METHOD OF RETENTION

The federal FMLA generally does not prescribe the form of FMLA records.[29] Employers are permitted to keep FMLA records in electronic form provided that in the event of a DOL inspection

- adequate projection or viewing equipment is available;
- clear reproductions can be made and are identifiable by date or pay period; and
- extensions or transcriptions of the information required by the DOL regulations can be made available upon request.[30]

FMLA medical records must be maintained as confidential medical records separate from the employee's general personnel file.[31] The FMLA does not prescribe how nonmedical FMLA records must be kept. Many employers keep nonmedical FMLA records in the employee's general personnel file. Covered employers must keep and maintain all FMLA records for at least three years.[32]

12.05 DISCLOSURE OF FMLA RECORDS

The FMLA requires covered employers to make the required FMLA records available to representatives of the DOL, at their request, for inspection, copying, and transcription.[33] Absent such a request, employers are not required to submit any FMLA records to the DOL.[34] Generally, the DOL cannot require an employer to submit FMLA records more than once during any 12-month period.[35] If, however, the DOL has reasonable cause to believe a violation of the Act exists or the DOL is investigating a complaint, the DOL may require employers to submit FMLA records more than once during any 12-month period.[36]

12.06 DOCUMENT-DESTRUCTION POLICIES

The FMLA does not address the disposal of FMLA-related records after the requisite retention periods have passed. However, the disposal of FMLA records is affected by the Fair and Accurate Credit Transactions Act of 2003 (FACT Act). A detailed analysis of the FACT Act is beyond the scope of this work. What follows is an overview of the provisions that may apply to the disposal of FMLA-related employment information.

The FACT Act was signed into law on December 4, 2003.[37] It amends the Fair Credit Reporting Act (FCRA)[38] by requiring that any person who maintains or otherwise possesses or maintains, for business purposes, consumer information derived from consumer reports must properly dispose of such information. The Federal Trade Commission adopted regulations, effective June 1, 2005, implementing the record-disposal requirements of the FACT Act.[39]

The FACT Act disposal rules apply to any person that, for a business purpose, maintains, obtains, or otherwise possesses consumer information, or any compilation of consumer information, including employers and government agencies. "Consumer information" means any record about an individual, whether in electronic or other form, that is a consumer report or is derived from a consumer report.[40] In pertinent part, a "consumer report" means any written, oral, or other communication of any information by a consumer reporting agency bearing on a consumer's character, general reputation, or personal characteristics that is used or collected in whole or in part for purposes of establishing a consumer's eligibility for employment.[41] An employee's exercise of FMLA rights may be reflected in such consumer reports, and therefore, FMLA-related records will very likely be subject to the FACT Act.

The FACT Act regulates the disposal of consumer information. "Disposal" means the discarding or abandoning of consumer information or the sale, donation, or transfer of any medium, including equipment, upon which consumer information is stored.[42] That includes computer tapes, computer disks, CDs, and other electronic means of storing consumer information, including the hard drives of computers. Under the FACT Act, persons who maintain or otherwise possess consumer information for business purposes must properly dispose of such information by reasonable measures to protect against unauthorized access to or use of the information in connection with its disposal.[43] The regulations give the following as examples of reasonable measures to protect against unauthorized access of consumer information in connection with its disposal:[44]

- Implementing and monitoring compliance with policies and procedures that require the burning, pulverizing, or shredding of papers containing consumer information so that the information cannot practically be read or reconstructed
- Implementing and monitoring compliance with policies and procedures that require the destruction or erasure of electronic media containing consumer information so that the information cannot practically be read or reconstructed
- After due diligence, entering into and monitoring compliance with a contract with another party engaged in the business of record destruction to dispose of material, specifically identified as consumer information, in a manner consistent with this rule

Schools would be well advised to consult with counsel regarding the disposal of FMLA-related employment records in compliance with the FACT Act and any other applicable state or local laws.

12.07 RECORD KEEPING UNDER STATE FAMILY AND MEDICAL LEAVE LAWS

State family and medical leave laws generally do not include record-keeping requirements. A few do, but the vast majority of the laws do not—at least not in the body of the law itself. In some cases, family and medical leave records may be governed by other state laws requiring employers to retain employment records. For example, Alaska's family and health leave law requires each department, office, institution, and agency of the state government to keep for its files a complete leave record, covering each of its officers and employees, on forms prepared and supplied by the Department of Administration. The records are subject to annual audit and approval by the director of personnel of the

Department of Administration.[45] The California Family Rights Act does not include record-keeping requirements. Generally, California law makes it an unlawful practice for covered employers, labor organizations, and employment agencies to fail to maintain and preserve any and all employment applications and personnel, membership, or employment-referral records and files for a minimum period of 2 years after the records and files are initially created or received, or for employers to fail to retain personnel files of applicants or terminated employees for a minimum period of 2 years after the date of the employment action taken.

Connecticut's private sector Family and Medical Leave Act provides that records and documents relating to medical certifications, recertifications, or medical histories of employees or employees' family members must be maintained as medical records pursuant to Connecticut's personnel file law, except that (1) supervisors and managers may be informed regarding necessary restrictions on the work or duties of an employee and necessary accommodations; (2) first aid and safety personnel may be informed, when appropriate, if the employee's physical or medical condition might require emergency treatment; and (3) government officials investigating compliance with Connecticut's Family and Medical Leave Act must be provided with relevant information upon request.[46]

12.08 INTERACTION OF THE FEDERAL FMLA WITH STATE FAMILY AND MEDICAL LEAVE LAWS: RECORD-KEEPING REQUIREMENTS

The federal FMLA does not supersede any provision of any state or local law that provides greater family or medical rights than the rights under the FMLA.[47] An employer covered by one law and not the other has to comply only with the law under which it is covered.[48] Where, however, a school employer is covered by both the federal FMLA and a state family and medical leave law and the laws contain differing provisions, school employers must apply the standard providing the greater right or more generous benefit to the employee.[49] According to the DOL, both procedural and substantive provisions of the federal FMLA are subject to the provision-by-provision analysis to determine which law, the federal FMLA or applicable state law, provides greater rights or benefits.[50]

Assuming that the federal FMLA's record-keeping requirements for employers constitute a benefit to employees, to be safe school employers should retain all records required under both the federal FMLA and any applicable state family and medical leave laws. Unless advised by counsel to do otherwise, school employers should not attempt to pick and choose which record-keeping provisions, the federal FMLA or state law, provide the greater benefit to employees.

NOTES

1. 29 U.S.C. §§ 201–19.
2. 29 U.S.C. § 203(d), (x); 29 C.F.R. § 553.3
3. 29 U.S.C. § 203(e)(2)(C).
4. 29 C.F.R. § 516.3.
5. 29 C.F.R. § 516.2.
6. 29 C.F.R. § 516.5.
7. 29 C.F.R. § 516.6.
8. 29 U.S.C. § 2616(b); 29 C.F.R. § 825.500(a).
9. 29 C.F.R. § 825.500(c)(1), (d).
10. Comments on Regulations Implementing the Family and Medical Leave Act of 1993 (§ 825.500), 60 Fed. Reg. 2180, 2228–29 (Jan. 6, 1995).
11. 29 C.F.R. § 825.500(c).
12. *Slaughter v. American Building Maintenance Co. of New York*, 64 F. Supp. 2d 319, 330 n.9 (S.D.N.Y. 1999).
13. *Kosakow v. New Rochelle Radiology Associates, P.C.*, 88 F. Supp. 2d 199, 207 (S.D.N.Y. 2000), *vacated and remanded on other grounds*, 274 F.3d 706 (2d Cir. 2001).
14. 29 C.F.R. § 825.500(f).
15. See 29 C.F.R. § 825.110(c).
16. 29 C.F.R. § 825.500(g).
17. *Id.*
18. 29 C.F.R. § 1630.14(c)(1), (d)(1).
19. 29 C.F.R. § 825.500(g).
20. 29 C.F.R. § 1630.14(c)(1), (d)(1).
21. *Dodge v. Trustees of the National Gallery of Art*, 326 F. Supp. 2d 1, 17 (D.D.C. 2004).

22. Privacy Act of 1974, as amended, 5 U.S.C. § 552a; see *Doe v. U.S. Postal Service*, 317 F.3d 339, 342 (D.C. Cir. 2003).

23. 29 C.F.R. § 825.106(a).

24. 29 C.F.R. § 825.106(b).

25. 29 C.F.R. § 825.106(c).

26. *Id.*

27. 29 C.F.R. § 825.500(e).

28. *Id.*

29. 29 C.F.R. § 825.500(b).

30. 29 C.F.R. § 825.500(e).

31. 29 C.F.R. § 825.500(g).

32. 29 C.F.R. § 825.500(b).

33. 29 U.S.C. § 2616(c); 29 C.F.R. § 825.500(b).

34. 29 C.F.R. § 825.500(a).

35. 29 U.S.C. § 2616(c); 29 C.F.R. § 825.500(a).

36. 29 U.S.C. § 2616(c); 29 C.F.R. § 825.500(a).

37. Fair and Accurate Credit Transactions Act of 2003, Pub. L. No. 108-159, 117 Stat. 1952 (2003).

38. 15 US.C. §§ 1681–1681t.

39. 16 C.F.R. pt. 682.

40. 16 C.F.R. § 682.1(b).

41. 15 U.S.C. § 1681a(d).

42. 16 C.F.R. § 682.1(c).

43. 16 C.F.R. § 682.3(a).

44. 16 C.F.R. § 682.3(b)(1)–(3).

45. Alaska Stat. § 39.20.330.

46. Conn. Gen. Stat. § 31-51oo; Conn. Agencies Regs. § 31-51qq-38.

47. 29 U.S.C. § 2651(b); 29 C.F.R. § 825.701(a).

48. 29 C.F.R. § 825.701(a).

49. Comments on Regulations Implementing the Family and Medical Leave Act of 1993 (§ 825.701), 60 Fed. Reg. 2180, 2230 (Jan. 6, 1995).

50. *Id.* at 2231.

CHAPTER 13

Coordination of the FMLA with Other Employee Rights and Benefits

13.01 OVERVIEW

FMLA rights and benefits do not exist, and therefore should not be considered, in a vacuum. The FMLA sets the minimum standard of family and medical leave that covered school employers must provide eligible employees. School employers may, however, be required to observe more generous family and medical leave benefits required by other federal, state, or local laws or by the terms of a collective bargaining agreement or school policy. The FMLA also does not modify or affect an employer's obligation to abide by federal or state antidiscrimination laws. While the requirements of the FMLA are separate and distinct from the requirements of other federal, state, and local laws, this is not to say that the FMLA does not interact with those laws. FMLA rights and benefits frequently affect or are affected by employee rights and benefits under other laws. This chapter addresses the coordination of FMLA rights with other employee rights and benefits.

Section 13.02 addresses the interaction of the FMLA with other federal laws, including the Americans with Disabilities Act of 1990, Title VII of the Civil Rights Act of 1964, and the Pregnancy Discrimination Act of 1978. Section 13.03 addresses the coordination of the FMLA with state and local laws, including workers' compensation laws. Section 13.04 discusses the integration of the FMLA with collective bargaining agreements. Section 13.05 addresses the effects of more generous employer leave benefits on the FMLA. Section 13.06 reviews state family and medical leave laws regarding their interaction with other laws, collective bargaining agreements, and employer practices.

13.02 INTERACTION OF THE FMLA WITH OTHER FEDERAL LAWS

[1] General Rule

Employers may be required by other federal laws to provide leave to employees in the same circumstances as required by the FMLA. To avoid violating either the FMLA or other federal laws, school employers must know how the FMLA interacts with these other federal laws. Generally, the FMLA does not modify or affect other federal laws prohibiting discrimination on the basis of race, religion, color, national origin, sex, age, or disability.[1] The FMLA's legislative history makes it clear that the FMLA was not intended to affect or amend Title VII of the Civil Rights Act of 1964, as amended, the Pregnancy Discrimination Act of 1978 (PDA), or the Americans with Disabilities Act of 1990 (ADA).[2] The "purpose of the FMLA is to make leave available to eligible employees and employers within its coverage and not to limit already existing rights and protections."[3]

In light of that legislative history, the DOL has interpreted the FMLA as requiring covered employers to "provide leave under whichever statutory provision provides the greater benefits to employees."[4] The DOL explained its adoption of the "greater benefits" requirement as follows:

> Comments from U.S. Senators Dodd and Kerry (sponsors of both FMLA and ADA), in a letter to the EEOC dated November 22, 1993, make clear that congressional intent was for both Acts to be applied with whichever statutory provision provides the greater rights to employees. In keeping with the statutory intent, FMLA § 401 should not be interpreted in any way as limiting or forcing an election of rights under FMLA or ADA. Similarly, comments from U.S. Representatives Williams and Ford (Committee on Education and Labor), in a letter to the EEOC dated November 19, 1993, explained that congressional intent, in the case of an employee with a serious health condition under FMLA who is also a qualified individual with a disability under ADA, was for the FMLA and ADA to be applied in a manner that assured the most generous provisions of both would apply. The statutes provide simultaneous protection and at all times an employer is required to comply with both laws. The Department concurs with this interpretation of

> the FMLA as it relates to the ADA and other discrimination laws. In summary, providing the "more beneficial" rights or protections does not undermine an employer's obligation to observe the requirements of both statutes. Satisfying any or all FMLA requirements, including granting an employee 12 weeks of leave and restoring the employee to the same job, does not absolve an employer of any potential ADA responsibilities to that employee (and vice versa).[5]

The "greater benefits" mandate of the federal FMLA requires school employers to carefully consider all federal employment rights that may apply to a given leave situation. School employers do not have to make an election between the FMLA and other federal leave rights. Rather, the leave rights of the FMLA must be considered separately from leave rights provided under, for example, the ADA or the PDA. Compliance with the requirements of the ADA or the PDA will not guarantee compliance with the FMLA, and vice versa.

An added incentive for school employers to exercise great care where FMLA rights are entangled with rights under antidiscrimination laws is legal liability. If an employer violates both the FMLA and an antidiscrimination law, the aggrieved employee may be able to recover under either or both of the statutes.[6] While double recovery for the same loss is not permitted, an aggrieved employee is allowed to elect the avenue of relief.[7]

[2] Americans with Disabilities Act of 1990

The FMLA interacts with the ADA in two ways. First, the FMLA incorporates by reference some of the requirements of the ADA. For example, the definition of an FMLA-covered son or daughter over the age of 18 requires that the individual have a "physical or mental disability" within the meaning of the ADA regulations.[8] The FMLA similarly incorporates the ADA definition of "essential functions of the employee's position" to determine whether the employee has an FMLA-covered serious health condition.[9] FMLA medical records, which are confidential, must be kept separate from the employee's personnel records and if the ADA also applies, must also be kept in conformance with ADA confidentiality requirements.[10] The ADA requirements that a medical examination must be job related and consistent with business necessity apply to FMLA return-to-work medical certifications.[11]

The second way that the FMLA interacts with the ADA is where a covered "serious health condition" also constitutes a physical or mental disability within the meaning of the ADA. Of course, it will not always be the case that an FMLA "serious health condition" will qualify as an ADA disability. The reverse is also true: not all ADA-covered disabilities will meet the definition of an FMLA-covered serious health condition. Generally, employers must separately comply with the requirements of the ADA and the FMLA. Compliance with the requirements of the ADA will not ensure compliance with the FMLA, and vice versa.

What follows is a brief overview of pertinent provisions of the ADA, followed by a review of how the ADA requirements commonly interact with the FMLA in terms of leave.

(i) ADA Basics

The ADA applies to private sector employers with 15 or more employees, including state and local government employers.[12] The ADA generally prohibits discrimination against qualified individuals with disabilities regarding job application procedures; the hiring, advancement, or discharge of employees; employee compensation; job training; and other terms, conditions, and privileges of employment.[13] A qualified individual with a disability is an individual who meets the prerequisites for the job and can perform the essential functions of the position with or without reasonable accommodation.[14] The ADA defines an individual with a disability as one who (1) has a physical or mental impairment that substantially limits one or more of the individual's major life activities, (2) has a record of such impairment, or (3) is regarded as having such an impairment.[15] "Major life activities" are functions such as caring for oneself, performing manual tasks, walking, seeing, hearing, speaking, breathing, learning, and working.[16]

The ADA requires employers to make reasonable accommodation to the known physical or mental limitations of an otherwise qualified employee with a disability unless the employer can show that the accommodation would impose an undue hardship on the operation of its business.[17] Reasonable accommodation may include job restructuring, part-time employment, or modified work schedules.[18] Allowing an employee to use accrued paid leave and providing additional unpaid leave are also acceptable forms of reasonable accommodation, at least where there is no accommodation that would allow the employee to do the job currently.[19] The amount of leave that an employer may be required to provide an employee as a reasonable accommodation technically is not capped.

While leave is a permissible form of reasonable accommodation, it is not a favored one. As indicated above, the EEOC regulations require that an employer first attempt to accommodate the employee in his or her current position before considering leave as a reasonable accommodation. Leave as a reasonable accommodation has met with a less than enthusiastic reception by the courts. Many courts have found that leave is not a reasonable accommodation because regular and predictable attendance is an essential function of most jobs and, therefore, is not required to be accommodated.[20] Notwithstanding this presumption, a number of courts have found that the ADA required an employer to provide temporary leave as a reasonable accommodation.[21] However, the ADA does not require employers to provide employees with indefinite leave as a reasonable accommodation.[22] One court has suggested that leave of up to a year pursuant to the employer's short-term disability policy could be an ADA-required reasonable accommodation.[23]

(ii) ADA and FMLA Interactions

There are many similarities and differences between the ADA and the FMLA. For example, there are significant differences in the scope of coverage between the FMLA and the ADA. The FMLA applies to all public and private sector school employers with 50 employees during 20 or more calendar weeks in the current or preceding calendar year.[24] The ADA, in contrast, applies to employers (including public sector employers) with 15 or more employees.[25] The ADA applies to all disabled employees of a covered employer. The FMLA, on the other hand, applies only to eligible employees of a covered employer.

The FMLA requires employers to grant leave to an eligible employee to care for a covered family member with a serious health condition. The ADA, by comparison, does not require an employer to provide job-protected leave to an employee to care for a covered family member with a disability. The ADA does, however, protect employees who have a relationship with an individual with a known disability. Such protection would ensure that an employee would be entitled to leave to address the need of an individual with a disability to the same extent that others were entitled to take leave to care for other persons.

The FMLA requires employers to maintain an employee's group health plan coverage during FMLA leave on the same conditions as coverage would have been provided if the employee had been continuously employed during the leave period. The ADA, in contrast, does not require maintenance of health benefits unless other employees receive health benefits during leave under the same circumstances.[26]

The ADA's "disability" and the FMLA's "serious health condition" are different concepts and must be analyzed separately. Not all FMLA "serious health conditions" will rise to the level of an ADA "disability." Conversely, not all ADA "disabilities" will be "serious health conditions" within the meaning of the FMLA (although it is more likely than the reverse). For example, the ADA defines "disability" to include having a record of a disability and being regarded as disabled (even if the employee is, in fact, not disabled). A "serious health condition" within the meaning of the FMLA requires actual incapacity. It does not recognize being regarded as having or having a record of a serious health condition as a legitimate serious health condition. Conversely, the FMLA recognizes pregnancy as a serious health condition. Absent unusual complications, because it is transitory, pregnancy is usually not considered to be an ADA disability.[27]

The ADA relieves employers of the obligation to reasonably accommodate an employee's disability where accommodation would cause undue hardship to the employer. The FMLA, in contrast, does not excuse an employer's obligation to grant an employee leave because it would cause the employer "undue hardship." Under the FMLA, if an employee is eligible and otherwise entitled to leave, the employer has to provide it, notwithstanding the hardship that granting the employee leave will cause. The FMLA attempts to mitigate the hardships imposed on employers by requiring the employee to provide advance notice of the need for leave, where possible, and to schedule planned medical appointments to minimize disruptions.

The FMLA permits an employer to temporarily transfer an employee who is taking leave intermittently or on a reduced leave schedule basis to an alternative position that better accommodates the employee's leave. The ADA, in contrast, allows an accommodation of reassignment to an equivalent vacant position only if the employee cannot perform the essential functions of the employee's present position and an accommodation is not possible in the employee's present position without undue hardship.

If an employee is a qualified individual with a disability within the meaning of the ADA, the employer must make reasonable accommodations, barring undue hardships, in accordance with the ADA. At the same time, if the employee also has a "serious health condition" within the meaning of the FMLA, the employer must afford an employee the FMLA right to take up to 12 workweeks of job-protected leave each leave year. The leave provisions of the FMLA are wholly distinct from the reasonable accommodation obligations of employers covered under the ADA.[28] An employer must provide leave under whichever statutory provision (the ADA or FMLA) provides the greater rights to employees.[29]

> The leave provisions of the FMLA are wholly distinct from the reasonable accommodation obligations of employers covered under the ADA. An employer must provide leave under whichever statutory provision (the ADA or FMLA) provides the greater rights to employees.

The DOL illustrates the rules summarized above with several examples worth repeating:

> A qualified individual with a disability who is also an "eligible employee" entitled to FMLA leave requests 10 weeks of medical leave as a reasonable accommodation, which the employer grants because it is not an undue hardship. The employer advises the employee that the 10 weeks of leave is also being designated as FMLA leave and will count toward the employee's FMLA leave entitlement. This designation does not prevent the parties from also treating the leave as a reasonable accommodation and reinstating the employee into the same job, as required by the ADA, rather than an equivalent position under the FMLA, if that

is the greater right available to the employee. At the same time the employee would be entitled under FMLA to have the employer maintain group health plan coverage during the leave, as that requirement provides the greater right to the employee.[30]

If the same employee needed to work part-time (a reduced leave schedule) after returning to his or her same job, the employee would still be entitled under FMLA to have group health plan coverage maintained for the remainder of the two-week equivalent of FMLA leave entitlement, notwithstanding an employer policy that part-time employees do not receive health insurance. This employee would be entitled under the ADA to reasonable accommodations to enable the employee to perform the essential functions of the part-time position. In addition, because the employee is working a part-time schedule as a reasonable accommodation, the employee would be shielded from FMLA's provision for temporary assignment to a different alternative position. Once the employee has exhausted his or her remaining FMLA leave entitlement while working the reduced (part-time) schedule, if the employee is a qualified individual with a disability, and if the employee is unable to return to the same full-time position at that time, the employee might continue to work part-time as a reasonable accommodation, barring undue hardship; the employee would then be entitled to only those employment benefits ordinarily provided by the employer to part-time employees.[31]

School employers must also be aware of differences between the FMLA and the ADA regarding reinstatement of an employee from leave. Again, we will assume that the employee is eligible and has an FMLA-covered serious health condition that is also an ADA-covered disability. We will also assume that the employee is a full-time employee. At the end of the FMLA leave, an employer is required under the FMLA to restore the employee to the same or an equivalent full-time position. The employer's FMLA obligations would be satisfied if the employer offered the employee an equivalent full-time position. Under the ADA, employers are generally required to return the employee to the same position the employee held before ADA reasonable accommodation leave began, unless the employee is no longer qualified for the position or the employee is unable to perform the essential functions of the position with a reasonable accommodation or the accommodation would cause undue hardship.

Similarly, the FMLA does not obligate an employer to reinstate from FMLA leave a disabled employee who cannot perform the essential functions of the preleave position. The employer's FMLA obligations would cease at that point. However, the ADA may require the employer to make a reasonable accommodation at that time by allowing the employee to work part-time or by reassigning the employee to a vacant position, barring undue hardship.[32] Here, the employer would have to provide the employee with the greater return-to-work benefits provided by the ADA.

If an employee is entitled to FMLA leave, an employer may not, in lieu of granting FMLA leave, *require* the employee to take a job with a reasonable accommodation. However, the ADA may require that an employer *offer* an employee the opportunity to take such a position as a reasonable accommodation. An employer may not change the essential functions of a job in order to deny FMLA leave.[33]

The complexities resulting from the similarities and differences between the ADA and the FMLA make compliance with both statutes very complex. School employers would be well advised to consult with counsel when addressing situations that are within the scope of both the ADA and the FMLA.

[3] Pregnancy Discrimination Act of 1978

The PDA interacts with the FMLA where the need for leave involves childbirth, pregnancy, or pregnancy-related conditions. The FMLA requires covered employers to provide eligible employees with up to 12 workweeks of job-protected leave each leave year for, among other conditions, childbirth, pregnancy, and prenatal care. Moreover, pregnancy-related ailments may also satisfy the definition of an FMLA serious health condition. The PDA, in contrast, does not require employers to grant employees leave for childbirth, pregnancy, or pregnancy-related illnesses. Rather, the PDA merely requires that employers treat employees who are pregnant or have pregnancy-related impairments no differently from other similarly situated employees who are not pregnant in terms of leave and other employment benefits.

The PDA amended Title VII of the Civil Rights Act of 1964 to include discrimination based on childbirth, pregnancy, or related health conditions within the meaning of prohibited sex discrimination.[34] The

PDA requires that women affected by pregnancy and related conditions must be treated in the same manner for all employment-related purposes as other similarly situated persons who are not pregnant or suffering from pregnancy-related health conditions.[35] The PDA does not, however, require an employer to grant leave to an employee due to pregnancy, childbirth, or related conditions.[36] Rather, the PDA requires employers to treat pregnancy and pregnancy-related conditions the same as non-pregnancy-related conditions under employer policies and practices.[37] As one court put it, "the PDA does not require employers to make accommodations for its pregnant employees; employers can treat pregnant women as badly as they treat similarly affected but nonpregnant employees."[38]

Remember, the FMLA does not modify or affect the leave requirements imposed on employers by Title VII of the Civil Rights Act of 1964, as amended by the PDA.[39] An employer must provide leave under whichever statutory provision provides the greater rights to employees.[40] Given the limited mandate of the PDA, the interaction of the PDA with the FMLA frequently boils down to whether the employer has leave policies more generous than those provided by the FMLA. If not, the FMLA policies prevail. If so, the more generous leave policies regarding pregnancy, childbirth, and pregnancy-related conditions would prevail.

[4] Title VII of the Civil Rights Act of 1964

The FMLA does not modify or affect federal or state laws prohibiting discrimination on the basis of race, religion, color, national origin, sex, or age (e.g., Title VII of the Civil Rights Act of 1964, as amended, and the Age Discrimination in Employment Act of 1973 (ADEA), as amended).[41] Neither Title VII, the ADEA, nor its state law equivalents affirmatively grant an employee a right to job-protected leave. Rather, these antidiscrimination laws generally prohibit employers from discriminating against employees regarding terms and conditions of employment, including leave, on the basis of race, religion, color, national origin, sex, or age. The EEOC explained these protections as follows:

> 22. Q: Does Title VII require covered employers to give employees leave to care for an ill child or family member?

A: Title VII in itself does not require employers to give employees leave to care for an ill child or family member. However, Title VII prohibits covered employers from discriminating on the basis of race, color, religion, sex, or national origin when they administer family leave.

For example, if an employer allowed a woman but not a man to take 12 weeks of leave to care for a newly adopted or placed child, the man would have a Title VII cause of action because the employer administered family leave in a discriminatory way based on gender.

As another example, if an employer allowed a woman to take 3 weeks of childcare leave in addition to leave necessary to recuperate from childbirth but declined to permit a man to take 3 weeks of childcare leave, the man would have a Title VII cause of action because the employer administered family leave in a discriminatory way based on gender.[42]

Note that the FMLA provides that the right to take leave under the FMLA applies equally to male and female employees.[43]

[5] Uniformed Services Employment and Reemployment Rights Act of 1994

The Uniformed Services Employment and Reemployment Rights Act of 1994 (USERRA) is a federal law that prohibits discrimination against veterans and members of the National Guard and Reserve following qualifying military service with respect to hiring, retention, promotion, or reemployment.[44] The USERRA applies to all employers in the United States, public or private and regardless of size.[45]

The USERRA interacts with FMLA eligibility. The DOL has interpreted the USERRA's entitlement to "all benefits of employment" upon return from military service to include the accrual of time toward the 12-month and 1,250-hours-worked FMLA eligibility requirements. The DOL addressed this issue in a memorandum providing questions and answers regarding the interaction of the USERRA and the FMLA, a copy of which is included in Appendix B. In pertinent part, the memorandum provides:

5. How should the 12-month FMLA requirement be calculated for returning service members?

USERRA requires that a person reemployed under its provisions be given credit for any months he or she would have been employed *but for* the military service in determining eligibility for FMLA leave. A person reemployed following military service should be given credit for the period of military service toward the months-of-employment eligibility requirement. Each month served performing military service counts as a month actively employed by the employer. For example, someone who has been employed by an employer for 9 months is ordered to active military service for 9 months after which he or she is reemployed. Upon reemployment, the person must be considered to have been employed by the employer for more than the required 12 months (9 months actually employed plus 9 months while serving in the military service) for purposes of FMLA eligibility. It should be noted that the 12 months of employment do not have to be consecutive to meet this FMLA requirement.

6. How should the 1,250 hours-of-service requirement be calculated for returning service members?

An employee returning after military service should be credited with the hours-of-service that would have been performed *but for* the period of military service in determining FMLA eligibility. Accordingly, a person reemployed following military service has the hours that would have been worked for the employer added to any hours actually worked during the previous 12-month period to meet the 1,250-hour requirement. In order to determine the hours that would have been worked during the period of military service, the employee's preservice work schedule can generally be used for calculations. For example, an employee who works 40 hours per week for the employer returns to employment following 20 weeks of military service and requests leave under the FMLA. To determine the person's eligibility, the hours he or she would have worked during the period of military service ($20 \times 40 = 800$ hours) must be added to the hours actually worked during the 12-month period prior to the start of the leave to determine if the 1,250-hour requirement is met.[46]

13.03 COORDINATION OF THE FEDERAL FMLA WITH STATE AND LOCAL LAWS

[1] General Rule

As with the interaction of the FMLA and other federal laws, nothing in the FMLA "shall be construed to modify or affect any . . . State law prohibiting discrimination on the basis of race, religion, color, national origin, sex, age, or disability."[47] The reader is referred to section 13.02

above for the rules governing the interaction of the FMLA with federal antidiscrimination laws.

As discussed throughout this book, the FMLA also provides that nothing in the Act shall be construed to supersede any provision of any state or local law that provides greater family or medical leave rights than the rights established by the FMLA.[48] The DOL explained: "The determination of which law provides the greater benefits, State or Federal, is determined on a provision-by-provision basis."[49] The DOL continued:

> Where the requisite coverage or applicability standards of both laws are met and the laws contain differing provisions, an analysis must be made of both laws, provision-by-provision, to determine which standards from each law will apply to the particular situation. The more generous benefit to the employee from each law (provision-by-provision) will apply.[50]

The "greater benefits" requirement does not lower the bar for employer coverage under the FMLA or any state or local family and medical leave laws. An employer covered by one law and not the other has to comply only with the law under which it is covered.[51] An employee eligible under one law must receive benefits in accordance with that law, but only if the employer is covered by that law.[52] For example, if a state family and medical leave law applies to private sector employers with 10 or more employees and the school has 15 employees, only the state family and medical leave law applies to the school because the FLMA applies to private sector employees with at least 50 employees. A provision-by-provision comparison with the federal FMLA is unnecessary because the federal FMLA does not apply to this employer.

Employers are also not required to determine which law, federal or state or local, provides the greater benefit where the reason for leave is not covered by both family and medical leave laws. If an employee takes leave for a purpose that is recognized under only one of the laws, rights and obligations are governed by that law alone, and the amount of leave taken cannot be charged against the amount of leave that may be allowed under the other law.[53] For example, if a state family and medical leave law allows an employee to take job-protected leave to care for an in-law, only that state law would apply. The federal FMLA does not provide for leave to care for an in-law. The "greater benefits" theory would not apply because the reason for the leave is not covered by both the federal and state family and medical leave laws.

Where, however, an employee of a covered employer under both federal and state family and medical leave laws takes leave for a purpose that is recognized under both the federal FMLA and state law, the employee is entitled to the benefits of whichever law is the most favorable to the employee, and the amount of leave taken is charged against the amount that is allowed under each law.[54] The DOL provides the following examples to illustrate the interaction of the federal FMLA and state family and medical leave laws:

> (1) If State law provides 16 weeks of leave entitlement over two years, an employee would be entitled to take 16 weeks one year under State law and 12 weeks the next year under FMLA. Health benefits maintenance under FMLA would be applicable only to the first 12 weeks of leave entitlement each year. If the employee took 12 weeks the first year, the employee would be entitled to a maximum of 12 weeks the second year under FMLA (not 16 weeks). An employee would not be entitled to 28 weeks in one year.
> (2) If State law provides half-pay for employees temporarily disabled because of pregnancy for six weeks, the employee would be entitled to an additional six weeks of unpaid FMLA leave (or accrued paid leave).
> (3) A shorter notice period under State law must be allowed by the employer unless an employer has already provided, or the employee is requesting, more leave than required under State law.
> (4) If State law provides for only one medical certification, no additional certifications may be required by the employer unless the employer has already provided, or the employee is requesting, more leave than required under State law.
> (5) If State law provides six weeks of leave, which may include leave to care for a seriously-ill grandparent or a "spouse equivalent," and leave was used for that purpose, the employee is still entitled to 12 weeks of FMLA leave as the leave used was provided for a purpose not covered by the FMLA. If FMLA leave is used first for a purpose also provided under State law, and State leave has thereby been exhausted, the employer would not be required to provide additional leave to care for the grandparent or "spouse equivalent."

(6) If State law prohibits mandatory leave beyond the actual period of pregnancy disability, an instructional employee of an educational agency subject to the special FMLA rules may not be required to remain on leave until the end of the academic term, as permitted by FMLA under certain circumstances.[55]

The DOL will not enforce state family or medical leave laws, and states may not enforce the federal FMLA.[56] Employees are not required to designate whether the leave they are taking is FMLA leave or leave under state law, and an employer must comply with the appropriate (applicable) provisions of both.[57]

[2] Workers' Compensation

An FMLA-covered "serious health condition" may result from injury to the employee "on or off" the job.[58] Where a "serious health condition" within the meaning of the FMLA results from an on-the-job injury, an eligible employee's FMLA leave entitlement may run concurrently with a workers' compensation absence.[59] The period of time the employee is out on workers' compensation leave may be counted against the eligible employee's annual 12-workweek FMLA leave entitlement, provided that all other requirements of the FMLA are complied with during the period of absence. For example, to count workers' compensation leave against the employee's 12-week FMLA leave entitlement, the employer would have to maintain health benefits during the leave under the same terms and conditions as if the employee continued to work.[60]

Workers' compensation is governed by state law. Workers' compensation is not an antidiscrimination law. Rather, it is an entitlement program that provides monetary compensation, medical care and assistance, vocational rehabilitation, and reemployment rights to employees injured on the job in lieu of allowing the injured employee to sue the employer in tort. Because it is not an antidiscrimination law, employers are not required to compare the FMLA and the applicable state workers' compensation law to determine which provisions provide the greater benefit to employees. Rather, employees who incur a workplace injury must separately satisfy the requirements of the applicable state workers' compensation law and the FMLA in order to obtain the benefits and protections of either or both of the laws.

While the workers' compensation laws of each state are different, there are several common areas of interaction with the FMLA. Workers' compensation is paid leave. As such, the FMLA provisions allowing the substitution of paid leave for unpaid leave do not apply when FMLA leave is taken for an injury also covered by workers' compensation. This prevents a double recovery by the employee (receipt of workers' compensation plus accrued paid leave). Once the employee's workers' compensation benefits cease, however, the paid leave substitution provisions of the FMLA may be applied.[61]

The FMLA requires employers to maintain group health benefits at the same levels and on the same terms and conditions, including the employee's responsibility to pay his or her share of health benefit plan premiums, during an employee's FMLA leave. If an employee is receiving payments as a result of an on-the-job injury covered by workers' compensation, the employee must make arrangements with the employer for payment of group health plan benefits when simultaneously taking FMLA leave.[62]

Another area where the FMLA intersects with state workers' compensation laws involves the right of an employer to require an employee to provide medical certification substantiating that the employee has a "serious health condition" within the meaning of the FMLA. The FMLA strictly prescribes the timing and content of medical information that an employer is entitled to receive. Employers are prohibited, absent the prior consent of the employee, from contacting the employee's health care provider regarding the content of a medical certification. An exception to that general prohibition exists where the employee's leave is also covered by a state workers' compensation law. An employer is entitled to have direct contact with the employee's workers' compensation health care provider if an employee is simultaneously taking FMLA leave and workers' compensation leave and the provisions of the workers' compensation statute permit such direct contact.[63] Of course, under the ADA, such contact must be job related and consistent with business necessity.[64]

Employers may not require an employee whose absence is covered by both the FMLA and a state workers' compensation law to take a light-duty position offered pursuant to workers' compensation in lieu of FMLA leave.[65] If the employee declines to take the light-duty position, the employee may no longer qualify for payments for workers' compensation. However, the employee remains entitled to continue on FMLA leave until the employee is either able to return to the same or equivalent position or until the 12-week FMLA entitlement is exhausted.[66]

Job restoration is the final area we will address where the federal FMLA may interact with state workers' compensation laws. For an employee to be entitled to job restoration, the FMLA generally requires that the employee return before the expiration of the 12-week FMLA entitlement and be able to perform all essential job functions upon return. If the employee is unable to perform all job functions and return to work until after the expiration of the employee's 12-workweek FMLA leave entitlement, the employee's return to work is governed by workers' compensation law, the ADA, other state laws, or the school employer's policies—not the FMLA.[67] If, for example, the applicable state workers' compensation law required the employee to be returned to work even though the employee was unable to perform all essential job functions, the employer would have to return the employee to work in conformance with the workers' compensation requirements. Those requirements may or may not require the employer to return the employee to the same or an equivalent job.[68]

13.04 INTEGRATION OF THE FMLA WITH MORE GENEROUS EMPLOYER LEAVE POLICIES

The FMLA sets the minimum requirements for family and medical leave for covered employers. The FMLA does not discourage employers from adopting or retaining leave policies that are more generous than any policies that comply with the requirements of the FMLA.[69] Covered employers that adopt policies that provide greater family or medical leave rights to employees than the minimum required by the FMLA must comply with those more generous leave policies.[70] Conversely, the rights established by the FMLA may not be diminished by any less generous employer leave policy or employment benefit program.[71]

A covered employer's "more generous" leave policies may extend family or medical leave benefits by, for example, lowering employer coverage or employee eligibility requirements or broadening the circumstances that entitle an employee to take leave beyond those covered by the FMLA. While the FMLA permits employers to adopt or retain more generous family or medical leave rights, leave granted under circumstances that do not meet the FMLA's employer coverage or employee eligibility requirements or that otherwise are not FMLA-qualifying is not FMLA leave and, therefore, may not be counted against the employee's annual 12-workweek FMLA leave entitlement.[72] For example, a private sector vocational school with less than 50 employees is not covered by the FMLA. The school could, if it wanted, adopt a family and medical leave program that incorporates by reference all of the requirements of the FMLA. The school employer would, as a matter of policy and contract, be obligated to comply with the provisions of its own family or medical leave policy. Because, however, the school does not meet the definition of a covered employer, its adoption of the FMLA as part of its leave policy does not render the school subject to the FMLA. Violation of the school's FMLA policy might be fodder for a grievance or breach of contract suit, but an employee would not be able to sue the school for violation of the FMLA.

Similarly, an employer policy that lowers eligibility for family or medical leave to 9 months of employment and 900 hours of work is more generous than the FMLA. An employee who met those lowered eligibility requirements would be entitled to family or medical leave pursuant to the employer's policy. However, unless the employee also met the eligibility requirements of the FMLA, the leave would not be covered by the FMLA and could not be counted against the employee's annual 12-workweek FMLA leave entitlement. If the employee did not meet the eligibility requirements of the FMLA, the employer's obligation, if any, to maintain group health benefits, protect the employee's job, and restore the employee to the same or an equivalent position upon the conclusion of leave would be governed by the employer's policy (or other federal, state, or local laws), not the FMLA.[73]

A typical form of more generous employer family or medical leave policy grants employees more than 12 weeks of leave each leave year. For example, an employer's short-term disability policy may allow an employee to take up to 20 weeks of leave a year. If the reason for the leave is covered by the FMLA and if all other FMLA prerequisites (e.g., employer coverage, eligibility, notice) are met, the employer could count 12 of those weeks against the employee's annual FMLA leave entitlement. Once those 12 weeks have been exhausted, all entitlements and rights under the FMLA cease. The employer is no longer obligated by the FMLA to continue to maintain health benefits, provide leave, or ensure job restoration. The employer's obligations, if any, to do those things would be governed by the employer's own leave policies.[74] Of course, the discrimination prohibition in the FMLA would prevent an employer from terminating employees who have used FMLA leave and do not return to work after 12 weeks if the employer does not treat similarly situated employees who have not used FMLA leave in the same manner.[75]

School employees do not have a viable cause of action under the federal FMLA against a school for violation of a more generous school leave policy to the extent that policy falls outside of the protections of the FMLA. Courts have consistently rejected employee attempts to use 29 C.F.R. § 825.700(a) as a basis for an FMLA claim against an employer for violation of a more generous family or medical leave policy in circumstances where the FMLA did not otherwise apply to the employer, the employee, or the reason for leave.[76]

An employer's more generous leave polices do not always render the employee outside of the benefits and protections of the FMLA. As discussed throughout this book, more generous employer leave policies may also lower certain FMLA requirements. Employers are prohibited from requiring compliance with stricter FMLA employee notice requirements where the provisions of a collective bargaining agreement or applicable leave plan allow less advance notice to the employer.[77] For example, if an employee or employer elects to substitute paid vacation leave for unpaid FMLA leave and the employer's paid vacation leave plan imposes no prior notification requirements for taking such vacation leave, no advance notice may be required for FMLA leave taken in these circumstances.[78] Similarly, if the school employer's sick or medical leave plan imposes medical certification requirements that are less stringent than the certification requirements of the FMLA and the employee or employer elects to substitute paid sick, vacation, personal, or family leave for unpaid FMLA leave where authorized, only the employer's less stringent sick leave certification requirements may be imposed.[79]

School employers must carefully review their current policies to determine whether they are more or less generous than the requirements of the FMLA. If they are less generous, they probably need to be changed as they have been superseded by the FMLA. If they are more generous, school employers must determine whether leave pursuant to those more generous policies is covered by the FMLA. If not, the leave is not governed by the FMLA. Rather, the leave would be governed by the school employer's more generous leave policies and any other applicable federal, state, or local laws. If the leave is covered both by the employer's more generous leave policies and the FMLA, the more generous leave policies will apply in lieu of the more stringent FLMA requirements.

Finally, as a condition for exercising certain employer rights, the FMLA requires the existence of certain school policies. For example, to exercise the FMLA right to require an employee to submit a fitness-for-duty report as a condition of job restoration, school employers must have a uniformly applied policy or practice that requires all similarly situated employees who take leave for such conditions to obtain and present a medical certification from the employee's health care provider that the employee is able to resume work.[80] A school employer that does not have such a uniformly applied policy or practice is not permitted by the FMLA to condition job restoration from FMLA leave on the submission of a fitness-for-duty report.

13.05 INTERACTION OF THE FMLA WITH COLLECTIVE BARGAINING AGREEMENTS

School leave policies and practices include the terms of any collective bargaining agreements. In that sense, the rules (discussed above) governing employer leave policies and practices that are more or less stringent than required by the FMLA apply with equal force to the terms of collective bargaining agreements. Nevertheless, both the Act and the

DOL implementing regulations specifically address the interaction of the FMLA with collective bargaining agreements.

FMLA rights may not be waived by the collective bargaining representative of an employee as a "trade-off" for other benefits.[81] Nor may employees waive their rights under the FMLA.[82] In addition to circumscribing the scope of collective bargaining regarding family or medical leave policies, the prohibition against waiver of FMLA rights would also appear to impact the settlement of grievances. Grievance settlements that waive the minimum rights guaranteed by the FMLA are forbidden and would constitute a violation of the FMLA. Waiver of FMLA rights is addressed in Chapter 14, *Prohibited Acts, Enforcement, and Remedies*.

The FMLA mentions the impact of collective bargaining agreements on other FMLA rights. For example, the right to assign an employee to an alternative position during a period of intermittent or reduced schedule leave "may require compliance with any applicable collective bargaining agreement."[83] An employer's FMLA obligation to continue leave, maintain health benefits, or reinstate a laid-off employee ceases at the time the employee is laid off, unless the employer has a continuing obligation under a collective bargaining agreement.[84] The terms of a collective bargaining agreement govern an employee's return to work from FMLA leave.[85] Finally, under the special school rules, the restoration of an instructional employee to an equivalent position upon return from FMLA leave is made on the basis of "established school board polices and practices, private school policies and practices, and collective bargaining agreements."[86]

13.06 INTERACTION OF STATE FAMILY AND MEDICAL LEAVE LAWS WITH OTHER LAWS, EMPLOYER POLICIES, AND COLLECTIVE BARGAINING AGREEMENTS

Like the federal FMLA, some state family and medical leave laws address how those laws interact with other federal or state laws, the terms of collective bargaining agreements, and employer practices. Many state family and medical leave laws do not address the issue, including the laws in Arizona, California, Colorado, Florida, Kentucky, Massachusetts, Ohio, and Texas. A few states, however, do address the interaction of state family and medical leave laws and other federal and state laws.

Alaska's family and health leave law provides an exception that exempts school districts from the requirements of the law. Under the law, the Commissioner of Education and Early Development may approve a collective bargaining agreement entered into between a school district and a bargaining organization that does not meet the requirements of Alaska's family and health leave law if the district establishes to the satisfaction of the Commissioner that a variance from the requirements of the law is necessary to avoid hardship on the school district based on the lack of qualified, available substitute teachers to replace teachers on family and health leave or the lack of available housing for replacement teachers who do not live in the community.[87] The provisions of Alaska's law are generally subject to collective bargaining, except that a collective bargaining agreement that does not contain benefit provisions at least as beneficial to the employee as those provided by Alaska's law are considered to contain the benefit provisions of Alaska's family and health leave law.[88] Alaska's family and health leave law also provides that its provisions do not affect other provisions of law relating to sex discrimination, pregnancy, or parenthood.[89]

The District of Columbia Family and Medical Leave Act provides that nothing in the family and medical leave law supersedes any provision of law that provides greater employee family or medical leave rights than the family or medical leave rights established under the family and medical leave law.[90] The Act does not diminish an employer's obligation to comply with any collective bargaining agreement or any employment benefit program or plan that provides greater family or medical leave rights to an employee than the family or medical leave rights provided under the Act.[91] The rights provided to an employee by the Act also may not be diminished by any collective bargaining agreement or employment benefit program or plan. The District of Columbia law allows family and medical leave rights to be temporarily suspended for certain public safety employees if the employee is required by rules or regulations of the agency or by the provisions of a collective bargaining agreement to return to duty because of an emergency declared by the agency head or the mayor.[92]

The New Jersey Family Leave Act provides that

> No provision of this act shall be deemed to justify an employer in reducing employment benefits provided by the employer or required by a collective bargaining agreement which are in excess of those required by this act. Nor shall any provision of this act, or any regulations promulgated to implement or enforce this act, be construed to prohibit the negotiation and provision through collective bargaining agreements of leave policies or benefit programs which provide benefits in excess of those required by this act. This provision shall apply irrespective of the date that a collective bargaining agreement takes effect.[93]

Family leave granted under New Jersey law is in addition to, and does not abridge or conflict with any rights under New Jersey's Temporary Disability Benefits Law.[94]

NOTES

1. 29 U.S.C. § 2651(a); 29 C.F.R. § 825.702(a); DOL WH FMLA Advisory Opinion No. 82 (July 31, 1996); DOL WH FMLA Advisory Opinion No. 47 (Oct. 17, 1994); DOL WH FMLA Advisory Opinion No. 29 (Feb. 7, 1994); DOL WH FMLA Advisory Opinion No. 27 (Jan. 31, 1994).
2. 29 C.F.R. § 825.702(a).
3. S. Rep. No. 103-3, at 38 (1993), as reprinted in 1993 U.S.C.C.A.N. 3, 40.
4. 29 C.F.R. § 825.702(a); DOL WH FMLA Advisory Opinion No. 82 (July 31, 1996); DOL WH FMLA Advisory Opinion No. 55 (Mar. 10, 1995); DOL WH FMLA Advisory Opinion No. 29 (Feb. 7, 1994).
5. Comments on Regulations Implementing the Family and Medical Leave Act of 1993 (§ 825.702), 60 Fed. Reg. 2180, 2232 (Jan. 6, 1995).
6. 29 C.F.R. § 825.702(a).
7. *Id.*
8. 29 C.F.R. § 825.113(c)(2).
9. 29 C.F.R. § 825.115.
10. 29 C.F.R. § 825.500(g).
11. 29 C.F.R. § 825.310(b).
12. 42 U.S.C. § 12111(5)(A); 29 C.F.R. § 1630.2(e)(1).
13. 42 U.S.C. § 12112(a).
14. 42 U.S.C. § 12111(8).
15. 42 U.S.C. § 12102(2).
16. 29 C.F.R. § 1630.2(i).

17. 42 U.S.C. § 12112(b)(5).

18. 42 U.S.C. § 12111(9)(B).

19. 29 C.F.R. § 1630.2(o).

20. See *Waggoner v. Olin Corp.*, 169 F.3d 481, 487 (7th Cir. 1999); *Nesser v. Trans World Airlines, Inc.*, 160 F.3d 442 (8th Cir. 1998); *Hypes v. First Commerce Corp.*, 134 F.3d 721, 727 (5th Cir. 1998).

21. See *Rascon v. US West Communications, Inc.*, 143 F.3d 1324, 1334 (10th Cir. 1998); *Myers v. Hose*, 50 F.3d 278, 284 (4th Cir. 1995); *Powers v. Polygram Holdings, Inc.*, 40 F. Supp. 2d 195, 200–01 (S.D.N.Y. 1999).

22. See *Gantt v. Wilson Sporting Goods Co.*, 143 F.3d 1042, 1047 (6th Cir. 1998); *Hudson v. MCI Telecommunications Corp.*, 87 F.3d 1167, 1169 (10th Cir. 1996).

23. See *Nunes v. Wal-Mart Stores, Inc.*, 164 F.3d 1243, 1245–46 (9th Cir. 1999); *Gantt*, 143 F.3d at 1047.

24. 29 U.S.C. § 2611(2)(A).

25. 42 U.S.C. § 12111(5).

26. 29 C.F.R. 825.702(b).

27. Compare 29 C.F.R. § 825.114(a)(2)(ii), with 29 C.F.R. § 1630.2(h).

28. 29 C.F.R. § 825.702(a).

29. *Id.*

30. 29 C.F.R. § 825.702(c)(2).

31. 29 C.F.R. § 825.702(c)(3).

32. 29 C.F.R. § 825.702(c)(4).

33. 29 C.F.R. § 825.702(d)(1).

34. 42 U.S.C. § 2000-e(k).

35. 42 U.S.C. § 2000-e(k); 29 C.F.R. pt 1604; 29 C.F.R. § 825.702(f).

36. U.S. Equal Opportunity Employment Commission, EEOC Fact Sheet: The Family and Medical Leave Act, the Americans with Disabilities Act, and Title VII of the Civil Rights Act of 1964, question 22 (Nov. 1995), available at http://www.eeoc.gov/policy/docs/fmlaada.html [hereinafter EEOC Fact Sheet].

37. 29 C.F.R. 825.702(f); EEOC Fact Sheet, *supra* note 36, question 22.

38. *Cabrera v. Trataros Construction Inc.*, 184 F. Supp. 2d 149, 156 (D.P.R. 2002).

39. S. Rep. No. 103-3, at 38 (1993), as reprinted in 1993 U.S.C.C.A.N. 3, 40; 29 C.F.R. § 825.702(a).

40. 29 C.F.R. § 825.702(a).

41. 29 U.S.C. § 2651(a); 29 C.F.R. § 825.702(a).

42. EEOC Fact Sheet, *supra* note 36.

43. 29 C.F.R. § 825.112(b).

44. 38 U.S.C. §§ 4301–4333.

45. 38 U.S.C. § 4303(4)(A)(i)–(iv); 38 C.F.R. § 1002.34(a).

46. U.S. Department of Labor, USERRA-FMLA Questions and Answers: The Effect of the Uniformed Services Employment and Reemployment Rights Act on Leave Eligibility Under the Family and Medical Leave Act (July 25, 2002), available at http://www.dol.gov/vets/media/fmlaq-a.pdf.

47. 29 U.S.C. § 2651(a); see also 29 C.F.R. § 825.702(a).

48. 29 U.S.C. § 2651(b); 29 C.F.R. § 825.701(a).

49. Comments on Regulations Implementing the Family and Medical Leave Act of 1993 (§ 825.701), 60 Fed. Reg. 2180, 2230 (Jan. 6, 1995).

50. *Id.* at 2231.

51. 29 C.F.R. § 825.701(a).

52. *Id.*

53. Comments on Regulations Implementing the Family and Medical Leave Act of 1993 (§ 825.701), 60 Fed. Reg. at 2230.

54. 29 C.F.R. § 825.701(a); Comments on Regulations Implementing the Family and Medical Leave Act of 1993 (§ 825.701), 60 Fed. Reg. at 2230.

55. 29 C.F.R. 825.701(a).

56. *Id.*

57. *Id.*

58. 29 C.F.R. § 825.207(d)(2).

59. *Id.*; DOL WH FMLA Advisory Opinion No. 42, question 5 (Aug. 23, 1994).

60. DOL WH FMLA Advisory Opinion No. 42, question 5 (Aug. 23, 1994).

61. The substitution of paid leave for unpaid FMLA leave is addressed in Chapter 9, *Paid Leave Substitution*.

62. Maintenance of health benefits during FMLA leave is addressed in Chapter 10, *Maintenance of Employment Benefits*.

63. 29 C.F.R. § 825.307(a).

64. FMLA rules governing the medical certification process are discussed in Chapter 7, *Documentation Requirements*.

65. 29 C.F.R. §§ 825.207(d)(2), 825.220(d), 825.702(d)(2); DOL WH FMLA Advisory Opinion No. 75 (Nov. 14, 1995); DOL WH FMLA Advisory Opinion No. 55 (Mar. 10, 1995); DOL WH FMLA Advisory Opinion No. 38 (July 21, 1994).

66. 29 C.F.R. §§ 825.207(d)(2), 825.702(d)(2); DOL WH FMLA Advisory Opinion No. 75 (Nov. 14, 1995); DOL WH FMLA Advisory Opinion No. 55 (Mar. 10, 1995); DOL WH FMLA Advisory Opinion No. 38 (July 21, 1994).

67. 29 C.F.R. § 825.216(d).

68. Return to work issues under the FMLA are addressed in Chapter 11, *Return to Work from Family Medical Leave*.

69. 29 U.S.C. § 2653; DOL WH FMLA Advisory Opinion No. 91 (Dec. 9, 1997).

70. 29 U.S.C. § 2652(a); 29 C.F.R. § 825.700(a); DOL WH FMLA Advisory Opinion No. 91 (Dec. 9, 1997).

71. 29 U.S.C. § 2652(b); 29 C.F.R. § 825.700(a); DOL WH FMLA Advisory Opinion No. 91 (Dec. 9, 1997).

72. Comments on Regulations Implementing the Family and Medical Leave Act of 1993 (§ 825.700), 60 Fed. Reg. 2180, 2230 (Jan. 6, 1995).

73. DOL WH FMLA Advisory Opinion No. 91, question 2 (Dec. 9, 1997).

74. *Id.* question 3; see also *Panto v. Palmer Dialysis Center/Total Renal Care*, No. 01-6013, 2003 U.S. Dist. LEXIS 5663, at *20 (E.D. Pa. April 7, 2003).

75. DOL WH FMLA Advisory Opinion No. 91, question 3 (Dec. 9, 1997).

76. See *Rich v. Delta Airlines, Inc.*, 921 F. Supp. 767, 773–74 (N.D. Ga. 1996); accord *Dolese v. Office Depot, Inc.*, 231 F.3d 202, 203 (5th Cir. 2000); *Fulham v. HSBC Bank USA*, No. 99-Civ. 11054 (JGK), 2001 U.S. Dist. LEXIS 13570, at *26–*29 (S.D.N.Y. Sept. 6, 2001); *Holmes v. E. Spire Communications, Inc.*, 135 F. Supp. 2d 657, 666–67 (D. Md. 2001).

77. 29 C.F.R. §§ 825.302(g), 825.207(h).

78. 29 C.F.R. §§ 825.302(g), 825.207(h).

79. 29 C.F.R. §§ 825.305(e), 825.207(h).

80. 29 C.F.R. § 825.310(a).

81. 29 C.F.R. § 825.220(d).

82. *Id.*

83. 29 C.F.R. § 825.204(a)–(b).

84. 29 C.F.R. § 825.216(a)(1).

85. 29 C.F.R. § 825.310(b).

86. 29 C.F.R. § 825.604.

87. Alaska Stat. § 39.20.530(c).

88. Alaska Stat. § 39.20.530(b).

89. Alaska Stat. § 39.20.530(a).

90. D.C. Code Ann. § 32-512.

91. D.C. Code Ann. § 32-513(a).

92. D.C. Code Ann. § 32-513(c).

93. N.J. Stat. Ann. § 34:11B-14.

94. N.J. Stat. Ann. § 34:11B-13. The New Jersey Temporary Disability Benefits Law provides cash benefits to employees who cannot work because of sickness or injury not caused by the employee's job. New Jersey is only one of five states that provides compulsory temporary disability insurance for workers.

CHAPTER 14

Prohibited Acts, Enforcement, and Remedies

14.01 OVERVIEW

The FMLA prohibits a broad range of conduct by employers that interferes with or discriminates against the exercise of an employee's FMLA rights. An employee may enforce his or her FMLA rights by filing a complaint with the DOL or by filing a private civil lawsuit against the offending employer. The FMLA does not, however, permit employers to sue employees for FMLA violations. Aggrieved employees are entitled by the FMLA to receive economic damages resulting from violations, including double damages for "willful" violations, plus attorneys' fees, costs, and interest. Given the inherent delays and expense of litigation, an FMLA lawsuit can easily cost school employers hundreds of thousands of dollars.

> **An FMLA lawsuit can easily cost school employers hundreds of thousands of dollars.**

Section 14.02 addresses prohibited employer conduct. Section 14.03 discusses the avenues available to enforce FMLA rights. Section 14.04 reviews the remedies available to employees for FMLA violations. Section 14.05 discusses noteworthy FMLA litigation issues. Section 14.06 addresses prohibited acts, enforcement, and remedies available under state family and medical leave laws.

14.02 PROHIBITED ACTS

[1] Introduction

The FMLA establishes three forms of prohibited acts that may be the basis of a DOL complaint or private civil lawsuit against an employer for violation of the FMLA. First, the FMLA prohibits interfering with, restraining, or denying an employee rights guaranteed under the FMLA.[1] Second, employers are prohibited from discriminating against an employee for opposing any practice deemed illegal under the FMLA.[2] Third, the FMLA prohibits employers from discharging or in any other manner discriminating against any individual because such individual has filed any charge, has instituted or caused to be instituted any proceedings, has given or is about to give any information in connection with any inquiry or proceeding, or has testified or is about to testify in any inquiry regarding FMLA rights.[3] This third form of prohibited action protects employees who try to protect and enforce their FMLA rights. The three forms of prohibited acts are addressed below. To constitute an actionable FMLA violation, the disputed employer activity must fall within the meaning of at least one of these three prohibited acts. The burden of proof to establish an FMLA violation varies depending on which form of prohibited activity is being asserted.

[2] Interference Claims

The FMLA prohibits employers from interfering with, restraining, or denying the exercise of or the attempt to exercise any right provided under the FMLA. The statute does not define the meaning of "interfering with, restraining, or denying the exercise of or the attempt to exercise" FMLA rights.[4] The DOL regulations do, however, broadly define these terms:

> Any violations of the Act or of these regulations constitute interfering with, restraining, or denying the exercise of rights provided by the Act. "Interfering with" the exercise of an employee's rights would include, for example, not only refusing to authorize FMLA leave, but discouraging an

employee from using leave. It would also include manipulation by a covered employer to avoid responsibilities under the FMLA, for example:

(1) transferring employees form one worksite to another for the purpose of reducing worksites, or to keep worksites below the 50-employee threshold for employee eligibility under the Act;
(2) changing the essential functions of the job in order to preclude the taking of leave;
(3) reducing hours available to work in order to avoid FMLA eligibility.[5]

Neither the Act nor the DOL regulations address the standard used to judge whether an employer has "interfered with" the exercise of an employee's FMLA rights. The Ninth Circuit has looked to interpretations of the National Labor Relations Act, which similarly prohibits employer interference with the exercise of collective bargaining rights, for guidance in determining whether an employer has interfered with an employee's FMLA rights.[6] Most courts simply make the determination on an ad hoc basis on the facts at issue.

Because the DOL broadly defines "interfering with" as any violation of the Act or DOL regulations, actionable interference with FMLA rights has been found in cases involving virtually every DOL regulation. Clearly, where all requirements are met, an employer that denies FMLA leave to an eligible employee has interfered with that employee's FMLA rights.[7] Of course, the denial of FMLA leave does not always "interfere with" an employee's FMLA rights. For example, one court held that an employer did not violate the anti-interference provisions of the FMLA by refusing to allow the employee to remain on FMLA leave in lieu of being laid off. Because the employee would have been laid off had FMLA leave not been taken, the employee was not entitled to remain on FMLA leave in lieu of being laid off.[8] Similarly, another court held that the termination of an employee while on FMLA leave (which effectively denied the employee the use of additional FMLA leave) did not "interfere with" the employee's FMLA leave rights where the termination was for reasons independent of the FMLA.[9] The failure to return an employee to the same or an equivalent position at the end of FMLA leave may constitute actionable interference with FMLA rights.[10]

An employer's failure to satisfy the various employee FMLA notice obligations has been found to constitute actionable interference.[11] To assert a viable interference claim, however, employees are generally required by courts to demonstrate that they were prejudiced by the employer's failure to properly notify them of their FMLA rights and responsibilities.[12] FMLA notice requirements are discussed in Chapter 6, *Notice Requirements*. The courts are split on whether an employee must have adequately notified his or her employer of the need for FMLA leave in order to maintain a viable interference claim.[13]

The federal FMLA does not define what it means for an employer to "discourage" an employee from exercising FMLA rights. Discipline for the use of FMLA leave has been found to "discourage" employees from exercising FMLA rights in violation of the Act.[14] Threatening an employee with the forfeiture of accrued but unused vacation or sick leave may discourage an employee's use of FMLA leave and, therefore, constitute a violation of the Act.[15] The courts are split on whether derogatory remarks and attempts to talk an employee out of taking FMLA leave "discourage" an employee's exercise of FMLA rights. Some courts have held that such conduct does not discourage an employee's use of FMLA leave where the employer eventually granted all of the employee's requests for FMLA leave.[16] Other courts have held that an employer's threats and initial denial of FMLA leave constituted actionable discouragement in violation of the FMLA, even where the employer granted the employee FMLA leave retroactively.[17] Comments that the employee should take leave at a different time and subsequent denial of leave was found to "chill" the employee's exercise of FMLA rights.[18]

To avoid federal FMLA violations, school employers should train managers, supervisors, and employees to refrain from making adverse comments regarding an employee's exercise of FMLA rights. Because violation of any of the myriad of DOL regulations may constitute an expensive FMLA interference claim, school employers should ensure that those responsible for administering FMLA rights are well grounded in the requirements of the FMLA and receive periodic training in order to stay current with FMLA developments. This is particularly true given that the FMLA permits aggrieved employees to sue individual school administrators for violations of the FMLA, whether intentional or not, in addition to suing the school employer.

[3] Discrimination Claims

The FMLA prohibits three types of discrimination: (1) discrimination for use of FMLA leave, (2) discrimination for opposition to unlawful practices, and (3) discrimination for participation in protected activities. An examination of each of these forms of discrimination follows.

(i) Use of FMLA Leave and No-Fault Attendance Policies

Employers are prohibited from discriminating against employees or prospective employees who have used FMLA leave.[19] It is unclear what standard is used to determine "discriminating against." The lack of clarity is due to the absence of statutory and regulatory guidance on this issue. By its terms, the Act does not explicitly make it unlawful to discriminate against an employee for the use of FMLA leave.[20] The DOL regulations also fail to define the meaning of "discriminating against." The absence of clear guidance has lead to some confusion in the courts regarding the standard for determining whether an employer has discriminated against an employee for use of FMLA leave. Some courts have applied the well-known Title VII standards for determining intentional discrimination.[21] Other courts have held that § 825. 220(c) discrimination claims for use of FMLA leave are really interference claims.[22] These courts apply the lower burden of proof standard for interference claims, which does not require a demonstration of employer intent. I agree that § 825. 220(c) discrimination claims should be analyzed as interference claims.

The DOL illustrates the prohibition against discrimination for use of FMLA leave with three examples:[23]

- If an employee on leave without pay would otherwise be entitled to full benefits (other than health benefits), the same benefits must be provided to an employee on unpaid FMLA leave.

- Employers cannot use the taking of FMLA leave as a negative factor in employment actions such as hiring, promoting, or disciplining employees.
- FMLA leave cannot be counted under "no fault" attendance policies.

The examples confirm that employers are prohibited from treating employees who invoke their right to take FMLA leave differently from employees who take other paid or unpaid leave and that the taking of FMLA leave may not be used against the employee.

Schools must take great care to screen out FMLA leave usage from all employment decisions. FMLA leave usage cannot be used as a negative factor against the employee taking the leave or against the employee's supervisor. For example, the absence record of subordinate employees is frequently factored into the performance evaluation of supervisors. Such performance evaluations may have a direct impact on bonuses and annual salary increases. If FMLA leave usage is not excluded from the absentee record, supervisors could be penalized in the form of lower bonuses or pay raises. The FMLA prohibits such conduct by employers.

A "no fault" attendance policy that counts FMLA leave as an absence or "an occurrence" violates the FMLA.[24] Generally, a "no fault" attendance policy is one that attaches penalties to absences or tardiness, which are generally recorded as "occurrences" no matter what the reason for the absence. Discipline usually results as an employee accumulates absences or occurrences. Conversely, the number of absences or occurrences an employee has accumulated is reduced when an employees goes for a designated period of time without an absence or occurrence. While FMLA absences can never be counted against the employee for purposes of a no-fault attendance policy, whether a period of FMLA leave counts for purposes of reducing the number of non-FMLA absences or occurrences will depend on the employer's paid and unpaid leave policies. The DOL explained the interaction of FMLA leave with the reduction of non-FMLA occurrences pursuant to employer no-fault attendance policies as follows:

> If the employee was on unpaid FMLA leave and the employer's policy does not permit the accrual of benefits or seniority during any unpaid

> leave, upon return to work the employer would only be obligated to restore the employee to the same or an equivalent position to what the employee had prior to the start of leave. If the employee had 45 days without a recordable incident at the time the unpaid FMLA leave commenced, the employer would be obligated to restore the employee to this number of days credited without an incident. The employer could neither count the FMLA leave period toward an attendance control policy for potential termination, nor credit the unpaid FMLA leave toward the recordable time for dropping such points.
>
> If FMLA leave was covered by paid leave (or unpaid leave) that provides for the accrual of benefits and seniority, then the FMLA leave could be credited toward the time free of a recordable incident. In this example, the FMLA leave could not be counted as an occurrence or incident pursuant to a "no fault" attendance policy.[25]

Attendance-based bonuses are a related area requiring school employers to exercise caution where FMLA leave is involved. Here, rather than accumulating points or occurrences for discipline, employees are rewarded for attaining perfect or near-perfect attendance.[26] As discussed more fully in Chapter 10, *Maintenance of Employment Benefits*, employers cannot count FMLA leave against an employee's entitlement to an attendance-based bonus. Rather, upon return to work from FMLA leave, an employee is entitled to any accrued benefits he or she had prior to taking leave, including whatever points or nonoccurrences the employee had accumulated toward an attendance-based bonus. If, prior to taking FMLA leave, the employee had perfect attendance, the employee must be restored to work following FMLA leave with a perfect attendance record. As a result, an employee who took his or her entire annual 12-week FMLA leave entitlement could have the right to a bonus for perfect attendance.

Note that the prohibition applies to discrimination against employees and prospective employees. As discussed more fully in section 14.03 below, the means of enforcing that broad prohibition are more limited. For example, the Act authorizes eligible employees to initiate a private civil lawsuit for violation of the FMLA. The FMLA, however does not allow noneligible employees or prospective employees to file a private lawsuit for violation of the FMLA. Some courts have allowed suit by prospective employees for FMLA violations. Noneligible and prospective employees may seek relief by filing an administrative complaint with the DOL.

(ii) Opposition to Unlawful Practices

The FMLA also prohibits an employer from discharging or discriminating against individuals for opposing unlawful FMLA practices.[27] The prohibition applies to any "person," including employees and nonemployees.[28] The Act does not define who is an "individual" for purposes of this prohibition. The DOL regulations define a "person" to include an individual, partnership, association, corporation, business trust, legal representative, or any organized group of persons.[29] As so broadly defined, "person" would appear to protect prospective employees and unions from retaliation for opposing unlawful FMLA practices.

The provisions of the FMLA governing discrimination for opposing unlawful practices are derived from Title VII of the Civil Rights Act of 1964 and were intended to be construed in the same manner.[30] An employee is protected against employer retaliation for opposing any practice that he or she reasonably believes to be a violation.[31] The FMLA provides the same sorts of protections to workers who oppose, protest, or attempt to correct alleged violations of the FMLA as are provided under Title VII.[32] The scope of the protection, however, is not clear. For example, the Sixth Circuit declined to decide whether an employee's profanity-laced verbal confrontation with her supervisors regarding the propriety of a return-to-work fitness-for-duty evaluation was a "complaint" within the meaning of the opposition provisions of the FMLA.[33] In addition to consulting FMLA case law, school employers should consult case law interpreting Title VII regarding the scope of the FMLA's antiretaliation provision.

Note that the protection extends to persons who reasonably believe that a practice violates the Act. It follows that if the individual's belief is not reasonable, opposition conduct would not be protected. Conversely, opposition activity would be protected where the individual reasonably believes that the employer's actions violate the FMLA, even if the individual is ultimately mistaken in that belief. For example, if an employee files a complaint or grievance alleging an FMLA violation that is reasonably based, the employee would be protected by the opposition provisions of the FMLA even if the complaint is ultimately determined to lack merit.[34]

While the FMLA opposition provisions apply to all "persons," the Act limits the enforcement avenues available to the aggrieved. By the terms of the FMLA, only eligible employees may sue an employer for violation of the antiretaliation provisions of the FMLA. Noneligible employees, prospective employees, and other "persons" who are not eligible employees may file a complaint with the DOL regarding a violation of the antiretaliation provisions. Most courts have found that such noneligible employees do not enjoy the right to sue the offending employer in court.[35]

(iii) Participation in Protected Activities

It is unlawful under the FMLA for any person to discharge or in any other manner discriminate against any individual because such individual

- has filed any charge, or has instituted or caused to be instituted any proceeding under or related to the FMLA;
- has given, or is about to give, any information in connection with any inquiry or proceeding relating to any FMLA rights; or
- has testified, or is about to testify, in any inquiry or proceeding relating to any right provided under the FMLA.[36]

Note that the protection extends to any "person," not just employees, and the prohibition applies to all persons, not just FMLA-covered employers. Here again, however, the Act permits only eligible employees to initiate a private suit for FMLA violations. Individuals who are not eligible employees may enforce the protections afforded by the Act only by filing a complaint with the DOL.

[4] Waiver of FMLA Rights

The FMLA prohibits the waiver of FMLA rights. Employees are prohibited from waiving their rights under the FMLA.[37] Collective bargaining representatives may not diminish or waive employee FMLA rights.[38] And employers are prohibited from inducing employees to waive their rights under the FMLA.[39] For example, employees (or their collective bargaining representatives) may not "trade off" the right to take FMLA leave against some other benefit offered by the employer.[40]

The FMLA does not identify which FMLA "rights" are subject to the antiwaiver provisions. The scope of the antiwaiver prohibition is important, as it may impact the ability of employees and employers to settle FMLA claims. Not surprisingly (given the absence of DOL guidance), courts are split on the effect of the antiwaiver provisions on the settlement of FMLA claims. The Fifth Circuit has held that the antiwaiver provisions apply only to "substantive rights" under the FMLA, such as the right to leave and reinstatement, rather than "procedural rights," such as the right to sue for damages for retaliation for the exercise of those substantive rights.[41]

In the case before the Fifth Circuit, the employee signed a release of all claims in exchange for the equivalent of one month's salary at the time of her termination for poor performance. The employee was given 45 days to consider the release and 7 days to revoke it after she signed it. The employee signed the release, received the money, and subsequently sued the employer for violation of the FMLA. She did not return the release payment.

Relying on the antiwaiver provisions of the FMLA, the district court refused to enforce the release and dismiss the case. On appeal, the Fifth Circuit reversed the decision of the district court. The court held that the antiwaiver provisions prohibit the waiver of substantive rights, such as leave and reinstatement, not the waiver of a cause of action for damages. The court also noted the public policy favoring settlement of employment claims. Because the employee had not returned the release payment, the court found that the release had been ratified. The court awarded summary judgment to the employer.

A very different result was reached by the Fourth Circuit in *Taylor v. Progress Energy, Inc.*[42] In that case, the employee was offered the opportunity to receive additional benefits, including monetary compensation, if she signed a general release and severance agreement within 45 days of her removal—ostensibly for poor performance. The release generally waived all employment claims under federal law Taylor may have had against the employer. Taylor received $12,000 pursuant to the release. She kept the money and subsequently filed suit against her former employer alleging violation of the federal FMLA. The district court, relying on *Faris*, awarded summary judgment to Progress Energy, finding that 29 C.F.R. § 825. 220(d) did not render the release unenforceable. Taylor appealed.

The Fourth Circuit reversed the award of summary judgment to Progress Energy. According to the court:

> We disagree with the district court's interpretation of § 825. 220(d). The regulation's plain language prohibits both the retrospective and prospective waiver or release of an employee's FMLA rights. In addition, the regulation applies to all FMLA rights, both substantive and proscriptive (the latter preventing discrimination and retaliation). Finally, the DOL, by recognizing that the FMLA's enforcement scheme is analogous to that of the Fair Labor Standards Act (FLSA), 29 U.S.C. § 201 *et seq.*, has indicated that § 825.220(d) permits the waiver or settlement of FMLA claims only with the prior approval of the DOL or a court.[43]

The court went on to find that the antiwaiver provisions of § 825.220(d) rendered the release unenforceable. Because FMLA claims are not waivable by agreement, the court also rejected the employer's argument that they were waivable by ratification due to Taylor's retention of the release money.

School employers would be well advised to confirm the state of the law regarding the release of FMLA or FLSA claims in their jurisdiction before settling FMLA claims. In the Fourth Circuit (North Carolina, South Carolina, West Virginia, Virginia, and Maryland), school employers must obtain the prior approval of a court or the DOL regarding the settlement of any FMLA claim.

14.03 ENFORCEMENT

The FMLA provides two avenues of relief for individuals who believe that an employer has violated their FMLA rights. Both avenues, however, are not available to all aggrieved persons. Any aggrieved person may file an administrative complaint with the DOL.[44] Eligible employees may maintain a private civil action in court for FMLA violations.[45]

These two avenues of enforcement are not exclusive. Employees may also use internal grievance or complaint mechanisms available pursuant to a collective bargaining agreement or school policy to resolve their FMLA complaints.

[1] Filing an Administrative Complaint with the U.S. Department of Labor

The Act empowers the DOL to receive, investigate, and attempt to resolve FMLA complaints.[46] The DOL's regulations in this regard are modeled on the enforcement scheme of the Fair Labor Standards Act.[47]

(i) Effect of Filing an Administrative Complaint on Maintenance of Private Lawsuit

The DOL administrative complaint process is a freestanding avenue of enforcement. An administrative complaint is not required as a prerequisite for an employee to file a private civil suit.[48] Similarly, the filing of an administrative complaint with the DOL does not preclude an employee from concurrently filing a private civil action regarding the same issue.[49]

(ii) Process for Filing Administrative Complaints

An employee or another person on behalf of the employee may file an administrative complaint with the DOL.[50] "Person" is a defined term that includes an individual, partnership, association, corporation, business trust, legal representative, or any organized group of persons.[51] In comments accompanying the final FMLA regulations, the DOL noted that for purposes of the FLSA, the DOL has accepted complaints from employees as well as other persons who may have knowledge of the circumstances, including "a relative of the employee, a Collective Bargaining Unit representative, a competitor, etc."[52]

Note that only employees and persons filing on behalf of an employee may file administrative complaints with the DOL for FMLA violations. The FMLA defines "employee" as that term is defined by the FLSA.[53] Applicants and other nonemployees are not included within the FMLA definition of "employee." As such, notwithstanding the FMLA's proscriptions against certain employer conduct toward non-employees, if the aggrieved individual is not an "employee" he or she technically does not have standing to file an administrative compliant with the DOL unless that individual is doing so on behalf of an employee. School employers should review FLSA case law to determine how the DOL handles complaints from nonemployees where such complaints are not on behalf of employees.

An administrative complaint must be filed within a reasonable time of the discovery that an employee's FMLA rights have been violated.[54] In no event may an administrative complaint be filed more than 2 years after the alleged violation occurred, or more than 3 years after in the case of a willful violation.[55] These are the same temporal periods as govern the initiation of a civil action.[56] Statute of limitations issues are addressed later in this section.

Note that an administrative complaint must be filed within a reasonable period of time after the employee discovers that his or her FMLA rights may have been violated. This may be a significantly shorter period of time than the 2- or 3-year period permitted. That is, an employee who files an administrative complaint within the 2- or 3-year period may nevertheless be untimely if he or she did not file within a reasonable period of time after learning of the potential violation. School employers who are contacted as part of a DOL investigation will want to explore this issue with the investigator. Where warranted, school employers will want to argue that the complaint is untimely and should be dismissed. Dismissal of the administrative complaint as untimely does not prevent the employee from filing a private civil suit.

The administrative complaint must be reduced to writing and include a full statement of the alleged unlawful acts or omissions, with pertinent dates.[57] The FMLA does not mandate that administrative complaints be on a particular form. The complaint may be filed in person, by mail, or by telephone with the national or any local office of the Wage and Hour Division, Employment Standards Administration, U.S. Department of Labor.[58] Addresses and telephone numbers of local DOL Wage and Hour offices may be found in the government pages of the telephone book or on the DOL's website: www.dol.gov.

(iii) Administrative Complaint Process

After an administrative complaint is filed, it is assigned to a Wage and Hour Division investigator. Generally, such assignments are not made on a first come, first served basis but on an assessment of the seriousness of the alleged violations. The investigator frequently begins the investigation by clarifying the complaint with the complainant and gathering supporting evidence. The employer is contacted after the investigator is satisfied, based on his or her preliminary investigation, that the FMLA may have been violated. More often than not the preliminary investigation involves little more than a conversation with the complainant and review of any documents presented. The DOL's considerable investigatory powers are addressed more fully in the next subsection.

The DOL investigator subsequently contacts the employer and explains the nature of the FMLA administrative complaint. At this time the investigator will often offer his or her preliminary findings. The employer will be afforded a reasonable opportunity to respond and submit information to the investigator to establish the employer's position—usually that the FMLA was not violated. The investigator reviews the information submitted by the employer to make a final determination on the complaint. If the investigator is satisfied that a violation did not occur, the investigator usually communicates that to the complainant and the employer and closes the investigation. The complainant, of course, may initiate a private civil lawsuit even if the investigator has concluded that the FMLA was not violated.

If the DOL investigator concludes that an FMLA violation did occur, the investigator informs the complainant and the employer of this determination. Note that there has not been a hearing or a finding by an administrative judge or other hearing officer. There is no administrative hearing regarding the FMLA complaint. Rather, the investigator will attempt to resolve the complaint with the employer informally.

At the conclusion of the investigation, the DOL investigator holds a conference with the employer to discuss his or her findings. The DOL investigator identifies what he or she believes to be violations and proposes the actions the employer would need to take to come into compliance with the FMLA. The employer may provide additional facts, clear up discrepancies, and assert defenses. More than one closing conference is possible. Frequently, at this conference the DOL will propose a settlement to resolve the FMLA complaint. If the employer agrees, the DOL will frequently supervise settlements between the employer and the employee. DOL-supervised settlements are addressed in subsection (vi) below. Employers are not obligated to agree to settle the complaint.

If the employer is reluctant to settle the matter, the DOL will likely threaten to sue the employer on behalf of the employee to enforce the employee's FMLA rights. As discussed later in this section, the DOL has the authority to bring a civil action against an employer on behalf of an aggrieved employee for FMLA violations. The prospect of litigating against the deep pockets of the federal government is, unquestionably, intimidating for most school employers. The DOL, however, very rarely files civil actions on behalf of employees. More typically, the threat is designed to compel the employer to settle with little prospect that the DOL will actually initiate a civil action. In the overwhelming majority of cases, if an employer does not settle, the DOL issues a letter indicating that the DOL has found a violation and informing the employee of his or her right to file a civil action. In essence, the employee is cut loose and must timely initiate and finance a civil action against the employer.

(iv) DOL Investigative Authority

The DOL is authorized to investigate employers to ensure compliance with the FMLA.[59] While the majority of DOL investigations are informal, school employers need to be aware of the full extent of the DOL's investigatory authority.

The DOL's authority to investigate FMLA compliance is governed by section 11(a) of the FLSA, 29 U.S.C. § 211(a).[60] Pursuant to that authority, the DOL may conduct so-called routine investigations or investigations prompted by FMLA complaints. Because of the scarcity of resources, the DOL rarely conducts routine investigations that are not prompted by a complaint of an FMLA violation. The overwhelming majority of DOL investigations are conducted as a result of employee or union complaints of suspected violations of the FMLA.

To investigate a complaint of a suspected FMLA violation, the DOL is legally authorized to conduct an on-site inspection. The DOL is authorized to enter the employer's premises to obtain records, question employees, and otherwise gather facts as part of the investigation. In practice, however, on-site inspections by the DOL are the exception rather than rule. In the case of a typical complaint by a single employee, the DOL investigator more often than not will contact the employer by telephone, explain the nature of the complaint, and afford the employer a reasonable opportunity to respond. On-site inspections are more likely to occur where the complaint involves an ongoing systemic FMLA violation of a serious nature (e.g., systemic denial of FMLA leave, refusal to return employees to work, discipline or termination of employees).

Where an on-site inspection is conducted, the DOL may simply show up and demand entry to review records and interview employees as part of an FMLA investigation. The DOL is not obligated to make prior arrangements with the employer for a time and place to conduct the on-site inspection, although this is often the practice. School employers would be well advised to plan ahead with counsel regarding the procedures the school will follow in the event a DOL investigator shows up at the facility demanding access to files and employees as part of the investigation of an FMLA complaint. The DOL investigator may understand the need for a short delay for the school to contact counsel before allowing the investigation to proceed, but long delays will likely not be tolerated and may result in obstruction charges.

School employers would be well advised to plan ahead with counsel regarding the procedures the school will follow in the event a DOL investigator shows up at the facility demanding access to files and employees as part of the investigation of an FMLA complaint.

As part of an FMLA investigation, whether routine or initiated by an administrative complaint, a DOL investigator has the right to inspect and copy relevant records maintained by the employer regarding the FMLA.[61] The FMLA records an employer must keep are addressed in Chapter 12, *Record-Keeping Requirements*. The records subject to such an inspection are limited by relevance and reasonableness based on the facts of each case. The DOL is not authorized to simply go on a fishing expedition to look for an FMLA violation. On the other hand, the facts of an FMLA complaint may warrant a very broad inspection of employer records.

The DOL investigator may interview employees, including members of management, as part of the on-site investigation. Employers may, but are not required to, make employees available to the DOL investigator on the premises during work hours. Most employers elect not to make employees, particularly management employees, available to the DOL investigator during work hours. Management employees are viewed as speaking for the employer. As such, most employers want to maintain as much control as possible over the information that is being provided to the DOL investigator by management. Schools would be well advised to have counsel involved with all management communications with the DOL during an FMLA investigation. Most employers do not agree to permit the DOL investigator to interview nonmanagement employees during work hours because it disrupts operations. As a result, most DOL interviews with nonmanagement employees take place off premises and off the clock.

Employers generally have the right to be present during a DOL investigator's interview with a management representative (assuming that the school employer agrees to such interview). Employers generally do not have the right to attend interviews of the complaining party or of nonmanagement employees.

(v) DOL Subpoena Power

The DOL is authorized to subpoena FMLA records and witnesses as part of its investigation (whether routine or prompted by a complaint).[62] This is accomplished by DOL's service of an administrative subpoena on the employer. In the case of records, the DOL subpoena must be limited in scope to what is reasonable and relevant and must describe with sufficient specificity the documents to be provided.[63] The DOL is prohibited from issuing the administrative subpoena arbitrarily or capriciously.[64]

Employers who believe that the administrative subpoena is unreasonable may refuse to comply. In that case, the DOL may seek to enforce the subpoena in the federal courts.[65] The subpoenaed employer is entitled to question the reasonableness of the subpoena before suffering any penalties for refusal to comply, and objections to the subpoena may be raised in an action filed in response to the enforcement action filed in federal court.[66]

If the federal court rules against the employer's challenge to the DOL administrative subpoena, it will issue an order enforcing the subpoena. An employer that refuses to obey an order of a federal court enforcing the DOL's subpoena may be cited for civil contempt.[67] Employers in civil contempt of a federal court can be subject to substantial fines and managers may face imprisonment.

(vi) DOL-Supervised Settlements

The FMLA authorizes the DOL to resolve FMLA complaints in the same manner as it resolves complaints under the FLSA.[68] Under the FLSA, if the DOL supervises a settlement, the employee waives any right to sue the employer for further damages in a private civil action.[69] Where the DOL supervises settlement of an employee's FLMA claim, the settlement is binding on the employee and the employee will be deemed to have waived the right to pursue a claim by way of a private civil action.[70] DOL settlements may be for less than the full amount the employee could have claimed.[71] As will be discussed in the next subsection, given the uncertainties of non-DOL FMLA settlements, the finality gained in DOL-supervised settlements should make this an attractive method for school employers to settle FMLA disputes.

Three factors govern whether the DOL will be considered to have supervised the resolution of an FMLA claim: (1) DOL supervision, (2) resolution of the claim, and (3) acceptance of the DOL-supervised resolution by the employee.[72] Indicia of DOL supervision has been found where the employer and the DOL held meetings and exchanged correspondence, telephone calls, and memos, and the DOL supplied WH-58 release forms.[73] In one case, the court held that the cashing of a check issued pursuant to a DOL-supervised settlement did not constitute acceptance by the employee where the DOL did not send out the release forms.[74] Where the DOL sends out the release forms and the employee cashes the check, the employee has accepted the DOL-supervised settlement, thereby waiving his or her right to sue the employer—even if the employee does not sign the release forms.[75] An employee's private civil action will be dismissed if the employee waived the right to sue for FMLA violations pursuant to a DOL-supervised settlement.[76]

(vii) Civil Actions Brought by the DOL

Where the investigator believes that the FMLA has been violated and the employer refuses to settle, the matter may be referred to the Solicitor of Labor. The Solicitor may initiate a private civil action for damages against the employer in any court of competent jurisdiction.[77] The Solicitor may also seek injunctive relief.[78] If the DOL initiates a civil action on behalf of an employee, the employee is precluded from bringing or maintaining a private civil action for violation of the FMLA unless and until the DOL's suit is dismissed.[79]

The Solicitor must initiate a civil action against an employer within 2 years after the date of the last event constituting the alleged violation, or within 3 years in the case of a willful violation.[80] Any monies recovered by the Solicitor must be held in a special deposit account and be paid directly to each affected employee.[81] After 3 years, if such deposited monies have not been paid out, they are deposited into the Treasury of the United States.[82]

Again, civil actions for FMLA violations have rarely been advanced by the Solicitor of Labor. More commonly, the DOL investigator issues a letter setting forth the investigation findings and notifies the employee of his or her right to initiate a civil action for the employer's alleged violation of the FMLA. At that point, the DOL's participation in the FMLA complaint ends.

(viii) Injunctive Relief

The Secretary of Labor may also seek injunctive relief in the federal courts to (1) restrain violations of the FMLA, including an employer's withholding of payment of wages, salary, employment benefits, or other compensation found by the court to be due to the eligible employee or (2) award such other equitable relief as may be appropriate, including employment, reinstatement, and promotion.[83] Courts give the DOL some, although not unbridled, discretion in requesting injunctive relief.[84] The fact that an employer is currently in compliance with the FMLA is not, alone, sufficient grounds to deny the DOL's request for injunctive relief to prevent future violations.[85]

(ix) Posting Violations

The DOL has developed some special rules governing the imposition and appeal of a civil penalty for failing to post the required FMLA notice. As discussed in Chapter 6, *Notice Requirements*, every covered employer is required to post and keep posted on its premises, in conspicuous places where employees are employed, a notice explaining the Act's provisions and providing information concerning the procedures for filing FMLA complaints with the DOL Wage and Hour Division.[86] An employer that willfully violates the posting requirement may be assessed a civil money penalty not to exceed $100 for each separate offense.[87]

If a DOL representative determines that an employer has committed a willful violation of the posting requirement and the imposition of a civil money penalty for such violation is appropriate, the DOL representative serves a notice of penalty on the employer by certified mail or in person.[88] Where service by certified mail is not accepted, notice will be deemed to have been received on the date of attempted delivery.[89] Where personal service or service by certified mail is not accepted, the DOL may serve the notice by regular mail.[90]

An employer may obtain review of the civil penalty from the Wage and Hour Regional Administrator for the region in which the alleged violation(s) occurred.[91] If the employer does not seek timely review, the notice of the penalty constitutes the final ruling of the Secretary of Labor.[92] That means that the employer has no other means of challenging the civil penalty.

To appeal the civil penalty, an employer must file a petition with the Wage and Hour Regional Administrator for the region in which the alleged violation occurred.[93] The petition must be mailed to the

Regional Administrator within 15 days of the notice of penalty.[94] The petition must be in writing and contain the legal and factual bases for the petition.[95] No particular form of petition is prescribed. A petitioning employer may also request an oral hearing to appeal the civil penalty.[96] If the employer's request for an oral hearing is granted, such appeal will be heard telephonically.[97]

The decision of the Regional Administrator on the civil penalty appeal constitutes the final order of the Secretary of Labor.[98] There is no further avenue of appeal after the final decision of the Regional Administrator.

[2] Private Civil Actions

(i) General Rule

The second avenue of redress available to enforce FMLA rights is by filing a private civil lawsuit against the offending employer. The FMLA, however, is not a model of clarity regarding who has the right to file such private civil actions. Specifically, it is less than clear whether the right to file a civil action is limited to eligible employees or whether others may also sue for FMLA violations.

By its terms, the FMLA permits civil actions "by any one or more employees" for or on behalf of the employees or similarly situated employees of a covered employer in any federal or state court of competent jurisdiction to recover damages or for equitable relief for violation of the FMLA.[99] The term "employee" is defined in the statute and DOL regulations.[100] Applicants, prospective employees, and former employees are not included within the FMLA definition of "employee." FMLA claims may proceed as class actions.[101]

Moreover, the FMLA expressly limits employer monetary and equitable liability for FMLA violations to eligible employees.[102] Several courts have dismissed lawsuits where the individual bringing the suit was not an eligible employee.[103] Because the plaintiff was not an eligible employee within the meaning of the FMLA, another court dismissed an FMLA suit initiated by a union on behalf of its bargaining unit members.[104]

Notwithstanding the statutory language, several courts have permitted lawsuits by nonemployees for violations of the FMLA.[105] These courts relied on the prohibition against employer discrimination of employees and prospective employees contained in the DOL regulations (29 C.F.R. §825.220(a)(2)–(3), (c)).

It is not required that an employee exhaust administrative remedies before initiating a private civil action against a covered employer for violation of the FMLA.[106] Exhaustion of administrative remedies is a concept embedded in other employment laws that requires employees to exhaust available administrative dispute-resolution processes before filing a lawsuit. Although the FMLA permits an aggrieved employee to file an administrative claim, it does not require an employee to do so. As a result, the employee need not file an administrative complaint with the DOL before proceeding to court. An employee may, if he or she desires, file an administrative complaint with the DOL and simultaneously initiate a lawsuit, or dispense with the administrative complaint altogether before initiating a civil action.

Note that an employee may initiate the civil action in a federal or state court. Because the FMLA is a federal law, if, as is often the case, the employee files suit in state court, the employer may be able to "remove" the case (have the case transferred) from state to federal court.[107] Employers frequently seek to remove FMLA suits from state to federal court.

(ii) When Must a Private Civil Action Be Initiated?

A private civil action to enforce FMLA rights must generally be filed within 2 years after the date of the last event constituting the alleged violation.[108] In the case of a "willful" violation, a civil action may be brought within 3 years of the date of the last event constituting the alleged violation.[109] Unfortunately, the FMLA does not provide a standard for determining willfulness.[110] Courts have applied standards for determining willfulness developed for purposes of the FLSA and the ADEA.[111] The standards are similar. Under the ADEA "willful" standard, an employer that intentionally or recklessly violates the FMLA is deemed to have acted willfully. The FLSA standard of willfulness is that the employer either knew its conduct violated the FMLA or showed reckless disregard for compliance with the FMLA. Under either standard, mere negligence on the part of the employer is insufficient to establish willfulness.[112] Failure to file before the expiration of the requisite statute of limitations bars the action or claims as untimely.[113]

(iii) Who Is the Defendant in a Private Civil Action?

A private civil action to recover damages for violation of the FMLA may be brought against an "employer."[114] Who is an FMLA-covered employer is addressed in Chapter 2, *Schools as FMLA-Covered Employers*. All public school employers and certain private sector school employers are covered by the federal FMLA. The Supreme Court has ruled that states can be sued as employers for violation of the FMLA.[115] For purposes of this subsection, it is important to remember that the FMLA defines covered school "employers" to include any person who acts, directly or indirectly, in the interest of an employer to any employee of the employer.[116] That means individual managers and supervisors are "employers" who, in addition to the school, can be sued for FMLA violations.

> Individual managers and supervisors may be sued for monetary damages as FMLA-covered "employers."

The overwhelming majority of courts have concluded that managers or supervisors of private sector employers who violate the FMLA may be individually liable for monetary damages.[117] The courts are split regarding individual liability of managers and supervisors of public agencies including schools. The majority of courts have found in favor of individual liability for public sector managers and supervisors who violate the FMLA.[118] A minority of courts have concluded that individual managers and supervisors of public agency employers are not individually liable for FMLA violations.[119] For a further discussion of this issue, see Chapter 2, *Schools as FMLA-Covered Employers*.

[3] State Law Public Policy Claims Based on FMLA Violations

Employees will sometimes attempt to enforce their FMLA rights indirectly, initiating private civil actions on grounds other than the

FMLA. Frequently, these suits are brought pursuant to other state statutes or common law. Generally, employees do this because of the availability of greater monetary damages than are available under the FMLA. Employers faced with these derivative suits often seek to have them dismissed, arguing that the FMLA provides the exclusive remedy for FMLA violations. Courts have split on the exclusivity of the FMLA as the sole means of enforcing FMLA rights.

> School employers should consult with counsel to determine the availability of indirect enforcement of FMLA claims under state law or common law.

Some courts have found that the FMLA provides the exclusive remedy for claims constituting violations of the FMLA and will dismiss these indirect state law claims.[120] Other courts have permitted such indirect claims to proceed.[121] School employers should consult with counsel to determine the availability of indirect enforcement of FMLA claims under state law or common law. Generally, however, employees must meet the requirements of the FMLA in order to gain the right to maintain an indirect lawsuit for violation of the FMLA. Where an employee, for example, fails to meet the eligibility requirements of the FMLA, an indirect civil action would not be available.[122] Employees who file suit for violations of the federal FMLA will frequently add a separate state public policy claim.

[4] Mandatory Arbitration of FMLA Claims

In addition to the avenues provided by the Act, FMLA rights may also be enforced through the arbitration process. Arbitration is an alternative method of dispute resolution that, in practice, closely resembles a court trial, albeit at a greatly reduced level of formality. The arbitrator is neutral and jointly selected by the parties to hear the complaint. Witnesses testify under oath, and the parties present evidence to support their respective positions. The complex rules of evidence that govern court trials, however, are generally dispensed with. After hearing the evidence and arguments, the arbitrator issues a binding decision.

The arbitration process should be familiar to school administrators with collective bargaining agreements. Arbitration of labor and employment disputes has also made inroads into individual employment contracts outside of the union environment. The increased popularity of arbitration as an alternative to going to court is attributable to the quicker (and therefore cheaper) resolution of employment disputes. In addition, employers prefer arbitration to court litigation because of the perception that arbitrators are less likely than juries to award large judgments. Arbitration as an alternative to court litigation of employment disputes has been given a boost by several decisions of the U.S. Supreme Court.[123]

Whether an employer can compel an employee to arbitrate an FMLA claim in lieu of filing a private lawsuit is a frequently litigated issue. The situation typically arises where an employee subject to an arbitration clause files suit against the employer alleging violation of the FMLA rather than use the arbitration process. The employer moves to dismiss the lawsuit and compel the employee to arbitrate the claim. Whether an employer will be successful in compelling arbitration will initially depend on whether the arbitration clause is contained in an individual employment contract or a collective bargaining agreement. The law is well settled that an agreement to arbitrate FMLA claims contained in an individual employment contract is enforceable and effectively waives the employee's right to sue the employer in court for violation of the FMLA. The law is unsettled as to whether an employee's right to sue an employer in court may be waived by a union in a collective bargaining agreement.

The distinction between individually negotiated waivers of the right to sue an employer for FMLA violations (in favor of arbitration) and those contained in a collective bargaining agreement rests on a divergent line of Supreme Court cases addressing the arbitrability of statutory employment claims.[124] The first line of cases is represented by *Alexander v. Gardner-Denver Co.*, in which the Supreme Court held that an employee who submits a grievance under a nondiscrimination clause in a collective bargaining agreement to arbitration does not forfeit the right to bring a Title VII claim in federal court.[125] Notably, the Court held that "there can be no prospective waiver of an employee's rights under Title VII."[126] In reaching this conclusion, the Court reasoned that an individual's right to be free from discrimination is unlike other rights, such as the right to strike, which may be collectively waived by the union. The Supreme Court has followed the holding of *Gardner-Denver* against the prospective waiver of employee statutory rights in collective bargaining agreements under other statutes—but not the FMLA.[127]

The second line of authority is represented by the decision of the Supreme Court in *Gilmer v. Interstate/Johnson Lane Corp.*[128] In *Gilmer*, the Court held that an age discrimination claim brought under the Age Discrimination in Employment Act of 1967 could be subject to compulsory arbitration pursuant to an arbitration provision contained in an individually negotiated employment contract.[129] The Supreme Court distinguished the situation from that in *Gardner-Denver*, where there was a "tension between the collective representation and individual statutory rights," which was not a concern in *Gilmer*.[130]

Following *Gilmer*, lower courts have focused on the party negotiating the waiver of rights. When the arbitration provision has been negotiated individually by an employee, the courts have found such provisions to be enforceable, thereby precluding the employee from seeking to enforce an FMLA claim in federal court. This is still the law.[131] Because it is settled that individually negotiated employment contracts are capable of waiving an employee's right to file a civil suit for FMLA violations, the focus in this area is on whether a proper waiver of the right to sue the employer has, in fact, occurred.[132] For example, an arbitration provision that required the employee to split costs would be unenforceable if the cost was such that it effectively denied the employee a forum in which to vindicate her statutory rights (a requirement to enforce an arbitration provision).[133]

After *Gardner-Denver*, most courts held that an employer may not compel a bargaining unit employee to arbitrate federal statutory employment claims even though the collective bargaining agreement required arbitration.[134] Only the Fourth Circuit concluded that a collective bargaining agreement requiring arbitration of a union member's statutory discrimination claims was enforceable.[135] Most courts similarly applied *Gardner-Denver* and rejected mandatory arbitration of FMLA claims as required by the terms of a collective bargaining agreement.[136] This relatively clear statement of the law lasted until the Supreme Court's 1998 decision in *Wright v. Universal Maritime Service Corp.*[137]

In *Wright*, the issue before the Supreme Court was whether an employee could be compelled to arbitrate an ADA claim pursuant to the terms of a collective bargaining agreement in lieu of proceeding with a private civil action in court. Although it noted the tension between its earlier holdings in *Gardner-Denver* and *Gilmer*, the court declined to resolve the question of the validity of a union-negotiated waiver. However, the Court proceeded to hold that even if such a clause were enforceable (although the court declined to decide whether it was enforceable), the waiver language must be "clear and unmistakable," which, the court found, was not the case.[138] The court opined that a general arbitration clause governing "all matters under dispute" was not a "clear and unmistakable" waiver of statutory rights because it did not explicitly incorporate the statutory rights to be arbitrated.[139] The court noted that the "clear and unmistakable" standard is not applicable where an individual employee waives his or her own right to a judicial forum in favor of arbitration.[140]

The decision of the Supreme Court in *Wright* injected a degree of uncertainty in the area of the enforceability of union-negotiated waivers of federal statutory claims.[141] Lower courts have split on the meaning of *Wright.* The Fourth Circuit has held that an arbitration clause in a collective bargaining agreement that specifically incorporates claims under the FMLA amounts to a "clear and unmistakable" waiver of the employee's right to a federal forum.[142]

Other courts have pledged varying degrees of allegiance to the *Gardner-Denver* standard to find that the waiver of the right to sue to enforce statutory rights contained in a collective bargaining agreement is not enforceable. Generally, these courts have initially noted that they follow the *Gardner-Denver* rule that collectively bargained waivers of individual statutory forum rights remain unenforceable. These courts nonetheless have then applied the *Wright* "clear and unmistakable" waiver test and found, based on the language of the collective bargaining agreement at issue, the waiver language deficient.[143] One court applied *Gardner-Denver* and declined to address *Wright* in the alternative.[144]

Finally, several courts have disregarded *Gardner-Denver* and decided the case based on whether the clause of the collective bargaining agreement constituted a "clear and unmistakable" waiver as contemplated by *Wright*.[145]

The Second and Fourth Circuits have developed a two-part test to determine whether a waiver is "clear and unmistakable."[146] First, a waiver is sufficiently explicit if the arbitration clause contains a provision whereby employees specifically agree to submit all federal causes of action arising out of their employment to arbitration.[147] Second, if the first test is not satisfied, a waiver may still be sufficiently clear and unmistakable if the collective bargaining agreement contains an explicit incorporation of the statutory antidiscrimination clause and makes unmistakably clear that the discrimination statutes at issue are part of the agreement and that employees will be bound to arbitrate their federal claims.[148] Thus, "if another provision, like a nondiscriminatory clause, makes it unmistakably clear that the discrimination statute at issue is part of the agreement, employees will be bound to arbitrate their federal claims."[149] Courts agree that specific incorporation requires identifying the federal statute by name or citation. Moreover, the collective bargaining agreement should make compliance with the named or cited statute a contractual commitment that is subject to the arbitration clause.[150]

A broad arbitration clause that encompassed "any dispute concerning the interpretation, application, or claimed violation" of the collective bargaining agreement and that did not contain a provision whereby employees explicitly agreed to submit all federal statutory claims to arbitration failed to satisfy these criteria.[151] In another case, a "clear and unmistakable" waiver was found not to exist even though the collective bargaining agreement specifically incorporated the FMLA, because the agreement did not explicitly state that any grievance arising out of a right under the FMLA was subject to arbitration.[152] Another court similarly observed that the combination of a broad arbitration clause, specific mention of the FMLA, and discussion of some of the employees' rights and duties under the FMLA in the collective bargaining agreement did not constitute a "clear and unmistakable" waiver of a judicial forum in favor of arbitration.[153]

A "clear and unmistakable" waiver of FMLA rights was found by one court based on the following language:

> The Company and the Union agree to comply with the Family and Medical Leave Act of 1993 (FMLA) as it may be amended from time to time. The parties further agree that the Company reserves all rights and privileges granted to it under the FMLA.
>
> Any dispute concerning the interpretation or application of the FMLA shall be subject to the terms of the grievance and arbitration procedure, the last step of which is final and binding arbitration.[154]

Schools that are looking to avoid jury trials should, in consultation with counsel, seriously consider including a "clear and unmistakable" waiver of a judicial forum in favor of arbitration in collective bargaining agreements (at least to the extent employees are represented by unions). Schools should review their current agreements to determine whether the language meets the "clear and unmistakable" standard. If not, the school will have to bargain with the union before implementing such a change.

14.04 REMEDIES FOR FLMA VIOLATIONS

The FMLA permits prevailing eligible employees in private litigation to recover monetary damages, equitable relief, and attorneys' fees and costs from employers for harm resulting from FMLA violations. A review of each of these categories follows.

[1] Monetary Damages

The FMLA recognizes five types of monetary damages that are recoverable by a prevailing eligible employee:[155]

- lost wages and salary
- employment benefits
- other compensation
- actual monetary losses (where there are no lost wages, salary, employment benefits, or other compensation)

- interest
- liquidated damages (for willful violations)

Monetary damages are recoverable only if they fit within one of these five categories.

(i) Lost Wages and Salary

The FMLA does not define what constitutes "lost wages and salary." Back pay is the most common form of lost wages or salary. The back pay amount cannot be speculative but must be clearly ascertainable.[156] In calculating the back pay award, the period of time an employee was on unpaid FMLA leave is not included.[157] An employer's back pay liability can be cut off by events subsequent to the FMLA violation. For example, the discharge of an employee for reasons independent of the benefits and protections of the FMLA terminates the requisite continuing employment relationship, including the obligation to pay wages and salary.[158] The same would be true if an employee were laid off due to a reduction in force or was unable to return to work before the conclusion of 12 weeks of FMLA leave. An employer's liability for back wages may also be terminated subsequent to an employer's FMLA violation by a discharged employee's unreasonable rejection of the employer's unconditional offer of reinstatement.[159]

An employer's back pay liability may also be limited where a wrongfully terminated employee fails to mitigate his or her damages. To mitigate damages, an employee wrongfully terminated in violation of the FMLA must exercise reasonable diligence to secure comparable alternative employment during the back pay period (i.e., the period beginning from the termination and ending with the favorable jury verdict).[160] Where an employee fails to mitigate damages, the employer's back pay liability may be reduced or eliminated entirely. The employer bears the burden of proving that the employee failed to exercise such reasonable diligence.[161]

The employer's violation of the FMLA must have caused the employee's lost wages and salary. Where the FMLA violation did not cause the employee to lose wages, monetary damages in the form of back pay is not warranted. For example, in one case an employee quit because the employer allowed medical coverage to lapse during FMLA leave. The employee sued, claiming three weeks of lost wages for the period it took the employee to find another comparable paying job. In finding against an award of monetary damages, the court noted that the employer's FMLA violation (failure to maintain health insurance during FMLA leave) did not cause the employee's lost wages. Rather, the employee's lost wages were due to the employee's independent resignation.[162]

(ii) Employment Benefits

The FMLA defines "employment benefits" to mean all benefits provided or made available to employees by an employer, including group life insurance, health insurance, disability insurance, sick leave, annual leave, educational benefits, and pensions, regardless of whether such benefits are provided by a practice or written policy of an employer or through an employee benefit plan. The term does not, however, include non-employment-related obligations paid by employees through voluntary deductions, such as supplemental insurance.[163] Courts have awarded employees monetary damages for the employer's portion of health plan premiums paid by the employee in order to continue health plan coverage during FMLA leave.[164] Similarly, lost vacation time that an employee was forced to use as a result of the denial of FMLA leave was held to constitute lost employment benefits recoverable as damages for an employer's violation of the FMLA.[165]

(iii) Other Compensation

The FMLA permits eligible employees to recover "other compensation" lost to the employee as a result of the employer's FMLA violation. The term "other compensation" is not, however, defined by the Act or the DOL regulations. Courts have interpreted "other compensation" narrowly, limiting the remedy to economic benefits like wages, salary, or employment benefits resulting or arising out of the employment relationship.[166] Commissions earned on sales while an employee is on FMLA leave have been found to be a form of "other compensation" recoverable as damages for violation of the FMLA.[167] Damages for lost profit sharing pursuant to the company's profit sharing plan have been found recoverable as "other compensation."[168] A stay bonus paid to employees who remained employed and actively working during a transition in company ownership has also been held to be recoverable as "other compensation."

Consequential damages resulting from an FMLA violation that do not arise out of the employment relationship are not recoverable as "other compensation" where the employee is entitled to some back wages, salary, or benefits. For example, out-of-pocket expenses for moving and a job search incurred by an employee terminated in violation of the FMLA were not recoverable as "other compensation" because they did not arise out of the employment relationship.[169] Similarly, child care and parental care costs incurred as a result of an FMLA violation, but that otherwise were not paid for by an employer, were not recoverable as "other compensation" as they did not result from the employment relationship.[170] Courts have also rejected employee claims for emotional distress damages as "other compensation."[171] As addressed in subsection (v) below, child care, parental care, moving, and job-search expenses may be recoverable as actual costs where the employee does not have a claim for lost wages, salary, benefits, or other compensation.

(iv) Punitive and Emotional Distress Damages

The overwhelming majority of courts have held that punitive damages and damages for mental or emotional distress are not recoverable as wages, salary, employment benefits, or other compensation by eligible employees as a result of employer violations of the FMLA.[172] A few courts, however, have opined that employees may recover damages (as other compensation) for the emotional distress they suffered as a result of an employer's violation of the FMLA.[173]

(v) Actual Monetary Losses

Where the employee has not suffered lost wages, salary, employment benefits, or other compensation, an eligible employee is entitled to recover actual monetary losses sustained as a direct result of the employer's violation of the FMLA.[174] The amount of actual monetary losses that are recoverable is capped at a sum equal to 12 weeks of the employee's wages or salary.[175] Again, actual monetary damages are only available where the employee is not claiming lost wages, salary employment benefits, or other compensation.[176]

As an example, the Act cites the expense of providing care to a family member when leave is denied as the type of actual monetary loses that would be recoverable.[177] The claimed actual costs must have been directly caused by the FMLA violation. Actual costs are not recoverable if the employee would have incurred the costs notwithstanding the FMLA violation. For example, one court held that an employee was not entitled to damages reflecting out-of-pocket medical expenses incurred when the employee's health benefits were cut off as a result of the employer's wrongful denial of unpaid FMLA leave because the employee, who did not pay her share of health benefits premiums during leave, would have lost health insurance coverage even if she had been granted FMLA leave.[178]

(vi) Interest

The FMLA mandates that interest at the prevailing rate be added to any award of monetary damages.[179] The method courts use to calculate the prevailing rate of interest varies.[180]

(vii) Liquidated Damages

Employees may also be entitled to recover "liquidated damages" equal to the sum of the damages for lost wages, salary, employment benefits, or other compensation, or actual monetary losses, and interest.[181] Liquidated damages effectively double the size of the monetary award.[182] Liquidated damages are not available in the absence of monetary loss resulting from a violation of the FMLA.[183] Absent the establishment of a good faith and reasonable belief defense (discussed below), employers are liable for liquidated damages in every case.[184] There is a strong presumption in favor of liquidated damages.[185]

The FMLA includes a good faith exception that relieves employers who have engaged in acts prohibited by the FMLA from liability for

An award of liquidated or double damages is the norm in FMLA cases involving monetary damages, unless the employer can prove that it acted in good faith and had an objective belief that its conduct did not violate the FMLA.

liquidated damages. Pursuant to that exception, employers may avoid liquidated damages where they can establish that the prohibited act or omission was in good faith and that they had reasonable grounds for believing that the act or omission was not a violation of the FMLA.[186] An employer must establish both that it acted in good faith and that it had reasonable grounds for believing that its actions did not violate the FMLA in order to perfect its right to this exception.[187] If the employer satisfies this good faith and reasonable belief requirement, a court, in its discretion, may reduce the employer's liability to the amount of actual damages.[188] Of course, an employer that does establish the good faith and reasonable belief defense is still liable for monetary damages resulting from its violation of the FMLA.[189]

The FMLA does not define what constitutes "good faith" or "reasonable grounds for believing" that the employer's conduct did not violate the FMLA.[190] Courts have looked to case law interpreting a similar liquidated damages provision of the FLSA for guidance regarding liquidated damages under the FMLA.[191] Good faith has both an objective and a subjective component. It requires both that the employer subjectively believed it acted in good faith and that such belief was objectively reasonable.[192] To be found to have acted in good faith, an employer must demonstrate that it took proactive steps to ascertain the dictates of the law and then acted to comply with those requirements.[193] An employer's claim of ignorance of the requirements of the FMLA does not establish that it acted in good faith.[194] It is not enough to show that the violation was not purposeful.[195] Nor is good faith demonstrated by the absence of complaints on the part of employees or conformity with industry-wide practice.[196] A misunderstanding of the Act's requirements, without more, was found insufficient to apply the good faith exception to liquidated damages.[197]

Courts have cited a variety of factors in finding that an employer acted in good faith and had reasonable grounds for believing that its actions were not in violation of the Act and denying an award of liquidated damages. For example, one court favorably cited an employer's attempt to review the DOL FMLA regulations and opinion letters as evidence that the employer acted in good faith and reasonably.[198]

(viii) Special School Exception to Liquidated Damages

The FMLA provides a special exception to liability for liquidated damages for local educational agencies and private elementary and secondary schools.[199] If a local educational agency or a private elementary or secondary school that has violated the FMLA proves to the satisfaction of the court that the agency, school, or department had reasonable grounds for believing that the underlying act or omission was not a violation of the Act, such court may, in its discretion, reduce the amount of liability to monetary damages (i.e., backpay or actual monetary losses).[200]

The FMLA does not explain the meaning of "reasonable grounds for believing" that the underlying act or omission was not a violation of the Act. The legislative history of this provision, however, provides some insight into the exception. According to the legislative history, factors indicating that a covered school had reasonable grounds for believing that its actions or omission did not violate the FMLA include acting on the advice of counsel, following the terms of a collective bargaining agreement, complying with valid state and local laws, and complying with other federal laws (e.g., the Individuals with Disabilities Education Act, section 504 of the Rehabilitation Act of 1973, or Title VII of the Civil Rights Act of 1964) or regulations or policies promulgated by the DOL.[201] These factors would also appear relevant for purposes of the general good faith and reasonable grounds for believing exception to liability for liquidated damages.

Note that the standard differs from the general exception for liquidated damages, which requires both good faith and reasonable grounds for believing that conduct did not violate the FMLA. The special school rule exception does not require good faith, only reasonable grounds for believing.

[2] Equitable Relief

Eligible employees may obtain equitable relief against an employer who engages in acts prohibited by the FMLA.[202] Equitable relief, including injunctive relief, requires an employer to do something (e.g., rehire or promote an employee) or to stop doing something that it is currently doing (e.g., to stop applying a policy that violates the FMLA).[203] One court has held that equitable relief is not available where the employee has not suffered any actual damages as a result of the employer's violation of the FMLA.[204]

The legislative history indicates that the FMLA was intended to provide employees with the right to pursue all varieties of equitable relief, including injunctive relief.[205] The Act cites as examples of equitable relief employment, reinstatement, and promotion.[206] Another common form of equitable relief involves "front pay." Front pay compensates the employee for the value of future lost wages and salary.[207] Although reinstatement is generally preferred, the equitable remedy of front pay is appropriate when reinstatement is not feasible or practicable.[208] It is well established that employers may be liable to eligible employees for front pay for violations of the FMLA.[209]

As an equitable remedy, the calculation and award of front pay is at the discretion of the court, not the jury.[210] The court may, however, make its determination of whether to award front pay with the assistance of an advisory jury.[211] To qualify for front pay, an employee must have been diligent in seeking comparable employment, and under no circumstances may an award of front pay be based on speculation.[212] A request for front pay may be denied if the court finds that the back pay award combined with liquidated damages is sufficient to make the plaintiff whole.[213]

[3] Attorneys' Fees and Costs

The FMLA permits a court to award a prevailing employee reasonable attorneys' fees, reasonable expert witness fees, and other costs of the action against the defendant employer.[214] The award of attorneys' fees and costs is in addition to any award of damages or equitable relief. According to the legislative history, this provision was modeled after section 316(b) of the FLSA, 29 U.S.C. § 216(b).[215] The award of attorneys' fees and costs is mandatory where violation of the FMLA is established.[216] The court, however, retains broad discretion in determining the actual amount of the award.[217]

An employee who fails to establish a violation of the FMLA is not entitled to attorneys' fees.[218] The FMLA violation, moreover, must result in actual harm to the employee. Statutory damages are a prerequisite to an award of interest, liquidated damages, and attorneys' fees.[219] Absent actual harm, mere technical violations of the Act will not support a claim for attorneys' fees and costs.[220] On the other hand, attorneys' fees have been awarded where an employee won only modest damages as a result of an employer's violation of the FMLA. In one case, an employee who won $720 in damages for the employer's violation of the FMLA was awarded $129,663.60 in attorneys' fees.[221] Another court awarded a prevailing plaintiff $391,279.78 in attorneys' fees alone.[222] In many FMLA cases, attorneys' fees will often equal or exceed the damage award.

In one case, an employee who won $720 in damages for the employer's violation of the FMLA was awarded $129,663.60 in attorneys' fees.

The FMLA does not authorize an award of attorneys' fees to a prevailing employer, only to a successful plaintiff-employee.[223] Attorneys' fees may be awarded to prevailing defendant-employers, however, by operation of the rules governing litigation in the federal and state courts, such as 28 U.S.C. § 1927.[224]

Employers who have been found to have violated the FMLA are also liable for reasonable costs to the prevailing plaintiff.[225] In federal court, by operation of Rule 54(d) of the Federal Rules of Civil Procedure, courts have awarded costs in FMLA cases to the prevailing party, whether the plaintiff-employee or the defendant-employer.[226] As in the case of attorney's fees, the award of costs to a prevailing party is mandatory.[227] Trial courts, however, possess wide discretion in determining whether the expenses claimed by the prevailing party are actually reimbursable costs.[228] Costs that a prevailing party may recover include fees for court conferences, court reporter costs, photocopying expenses, transcript fees, filing fees, and fees for service of the summons and subpoenas.[229]

The FMLA provides for the recovery of expert witness fees.[230] Expert witness fees have been found to be exempt from the witness reimbursement restrictions of Rule 54(d) of the Federal Rules of Civil Procedure and 28 U.S.C. § 1920, including the $40 per day cap.[231] That means that employers may be required to pay the full cost of expert witness fees rather than the normally capped rate at which witness are reimbursed pursuant to federal or state law.

14.05 FMLA LITIGATION ISSUES

[1] Burden of Proof

Courts have generally recognized two theories of recovery for prohibited conduct in violation of the FMLA: (1) interference or entitlement claims and (2) retaliation and discrimination.[232] These theories have been found to be broad, interrelated, and nonexclusive.[233] The lines between the two categories are not hard and fast.[234] The two types of claims can be asserted simultaneously.[235] There are, however, important differences between the two types claims.

(i) Interference or Entitlement Claims

The entitlement or interference theory is based on the FMLA's creation of substantive rights.[236] The theory arises from the provisions of 29 U.S.C. § 2615(a)(1), which makes it unlawful "for an employer to interfere with, restrain, or deny the exercise of or the attempt to exercise, any right provided in this subchapter."[237] An employer may be found to have interfered with an employee's substantive FMLA rights in violation of § 2615(a)(1) regardless of the employer's intent.[238] That is, an employer may be found to have violated the FMLA by interfering with an employee's prescriptive rights even if the employer did not intend to do so. Intent is simply not a necessary element of an FMLA interference claim. The burden of proof for interference claims has been described as being a much simpler standard than for FMLA discrimination-retaliation claims.[239]

To prevail on an FMLA interference/entitlement claim, an employee need only establish by a preponderance of the evidence that the employee was entitled to the FMLA right being claimed.[240] Courts have come up with different formulations for an employee's prima facie case of interference with FMLA rights depending on the deprivation of rights at issue. At the most basic level, an employee must establish (1) entitlement to the FMLA right, (2) that the employee experienced an adverse employment action, and (3) a causal connection between the protected activity and the adverse action.[241] An employee who fails to establish all three elements will not have a viable interference claim. For example, an employee who has failed to give timely and adequate notice of the need for FMLA leave has failed to establish an interference claim because he or she cannot establish entitlement to FMLA leave.[242] Similarly, if the employee cannot establish a causal connection between the exercise of FMLA rights (e.g., requesting leave) and the adverse employment action, the claim will fail. Where, for example, an employer's investigation of an employee's conduct or performance began prior to the request for FMLA leave, courts have been less willing to find interference where an employer terminated the employee after the leave request.[243]

(ii) Retaliation and Discrimination Claims

Retaliation and discrimination claims are the second FMLA theory of recovery. This theory is grounded in 29 U.S.C. § 2615(a)(2), which provides that "it shall be unlawful for any employer to discharge or in any other manner discriminate against any individual for opposing any practice made unlawful by this subchapter."[244] This theory has been characterized as proscriptive in nature, as it is based on the provisions of the FMLA that proscribe or prohibit employer discriminatory conduct.[245]

The intent of the employer matters in FMLA discrimination or retaliation claims. Accordingly, most courts analyze FMLA retaliation and discrimination claims pursuant to the burden of proof scheme initially developed by the Supreme Court for Title VII cases in *McDon-*

nell Douglas v. Burdine, 411 U.S. 792 (1973), and *Price Waterhouse v. Hopkins*, 490 U.S. 228 (1989).[246] The Ninth Circuit has reserved judgment on whether the *McDonnell Douglas* proof scheme applies, preferring instead to apply a modified *McDonnell Douglas* approach.[247] Under this approach, an employee alleging that he or she was discriminated against in violation of § 2615(a)(2) may establish a violation with either direct or indirect evidence.[248] In the absence of direct evidence of the employer's intent to retaliate or discriminate, courts apply the *McDonnell Douglas* burden-shifting formula.[249]

Generally, under the *McDonnell Douglas* burden-shifting framework, courts apply a three-prong test. To establish a prima facie case of retaliation or discrimination, a plaintiff must demonstrate that (1) he or she engaged in protected activity, (2) he or she suffered an adverse employment action, and (3) a causal connection exists between the protected activity and the adverse action.[250] If the employee establishes his or her prima facie case, the burden of proof shifts to the employer to articulate some legitimate, nondiscriminatory reason for the action taken against the employee that is sufficient to raise a genuine issue of fact as to whether the employer discriminated against the employee.[251] If the employer's evidence creates a genuine issue of fact, the presumption of discrimination drops from the case, and the employee retains the ultimate burden of showing that the employer's stated reason for taking the adverse action was in fact pretext for retaliating against the employee for engaging in FMLA-protected activity.[252]

The courts are split regarding the appropriate proof scheme that applies where negative consequences result from an employee's use of FMLA leave. The split results from the absence of clear language in the statute prohibiting discrimination for an employee's use of FMLA leave. The antidiscrimination provisions of § 2615(a)(2) and § 2615(b) prohibit discrimination and retaliation for opposing unlawful practices or participating in FMLA inquiries. The Second, Sixth, and Tenth Circuits have held that an employee's claim that he or she was subjected to adverse consequences as a result of using FMLA leave is analyzed pursuant to the retaliation theory of § 2615(a)(2).[253] The First, Third, Seventh, Ninth, and Eleventh Circuits apply the burden of proof standard used for interference claims to analyze discrimination and retaliation claims arising out of the use of FMLA leave.[254]

[2] Honest Belief Defense

A growing number of courts have recognized a defense to a claim of unlawful discrimination or retaliation based on the employer's honest, albeit mistaken, belief that the action it took was for legitimate, nondiscriminatory reasons.[255] Where the "honest belief" defense is established, the employee's FMLA discrimination or retaliation claim fails even if the employer, in fact, violated the FMLA. The "honest belief" defense negates the requisite retaliatory or discriminatory intent necessary for an employee to establish a § 2615(a)(2) discrimination claim. The defense would not, however, be available for an FMLA interference claim, because the employer's intent is not relevant to establishing an interference violation.

14.06 STATE FAMILY AND MEDICAL LEAVE LAWS

Most, but not all, state family and medical leave laws identify prohibited acts and provide a mechanism for enforcement. States with a general family and medical leave law may also address the remedies available for violations. Of the state laws that address prohibited acts, most closely resemble the prohibited acts provisions of the federal FMLA. The enforcement alternatives and remedies available for violation of state family and medical leave laws, however, frequently differ from those provided under the federal FMLA. The DOL does not enforce state family or medical leave laws, and states may not enforce the FMLA.[256]

The California Family Rights Act makes it an unlawful employment practice for an employer to refuse to grant a request by an eligible employee to take up to 12 workweeks of leave in any 12-month period for family care and medical leave.[257] It is an unlawful employment practice for an employer to refuse to hire, or to discharge, fine, suspend, expel, or discriminate against any individual because of any of the following: (1) an individual's exercise of the right to family care and medical leave or (2) an individual's giving information or testimony as to his or her own family care and medical leave, or another person's family care and medical leave, in any inquiry or proceeding related to rights guaranteed under this section.[258] The California Family Rights Act does not address how the Act is enforced or remedies available to employees for its violation.

Colorado's family and medical leave provisions for state employees provide that the use of family or medical leave cannot be considered in evaluating performance. If the performance plan includes an attendance factor, any time the employee was on family or medical leave cannot be considered.[259] On the other hand, Colorado law also recognizes that family and medical leave does not prohibit any adverse action that would have otherwise occurred had the leave not been taken.[260] Colorado's family and medical leave law does not address enforcement or remedies available for violation.

The Maine Family Medical Leave Act makes it unlawful for an employer to (1) interfere with, restrain, or deny the exercise of or the attempt to exercise any right provided by the Act; (2) discharge, fine, suspend, expel, discipline, or in any other manner discriminate against any employee for exercising any right provided by the Act; or (3) discharge, fine, suspend, expel, discipline, or in any other manner discriminate against any employee for opposing any practice made unlawful by the Act.[261] Maine allows an employee to bring a civil action in an appropriate court against any employer to enforce the Maine Family Medical Leave Act. The court may enjoin any act or practice that violates or may violate the Act and may order any other equitable relief that is necessary and appropriate to redress the violation or to enforce the Act. The court may also order the employer to pay as liquidated damages $100 to the employee for each day the violation continues.[262]

NOTES

1. 29 U.S.C. § 2615(a)(1); 29 C.F.R. § 825.220(a)(1).
2. 29 U.S.C. § 2615(a)(2); 29 C.F.R. § 825.220(a)(2).
3. 29 U.S.C. § 2615(b); 29 C.F.R. § 825.220(a)(3).
4. *Sherrod v. Philadelphia Gas Works*, No. 02-2153, 2003 U.S. App. LEXIS 1428, at **9 (3d Cir. Jan. 29, 2003).
5. 29 C.F.R. § 825.220(b).

6. See 29 U.S.C. § 158(a)(1) (providing that it is an unfair labor practice for an employer "to interfere with, restrain, or coerce employees in the exercise of the rights guaranteed" by section 7 of the NLRA; *Bachelder v. America West Airlines, Inc.*, 259 F.3d 1112, 1123 (9th Cir. 2001).

7. 29 U.S.C. § 2615(a)(1); 29 C.F.R. § 825.220(a)(1); see also *Liu v. Amway Corp.*, 347 F.3d 1125, 1133 (9th Cir. 2003).

8. See *Regan v. Natural Resources Group, Inc.*, 345 F. Supp. 2d 1000, 1010 (D. Minn. 2004).

9. See *Geromanos v. Columbia University*, 322 F. Supp. 2d 420, 428 (S.D.N.Y. 2004).

10. See *Hoge v. Honda of America Manufacturing, Inc.*, 384 F.3d 238 (6th Cir. 2004).

11. See *Wilson v. Lemington Home for the Aged*, 159 F. Supp. 2d 186, 194 (W.D. Pa. 2001); *Goodwin-Haulmark v. Menninger Clinic, Inc.*, 76 F. Supp. 2d 1235, 1241 (D. Kan. 1999).

12. See *Conoshenti v. Public Service Electric & Gas Co.*, 364 F.3d 135, 141 (3d Cir. 2004); *Geromanos*, 322 F. Supp. 2d at 428.

13. Compare *Bones v. Honeywell International Inc.*, 366 F. 3d 869, 877 (10th Cir. 2004) (explaining that whether employee properly notified employer of need for FMLA leave is separate from analysis of anti-interference claim), with *Cavin v. Honda of America Manufacturing, Inc.*, 346 F. 3d 713, 719–22 (6th Cir. 2003) (asserting that employee must provide timely and adequate notice of need for FMLA leave to establish viable anti-interference claim).

14. *Liu v. Amway Corp.*, 347 F. 3d 1125, 1133 (9th Cir. 2003); *Sabbrese v. Lowe's Home Centers, Inc.*, 320 F. Supp. 2d 311, 326, 331 (W.D. Pa. 2004).

15. *Mardis v. Central National Bank & Trust of Enid*, No. 98-6056, 1999 U.S. App. LEXIS 7261 (10th Cir. Apr. 15, 1999).

16. See *Keller v. Putnam Fiduciary Trust Co.*, 238 F.3d 5, 10 (1st Cir. 2000) (asserting that not every comment about problems created by the use of FMLA leave can fairly be treated as an adverse employment action violative of the FMLA); *Dittle v. U.S. Postal Service*, No. 04-146 (PAM/RLE), 2005 U.S. Dist. LEXIS 1487, at *23 (D. Minn. Feb. 2, 2005); *Alifano v. Merck & Co*, 175 F. Supp. 2d 792 (E.D. Pa. 2001).

17. See *Williams v. Shenango, Inc.*, 986 F. Supp. 309, 320–21 (W.D. Pa. 1997).

18. *Shtab v. Greate Bay Hotel and Casino, Inc.*, 173 F. Supp. 2d 255, 267–68 (D.N.J. 2001).

19. 29 C.F.R. § 825.220(c); see also *Conoshenti v. Public Service Electric & Gas Co.*, 364 F. 3d 135, 141 (3d Cir. 2004); *Geromanos v Columbia University*, 322 F. Supp. 2d 420, 428 (S.D.N.Y. 2004).

20. *Hodgens v. General Dynamics Corp.*, 144 F.3d 151, 160 n.4 (1st Cir. 1998); *Dodgens v. Kent Manufacturing Co.*, 955 F. Supp. 560, 565 (D.S.C. 1997).

21. See *Hurlbert v. St. Mary's Health Care Systems, Inc.*, 439 F.3d 1286, 1297 (11th Cir. 2006); *Chaffin v. John H. Carter Co.*, 179 F.3d 316, 319 (5th Cir. 1999); *King v. Preferred Technology Group*, 166 F.3d 887, 891–92 (7th Cir. 1999); *Hodgens*, 144 F.3d at 160; *Morgan v. Hilti, Inc.*, 108 F.3d 1319, 1323 (10th Cir. 1997).

22. See *Bachelder v. America West Airlines, Inc.*, 259 F. 3d 1112, 1124–25 (9th Cir. 2001); *Rankin v. Seagate Technologies, Inc.*, 246 F.3d 1145, 1148 (8th Cir. 2001).

23. 29 C.F.R. § 825.220(c).

24. *Id.*; DOL WH FMLA Advisory Opinion No. 31 (Mar. 21, 1994); DOL WH FMLA Advisory Opinion No. 2 (Aug. 16, 1993).

25. DOL WH FMLA Advisory Opinion No. 100 (Jan. 12, 1999).

26. DOL WH FMLA Advisory Opinion No. 31 (Mar. 21, 1994).

27. 29 U.S.C. § 2615(a)(2).

28. 29 C.F.R. § 825.220(a)(2).

29. 29 C.F.R. § 825.800 ("person" defined).

30. S. Rep. No. 103-3, at 34 (1993), as reprinted in 1993 U.S.C.C.A.N. 3, 36.

31. 29 C.F.R. § 825.220(e); see also S. Rep. No. 103-3, at 34, as reprinted in 1993 U.S.C.C.A.N. 3, 36.

32. 29 C.F.R. § 825.220(e); Comments on Regulations Implementing the Family and Medical Leave Act of 1993 (§ 825.220), 60 Fed. Reg. 2180, 2218 (Jan. 6, 1995).

33. *Hoffman v. Professional Med Team*, 394 F.3d 414 (6th Cir. 2005).

34. See *Jeremy v. Northwest Ohio Development Center*, 33 F. Supp. 2d 635, 639 n.4 n.4 (N.D. Ohio 1999), *aff'd*, 210 F.3d 372 (6th Cir. 2000).

35. See *Humenny v. Genex Corp., Inc.*, 390 F.3d 901, 905 (6th Cir. 2004); *Walker v. Elmore County Board of Education*, 379 F.3d 1249, 1253 (11th Cir. 2004).

36. 29 U.S.C. § 2615(b)(1)–(3); 29 C.F.R. § 825.220(a)(3).

37. 29 C.F.R. § 825.220(d).

38. 29 U.S.C. § 2652(b); 29 C.F.R. § 825. 220(d).

39. 29 C.F.R. § 825.220(d).

40. *Id.*

41. *Faris v. Williams WPC-1, Inc.*, 332 F.3d 316, 320–22 (5th Cir. 2003).

42. 415 F.3d 364 (4th Cir. 2005).

43. *Id.* at 368.

44. 29 U.S.C. § 2617(b); 29 C.F.R. § 825.400(a)(1).

45. 29 U.S.C. § 2617(a); 29 C.F.R. § 825.400(a)(2).

46. 29 U.S.C. §§ 2616, 2617(b).

47. S. Rep. No. 103-3, at 35 (1993), as reprinted in 1993 U.S.C.C.A.N. 3, 37.

48. Comments on Regulations Implementing the Family and Medical Leave Act of 1993 (§ 825.400), 60 Fed. Reg. 2180, 2228 (Jan. 6, 1995) ("The statute places no requirement that an employee exhaust administrative remedies before being authorized to file private suit.").

49. *Wilson v. Dallas Independent School District*, No. CA3: 97-CV-0281-BC, 1998 U.S. Dist. LEXIS 1415, at *11 (N.D. Tex. Jan. 30, 1998).

50. 29 C.F.R. § 825.400(a)(1).

51. 29 C.F.R. §§ 825.203(a), 825.800 ("person" defined).

52. Comments on Regulations Implementing the Family and Medical Leave Act of 1993 (§ 825.400), 60 Fed. Reg. 2180, 2228 (Jan. 6, 1995).

53. 29 U.S.C. § 2611(3) (citing the FLSA as codified at 29 U.S.C. § 203(e)); 29 C.F.R. § 825.800 ("employee" defined).

54. 29 C.F.R. § 825.401(b).

55. *Id.*

56. 29 U.S.C. §§ 2617(b)(3), (c)(1)–(2).

57. 29 C.F.R. § 825.401(c).

58. 29 C.F.R. § 825.401(a).

59. 29 U.S.C. § 2616(a).

60. *Id.*

61. 29 U.S.C. §§ 2616(a), 2717(b)(1); 29 C.F.R. § 825.500(b).

62. 29 U.S.C. § 2616(c).

63. *Donovan v. Lone Steer, Inc.*, 464 U.S. 408, 415 (1984).

64. See *Newmark & Co. v. Wirtz*, 330 F.2d 576, 578 (2d Cir. 1964).

65. *Oklahoma Press Publishing Co. v. Walling*, 327 U.S. 186, 200 (1946).

66. *Donovan*, 464 U.S. at 415.

67. See *Durking v. Fisher*, 204 F.3d 930 (7th Cir. 1953), *cert. denied*, 346 U.S. 897 (1953).

68. 29 U.S.C. § 2617.

69. 29 U.S.C. § 216(c).

70. *Mion v. Aftermarket Tool & Equipment Group*, 990 F. Supp. 535, 540–41 (W.D. Mich. 1997).

71. *Id.*

72. *Id.*

73. See *Cuevas v. Monroe Street City Club*, 752 F. Supp. 1405, 1416 (N.D. Ill. 1990); *Torreblanca v. Naas Foods, Inc.*, No. F78-163, 1980 U.S. Dist. LEXIS 13893, at *9 (N.D. Ind. Feb. 25, 1980).

74. *Mion*, 990 F. Supp. at 540–41.

75. *Id.*

76. *Id.*

77. 29 U.S.C. § 2617(b)(2), (e).

78. 29 U.S.C. § 2617(d).

79. 29 U.S.C. § 2617(a)(4).

80. 29 U.S.C. § 2617(c)(1)–(3).

81. 29 U.S.C. § 2617(b)(3).

82. *Id.*

83. 29 U.S.C. § 2617(d)(1)–(2).

84. *Reich v. Midwest Platic Engineering, Inc.*, 934 F. Supp. 266, 268 (W.D. Mich. 1996), *aff'd without opinion*, 113 F.3d 1235 (6th Cir. 1997).

85. *Id.*

86. 29 C.F.R. § 825.300(a).

87. 29 C.F.R. § 825.300(b).

88. 29 C.F.R. § 825.402.

89. *Id.*

90. *Id.*

91. 29 C.F.R. § 825.403(a).

92. *Id.*

93. *Id.*

94. 29 C.F.R. § 825.403(b).

95. *Id.*

96. *Id.*

97. *Id.*

98. 29 C.F.R. § 825.403(c).

99. 29 U.S.C. § 2617(a)(2).

100. 29 U.S.C. § 2611(3); 29 C.F.R. § 825. 800 ("employee" defined).

101. *Bond v. Abbott Laboratories*, 188 F.3d 506, *reported in full in* 1999 U.S. App. LEXIS 22242 (6th Cir. 1999) (allowing case to proceed as class action on whether employer's attendance control policy violated FMLA); *Cox v. Autozone, Inc.*, 990 F. Supp. 1369, 1373 n.7 (M.D. Ala. 1998) (asserting that class actions are possible under the FMLA), *aff'd, McGregor v. Autozone, Inc.*, 180 F.3d 1305 (11th Cir. 1999).

102. 29 U.S.C. § 2617(a)(1)(A)–(B).

103. See *Humenny v. Genex Corp., Inc.*, 390 F.3d 901, 904 (6th Cir. 2004); *Walker v. Elmore County Board of Education*, 379 F.3d 1249, 1253 (11th Cir. 2004).

104. *New York Metro Area Postal Union v. Potter*, No. 00 Civ. 8538 (LTS)(RLE), 2003 U.S. Dist. LEXIS 4904 (S.D.N.Y. Mar. 31, 2003).

105. *Smith v. Bellsouth Telecommunications, Inc.*, 273 F.3d 1303, 1307–14 (11th Cir. 2001); *Duckworth v. Pratt & Whitney, Inc.*, 152 F.3d 1, 10–11 (1st Cir. 1998).

106. *Ogborn v. United Food and Commercial Workers, Local No. 881*, No. 98 C 4623, 2000 U.S. Dist. LEXIS 14092, at *31 (N.D. Ill. Sept. 25, 2000), *aff'd*, 305 F.3d 763 (7th Cir. 2002); *Krohn v. Forsting*, 11 F. Supp. 2d 1082, 1085 (E.D. Mo. 1998).

107. *Eastus v. Blue Bell Creameries, L.P.*, 97 F.3d 100 (5th Cir. 1996); *Ladner v. Alexander and Alexander, Inc.*, 879 F. Supp. 598 (W.D. La. 1995).

108. 29 U.S.C. § 2617(c).

109. 29 U.S.C. § 2617(c)(1).

110. *Williams v. Schuller international, Inc.*, No. 00-3614, 2002 U.S. App. LEXIS 2071, at **6 (6th Cir. Feb. 5, 2002); *Packard v. Continental Airlines, Inc.*, No. 01-4013, 2001 U.S. App. LEXIS 26984, at **5 (10th Cir. 2001), *cert. denied*, 536 U.S. 923 (2002).

111. See *Hoffman v. Professional Med Team*, 394 F.3d 414, 418 (6th Cir. 2005) (applying ADEA willful standard); *Williams*, 2002 U.S. App. LEXIS 2071, at **6 (applying FLSA reckless disregard standard); *Packard*, 2001 U.S. App. LEXIS 26984, at **5 (applying FLSA reckless disregard standard).

112. *Packard*, 2001 U.S. App. LEXIS 26984, at **5 ("willful" generally understood to mean conduct that is not merely negligent).

113. *Melvin v. Knoll, Inc.*, No. 01-1012, 2001 U.S. App. LEXIS 18588, at **5 (6th Cir. Aug. 9, 2001); *Porter v. NYU School of Law*, No. 99 Civ. 4693 (TPG), 2003 U.S. Dist. LEXIS 14674, at *21 (S.D.N.Y. Aug. 25, 2003), *aff'd*, 392 F.3d 530 (2d Cir. 2004).

114. 29 U.S.C. § 2617(a)(1)–(2).

115. *Nevada Department of Human Resources v. Hibbs*, 538 U.S. 721 (2003).

116. 29 U.S.C. § 2611(4)(A)(ii)(I); 29 C.F.R. § 825.104(d).

117. See *Longstreth v. Copple*, 101 F. Supp. 2d 776, 778–79 (N.D. Iowa 2000); *Buser v. Southern Food Service, Inc.*, 73 F. Supp. 2d 556, 561 (N.D. Iowa 2000); *Bryant v. Delbar Products, Inc.*, 18 F. Supp. 799, 807–08 (M.D. Tenn. 1998).

118. See *Hibbs v. HDM Department of Resources*, 273 F.3d 844, 871–72 (9th Cir. 2001), *aff'd on other grounds*, *Nevada Department of Human Resources v. Hibbs*, 538 U.S. 721 (2003); *Luder v. Endicott*, 253 F.3d 1020, 1022 (7th Cir. 2001); *Darby v. Bratch*, 287 F.3d 673, 680–81 (8th Cir. 2000).

119. See *Mitchell v. Chapman*, 343 F.3d 811, 826–33 (6th Cir. 2003), *cert. denied*, 542 U.S. 937 (2004); *Lizzi v. Alexander*, 255 F.3d 128, 136–38 (4th

Cir. 2001), *aff'd*, 534 U.S. 1081 (2002); *Wascura v. Carver*, 169 F.3d 683, 685–87 (11th Cir. 1999).

120. *Jakischa v. Central Parcel Express*, No. 03-3976, 2004 U.S. App. LEXIS 18965, at **10 (6th Cir. Sept. 1, 2004) (citing decision of Ohio Supreme Court finding that FMLA provides exclusive remedy for violations thereof and concluding therefore that wrongful discharge claim could not be supported in violation of public policy); *Sallis v. Prime Acceptance Corp.*, No. 05 C 1525, 2005 U.S. Dist. LEXIS 16693, at *9 (N.D. Ill. Aug. 10, 2005) (asserting that tort of retaliatory discharge under Illinois law cannot be based on FMLA claim); *Patterson v. Toyota Motor Manufacturing, Indiana, Inc.*, No. 3:05-cv-003 RLY-WGH, 2005 U.S. Dist. LEXIS 11398, at *4 (S.D. Ind. June 6, 2005) (holding that Indiana public policy exception to at-will employment does not permit a suit based on FMLA, which has adequate remedies); *Carver v. Electronic Data Systems, Corp.*, No. 1:03-cv-1033-DFH-VSS, 2005 U.S. Dist. LEXIS 3692, at *24 (S.D. Ind. Feb. 11, 2005) (same); *Handel v. Belevedere USA Corp.*, No. 00 C 50420, 2001 U.S. Dist. LEXIS 17357, at *12 (N.D. Ill. 2001) (asserting that the FMLA is exclusive remedy for violations thereof); *Callozzo v. Office Depot, Inc.*, No. 97 C 5308, 1998 U.S. Dist. LEXIS 2706, at *7 (N.D. Ill. 1998) (noting that action for retaliatory discharge under Illinois State law not recognized for violations of the FMLA); *Desrochers v. Hilton Hotels Corp.*, 28 F. Supp. 2d 693, 695 (D. Mass. 1998); *O'Hara v. Mount Vernon Board of Education*, 16 F. Supp. 2d 868, 893–94 (S.D. Ohio 1998); *Joliffe v. Mitchell*, 971 F. Supp. 1039, 1044–45 (W.D. Va. 1997).

121. See *Conoshenti v. Public Service Electric & Gas Co.*, 364 F.3d 135, 149 n.13 (3d Cir. 2004) (citing New Jersey case that found that FMLA can be basis for wrongful discharge of at-will employee in violation of clear mandate of public policy); *Liu v. Amway Corp.*, 347 F.3d 1125, 1138 (9th Cir. 2003) (asserting that FMLA can be basis of public policy claim under California law); *Danfelt v. Board of County Commissioners of Washington County*, 998 F. Supp. 606, 611 (D. Md. 1998).

122. *Humenny v. Genex Corp., Inc.*, 390 F.3d 901, 907 (6th Cir. 2004) (applying Michigan common law); *Moreau v. Air France*, 343 F.3d 1179, 1191 (9th Cir. 2003) (applying California common law).

123. See *Wright v. Universal Maritime Service Corp.*, 525 U.S. 70 (1998); *Gilmer v. Interstate/Johnson Lane Corp.*, 500 U.S. 20 (1991); *Alexander v. Gardner-Denver Co.*, 415 U.S. 36 (1974).

124. See, e.g., *Wright*, 525 U.S. at 75 (1998); *Hess v. Anheuser-Busch Companies, Inc.*, No. 2:01-CV-533, 2002 U.S. Dist. LEXIS 27362 (S.D. Ohio Mar. 27, 2002).

125. *Alexander v. Gardner-Denver Co.*, 415 U.S. 36 (1974); see also *Wright*, 525 U.S. at 75; *Neppl v. Signature Flight Support Corp.*, 234 F. Supp. 2d 1016 (D. Minn. 2002); *Hess*, 2002 U.S. Dist. LEXIS 27362, at *9.

126. *Gardner-Denver*, 415 U.S. at 51.

127. *Wright*, 525 U.S. at 76 (citing *McDonald v. West Branch*, 466 U.S. 284 (1984) (§ 1983 claim)); *Barrentine v. Arkansas-Best Freight System, Inc.*, 450 U.S. 728 (1981) (FLSA claim).

128. 500 U.S. 20 (1991).

129. *Gilmer*, 500 U.S. at 34–35; see also *Wright*, 525 U.S. at 76.

130. *Gilmer*, 500 U.S. at 35; *Wright*, 525 U.S. at 80–81.

131. *O'Neil v. Hilton Head Hospital*, 115 F.3d 272, 275 (4th Cir. 1997); *Darrah v. Friendly Ice Cream Corp.*, 328 F. Supp. 2d 319, 323 (N.D.N.Y. 2004); *Mandel v. SCI Illinois Services, Inc.*, No. 02 C 8979, 2003 U.S. Dist. LEXIS 13408, at *4–*6 (N.D. Ill. Aug. 1, 2003); *Blocker v. Providian Life & Health*, No. 99-2201, 2001 U.S. Dist. LEXIS 400, at *6 (E.D. Pa. Jan. 2, 2001); *Jones v. Fujitsu Network Communications, Inc.*, 81 F. Supp. 2d 688 (N.D. Tex. 1999); *O'Hara v. Mt. Vernon Board of Education*, 16 F. Supp. 2d 868, 881 (S.D. Ohio 1998) ("In the context of a private employment agreement, it is not surprising to find decisions following *Gilmer* holding that FMLA claims covered by an arbitration agreement must be submitted to arbitration and not brought in court."); *Shaw v. Walsh Services, Inc.*, No. 3:96-CV-1772-D, 1997 U.S. Dist. LEXIS 23464 (N.D. Tex. Jan. 22, 1997); *Satarino v. A.G. Edwards & Sons, Inc.*, 941 F. Supp. 609, 613 (N.D. Tex. 1996); *Hoffman v. Aaron Kamhi, Inc.*, 927 F. Supp. 640 (S.D.N.Y. 1996).

132. See *Kunkel v. D.R. Horton-Texas, Ltd.*, No. 3:05-CV-0381-D, 2005 U.S. Dist. LEXIS 15860 (N.D. Tex. Aug. 3, 2005); *Darrah*, 328 F. Supp. 2d 319 (holding that arbitration provision did not clearly cover FMLA claims); *Parker v. Hahnemann University Hospital*, No. 00-4173(JBS), 2001 U.S. Dist. LEXIS 10661 (D.N.J. June 15, 2001) (holding that defective waiver did not preclude employee's FMLA civil suit); *Fujitsu*, 81 F. Supp. 2d 688, 691 (N.D. Tex. 1999) (holding fee-spitting portion of arbitration policy unenforceable); *Satarino*, 941 F. Supp. at 611–13; *Hoffman*, 927 F. Supp. 640, 642–45 (S.D.N.Y. 1996) (holding that arbitration provision not sufficiently broad to encompass FMLA claim).

133. *Baugher v. Dekko Heating Technologies*, 202 F. Supp. 2d 847, 851 (N.D. Ind. 2002).

134. *Rogers v. New York University*, 220 F.3d 73, 75 & n.1 (2d Cir. 2000), *cert. denied*, 531 U.S. 1036 (2000).

135. *Id.* (citing *Austin v. Owens-Brockway Glass Container, Inc.*, 78 F.3d 875, 880–86 (4th Cir. 1996)). The Fourth Circuit covers North Carolina, South Carolina, Virginia, West Virginia, and Maryland.

136. See *O'Hara v. Mt. Vernon Board of Education*, 16 F. Supp. 2d 868, 882–83 (S.D. Ohio 1998); *McGinnis v. Wonder Chemical Co.*, No. 95-4384, 1995 U.S. Dist. LEXIS 18909, at *5 n.1 (E.D. Pa. Dec. 21, 1995). But see *Smith v. CPC Foodservice*, 955 F. Supp. 84, 87 (N.D. Ill. 1997) (enforcing arbitration of FMLA claim contained in a collective bargaining agreement). The decision was overruled on reconsideration based on a subsequent adverse decision of the Seventh Circuit. *Smith v. CPC Foodservice*, 1997 U.S. Dist. LEXIS 9041 (N.D. Ill. June 23, 1997).

137. 525 U.S. 70 (1998).

138. *Wright*, 525 U.S. at 80; *Kelly v. Classic Restaurants Corp.*, No. 01 cv 09345 (GBD), 2003 U.S. Dist. LEXIS 15211, at *9 (S.D.N.Y. Sept. 2, 2003).

139. *Wright*, 525 U.S. at 80.

140. *Jones v. Fujitsu Network Communications, Inc.*, 81 F. Supp. 2d 688, 691 (N.D. Tex. 1999).

141. *Hess v. Anheuser-Busch Companies, Inc.*, No. 2:01-CV-533, 2002 U.S. Dist. LEXIS 27362, at *19 (S.D. Ohio Mar. 27, 2002).

142. *Wilkie v. CNA Holdings, Inc.*, No. 01-1119, 2001 U.S. App. LEXIS 8440, at **3 (4th Cir. May 4, 2001) (citing *Carson v. Giant Food, Inc.*, 175 F.3d 325, 332 (4th Cir. 1999)).

143. See *Rogers v. New York University*, 220 F.3d 73, 75 (2d Cir. 2000), *cert. denied*, 531 U.S. 1036 (2000); *Kelly*, 2003 U.S. Dist. LEXIS 15211, at *6–*13; *Ozolins v. Northwood-Kensett Community School District*, 40 F. Supp. 2d 1055, 1066–67 (N.D. Iowa 1999).

144. *Neppl v. Signature Flight Support Corp.*, 234 F. Supp. 2d 1016, 1023–25 (D. Minn. 2002) (asserting that *Gilmer* and *Wright* did not reverse the *Gardner-Denver* line of cases and those cases remain binding precedent).

145. See *Mitchell v. Chapman*, 343 F.3d 811, 824 (6th Cir. 2003), *cert. denied*, 542 U.S. 937 (2004); *Dearinger v. Racing Association of Central Iowa*, No. 4:03-cv-40284, 2004 U.S. Dist. LEXIS 19543, at *11–*12 (S.D. Iowa Sept. 24, 2004); *Hess*, 2002 U.S. Dist. LEXIS 27362, at *17 (declining to apply *Wright* test even though waiver was clear and unmistakable and holding that *Gardner-Denver* remains good law).

146. *Neppl*, 234 F. Supp. 2d at 1023–25; *Pichon*, 2001 U.S. Dist. LEXIS 7379.

147. *Rogers*, 220 F.3d at 76.

148. *Id.*

149. *Id.*

150. *Id.*

151. *Id.*; *Kelly v. Classic Restaurants Corp.*, No. 01 cv 09345 (GBD), 2003 U.S. Dist. LEXIS 15211, at *11–*13(S.D.N.Y. Sept. 2, 2003); *Bonilla v. Small Assemblies Co.*, No. 99 C 6675, 2001 U.S. Dist. LEXIS 7342, at *11–*16(N.D. Ill. May 31, 2001) (finding that grievances limited to terms of collective bargaining agreement and did not extend to statutory claims).

152. *Dearinger v. Racing Association of Central Iowa*, No. 4:03-cv-40284, 2004 U.S. Dist. LEXIS 19543, at *13 (S.D. Iowa Sept. 24, 2004).

153. *Neppl v. Signature Flight Support Corp.*, 234 F. Supp. 2d 1016, 1025 n.13 (D. Minn. 2002), *vacated on other grounds*, 2002 U.S. App. LEXIS 6286 (5th Cir. 2002).

154. *Hess v. Anheuser-Busch Companies, Inc.*, No. 2:01-CV-533, 2002 U.S. Dist. LEXIS 27362, at *6 (S.D. Ohio Mar. 27, 2002).

155. 29 U.S.C. § 2617(a)(1)(A).

156. *Thorson v. Gemini, Inc.,* 205 F.3d 370, 384 (8th Cir. 2000) (rejecting employee's challenge to back pack award as insufficient because it did not include overtime and noting that employee's overtime claim was speculative), *cert. denied*, 531 U.S. 871 (2000).

157. *Barrileaux v. Thayer Lodging Group, Inc.*, No. 97-3252 E/5, 1998 U.S. Dist. LEXIS 14597 (E.D. La. Sept. 11, 1998).

158. *Lapham v. Vanguard Cellular Systems, Inc.*, 102 F. Supp. 2d 266, 270 (M.D Pa. 2000); *Hite v. Biomet, Inc.*, 53 F. Supp. 2d 1013, 1025–26 (N.D. Ind. 1999).

159. *Barrileaux*, 1998 U.S. Dist. LEXIS 14597, at *7–*9.

160. *Taylor v. Invacare Corp.*, Nos. 01-3824, 01-3827, 2003 U.S. App. LEXIS 10318, at **18–**20 (6th Cir. May 21, 2003); *Nichols v. Ashland Hospital Corp.*, 251 F.3d 496, 503 (4th Cir. 2001); *Thorson v. Gemini, Inc.*, 205 F.3d 370, 384 (8th Cir. 2000), *cert. denied*, 531 U.S. 871 (2000).

161. *Snow v. Health South Corp.*, No. IPOO-0151 C-M/S, 2001 U.S. Dist. LEXIS 5534, at *76–*81 (S.D. Ind. March 21, 2001).

162. *Tornberg v. Business Interlink Services, Inc.*, 237 F. Supp. 2d 778, 789 (E.D. Mich. 2002).

163. 29 U.S.C. § 2611(5); 29 C.F.R. § 825. 800 ("employment benefits" defined).

164. *Herman v. Princeton City School*, No. 1-C-96-358, 1997 U.S. Dist. LEXIS 22250, at *7 (S.D. Ohio Sept. 23, 1997).

165. *Carlsen v. Green Thumb, Inc.*, No. 01-2076 (JRT/RLE), 2004 U.S. Dist. LEXIS 12497, at *13 (D. Minn. May 21, 2004).

166. See *Nero v. Industrial Molding Corp.*, 167 F.3d 921, 930 (5th Cir. 1999). See generally Kelly N. Honohan, Note, *Remedying the Liability Limitation under the Family and Medical Leave Act*, 70 B.U. L. Rev. 1043 (1999).

167. *Estes v. Meridian One Corp.*, No. 99-2662, 2001 U.S. App. LEXIS 4443, at **13 (4th Cir. 2001).

168. *Thorson v. Gemini, Inc.*, 205 F 3d 370, 384–85 (8th Cir. 2000), *cert. denied*, 531 U.S. 871 (2000).

169. *Nero*, 167 F 3d at 930.

170. *Barrileaux v. Thayer Lodging Group, Inc.*, No. 97-3252 E/5, 1998 U.S. Dist. LEXIS 14597, at *6 (E.D. La. Sept. 11, 1998).

171. *Lloyd v. Wyoming Valley Health Care System, Inc.*, 994 F. Supp. 288, 291 (M.D. Pa. 1998).

172. See *Montgomery v. State of Maryland*, 266 F.3d 334, 341 (4th Cir. 2001), *vacated and remanded on other grounds*, 535 U.S. 1075 (2002); *Graham v. State Farm Mutual Insurance Co.*, 193 F.3d 1274, 1284 (11th Cir. 1999); *Nero*, 167 F.3d at 930; *Coleman v. Potomac Electric Power Co.*, 281 F. Supp. 2d 250, 254 (D.D.C. 2003); *Rogers v. AC Humko Corp.*, 56 F. Supp. 2d 972, 979 (W.D. Tenn. 1999).

173. See *Duty v. Norton-Alcoa Proppants*, 293 F.3d 481, 496 (8th Cir. 2002); *Billings v. Cape Cod Child Development Program, Inc.*, 270 F. Supp. 2d 175 n.1 (D. Mass. July 15, 2003); *Beyer v. Elkay Manufacturing Co.*, No. 97 C 50067, 1997 U.S. Dist. LEXIS 14459, at *9 (N.D. Ill. Sept. 19, 1997).

174. 29 U.S.C. § 2617(a)(1)(A)(i)(II).

175. *Id.*

176. *Barrileaux v. Thayer Lodging Group, Inc.*, No. 97-3252 E/5, 1998 U.S. Dist. LEXIS 14597, at *4 (E.D. La. Sept. 11, 1998).

177. 29 U.S.C. § 2617(a)(1)(A)(i)(II).

178. *Ammons-Lewis v. Metropolitan Water Reclamation District of Greater Chicago*, No. 03 C 0885, 2004 U.S. Dist. LEXIS 21917, at *27 (N.D. Ill. Nov. 1, 2004).

179. 29 U.S.C. § 2617(a)(1)(A)(i)(II); *Brenlla v. LaSorsa Buick Pontiac Chevrolet, Inc.*, No. 00-Civ. 5207 (JCF), 2002 U.S. Dist. LEXIS 9358, at *37–*38 (S.D.N.Y. May 28, 2002).

180. See *Rice v. Sunrise Express, Inc.*, 237 F. Supp. 2d 962, 969 (N.D. Ind. 2002) (using prime rate to calculate interest on monetary damages); *Brenlla*, 2002 U.S. Dist. LEXIS 9358, at *38 (calculating interest based on rate governing awards for postjudgment interest in 28 U.S.C. § 1961).

181. 29 U.S.C. § 2617(a)(1)(A)(ii), (b)(2); 29 C.F.R. § 825.400(c).

182. *Smith v. Diffee Ford-Lincoln-Mercury, Inc.*, 298 F.3d 955, 964 (10th Cir. 2002).

183. *Tornberg v. Business Interlink Services, Inc.*, 237 F. Supp. 2d 778, 789 (E.D. Mich. 2002).

184. *Nero v. Industrial Molding Corp.*, 167 F.3d 921, 930 (5th Cir. 1999).

185. *Palma v. Pharmedica Communications, Inc.*, No. 3:00CV1128 (HBF), 2003 U.S. Dist. LEXIS 21227, at *2–*3 (D. Conn. Sept. 30, 2003).

186. 29 U.S.C. § 2617(a)(1)(A)(iii); 29 C.F.R. § 825.400(c).

187. *Taylor v. Invacare Corp.*, Nos. 01-3824, 01-3827, 2003 U.S. App. LEXIS 10318, at **11–**12 (6th Cir. May 21, 2003).

188. 29 U.S.C. § 2617(a)(1)(A)(iii).

189. *Bachelder v. America West Airlines, Inc.*, 259 F.3d 1112, 1130 (9th Cir. 2001).

190. *Nero v. Industrial Molding Corp.*, 167 F.3d 921, 928 (5th Cir. 1999).

191. *Id.*; *Frizzell v. Southwest Motor Freight*, 154 F.3d 641, 644 (6th Cir. 1998) (noting that the FMLA legislative history indicates that FMLA remedial provisions parallel those of the FLSA).

192. *Morris v. VCW, Inc.*, No. 95-07370CV-W-3-6, 1996 U.S. Dist. LEXIS 19201, at *13 (W.D. Mo. Dec. 26, 1996).

193. *Palma v. Pharmedica Communications, Inc.*, No. 3:00CV1128 (HBF), 2003 U.S. Dist. LEXIS 21227, at *7 (D. Conn. Sept. 30, 2003).

194. *Chandler v. Specialty Tires of America (Tennessee), Inc.*, 283 F.3d 818, 827 (6th Cir. 2002); *Palma*, 2003 U.S. Dist. LEXIS 21227, at *7–*13; *Miller v. G.B. Sales & Service, Inc.*, No. 02-70758, 2003 U.S. Dist. LEXIS 19450, at *7–*12 (E.D. Mich. Sept. 29, 2003); *Morris*, 1996 U.S. Dist. LEXIS 19201, at *10.

195. *Nero*, 167 F.3d at 928 ("good faith" is not the same as "willful"); *Palma*, 2003 U.S. Dist. LEXIS 21227, at *8–*13.

196. *Palma*, 2003 U.S. Dist. LEXIS 21227, at *8–*13.

197. *Morris*, 1996 U.S. Dist. LEXIS 19201, at *10.

198. *Thorson* v. *Gemini, Inc.*, 96 F. Supp. 2d 882 (N. D. Iowa 1999), *aff'd*, 205 F.3d 370 (8th Cir. 2000) (finding that the employer acted in good faith when it fired employee for excess absenteeism due to minor ulcers and gastritis as FMLA was only six months old at the time of termination, employer made active effort to learn law and comply with it, and employer's mistake about the law was only determined when the Secretary of Labor issued an advisory opinion during pendency of employee's appeal).

199. 29 U.S.C. § 2618(f).

200. *Id.*

201. S. Rep. No. 103-3, at 37 (1993), as reprinted in 1993 U.S.C.C.A.N. 3, 39; see also 29 U.S.C. § 2618(b).

202. 29 U.S.C. § 2617(a)(1)(B).

203. *Walker v. UPS, Inc.*, 240 F.3d 1268, 1277 (10th Cir. 2001); *Herman v. Princeton City School*, No. 1-C-96-358, 1997 U.S. Dist. LEXIS 22250 (S.D. Ohio Sept. 23, 1997).

204. *Walker v. UPS*, 240 F.3d at 1277.

205. S. Rep. No. 103-3, at 36, as reprinted in 1993 U.S.C.C.A.N.3, 38.

206. 29 U.S.C. § 2617(a)(1)(B).

207. *Smith v. Diffee Ford-Lincoln-Mercury, Inc.*, 298 F.3d 955, 964 (10th Cir. 2002); *Palma v. Pharmedica Communications, Inc.*, No. 3:00CV1128 (HBF), 2003 U.S. Dist. LEXIS 21227, at *15–*20 (D. Conn. Sept. 30, 2003).

208. *McCoy v. Orleans Parish School Board*, No. 02-2510 Section "R" (3), 2004 U.S. Dist. LEXIS 6843, at *6 (E.D. La. Apr. 19, 2004); *Palma*, 2003 U.S. Dist. LEXIS 21227, at *21.

209. *Diffee Ford-Lincoln Mercury*, 298 F.3d at 964; *Nichols v. Ashland Hospital Corp.*, 251 F.3d 496, 503–04 (4th Cir. 2001); *Thorson v. Gemini, Inc.*, 205 F.3d 370, 384 (8th Cir.), *cert. denied*, 531 U.S. 871 (2000).

210. *Taylor v. Invacare Corp.*, Nos. 01-3824, 01-3827, 2003 U.S. App. LEXIS 10318, at **19 (6th Cir. May 21, 2003); *Diffee Ford-Lincoln Mercury*, 298 F.3d at 964; *Nichols*, 251 F.3d at 503–04 (4th Cir. 2001); *Thorson*, 205 F.3d at 384.

211. *Passauer v. Quest Diagnostics, Inc.*, No. CCB-03-159, 2004 U.S. Dist. LEXIS 6966 (D. Md. Apr. 22, 2004).

212. *Thorson*, 205 F.3d at 384; *Palma*, 2003 U.S. Dist. LEXIS 21227.

213. *Palma*, 2003 U.S. Dist. LEXIS 21227, at *8–*12.

214. 29 U.S.C. §§ 2617(a)(1)(B)(3), 2617(b)(2); 29 C.F.R. § 825.400(c).

215. S. Rep. No. 103-3, at 36 (1993), as reprinted in 1993 U.S.C.C.A.N. 3, 38.

216. *Estes v. Meridian One Corp.*, No. 99-2662, 2001 U.S. App. LEXIS 4443, at **9–**10 (4th Cir. 2001); *Bond v. Abbott Laboratories*, 188 F.3d 506, *reported in full in* 1999 U.S. App. LEXIS 22242, at *12 (6th Cir. 1999); *Sherry v. Protection, Inc.*, 14 F. Supp. 2d 1055, 1057 (N.D. Ill. 1998).

217. *Estes*, 2001 U.S. App. LEXIS 4443, at **9.

218. *Bond*, 188 F.3d 506, *reported in full in* 1999 U.S. App. LEXIS 22242, at *12.

219. *Coleman v. Potomac Electric Power Co.*, 281 F. Supp. 2d 250, 254 (D.D.C. 2003).

220. *Bond*, 188 F.3d 506, *reported in full in* 1999 U.S. App. LEXIS 22242, at *12.

221. *Rice v. Sunrise Express, Inc.*, 237 F. Supp. 2d 962, 971–78 (N.D. Ind. 2002).

222. *Mora v. Chem-Tronics, Inc.*, No. 97-CV-0851-J (JFS), 1999 U.S. Dist. LEXIS 10752 (S.D. Cal. 1999).

223. *Billings v. Cape Cod Child Development. Program, Inc.*, 270 F. Supp. 2d 175 (D. Mass. July 15, 2003).

224. See *Id.*

225. 29 U.S.C. § 2617(a)(3).

226. See *Ogborn v. United Food and Commercial Workers, Local No. 881*, 305 F.3d 763, 769–70 (7th Cir. 2002); *Billings*, 270 F. Supp. 2d 175.

227. S. Rep. No. 103-3, at 36 (1993), as reprinted in 1993 U.S.C.C.A.N. 3, 38 ("[T]he award of attorney's fees under the FLSA is unconditional. A court has no discretion to deny fees to a prevailing plaintiff; its discretion extends only to the amount allowed.")

228. *Rice v. Sunrise Express, Inc.*, 237 F. Supp. 2d 962, 979 (N.D. Ind. 2002).

229. See *Id.*

230. 29 U.S.C. § 2617(a)(3).

231. See *Brenlla v. LaSorsa Buick Pontiac Chevrolet, Inc.*, No. 00-Civ. 5207 (JCF), 2002 U.S. Dist. LEXIS 9358, at *48 (S.D.N.Y. May 28, 2002) (awarding $2,000 expert witness fee); *Shepard v. Honda of America Manufacturing, Inc.*, 160 F. Supp. 2d 860, 875–76 (S.D. Ohio 2001) (awarding $3,122.50 in expert fees)

232. See *Hoge v. Honda of America Manufacturing, Inc.*, 384 F.3d 238, 244 (6th Cir. 2004); *Walker v. Elmore County Board of Education*, 379 F.3d 1249, 1251 (11th Cir. 2004); *Liu v. Amway Corp.*, 347 F.3d 1125 (9th Cir. 2003); *Smith v. Diffee Ford-Lincoln-Mercury, Inc.*, 298 F 3d 955, 960 (10th Cir. 2002); *King v. Preferred Technical Group*, 166 F.3d 887, 891 (7th Cir. 1999); *Hodgens v. General Dynamics Corp.*, 144 F.3d 151, 159–60 (1st Cir. 1998).

233. *Diffee Ford-Lincoln-Mercury*, 298 F.3d at 960; *Bachelder v. America West Airlines, Inc.*, 259 F.3d 1112, 1122 (9th Cir. 2001).

234. *Dillaway v. Ferrante*, No. 02-715 (JRT/JSM), 2003 U.S. Dist. LEXIS 23468 (D. Minn. Dec. 9, 2003).

235. *Ash v. Aronov Homes, Inc.*, 354 F. Supp. 2d 1251, 1264 (M.D. Ala. 2004).

236. *Smith v. Diffee Ford-Lincoln-Mercury, Inc.*, 298 F.3d 955, 960 (10th Cir. 2002).

237. *Hoffman v. Professional Med Team*, 394 F.3d 414, 415 (6th Cir. 2005); *Hoge v. Honda of America Manufacturing, Inc.*, 384 F.3d 238, 244 (6th Cir. 2004); *Potenza v. City of New York*, 365 F.3d 165, 167 (2d Cir. 2004); *Diffee Ford-Lincoln-Mercury*, 298 F.3d at 960.

238. *Professional Med Team*, 394 F.3d at 415; *Hoge*, 384 F.3d at 244; *Potenza*, 365 F.3d at 167; *Diffee Ford-Lincoln-Mercury*, 298 F.3d at 960; *Strickland v. Water Works and Sewer Board*, 239 F.3d 1199, 1206–07 (11th Cir. 2001); *King v. Preferred Technical Group*, 166 F.3d 887, 891 (7th Cir. 1999); *Hodgens v. General Dynamics Corp.*, 144 F.3d 151, 159–60 (1st Cir. 1998).

239. *Zsenyuk v. City of Carson*, No. 03-15746, 2004 U.S. App. LEXIS 10192, at **3 (9th Cir. May 21, 2004).

240. *Professional Med Team*, 394 F.3d at 415; *Hoge*, 384 F.3d at 244; *Diffee Ford-Lincoln-Mercury*, 298 F.3d at 960; *Bachelder v. America West Airlines, Inc.*, 259 F.3d 1112, 1122 (9th Cir. 2001); *Diaz v. Ft. Wayne Foundry Corp.*, 131 F.3d 711, 713 (7th Cir. 1997).

241. *Hulbert v. St. Mary's Health Care System, Inc.*, 439 F.3d 1286, 1297 (11th Cir. 2006); *Dry v. Boeing Co.*, No. 01-3294, 2004 U.S. App. LEXIS 2953, at **10 (10th Cir. Feb. 19, 2004); *Strickland*, 239 F.3d at 1206–07.

242. See *Cagle v. FinishMaster, Inc.*, No. 1:03-cv-0265-JDL-WTL, 2004 U.S. Dist. LEXIS 26714, at *30–*32 (S.D. Ind. Dec. 23, 2004).

243. See *Zsenyuk*, 2004 U.S. App. LEXIS 10192, at **4–**5; *Cagle*, 2004 U.S. Dist. LEXIS 26714, at *35 (opining that sequence of events was "fatal" to employee's interference claim where decision to terminate employee was made before initial request for FMLA leave was made).

244. *Hoffman v. Professional Med Team*, 394 F.3d 414, 420 (6th Cir. 2005); *Dry*, 2004 U.S. App. LEXIS 2953, at **9 (10th Cir. Feb. 19, 2004).

245. *Hoge*, 384 F.3d at 244; *Shaeffer v. County of Chatham*, 337 F. Supp. 2d 709, 726 (M.D.N.C. 2004); *McCoy v. Orleans Parish School Board*, No. 02-2510 Section "R" (3), 2004 U.S. Dist. LEXIS 6843, at *8 (E.D. La. Apr. 19, 2004).

246. See *LePore v. LanVision Systems, Inc.*, No. 03-3619, 2004 U.S. App. LEXIS 21742, at **9 (3d Cir. Oct. 19, 2004); *Slaughter-Cooper v. Kelsey Seybold Medical Group, P.A.*, 379 F.3d 285, 291 n.13 (5th Cir. 2004); *Potenza v. City of New York*, 365 F.3d 165, 167 (2d Cir. 2004); *Strickland*, 239 F.3d at 1206–07; *Doebele v. Spring/United Management Co.*, 342 F.3d 1117, 1135 (10th Cir. 2003); *King v. Preferred Technical Group*, 166 F.3d 887, 891 (7th Cir. 1999); *Hodgens v. General Dynamics Corp.*, 144 F.3d 151, 159–60 (1st Cir. 1998).

247. See *Liu v. Amway Corp.*, 347 F.3d 1125, 1133 (9th Cir. 2003).

248. *Buie v. Quad/Graphics, Inc.*, 366 F.3d 496, 503 (7th Cir. 2004); *Skrjanc v. Great Lakes Power Service Co.*, 272 F.3d 309, 315 (6th Cir. 2001); *Bila v. Radio Shack Corp.*, No. 03-10177-BC, 2004 U.S. Dist. LEXIS 24649, at *27 (E.D. Mich. Nov. 23, 2004); *Schrieber v. Chicago Mercantile*

Exchange, Inc., No. 03 C 8568, 2004 U.S. Dist. LEXIS 23108, at *9 (N.D. Ill. Nov. 14, 2004).

249. See *Spurlock v. Peterbilt Motors Co., Inc.*, No. 01-6544, 2003 U.S. App. LEXIS 3185, at **4 (6th Cir. Feb. 19, 2003); *Smith v. Memorial Hospital Corp.*, 302 F.3d 827, 832 (8th Cir. 2002); *Nichols v. Ashland Hospital Corp.*, 251 F.3d 496, 502 (4th Cir. 2001); *Hunt v. Rapides Healthcare Sytems, LLC*, 277 F.3d 757, 768 (5th Cir. 2001); *Strickland*, 239 F.3d at 1206–07; *King*, 166 F.3d at 891; *Hodgens*, 144 F.3d at 159–60.

250. *LePore*, 2004 U.S. App. LEXIS 21742, at **9; *Doebele v. Spring/United Management Co.*, 342 F.3d 1117, 1135 (10th Cir. 2003); *Strickland*, 239 F.3d at 1206–07; *King*, 166 F.3d at 891.

251. *McDonnell Douglas*, 411 U.S. at 802; *Smith v. BellSouth Telecommunications, Inc.*, 273 F.3d 1303, 1314 (11th Cir. 2001); *King*, 166 F.3d at 891.

252. *Texas Department of Community Affairs v. Burdine*, 450 U.S. 248, 252–53 (1981); *King*, 166 F.3d at 891; *Hodgens*, 144 F.3d at 159–60.

253. *Conoshenti v. Public Service Electric & Gas Co.*, 364 F.3d 135, 141 (3d Cir. 2004); *Potenza v. City of New York*, 365 F.3d 165, 167 (2d Cir. 2004); *Arban v. West Publishing Corp.*, 345 F. 3d 390, 401 (6th Cir. 2003); *Smith v. Diffee Ford-Lincoln-Mercury, Inc.*, 298 F.3d 955, 960 (10th Cir. 2002).

254. *Conoshenti*, 364 F.3d at 141; *Strickland*, 239 F.3d at 1206–07; *Bachelder v. America West Airlines, Inc.*, 259 F.3d 1112, 1123 (9th Cir. 2001); *King*, 166 F.3d at 891; *Hodgens*, 144 F.3d at 159–60.

255. See *Hoffman v. Professional Med Team*, 394 F.3d 414 (6th Cir. 2005); *Slaughter-Cooper v. Kelsey Seybold Medical Group, P.A.*, 379 F.3d 285, 291 n.13 (5th Cir. 2004); *Medley v. Polk Co.*, 260 F. 3d 1202, 1207–08 (10th Cir. 2001); *Kariotis v. Navistar International Transportation Corp.*, 131 F 3d 672, 680–81 (7th Cir. 1997).

256. 29 C.F.R. § 825. 701(a).

257. Cal. Govt. Code § 12945.2(a).

258. Cal. Govt. Code § 12945.2(l)(1)–(2).

259. 4 Colo. Code Regs. § 801-5-36.

260. 4 Colo. Code Regs. § 801-5-35.

261. Me. Rev. Stat. Ann. tit. 26, § 847.

262. Me. Rev. Stat. Ann. tit. 26, § 848.

APPENDIX A

FMLA Poster

Your Rights under the Family and Medical Leave Act of 1993

FMLA requires covered employers to provide up to 12 weeks of unpaid, job-protected leave to "eligible" employees for certain family and medical reasons. Employees are eligible if they have worked for their employer for at least one year, and for 1,250 hours over the previous 12 months, and if there are at least 50 employees within 75 miles. The FMLA permits employees to take leave on an intermittent basis or to work a reduced schedule under certain circumstances.

Reasons for Taking Leave:

Unpaid leave must be granted for *any* of the following reasons:

- to care for the employee's child after birth, or placement for adoption or foster care;
- to care for the employee's spouse, son or daughter, or parent who has a serious health condition; or
- for a serious health condition that makes the employee unable to perform the employee's job.

At the employee's or employer's option, certain kinds of *paid* leave may be substituted for unpaid leave.

Advance Notice and Medical Certification:

The employee may be required to provide advance leave notice and medical certification. Taking of leave may be denied if requirements are not met.

- The employee ordinarily must provide 30 days advance notice when the leave is "foreseeable."
- An employer may require medical certification to support a request for leave because of a serious health condition, and may require second or third opinions (at the employer's expense) and a fitness for duty report to return to work.

Job Benefits and Protection:

- For the duration of FMLA leave, the employer must maintain the employee's health coverage under any "group health plan."
- Upon return from FMLA leave, most employees must be restored to their original or equivalent positions with equivalent pay, benefits, and other employment terms.
- The use of FMLA leave cannot result in the loss of any employment benefit that accrued prior to the start of an employee's leave.

Unlawful Acts by Employers:

FMLA makes it unlawful for any employer to:

- interfere with, restrain, or deny the exercise of any right provided under FMLA:
- discharge or discriminate against any person for opposing any practice made unlawful by FMLA or for involvement in any proceeding under or relating to FMLA.

Enforcement:

- The U.S. Department of Labor is authorized to investigate and resolve complaints of violations.
- An eligible employee may bring a civil action against an employer for violations.

FMLA does not affect any Federal or State law prohibiting discrimination, or supersede any State or local law or collective bargaining agreement which provides greater family or medical leave rights.

For Additional Information:

If you have access to the Internet visit our FMLA website: **http://www.dol.gov/esa/whd/fmla.** To locate your nearest Wage-Hour Office, telephone our Wage-Hour toll-free information and help line at 1-866-4USWAGE (1-866-487-9243): a customer service representative is available to assist you with referral information from 8am to 5pm **in your time zone**; or log onto our Home Page at **http://www.wagehour.dol.gov.**

U.S. Department of Labor
Employment Standards Administration
Wage and Hour Division
Washington, D.C. 20210

WH Publication 1420
Revised August 2001

*U.S. GOVERNMENT PRINTING OFFICE 2001-476-344/40051

APPENDIX B

FMLA-USERRA Memos

U.S. Department of Labor

Assistant Secretary for
Veteran's Employment and Training
Washington D.C. 20210

JUL 22 2002

MEMORANDUM FOR:	**REGIONAL SOLICITORS; VETERANS' EMPLOYMENT AND TRAINING SERVICE REGIONAL ADMINISTRATORS AND DIRECTORS; WAGE AND HOUR DIVISION REGIONAL ADMINISTRATORS AND DISTRICT DIRECTORS**
FROM:	**EUGENE SCALIA** **Solicitor of Labor**
	FREDERICO JUARBE JR. **Assistant Secretary** **Veterans' Employment and Training**
	TAMMY D. MCCUTCHEN **Administrator** **Wage and Hour Division**
SUBJECT:	**Protection of Uniformed Service Members' Rights to Family and Medical Leave**

The purpose of this memorandum is to advise staff of the three agencies regarding the rights of reemployed members of the uniformed services to family and medical leave under the provisions of the Family and Medical Leave Act of 1993, 29 U.S.C. §§ 2601-2654 (FMLA), and the Uniformed Services Employment and Reemployment Rights Act of 1994, 38 U.S.C. §§ 4301-4333 (USERRA). This memorandum also provides guidance regarding coordination between the Department of Labor's Wage and Hour Division field staff (WHD) and the Veterans' Employment and Training Service (VETS) field staff on cases involving this issue.

Over 90,000 members of the National Guard and Reserve have been called up since the President's declaration of a national emergency following the attacks of September 11, 2001. As these service members conclude their tours of duty and return to civilian employment, it is important for employers to recognize that USERRA requires that returning veterans receive all benefits of employment that they would have obtained if they had been continuously employed. One such benefit is eligibility for leave under the FMLA.

Under the FMLA, an "eligible employee" is entitled to 12 workweeks of leave during any 12-month period because of childbirth, adoption or foster care, or a serious health condition of the employee or certain family members. The FMLA provides that, to be eligible for family or medical leave, an employee must work for a covered employer, must have worked for the

employer for at least 12 months and must have worked at least 1250 hours for that employer during the 12-month period prior to the start of the leave. The requirement of 1250 hours worked applies to persons employed by private employers, state and local governments, and the Postal Service.

A member of the National Guard or Reserve who is absent from employment for an extended period of time due to military service and who requests FMLA leave shortly after returning to civilian employment may not have actually worked for his or her employer for a total of 12 months or may not have performed 1250 hours of actual work with the employer in the 12 months prior to the start of the FMLA leave. Thus, the question may arise as to whether the time and hours that the employee would have worked but for his or her military service should be combined with the time employed and the hours actually worked for an employer to meet the 12-months of employment and the 1250 hours eligibility requirements.

For example, suppose that an employee who normally works a 40-hour week leaves civilian employment on November 5, 2001, to serve a tour of duty in Afghanistan, and is reemployed by the same civilian employer on June 10, 2002. On July 1, 2002, the employee begins FMLA leave, at which time the employee has only 840 hours of actual work performed for the civilian employer in the twelve months prior to the leave request (18 weeks prior to the military service, and 3 weeks following reemployment, at 40 hours per week). If the employee is otherwise eligible for FMLA leave, the 1240 hours that the employee would have worked but for his or her service in Afghanistan (31 weeks at 40 hours per week) should be added to the 840 hours actually worked, for a total of 2080 hours for purposes of determining FMLA eligibility.

Under USERRA, a person who is reemployed is entitled to the rights and benefits that he (or she) would have attained if he had remained continuously employed.[1] The "rights and benefits" protected by USERRA include those provided by employers and those required by statute, such as the right to leave under FMLA. Accordingly, a returning service member would be entitled to FMLA leave if the hours that he or she would have worked for the civilian employer during the period of military service would have met the FMLA eligibility threshold. Therefore, in determining whether a veteran meets the FMLA eligibility requirement, the months employed and the hours that were actually worked for the civilian employer should be combined with the months and hours that would have been worked during the twelve months prior to the start of the leave requested but for the military service.

Recognition of the rights and responsibilities established by USERRA will facilitate reentry into the workforce by those who stood ready to serve our nation. To assure that reemployed service members receive family and medical leave benefits that they are entitled to, all WHD and VETS investigators should follow the guidance in this memorandum when dealing with inquiries involving family and medical leave rights for such service members. WHD will refer to VETS any complaint in which this interpretation may be determinative along with a written determination that the information provided by the complainant appears, on its face, to indicate that: 1) the reason for leave qualifies as leave under the FMLA; 2) the employer is covered by

---

[1] However, a service member would not be entitled to rights and benefits that are considered as a form of short-term compensation, such as accrued vacation.

the FMLA; and 3) the service member would have been eligible for FMLA but for his or her military service. If the complainant in such a case meets USERRA's eligibility criteria (i.e., notice given, duration and nature of service, timely return/application), VETS will open a USERRA case. For cases opened directly with VETS in which the USERRA eligibility criteria are met, VETS will seek a written determination from WHD regarding the FMLA eligibility issues. With respect to cases opened directly by VETS or cases opened upon referral from WHD, VETS State Directors and WHD District Directors will coordinate as necessary to investigate and resolve these complaints. A request for assistance from one Director to another will constitute a delegation of authority to the other to assist in the conduct of the investigation.

APPENDIX C

DOL FMLA Fact Sheets

U.S. Department of Labor
Employment Standards Administration
Wage and Hour Division

Fact Sheet #28: The Family and Medical Leave Act of 1993

THE FAMILY AND MEDICAL LEAVE ACT OF 1993 See The CFR

The U.S. Department of Labor's Employment Standards Administration, Wage and Hour Division, administers and enforces the Family and Medical Leave Act (FMLA) for all private, state and local government employees, and some federal employees. Most Federal and certain congressional employees are also covered by the law and are subject to the jurisdiction of the U.S. Office of Personnel Management or the Congress.

FMLA became effective on August 5, 1993, for most employers. If a collective bargaining agreement (CBA) was in effect on that date, FMLA became effective on the expiration date of the CBA or February 5, 1994, whichever was earlier. FMLA entitles eligible employees to take up to 12 weeks of unpaid, job-protected leave in a 12-month period for specified family and medical reasons. The employer may elect to use the calendar year, a fixed 12-month leave or fiscal year, or a 12-month period prior to or after the commencement of leave as the 12-month period.

The law contains provisions on employer coverage; employee eligibility for the law's benefits; entitlement to leave, maintenance of health benefits during leave, and job restoration after leave; notice and certification of the need for FMLA leave; and, protection for employees who request or take FMLA leave. The law also requires employers to keep certain records.

EMPLOYER COVERAGE

FMLA applies to all:

- public agencies, including state, local and federal employers, local education agencies (schools), and
- private-sector employers who employed 50 or more employees in 20 or more workweeks in the current or preceding calendar year and who are engaged in commerce or in any industry or activity affecting commerce — including joint employers and successors of covered employers.

EMPLOYEE ELIGIBILITY

To be eligible for FMLA benefits, an employee must:

1. **work for a covered employer;**
2. **have worked for the employer for a total of 12 months*;**
3. **have worked at least 1,250 hours over the previous 12 months*; and**
4. **work at a location in the United States or in any territory or possession of the United States where at least 50 employees are employed by the employer within 75 miles.**

*** See special rules for returning reservists under USERRA.**

LEAVE ENTITLEMENT

A covered employer must grant an eligible employee up to a total of 12 workweeks of unpaid leave during any 12-month period for one or more of the following reasons:

- for the birth and care of the newborn child of the employee;
- for placement with the employee of a son or daughter for adoption or foster care;
- to care for an immediate family member (spouse, child, or parent) with a serious health condition; **or**
- to take medical leave when the employee is unable to work because of a serious health condition.

Spouses employed by the same employer are jointly entitled to a **combined** total of 12 work-weeks of family leave for the birth and care of the newborn child, for placement of a child for adoption or foster care, and to care for a parent who has a serious health condition.

Leave for birth and care, or placement for adoption or foster care must conclude within 12 months of the birth or placement.

Under some circumstances, employees may take FMLA leave intermittently — which means taking leave in blocks of time, or by reducing their normal weekly or daily work schedule.

- If FMLA leave is for birth and care or placement for adoption or foster care, use of intermittent leave is subject to the employer's approval.
- FMLA leave may be taken intermittently whenever **medically necessary** to care for a seriously ill family member, or because the employee is seriously ill and unable to work.

Also, subject to certain conditions, employees **or** employers may choose to use accrued **paid** leave (such as sick or vacation leave) to cover some or all of the FMLA leave.

The employer is responsible for designating if an employee's use of paid leave counts as FMLA leave, based on information from the employee.

"**Serious health condition**" means an illness, injury, impairment, or physical or mental condition that involves either:

- any period of incapacity or treatment connected with inpatient care (i.e., an overnight stay) in a hospital, hospice, or residential medical-care facility, and any period of incapacity or subsequent treatment in connection with such inpatient care; **or**
- Continuing treatment by a health care provider which includes any period of incapacity (i.e., inability to work, attend school or perform other regular daily activities) due to:

(1) A health condition (including treatment therefor, or recovery therefrom) lasting more than three consecutive days, and any subsequent treatment or period of incapacity relating to the same condition, that **also** includes:

- treatment two or more times by or under the supervision of a health care provider; **or**
- one treatment by a health care provider with a continuing regimen of treatment; **or**

(2) Pregnancy or prenatal care. A visit to the health care provider is not necessary for each absence; **or**

(3) A chronic serious health condition which continues over an extended period of time, requires periodic visits to a health care provider, and may involve occasional episodes of incapacity (e.g., asthma, diabetes). A visit to a health care provider is not necessary for each absence; **or**

(4) A permanent or long-term condition for which treatment may not be effective (e.g., Alzheimer's, a severe stroke, terminal cancer). Only supervision by a health care provider is required, rather than active treatment; **or**

(5) Any absences to receive multiple treatments for restorative surgery or for a condition which would likely result in a period of incapacity of more than three days if not treated (e.g., chemotherapy or radiation treatments for cancer).

"Health care provider" means:

- doctors of medicine or osteopathy authorized to practice medicine or surgery by the state in which the doctors practice; or
- podiatrists, dentists, clinical psychologists, optometrists and chiropractors (limited to manual manipulation of the spine to correct a subluxation as demonstrated by X-ray to exist) authorized to practice, and performing within the scope of their practice, under state law; or
- nurse practitioners, nurse-midwives and clinical social workers authorized to practice, and performing within the scope of their practice, as defined under state law; or
- Christian Science practitioners listed with the First Church of Christ, Scientist in Boston, Massachusetts; or
- Any health care provider recognized by the employer or the employer's group health plan benefits manager.

MAINTENANCE OF HEALTH BENEFITS

A covered employer is required to maintain group health insurance coverage for an employee on FMLA leave whenever such insurance was provided before the leave was taken and on the same terms as if the employee had continued to work. If applicable, arrangements will need to be made for employees to pay their share of health insurance premiums while on leave.

In some instances, the employer may recover premiums it paid to maintain health coverage for an employee who fails to return to work from FMLA leave.

JOB RESTORATION

Upon return from FMLA leave, an employee must be restored to the employee's original job, or to an equivalent job with equivalent pay, benefits, and other terms and conditions of employment.

In addition, an employee's use of FMLA leave cannot result in the loss of any employment benefit that the employee earned or was entitled to **before** using FMLA leave, nor be counted against the employee under a "no fault" attendance policy.

Under specified and limited circumstances where restoration to employment will cause substantial and grievous economic injury to its operations, an employer may refuse to reinstate certain highly-paid **"key"** employees after using FMLA leave during which health coverage was maintained. In order to do so, the employer must:

- notify the employee of his/her status as a "key" employee in response to the employee's notice of intent to take FMLA leave;
- notify the employee as soon as the employer decides it will deny job restoration, and explain the reasons for this decision;
- offer the employee a reasonable opportunity to return to work from FMLA leave after giving this notice; and
- make a final determination as to whether reinstatement will be denied at the end of the leave period if the employee then requests restoration.

A **"key"** employee is a salaried "eligible" employee who is among the highest paid ten percent of employees within 75 miles of the work site.

NOTICE AND CERTIFICATION

Employees seeking to use FMLA leave are required to provide 30-day advance notice of the need to take FMLA leave when the need is foreseeable and such notice is practicable.

Employers may also require employees to provide:

- medical certification supporting the need for leave due to a serious health condition affecting the employee or an immediate family member;
- second or third medical opinions (at the employer's expense) and periodic recertification; and
- periodic reports during FMLA leave regarding the employee's status and intent to return to work.

When intermittent leave is needed to care for an immediate family member or the employee's own

illness, and is for planned medical treatment, the employee must try to schedule treatment so as not to unduly disrupt the employer's operation.

Covered employers must post a notice approved by the Secretary of Labor explaining rights and responsibilities under FMLA. An employer that willfully violates this posting requirement may be subject to a fine of up to $100 for each separate offense.

Also, covered employers must inform employees of their rights and responsibilities under FMLA, including giving specific written information on what is required of the employee and what might happen in certain circumstances, such as if the employee fails to return to work after FMLA leave.

UNLAWFUL ACTS

It is unlawful for any employer to interfere with, restrain, or deny the exercise of any right provided by FMLA. It is also unlawful for an employer to discharge or discriminate against any individual for opposing any practice, or because of involvement in any proceeding, related to FMLA.

ENFORCEMENT

The Wage and Hour Division investigates complaints. If violations cannot be satisfactorily resolved, the U.S. Department of Labor may bring action in court to compel compliance. Individuals may also bring a private civil action against an employer for violations.

OTHER PROVISIONS

Special rules apply to employees of local education agencies. Generally, these rules provide for FMLA leave to be taken in blocks of time when intermittent leave is needed or the leave is required near the end of a school term.

Salaried executive, administrative, and professional employees of covered employers who meet the Fair Labor Standards Act (FLSA) criteria for exemption from minimum wage and overtime under Regulations, 29 CFR Part 541, do not lose their FLSA-exempt status by using any unpaid FMLA leave. This special exception to the "salary basis" requirements for FLSA's exemption extends only to "eligible" employees' use of leave required by FMLA.

The FMLA does not affect any other federal or state law which prohibits discrimination, nor supersede any state or local law which provides greater family or medical leave protection. Nor does it affect an employer's obligation to provide greater leave rights under a collective bargaining agreement or employment benefit plan. The FMLA also encourages employers to provide more generous leave rights.

FURTHER INFORMATION

The final rule implementing FMLA is contained in the January 6, 1995, Federal Register. For more information, please contact the nearest office of the Wage and Hour Division, listed in most telephone directories under U.S. Government, Department of Labor.

U.S. Department of Labor
Frances Perkins Building
200 Constitution Avenue, NW
Washington, DC 20210

1-866-4-USWAGE, TTY: 1-877-889-5627
Contact Us

APPENDIX D

DOL WH-380: Medical Certification Form

Certification of Health Care Provider
(Family and Medical Leave Act of 1993)

U.S. Department of Labor
Employment Standards Administration
Wage and Hour Division

(When completed, this form goes to the employee, Not to the Department of Labor.)

OMB No.: 1215-0181
Expires: 07/31/07

1. Employee's Name	2. Patient's Name *(If different from employee)*

3. Page 4 describes what is meant by a "serious health condition" under the Family and Medical Leave Act. Does the patient's condition[1] qualify under any of the categories described? If so, please check the applicable category.

(1)______ (2) ______ (3) ______ (4)______ (5)______ (6) ______ , or None of the above ______

4. Describe the medical facts which support your certification, including a brief statement as to how the medical facts meet the criteria of one of these categories:

5. a. State the approximate date the condition commenced, and the probable duration of the condition (and also the probable duration of the patient's present incapacity[2] if different):

b. Will it be necessary for the employee to take work only intermittently or to work on a less than full schedule as a result of the condition (including for treatment described in Item 6 below)?

If yes, give the probable duration:

c. If the condition is a chronic condition (condition #4) or pregnancy, state whether the patient is presently incapacitated[2] and the likely duration and frequency of episodes of incapacity[2]:

[1] Here and elsewhere on this form, the information sought relates only to the condition for which the employee is taking FMLA leave.

[2] "Incapacity," for purposes of FMLA, is defined to mean inability to work, attend school or perform other regular daily activities due to the serious health condition, treatment therefor, or recovery therefrom.

6. a. If additional treatments will be required for the condition, provide an estimate of the probable number of such treatments.

If the patient will be absent from work or other daily activities because of treatment on an intermittent or part-time basis, also provide an estimate of the probable number of and interval between such treatments, actual or estimated dates of treatment if known, and period required for recovery if any:

b. If any of these treatments will be provided by another provider of health services (e.g., physical therapist), please state the nature of the treatments:

c. If a regimen of continuing treatment by the patient is required under your supervision, provide a general description of such regimen (*e.g.*, prescription drugs, physical therapy requiring special equipment):

7. a. If medical leave is required for the employee's absence from work because of the employee's own condition (including absences due to pregnancy or a chronic condition), is the employee unable to perform work of any kind?

b. If able to perform some work, is the employee unable to perform any one or more of the essential functions of the employee's job (the employee or the employer should supply you with information about the essential job functions)? If yes, please list the essential functions the employee is unable to perform:

c. If neither a. nor b. applies, is it necessary for the employee to be absent from work for treatment?

8. a. If leave is required to care for a family member of the employee with a serious health condition, does the patient require assistance for basic medical or personal needs or safety, or for transportation?

b. If no, would the employee's presence to provide psychological comfort be beneficial to the patient or assist in the patient's recovery?

c. If the patient will need care only intermittently or on a part-time basis, please indicate the probable duration of this need:

Signature of Health Care Provider | **Type of Practice**

Address | **Telephone Number**

Date

To be completed by the employee needing family leave to care for a family member:

State the care you will provide and an estimate of the period during which care will be provided, including a schedule if leave is to be taken intermittently or if it will be necessary for you to work less than a full schedule:

Employee Signature | **Date**

A "Serious Health Condition" *means an illness, injury impairment, or physical or mental condition that involves one of the following:*

1. <u>Hospital Care</u>

   Inpatient care (*i.e.*, an overnight stay) in a hospital, hospice, or residential medical care facility, including any period of incapacity[2] or subsequent treatment in connection with or consequent to such inpatient care.

2. <u>Absence Plus Treatment</u>

   (a) A period of incapacity[2] *of* more than three consecutive calendar days (including any subsequent treatment or period of incapacity[2] relating to the same condition), that also involves:

   (1) Treatment[3] two or more times by a health care provider, by a nurse or physician's assistant under direct supervision of a health care provider, or by a provider of health care services (*e.g.*, physical therapist) under orders of, or on referral by, a health care provider; or

   (2) Treatment by a health care provider on at least one occasion which results in a regimen of continuing treatment[4] under the supervision of the health care provider.

3. <u>Pregnancy</u>

   Any period of incapacity due to pregnancy, or for prenatal care.

4. <u>Chronic Conditions Requiring Treatments</u>

   A chronic condition which:

   (1) Requires periodic visits for treatment by a health care provider, or by a nurse or physician's assistant under direct supervision of a health care provider;

   (2) Continues over an extended period of time (including recurring episodes of a single underlying condition); and

   (3) May cause episodic rather than a continuing period of incapacity[2] (*e.g.*, asthma, diabetes, epilepsy, etc.).

5. <u>Permanent/Long-term Conditions Requiring Supervision</u>

   A period of incapacity[2] which is permanent or long-term due to a condition for which treatment may not be effective. The employee or family member must be under the continuing supervision of, but need not be receiving active treatment by, a health care provider. Examples include Alzheimer's, a severe stroke, or the terminal stages of a disease.

6. <u>Multiple Treatments (Non-Chronic Conditions)</u>

   Any period of absence to receive multiple treatments (including any period of recovery therefrom) by a health care provider or by a provider of health care services under orders of, or on referral by, a health care provider, either for restorative surgery after an accident or other injury, or for a condition that would likely result in a period of incapacity[2] of more than three consecutive calendar days in the absence of medical intervention or treatment, such as cancer (chemotherapy, radiation, etc.), severe arthritis (physical therapy), and kidney disease (dialysis).

This optional form may be used by employees to satisfy a mandatory requirement to furnish a medical certification (when requested) from a health care provider, including second or third opinions and recertification (29 CFR 825.306).

***Note:* Persons are not required to respond to this collection of information unless it displays a currently valid OMB control number.**

---

[3] **Treatment includes examinations to determine if a serious health condition exists and evaluations of the condition. Treatment does not include routine physical examinations, eye examinations, or dental examinations.**

[4] **A regimen of continuing treatment includes, for example, a course of prescription medication (*e.g.*, an antibiotic) or therapy requiring special equipment to resolve or alleviate the health condition. A regimen of treatment does not include the taking of over-the-counter medications such as aspirin, antihistamines, or salves; or bed-rest, drinking fluids, exercise, and other similar activities that can be initiated without a visit to a health care provider.**

Public Burden Statement

We estimate that it will take an average of 20 minutes to complete this collection of information, including the time for reviewing instructions, searching existing data sources, gathering and maintaining the data needed, and completing and reviewing the collection of information. If you have any comments regarding this burden estimate or any other aspect of this collection of information, including suggestions for reducing this burden, send them to the Administrator, Wage and Hour Division, Department of Labor, Room S-3502, 200 Constitution Avenue, N.W., Washington, D.C. 20210.

DO NOT SEND THE COMPLETED FORM TO THIS OFFICE; IT GOES TO THE EMPLOYEE.

Page 4 of 4

*U.S. GPO: 2009-481-664/28606

APPENDIX E

DOL WH-381: Employer Response to Employee Request for FMLA

Employer Response to Employee Request for Family or Medical Leave
(Optional Use Form – See 29 CFR § 825.301)

U.S. Department of Labor
Employment Standards Administration
Wage and Hour Division

(Family and Medical Leave Act of 1993)

OMB No. : 1215-0181
Expires : 08-31-07

Date:

To: ______________________________
(Employee's Name)

From: ______________________________
(Name of Appropriate Employer Representative)

Subject: REQUEST FOR FAMILY/MEDICAL LEAVE

On ____________ *(Date)*, you notified us of your need to take family/medical leave due to:

☐ The birth of a child, or the placement of a child with you for adoption or foster care; or

☐ A serious health condition that makes you unable to perform the essential functions for your job: or

☐ A serious health condition affecting your ☐ spouse, ☐ child, ☐ parent, for which you are needed to provide care.

You notified us that you need this leave beginning on ____________ *(Date)* and that you expect leave to continue until on or about ____________ *(Date)*.

Except as explained below, you have a right under the FMLA for up to 12 weeks of unpaid leave in a 12-month period for the reasons listed above. Also, your health benefits must be maintained during any period of unpaid leave under the same conditions as if you continued to work, and you must be reinstated to the same or an equivalent job with the same pay, benefits, and terms and conditions of employment on your return from leave. If you do not return to work following FMLA leave for a reason other than: (1) the continuation, recurrence, or onset of a serious health condition which would entitle you to FMLA leave; or (2) other circumstances beyond your control, you may be required to reimburse us for our share of health insurance premiums paid on your behalf during your FMLA leave.

This is to inform you that: *(check appropriate boxes; explain where indicated)*

1. You are ☐ eligible ☐ not eligible for leave under the FMLA.

2. The requested leave ☐ will ☐ will not be counted against your annual FMLA leave entitlement.

3. You ☐ will ☐ will not be required to furnish medical certification of a serious health condition. If required, you must furnish certification by ____________ *(insert date)* (must be at least 15 days after you are notified of this requirement), or we may delay the commencement of your leave until the certification is submitted.

4. You may elect to substitute accrued paid leave for unpaid FMLA leave. We ☐ will ☐ will not require that you substitute accrued paid leave for unpaid FMLA leave. If paid leave will be used, the following conditions will apply: *(Explain)*

Form WH-381
Rev. June 1997

5. (a) If you normally pay a portion of the premiums for your health insurance, these payments will continue during the period of FMLA leave. Arrangements for payment have been discussed with you, and it is agreed that you will make premium payments as follows: *(Set forth dates, e.g., the 10th of each month, or pay periods, etc. that specifically cover the agreement with the employee.)*

(b) You have a minimum 30-day *(or, indicate longer period, if applicable)* grace period in which to make premium payments. If payment is not made timely, your group health insurance may be cancelled, *provided* we notify you in writing at least 15 days before the date that your health coverage will lapse, or, at our option, we may pay your share of the premiums during FMLA leave, and recover these payments from you upon your return to work. We ☐ will ☐ will not pay your share of health insurance premiums while you are on leave.

(c) We ☐ will ☐ will not do the same with other benefits (*e.g.*, life insurance, disability insurance, etc.) while you are on FMLA leave. If we do pay your premiums for other benefits, when you return from leave you ☐ will ☐ will not be expected to reimburse us for the payments made on your behalf.

6. You ☐ will ☐ will not be required to present a fitness-for-duty certificate prior to being restored to employment. If such certification is required but not received, your return to work may be delayed until certification is provided.

7. (a) You ☐ are ☐ are not a "key employee" as described in § 825.217 of the FMLA regulations. If you are a "key employee:" restoration to employment may be denied following FMLA leave on the grounds that such restoration will cause substantial and grievous economic injury to us as discussed in § 825.218.

(b) We ☐ have ☐ have not determined that restoring you to employment at the conclusion of FMLA leave will cause substantial and grievous economic harm to us. *(Explain (a) and/or (b) below. See §825.219 of the FMLA regulations.)*

8. While on leave, you ☐ will ☐ will not be required to furnish us with periodic reports every ________________________________ *(indicate interval of periodic reports, as appropriate for the particular leave situation)* of your status and intent to return to work *(see § 825.309 of the FMLA regulations)*. If the circumstances of your leave change and you are able to return to work earlier than the date indicated on the reverse side of this form, you ☐ will ☐ will not be required to notify us at least two work days prior to the date you intend to report to work.

9. You ☐ will ☐ will not be required to furnish recertification relating to a serious health condition. *(Explain below, if necessary, including the interval between certifications as prescribed in §825.308 of the FMLA regulations.)*

This optional use form may be used to satisfy mandatory employer requirements to provide employees taking FMLA leave with Written notice detailing specific expectations and obligations of the employee and explaining any consequences of a failure to meet these obligations. (29 CFR 825.301(b).)

Note: Persons are not required to respond to this collection of information unless it displays a currently valid OMB control number.

Public Burden Statement

We estimate that it will take an average of 5 minutes to complete this collection of information, including the time for reviewing instructions, searching existing data sources, gathering and maintaining the data needed, and completing and reviewing the collection of information. If you have any comments regarding this burden estimate or any other aspect of this collection of information, including suggestions for reducing this burden, send them to the Administrator, Wage and Hour Division, Department of Labor, Room S-3502, 200 Constitution Avenue, N.W., Washington, D.C. 20210.

DO NOT SEND THE COMPLETED FORM TO THE OFFICE SHOWN ABOVE.

Index

About the Author

Carl C. Bosland, Esq., is a Denver-based attorney and consultant who has written and trained extensively on the FMLA. For free updates on FMLA developments, visit Bosland's website, the FMLA Blog, at http://federalfmla.typepad.com/_fmla_blog.

www.ingramcontent.com/pod-product-compliance
Lightning Source LLC
LaVergne TN
LVHW020138280526
839948LV00003B/475